ECONOMIC MODELS AND QUANTITATIVE METHODS
FOR DECISIONS AND PLANNING IN AGRICULTURE /
Proceedings of an East-West Seminar

ECONOMIC MODELS

FOR DECISIONS AND

The Iowa State University Press / AMES, Iowa, U.S.A.

AND QUANTITATIVE METHODS

PLANNING IN AGRICULTURE /

Proceedings of an East-West Seminar

Edited by EARL O. HEADY

CONTENTS

v

FOREWORD

THE SEMINAR reported in this volume was initiated as a result
of interactions among members of the committee listed below
and from contacts of committee members with other international
colleagues in the agricultural economics profession. We found that a
large number of agricultural economists in a wide range of countries
were turning to use of recent models and methods for analyzing or directing decisions and planning of agriculture. There was great and
wide interest in a seminar or congress to further develop, apply, and
evaluate these methods and their possibilities. Interest was expressed
in a seminar which could treat the topics intensively, with the number
of participants restricted to persons particularly interested in the subject matter and to those who could interact deeply and continuously
over a period of time in extending, illustrating, and evaluating modern
methods for decisions and planning in agriculture. A grant from the
Ford Foundation allowed us to assemble as a planning committee,
evaluate potential interest, and formulate a seminar program. The
proceedings reported are the result of these initial interests and
efforts.

In planning the conference, we found that many persons from
countries of both East and West were using or experimenting with recent and prospective decision and planning models. Hence we constructed a seminar program which would bring together approximately
equal numbers of professional persons from Eastern European countries and Western European and North American countries. While
persons from many other countries would have been interested in attending the seminar, participants were restricted thus to maintain the
seminar nature of the meeting. We also found important reasons for
composition of the seminar as outlined.

As a basis for improvement in the agricultural sector, all countries represented have fairly elaborate agricultural policies, planning
organizations, and extension or advisory services. Facilities for
guidance or planning of agriculture prevail at national, regional, and
individual farm levels. In some cases, national guidance and planning
involve production goals or quotas, support prices, compensation
payments, resource subsidies, research and education, and national
projections of food demand aimed at balancing the overall use of farm

resources relative to national needs. In other cases, national planning is somewhat parallel but involves a more formal set of tools for establishing balances and plans in the agricultural industry. As a step in attaining national balance in the use of resources and food production, all countries of East and West devise plans and programs which relate to agricultural or economic regions differing in climate, soil, location, and interrelations with other sectors.

Finally, all of the Eastern and Western countries represented have public machinery to aid planning of individual farms. In countries where agriculture performs largely through the market mechanism, planning aids are provided through agricultural extension or advisory services, mainly in the form of budgeting or related techniques but frequently through modern mathematical models. In Eastern Europe the range also is great: the majority of individual farms are planned by traditional techniques, but in a few cases by mathematical programming methods. While systematic and advanced models exist for the projection, planning, and development of agriculture and its policies, they are not widely used in countries of either the East or West. Need exists to evaluate and establish the potential of these models and devise means for their application where they are most relevant. Recent advances in economic and econometric methods provide potential techniques or models which can greatly improve and integrate decisions for agriculture. These techniques promise to provide methods which improve the allocation of resources and management decisions within farms, in the regional and interregional development of agriculture, and in the functioning of agriculture in national economies. Other less formal techniques for decision procedures and planning in agriculture exist and are widely used. Frequently, however, these simpler methods can be applied effectively only if greater information is provided relative to national food demand structure, resource supplies and mobility, and the interaction of product supply and resource use at the individual farm and national levels. Several national econometric models are being developed and applied which allow integration of the development or structural adjustment of the agricultural sector with other sectors of national economies. However, to this point in time, national models have incorporated insufficient details of agriculture. Similarly agricultural planning and policy often have been insufficiently related to national economies and economic development. While the agricultural sectors of Eastern Europe, Western Europe, and North America operate under a range of economic and social systems, models available for decision and planning appear to have equal potential and applicability for improving the functioning of the agricultural sector. With adaptations to meet the conditions of resource restraints, agricultural organization, methods of demand reflection, farm objectives or objective functions, national policy, consumer welfare, and similar conditions, it appears that many existing and potential decision and planning models can have equal usefulness and relevance in all countries.

With this common background in methods, agricultural problems,

and planning or policy needs, the seminar was developed with these objectives:

1. To review the decisions and planning concepts and methods now in
   use and evaluate their evolution.
2. To review recent economic decision and planning models which are
   available, are being developed, or can be formulated for improved
   functioning of agriculture at farm, regional, and national levels.
3. To illustrate and evaluate the application of these methods in problems of resource allocation and efficiency in the farm sectors.
4. To examine adaptations in existing models and develop new theories
   relevant to the decision, planning, and policy problems unique to agriculture.
5. To evaluate planning and decision models in terms of the potentials
   which they pose and their actual application of improved planning
   and policy.
6. To evaluate the gap or divergence between optimum plans and planning techniques for the guidance of the agricultural sector (as devised by modern decision models) against decision, plans, and policies actually used at various levels of farm production and resource
   use.
7. To acquaint extension and administrative personnel with newer decision and planning models which have potential in improving management at the individual farm level and policy at the national level.

The seminar was organized to review traditional planning methods
and to evaluate new methods as they apply at the farm, regional, and
national levels. In the implementation of the seminar, participants
prepared their papers in advance. The papers were then translated
into English and Russian. A major discussant was named for each paper
or set of papers; a half-day was devoted to each paper. The person
presenting the paper was given 20 minutes to summarize it, the formal
discussant was given 20 minutes to open the discussion, and the remainder of time was devoted to dialogue and participation on the specific
paper and related methods and problems by the entire seminar membership.

Each person entering the dialogue made a summary of his remarks
and submitted it to the session chairman and secretary at the end of the
half-day. Initial plans were to publish these contributions from the
seminar membership. However, when they were summed, the total of
these contributions was greater than that of the original papers. Hence
the papers and formal discussions are being published first as a separate set. It is hoped that a second summary publication can contain
other discussions of the seminar.

This volume deals with plans and their attainment. The committee
named below planned a seminar with a distinct system to it: the review,
development, and evaluation of modern methods at the interwoven levels
of farms, regions, and nations, with a summary of national models now
being applied for agriculture. One section of the program dealt with

the divergence between plans and realization. It is possible that the planning committee experienced some divergence between plans and realization. Perhaps, in a few instances, papers were written on topics other than those initially assigned, or perhaps a few formal discussants detoured the paper they were assigned and took a different road. But even though there were some divergences between plans and realization, the majority of persons assigned papers and discussions dealt with their topics in a manner to maintain the central theme of the seminar. We wish to thank all persons who devoted so much effort to prior preparation of papers and the entire seminar membership for their intense interest and participation in it.

The seminar not only was successful in its specified scientific objectives but it also brought us together as individuals and broadened our acquaintances and perspectives. The seminar, held at Lake Balaton at Keszthely, Hungary, extended for ten days during the summer of 1968. Attendance by all persons was continuous for this entire period, and the discussion was as spirited at the final as at the first session.

The seminar was possible only through the donation of time, funds, professional personnel, and facilities of many organizations and several countries. The Ford Foundation made an initial grant to allow convening of the planning committee. It then provided a large grant to finance the major costs of the seminar, including the travel and subsistence costs of designated participants and other necessary expenses. The Hungarian Academy of Science also made an important grant to the seminar which covered professional aid in organization, implementation, typing, and translation of original papers and in many other facilities insuring success of the seminar. Various institutions of the U.S.S.R. contributed to the seminar in providing travel grants and professional services for translations. Also, Czechoslovakian institutions came to the rescue in providing badly needed translation services under the initial deluge of papers. Finally, the Center for Agricultural Development of Iowa State University provided funds and personal services for typing, translating, and preparing final papers and for covering part of the costs of this publication.

On behalf of the seminar participants, we express sincere appreciation to the persons and institutions who contributed to and made possible this seminar. Special appreciation is due Stanley Gordon and other officials of the Ford Foundation who provided both professional ideas and guides for overall financing through the Ford Foundation. We are particularly indebted to President Rusnyak, Vice President Erdei, and other officers of the Hungarian Academy of Science who encouraged us, invited us to hold the seminar in Hungary, and provided implementation means and facilities. We are particularly indebted to Rector Lang, Vice Rector Potsubay, and others of the staff at the College of Agriculture, Keszthely, who provided us with excellent organization and facilities for the seminar proper and with other amenities which enhanced our enjoyment at Keszthely. Finally, Dr. Lazlo Enese of the Hungarian

Research Institute for Agricultural Economics served as coordinator for the planning committee and spent long days, both before and during the seminar, in insuring the smooth functioning of the activity.

Planning Committee

Earl O. Heady (U.S.A.), Chairman
Michele de Benedictis (Italy)
Vladimir Kadlec (Czechoslovakia)
Rostislav G. Kravtchenko (U.S.S.R.)
Danilo Pejin (Yugoslavia)
Joseph Sebestyen (Hungary)

ECONOMIC MODELS AND QUANTITATIVE METHODS
FOR DECISIONS AND PLANNING IN AGRICULTURE /
Proceedings of an East-West Seminar

Chapter 1 ∽ WELCOME: PROSPECTS IN IMPROVED ECONOMIC
FUNCTIONING AND METHODS FOR THE AGRICULTURAL ECONOMY

Ferenc Erdei, *Director, Research Institute for Agricultural Economics,
and Vice President, Hungarian Academy of Sciences* (Hungary)

O N BEHALF of the Presidency of the Hungarian Academy of Sciences and also myself, I have the honor of greeting you at the
International Seminar which will discuss the problems of economic models and quantitative methods for decisions and planning in
agriculture.

The topics of our present consultations have a particular importance in the sphere of agricultural economics and bear the marks of a
discipline in full evolution. We might say that this field of scientific
activity is really representative for our century, and a period is mani-
fested in it where science becomes an ever more and more efficient
productive force in the hands of mankind. Scientists of this century
have reached impressive results in several disciplines, and these scientific achievements have opened up new prospects for the human nation. The achievements of scientists essentially contributed to the development and increasing welfare of humanity. Certain scientific
issues, however, were wrenched from the hands of scientists and
transformed to means of destruction. Up-to-date scientific results in
agricultural economics are not, and due to their nature they even cannot become, issues of this kind. Our science is instrumental for the
conversion of natural forces to the benefit of the human race, for increasing agricultural production, and for the improvement of labor
productivity. Scientific achievements in agricultural economics contribute to a more copious and more economical satiation of human
needs and demands.

Although our discipline cannot be converted to means of destruction, if its findings do not become the real incentives of more efficient
agricultural production, then we let hunger — one of the most menacing
dangers for mankind — to be preponderant. It is well known that a significant part of mankind is inadequately nourished or starving and cannot even cover its everyday needs. This represents a constant danger,
the effect of which can surpass that of any other means of destruction.
Hence double responsibility rests upon us. On the one hand, we have to
achieve results which are suitable to contribute to the abundance of
foodstuffs and other agricultural products and, on the other hand, to
find a way for scientific issues to be turned into production practice.
Consequently I think that the seminar to be opened today also has a
double task. One is to discuss, based on the papers of excellent representatives of our discipline who are present here, achievements

1

already performed and the opportunities for further development while the other will be — and this is what I particularly should like to emphasize — to select the most appropriate methods for the practical realization of these achievements, the aggregation of which represents already a considerable potentiality. Even among agricultural economists, the partisans of econometrics are frequently subjected to remarks claiming that their scientific activity is alien from the realities of life. I do not agree with this opinion because I appreciate that the rational efforts of our age are involved. Unfortunately, however, we can observe — and this is expressed also in several papers presented for discussion in this seminar — that the practice of agriculture not only does not apply the most outstanding issues of this discipline but even the so-called simple mathematical methods of economic procedures could not find an everyday application. Therefore I think that a task of this seminar, at least equal to the discussion of new issues or even more important than that, is to explore the methods of practical application and the possibilities of efficient extension of methods in research. This is one way we can meet the danger of hunger and improve the outlook for establishing abundance in order to assist in the prosperity of mankind.

There is yet another characteristic of our consultations about which I should like to speak. Already the bringing about of this seminar is the result of a collaboration realized among scientists of very different nations and of countries having the most divergent social organization. The initiation made by several scientists to suggest such a creative consultation, has originally been international. Preparatory activities were international too, carried out by the closest cooperation of six colleagues representing six foreign countries, and financial means needed for the realization of the seminar were also established by joining of international forces. Colleagues of the United States of America, of the Soviet Union, of Czechoslovakia, and of Hungary afforded particularly valuable assistance in procuring the support of respective institutions in their countries; and I am convinced that several other participants present in this room are enjoying the assistance of many other institutions in other countries in creating conditions for their resultful activities in this seminar.

I take this opportunity to express the fullest acknowledgment and most sincere thanks to Curtiss Distinguished Professor Earl O. Heady of Iowa State University and Honorary Member of the Hungarian Academy of Sciences for all his activities developed in the realization of this seminar as the Chairman of the Planning Committee and also to our colleagues Michele de Benedictis from Italy, Vladimir Kadlec from Czechoslovakia, Rostislav Kravtchenko from the U.S.S.R., Danilo Pejin from Yugoslavia, Ulf Renborg from Sweden, and Joseph Sebestyen from Hungary who laboriously and selflessly acted as the members of the Planning Committee. Tribute also is due Lazlo Enese of Hungary who served as coordinator for the Planning Committee and special implementation activities in our country.

Following the wishes of the Planning Committee, the Commission of the Hungarian Academy of Sciences for Agricultural Economics and Farm Management took care of preparations for this seminar. The Governing Body of the Agricultural College in Keszthely, the site of our consultations, has taken utmost pains to create all the conditions needed for our resultful activity.

Feelings of sincere friendship and appreciation inspire us in welcoming you and we wish you an enjoyable and productive time in Hungary. Constructive results should accompany your consultations. In the spirit of these remarks I declare the seminar open.

Part I ✒ FOUNDATION AND BACKGROUND
IN PLANNING MODELS

Chapter 2 ᚙ SYNTHESIS OF DECISION AND
PLANNING TOOLS AND ENVIRONMENT

Earl O. Heady, *Iowa State University* (U.S.A.)

F ARM PLANNING and decisions occur in all countries regardless
of economic and social systems. In some countries decisions and
plans originate dominantly at the farm level, and the planning direction is "upward and outward" from them; in other countries the
planning and decisions for agriculture originate dominantly at the aggregative level by central administrators, and the direction is "downward and inward" to farms. This difference does not obviate the fact
that farm planning and decisions prevail in all countries and that procedures, whether naive or sophisticated and whether systematic or
otherwise, exist and are used. In capitalistic countries where the orientation and meshing of production, investment and consumption is
mainly or importantly through the market mechanism, the greatest
amount of planning is done at the individual farm level and by its manager. But even in socialist countries where national balances are distributed among regions and regional balances among areas and farms,
largely apart from a direct market mechanism, farm managers do
make decisions within plan constraints extended down through administrative planning.

While major planning is mainly an off-farm activity by government
administrators in socialist countries, policy as a degree of overall
planning is also a fact in capitalistic or market economies and is man-
ifested in the form of agricultural policies relating to inputs (e.g., research, education, irrigation, soil improvement, price subsidies) and
to outputs (e.g., production quotas, support prices, subsidies). The
methods of implementing "plans" on the one hand and "policies" on the
other hand do differ somewhat (although the signs connecting policies
and plans are as often equal as not equal). Plans may be implemented
mainly by mandates from planners who are in administrative authority
— supplemented by some price relatives and material incentives. In the
other case, policies may be implemented mainly by support prices,
subsidies, and direct payments directly motivating farmers to shift
their resources among crops — supplemented by some mandates of
market quotas or other direct restraints. There are countries in
which the policies and plans fall in between these "somewhat extremes" and both are used, especially where there is a mixture of private, state, and collective farms. While organization of agriculture by
state or private farms is a distinguishing characteristic, it does not
obviate the fact that in all countries planning is conducted at various
levels of government administration and farming. In one case,

restraints in planning may be more restrictive on the farm manager; and in another case on the public administrator. But these differences do not negate the fact that plans are made and implemented, and planning procedures are used, in all countries.

We are just emerging from the period in which planning techniques, both at the farm and national level, were rather simple and naïve, partly because economic science had not yet developed more powerful and useful models and partly because the services of economists were not assigned this task. While denoted by different terms and jargon in different countries, these older planning methods frequently were similar, even when applied mainly at the farm level in some countries and at the national level in other countries. The rather simple budgeting technique used up to the advent of linear programming in capitalistic countries (and still the dominant planning technique at the farm level in both socialist and capitalist countries) was quite similar to the systems of balances used at the national level in socialist countries, or to the capacity studies of some capitalist countries, except that the task of meshing production items with consumption items was not involved at the farm level. Otherwise the technique of budgeting or balances is the same in principle, arithmetic approach, meshing input requirements with projected output, and so on. The technique applied at the two levels and places had advantage in arithmetic simplicity, in ease of application by persons with little knowledge of economics and mathematical methods, and in results readily communicated and understood by non-professional persons. Both methods, budgeted planning at the farm level in capitalist countries and systems of balances at the national and other levels in socialist countries, also had similar limitations. Both were generally devoid of marginality concepts necessary for determining most efficient allocations; lacked computing capacity to handle the full number of relationships necessary for realistic and practical alternatives at either the farm or national level; did not represent models formulated to consider sufficient interdependent relationships and variables with simultaneous and endogenous solution of allocations in an optimizing manner; and were deficient in other areas.

PLANNING ENVIRONMENT

The environment of farm planning and decision making has many homogeneous characteristics over the world. This homogeneity, at least for possibilities of applying modern planning and decision models, is greater than realized by the typical person or administrator, even though the planning is done at different levels of agriculture and different economic and social organizations of agriculture prevail over the world. The planning environment, in the applicability of modern planning methods, would be even more homogeneous if models widely used were made more systematic and logical in relation to the goals for agriculture in different countries. Homogeneity in the planning environment exists among countries in these respects:

1. All farms have plans, whether they are operated by individuals planning relative to their own goals in a market economy, administered by central planners who prescribe relative to national food balances, or are operated by subsistence cultivators attempting only to guarantee their annual food requirements.
2. All farms have several limited physical resources such as land, labor, buildings, machinery, and capital in other forms which restrain the range of plans or optimal programs which are feasible.
3. In addition, all farms have institutional or subjective restraints which restrict the range of feasible plans considered or put into actual operation. These institutional or subjective restraints may even relate to uncertainty of various types, the objective function or goals of the planners or managers, and related phenomena.
4. All farms have an objective function of some type to be maximized or goal to be approached. This function may include any one or a mixture of quantities such as profit, utility of the manager or planner, physical expression of food output, or other units. The objective function must be maximized, or the goals attained, subject to the resource and other restraints of the farm.
5. Weights must and do exist to evaluate or express the contribution of alternative feasible plans toward objective function maximization or goal attainment. For the individual farmer operating in a competitive market with an objective of maximum profit, the weights are price constants or parameters reflected to him from the market. For a centrally planned farm with minimum goals stated as restraints through the system of allocating national and regional balances, but with some range of alternatives allowed in management, weights may simply be prices prescribed by the central planners. Or they may be "equivalents" in which one crop is used as the "common denominator." The subsistence farmer will have, even though crude and subjective, weights relating to maximizing or attaining the family food supply subject to some mix of proteins, carbohydrates, and vitamins. The weights will be physical characteristics or coefficients of food. An objective function could be formulated to minimize variance or other stochastic properties of income. The weights then would represent the variance functions of different products or enterprises.
6. Farms in all countries and under all organizations of agriculture have enterprises, technologies, or activities which are competitive in the use of resources. For purposes of practical application, they also have a finite number of enterprises and technologies that are reasonable within the confines of knowledge and natural conditions.

Since all farms have these characteristics or properties, modern planning models which are appropriate under one condition of agriculture also are appropriate for farming under other conditions in other countries. Differences in size, economic or social organization, market orientation, ownership, goals, and other attributes of farms do not cause modern planning or decision models to be less appropriate in one case than in the other. The models are general and are applicable under all of these conditions. The imagination and ingenuity of the analyst who can apply them under conditions in one country can modify them to make them applicable in another country under other conditions. It is the ability of the analyst, not the differences or similarities of agriculture, which cause them to have general application. The task and challenge is that of adapting the general models to the specific conditions or properties of agriculture in any country, whether decisions or plans for individual farms are mostly by individual managers or by administrative planners at various levels of regional and central administration. The same general model can or does apply to an individually owned farm in Canada, a state farm in the U.S.S.R., a cooperative farm in Hungary, a rented farm in England, or a subsistence farm in India. The problem is not one of the applicability of modern models to farms in these different environments but of specifying or formulating the model in a manner which is consistent with the planning environment and market conditions surrounding agriculture, the unique restraints of the farm, the objective function which is applicable in the particular case, and the activities (enterprises, technologies, and transactions) which are appropriate.

SIMILARITY OF MODELS UNDER DIFFERENT OBJECTIVE FUNCTIONS

While objectives for farms operated under dissimilar conditions do vary, the difference does not negate the explicit or implicit existence of an objective function. It means only that the weights in the function are of a different nature. The existence of different types of weights does not invalidate any other properties, relationships, and functions of planning or optimizing models. In a general model of the farm, production functions for each commodity exist whether agriculture is socialized and planned completely from above or whether it is of a capitalistic economy with plans made by individual managers. Costs, scarcity values, and/or limited quantities of resources exist in both cases. The mathematical and economic conditions under which the objective function is maximized are identical; hence the same general knowledge and data are needed for planning. The existence of different types and magnitudes of weights in the objective function does not alter the fact that all farms, regardless of the social and economic organization of agriculture, can be represented by a set of equations in which (a) the left-hand sides represent a vector of resource supplies or other constraints, defining the maximum and minimum quantities of commodities which the farm can or must produce, while (b) the right-hand sides contain technical coefficients of requirements for these resources and restraints, multiplied by variables representing the commodities to be produced, the technologies to be used, or the transactions to be conducted by the farm. The assignment of values to the variables on the right-hand sides of the equations to maximize the objective function, given the parameters represented by the technical coefficients, the restraints of the left-hand sides, and the weights of the objective function, is precisely the same activity for an optimal plan of a state farm, a collective farm, or an individual entrepreneur. The mathematical steps in attaining the optimal plan and the mathematical and economic conditions which define it are exactly the same. In this sense, formal planning models directed towards optimization of an objective function are the same for all farms whether they are directed by planners or oriented to the market, relate to socialized or private agriculture, are big or small, or have other differentiating conditions and characteristics.

It is this fact which causes the current symposium to have broad interest and important implications. While we come from countries with different economic and social organizations of agriculture, we can study, perfect, and adapt the same set of tools because they are generally applicable in all countries. And these general models will have interest and application for planners and managers in other countries with still different agricultures, because they have universal applicability.

There are obvious differences in the agricultures of the countries represented by participants in the seminar. Some agricultures are composed only of private farms, some mostly of state farms, and some have a mixture of socialized and private farms. Recently or still, the major planning for farms in some countries has been highly centralized, even if only at the district level but usually with balances passed down to the district from central planners. The response at the farm level then is to aggregate or national plans. In other countries, planning is purely decentralized and the aggregate response at the national level is to that of many individual planners. For the agricultures of some countries the prices which serve as weights in the objective function are expressions directly from consumers reflecting their desires of how resources should be used to maximize utility from scarce resources. For other agricultures the prices for the same purpose are informal estimates (but ordinarily with some empirical basis in attempt to simulate a restricted market) by central planners, administrators, and clerical workers of the relative magnitudes which will balance the output of farms with demand quantities of consumers. Under certain national planning procedures, especially where food supply tends to be light relative to demand, minimum delivery or acreage quotas are provided every farm as a spinoff from the national or central plan. In countries where food supply is large relative to market demand, farms may have upper limits or quotas reflecting national agricultural policies.

These variations provide different environments of farm planning among countries for adapting models. However the principles of optimization are the same in mathematical steps of computation, in mathematical specification of optima, and in specification of the economic or marginality conditions which define an optimal use of resources. The problem of efficient planning is not of the models per se, but of ability to obtain appropriate data and adapt universal planning models and principles to the farm environment so that they serve most appropriately. The optimization principle for a farm operated under a particular social objective and economic environment is the same whether price weights are reflections directly from consumers, or indirectly as judgments of administrators. The dominance, among nonphysical constraints, of minimum restraints in some cases and maximum restraints in other countries does not change the general method. A farm with a minimum obligatory quota for wheat in Poland simply has an additional relation or equation specified for its planning model, just as does a farm with an upper quota for wheat in Canada or milk in the United States. In the first case, with the minimum restraint on the left-hand side, the sign of the relation is $\geq$; in the second case, the sign is $\leq$. The relation for the first will be converted to an equation by the addition of a variable x_j with a coefficient of -1; the relation for the second becomes an equation with addition of variable x_j having a coefficient of +1. True, these are differences, but they are of arithmetic details rather than scientific conceptualization in the process of specification and application of models.

These same differences in arithmetic detail and model specification exist even within countries. They are of the same order as variations in technical coefficients to express differences in soil and climatic conditions; or to represent lower and upper bounds on acreages of various crops to maintain soil productivity, prevent alkalinity, or conform with the preferences of the manager. The range in types of models, and variations of each of these to reflect the unique natural, economic, sociological, and geographic environments of individual farms, needs to be equally as great within countries as between countries. Since this is true, the expert analyst who is acquainted with and applies modern farm planning and decision models in one country should be able to do so equally well in any other country.

Regionalism does not negate the efficacy of modern models as either conceptual or practical tools in farm planning. Regionalism, however, evidently has somewhat conditioned the terms used in describing characteristics or application of models. Linear programming is a rather universally accepted term and connotes exactly the same model and approach in all countries. But we still find that such terms as program planning, budgeting, mathematical methods, econometrics, systems of balances, marginality, and resource allocation to have provincial meanings and connotations. Over the long run, as a further step to reflect the universality of modern scientific methods for planning and decisions, it would be useful if we could develop a common set of terminology and notation. Especially for young scholars, this step not only would hasten the understanding of the models and principles but also would better emphasize the broadness of their application.

COMMONALITY OF MODELS WITH
APPROPRIATE SPECIFICATIONS

The equivalence and modification of planning models at the farm level can be further emphasized with illustrations. Since there is some objective for all farms, weights or criteria must exist to evaluate approach or optimization of this objective. Since all farms have some limited resources to be transformed into a finite set of commodities and transactions at rates defined by alternative technologies, a programming model which applies under one condition of farming also applies or can be adapted under other conditions. Consider the collective farm in Czechoslovakia or the family farm in Holland where each has limited land, labor, and capital resources. (We could consider the limited capacity of buildings, power units, and machinery. However we "keep our problem small" by not doing so at this point.) The collective farm has a limited supply of labor represented by that available in the village; the family farm by that represented in the family. (Both might hire seasonal labor, with an activity specified accordingly.) For simplicity, suppose that each farm produces only wheat and potatoes. At this stage in model specification the resource restrictions and the feasible set of plans will be similar for both, as represented by A in Figure 2.1, even though the magnitude of the i-th resource represented on the collective farm is r_i times that represented on the family farm. Initially, with only the three resources constraining feasible plans, the planning possibilities are those of A in Figure 2.1 where the location of the resource restraints for the collective farm extend over the commodity plane by r_i times those for the family farm. With the requirement on feasible plans that

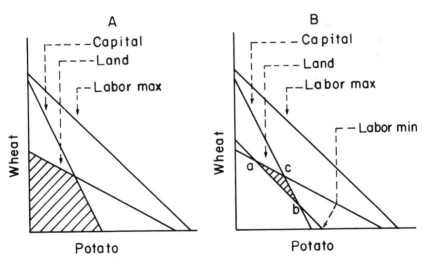

Fig. 2.1. Feasible planning sets with (A) maximum restraints only and (B) minimum and maximum restraints.

$$s_i \geq \sum_j a_{ij}x_j \text{ and } x_j \geq 0 \tag{1}$$

we denote (a) that the requirements of the plan for the i-th resource, s_i (as reflected in the sum of products of technical coefficients, a_{ij}, multiplied by the quantity of the jth commodity, x_j) cannot exceed the availability of the i-th resource, and (b) no variable or commodity can be negative. With only land and capital providing upper bounds on possibilities, the set of feasible plans is that represented by the shaded area in Figure 2.1A. While the farm plan or value of variables at the origin is feasible, we have economic interest only in the other three corner or extreme points of the set bounded by the land and capital restraints. If the weights in the objective function are c_w and c_p, respectively, for wheat and potatoes, representing perhaps net prices or coefficients expressing the caloric content of each product, the optimal or maximizing plan will include (a) only potatoes if the ratio $c_p c_w^{-1}$ is greater than the slope of the capital restraint, (b) only wheat if $c_p c_w^{-1}$ is less than the slope of the land restraint, or (c) the combination of wheat and potatoes denoted at the intersection of land and capital restraints if $c_p c_w^{-1}$ has a value between the two slopes. The quantity for the family farm will always be an r_i^{-1} proportion of that for the collective farm, but the two farms will have the same plan in terms of the mix of the two products for a given $c_p c_w^{-1}$ ratio if we assume constant returns to scale for each resource transformed into each commodity. (While production elasticities different from unity are realistic, especially for capital, we need not deal with this problem at the moment.) The same arithmetic or computational technique will define the optimum plan for either farm, even if c_w and c_p refer to prices for one farm and food quantities for the other.

We can examine other characteristics of the planning environment, to illustrate further the applicability and modification of given models when other facets are added to the planning problem. Now suppose that a required employment restraint is added for the collective farm and is represented by the minimum labor isoquant in Figure 2.1B where other resource isoquants are the same as in Figure 2.1A.[1] The set of feasible plans then becomes the smaller shaded area in Figure 2.1B. The number of feasible plans has been shrunk greatly since the shaded area in Figure 2.1B is smaller than that in area 2.1A. Too, it is apparent, even for extreme ranges of the ratio $c_p c_w^{-1}$, the farm will always be forced to produce a mix of the two commodities represented at points a, b, or c

---

1. Alternative commodities, such as livestock in comparison with crops, would be more relevant in practical application to indicate restraints providing minimum employment levels for workers. Also, we would expect that labor restraints should be defined by periods of the year to provide employment minima. In some cases, one product may provide employment in January but the second will not. In this case, the minimum employment restraint will be perpendicular to the axis of the relevant commodity. A similar minimum employment restraint in another period for the second product will result in a rectangular feasible set of plans in the "middle" of the commodity plane, bounded on the lower sides by the two minimum employment restraints and on the upper sides by the restraints of labor availability. Other maximum and minimum labor restraints would "fall between" this rectangular set and the type illustrated in Figure 2.2B.

(depending on whether $c_p c_w^{-1}$ is, respectively, smaller than the slope of the land line, greater than the slope of the capital line, or between these two levels). If $c_p c_w^{-1}$ is smaller than the slope of the land restraint or greater than the slope of the capital line, the objective function for the farm would always be greater if the employment restraint were not included. In other words, the farm would have a greater payoff with less work.[2] We have, then, one of those rare welfare economic situations where all members could be made better off (more product or products would be available for distribution) through a broader opportunity in plans and the aggregate welfare of the cooperative farm necessarily would be increased. If the ratio $c_p c_w^{-1}$ accurately reflects consumer preference for the two products, consumers also will have higher utility in the absence of the minimum employment restraint. (Not every labor or employment minimum forces more work with a smaller farm payoff, but there are numerous conditions under which they do.)

Other minimum restraints also may be provided the collective farm. Suppose it is given a minimum delivery goal of op of potatoes and ow of wheat, as in Figure 2.2A. The vertical line originating at p is the new lower bound for potatoes and horizontal line originating at w

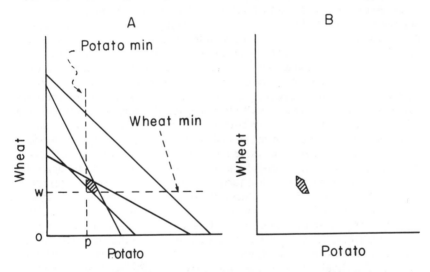

Fig. 2.2. Feasible planning set with wheat and potato minimum restraints.

2. The level of payoff (profit or food production, depending on the objective function) without the employment restraint would be denoted by an isopayoff line intersecting the wheat axis at the same point as the land restraint line while the income level with the employment restraint is denoted by an isopayoff line tangent to point a. The labor required without the minimum employment restraint would be denoted by an isolabor line of the same slope as the isoemployment line but intersecting the wheat axis at the same point as the land restraint line. In this case the payoff without the restraint is higher and the labor input is smaller without the employment restraint. The same would be true for an isopayoff line (objective function) with a slope such that it denotes an optimum by intersecting the potato axis at the same point as the capital restraint.

is the new one for wheat. With other restraints remaining the same as in Figure 2.1B, the two new minimum restraints cause the convex set of feasible plans to be the shaded area in Figure 2.2A. Or, if we lift this set of feasible plans out by itself, abstracting it from irrelevant portions of isorestraint lines which denote nonfeasible values of variables, the planning set is that represented in Figure 2.2B. The optimal plan falls at one of the three "upper corners," depending on the ratio of $c_p c_w^{-1}$ for the objective function, although any point within the boundaries of this convex set represents a feasible plan. The set of feasible plans now is much smaller than the initial set in Figure 2.1A, a general result in adding minimal restraints. The manager of the farm now has a larger mathematical problem before him (more corners in the set) but he is faced with a smaller set of feasible plans than in Figure 2.1B and a much smaller set than in Figure 2.1A. The optimal feasible plans in Figure 2.2B denote an even smaller objective function than those in Figure 2.1B if the ratio $c_p c_w^{-1}$ is greater than the slope of the capital restraint and less than the slope of the land restraint.

Yet the optimizing principle for the feasible plans of Figure 2.2B is the same as for those in 2.1B and 2.1A. (The solution, geometrically apparent, is denoted by tangency of an isopayoff line with the slope $c_p c_w^{-1}$ to one of the three corners on the "upper side" of the shaded area or feasible set, in this simple problem.) And the same general planning set may characterize choices available to an individual or private farm manager operating mainly in a market economy. He may arbitrarily decide to produce a minimum of one or more products because he "likes to grow them" (as may also the manager of a collective or state farm). He also may select such minima because of weather and price uncertainty and his aversion to risk. (A stochastic model relating to minimum income variance or an optimal proportion of stability and income might then be a more relevant planning model.) Or he may sign a contract with a food processor for minimum delivery of one or more commodities. Under these conditions the specification of the model for the individual farm will be the same as for a collective or state farm which has administratively imposed lower bounds for some products. The process of specification and the principle of optimization then is the same for the individual farm as for the collective farm in Czechoslovakia or the state farm in U.S.S.R. The addition of the minimum restraints does not change the method, only the specification of the model. Hence it adds to the challenge in model construction.

In simple illustration of the equivalence or adaptation of planning models for farms whether operated under individual, cooperative, or state orientation, emphasis has been on physical, institutional, contractual, and social restraints. While the feasible plan set is altered by addition of restraints, the principle of optimization is the same whether the goal is food production, profit, or other payoff measures. From a social standpoint the relevant problem in national planning or policy frequently is the ratio of the weights in the objective function, $c_p c_w^{-1}$, and how they are determined. The organization and direction of agriculture in some countries calls for different weights for the same commodity on a given farm. An example is different prices for obligatory delivery, contract delivery, and free market sales in Poland. Certain price policy programs such as those in the United States also result in different prices for the same commodity on the individual farm. Again, such modifications do not change the basic nature or application of a planning model; they only change its specification so that the operational model is consistent with the environment of application. The adaptation of models to meet these conditions is the same for individual farms operating in a market economy, or collective and state farms operating under administered price constants.

In fact one general model can be devised which can conform with an individual farm operating under market prices or state and collective farms. To cover all of these organizations and the fact that some or all of such farms may operate under market, obligatory, or contract prices, we can state a general objective function as

$$\phi = C'X = C_1'X_1 + C_2'X_2 + C_3'X_3 \tag{2}$$

where C_1 is a subvector of obligatory prices, C_2 is a subvector of contract prices, C_3 is a subvector of market prices, and $C' = (C_1'\ C_2'\ C_3')$. For the individual farm operating only under market prices, the model applies with $C_1 = 0$, $C_2 = 0$, and $C_3 \neq 0$. For a collective or other farm which operates under all three types of prices, none of the price subvectors is null. If sales are all under obligatory delivery, then $C_2 = C_3 = 0$. The system of relations representing production possibilities is

$$AX \leq S, \text{ or } \begin{bmatrix} A_{11} & A_{12} & A_{13} \\ A_{21} & A_{22} & A_{23} \\ A_{31} & A_{32} & A_{33} \end{bmatrix} \begin{bmatrix} X_1 \\ X_2 \\ X_3 \end{bmatrix} \leq \begin{bmatrix} S_1 \\ S_2 \\ S_3 \end{bmatrix} \tag{3}$$

where A is the matrix of technical coefficients, X is the vector of activity levels, and S is the vector of resource restraints which are partitioned as shown to the right; A_{11} and S_1 are submatrices conforming with X_1, a subvector of activities for obligatory delivery; A_{22} and S_2 conform with X_2, a subvector of activities for contractual delivery; and A_{33} and S_3 conform with X_3, a subvector of activities sold at market prices. For all farms where $i \neq j$, we have $A_{ij} = 0$. For a farm with obligatory and contract deliveries, $A_{11} = I$, $X_1 = S_1 \neq 0$, $A_{22} = I$, and $X_2 = S_2 \neq 0$. For a farm responding only to market prices, $S_1 = 0$ and $S_2 = 0$. Formulated in this fashion with a subvector S_i in S_3 to represent minimum output or employment levels but where $S_i = 0$ for the individual farm without these lower bounds imposed on it, exactly this same model can be applied to the individual, collective, or state farm. (Computations can be saved, of course, by dropping all but A_{33}, X_3, and S_3 from the model of the individual farm.) In formulating the model, variables x_{i1}, x_{i2}, and x_{i3} representing the i-th product, respectively, for obligatory contractual and market prices and delivery can express the actual growing of the crop such as wheat; or they may represent only a sales or transactions activity for the crop while another element of X_3 represents the actual growing of wheat and has a -1 coefficient in an equation conforming to an element of S_3 representing the total supply of wheat produced on the farm.

Other details of a general model applicable to different economic and social organizations of farms could be outlined. However we have gone far enough to illustrate that planning models can be universal and that the organization of agriculture and farms in a particular country has no bearing on the general applicability of the models. The extent to which decisions are made by the farm manager or administrative planners will of course depend on the magnitudes of S_1. If $S_1 = 0$, all decisions are left to the individual manager, the farm responds only to the market, and the manager can assign "full" values to the x_{ij} of X_3 to conform with the resource restrictions in S_3. If the elements in S_1 $\equiv X_1$ are large, then the decisions are entirely by the administrative or off-farm planners and the farm manager only implements these plans. If the elements in S_1 are modest, then the farm manager has a greater range of values which he can assign to the x_{i3} in X_3 — his range of actual decision making is greater.

The linear programming or planning models discussed above can be formulated to accommodate all important variants of the individual farm and the economic and social organization of farms. There are of course numerous instances when a model which is quadratic in the objective function would be more applicable. Examples are large-scale individual farms operating under market demand and producing a highly specialized product consumed in the community and large state or cooperative farms supplying all or most of the milk or vegetables for a given city. Application of a model of this type requires quantitative estimates of the consumer demand functions in the relevant market. Otherwise it is general and applies equally to individual farms or those under collective and state operation.

MORE GENERAL MODELS

Mathematical programming models are quite general and do cover most of the relevant farm planning situations. Other more general models are less widely used (except for microprescriptions such as optimal fertilizer rates based on estimated production functions) because data in appropriate forms and quantities are not available. As time progresses, added data may allow application of more general models which consider technical relations in the vein of continuous production functions related to the magnitude of commodity output, rather than as constants unrelated (at least over a range) to output level. The more general models are conceptually equivalent for individual, collective, and state farms and can be stated as follows.

$$\pi = \sum_{i=1}^{m} p_i y_i - \sum_{j=1}^{n} p'_j x_j \tag{4}$$

$$y_i = f_i (x_{i1}, x_{i2}, \ldots, x_{ij}, \ldots, x_{in}); \ (j = 1, 2, \ldots, n) \ (i = 1, 2, \ldots, m) \tag{5}$$

$$\frac{\partial \pi}{\partial x_{11}} = p_1 \frac{\partial y_1}{\partial x_{11}} - p'_1 = 0, \ldots, \frac{\partial \pi}{\partial x_{1n}} = p_i \frac{\partial y_1}{\partial x_{1n}} - p'_n = 0$$

$$\vdots$$

$$\frac{\partial \pi}{\partial x_{i1}} = p_i \frac{\partial y_i}{\partial x_{i1}} - p'_1 = 0, \ldots, \frac{\partial \pi}{\partial x_{in}} - p'_n = 0 \tag{6}$$

$$\vdots$$

$$\frac{\partial \pi}{\partial x_{m1}} = p_n \frac{\partial y_n}{\partial x_{m1}} - p'_1 = 0, \ldots, \frac{\partial \pi}{\partial x_{mn}} = p_m \frac{\partial y_m}{\partial y_{mn}} - p'_n = 0$$

Equation (4) is an objective function where π is profit or other quantity to be maximized, y_i is the quantity of the i-th product, x_j is the quantity of the j-th resource, p_i is the price of the i-th commodity (or food or other coefficient of the i-th product where the goal is other than profit), and p'_j is the price per unit of the j-th resource. The objective function is maximized under the first-order conditions that

$$\frac{\partial \pi}{\partial x_{ij}} = p_i \frac{\partial y_i}{\partial x_{ij}} - p'_j = 0 \ \text{or} \ \frac{\partial y_i}{\partial x_{ij}} = p'_j \, p_i^{-1}$$

where both p'_j and p_i are constants or parameters for the farm.

We present this "general model" because as a concept it is equally relevant for agricultures dominated by individual, collective, or state farms. Perhaps it is even more useful for the highly planned economies of socialized countries, including state and collective farms, than in economies where farms operate under individual planning and market conditions. The model is significant since it emphasizes the marginal productivity of resources, a concept and quantity which has not frequently prevailed in farm planning generally but which should have even greater applicability for agriculture where planning is more from central managers or administrative origin and less by individual farm (and could even be expressed in some physical units of measurement). It also is significant since it emphasizes $p'_j \, p_i^{-1}$ as a relative weight which must be "determined" carefully to reflect resource scarcities and related to marginal resource productivities in prescribing the optimal plan and resource quantities to be used by individual farms. Finally, if we consider the "second-order conditions," that all second derivatives must be negative, we begin to analyze and pose questions of optimal farm size. This determination mostly is yet to be attained in farm planning for developed countries such as those we represent.

Under prevailing short-run conditions, farms do not have unlimited access to resources. Hence we can modify the objective function in (4) by placing a budget restraint, $\lambda \, (B - \sum_{j=1}^{n} p'_j x_j)$, on resource acquisition where λ is the La Grange multiplier and an optimal farm plan now uses the j-th resource and produces the i-th product in quantities such that the marginal productivity of the former used for the latter exceeds the ratio $p'_j \, p_i^{-1}$ by the proportion $1 + \lambda$, or for all resources and products:

$$\frac{\partial y_i}{\partial x_{ij}} = (1 + \lambda) \, p'_j \, p_i^{-1} \tag{7}$$

If the magnitudes of some x_j are given, as the supply of labor, land, and buildings available to the farm, then the production function in (5) will be estimated only for resources which are variable in supply and availability. The conditions of optimality specified in (6) still prevail regardless of the economic or social system and the structural organization of farms (restraints also can be placed on individual x_{ij} in this model).

Modifications of the model to accommodate limited resource supplies is worthy of mention because it emphasizes both conceptual and quantitative structures which also are important in interfarm planning and resource allocation. The concepts and conditions of the model, based on marginal productivities, probably are more relevant guides, even though the quantities may be available only in "rough" arithmetic form, in socialist or "centrally planned" agricultures than in capitalist or "decentrally planned" agricultures. This is true since quantities of certain resources such as machines and chemicals are usually given as fixed, and predetermined quantities are not distributed through market mechanisms but through administrative allocations. Hence, with a limited supply of fertilizer, at least for farms within regions where price and transportational differentials are unimportant, chemicals should be allocated among farms in the manner of (6) and (7). The objective function can be one of profit, or it can be one of food production with caloric or other nutritional weights, c_i, replacing p_i. Given different products and different farms among which the fixed supply of chemicals or other transferable resources can be used, some commodity and resource weights in an objective or criterion function are necessary. Otherwise there is no efficient means for planning of interfarm resource allocation as in the simple case of given supplies of fertilizer and machines. With a set of prices or other appropriate weights, expressing the relative value (utility) or scarcity of the different commodities, we have the combined problem of determining x_{ij}^g, the amount of the j-th resource (e.g., nitrogen) to be used for the i-th product, y_i^g, on the g-th farm. An optimal interfarm plan allocates the n fixed resources among the m products and r farms, so that the marginal productivity of

$$\frac{\partial y_i^g}{\partial x_{ij}^g} = (1 + \lambda) \, p'_j \, p_i^{-1} \tag{8}$$

x_{ij}^g (i.e., the marginal product of the j-th resource used in the production of the i-th product on the g-th farm) satisfied (8) for each farm. An optimal plan further requires that the budget restraint in the form of (9) be satisfied, where B is the total value to be allocated. Not

$$B - \sum_i^m \sum_j^n \sum_g^r p_j' x_{ij}^g = 0 \qquad (9)$$

only does this general model produce, against the given weights or prices prescribed for the area, the optimum allocation of material inputs among farms and crops, it also provides a numerical basis for the allocation of the fixed budget B among the different individual input categories, x_j. In overall central planning, this is a problem no less important than determining x_{ij}^g.

While the above is a preferred technique for determining the x_j and x_{ij}^g, the supply of each individual input category, x_j, is sometimes fixed for a period of years until more facilities can be built for fabrication. An adaptation of the above model and principle is then applicable and is meaningful at the present in some countries because the x_j values are given for the short run. We then have to plan the allocation of resources separately so that for each (the j-th) of the n resources fixed in supply but allocable among the m products and r farms:

$$x_{1j}^1 + x_{2j}^1 + \ldots + x_{1j}^2 + x_{2j}^2 + \ldots + x_{ij}^g + \ldots + x_{mj}^r = x_j \qquad (10)$$

With fixed supplies of each x_j and weights in the criterion function only expressed as the nutritive value of food, c_i, optimal interfarm planning requires that values of x_{ij}^g be established so that the given amount x_j is allocated as in (11) where c_i is the food (or price) weight for the i-th product in the region and k is an unknown constant to be determined. For certain forms of production functions

$$\frac{\partial y_i^g}{\partial x_{ij}^g} = k \, c_i^{-1} \qquad (11)$$

(i.e., linear partial derivatives), we could determine the optimal allocation of the given supply of the resource, x_j, simultaneously among all farms and products through solution (12) where M is a square matrix, containing an upper-left submatrix of mr rank with the coefficients of

$$MX = A \qquad (12)$$

x_{ij}^g from the mr individual equations (11), a bottom row of mr unit values and a zero, and a right-hand column containing mr unit values and a zero. The vector X contains mr elements x_{ij}^g and one element k, while vector A contains mr elements, constants, and one element for x_j.

The solution to this set of equations specifies the optimal interfarm plan or allocation, measuring[3] the amount of a particular resource of

---

3. While we expect prices to be approximately the same in small regions, comparisons among distant regions would imply variations in the c_j values. Or, in the context of a complete model, we would wish to insert demand functions for the weights.

fixed quantity, x_j, which should be allocated to each crop, x_{ij}^g, and farm, $\sum_n^m{}^g x_{ij}$.

This type of model applies equally among soil types within a farm in countries where allocative decisions are the function of the individual manager, or among farms of a region in countries where allocative decisions are the function of administrative planners. While the vast void in data does not allow its application to all farm resources, the concept and procedure are practical and operational for such inputs as fertilizers where the farm or country has a limited quantity to allocate and some useful estimates of functions are now being generated. Some restraint in knowledge will keep such procedures from being used widely for some time. Hence we are likely to turn to programming models, using constants to represent marginal productivities and neglecting the fact that while we should know the marginal productivities, we do not. Yet it is extremely important to keep such conceptual models before us. We are reminded that we need the marginal productivities if we are to have any precise form of resource allocation and interfarm plans. Biological and physical research then can be organized to provide data so badly needed for both interfarm and individual farm allocations and decisions. We also are reminded that the general concepts are highly useful and could and should be used in planned allocations to farms even where the estimates are "rough" and are expressed as arithmetic increments. While the terminology and conceptual importance of these marginal quantities are not widely understood by government administrators in charge of allocating supplies of fertilizer, machinery, and other inputs among farms, they must either (a) implicitly and unwittingly use the concept or (b) have no economically systematic basis for the allocation.

Again, we can point out the equivalence of these more general models in planning both farms of capitalist countries with managers oriented to market response and farms of socialist countries with allocations oriented towards administrative decisions. The fact that market prices serve as the weights, c_i, in the first case while administratively specified prices or quantities serve as the weights in the other case does not negate the equal applicability of the concepts to the two organizations of agriculture. While the functions and coefficients are not widely available for the overall application of such general models, they now are becoming available in some countries for smaller allocation problems (such as those relating to fertilizer response and supplies). Until the time of "sufficient availability," however, general models are useful overall constructs within which approximations such as linear models can be applied. The evolution of programming models, as they progress from those of purely linear relationships to those with quadratic properties, will always be towards the general models. And this evolution will be equally useful for policies and planning of agriculture for either market-oriented individual farms or administratively directed socialized farms.

The models we have used in discussing their equivalent applicability among different social and economic organizations of agriculture appear complicated in structure and data needs. Actually they are overly simple relative to real world problems of farm planning (but are more realistic than the simple systems of budgets and balances). They omit entirely those important interperiod problems which relate to the development, growth, and uncertainty of farms. Conceptually these models can be rather easily extended, under either private or socialized farms, from the "static" base in planning outlined above. However they quickly expand in algebraic, arithmetic, and computational scale as variables and equations are dated for different plan periods and transfer restraints. Several categories of "continuous function" models and dynamic or recursive programming models can be formulated to accommodate plans relating to time and farm development. Yet, aside from previously illustrated modifications in equations and variables to conform with particular resource, institutional, sociological, and economic variations, specific models are equally appropriate for dynamic planning of individual, collective, or state farms or for farms under any other organization of agriculture. So too are models which incorporate stochastic properties to cope with problems of variability in weather, demand, and similar phenomena.

REGIONAL AND INTERREGIONAL PLANNING

Interregional allocation and competition prevails in agricultures of both individual and central planning. In market-oriented and individually planned agricultures, farms in each region compete with each other and with farms of other regions. Market forces reflecting price equilibrium, transportation rates, and the corresponding interregional price differentials cause comparative advantage eventually to prevail in the spatial allocation of agricultural products and resources. The plan of one farm is not linked quantitatively to that of farms in other regions. Yet effort is made by the public (through communication media, economic analysis, and extension education programs) to share knowledge of developments and potentials with farmers of other regions so that adjustments can be adapted accordingly in the market-enforced interregional meshing of farm plans. Obviously the adjustment occurs only with a distributed lag in the plans of individual farmers. Hence economists have long sought quantitative means of predicting interregional interdependencies and a forward means of guiding adjustments among regions. The first major empirical attempt in this direction was by Black and others.[4] Rather simple budgeting techniques were used, wherein an "improved plan" was made up for each individual farm in a sample. The results then were aggregated to provide indications of

4. See Mighell, R. L., and Black, J. D. *Interregional Competition in Agriculture* (Cambridge, Mass.: Harvard Univ. Press, 1951).

regional response and supply functions. This study, initiated in the 1930s, was until the 1950s the only quantitative one linking plans and response of market-oriented farms in one region with those of another region. With the advent of programming models and computers, the attempt was taken up more vigorously, and numerous locational and interregional models have been made operational. Applied to agricultures of individually planned farms, the purpose of these studies has been projection of supply possibilities, estimating production potentials, prescribing the optimal spatial distribution of production to improve efficiency or lower public costs, analyzing interregional competition, etc. In some linear programming models, such as those we relate in Chapter 12, entire regions serve as the producing units for which variables or activities are specified and resource restraints are defined. Linked by transportation matrices and demand variables and restraints, optimal interregional allocations of production and commodity flows have then been computed. In a somewhat contrasting model, optimal plans also have been estimated for samples of farms of individual regions, with these then aggregated to provide regional estimates for a number of regions. While the models could so serve, they have not yet been applied in specifying and analyzing interrelationships among regions.

A third type of model combines the above two, with restraints and activities defined both for "samples" of farms and for the regions which they compose. Most models have represented food demand by regions as a "bill of goods," wherein fixed demand restraints are equated with supply (generated internally or by imports). Some models have used only soil types by regions as producing restraints. Others have used land, labor supplies, and capital items of individual farms as the restraints limiting the magnitude of production activities. Because of the sheer size of any interregional model, most models have been static and refer to a given production period or year. Some smaller models, applied to a single region, have been of multiperiod nature, usually with recursive characteristics and restraints used to limit the rate of change among years. Finally, as we outline in Chapter 12, quadratic models incorporating demand functions into the objective equation (with price and demand quantities determined endogenously along with supplies for producing and consuming regions) are now possible.

These programming models, prescribing an optimal interregional distribution of production, land use, and commodity flows, have not been used to impose or implement plans for individual farms of regions. Rather they are used to forecast and interpret optimal or likely shifts among regions. Mechanisms of extension education then are used in influencing farmers to adapt production and resource use accordingly. In a few instances the interregional models have been used to suggest national policies with interregional implications.

Models designed for these purposes in countries of individually planned farms have equal or greater applicability in countries of administratively planned farms. In the latter countries there has always been some allocation of national targets or balances among regions, and then to farms. This allocation, based on traditional balances and allocating methods at the national and district level, represents active interregional plans and planning. However the traditional methods (a few programming models have been applied) are unable to handle effectively the many interrelationships and interdependencies of the large number of agricultural regions and subregions of any country.

While the methods of implementation differ, the quantitative interregional models which best serve (a) as guidance for individual farmers in countries where response is a function mainly of the market through individual planning and (b) for interregional allocation of production targets in countries of central plan specification, appear to be equally applicable. The formal models, such as those outlined in Chapter 12, are important in both cases because they provide a quantitative base for the large-scale computations necessary in full expression of simultaneous interrelationships among producing and consuming regions. The conventional methods of analysis, planning, and allocation based on traditional balances and budgeting methods, just do not have the scope and capacity to handle enough endogenous relationships on a sufficiently large and realistic interregional basis. While the past could be survived with conventional methods, the future can be improved greatly through development and application of modern models.

Optimal for both types of agriculture would be a model which incorporates empirically estimated supply and demand functions by regions and transportation equations. The model then could be solved for equilibrium prices and quantities by regions, as well as resource and commodity flows among regions. In the framework of a competitive market it also would specify the optimal or least-cost distribution of production on a spatial or interregional basis. The empirical problem, of course, is that of obtaining appropriate regional estimates of demand and supply functions. Based on time series regression models, assuming proper identification of the relationships involved, the demand estimates may be fairly reliable for future predictions, but we expect to have problems with supply shifters. The availability of data also diverts effort from this type of detailed regional analysis. (Time series data are available on a civil basis rather than in terms of other more meaningful spatial characteristics of consuming and producing regions.) If these obstacles in estimation could be overcome, the general model would be equally as relevant in a socialist as in a capitalist economy. It would solve directly the problem of interregional balances, product allocation, and transportation flows. Too, it implies knowledge of consumer demand functions, which is no less important in a socialist than in a capitalist economy if maximum welfare or utility of consumers is to be approached. Supposing the supply function expresses the same, it is as useful for planners to know the supply response of managers on state and collective farms in a socialist economy as to know the aggregate supply response of individual farmers in a capitalist economy.

However this detail in knowledge by regions is not in prospect for any country or economy. If we turn to "next best" alternatives without knowledge of demand functions, the model which immediately presents itself is interregional linear programming which supposes a "fixed bill of goods" for national and regional demands. Models of this type have great relevance for policy and planning in all highly developed countries where price and income elasticities of demand are low. They are especially relevant in countries of central planning where the traditional system of balances, computed against a given per capita quantity of each product, is used. The linear programming model simply retains this formulation of demand, but it can improve greatly the specification of interregional product allocation and transport distribution (even with the data now used in the traditional system of balances).

Such models are equally applicable between the two types of economies for the majority of analyses and planning now conducted on a national and interregional basis. However there are "better than" alternatives in programming models, with equal potential applicability in the two economic systems. The first step away from a purely linear model, including fixed regional food demands, is one which incorporates demand functions in the objective equation to provide a nonlinear model. Certainly a rapid advance will occur with these types of models for agricultures where the targets of response are those implied in consumer preference and market prices. It is in this sense that they become highly relevant in socialist economies where current reforms call for an increased orientation of production to consumer demand. They may be more applicable for these purposes than for policies in countries where agricultural production already is mainly market oriented and planning is by individual farmers. Adoption of these models implies intensive work on demand function estimates. Some knowledge of demand functions does exist in socialist countries. The application of arithmetic balances, and previous knowledge of apparent "overages" and "underages" in the product mix relative to consumer requests or pressures, implies some knowledge of demand functions relative to price response. (Most demand function estimates in socialist countries are based on household surveys or budget data and reflect mainly income elasticities and demographic variables.) However this knowledge does not provide "workable quantities" which can be inserted into a quadratic model for solving equilibrium prices and quantities, the allocation of production among regions, and the transportation of outputs to consumer destinations which is unique to a country. Application of full-scale quadratic programming models as a major planning tool, to ascertain national equilibrium or balances and interregional or spatial allocations, will require estimation of demand functions with emphasis on price variables as well as those of income, population, age, and sex. These types of demand estimates can be obtained only from time series data accumulated over a sufficiently long period to adequately reflect consumer response to price variations.

Equality of potential application and usefulness seems to exist in socialist countries where central planning has dominated but economic reforms are directed toward more market orientation, and in capitalist economies where production and consumption is already so oriented. Problems of data and model formulation exist in both. The urgency and task of improving data on the demand side is greater in socialist countries, since they already are available in more detail in the market-oriented countries. The task of improving data on the production side may be greater in capitalist countries, since a vast amount of data on a farm-by-farm and region-by-region basis has been accumulated in socialist countries.

NATIONAL AND OTHER MODELS

Other planning and decision models could be examined as they relate to different organizations of agriculture. Strategies are used to meet uncertainties of weather and other phenomena at both the farm and national levels in both capitalist and socialist countries. Because of the smaller sample in time and space available to them, managers of individual farms in both cases must use different strategies than those possible at the national level. As well as conventional approaches to lessen yield and income variance, individual managers could employ stochastic programming and game theoretic models to select strategies under the assumption of absolute uncertainty. Such models may be applied easier on individual farms of socialist countries because the main uncertainty is in yields, prices typically being reflected as parameters from central administrators.

Yield variance is the main uncertainty at the national level of all countries since regression models or central planning can provide sufficiently accurate predictions on rates of technological advance, population growth, and income advance. While my knowledge is not complete, I believe no country has a sufficiently detailed and recent model for efficient storage policy. The interyear surpluses and shortages of the last decade provide empirical indication of this fact. Yet with the amount of yield and climatological data available to establish probabilities, the refined application of national models for these purposes would appear readily attainable in all countries of Europe and North America. The models would be equally as useful for national policies and plans in countries where the tendency is toward large production and low market prices for farmers and those where it is toward frequent short falls and higher prices or smaller supplies for consumers.

At the level of national planning and policy the two general approaches available are regression and programming models. The two can be welded together, of course, through quadratic programming models which incorporate demand functions. The programming models provide normative estimates of the best plan or policy to be followed. Regression models have the potential of predicting outcomes when different policies are implemented. The full range of models can be applied in capitalist countries where supply quantities, demand quantities, and equilibrium prices are determined simultaneously and endogenously

by the market. However in socialist countries where prices are given
as exogenously determined parameters, to which supply and demand
quantities may respond within the restraints of plans, national models
must rest largely on linear programming. Economic reforms directed
towards greater consumer orientation and manager supply response,
with simultaneous determination of market prices, eventually would
allow models which incorporate the endogenous variables, as well as
the exogenous set relating to population, age, climate, government policies, and the like. In fact such models are exactly those needed in reforms directed towards market orientation. However, even though ur-
gently needed for these purposes, the models cannot be implemented
until reforms have been in effect for a sufficient period to provide adequate time series observations.

PRESENT PROCEDURES AND POTENTIAL MODELS

As mentioned at the outset of this paper, planning and decision procedures are used at all levels of agriculture in all countries. The procedures used range from informal budgeting at the farm level to traditional systems of balances at the national level. These procedures, in
wide use, are highly informal in terms of economic principle and un-
systematic in terms of mathematical possibilities and computing capacities. For these reasons the traditional methods are greatly inefficient relative to the power of present-day planning and decision models.
While data are lacking for some of the more sophisticated models, the
data now being used for traditional methods can be converted and are
sufficient for the application of many modern models. The models
which can be applied with these data may not be optimal, but they can
provide better plans with the same data than can present arithmetic and
informal methods.

Chapter 2 ᏕᎿᎨ **DISCUSSION**

Tadeus Rychlik, *Institute of Agricultural Economics* (Poland)

P ROFESSOR HEADY'S ideal report can be properly considered to
disclose the subject of our whole seminar. He has explained the
basic principles of mathematical methods, of putting them into
practice, of projecting, and of decisions relating to objectives, from the
level of farming to the height of management factors. In this point of
view, mathematical methods are presented as some generalized patterns

which result in planning and universal maxima which are characterized as nonpolitical ones and remain far beyond any sociopolitical structure, and can become a decent terrace for our international meeting.

In such a case, one may say that it would be worthwhile to come together in organized encounters to exchange methods and models, using the properties and experiences of one another in order to gain mutual advantages. In addition, these factors allow "beyond sociopolitical structure" complexities in general projecting patterns and in the decision environment.

PRODUCTION PROCESS

An agricultural farm in any country has a simple rule: to realize some production, one needs not only farmland but a labor force and material production means (or their financial equivalents).

The contents of this rule concern the truth that all three factors appear as some quantitatively limited resources. So the organizers or farm operators' duties include joining resources in such a way that it becomes possible to purchase and, of most importance, to realize the objectives or designs of the economic farm.

This simple principle of economic activity is expressed in the equation,

$$\Sigma a_{ij} x_j \leq s_i$$

where a_{ij} means the amount of the i-th resource used per unit of the j-th activity, while x_j is the quantity of the j-th activity.

In the production process, some activity restrictions also may occur "from underneath" or "from upwards." They result most frequently from the combined moods of the farm unit or its connections with the "external world." These are the ordinary farm obligations such as contracts, compacts, and obligatory deliveries. The contents of these obligations depend on both a sociopolitical structure and on the socialized farming development. Therefore they may be highly differentiated. However the mathematical recording will follow the same pattern:

$$\Sigma a_{ij} x_j \geq s_i$$

It is most evident, as has been rigidly pointed out by Professor Heady, that the more there are of such limitations, the less freedom and independence in choice will exist. Consequently there will be a lessened field of competition among some activities. It must be said here that if those limitations have a real influence on the choice of activities, they also would cause a lessened value of some optimized objective function.

As to the economic efficiency objective, one can mention that it seems to have entirely a structural character. It will probably present some reassuring of the maximum needs in a family farm, a maximum

of relevant benefits for the producer in a capitalist enterprise, the
maximal satisfying of the whole nation's necessities in a socialistic
economy, and/or some other aims of more limited nature with regard
to the concrete, variegated, and projected tasks or decisions.

If that objective has a quantitatively measurable character—or if it
can be evaluated by means of numbers and, in the case of a possibility
of weighting, taxing or appreciating the amount of a unit in the efficiency of the objective function—then we'll be able to perform some
choice between activities and be in a state of choice optimizing. Let us
note it in the form of an equation:

$$Z = \Sigma c_j x_j$$

It would appear to change among efficiencies (activities), the existence of weights, and objective function parameters. It has to be a
product of historical farming development. Subsistence farming which
does not partake in goods exchange or is detached from some market
also must meet a demand *in natura* of the most important and tradition-
formed needs of a family. It is not easy to speak here of mathematical
optimization. While one cannot, the clothes need requires flax cultivation, and consumption requires milk. Each need appears independently
here and it must be separately filled by production. Just as much as
distinct needs must be met, there also are mutual replacement objectives which must be realized. Evidently the individual needs can be accomplished in a larger or smaller degree, depending on the whole
farming level and on traditionally formed preferences. So subsistence
farming is followed by a gradual transformation in production structure. The development of goods exchange and the pecuniary economy
make possible a common denominator—prices or weights—expressing
the various needs of farm people which are stated for the individual
producers.

The ability to use some mathematical methods thus depends simultaneously on the separate (individual) farm development level and on the
general level of the economy. Furthermore the farm must have the
ability to participate in the goods-pecuniary economy (i.e., the family
farm must be fully included in the industrialized goods turnover). If the
gross national economy is not being developed to the extent of goods-
adjusted farms which serve the marketplace, the environment may not
exist for using these methods for capitalist farm enterprises and, above
all, for the largest socialistic farm enterprises.

Let us return to the objective function. If one could pass over the
tasks of the above limited, partial, activity sphere and of the responding
fragmentary objective functions for the farm enterprise as a whole, then
probably the most suitable measure is the maximization, in this or in
another way, of the clear gain profitability, and so on. One can refer
to it, I think, in both capitalistic and socialistic enterprises. However
it does not mean at all that the aims of those two antagonistic structural
field enterprise types are identical, or that the socialistic enterprises
are realizing the capitalistic production aims.

This is simply to say that each society, irrespective of sociopolitical structure, for an enlargement of its productiveness and production possibilities and to develop production beyond limited activity spheres, has to attain a surplus value of production (in respect to material goods) over production costs and relevant consumption of material outlays. The scale of such an excess appears to be some peculiar reflection of the total labor (living and materialized) engaged in the production process. The policies (structures) differentiate among them with respect to surplus according to whom it belongs, who is disposing of it, and for what objective it is destined. (I am making appropriately some abstraction of the concrete rule to reckon with that surplus in programming; otherwise I would deal with it in a more generalized manner.) Profit maximization in a capitalist enterprise seems to be, in some measure, a natural for that enterprise or production scope. There are perhaps some enterprises not characterized by immediate gain maximization. They are, however, merely an exception. There exists nevertheless some doubt connected with an optimum projection in a capitalist-socialist political structure. A farm's plan resists (stands) against the projectionless market. There seems to exist a determined correlation between an enterprise and the "outside (external) world," called here "a symbolical market." Not only does the enterprise depend on the environment but it helps to form it. The optimum plan is delineated according to some optimum fitting of an enterprise to an external environment (saying in a simplified way, to a market). If it can be done by a single socialist enterprise, it will derive significant profit from it. However the market situation, expressing demand and prices, is adapted to the nonoptimally organized enterprises. The infrastructure adjusts to such enterprises. In case all enterprises adequately tune their farms and establish the optimum production plan, then of course the demands and market price must be changed and the plans and the production organization will automatically have become nonoptimal. Knowledge of some production (supply) and demand functions does not provide any solution even in such a case. If the functions were known, the market background still is composed of a disorganized and separately acting producer mass.

A similar question can be posed in capitalistic countries. Taking this phenomenon into formal consideration here, one could state this problem to be even more severe there, not for a producer and to the state but to a society. The price system in the socialistic countries has been formed, in a significant degree, by decisions of central planning organs. Prices in this case are of a stabilized character.

Mass socialist enterprises adjusting themselves to the drastic use of all the preferences in this price system would cause some market perturbations. In socialism, however, such a threat seems to be more potential than actual, for there are influences and methods beyond market variables which press on the producer's decisions. If those methods are not yet used enough, they can be under some realized need.

Under socialistic economic conditions, there steps forth a

somewhat different difficulty. The farm enterprise objective function is one of meeting maximum social needs. It means, in practice, gaining the maximum surplus above outlays on consumption; that is, expressed in respect to some value, the maximum of the otherwise established aim of clear profit, or the like. It concerns, of course, the maximum in the gross national economy, not the enterprise scale only. If the sum of partial maxima is equal to the whole maximum, the cause has a simple character. It would be satisfied if each enterprise realized its optimum plan and their sums gave the optimum gross national economy plan, but so far this is not true. Therefore the connection problem between the plans of some enterprises and the central plan appears of most importance.

Hence one observes a strong interest in the field of optimum locational production methods and in being able to institute some solution. I will return to this subject later.

The above questions are a part of more generalized uncertainty of planning conditions. In the planning of production proportions, we do not know the concrete market situation for which we are forming this plan. The uncertainty around planning conditions not only relates to some unrestrained and spontaneous price changes but also to powerful changes in production partly related to climatic conditions. This uncertainty bound to climatic conditions depends, among others, on the intensity level and on technological farm culture, and not on social structure. One could limit it by material insurance (reserves) or by the patterns used in undertaking buildings.

Fluctuating prices, as an uncertainty source, are important, mainly for capitalistic farm enterprises. The socialistic enterprises act, up to this moment, in the frames of a fixed price system. For this reason, the plan and the plan technique, taking into account or foreseeing price changes, are more understood and of greater interest in the capitalistic countries than in the socialistic ones.

In the near future, perhaps, when the supply for the majority of products exceeds local and export demands, there will be some unstable prices as well in the socialist countries.

We have been speaking till now about planning similarity, considered irrespective of different sociopolitical structures of countries and which result from the technoeconomical production conditions. It agrees with a simple static pattern; for instance, linear programming, the most frequently used and best understood of all. Now we will turn to the reproduction theme.

REPRODUCTION PROBLEM

In order to perform production processes in a continual and unceasing way, an enterprise has to reproduce all the production conditions (the production means, the labor force, some resources, the current ready money) in each production cycle. In case all the production conditions are reproduced at the same level as at the beginning of the production cycle, one can say that simple, natural, or disextended reproduction has been attained. If some extension of the production abilities occur, we can speak of an extended reproduction. The extended reproduction appears as an accumulation. The reproduction process is a dynamic one. Some internal transformations occur in techniques, organization, and enterprise economics.

In a capitalistic economy the extended reproduction basically takes place at the cost and billing of some individual who develops the enterprise. An enterprise evidently can derive some profit from interest paid outside. However it must arrange such credit. Appropriate production and financial patterns must be arranged (taking into account the durable and rotation means turnover, capital circulation, and an economically managed surplus share) for the reproduction process.

In a socialistic economy, reproduction in cooperatives occurs according to this same maxim. In the origin of some cooperatives the state authority supports some of the reproduction through endowments which do not have to be returned through the investment cooperative and the establishment of amortized debts. Nevertheless, when a farm is established and initial investing money has been provided, the further reproduction process ought to be led by the farm on its own account. In this way there also can be some financial accounts whose mathematical expression may be like those for a capitalistic enterprise, although the sociopolitical structure contents will be different.

Primarily, using such financial accounts, we reproduce the capitalistic enterprise and its capitalistic relations based on private production, means, and ownership principles; secondly, the socialistic cooperative farm with its proper social relations can be retained.

For state farms the enlarged, widened, and extended reproduction process takes place through the central budget like other state enterprises. The central budget encompasses the whole of state enterprise accumulation (and some part of the cooperative farms). At the center, a basic share is allocated among the various social needs and between many reproduction branches. Then, in such a way, limited resources are next divided in a "downstairs" fashion among the investment proposals of the enterprises who are endeavoring to move "upstairs." Hence, for state enterprises of many years standing, plans can be represented in simple, static production models having definite investment limits. By solving the optimum production structure, various investment possibilities can be considered and optimum investment directions can be determined. Various planning stages can be investigated in determining the optimum allocation of investment means. These problems are being solved by traditional planning methods under several alterable variants.

In the socialistic economy, need exists for elastic allocation or distribution patterns. The state farm organization is now endeavoring some self-dependent directions in enterprises enlargement, as well as use of outside investment sources and credits. One ought to suppose,

however, that there still will be some central distribution methods
which will require the usual patterns.

MAKING MACROSCALE PLANS

Planning at higher stages takes place permanently in socialistic
countries only. These plans are constructed at individual stages of the
state administration as one-year and multiyear plans. They relate to
relevant activities in economic life and use the political economy mechanisms. In respect to this principle, plans are of the normative character. Besides the normative plans contain economics fields, surren-
dering themselves immediately to the projected human efficiency. One
elaborates varied projections concerning elements of economic life
which in evident measure depend on powerful phenomena. One can designate the following kinds of projections: demographic, consumption
structure, migration of the labor force, agricultural structural changes,
market character (as those in the meat market sphere), foreign trade in
several products, and the like. The projections are being used in the
normative plans and also to adapt current regulation to the course of
economic life for attaining concrete decisions.

Under capitalistic conditions there are no possibilities for direct
planning of the whole national economy or even any of its sections.
Even if the plans are worked out, they have some projection features.
Administrative instructions with political economy aims, or with some
indications, can orient private producers in proposed development directions. This type of plan does not have normative characteristics.
This does not mean that an administration or some economic organization does not influence the course of life. To be sure, this political
economy process seems to be distantamount with planning. Through the
mechanisms (prices, credits, subsidies, finances, taxes) of the concrete
political economy, one influences decisions.

A plan has some concrete measurable nature. It determines magnitude or size and proportions, outlays, and their consequences. It has
to be inwardly conformable, not merely in the direction of activities but
also in immediate magnitudes of materials and services streams, processing power, energies, labor force, and so on. The objectives specify
the quantitative determined figures. Economic policies have none of
those features. Political economy methods rather delineate an activity,
adjusting it in terms of long-term objectives and assumptions on multiyear plan principles. The annual plans can be for implementation of
long-term political economy realization. Current policies are necessary over many years for performance.

In socialistic countries as well there is a determined economy direction, and plans can be its composition parts. This way there is no
absolute analogy between socialistic and capitalistic economies as concerns regional and land use planning. There are, however, many activities where one could profitably use the same or similar methods and

plans for undertaking decisions. For example, one could mention here such problems as the optimum reproduction enterprise, location of production and transport means, optimum stores locations, the optimization of individual agricultural products, mass goods transportation, adaptations in production stores, consumption center location, and the optimum magnitude of agricultural enterprises. Also there are common projection problems for short periods connected mainly with foreseeing the market situation. Examples are production and supply fluctuations (a typical example being meat), farm population and its professional and age structure, the farm structure (in socialistic agriculture it can concern the cooperatives), farm size, animal husbandry quantity and quality, and milk production.

For the examples given here there exists or have been elaborated more or less accomplished models which can be used in both capitalistic and socialistic countries. Thanks to this fact, for they possess and imply some processes and phenomena whose bases are determined by natural, technological, and structural meanings and phenomena. The essential model compositions can be identical, while the structural specification will vary with the economic development level or those traditions and customs which find their reflection in detailed adaptations to some concrete needs in establishing parameters and restraints. One can especially use common methodology for regional plans and for production location. I shall elaborate on both.

REGIONAL PROJECTS

Independent of more or less normative plans submitted in the national economy balance sheet, plans are being made (plans-studies) for chosen economic regions. Usually these regions have some specific features, deviate from the average, often are loaded with deficits in respect to agricultural production, or have rich agricultural soils but are in a disadvantageous economic situation, and so on. For such plans one makes research to solve major difficulties, specify investment directions, or outline optimal investment possibilities. These plans are elaborated for relatively long periods, as 15 to 20 years. They do not have a normative character. They are projections for which direction is given to development, types of expenses, political considerations, and economic variables. They consequently set guiding principles for policies of regional administration centers and an orientation for the central projecting organizations. These species of regional "plans-studies" are being worked out in both socialistic and capitalistic countries and surely also in "Third World" countries.

Preserving their several common variants, one could unquestionably use mathematical programming in an enlarged sphere for these problems. Some trials, experiments, and research investigations at least are being made in different countries.

One can state the existence of some definite possibilities for this

kind of problem. Not engaging in details or particulars, one could indicate the following (among others) directions.

1. Dealing with a region as if it were one farm of specified soils, material resources, and labor force. If both the technoeconomic parameters, as well as those for the objective function, are accepted
   for the whole region, some average coefficients can be used in which
   technological advance (progress) is taken into account. One can use,
   for instance, data from leading farms or highly realistic information
   concerning the region from abroad. Also certain rules and standards, elaborated by the scientific institutes or certain other factors,
   can be used. Yet one still must undertake a certain number of arbitrary decisions. Examples relate to the investment magnitudes,
   prices, the objective function, production maximization, cost minimization, and the like.
2. This model seems to be most simple. Its main deficiencies are the
   schematic stratagem toward a region, an exhorbitant (excessive) aggregation, and a limited information stock. One assumes here, as if
   passing over it in silence, that differentiated territories can develop
   at the same rate (thus allowing one to use some mediocre parameters).
3. One could likewise construct a dynamic model, simulating future regional development. Since the matrix of technoeconomic parameter
   transformations as yet seems not to be solved in a methodical way,
   one ought to look to a decade in programming and change the technological coefficient matrix in several periods, such as every five
   years. Nearer to real conditions would be a model in which we also
   take into account subregions, with different natural and economic
   features which influence the pace and direction of development. It
   would be a block matrix, in which the intersubregion connections
   would follow the form of a common block, implying some limitations
   for the whole region and a joint objective function. It would include
   transfer activities, production means, labor force relocation, and
   product transport.
4. One could also work out a version of this model through decomposed
   recognition of subregions and different enterprise sectors.
5. Finally one could elaborate a model on the basis of various farm
   types within the region. If one chose some admissible farm types,
   with parameters conforming to individual conditions or subregions,
   then we could designate not the sown area of the region or its production magnitude but the farm types. The separate farm types
   should be elaborated in such a way that they express the future of an
   economy. One could perform the task, for instance using future
   technoeconomic parameters or developing from present farm types
   some dynamic programming model.

AGRICULTURAL PRODUCTION LOCATION

The task here is in space location of a determined production relative to location of a definite requirement (demand). Under socialistic economic conditions these tasks are solved in every five-year plan. Under capitalistic economic conditions, the location patterns are characterized by projected plans and are performed most frequently as definite studies of scientific centers. Perhaps political economics specifies the approach in either case. In any case, programming of production location is giving rise to permanent interest among economists of both sociopolitical structures.

If one investigates publications devoted to this question all over the world, one cannot find any differences in model construction among countries. Existing models vary according to specific features connected with the economy of the given country or differentiations in economic organization. In the production location models in the socialist countries, known by me, one does not take into account either distance or transportation as forces affecting production location. This results from the fact that the agricultural products are destined for specific centers and are articles for industrial sale. In all market centers, irrespective of their distance from a center, equal prices prevail. As the state authority takes transportation costs on itself, these costs do not encumber the producer, and do not act on him as a force creating location phenomenon. In models worked out in the capitalistic countries, transportation plays an essential role. In patterns elaborated in capitalistic countries, one can find models based on the varied natural resources and objective functions.

I pass over existence of some regional prices for agricultural products, for instance in the Soviet Union, as they are stable within the limits of the given region and the other transport costs are their cause.

The difference results from some lack of confidence, entertained by some economists, towards the price system created by central planners. There are prevailing models which lean in whole on the value system and take into an account, in an objective function, product value maximization, clear income maximization, or cost minimization.

In those models formed in the United States one takes into account the more significant internal connections and proportions between the branches and production sections. These models are concerned not only with the location pattern but also with individual farms. However these models result not from structural causes, but from the traditional farming where specialization has not increased.

The production location models in capitalistic countries rest on some ideal assumptions of perfect competition among producers, on an acting market rationalization principle, and on correct information on production costs and sales conditions. These assumptions are unnecessary in a socialistic economy where production location projects can be used as the space plan variant, in some frame of the planned agriculture

management. Possibilities of practice realization undoubtedly bring a
great satisfaction to an economist working out an optimum pattern. But
it also sets before him a great responsibility, and for the economy it
seems to mean a determined risk. Therefore one is noting a tendency
for some "disenlargement" of that risk. For this reason the economists
of socialistic countries incorporate less elegance into the constructed
models, while they lay stress and set store by practical parts of the
problem; by the model realization possibility, by the possibility of receiving useful information, and by the adaptation of some theoretical
pattern to extremely complicated and actual economic life.

GENERAL VIEWS

Mathematical programming, as the basic method of a planning at
the farm level or higher stages, is not used in a mass manner in either
capitalist or socialist countries. Application of mathematical methods
should determine and undoubtedly result in some enormous progress.
One has to hope that some great economy or profits in socialistic countries, where the whole economy rests on the planning rules (bases) and
some implementation is performed as an economic practice, can be realized from these methods. More perfect plans, possessing more complicated connections of economic dependencies and expressing improved
economic objectives, ought to have a significant and positive influence
on the national economy. For this reason, one observes an increasing
interest in mathematical methods among managing organs of economic
life. Every year an enlarged number of enterprises are founding their
multiyear projects on the basis of linear programming results. But the
models are still simple, static ones. For use of dynamic programming,
one still lacks verified and working models; above all, scarcity of suitable and adequate information prevails.

The exchange of experiences, methods, results, and models among
countries is useful for us and for each other. The mathematical
methods are, as is known, of a "beyond structural" character, and those
used in one country can be used, developed, and adapted in other countries. It seems, indeed, of most importance to make practical use of
models already elaborated, and I suppose the main effort has to be
dedicated in this direction.

Correctable, generalized mathematical model formulation is merely
in the initial stages. There is still need for a great and varied amount
of work, in order to realize a transition from a general pattern to the
working models of practical use.

I already mentioned "variableness in the universal optimization" of
the farm enterprises under capitalistic as well as under socialistic conditions. I desire to develop this question. It has a basic meaning in the
theoretical and practical spheres in capitalistic economies as well as
under socialistic economic planning. Under capitalistic conditions the
farmer maximizes his objective function—under the basic assumptions

of the activity analysis mechanism. Hence he should not be shown any
solicitude. Nor should he grieve at the results nor alarm his neighbors
or dispute with society as a whole if his plan proves to be nonoptimal
relative to his selections. But due to the markets, results may ricochet
and frustrate the optimized effects initially specified. Capitalistic society as a whole either does not own or apply highly limited means of
conscious, methodical aversion to these negative consequences. It
leaves these questions to be solved by a powerful market mechanism.
In contrast to the automized economy of capitalistic agriculture, the
socialistic planned economy has fixed prices, tending to social integration through economic mechanisms for production elements. In a methodological sense, this problem enjoys a basic importance in the views
of this economy. The above indicated problem is an association question of the individual interests with a society's interest as a whole. The
optimization manner and consequences of the given farm enterprise,
then, are not just a private matter but become a more social problem.
Yet it is still true that optimization or gain for one unit or object comes
at a cost or lower optimization for another unit or object. The enlargement of fertilizers for state farms beats back on the possibility of purchasing these inputs by farm cooperatives or by private farms. The
more investment credits used by region or farm A, the smaller the
quantity available for region or farm B, and so on.

National income maximization might be attained equally well from
agricultural production and industrial production. Chemistry factories
can produce more fertilizers, nylon stockings, or nitroglycerine. The
central plan specifies some concrete production tasks, measured not by
their value (or price) but *in natura* for some categories. So the problem lies in fact: how ought it confront and harmonize the optimum central procedure, both in a value scheme—the national income—as in a "use
system" (some concrete amounts of cereals, meat, milk, shoes, steel,
fertilizers) with an optimized procedure for individual production links?

We should be able to imagine the national economy in the form of a
great input-output matrix, constructed with a first-place submatrix
(e.g., regions or economic sections) and successively with a second-
place submatrix (e.g., enterprises). Both the main matrix and the submatrices have their own objective functions which are to be maximized.
They also have their own restraints which limit the optimized field.
Some complications arise since these matrices are dependent on each
other. Some definite connections exist among them of complementary
and competitive types and they are mutually able to substitute to a determined degree. We are therefore dealing with a category which in a
cybernetic term is called a system (a composition) of an extended structure, or of a maneuverable interconnection network between elements.
The maximized effects of some matrices enter together with the coefficient 1, as the outlays for other ones become their limitation, or vice
versa. Methodologies for solving such schemes, however, are still far
away from perfect elaboration. The formulation demands some theory
and cybernetic methodology based on the use of optimization procedures.

Let me raise here some thoughts derived from Professor A. Brzoza, in "The Agriculture Economist and Cybernetics." The starting point of his reasonsing is the formulation of Professor Lange:

> The arrangement action mode (of an economic organism, A,B) as a whole depends not only upon the individual element's action, but also on the structure of compromise or agreement, i.e., upon the interconnection network amongst some rudimentary elements. . . . The structure confers upon the arrangement a character of the whole. . . . The same elements, with the same action modes, interconnected in a changeable way, make another whole with another action mode. . . . So the most general and most elementary conclusion resulting from the above mentioned contents, lies in a fact that in a creative process a man has in some measure a right to choose; a choice of some elements, from which he builds the arrangement and choice of their interconnection mode, i.e., the disposition structure.

As to this moment, both in theory as in practice, that second choice possibility has been becoming significantly less understood, esteemed, and used.

Continuing the thought, implied in Lange's formulation, there is not only the cause explained, for which two economic organisms (two lands, regions, or farms) dispose of the same material-power elements, but also variable results depending upon the connection mode of these elements.

Simultaneously there results from the above logical conclusion some rudimentary economic importance; namely, the material-power elements have, thanks to a structure, a substitution possibility. This possibility allows, among others, the moderation of the material-power limitations in an optimization of farming modes, and additional savings or minimization in costs. Such an arrangement of optimization is neither "downwards" from the hierarchic higher level objectives to lower level objectives, nor "upwards" from lower to higher level. It is impossible to prevail as a single direction procedure. However, simultaneously, some action mode of an economic organism as a whole appears not to be a sum of the efficiency of the individual elements.

An optimization arrangement as a whole is not on the level with the sums of the optimized partial plans. In a similar vein, social cost minimization cannot be reached if cost minimization possibilities of the separate elements are excluded. This result stems from the limitation of production factors and interdependence among economic organisms.

One has to state that in both capitalistic and socialistic countries cybernetic theory and methodology for economic optimization arrangements are still in an introductory or structural phase. Practical use is still far away. One should think that future techniques and computers will allow use and practice of cybernetic models which have a theme of interbranch flow (input-output) properties. (I am aware of such efforts in the Economic Institute of the Soviet Union.) The central plan can then be best linked with the enterprises. A discussion on this question and a further sharing of views and information during our seminar would be of reciprocal interest and would be rewarding.

Chapter 3 ⚭ HISTORIC EVOLUTION OF PLANNING AND DECISION MODELS

C. B. Baker, *University of Illinois* (U.S.A.)

THE SUGGESTED TITLE is not specific as to level of the economic unit to be planned. However the assignment was specific. Following the outline suggested in the program outline, I will discuss old and new methods of farm planning, including an interpretation and evaluation of the evolution now apparently under way, identifying newer planning methods as extensions of older planning methods. In particular, I will emphasize a computerized planning system now partially designed for use on individual farms. Excellent literature reviews (6, 10, 15) make it possible to summarize the evolution of planning methods in North America and Western Europe. In the following section I will supplement such a summary as necessary to provide a context for the planning system elaborated later.

OLDER METHODS OF FARM PLANNING

It is plausible to suppose that the oldest method used to plan a farm firm (or other economic organism) is that of comparison. In its simplest use, a farmer casts a neighboring farm as a model to be studied for suggested courses of action. The farm may or may not be chosen for its performance level, either superior or inferior to that of the curious and plan-conscious farmer. It is chosen simply because it is convenient for observation and has behavioral content obviously transferable because of locational proximity. In such elementary use the analytical procedures used likewise can be supposed to be simple, with inferences limited, hazardous, or both. Similarities of site do not guarantee success for a change in practices, investment, or enterprise simply because the change appeared successful on the neighboring farms. Yet to extend the simple analytical practices clearly exceeds the capability of the unaided farmer using the comparative method. We return later to modern extensions of the method.

A more directly applicable planning method is found in the process of "budgeting." We define a farm *production* budget as a set of expectations on resource use for the farm. A *whole* farm budget describes a plan projected for the entire mix of products and resources, and includes marketing and finance as well as production. A "farm production

Thanks are due to Professors John T. Scott and Ian W. Marceau, Departments of Agricultural Economics and Computer Science, respectively, University of Illinois, for their help on and review of the discussion of a computer planning system for individual farms.

41

budget" can be defined as a subset of a farm budget. So also can a "production process budget." Other budgets can be defined for specific purposes: for example, a "capital budget," either with or without intertemporal specifications. It is clear that budgets are flexible in use. They gain content only by specifications in a given use. However defined, they constitute planning models for the economic organism or subsystem of the organism for which they are defined. In contrast with the method of comparison, the budgeting method casts the farm or the part of the farm to be planned as the model to be studied. Yet if a budget includes an enterprise which has not been on the farm before, exogenous information is needed.

Educators have always been skeptical of working in detail with a large number of individual farmers on planning problems (15). The scarcity of trained professional personnel has precluded such activity except on a "pilot project" basis. Perhaps the most outstanding example of a continued program is associated with the lending program of the U.S. Farmers Home Administration. Budgeting with individual and personal contact between FHA client and the farm planning consultant has by most accounts been a successful program.

However the cost of the practice suggests strong reasons for failure to expand it to a wider range of farm families. In the Soil Conservation Service, failure of comparable planning procedures, developed with superior information but with less budgeting skill, attests to the demanding requirements for success in personal budgeting.

Aware of these limitations, the educator has sought alternatives. The first alternative was to turn to research personnel for budgets with *substantive* generality. That is, planning was made a research objective. Considerable U.S. literature in the 1920s and the 1930s centered on debates about the utility of such studies. As the debates continued, farmers themselves were demonstrating that the substance containing empirical generality bordered on the trivial. Hence emphasis was returned to the individual farm with hope for progress in *methodological* generality. An extension program in Farm and Home Development, developed in the 1950s, abandoned hope for empirical generality in the substantive results from farm planning (8). It shifted rather quickly also from methodological instruction of individual farmers to interesting experiments with groups of farmers. The more promising results remain today as a part of U.S. educational programs with farmers.

A strong interest developed during the 1940s and 1950s in estimates of whole-farm production functions (5). Output, usually expressed in value terms, was related to inputs, usually expressed in such aggregates as land, labor, and machine inputs. Coefficients were inferred from functions fitted by regressions with data from individual farms sampled in survey or included in a record-keeping panel. The coefficients could be used as a basis for appraising the use of inputs by a reference to a norm (for example, equal returns at the right margin). They also could be used, with respect to an individual farm, in the population represented by the sample or panel, to deduce an optimum use of resources in the categories expressed in the fitted function. Clearly such a procedure represents a modern extension of the method of comparison.

Throughout the evolution sketched so briefly in this section, the economist has held two objectives. On the one hand he has sought to better understand and predict the behavior of farmers and organizations of farms. On the other he has been concerned with improvement in methods by which the farmer can plan and make decisions consistent with his goals. The two objectives are not entirely competitive. Progress toward one contributes toward progress in the other. However, if oriented to behavioral objectives, the investigator is absorbed by analytical problems: sorting out causal relationships. If oriented to planning objectives, he is more concerned with problems of synthesis: integrating elements of the farm firm into an articulated plan.

We now see a renewed interest in the possibility of substantive budget planning on an individual farm basis (12). The opportunity arises from computer facilities for data handling. However interesting innovations also have been made that do not require high-speed computers (2). The educational motivation, rooted in the past, now is reinforced by commerical incentive on the part of farm-related firms. Indeed, so strong are the commercial complementarities between sale of supplies and provision of planning services that farm-related firms may soon assume major responsibilities in the planning area. However the exciting element in current activity is the shift from analytical to planning objectives that appears to be just on the horizon.

MODERN DEVELOPMENTS

Linear programming (and other operations research) methods have been widely used by agricultural economists for the past 20 years (6). Despite their analytical limitations, they have been used principally by research personnel. They may be ill-adapted for developing empirical generalizations. Because of their synthetic power, they appear well adapted for problems of the planning consultant (12). Their solutions provide few of the properties required to test hypotheses, a principal objective of the research investigator. However they are remarkably adaptable to the formulation of numerous problems faced by individual decision makers. And the lack of substantive generality can safely be ignored in most of such applications.

Commercial attempts to program individual farms cannot yet be characterized as successful. Early U.S. attempts were made by Doane Agricultural Service, International Mining and Mineral Corporation, and others (14). These pioneering attempts have been most interesting and instructive but also too costly to survive commercially. While these efforts may have been premature, the evidence suggests that others may succeed in a future now near at hand. The problem is to design a planning system capable of answering useful questions at a cost recognizably lower than the value of the answers.

To be commercially successful the planning consultant must reduce costs in three areas: data collection, data use, and interpretation of results. The first and last areas are perhaps the most costly. Despite progress in *processing* record data, the cost of *acquiring* data relevant for planning remains high in terms of time and in terms of skill requirements for the data collector. The same is true for interpreting results. The output from a linear programming solution cannot well be entrusted to an untrained salesman or a production technologist without considerable advance in making the linear programming report more intelligible at the outset.

Inferences from Programmed Representative Farms

An interesting suggestion by Brant and Walker (1) would reduce the cost of data collection and data use. In some locations research investigators have provided optimal solutions on representative farms (13). Can such solutions be used as the basis for organizational recommendations on an individual farm in the locality? Those who have attempted to adapt a solution for one farm to the resource base of another are aware of the problems that exist. Brant and Walker suggest using the optimal organization of each representative farm as an activity in a linear programming model with constraint levels relating to the individual farm to be planned. Elements of each activity budget reflect rates at which the resources are used by the optimally organized farm described by the activity budget. The solution of the model is comprised of levels at which, at an optimum, each (optimally organized) representative farm is activated within the resource constraints of the individual farm. These results then can be translated into activities for the farm to be planned by reference to the activity levels that are optimum in the representative farms used in constructing the individual-farm planning model. An example by the authors suggests that the approximation may be close to the solution found by conventional linear programming.

If we were supplied with a sufficient array of solutions for representative farms, the Brant-Walker procedure might offer considerable promise. Though the interpretation task might remain costly, the cost of data collection and data use certainly would be greatly reduced. It seems likely, however, that the method would be tolerably accurate for the farm to be planned only if the representative farms used deviated but slightly from that of the individual farm, in terms of constraint set and alternatives.

In summary, two obstacles seem important: (a) the research commitment required to provide a sufficient array of linear programming solutions for representative farms would appear beyond the research budget likely available to either public research institutions or commercial firms; (b) application of the method is restricted to farms for which it is appropriate to use a constraint set identical to that used (homogeneously) for relevant representative farms. However the idea may have merit for a food processor; for example, in consultation planning with farms from which he procures a product supply. The answer may well depend upon homogeneity of the area of the individual farm and the density of contracts of the procuring firm in the area.

Individual Farm Programming Matrices

Finley (3) has suggested the use of a standardized linear programming matrix to be stored in the computer for each farm in an array of farms. Data required for the input would come from farm records plus information supplied by the farmer in an interview with the planning consultant. Once stored, it would be simple (and inexpensive) to call the matrix and solve it by conventional means. The interpretation task would be the same as for the output of any conventional linear programming solution. The principal objection to this procedure lies in the highly specific form in which the data are stored for individual farms. They are so stored as to be specifically adapted to the requirements of a linear programming application. Hence the data may not be well adapted to the requirements of other operations research models more appropriate for such specialized problems as machine replacement, financial or marketing choices, and capital budgeting.

Data Storage, Retrieval, and Use in Individual Farm Planning Models

A third proposal (11) is a data storage program. Such a program stores *data* from individual farms on magnetic tape from which elements can be retrieved for use by a matrix-generator program. The only property that need be common to the matrix generated by the program for each of the several farms to be planned is the identity of rows and columns. Data input by the matrix-generator are specific to the individual farm. The appeal of this suggestion is the flexibility permitted in the formulation of the model to be solved and availability of data for other uses that might be devised. It does little to reduce the cost of collecting data and interpreting results. We return later to this point. For now we elaborate on the method itself.

To date the method has been used to generate a linear programming matrix for a crop farm and a linear programming matrix for a crop-livestock farm. For the crop farm the model accommodates a choice among eleven crops in each of 25 fields or other divisions useful in distinguishing among production conditions. Each crop is produced at a choice among three levels of fertilization or other technologically differentiated input choice. Land can be withdrawn in compliance with government programs. Each crop can be sold at harvest or stored for sale in any of the eleven following months. Labor constraints are specified at monthly levels. Other constraints specify the total of land that can be withdrawn and the total storage capacity. The objective function maximizes returns above costs not associated with resources in the constraint set. The model period is one year. Though simple, it can be seen that the model is capable of rather sophisticated choices within the crop system. However no land or capital purchases are involved. Nor are there constraints in terms of cash or machine capacity. Thus the model in its present form cannot be used in problems of finance or capital budgeting.

The crop-livestock model accommodates a choice among ten crops at two technological (for example, fertilizer) levels in each of 20 fields (or other farm divisions). The number of crop alternatives was reduced to allow model-space for livestock alternatives. Four cattle-feeding systems are arrayed with choice of month to start each system. The monthly purchase of shelled corn and other feed is added to marketing choices, as specified in the crop model. Also added are constraints in the form of nutritional requirements imposed monthly on the cattle systems: dry matter (maxima), digestible protein, total digestible nutrients, calcium, and phosphorus (minima), plus monthly maxima in urea. Thus again the model, while simple, does provide for rather sophisticated choices *within* the domain of its specification.

The efficiency of procedures to manipulate the data embodied in the data-storage and matrix-generator routines depends on the way in which the generalized linear programming matrices are specified. The definition of series of similar activities, such as cropping alternatives, results in a repetitive model structure, facilitating the generation of the model within the computer. Careful definition of activity units and restraint units produces many unitary matrix coefficients, correspondingly reducing the number of nonzero matrix coefficients which must be input to specify a matrix for a given farm.

The procedure followed in matrix formation takes advantage of the large number of unit coefficients created by the definition of units of activities and restraints. The matrix-generator routine is written to provide the capability of generating matrices composed of any subset of the activities defined in the generalized model. The specific activities required for an individual farm matrix are named on input parameter cards read by the matrix-generator routine. These parameters specify which crops are to be compared, the types of disposal activities to be considered, the types of feedstuffs to be compared, and the types of livestock to be considered. Only the columns of the model corresponding to the activities specified are generated for a matrix for a given farm. For each farm a separate set of parameter cards is input. The set is preceded by an identification card bearing the name and storage-location code for the farm in exactly the same format as is used in the data storage routine. (See Fig. 3.1 for a schematic description of the system.)

There is no limit to the number of farms which can be programmed in order by sequencing parameter decks. However in practice the amount of machine time available for a single computer run would form an upper limit. After reading the parameter input for a farm, the matrix-generator routine causes the machine to find the farm's data on the storage tape and to place these data in the appropriate locations in the matrix which is formed in core during the tape search procedure. The unit coefficients appropriate to the columns generated also are placed in the correct matrix locations.

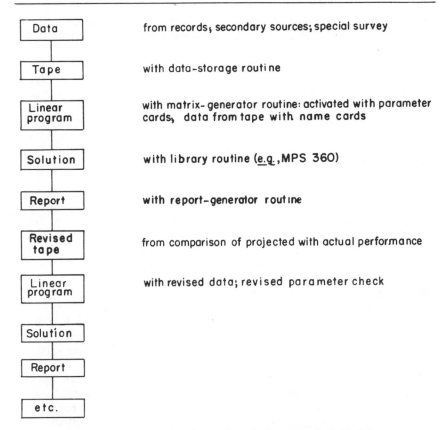

Data	from records, secondary sources; special survey
Tape	with data-storage routine
Linear program	with matrix-generator routine: activated with parameter cards, data from tape with name cards
Solution	with library routine (e.g.,MPS 360)
Report	with report-generator routine
Revised tape	from comparison of projected with actual performance
Linear program	with revised data; revised parameter check
Solution	
Report	
etc.	

Fig. 3.1. A computer-planning system designed for individual farms.

Following error checking, the matrix-generator is replaced in core by the linear programming routine. Iterations begin on the completed matrix, on call of a library routine available for finding an optimum solution. Results are output, following the attainment of an optimum solution for the first farm called. Solutions are obtained in sequence for all other farms specified by parameter decks. The end of a computer run is signified by a special parameter card following the last set of parameter cards.

For the two models tested so far, the nonunit coefficients required for an individual farm matrix are (a) the expected yields for each crop on each field or soil type and at each of the technologically different treatments; (b) the monthly labor requirements for all crops considered (a function of the type of machinery available); (c) the nutritional requirements of livestock, by rates of gain and body weight; (d) the amounts of labor available on the farm, by month; (e) production costs per acre and per head of livestock; (f) the capacities of crop storage and livestock feeding facilities; (g) the acreage constraints; and (h) the expected prices for products, by month. In summary, monthly labor requirements and livestock nutritional requirements are needed for each farm.

The small number of nonunit coefficients required to specify a matrix for each farm makes it feasible to use magnetic tape for storage of individual farm coefficients. The magnetic tape thus becomes a semipermanent record of the objective function, constraint, and matrix-coefficient data for each farm involved in the planning system. Initially the tape is established with data derived from each farm's record and from other sources when the specific farm data are not available. In a continuing commercial planning system, the data tape once established, can be updated each year from farm record data compiled by either the farmer, by a record service such as those found in some of the land grant colleges, or by a commercial firm. Without a record system the magnetic tape data storage system would require the collection of pertinent data from farms by trained personnel, with a resultant increase in operating costs. The other alternative is data from secondary sources. But this reduces precision for the farm to be planned.

The initial establishment of the data tape is accomplished by use of a computer routine written specifically for the data required by a given model. The subsequent retrieval of the data and formation of the linear programming matrix specific to a given farm are carried out by the linear programming matrix-generator routine, also specially written for the model in use. Therefore two routines are required for each model.

Data required to establish the semipermanent data storage tape are read from punched cards and stored on the tape in locations assigned to each of the farms by the computer program. The number of cards required to input these data is small, and the punching and verification costs are correspondingly low. Data for each farm are identified on the tape by the name and address of the farmer and can be retrieved at any time by use of a location code assigned by a computer program.

Coefficients for each type of data input (for example, objective function, constraints, labor requirements) are sequenced within each block of individual farm data and are assigned codes which are punched on the input cards. Thereafter the computer recognizes these codes. In order to make changes in the stored data, change cards are read into the computer as input for the matrix-generator routine.

NEEDS FOR FURTHER RESEARCH AND DEVELOPMENT

Results so far suggest perceptible progress in the problem of designing a computerized planning method adaptable to requirements of individual farmers. Indeed, it may be reasonable to conclude that a computerized planning method will yet be developed that will be feasible from a cost viewpoint and sufficiently enriched to be empirically useful for an individual farm. Assuming that the data-storage and matrix-generator programs survive the test of adaptability to empirically useful planning models, two problems remain to be solved: (a) reducing the cost of acquiring relevant data and (b) reducing the cost of interpreting solutions made available to the farmer.

Three sources of data are available: the farm to be planned, secondary sources, and an interview or mail questionnaire from the farmer. The first two are by far the least expensive. Most farmers keep at least minimal records for tax purposes. Hence data for planning are increments to data already available. Though far from negligible, the increments have at least a base in data already provided. Secondary data in the form of yields and other production coefficients are available from agricultural experiment stations and the U.S. Department of Agriculture, as well as from commercial firms. Much work remains to be done to test solutions from planning models for sensitivity to variations in values of objective function weights and technical coefficients, as well as in certain constraint levels. The most relevant sensitivity is in elements of the solution that are used as a basis for recommendations to the farmer and in the constraints that limit the solution achieved.

The cost of intepreting results for use by the farmer can be reduced by development of a "report-generator"—a computer program that would sort from the solution produced with library programs the essentials needed for (a) determining a course of action and (b) comparing results predicted by the solution with results actually obtained. It would seem that determination of a course of action could be developed with little difficulty. Such a program would include a listing of activities generated in an optimum solution, each reported at the level at which it is optimum. An additional useful feature would be the range that could be tolerated in value of the coefficient of the activity unit without changing the optimum level of the activity. Such information is produced in computer programs commonly used to obtain solutions to linear programming problems.

It is more difficult to provide in a report-generating program output that can be used later for comparing projected with actual results. The most obvious suggestion is an income and expense statement projected from the optimum solution. Ideally the statement would be expressed in terms comparable to an income and expense statement that can be summarized from records kept by the farmer. However this achievement alone would be insufficient. The projected statement is based on assumptions reflected in coefficients used in the linear programming model. The actual (ex post) statement reflects actual values for these coefficients. Hence a report-generator would be more useful for the farmer if it also produced a summary of assumptions on production and price coefficients that were used in activities chosen in the optimum solution.

SUMMARY AND EVALUATION

Past applications of linear programming to farm management decision and planning problems have involved the development of a model
for each farm, the acquisition of data to estimate coefficients and form
a matrix, the punching and checking of large numbers of cards, and the
formidable problems of interpreting results to farmers. These requirements have resulted in high costs per farm, making large-scale commercial applications infeasible. With the system described in the preceding section, the acquisition of data remains a serious problem, but
considerable reductions in costs can be achieved by use of the data-
storage and matrix-generator routine. It no longer is necessary to formulate a model for each farm, and the card punching and checking requirements have been reduced to a minimum.

Finally, a report-generator program might be developed, greatly
reducing the problems of interpreting results and thereby freeing valuable trained personnel for other work. The normal output of a linear
programming solution consists of a set of column numbers and activity
levels and other tables of numbers, which require interpretation before
presentation to participating farmers. Thus interpretation is costly.
However it seems possible that a report-generator procedure can be developed to interpret solutions in the computer and print out the farm solutions in the form of self-explanatory farm plans and financial statements which could be mailed directly to the farmer.

If or when computerized planning becomes commercially feasible,
the operation is likely to include at least some of the features of the
data-storage, matrix-generator system just described. Such a system
at once provides a solution of a modest planning model. To enrich the
model much more in alternatives would endanger the assumption of
profit maximizing as a plausible uniform objective. To add constraints
for greater individual relevance would seriously reduce the empirical
generality of the model. However the data stored on magnetic tape are
available for retrieval and use in models more elaborate and/or more
specific with respect to special problems and/or objectives. We hold
this potential of the system to be of considerable value. It allows the
special characteristics of the farmer to be taken into account for special problems. It would provide the basis also for a schedule of fees
consistent with planning costs.

The stored data might also provide a common data basis for use by
planning consultants from each of a variety of locations: educational institutions, financial intermediaries, market firms, and professional farm
managers. This would be no small accomplishment. It might, finally, be
one way in which to curtail what appears to be excess competition in the
race to obtain "participation rights" in the planning of individual farms.

COMPARISONS OF OLDER PROCEDURES AND NEWER METHODS

The methods of comparison and of budgeting are linked with the newer methods just described in an evolutionary manner. The method of comparison has evolved into use of whole-farm production function not described here. Competent reviews are available elsewhere (5). The lineage is clear, however, in that objectives sought are the same. Also, both old and new methods base prescriptions for decisions on results obtained from past experience on farms with properties assumed sufficiently in common with the subject farm to permit the inferences required for prescription.

The method of budgeting also has evolved into more sophisticated frames of reference. An example is linear programming, as described in preceding sections. Other examples could have been developed: non-linear, dynamic, multiperiod, and recursive programming models; inventory, replacement, and queueing models; and others (6). We chose to expand somewhat on linear programming models. They have proven most flexible in use (12) and are most clearly linked with the older budgeting methods. Many have noted that a perceptible change between old and new is that the latter are "optimizing" models. They are solved by maximizing or minimizing a function subject to constraints made explicit in the formulation of the model.

Budgeting also has given rise to an expanding range of simulation models (4, 6). We note that the optimizing models just identified can be subjected to simulation applications by varying parameters that specify the optimizing model. However the genus of simulation models also includes models that are not optimizing. They simply describe what "happens" in the operation of a system so simulated. The research objective in such a description is to provide the basis for varying a parameter suspected of causal relation with a phenomenon to be explained. If the simulation is capable of reproducing past behavior of the system under known conditions, the basis then is provided for introducing a change, then asking and answering a counterfactual question—the basis for research with explanatory objectives.

In planning frame of reference, simulation models are turned toward tests of alternative courses of action. Flexibility is facilitated in the formulation of the models because of freedom gained in a nonoptimizing application. Moreover numerous performance variables can be studied as they vary in response to alternative organizations of the system. It may be easy to overemphasize advantages on the latter point. Optimizing models also provide numerous outputs of interest to the decision maker.

REFERENCES

1. Brant, W. L., and O. L. Walker. Extending the Representative Farm Concept. Mimeo. Dept. Agr. Econ., Oklahoma State Univ., 1967.

2. Clark, G. B., and I. G. Simpson. A Theoretical Approach to Profit Maximization Problems in Farm Management. *J. Agr. Econ.*, vol. 13.
3. Finley, R. M. An Appraisal of Electronic Data Processing and Its Relationship to the Decision Making Process in Farm Management. Agr. Econ. Paper 1963-3. Dept. Agr. Econ., Univ. Missouri, 1966.
4. Halter, A. N., and G. W. Dean. Simulation of a California Range-Feedlot Operation. Giannini Foundation Res. Rept. 282. Univ. California, 1965.
5. Heady, Earl O., and John L. Dillon. *Agricultural Production Functions.* Ames: Iowa State Univ. Press, 1961.
6. Hutton, Robert F. Operations Research Techniques in Farm Management: Survey and Appraisal. *J. Farm Econ.*, vol. 43.
7. Kottke, Marvin W. Budgeting and Linear Programming Can Give Identical Solutions. *J. Farm Econ.*, vol. 43.
8. Loftsgaard, L. D., E. O. Heady, and H. B. Howell. Programming Procedures for Farm and Home Planning Under Variable Price, Yield and Capital Quantities. Iowa Agr. Exp. Sta. Res. Bull. 487.
9. McFarquhar, A. M. M. The Practical Use of Linear Programming in Farm Planning Involving Problems of Flexibility and Uncertainty in Seasonal Labor Inputs. *Farm Economist*, vol. 9.
10. ——. Research in Farm Management Planning Methods in Northern Europe. *J. Agr. Econ.*, vol. 15.
11. Marceau, Ian W. Linear Programming for Individual Farms: A Contribution Toward a Commercially Applicable System. Ph.D. diss., Univ. Illinois, 1968.
12. Renborg, Ulf. Studies on the Planning Environment of the Agricultural Firm. Uppsala: Almqvist & Wiksell, 1962.
13. Sundquist, W. B., et al. Equilibrium Analysis of Income-Improving Adjustments on Farms in the Lake States Dairy Region. Minnesota Agr. Exp. Sta. Tech. Bull. 246.
14. Swanson, Earl R. Programmed Solutions to Practical Farm Problems. *J. Farm Econ.*, vol. 43.
15. Westermarck, N. Interaction Between Farm Planning, Individual Advisory Services and the Farm Entrepreneur. *Acta Agr. Scand.*, vol. 16.

Chapter 3 ᏬᎧᎤ DISCUSSION

Bela Szikszai, *Research Institute for Agricultural Economics* (Hungary)

I SHOULD LIKE to speak briefly on horizontal, global farm comparisons. Horizontal, global farm comparisons could formerly be applied very suitably for Hungarian peasant farms. At present, however, no comparison exists among Hungarian large-scale farms. Even farms situated in a specific region cannot be compared with each other. This is the reason why the importance of horizontal comparison is considerably lessened under large-scale farming conditions. In course of comparison with a farm model, which is also called "relative horizontal farm comparison," input-output relations are united on the basis of causality in an

integrated entirety. Unfortunately, however, even causality principles
are not sufficiently grounded by production techniques. The elaboration
of an optimum plan for each large-scale farm is required by the considerable size of the farms and by the fact that similarity among different
farms, and even in a narrow sense within one farm, hardly exists. As
the saying goes: so many farms, so many types. The realization of this
task under conditions prevailing at present in Hungary is cumbered by
the great number of farming lines, by the high internal level of farm
performances, by difficulty in assessment of restricting factors, and by
the great qualitative differences in farm management.

As a starting point, one of the most important tasks in planning is
the correct formulation of the objective function. Mutual consent often
fails to exist in this respect. In certain cases these differences can be
accepted, but in several cases they seem to be unjustified. If the consideration that (a) direct costs vary with the restricting or extension of
existing farming lines or enterprises as well as from inaugurating new
ones, and (b) at the same time constant (i.e., fixed) costs are independent from the production lines and from the proper scope of the respective farm, is correct (and it is) then it can be admitted that the greatest
possible increase in production value, reduced by direct costs, will result in the maximum of total income. Thus the objective function should
not incorporate net incomes with small first costs but net production
value must be used.

In order to assess maximum net production value for the entire
farm, the first step should be the weighting of single farming lines, that
is, the determination of their relative profitability. In the course of estimating the relative profitability of different farming lines, real opportunities for the increasing output should be considered at the same time.
In Hungary this is one of the most important problems concerning the
improvement of profitability. Potential sources of output are so far not
at all exhausted. The combination of farming lines where mathematical
methods already have a broad field of application can only be performed
after these important professional preparations (i.e., the suitable formulation of the objective function, the correct weighting of farming
lines, and the real assessment of potentialities for increasing the output)
are all carried out. This labor can be accomplished well only if restricting factors are correctly determined, if production means and labor force available (as well as the demands for both in the single farming lines) are reasonably assessed for each season on the basis of
empirical local standards.

A number of objective and subjective factors must be taken into
consideration when selecting suitable farming lines or enterprises and
deciding on their combination. First of all, the personality of the manager comes into prominence and the role of his individual qualities will,
in large-scale farms, surpass that of the classical production factors.
This evaluation of personal qualities cannot be solved by mathematical
means. That is the reason why "stereotypization" and "uniformization"
cannot lead to success in Hungarian large-scale farms. An ample field

should be given to the manager's individual initiative in planning. The combination of farming lines and the determination of their size can be carried out after we take into account the correct weighting of the single lines, the real estimation of potentialities for increasing output, the establishment of restricting factors, assessing available production means and labor force, and demands of single farming lines for them.

Single farming lines are encouraged by mathematical models according to the totality of their input-output relations (i.e., ranked according to relative profitability within the limits of production means and labor force available). Since several alternatives can of course be considered in planning, decision obviously will be made on the most suitable one. But before decision is made for the suggested scope of production, the result of the proposed system should be compared with earlier factual data. It also should be compared with corrected figures of the schedule. Even the process of correction is not easy. These considerations are perhaps taken to mean that only the united activity of the agricultural expert and of the mathematician can be successful in use of new planning techniques.

Many questions of details also must be answered. One of them, in connection with the objective function referred to above can be mentioned: Production value reduced by direct costs and indicated in the objective function cannot be considered as a uniform index. It will be modified depending on the target of planning, on the character of the farm, and on whether it relates to a state farm or to a cooperative one. Neither can uniformity be maintained in planning, not only in various countries but even perhaps within one single country. Thus the value of the index depends also on the selected method of planning and on whether the farm in question is developing a one-line or a multiline production.

The importance of up-to-date planning of course cannot be diminished by these aspects. Since the steady role of production and of its influencing factors continues, the modification and eternal movement or change of factors requires an elasticity which can be realized only through the application of mathematical methods in the future.

Chapter 4 ∽ SYSTEMATIC PLANNING AND DECISION MODELS

Gerhardt Tintner, *University of Southern California* (U.S.A.)

I N CONTRADICTION to natural science, especially physics, economics is much more closely related to problems of applications. In any case, it is perhaps only during the present century that "pure" or positive economics has been studied for its own sake (66). This is not to say, of course, that analytical propositions have not been developed by economists primarily interested in practical problems.

The orientation towards policy explains especially the type of economic problems which were treated by economists at any given time. But the fact that many (perhaps all) great economists were interested in problems of policy or desired passionately the adoption of certain measures does not mean that they did not try to apply scientific methods objectively.

WELFARE ECONOMICS

The problems of economic policy, like all political problems, involve economics in questions of ethics and social philosophy. This preoccupation can be traced back to Plato and Aristotle. It is particularly obvious in the writings of the English classical economists who were under the potent influence of utilitarian philosophy. This influence has persisted to this day. The efforts of Pareto and his modern followers and of the writers in decision theory who are under the influence of game theory to emancipate economics from utilitarian ethics form an important part of the background of much of the modern literature in this field.

Thanks to a method proposed by Wald (75) we are able to approximate the static utility function or indifference system. Wald uses quadratic utility functions as approximations. The Engel curves, that is, relations between consumption and money income with constant prices, are then linear. We present a result due to Nordin (65). Our data refers to the United States for 1935, 1936, and 1941. The first study includes 300,000 families and the last study 3060 families. Let x be consumption of food and y be consumption of all other commodities and services. After fitting the linear Engel curves for both time periods, the author finds as an empirical approximation the following utility function for the American economy:

$$U = -0.000890x^2 + 0.022401xy + 0.0083SSy^2 + 104.572144x + 96.686771y$$

It is known from the modern theory of indifference curves (28, 47), that we might substitute for this utility function U any function:

$$V = f(U) \text{ as long as } dV/dU > 0$$

It should, however, be mentioned that according to Georgescu-Roegen (23), the very existence of indifference surfaces might be doubted. Following Aristotle and some ideas of the early Austrian writers, he puts forward the idea that utility is perhaps lexicographic (18, 60, 63). This implies the existence of a hierarchy of wants. The more urgent wants will be satisfied first, and less urgent wants only after the satisfaction of the most urgent ones. Georgescu-Roegen considers in an example the choice between butter and margarine. First, the desire for food (calories) will be fulfilled, then the desire of taste, finally the desire for entertainment. These three form a hierarchical order for choice and give rise to a lexicographical ordering: first, the need for food is decisive; for combinations which have the same satisfaction of this need, the one which satisfies taste better will be chosen; finally, combinations which satisfy the need for food and taste equally well will be ordered according to the satisfaction of the need for entertainment.

USE OF CONSUMER'S AND PRODUCER'S SURPLUS IN THE EVALUATION OF PROJECTS APPLIED TO INDIAN AGRICULTURE[1]

There has been a revival of interest in the Marshallian Theory of consumer's and producer's surplus (28, 40, 42). It provides a simple and manageable concept and method to form a rough idea of the welfare aspects of planning. Since the welfare aspects are frequently neglected, especially in planning for underdeveloped countries, we might propose them, at least tentatively, as a corrective for other goals which have been proposed. To give a justification of consumer's surplus, we consider a society which is composed of m individuals with similar tastes and preferences. The individual i has a utility function:

$$u_i = u_i (x_{i1} \ldots x_{in})$$

where x_{ik} is the amount of goods or service k available to individual i. Let his money income be M_i and consider static conditions. Equilibrium will exist if u_i is a maximum. The conditions for a maximum of utility are

$$\partial u_i / \partial x_{ij} = L_i P_j ; \quad j = 1, 2, \ldots, n$$

$$\sum_{k=1}^{n} P k \, x_{ik} = M_i$$

In these formulas P_k is the price of commodity or service k; L_i is the marginal utility of money. We may solve the system for the individual demand functions of the various commodities:

1. From Tintner and Patel (74).

$$x_{ik} = f_{ik} (P_1, \ldots, P_{n_9} M_i); \quad k = 1, 2, \ldots, n$$

The total demand functions are given by

$$X_k = \sum_{i=1}^{m} f_{ik} (p_1, \ldots, P_{n_9} M_i)$$

Assume all other prices and incomes, except P_j, constant, then we have:

$$u_i = L_i \int_0^x p_j \, dx_j$$

where we may not think of the expression p_j as a demand function. Also we assume L_i (marginal utility of money) constant. This excludes the income effects. By analogy, we might solve the collective demand functions in terms of the prices. The analogous expression

$$U = \int_0^{X_j} {}_jp \, dX_j$$

might under similar assumptions be considered an approximation of total utility.

Now consider a market of a given commodity. Denote the price of the commodity as p and its quantity as q. Also let s be a shift parameter: $p = f(q,s)$ is the demand function (78). For simplicity we assume it is continuously falling. The supply function is $p = g(q,s)$. It is assumed not falling. Define by $g(q,s) = 0$ a function $q_1 = q_1(s)$ which shows where the supply function crosses the q axis. Also we have $f(q,s) = g(q,s)$ which defines the equilibrium quantity $q_0 = q_0(s)$. The sum of consumer's and producer's rent or surplus is given by

$$R(s) = \int_0^{q_1} f(q,s) \, dq + \int_{q_1}^{q_0} [f(q,s) - g(p,s)] \, dq$$

We might identify the shift parameter s with a project. This project might lower the supply function $p = g(q,s)$, for example, because of the introduction of new production methods, training of labor, and so on. But it could also shift the demand function $p = f(q,s)$ (e.g., because of additional income created, propaganda, etc.).

Given an initial situation with $s = S_0$, we might compare the difference for $s = s_1$ as $R(s_1) - R(S_0')$ with the total cost of the shift s_1. Also we might compare the discounted value with the total discounted costs of bringing about the shift, and so on. We have estimated demand and supply functions for Indian agriculture (rice and wheat), 1946-64. The demand function for per capita quantity consumed of rice is

$$p = 0.985 - 6.77q$$

p is the real price, that is, harvest price per quintal discounted by the cost of living index.

Regarding the supply function, it was observed that until very recently the agricultural production in India depended largely on weather conditions. It has therefore been said that in India "agriculture is a gamble in rain." However empirical data show that price and quantity supplied are not systematically related, and for this reason we considered supply as completely price inelastic. The estimated supply function for rice is q = 0.06 + 0.036s. Here s is the shift parameter per capita quantity (in $1/10^3$ ton) of nitrogenous fertilizer[2] in production of rice. Here we have

$$R(s) = 0.047 + 0.019s - 0.0044s^2$$

Similarly we have demand and supply functions for wheat. The demand function is[3]

$$p = 0.71 - 12.17q$$

and the supply function is

$$q = 0.02 + 0.029s$$

and the consumer's and producer's surplus is

$$R(s) = 0.012 + 0.014s + 0.0051s^2$$

From these functions we can compute the surpluses with different amounts of fertilizer. Tables 4.1 and 4.2 show the estimated surpluses in rice and wheat respectively, where α is the same per capita quantity of fertilizer as in the year 1963-64. β is an increase by one half, γ a doubling, δ threefold increase, ϵ fourfold increase.

Based upon the utilitarian philosophers, many of whom made important contributions to positive economics, a tradition of doctrines of welfare economics has grown up and persisted in the writings of many economists. Pareto (47) was, for philosophical and political reasons, opposed to the utilitarian point of view and proposed another method which is still in the center of discussion. The Pareto optimum is defined as the state in which no individual can be made better off without making some individual worse off. Looked at as a prescription of economic policy, this amounts of course to a defense of the status quo.

Table 4.1. Consumer's and producer's surplus for rice

Fertilizer level	s	R(s)
α	0.498922	0.056
β	0.748383	0.060
γ	0.997844	0.062
δ	1.496766	0.067
ϵ	1.995688	0.069

2. As nitrogenous and phosphatic fertilizers are used in certain combinations, we use one of them (nitrogenous) as a shift parameter.

3. All the regression coefficients are significant at the 95 percent level of significance except for this coefficient, which is significant at the 90 percent level of significance.

Table 4.2. Consumer's and producer's surplus for wheat

Fertilizer level	s	R(s)
α	0.18943	0.014
β	0.284145	0.015
γ	0.37886	0.016
δ	0.56829	0.018
ϵ	0.75772	0.019

A most important contribution to welfare economics is due to Bergson (9), who introduced a welfare function which depends upon the utilities or satisfactions of all individuals in a given economy. But the welfare function which he proposes has been criticized most successfully by Arrow (4).

Starting from purely individualistic and atomistic assumptions, Arrow showed that if there are at least three alternatives which the members of a society are free to order in any arbitrary way, then a social ordering must be either imposed or dictatorial. The assumption here is that choices are comparable and transitive. The welfare function is conceived in such a fashion that individual preferences are taken into account and irrelevant alternatives play no part. Dictatorship means here that the choices of a single individual are decisive; imposition means that social welfare is independent of individual choices.

The trouble is that welfare economics considers economic phenomena in isolation. In this form modern welfare economics is decidedly inferior to the writings of the utilitarian philosophers who considered economics as only one of the aspects of the desirable social order. Much of welfare economics was conceived as a defense of unrestricted laissez-faire. This involves the idea of consumer's sovereignty, that is, each consumer is assumed to act in isolation, independently of all other consumers, in order to maximize his satisfaction. Whereas there is not much objection to this idea as a first approximation in the explanation of choice under static conditions, it becomes most questionable if it is made the basis of considerations in welfare economics. Is it really possible to consider the consumer as independent, atomistic, and sovereign, determining by his choice ultimately the totality of economic phenomena? This contradicts an old idea expressed by Aristotle, that man is "a political animal." A society of isolated atomistic individuals as conceptualized in much of modern welfare economics is hardly imaginable.

The questionable nature of the assumption of consumer's sovereignty, which is still often maintained as a foundation of welfare economics, might be indicated by an example. In an unpublished dissertation, Basmann has investigated the demand for tobacco and tobacco products in the United States, 1926-45 (66). He finds that the elasticity of demand for tobacco per head of population with respect to the real cost of advertising for tobacco is 0.085. If, ceteris paribus, the cost of advertising for tobacco and tobacco products increases by 1 percent, the demand for these products will increase by a little less than 0.10 percent.

The criticism of welfare economics by Albert (2) and earlier by Myrdal (45) is certainly not to be neglected. Perhaps, however, we might tentatively retain this idea and reform it in the direction indicated in an earlier article. Take collective wants into account, make the theory dynamic by taking historical factors into account, perhaps introduce stochastic (i.e., probability) considerations in order to deal with irrational elements, and pay serious attention to external economies and diseconomies in consumption. The last point involves the fact that the individuals in the society do not really live as isolated atoms but interact and that their preferences and tastes might be at least in part determined by this interaction.

MATHEMATICAL ECONOMICS IN WELFARE PROBLEMS

We want to illustrate the contribution of modern mathematical economics to welfare problems by an example. The method of linear programming can be generalized to short-term production in general. It can make a contribution to the interesting problem of whether rational calculation and decentralized decision is possible in a static collectivist or planned economy. Generalizing older contributions due to Pareto (47), Barone (6), Lange (32), Lerner (33), and Koopmans (30) has shown the following. Assuming an economic system which is essentially a generalization of the linear programming model, they prove again the proposition that under free competition no firm makes any profit. But what about a collectivist economy? Would all decisions have to be made by the central planning board? Koopmans proves that even under collective economies decentralized decisions are possible (see also Sweezy, 61, and Schumpeter, 54). Accounting or shadow prices are used.

Assume that there is a helmsman (central planning board), a custodian for each commodity, and a manager for each activity. A social optimum which corresponds exactly to the competitive optimum will be reached if the following rules are imposed:

1. For the helmsman: Choose a set of positive prices for all final commodities and inform the custodian of each commodity of his price.
2. For the custodians: Buy and sell your commodity from and to managers at a single price announced to all managers. Buy all that is offered at this price. Sell all that is demanded at the given price to the limit of the availability of your commodity.
3. For all custodians of final commodities: Announce to managers the price on your commodity by the helmsman.
4. For all custodians of intermediary commodities: Announce a tentative price on your commodity. If the demand by the managers falls

short of the supply by managers, lower the price. If demand exceeds
supply, raise the price.

5. For all custodians of primary commodities: Regard the available inflow from nature as part of the supply of commodity. Then follow
the rules for custodians for intermediary commodities except do not
announce a price lower than zero but accept a demand below supply
at zero price if necessary.

6. For all managers: Do not engage in activities with negative (shadow)
profits. Maintain activities of zero profitability at a constant level.
Expand activities with positive profits by increasing order for the
necessary inputs with the custodians of the pertinent commodities,
and by offers of the outputs in question to the custodians of the commodities concerned.

This is certainly an interesting contribution of mathematical economics to the most burning problem of our times. However it is important to realize that the result is subject to severe limitations. It is
completely static and tells us nothing about the more important economic problems which are dynamic (43). Even with the subject of static
economics, it should be realized that the result applies to a severely
idealized model of a competitive or collectivist economy. No indivisibilities are allowed. All coefficients of production are constant. There
are no increasing or decreasing returns to scale: if all inputs are increased or decreased in a fixed proportion, the outputs will also increase or decrease in the same proportion. Just like under ideal unrestricted free competition, the solution is optimal in the Pareto sense:
no more of any final commodity can be produced under the given assumptions without diminishing the production of some other final commodity.

Even within the compass of the model, the question of incentives is
not treated. But evidently the incentive of entrepreneurs to maximize
profits in a competitive market economy and the incentives of managers
in a collective economy to maximize bookkeeping profits are psycholog-
ically different. However it should be realized that there is perhaps not
much difference between the manager of a large capitalist corporation
and the manager of a state trust or a nationalized enterprise. It is very
likely that the problems faced by these managers are very similar (54).
It is deplorable that mathematical economists have not occupied themselves more with the most important problem of our time, the question
of the best economic regime—capitalism or socialism. One exception is
the interesting article of Tinbergen (64), which is a promising beginning
but does not come to very impressive conclusions.

The most important contribution of econometric methods to policy
questions is without doubt due to Theil (62), who bases himself upon
ideas of Tinbergen (64). First a quadratic welfare function is constructed. This is based upon consideration related to the modern theory of welfare economists.

The analogy with committee decisions is made and a method of
compromising different viewpoints is suggested. (See also 21.) The

theory of measurable utility of von Neumann and Morgenstern (46) plays a most important part: the expected value of utility is to be maximized (10, 55). Certain equivalents are introduced in order to deal with risk situations (56). This is to say, a probability distribution is replaced by the mean value of the variable in question. Rothenberg (51), who compares the essence of social decisions in a "going society" to actual choice as made in a typical family, also comes to similar conclusions. Hence the idea of a social welfare function perhaps might be retained and even used successfully in planning. Welfare considerations can surely only give a partial answer to problems of economic policy. For one thing, as Albert (2) emphasizes, economic welfare is only a part of general welfare, perhaps in some cases not even the most important part. Consider for example the modernization of agriculture in India, surely one of the most important aspects of economic development in this country (53). In the Indian villages modernization may break up the traditional Indian caste society and have a number of disagreeable consequences which cannot be overlooked in the general program. Great masses of landless peasants will come to the Indian cities and might form there an unemployed and restless, potentially revolutionary proletariat. This situation might also explain and to an extent justify the forced development of heavy industry in India.

Welfare economics is concerned with the ends of economic policy. Given these ends we might use modern decision theory in order to implement the chosen policy. Lange (32, p. 188), expresses himself as follows: "In view of the fact that rationality of action is now a feature of many fields of human activity, there arises the problem of discovering what is there that is common to all fields of rational activity. This has led to the general study of rational activity, *praxiology*." Lange goes on to include operations research, cybernetics, decision theory, and the marginal calculus into the field of praxiology.

One of the most interesting developments in mathematical economics was the introduction of game theory. (See also 11, 12, 65.) Here we find for the first time a mathematical model which is not borrowed from the models of classical (deterministic) physics but from the theory of games strategy. (See also 34). Games of chance (e.g., roulette, dice) have of course played a very important part in the development of theory of probability. But the theory of games of strategy is entirely different and has actually very little to do with games of chance. It deals, on the contrary, with games of strategy where each participant pursues his aim intelligently, like poker, bridge, and chess. Chance plays a very minor part in this theory but is not entirely absent (chance moves). We consider a simple example taken from the most satisfactory part of the theory, two-person, zero-sum games. Assume that A plays against B. What A wins, B loses, and vice versa (zero-sum). The totality of all possible moves of the game by A is called a strategy. The same is true for B. Assume for example that A has the strategies A_1A_2 and B the strategies $B_1B_2B_3$. We present in Table 4.3 the gains of A, which are at the same time the losses of B. If A uses strategy A_1, he will gain 21,

Table 4.3. Game matrix of A (loss matrix of B)

	B_1	B_2	B_3	Row minimum
A_1	21	11	31	11
A_2	32	0	4	0
Column maximum	32	11	31	...

11, or 31 if B uses B_1, B_2, or B_3, respectively. Since A knows that B
is an intelligent opponent and that A's gains are B's losses, B will minimize his loss (which is A's gain). Hence A can only count on winning
the minimum of the first row, 11, if he uses his strategy A_1. The equilibrium exists if the desire of A to maximize his minimum gain for
each strategy coincides with the aim of B to minimize his maximum
loss for each of his own strategies. This is a minimax or saddle point.
In our simple example it is evidently 11. Hence A will use A_1 and B
utilize B_2. This combination of strategies makes sure that A will gain
at least 11 and B will lose not more than 11. It is of course easy to
construct matrices which have no minimax. Table 4.4 provides an example. It is evident that in this case no minimax exists. But if we

Table 4.4. Gain of A (loss of B)

	B_1	B_2	B_3	Row minimum
A_1	9	10	11	9
A_2	11	10	9	9
Column maximum	12	10	11	...

change the problem slightly, we may consider the case where A and B
play the game not just once but many times. Suppose that A uses the
strategy A_1 with a probability p_1, the strategy A_2 with probability p_2,
and A_3 with probability p_3. Also B uses strategy B_1 with probability q_1,
B_2 with probability q_2, and B_3 with probability q_3. In a long series of
games played by A and B the average gain of A (loss of B) will be the
mathematical expectation:

$$E = 9p_1q_1 + 10p_1q_2 + 11p_1q_3 + 10p_2q_2 + 9p_2q_3 + 12p\ q_1 + 10p_3q_2 + 8p_3q_3$$

Assume now that A tries to maximize and B tries to minimize the mathematical expectation. Then A has the choice of two probability distributions: $p_1 = 2/3$, $p_2 = 0$, $p_3 = 1/3$; alternatively, $p_1 = 1/2$, $p_2 = 1/2$, $p_3 = 0$.
B has to choose the probability distribution: $q_1 = 0$, $q_2 = 1$, $q_3 = 0$; or q_1
$= 1/2$, $q_2 = 0$, $q_3 = 1/2$. If A and B choose their strategies with the indicated probabilities, the mathematical expectation of the gain of A (loss
of B) is $E = 10$; this is to say, by choosing the given probabilities, A can
make sure to gain at least 10 in a long series of games and B can make
sure to lose not more than 10 in a long series.

An interesting development in recent years is the theory of measurable utility by von Neumann and Morgenstern (46). The concept of utility has a long history which cannot be presented here. It might only be mentioned that Bernoulli (10) presented early a specific form of measurable utility, characteristically in connection with a problem in probability theory. The founders of modern utility theory also considered utility measurable. Since Pareto (47), however, it is recognized that measurable utility is not necessary for the purposes of static (timeless) economics, that is, in order to explain choice in consumption. We follow here the excellent presentation of Marschak (39), who in turn utilized some ideas of Ramsey (50) and Savage (52). Consider an individual who has the choice between two possible states of the world with state description in the Carnap (13) terminology, s_1 and s_2. Table 4.5

Table 4.5. Choices of the individual

Actions	States of the world	
	s_1	s_2
a_1	b	b
a_2	a	c

represents his position and the choices open to the individual. If the state of the world is s_1, then the consequence of his action will be b if he chooses a_1, a if he chooses a_2. If the state of the world is s_2, then his choice of action a_1 will have consequence b and action a_2 consequence c.

There is complete uncertainty about the state of the world. Assume that a is preferred to b and b to c. In order to fix an arbitrary scale of utility we assume u(c) = 0, u(a) = 1, and it follows that $0 \leq u(b) \leq 1$. Now we assume that the individual has a subjective probability p for the state s_1 and 1-p for the state s_2. Then assuming the principle of evaluation of actions by their average utility (mathematical expectation of utility) we have for action a_2, $u(a_2)$ = u(a)p + u(c) (1-p) = p; and similarly for action a_1, $u(a_1)$ = u(b)p + u(b) (1-p) = u(b). Now there should be a probability P_0 for the individual at which he is indifferent between actions a_1 and a_2. This is the utility of b: u(c) = 0, u(b) = P_0, and u(a) = 1. Hence we have now assigned measurable utility to a, b, and c. These utilities are unique up to a linear transformation. The zero point and the scale of utility can be assigned arbitrarily.

The von Neumann-Morgenstern concept of measurable utility has been criticized because utility of gambling and love of danger are excluded (25, 39). The case of risk concerns a situation in which the relevant probability distributions are known. This means in practice that we are dealing with a stable situation (unchanging tastes and technology), and that we have ample experience in the past in order to estimate accurately the relevant probability distributions. If this is not the case, if the underlying probability distributions are not known, we deal with a case of uncertainty.

Consider now the general problem of decisions (17, 65, 75). This is also called games against nature. We utilize a game theoretical set-up and assume that the strategies of nature are x = 0, 1, 2, 3. Also the possible strategies of the individual playing against nature are the actions a = 0, 1, 2, 3. If the individual for example chooses the action a=1 he will get -0.75 if nature plays the strategy x=0; 0.25 if nature is in the state x=1; the same amount also for x=2 or x=3.

According to the minimax criterion of Wald (75), the individual has to treat nature as if he was playing a two-person, zero-sum game. He has always to expect the worst. This is expressed in Table 4.6 as the

Table 4.6. Game against nature

Strategies of the individual	Strategies of nature				Row minimum	Row maximum
	x=0	x=1	x=2	x=3		
a=0	0*	0	0	0	0	0
a=1	-0.75	0.25	0.25	-0.75	-0.75	0.25
a=2	-1.50	-0.50	0.50*	-1.50	-1.50	0.50
a=3	-2.25	-1.25	-0.25	0.75*	-2.25	0.75

minimum for each row, that is, for each strategy. It is sensible, under such conditions, that the individual will maximize the row minimum, for example, choose the largest figure among the row minima. Thus in our case the individual will choose action a=0 since this is the maximum of all the figures in the column of row minima. This procedure has been criticized from the point of view of personalist probability by Savage (52). The regret matrix of Savage is formed by the following considerations: we might consider the regret of the acting individual as the loss occurring between the actual result for a given strategy and the result which could be obtained if the state of nature was known. In Table 4.6 we have starred for each column (strategy of nature) the maximum. Deducting this from each figure in the given column, we obtain the regret matrix of Savage (Table 4.7). Now we apply the minimax principle to

Table 4.7. Savage regret matrix

Strategies of the individual	Strategies of nature				Row minimum
	x=0	x=1	x=2	x=3	
a=0	0	-0.25	-0.50	-0.75	-0.75
a=1	-0.75	0	-0.25	-0.50	-0.75
a=2	-1.50	-0.75	0	-0.25	-1.50
a=3	-2.25	-1.50	-0.75	0	-2.25

the regret matrix. We are given a column of row minima, and among these the individual will choose the maximum. We see that in our case he is free to choose a=0 or a=1. Another criterion has been given by Hurwicz (34) (Table 4.8). Consider an individual who is influenced by the

Table 4.8. Hurwicz formulation

Strategy of the individual	Row minimum	Row maximum	0.5 min + 0.5 max	0.1 min + 0.9 max
a=0	0	0	0	0
a=1	-0.75	0.25	-0.25	0.15
a=2	-1.50	0.50	-0.50	0.30
a=3	-2.25	0.75	-0.75	0.45

worst (row minimum) and the best (row maximum) which could happen for each strategy. The weights chosen may be regarded as measures of optimism or pessimism of the individual. For instance, if he gives equal weight to the best and the worst for each strategy (0.5 min + 0.5 max) he will choose a=0 as the best strategy. If he is more optimistic and acts according to 0.1 min + 0.9 max, he will choose a=3. Another possibility is the criterion of Laplace (Table 4.9). We consider here all four

Table 4.9. Laplace criterion

Strategy of the individual	Expected profit
a=0	0
a=1	0
a=2	-0.25
a=4	-0.75

strategies of nature equally probable and compute the mathematical expectation for each strategy. In our example the individual who wants to maximize the expected profit (computed with the help of the Laplace assumption) will have the choice between strategies a=0 and a=1.

Here I want to show how one version of the probability theory of Carnap (13, 14) might be used in the face of complete uncertainty to construct a decision model. We are dealing with a perishable commodity and also an entirely new commodity where no past experience is possible. Consider, for instance, a man who contemplates constructing a rocket for travel to the moon (65, 69). This is a simple version of an inventory problem. His problem is how big a rocket should he construct. Assume that there are only two customers, C_1 and C_2. Each of these might buy 0, 1, or 2 tickets. In this little universe, we might construct the information as in Table 4.10, which shows us what could actually happen. Each line in Table 4.10 is a state description. In the first line, none of the customers buys a ticket. In the second, the first buys none, but the second buys one. In the third, the first buys one, the second none. In the fourth, the first buys no ticket, but the second two, and so on. Now, according to the theory of Carnap (13), we must treat the two individuals on a par. The entrepreneur does not care who buys

Table 4.10. Probabilities of outcomes in two-consumer,
three-choice economy

State description	C_1	C_2	a priori probability
1	0	0	1/6
2	0	1	1/12
3	1	0	1/12
4	0	2	1/12
5	2	0	1/12
6	1	1	1/6
7	1	2	1/12
8	2	1	1/12
9	2	2	1/6

the tickets, only how many are sold. Hence we see that a certain state
description may be obtained by permutation of the two individuals.
These are the structure descriptions which are classes of equivalent
state description. State description 2 and 3, then, form one structure
description. Also 4 and 5 another and 7 and 8 still another structure
description. State descriptions 1, 6, and 9 alone form a structure description.

According to one version of the probability theory of Carnap, we
give each structure description the same a priori probability. There
being 6 structure descriptions, each receives probability 1/6; within
each structure description each state description receives the same
probability. The a priori probabilities of the state descriptions are indicated in the last column of the information. Now assume that it
costs 1 money unit to construct one place in the rocket; and that each
ticket may be sold for 2 units. If a rocket of a place is available and x
places are sold, the profit is given by

$$P = 2x - a \qquad 0 \le x \le a$$
$$P = a \qquad\qquad x > a$$

For various sizes of the rocket (a) and for various numbers of places
sold (x) we obtain the data in Table 4.11. These data must be interpreted in the following way. The a priori probabilities are taken from
the previous set of information. Assume now that a = 2, that is, a

Table 4.11. Economic gains accruing to entrepreneur by rocket sizes
and possible levels of seat sales

Number of seats sold	a priori probability	Size of rocket				
		a=0	a=1	a=2	a=3	a=4
x	P_x	0	-1	-2	-3	-4
0	1/6	0	-1	-2	-3	-4
1	1/6	0	1	0	-1	-2
2	1/3	0	1	2	1	1
3	1/6	0	1	2	3	2
4	1/6	0	1	2	3	4
EP	. . .	0	2/3	1	2/3	0

rocket is constructed which holds 2 places. Assume x=0 seats are sold. Then the gain is -2. If x=1 seat is sold, the gain is 0. If x=2 seats are sold the gain is 2, also if x=3 or x=4 seats are sold. Using Carnap's probabilities in order to compute the mathematical expectation, we see that under the given circumstances it will be more profitable to construct a rocket which has a=2 places. The average gain, EP=1 unit, is the highest.

DETERMINISTIC MODELS OF ECONOMIC DEVELOPMENT

Since stochastic methods are still very little developed, we frequently have to utilize deterministic models. These may be justified by the idea that under some special circumstances we may replace the probability distributions involved by the mean values (arithmetic means) of the random variables involved. As an example for the more modern linear methods used in mathematical economics and operations research, let us consider linear programming. Consider the situation of a typical Iowa farm in Hancock County, Iowa, during the period of 1928-52 under simplifying assumptions. The data came from a sample survey, Babbar (5). We consider two activities, corn (x_1) and flax (x_2). The amounts produced are expressed in bushels. We consider the situation on the typical farm in the short run (27). Therefore we can neglect the fixed costs, that is, costs which are independent of the amounts produced, since in the short run they are incurred anyway. Also we assume that the farm produces under static conditions. The price of a bushel of corn is \$1.56 and of a bushel of flax is \$3.81. The "objective function" of the short-run profits the farmer wants to maximize is

$$f = 1.56x_1 + 3.81x_2$$

For the conditions of production in the short run, we make again the simplest possible assumptions, fixed coefficients of production. We assume that (approximately) outputs are proportional to inputs. The sample survey tells that it takes (on the average) 0.022740 acres of land to produce a bushel of corn and 0.92449 acres of land to produce a bushel of flax. The average farm we are investigating utilizes 148 acres of land. Similarly it takes on the average \$0.317720 of capital in order to produce a bushel of corn. Also one must use \$0.969500 of capital in order to produce a bushel of flax. The average capital available for a typical farm is \$1800. Again, for the sake of simplicity, we neglect other factors of production (e.g., labor). Now in the short run the farmer can use only the land (148 acres) and the capital (\$1800) available. But he is not obliged to utilize all the land and capital available. In the long run he might for example sell some land or borrow more capital. The conditions of production in our simple example are

$$0.022740x_1 + 0.092440x_2 \leq 148$$
$$0.317720x_1 + 0.969500x_2 \leq 1800$$

To these conditions of production in the short run we must also add the condition that it is impossible to produce negative amounts of corn and flax $x_1 \geq 0$ and $x_2 \geq 0$. The solution of the problem, found by the simplex method: In order to maximize profits the farmer ought to produce $x_1 = 5365.366$ bushels of corn and $x_2 = 0$ bushels of flax. Then his optimal profit will be $f = \$8837.971$. This maximum is achieved if the farmer uses all his available capital (\$1800) but only 128.83 of the total available 143 acres of land.

To each maximum problem in linear programming there exists a dual minimum problem. Consider again our example. The farmer in question will have to establish certain accounting (bookkeeping) or shadow prices for the two factors of production used. Let u_1 be the shadow price for an acre of land and u_2 the shadow price for \$1 of capital. It should be emphasized that these are merely accounting or shadow prices. They express the valuation of units of factors of production for the farmer in the short run and are not necessarily identical with market prices. Since the typical farm possesses in the short run 148 acres of land and \$1800 of capital, the farmer will try to minimize:

$$g = 148u_1 + 1800u_2$$

The inequalities imposed are now that for each activity (bushels of corn and flax produced) the imputed cost (using the accounting prices) must be at least as great as the net price of the activity (price of a bushel of corn or flax):

$$0.022740u_1 + 0.317720u_2 \geq 1.56$$
$$0.092440u_1 + 0.969500u_2 \geq 3.81$$

The last condition says that the accounting prices are not negative $u_1 \geq 0$ and $u_2 \geq 0$. The solution of this minimum problem: The imputed price of land is $u_1 = 0$. Land for the farmer in question is a free good, as shown by the fact that he used only 128.83 acres of the land available. (It would not directly cost him anything to use more of his own land.) The imputed price of capital is $u_2 = 4.91$. This very high price is explained by the scarcity of capital.

The total cost $g = \$8837.971$. Hence we see that the dual problem has the same solution (minimum value of imputed cost) as the original maximum problem (maximum of short-run profits). If the factors of production are correctly evaluated, they exhaust the profits and no extra profits are made, in equilibrium. In evaluating this example, the fundamental assumptions should be kept in mind. The model is static. We assume pure and perfect competition, that is, the farmer cannot in any way influence the prices at which he sells his products. We investigate production in the short run, that is, the farmer cannot increase or decrease in any way the amounts of the factors of production (land and capital) available. Also, for the sake of simplicity, we distinguish only two factors of production. In a more realistic investigation labor should be introduced and various types of labor, capital, and land distinguished.

Very strong is the assumption of constant coefficients of production.

The output of a given commodity (corn or flax) is strictly proportional to the inputs (land and capital). Finally, we assume that the farmer only tries to maximize his short-run profit or, equivalently, tries to minimize his accounting cost in the short run. In spite of these severe limitations, the method of linear programming has been applied with some success to concrete economic problems. It should be pointed out that certain generalizations are possible. We might generalize the method to nonlinear programming, where neither the objective function nor the inequalities need to be linear (26, 31). Sometimes the solutions are required to be integral numbers. Then we must use the method of integer programming. The method can also be generalized to deal with dynamic problems, that is, production over time. This leads us to dynamic programming (7, 8). Finally, we might even introduce probability considerations into a linear program. The methods of stochastic programming will be discussed below (16, 35).

AN INPUT-OUTPUT MODEL FOR THE PORTUGUESE ECONOMY, 1957[4]

We distinguish only four sectors in the Portuguese economy: (1) enterprise, (2) government, (3) foreign trade, (4) households. Sector 1 includes agriculture, fisheries, industry, commerce, and the like. Sector 2 is made up of the central government, local authorities, cooperative organizations, and the office of economic coordination. Sector 3 concerns all transactions with countries outside Portugal. Sector 4 includes consumers or the domestic economy. Table 4.12 refers to the

Table 4.12. Input-output matrix for Portugal, 1957

From	(1) Enter- prises	(2) Govern- ment	(3) Foreign Trade	(4) House- holds	Total
(1) Enterprises	...	3.49	10.97	45.34	59.80
(2) Government	2.14	...	1.79	3.08	7.01
(3) Foreign Trade	15.14	...	...	...	15.14
(4) Households	48.83	2.85	...	...	51.68
Total	66.11	6.34	12.76	48.42	...

Portuguese economy in 1957. Figures are in millions of escudos. In this table the entry in row 1 and column 2 is the value of the services of government to the enterprises; (1, 3) is the exportation of goods and services; (1, 4) is private consumption; (2, 1) is value of services rendered by the government to enterprises, measured by taxes collected from the productive sector; (2, 3) is import duties; (2, 4) is taxes paid by private individuals as a measure of the value of government services;

4. Based on Tintner and Murteira (72).

(3, 1) is importation of goods and services; (4, 1) is remuneration of productive factors by enterprises[5] and (4, 2) is payment of the public sector for personnel.[6]

We have a static model. Investment is not considered. Let X_i (i = 1, 2, 3, 4) be the net output of sector i, that is, the value delivered to the other sectors. Internal transactions are excluded. Let x_{ij} be the value of production of sector i absorbed by sector j. In static equilibrium the matrix of the fixed coefficients of productions is given by

$$a_{ij} = x_{ij}/x_j$$

$$\begin{bmatrix} \cdots & 0.498 & 0.725 & 0.877 \\ 0.036 & \cdots & 0.118 & 0.060 \\ 0.253 & 0.000 & \cdots & 0.000 \\ 0.817 & 0.407 & 0.000 & \cdots \end{bmatrix}$$

These technical coefficients have the following interpretation. In 1957 the sector of the enterprises (1) absorbed for each escudo of net product 0.036 escudos of government services from sector 2; 0.253 worth of imports from foreign trade (3); and 0.817 escudos worth of labor and services from sector 4 (households). The public sector (2) needed for each escudo of public services produced from sector 1 (enterprises) goods and services worth 0.498 escudos, and from households (sector 4) work worth 0.407 escudos. The sector foreign trade (3) needed for each escudo in 1957 from sector 1 (enterprises) 0.725 escudos, from the public sector 0.118 escudos in tariffs. With the help of the empirical data in the matrix we obtain for the economy of Portugal in 1957 the following equilibrium system:

$$\begin{aligned} + X_1 - 0.498X_2 - 0.725X_3 - 0.877X_4 &= 0 \\ -0.036X_1 + X_2 - 0.118X_3 - 0.060X_4 &= 0 \\ -0.253X_1 + X_3 &= 0 \\ -0.817X_1 - 0.407X_2 + X_4 &= 0 \end{aligned}$$

In addition to previous assumptions, we assume free competition. Hence the income which results from the sale of goods and services in each sector is equal to cost. This helps us to find a model which explains the prices. We denote by p_i (i = 1, 2, 3, 4) the prices (better = price indices) in each sector. The price of each good produced in a given sector is exactly equal to its cost of production. The system is again a linear system of equations and is homogeneous. Hence we cannot determine the absolute prices but only price ratios, for example, p_1/p_4, p_3/p_4 if we take p_4 (price of sector 4, i.e., wages) as numéraire. In our empirical case we have the system:

---

5. Estimated from the national income at market prices (57.42). We deduct 10 percent for amortization; of the remainder we attribute 2.85 to the payments of the public administration to the enterprises (1,2) and 48.83 to payment of salaries, rents, and dividends to private individuals by enterprises.

6. Sources for all data: Estadisticas Financeiras. INE, 1957. Estimates furnished by the Instituto Nacional de Estadistica.

$$p_1 \ -0.036p_2 \ -0.253p_3 \ -0.817p_4 = 0$$
$$-0.498p_1 + \quad p_2 \qquad\qquad -0.407p_4 = 0$$
$$-0.725p_1 \ -0.118p_2 \qquad + p_3 \qquad\quad = 0$$
$$-0.877p_1 \ -0.060p_2 \qquad\qquad\quad + p_4 = 0$$

This model explains the price formation in the Portuguese economy under the simplifying assumptions indicated.

In the closed Leontief model consumption is really an input, like consumption of fuel of a machine. We have no final demand, no primary productive factors.

In the open Leontief model, we consider now the final demand by the households for goods produced by the other sectors as given. Labor is the only primary productive factor. The autonomous and the exogenous final demand of the households for the goods of the various sectors is now $y_1 = x_{14}$ (goods produced by enterprises), $y_2 = x_{24}$ (government services), and $y_3 = x_{34}$ (imports). In our case, we have $y_3 = 0$, since all imports are obtained by the enterprises. This model may be used in order to estimate the influence of changes in final demand on the net output of the various sectors. Now we have for the Portuguese economy in 1957 the system:

$$X_1 = 1.276y_1 + 0.635y_2 + 1.000y_3$$
$$X_2 = 0.084y_1 + 1.042y_2 = 0.184y_3$$
$$X_3 = 0.323y_1 + 0.161y_2 + 1.253y_3$$

Let us assume a 1 percent increase in the final demand for goods produced by the first sector (enterprises). This demand by the consumers increases from 45.34 to 45.79 millions contos, but the final demand for the goods and services of other sectors remains constant. We insert $y_1 = 45.79$, $y_2 = 3.08$, $y_3 = 0$, into the linear system. We can say that the increase of 1 percent in the final demand by consumers for goods and services produced by the first sector (enterprises) necessitates, ceteris paribus, an increase of 0.96 percent of the net product of the same sector (enterprises), also an increase of 0.66 percent in the net product of the second sector (government), and finally an increase of 0.90 percent in the net product of the third sector (foreign trade). We make the hypothesis that the final demand of consumers for the services of the second sector (government) y_2 increases, ceteris paribus, by 1 percent. We assume that y_2 becomes 4.11 instead of 3.98 million contos, as before, but we maintain $y_1 = 45.34$ and $y_3 = 0$ as formerly. If we insert these figures into the system of linear equations we achieve these results. We conclude that a ceteris paribus increase of the final demand of consumers for government services by 1 percent has the following consequences. The net product of the first sector (enterprises) will increase by only 0.04 percent, the net product of the second sector itself (government) will increase by 0.56 percent, and the net product of the third sector (foreign trade) will remain unchanged.

Another interesting problem which can be treated in terms of the open Leontief model is the total value of labor. In the open model we have for E (value of labor):

$$E = 1.077y_1 + 0.943y_2 + 0.892y_3$$

This has the following interpretation. For each escudo that the final demand of households for goods and services of enterprises increases, the value of labor has to increase by 1.077 escudos. If, on the other hand, ceteris paribus, the demand for government services increases by one escudo, the value of total labor has to increase by 0.943 escudos. Finally, let, ceteris paribus, the demand for imports by consumers increase by one escudo; then the value of total labor must increase by 0.892 escudos. We investigate price formation in the open Leontief model. Let the cost of labor be w_1, w_2, and w_3 in the sectors 1, 2, and 3, respectively. Numerically we have in terms of the empirical results for Portugal in 1957:

$$p_1 -0.036p_2 -0.253p_3 = w_1$$
$$-0.498p_1 + p_2 = w_2$$
$$-0.725p_1 -0.118p_2 + p_3 = w_3$$

We solve for the prices:

$$p_1 = 1.276w_1 + 0.084w_2 + 0.323w_3$$
$$p_2 = 0.635w_1 + 1.042w_2 + 0.161w_3$$
$$p_3 = 1.000w_1 + 0.183w_2 + 1.253w_3$$

The system has the following interpretation. Assume that, ceteris paribus, the labor cost in the sector of enterprises (w_1) increases by one escudo. Then the price in the same sector (p_1) will increase by 1.276 escudos, prices for government services (p_2) by 0.635 escudos, prices for imports (p_3) by one escudo. Similar interpretations can be given for wage cost increase in other sectors.

Finally, we define a general wage cost index (w) in terms of our indices of wages in the three sectors (w_1, w_2, w_3):

$$w_1 = 0.817\,w, \quad w_2 = 0.407\,w, \quad \text{and} \quad w_3 = 0.102\,w.$$

We obtain a relation between the price indices (p_1, p_2, p_3) and the general wage index: $p_1 = 1.077\,w$, $p_2 = 0.943\,w$, and $p_3 = 0.892\,w$. This has to be interpreted as follows. If wages in general (W) increase by one escudo, then prices in the first sector (enterprises, p_1) will increase by 1.077 escudos; under the same assumption, prices in sector 2 (government, p_2) will increase by 0.943 escudos, and prices in the third sector (foreign trade, p_3) by 0.892 escudos. We have constructed a small static model for the United States, using national income data for the period 1948-60. The endogenous variables are variables which are simultaneously determined by the interaction of the equations of the system (C, personal nominal consumption; Y, nominal gross national product; P, price index of gross national product; X, real gross national product; D, total employment). It is realized that the system is also influenced by other (exogenous) variables. These are N, population; G, nominal public consumption; I, nominal gross asset formation; L, nominal increases in stock; E, nominal exports; M, nominal imports; W, nominal yearly wage per worker; T, time. It should be realized of course that

some of these variables are not really exogenous to the functioning of
the American economic system. They have been assumed as exogenous
and would become endogenous in a larger dynamic system. Our purpose
was to construct a small model which would be immediately comparable
to other similar models of Western European countries and Canada.

Using the method of simultaneous equations we derived the following
estimates of the equations in our system:

$$C_t / N_t P_t = 687.9 + 0.336 Y_t / N_t P_t$$

This Keynesian type consumption function relates linearly real consumption per head ($C_t / N_t P_t$) to real national income per head ($Y_t /
N_t P_t$). Our estimate of the marginal propensity to consume is 0.336.
This means that if, ceteris paribus, real national income per capita increases by \$1.00, real per capita consumption might be expected to in-
crease by about \$0.34. The next equation is just the bookkeeping defini-
tion of nominal national income:

$$Y_t = C_t + G_t + I_t + L_t + E_t - M_t$$

We have the obvious definition of real national income, $X_t = Y_t / P_t$.
Real national income is nominal national income divided by the price
level. The demand for labor is determined by the marginal productivity
of labor, $dX_t / dD_t = W_t / P_t$. This follows from the theory of production
under free competition and neglects the monopolistic elements in the
American economy. Under free competition it can be shown that if a
firm maximizes its profits with given prices and wages, the maximum
of profits implies the condition that the marginal productivity of each
factor of production is equal to the ratio between the price of this factor
and the price of the product. The next and last equation is a primitive
production function of the Cobb-Douglas type. (See also 66, 69.)

$$\log X_t = 6652 + 0.630 \log D_t$$

It has been estimated by the method of simultaneous equations, using the assumption of free competition. Here again we neglect the monopolistic elements, for example the existence of trade unions. It should
also be noted that in this static model capital has been neglected. The
estimated coefficient 0.633 is an elasticity. If, ceteris paribus, employment in the United States increases by 1 percent, we might expect an increase of production of about 0.63 percent.

In order to utilize this model for problems of economic policy (62,
64) we have considered the exogenous variables as policy variables and
asked the following question. Given an isolated autonomous increase in
a given exogenous variable 1 percent, what will be the simultaneous percentage change in the endogenous variables? The interpretation of Table 4.13 is as follows. Let us assume that, ceteris paribus, population
(N) increases by 1 percent, by immigration for example. Then we might
expect the following reaction of the endogenous variables: the price
level (P) will increase by about 1/5 percent; national income (Y) will increase by more than 1/2 percent; real national income (X) will increase

Table 4.13. Change in endogenous variables

Variable	N	W	G	I	L	E	M
P	0.21	0.76	0.12	0.11	0.01	0.04	-0.03
Y	0.56	0.35	0.32	0.30	0.02	-0.10	-0.03
X	0.35	-0.41	0.20	0.19	0.01	-0.06	-0.05
D	0.56	-0.65	0.31	0.30	0.02	0.10	-0.08
C	0.87	0.55	0.22	0.21	0.01	0.07	-0.06

by about 1/3 percent; employment (D) will increase by about 1/2 percent; nominal consumption (C) will increase by about 9/10 percent.
Consider now, ceteris paribus, an increase of nominal (money) wages
(C) by 1 percent. We might expect that the price level will increase by
about 3/4 percent and nominal national income by about 1/3 percent; but
real national income will decrease by about 4/10 percent and employment by almost 2/3 percent; nominal consumption will increase by
about 1/2 percent.

What are the effects of an increase in public consumption (G) by 1
percent, ceteris paribus? Such an increase might be due to public
works. The price level will increase by more than 1/10 percent, nominal national income by about 1/3 percent, real national income by 1/5
percent, employment by about 3/10 percent, and nominal consumption by
about 1/5 percent. The effects of an increase of nominal investment (I)
by 1 percent, ceteris paribus, are as follows. The price level will increase by about 1/10 percent, nominal national income by 3/10 percent,
real national income by about 1/5 percent, employment by 3/10 percent,
and nominal consumption by about 1/5 percent. The effects of changes
in stocks (L), imports (M), and exports (E) are very small.

This shows that these variables are not very suitable in order to
influence the endogenous variables by public policy. For the estimation
of our model, data from the period 1948-60 have been used. The model
is very simple and we cannot expect great accuracy in prediction. Nevertheless I have ventured to use the elasticities in Table 4.13 to predict
the changes in the U.S. economy for 1963-64. Table 4.14 gives the actual and computed predictions. Whereas there is of course no great

Table 4.14. Actual and predicted changes in endogenous variables

	Percentage change, actual	U.S. economy 1963-66, predicted
Price level	1.1	4.5
Nominal income	5.9	3.1
Real income	4.8	1.3
Employment	4.4	2.1
Nominal consumption	5.6	5.4

accuracy in prediction, the sign of the change and the order of magnitude have been correctly predicted. This shows that even a small and simple model is perhaps not completely useless. We have presented this model only as an example. Much larger models are necessary in order to achieve predictions which are really potentially useful in applications to economic policy.

ECONOMETRIC MODEL FOR ECUADOR[7]

Following the example of some Keynesian models constructed for the Western European countries, Canada, and the United States, we have endeavored to build a model for Ecuador. The model is based upon data collected by the Central Bank of Ecuador. Our variables are as follows. Endogenous variables: C = personal consumption, Y = nominal gross national product, P = price index of gross national product, X = real gross national product, D = total employment. Exogenous variables: N = population, G = public consumption (nominal), I = gross fixed asset formation (nominal), L = increases in stock (nominal), E = exports, M = imports, W = nominal yearly wage per worker, t = time.

The data for Y, C, I, P, G, E, M, N are taken from Memoria del Gerente General del Banco Central del Ecuador, Correspondente al Ejercisio de 1961. Quito, Ecuador, 1962, Annexes. Data for D, L, W, and X come from Republica del Ecuador, Informe al Consejo Interamericano y Social de la Organizacion de los Estados Americanos, Quito, Ecuador, Octubre 1962.

The consumption function is estimated by a variation of the method of simultaneous equations. We define $U_t = C_t + G_t + I_t + L_t + E_t - M_t$ and obtain empirically: $C_t/N_t P_t = 1840.1 + 0.9032 (U_t/N_t P_t)$, $Y_t/N_t P_t = 1840.1 + 1.9032 (U_t/N_t P_t)$. Hence our consumption function is estimated as $C_t/N_t P_t = 966.8453 + 0.4746 (Y_t/N_t P_t)$. For estimating the production function our computations give

$$\log X_t = 3.9037 - 0.4215 \log D_t$$

In application to policy, we have computed the elasticities of all endogenous variables in the Ecuadorian economy with respect to all the exogenous variables (Table 4.15). The results are interpreted in the following way. Assume that, ceteris paribus, population (N) in Ecuador increases by 1 percent. Then we expect the following percentage increases of the endogenous variables: price level (P) 0.73 percent, nominal national income (Y) 1.3 percent, real national income (X) 0.55 percent, employment (D) 1.3 percent, and nominal consumption (C) 1.5 percent. Assume on the other hand that money wages (W) increase, ceteris paribus, by 1 percent. Then the price level may be expected to increase by 0.74 percent; nominal national income will increase by 0.53 percent; real national income will decrease by 0.21 percent; employ-

7. Based on Tintner and Davila (70).

Table 4.15.　Elasticities of endogenous variables

Endogenous variables	N	W	G	I	L	E	M
P	0.7256	0.7385	0.2514	0.2876	0.3101	0.3713	-0.3423
Y	1.3009	0.5296	0.4351	0.4946	0.5335	0.6386	-0.5887
X	0.5483	-0.2089	0.1821	0.2071	0.2233	0.2673	-0.2464
D	1.3009	-0.4765	0.4320	0.4911	0.5296	0.6340	-0.5844
C	1.5300	0.6106	0.3518	0.4000	0.4314	0.5164	-0.4760

ment will decrease by 0.48 percent; consumption will increase by 0.61 percent. If we assume that, ceteris paribus, government consumption (C) increases by 1 percent, then other variables will increase as follows: price level by 0.25 percent, nominal income by 0.44 percent, real income by 0.18 percent, employment by 0.43 percent, and consumption by 0.35 percent. If, ceteris paribus, gross fixed asset formation (I) increases by 1 percent, this will have the following consequences: the price level will increase by 0.29 percent, nominal income by 0.49 percent, real income by 0.21 percent, employment by 0.49 percent, and consumption will increase by 0.40 percent. Let us now assume that, ceteris paribus, stocks (L) increase by 1 percent. This will have the following increases as a consequence: price level 0.31 percent, nominal income 0.53 percent, real income 0.22 percent, employment 0.53 percent, and consumption 0.43 percent.

Now we assume that, ceteris paribus, exports (E) from Ecuador increase by 1 percent. Then the following increases may be expected: price level 0.37 percent, nominal income 0.64 percent, real income 0.27 percent, employment 0.63 percent, and consumption 0.52 percent. Finally, a ceteris paribus increase of imports (M) into Ecuador will cause the following decreases: price level 0.34 percent, nominal income 0.59 percent, real income 0.25 percent, employment 0.58 percent, and consumption 0.48 percent. Let us finally indicate the limitations of this model. It is static, and dynamic factors are neglected. It is of course highly aggregated; the production function depends only upon one single factor (labor); all elasticities are computed on the assumption that, apart from an isolated 1 percent increase of some exogenous variable, things are on the average the same as in Ecuador during the period considered.

From this short-time static planning model a long-term dynamic model may be derived. Now all variables are in real terms per capita. Let x_t be real national income; c_t, real consumption; w_t, real wages; e_t, proportion of the population which is employed; k_t, real capital. These are the endogenous variables. The exogenous variables are i, real investment; h_{1t}, real government spending; h_{2t}, real exports; h_{3t}, real imports. The model is now

$$c_t = 497.2667 + 0.5699 \, x_t$$
$$x_t = c_t + i_t + h_{1t} + h_{2t} - h_{3t}$$
$$0.4119 x_t = w_t \, e_t$$
$$\log x_t = 1.32 + 0.00739t + 0.4119 \log e_t + 0.5881 \log k_t$$

The coefficient of log k_t in this equation follows from the assumption of a linear homogeneous production function.

$$k_t = 0.9714 \, k_{t-1} + i_t$$

From this model we may compute predictions of the endogenous variables given values of the exogenous variables. For predictions in the very long run we have from the difference equation for capital: $\lim\limits_{t \to \infty} k_t$ = $i/0.9714$. Here i is average investment. From this relation we may compute from the model the long-run elasticities of the endogenous with respect to the exogenous variables. We have for x (real income per capita): $Ex/Eh_1 = 0.2873$; $Ex/Eh_2 = 0.2262$; $Ex/Eh_3 = 0.2047$; $Ex/Ei = 0.330$. Similarly for c (real per capita consumption): $Ec/Eh_1 = 0.2288$; $Ec/Eh_2 = 0.1802$; $Ec/Eh_3 = -0.1723$; $Ec/Ei = -0.60$.

The negative value of the elasticity of real per capita consumption with respect to real per capita investment might be explained by the fact that the Ecuadorian economy is still quite primitive and the increase of capital will lead to decreased employment and hence less consumption: $Ec/Eh_1 = 0.7035$; $Ee/Eh_2 = 0.1802$; $Ee/Eh_3 = -0.5079$; $Ee/Ei = -0.6266$. The last negative value might be explained as before: $Ew/Eh_1 = -0.4110$ $Ew/Eh_2 = -0.3236$; $Ew/Eh_3 = 0.2967$; $Ew/Ei = 0.9566$.

The negative values of these elasticities show a decrease of real wages with increasing government expenditure. This may be explained by the fact that at the present time most of the government expenditure goes to the army and bureaucracy. Real investment, on the contrary, will increase real wages.

AN OPTIMAL POLICY OF ECONOMIC GROWTH FOR INDIA

In the context of economic planning for India, it has been repeatedly ascertained that the basic objectives are to provide employment for all those willing to work, to maintain at least a minimum standard of living, and to provide foundations for self-sustaining economic growth and the maintenance of its momentum. Hence the problems related to full employment as soon as possible and balanced growth thereafter, with the highest sustainable per capita consumption, would have to be dealt with.

Stoleru (58) developed a two-sector model designed to make the decision whether "to consume or to save." He considers his model to be appropriate for an economy in which the level of unemployment and capital/output ratio are high, and the capital goods sector is less capital intensive than the consumer goods sector. The Indian economy does not, however, have all these properties. Its capital goods sector is highly capital intensive compared to the consumer goods sector. It has a very high population though the rate of growth is small; it has a high capital/output ratio in the capital goods sector but not in the consumer goods sector. This article reports an experiment on the Stoleru model, since the objectives of the model are the same as those stated in the Indian economic plans.

The conclusions are not very encouraging, however. Without any change in the structure of industry, it would be possible to obtain full employment and balanced growth by 1972 if the present level of per capita income is allowed to fall by about one half. The optimal policy would then consist of investing in the capital goods sector alone until 1968 and then until 1972 in the consumer goods sector. If consumption is not allowed to fall by more than 10 percent of the present level, it would be possible to achieve full employment only by 1982. The optimal policy would then consist of investing in the capital goods sector alone for one year and then in both sectors until 1979. The proportion of investment going into the capital goods sector would increase from 0.72 to 0.93 and after 1979 would be concentrated in the consumer goods sector only. From the time when balanced growth and full employment are achieved, the economy tends to grow at the rate of growth of population and a hands-off policy will be optimal thereafter. This represents an unbalanced growth strategy with balanced growth in perspective.

We now present an outline of the model and the workings in the particular case; we conclude with certain observations about the structure and mechanics of the model. We have constructed our parameters from planning commission publications. Our I-sector contains (a) mining and factory establishments, (b) construction, and (c) transport and communications with an adjustment for including part of the "others" as classified by the p.p. division study. The rest of the sectors comprise our C-sector. The facts laid down here correspond to our base year 1960-61.[8]

I-sector: Y_I = output = 3950.66 RS crores;
            K_I = capital stock = 19973.0 RS crores;
            L_I = labor force = 11.2 millions.

C-sector: Y_c = output = 10237.44 RS crores;
            K_c = capital stock = 13581.64 RS crores;
            L_c = labor force = 162.98 millions.

Net national income = 14208.0 RS crores; C-sector output per capita = 233.15 RS crores. The other parameters of the model are

L = available labor force = $L_o e^{nt}$, where n = 0.01;
$1/\alpha$ = K_I/Y_I, where α = 0.1978;
σ = K_c/K_I = 0.68;
δ = c/b = 21.4, where b = K_I/L_I = 0.00056;
γ = K_c/L_c = 0.012;
$1/\beta$ = K_c/Y_c, where β = 0.7495;
l_o = L_o/L_I = 22.9.

Also A = 1.265533 and B = 1.010956.
The optimal policy of the no-constraint models is found to be

$$u(t) = 1 \text{ for } 0 \leq t \leq Z$$
$$0 \text{ for } Z \leq t \leq T$$

where t = 7.87 and T = 12 years. The results show the following:

---

8. Updated figures for capital stock are not available on print for latter years. We will revise the results when a detailed fourth-plan draft becomes available.

(a) The capital goods sector cannot be relied upon to absorb enough of the labor force. More than 90 percent will therefore have to find employment in the C-sector. It appears, then, that small enterprise and services will have to absorb most of the growth if agriculture has already attained a point of diminishing returns with respect to labor employed.

(b) Employment and per capita consumption will decrease considerably until 1968, which is not desirable with the low levels in view. Hence we reconsider the model with a minimum constraint on per capita consumption.

The Model with Constraint

If we want to maintain the level of per capita income at m percent of the original value, we introduce in the model a restriction $Ze^{-rt} \geq mp$. Stoleru (58) has shown that the following is an optimal policy under the restriction.

$$U(t) = 1 \text{ for } 0 \leq t \leq Z$$
$$= d(t) \text{ for } Z \leq t \leq \theta$$
$$= 0 \text{ for } \theta \leq t \leq T$$

where $d(r) = \{ (e^{\alpha t} - \delta) e^{r(t-Z) + 0.5 r \sigma} \} \div \{ (e^{\alpha Z} - \sigma) e^{r(t-Z) + \sigma} \}$

θ and T are determined by

$$1 - \alpha (T - \theta) = \sigma B^{-1} e^{-r(T - \theta + \alpha)}$$

$$(e^{\alpha t} - \delta) e^{r(T-Z)} + \sigma = A e^{r(T - \theta + Z)}$$

The optimal policy satisfies the following conditions: (a) m cannot be greater than 1 (i.e., until balanced growth is achieved, per capita consumption cannot be increased); (b) for $m \leq 1$, the optimal solution is unique and converges to the optimum without constraint as m decreases.

We have tabulated the time through which balanced growth is to be postponed if m is taken as greater than the minimum attained under no restriction. It can be observed that the Indian economy cannot achieve full employment and balanced growth even by 1980, unless it allows the present level of per capita consumption to fall to 80 percent. We chose 90 percent to represent our constraint to emphasize the following. Even if until 1964 the Indian economy had been giving heavy emphasis to in-dustrialization with a stepchild care for its C-sector, it is still not de-sirable to jump into agricultural and small industrial investments alone in the fourth and fifth plans just to provide higher employment. This may not help the economy in attaining balanced growth eventually. Under this restriction our optimal policy turned out to be

$$u(t) = 1 \text{ for } 0 \leq t \leq 0.958$$
$$= d(t) \text{ for } 0.958 \leq t \leq 19.40$$
$$= 0 \text{ for } 19.40 \leq t \leq 22.21$$

where d(t) is as specified earlier. The following observations can be made:

1. The prospects of the I-sector absorbing the increasing population are very small. The major emphasis still remains on services and small manufacturers.
2. The effective employment in both sectors together continues to increase beyond 1963 and hence we could eliminate the undesirability of reducing employment to an extent.
3. All along the second phase the per capita C-sector product remains constant at 90 percent of its original level and the I-sector achieves almost a 300 percent increase in its output.
4. The average growth rate during the transition is about 4 percent per year.
5. After 1982 the economy starts growing at the rate of population growth.

It is worth emphasizing that a much higher level of per capita consumption can be provided by merely shifting the C-sector investments into those with low capital/output ratio without altering capital intensity. The model could by simple extension provide a higher level of per capita income even without any change in structure though we have not analyzed the implications of the time necessary to meet a stated objective. The rate on the balanced growth path is low and can be improved by labor efficiency alone, within the context. During the transition between 1960-61 and 1963-64, the following occurred:[9]

I-sector: output 1960-61:   39.51 RS abja
                    1963-64:   61.80 RS abja
C-sector: output 1960-61: 102.37 RS abja
                    1963-64: 110.20 RS abja

That is, per capita consumption increased from 233.15 RS to 243.53 RS of the present model.

Observations on the Mechanics of the Model

Since the breakdown of the economy into the two sectors is arbitrary and our parameters approximate, we have not attempted any sensitivity analysis. Objectives of attaining the highest rate of growth are not compatible with investment in sectors with high capital/output ratios unless we expect them to generate external economies in other sectors and improve the overall rate of growth. Our model does not allow any such assumptions. They can, however, be easily incorporated using concepts of external economies of the factor-using type following Meade (41) and Morishima (43), who have proved in a different context that the absolute level at which balanced growth starts will be higher with the same rate of growth. For related models, see also Ramsey (50), Pugachev (49), and Stone (59).

9. Source: National Income Estimates, C.S.O., India.

STOCHASTIC PROCESSES APPLIED TO ECONOMIC DEVELOPMENT

There is not yet any very general and successful method of incorporating random influences in policy development. The following models should be regarded as very tentative, and it is hoped that they will soon be replaced by better models.

The methods of cybernetics and dynamic programming are most promising for the treatment of dynamic economic problems. We give here an example taken from Holt et al. (29). Denote by P_t production, by W_t work, by I_t inventories, by S_t orders; the cost function to be minimized is

$$V = E[A_1(W_t - W_{t-1})^2 + A_2(P_t - W_t)^2 + A_3(I_t - B)^2]$$

where E denotes the mathematical expectation (mean value) and A_1, A_2, A_3, and B are given constants. Also, $P_t - S_t = I_t - I_{t-1}$. Making the assumption that the variables follow stationary stochastic processes which have spectra and cross spectra, one can find the optimum policy. Another example is due to Phillips (48), Allen (3), and Whittle (76). Denote by y income or production per unit of time, by z aggregate demand or sales, by v policy demand (i.e., demand by the government), by x other demand; e is a random disturbance, the result of a stationary stochastic process. We have the following system:

$$dy/dt - a(z-y)$$

where production changes at a rate proportional to unsatisfied demand:

$$z = x + v$$

Nonpolicy demand is linearly related to income; a, c, d are constants. The criterion to be optimized is

$$V = E[(y - M)^2 + Lv^2]$$

where E denotes the mathematical expectation, y is the desired income level, and L is a constant. Assuming again that the random variable e follows a stationary stochastic process, we might find the optimal policy. Denote by Y national income, by C consumer spending, by S government spending, by I private investment; c is the constant marginal propensity to consume. We want to determine optimal government spending in this form:

$$S_t = M + \sum_{j=1}^{\infty} B_j I_{t-j}$$

where M and the B_j are constants to be determined. The aim is to minimize the function:

$$V = L[(Y - Y^*)^2 + L(S - S^*)^2]$$

In this formula Y^* is the desirable level of national income, S^* the desirable level of government spending. L is a constant and E denotes the mathematical expectation. Assuming that

$$Y_t = I_{t-1} + S_{t-1} + C_{t-1}$$

and that private investment follows a stationary stochastic process with a known spectral function, it is possible to determine the optimal policy. In presenting these cybernetic models we should realize that they tentatively use methods utilized in private enterprises (e.g., large corporations) or alternatively policy models for the whole economy. Methods of dynamic programming could be utilized.

GENERALIZED POISSON PROCESS FOR THE EXPLANATION OF ECONOMIC DEVELOPMENT WITH APPLICATIONS TO INDIAN DATA[10]

In the following we consider a very simplified system which yields a linear trend. We consider only steps upwards and no steps down in economic development. Consider a simple birth process, where only transitions from x to $x + u$ are possible without negligible probabilities. More formally we have a quantity x and consider its possible change in a small interval of time, from t to $t + \Delta t$. There are two possibilities: a transition from x to $x + u$ with probability $b(\Delta t)$ to (Δt); or no change, with probability $1 - b(\Delta t) + 0(\Delta t)$. All other transitions have probabilities of order $0(\Delta t)$.

$$p_x(t) = e^{-bt} (bt)^{(x-a)/u} / [(x-a)/u]!$$

$$x = a, \ a + u, \ a + 2u \ldots$$

This is surely the Poisson distribution of a variable which can only assume the values $a, a + u, a + 2u \ldots$. We derive the characteristics of the distribution: $M_t = a + ubt$, the mean of the distribution. This is a linear trend, $V_t = u^2 bt$, the variance of the distribution, a linear function of time. The skewness of the distribution is $\gamma_1 = 1/bt$ and the kurtosis is $\gamma_2 = 1/bt$. Since $\lim_{t \to \infty} \gamma_1 = \lim_{t \to \infty} \gamma_2 = 0$ we see that for large t our variable tends to be normally distributed with mean $a + ubt$ and variance $u^2 bt$.

Suggested Estimation Methods and Applications to India

We have the mean $M_t = a + ubt$. Using the method of least squares and minimizing $\sum_{t=1}^{k} (Y_t - M_t)^2$, we derive the following relations for the estimates of a and ub:

$$k \hat{a} + \hat{ub} \sum_{t=1}^{k} t = \sum_{t=1}^{k} Y_t$$

and

$$\hat{a} \sum_{t=1}^{k} t + \hat{ub} \sum_{t=1}^{k} t^2 = \sum_{t=1}^{k} t Y_t$$

---

10. Based on Tintner and Narayanan (73).

This yields the estimates a and ub. Further we have from this the variance:

$$V_t = u^2 \, bt = E \, (y_t - M_t)^2$$

Hence an estimate for $u^2 b$ is given by

$$\hat{u^2 b} = \frac{\sum\limits_{t=1}^{k} t \, (y - \hat{a} - \hat{ub}t)^2}{\sum\limits_{t=1}^{k} t^2}$$

Applying the method of least squares indicated above to the conforming data, we have the following trend:

$$M_t = 78.0385 + 4.270 \, t$$
$$(0.454)$$

The standard error of the coefficient of t is indicated in parentheses below. The correlation coefficient is 0.94. The estimate of u is $\hat{u}$ = 1.225, and the estimate of b is $\hat{b}$ = 3.485. We try to predict on the basis of our theory Indian national income for 1964-65. From the above formula M_{17} = 150.6285. According to the formula, national income is a Poisson variable, distributed with a parameter bt - 59.262. We use the normal approximation because of lack of tabulated values and determine the 95 percent confidence limits for national income in India in 1964-65 as 132.148 and 169.309. If we apply weighted regression to the problem of estimating the parameters, we minimize:

$$\sum\limits_{t=1}^{k} \frac{(y_t - M_t)^2}{t}$$

and the estimates are derived from the following system of equations:

$$\hat{a} \sum\limits_{t=1}^{k} (1/t) + \hat{ub} \cdot k = \sum\limits_{t=1}^{k} y_t /t$$

$$k \, \hat{a} + \hat{ub} \sum\limits_{t=1}^{k} t = \sum\limits_{t=1}^{k} y_t$$

$$V = \hat{u^2 b} = \frac{1}{(k=2)} \sum\limits_{t=1}^{k} \frac{1}{t} (y_t - M_t)^2$$

Applying this method to our data, we have for the simple linear trend:

$$M_t = 82.0598 + 3.734 \, t$$

The correlation coefficient is 0.95 and the estimates of the parameters are

$$\hat{u} = 0.474 \text{ and } \hat{b} = 7.873$$

Using this formula, we predict national income in India for 1964-65 as 145.378. Using again the normal approximation, we obtain the 95 percent confidence limits, 134.785 and 156.290.

Consider now a slight generalization of the Poisson Process. We consider the situation at time t. The probability of the transition from x to x + u is $b(t)(\Delta t) + 0(\Delta t)$. The probability of no change is now

$$1 - b(t)(\Delta t) + 0(\Delta t)$$

Note that now the birth rate $b(t)$ is a function of time. Also, as before, we assume that at time t=0 we have x = a with probability one. Now we have for $x > a$

$$p_x (t + \Delta t) = p_{x-u} (t)b(t)(\Delta t) + p_x (t) [1 - b(t)(\Delta t)]$$

and for x = a

$$p_a (t - \Delta t) = p_a (t) [1 - b(t)(\Delta t)]$$

The probabilities of x at time t are

$$p_x (t) = e \int_0^{-t} b(z)dz \, [\int_0^t b(z)dz]^{(x-a)/u}/[(x-a)/u]1! ;$$
$$x = a, \ a + u, \ a + 2u \ldots$$

The mean of the stochastic process is

$$M_t = a + u \int_0^t b(z)dz$$

and the variance is

$$V_t = u^2 \int_0^t [b(z)]dz$$

The skewness is

$$\gamma_1 = 1/\sqrt{} \int_0^t b(z)dz$$
$$\gamma_2 = 1/\int_0^t b(z)dz$$

It is evident that the distribution tends toward normal if the integral becomes infinite. As a special case, consider now the influence of government consumption G_t . We assume this influence linear and have

$$b(t) = b_0 + b_1 G(t)$$

We assume that G(t) is a step function. We have

$$\int_0^t b(z)dz = b_0 t + b_1 \sum_{r=1}^t G$$

Using the simple least-squares method, we compute the estimates for our stochastic process. The mean value is

$$M_t = 88.8026 - 3.141 t + 0.550 \sum_{r=1}^t G$$

The multiple correlation coefficient is 0.98. Other estimates are $\hat{a} = 88.8026$, $\hat{u} = 1.798$. The function b(t) which includes the linear influence of government consumption is

$$b(t) = 1.7467 + 0.306 G_t$$

We have again estimated some results for 1964-65 (t = 17). Assuming

G_t = 25 on the average in the three intervening years, we have for our estimate of the trend of Indian national income 179.671. The 95 percent limits are 154.618 and 204.724. If we assume that government consumption will be on the average 30 in the three years, we have an estimate of trend as 187.221. The 95 percent limits of this estimate are 161.755 and 214.087.

A LOG-NORMAL DIFFUSION PROCESS APPLIED TO THE ECONOMIC DEVELOPMENT OF INDIA[11]

The following tries to apply a log-normal diffusion process to the development of the Indian economy. The theory of difference processes has been very important in many applications. The use of the log-normal rather than the normal or the Pareto distribution (17, 24, 37, 47, 57) is suggested by a number of investigations which seem to point to its usefulness as a convenient approximation in a number of fields of economics.

Log-Normal Process

Let X(t), national income at time t, be a random variable of continuous process {X(t), t ≥ 0} of the Markovian type; that is, X(t) is a Markovian random variable depending on a continuous time parameter t, which assumes values in the state space. We assume the transition probability density for

$$f(\tau,x;\, t,y) = \Pr\left[X(t) = y \mid X(\tau) = x\right],\ 0 < y,\, x < \infty$$

exists for every τ and t, where $0 \le \tau < t$, and satisfies the backward and forward Kolmogorov equations. We also assume the random variable X(t) continuous with probability one. Consider the coefficients b(t,x) and a(t,x), the infinitesimal mean and variance of the change in X(t) during small interval Δt of time, that characterize a particular process of the diffusion type as

$$b(t,x) = b_t \cdot x;\quad a(t,x) = a_t \cdot x^2 > 0$$

where $b_t = b_0$ and $a_t = a_0$, where a_0, b_0 are constants, $a_0 > 0$. We thus assume that the expected change and its variance in national income are proportional to the instantaneous size of it. With a(t,x) > 0, it is certain that some change in national income will take place in any interval Δt and it will be small if Δt is small. This seems to well describe the plausible characteristic of economy. The probability density function satisfying these diffusion equations is then given by the log-normal density function (1).

---

11. From Tintner and Patel (74).

$$f(\tau,x;\ t,y) = \frac{1}{y_1\ \sqrt{2\pi\gamma\ (t-\tau)}}$$

$$\exp \frac{1}{2\ (t-\tau)} \{ \log y - \log x - \beta(t - \tau)\}^2$$

where $\gamma = a_0$ and $\beta = (b_0 - \dfrac{a_0}{2})$.

The characteristics of this distribution are easily derived from its moments. If we take $\tau = 0$ and assume $\Pr[X(0)] = 1$, then

$$\text{mean, } E[X(t)] = x_0 \cdot e^{b_0 t}$$

which is an exponential trend; and

$$\text{variance, } V[X(t)] = x_0^2 \cdot e^{2b_0 t} (e^{a_0 t} - 1)$$

which is also an exponential function of time. The coefficients of skewness and kurtosis are:

$$\gamma_1 = \frac{(e^{3\gamma t} - 3e^{\gamma t} + 2)}{(e^{\gamma t} - 1)^{3/2}}$$

$$\gamma_2 = \frac{(e^{6\gamma t} - 4e^{3\gamma t} - 6e^{\gamma t} - 3)}{(e^{\gamma t} - 1)^2}$$

Maximum Likelihood Estimates

If we assume that the observations are taken at equal intervals of time of unity, that is, $(t_j - t_{j-1}) = 1$, $j = 1, 2, \ldots, n$, and $t_0 = 0$, then the estimates and their sampling variances are

$$\hat{\beta} = \sum_{j=1}^{n} \frac{(\log x_j - \log x_{j-1})}{n}$$

$$\hat{\gamma} = \sum_{j=1}^{n} \frac{(\log x_j - \log x_{j-1})^2 - \hat{\beta}^2}{n^2}$$

$$V(\hat{\beta}) = \frac{\gamma}{n} \cdot \frac{1}{t} \longrightarrow 0 \text{ as } t \longrightarrow \infty$$

$$V(\hat{\gamma}) = \frac{2\gamma^2}{n}$$

and

$$V(\hat{a}_0) = \frac{2\gamma^2}{n}$$

$$V(\hat{b}_0) = \frac{\gamma^2}{2n} + \frac{\gamma}{n} \cdot \frac{1}{t} \longrightarrow \frac{\gamma^2}{2n} \text{ as } t \longrightarrow \infty$$

Empirical Illustrations

We now fit the above model to the data of real national income of India for the period 1948-61. Here $X(t)$ represents the real national income of India in the year t, in billions of rupees, and $Pr[X(0) = 86.5] = 1$. The maximum likelihood estimates and their variances are found as $\hat{\beta} = 0.0322$ and $\hat{\gamma} = 0.5947 \times 10^{-3}$.

$$V(\hat{\beta}) = 0.4956 \times 10^{-4} \cdot \frac{1}{t} \quad V(\hat{\gamma}) = 0.5895 \times 10^{-7}$$

Hence $\hat{b}_0 = 0.0325$ and $\hat{a}_0 = 0.5947 \times 10^{-3}$.

$$V(\hat{b}_0) = 0.1474 \times 10^{-7} - 0.4956 \times 10^{-4} \cdot \frac{1}{t}$$

and

$$V(\hat{a}_0) = 0.5895 \times 10^{-7}$$

The trend is given by

$$E[X(t)] = 86.5 \ e^{0.0325 t}$$

$$t = 0, 1, 2, \ldots$$

We try to predict the values of national income for 1965-66 (end year of third five-year plan), and for selected years of the fourth five-year plan period (to 1970-71). The results of prediction based on our theory are given in Table 4.16. We observe 3.25 percent growth rate during the fourth plan on the basis of our model.

Table 4.16. Estimates of the national income of India for selected years, based on trend

Year	t	E X(t)
1965-66	17	150.3
1967-68	19	160.4
1969-70	21	171.2
1970-71	22	176.8

Influence of Exogenous Factor

The influence of an exogenous factor like government expenditure on economic growth can be considered by taking the parameters of the process as function of such variable. Let us assume a linear effect of government expenditure $G(t)$ on βt; that is

$$\beta_t = \beta_0 + \beta_1 \ G(t)$$

We have then

$$\int_\tau^t \beta_t \ dt = \beta_0 \ (t - \tau) + \beta_1 \int_\tau^t G(t) dt$$

$$= \beta_0 \ (t - \tau) - \beta_1 \cdot (G)_\tau^t$$

where $\int_\tau^t G(t)dt = (G)_\tau^t$, say. With infinitesimal mean and variance of change in X(t) defined as

$$b(t,x) = b_t \cdot x \ \text{and} \ a(t,x) = a_t \cdot x^2 > 0$$

where $a_t = a_0 > 0$ and $b_t = b_0 + b_1 \cdot G(t)$, where a_0, b_0, $b_1 = 0$ are constants, we have the probability density function for X(t) satisfying the Kolmogorov equations as

$$f(\tau,x; t,y) = \frac{1}{y\sqrt{2\pi\gamma(t-\tau)^1}}$$

$$\exp - \frac{1}{2\gamma(t\tau)} [\log y - \log x - \beta_0(t-\tau) - \beta_1 (G)_\tau^t]^2$$

where $\gamma = a_0$; $\beta_0 = (b_0 - \frac{a_0}{2})$; and $\beta_1 = b_1$.

If observations are made at equal intervals of time of unity, that is, $(t_j - t_{j-1}) = 1$, $j = 1, 2, \ldots, n$, and if we assume G(t) a step function $G(t) = Gt_j$ for $t_{j-1} \le t \le t_j$, $j = 0, 1, 2, \ldots, n$, so that

$$\int_{t_{j-1}}^{t_j} G(r)dr = Gt_j \cdot (t_j - t_{j-1})$$

then our estimates are

$$\beta_0 = \sum_{j=1}^n \frac{(\log x_j - \log x_{j-1})}{n} = \hat{\beta}_1 \cdot \sum_{j=1}^n (G_j)$$

$$\hat{\beta}_1 = \frac{\sum_{j=1}^n [(G_j) \cdot \log(x_j/x_{j-1})] - \{\sum_{j=1}^n [\log(x_j/x_{j-1})] \cdot \sum_{j=1}^n [G_j]\}/n}{\sum_{j=1}^n (G_j^2) - \frac{\sum_{j=1}^n [(G_j)]^2}{n}}$$

and $\hat{\gamma} = \frac{1}{n} \cdot \sum_{j=1}^n [\log(x_j/x_{j-1}) - \hat{\beta}_0 - \hat{\beta}_1 G_j]^2$

The dispersion matrix of the estimates $(\beta_0, \beta_1, \gamma)$ is given by the inverse of the information matrix I:

$$I = \frac{n}{\gamma} \begin{bmatrix} t & \sum_1^t G_j & 0 \\ & (\sum_1^t G_j)^2/t & 0 \\ & & \\ 0 & & \frac{1}{2\gamma} \end{bmatrix}$$

Therefore

$$V(\beta_0) = \frac{\gamma}{n} \cdot \frac{1}{t} \longrightarrow 0 \text{ as } t \longrightarrow \infty$$

$$V(\beta_1) = \frac{\gamma}{n} \cdot \frac{1}{(\sum_1^t G_j)^2/t} \longrightarrow 0 \text{ as } t \longrightarrow \infty$$

when G_j is constant or increasing

$$V(\gamma) = \frac{2\gamma^2}{n}$$

Hence

$$V(\hat{a}_0) = \frac{2\gamma^2}{n}$$

$$V(\hat{b}_0) = \frac{\gamma}{n} \cdot \frac{1}{t} + \frac{\gamma^2}{2n} \longrightarrow \frac{\gamma^2}{2n} \text{ as } t \longrightarrow \infty$$

$$V(\hat{b}_1) = \frac{\gamma}{n} \frac{1}{(\sum_1^t G_j)^2/t} \longrightarrow 0 \text{ as } t \longrightarrow \infty$$

when G_j is constant or increasing.

The probability density function $X(t)$ with $t_0 = 0$ and $Pr[X(\theta) = x_0] = 1$ is

$$f(x_0, t, x) = \frac{1}{x\sqrt{2\pi\gamma t}} \exp - \frac{1}{2\gamma t} (\log x - \log x_0 - \beta_0 t - \beta_1 \cdot \sum_1^t G_j)^2$$

$$\text{mean, } E[X(t)] = X_0 \cdot e^{(b_0 t + b_1 \cdot \sum_1^t G_j)}$$

and

$$\text{variance, } V[X(t)] = X_0^2 \cdot e^{2(b_0 t + b_1 \sum_1^t G_j)} (e^{a_0 t} - 1)$$

Also the coefficients of skewness and kurtosis are

$$\gamma_1 = \frac{(e^{2\gamma t} - 3e^{\gamma t} + 2)}{(e^{\gamma t} - 1)^{3/2}}$$

$$\gamma_2 = \frac{(e^{6\gamma t} - 4e^{3\gamma t} + 6e^{\gamma t} - 3)}{(e^{\gamma t} - 1)}$$

Empirical Example

We now fit the generalized model with government expenditure G_t to the same Indian data. The maximum likelihood estimates and their variances are obtained as

$$\hat{\beta}_0 = 0.01118, \ \hat{\beta}_1 = 0.001623, \ \gamma = 0.5494 \times 10^{-3}$$

$$V(\hat{\beta}_0) = 0.4578^{-4} \cdot \frac{1}{t}, \ V(\hat{\beta}_1) = 0.4578 \times 10^{-4} \cdot \frac{1}{(\sum\limits_{1}^{t} G_j)^2/t}$$

$$V(\gamma) = 0.503 \times 10^{-7}$$

Hence

$$\hat{b}_0 = 0.01146, \ \hat{b}_1 = 0.001623, \ \hat{a}_0 = 0.5494 \times 10^{-3}$$

$$V(\hat{b}_0) = 0.1257 \times 10^{-7} + 0.4578 \times 10^{-4} \cdot \frac{1}{t}$$

$$V(\hat{b}_1) = \frac{0.4578 \times 10^{-4}}{(\sum\limits_{1}^{t} G_j)^2/t}, \ V(\hat{a}_0) = 0.503 \times 10^{-7}$$

The trend is given by

$$E[X(t)] = 86.5 \ e^{(0.01146 \ t + 0.001623 \sum\limits_{1}^{t} G_j)}$$

$$t = 0, 1, 2, \ldots$$

We find that the fit is better than the one without the influence of government expenditure. We now try to predict the values of national income for the same years chosen earlier under the following different hypotheses of G_t: (a) yearly 1.5 billion increase in G during third and fourth five-year-plan period; (b) yearly 2.0 billion increase in G during third and fourth plan period; (c) yearly 2.5 billion increase in G during third and fourth plan period; (d) yearly 2.0 billion increase in G during third plan and 3.0 billion increase in G during fourth plan. The results obtained are shown in Table 4.17. We observe the following growth rates under the different hypotheses of government expenditure and levels of income at the end of fourth five-year plan (1970-71) (Table 4.18). Thus, depending on what growth rate is desired, the levels of government expenditure may be maintained.

The method of log-normal diffusion processes has also been applied to Indian agriculture (74) data from 1951-52 to 1963-64 for real per capita agricultural production and real per capita government expenditure on agricultural production and agriculture. Table 4.19 indicates predictions for 1969-70 under the following hypotheses: (a) same real per capita government expenditure in the intervening years as in 1963-64; (b) an increase by one half; (c) a doubling; (d) two and a half times; (e) three times the expenditure of 1963-64. In 1963-64 the real per capita agricultural production (Table 4.20) was 0.9401. Table 4.20 shows that it would take a doubling of real per capita government expenditure in agriculture in order to maintain or slightly surpass the real per capita

Table 4.17. Estimates of the national income of India
for selected years, under four hypothesized levels
of government expenditure

Year	t	(a)	(b)	(c)	(d)
1965-66	17	167.7	168.5	168.6	168.5
1967-68	19	190.2	192.5	193.1	193.4
1969-70	21	217.8	222.8	224.8	226.5
1970-71	22	234.0	240.9	244.0	246.8

Table 4.18. Expected growth rates
during fourth plan

| | Hypothesis about G_t | | | |
	(a)	(b)	(c)	(d)
First two years	6.7	7.1	7.2	7.3
Next two years	7.2	7.8	8.2	8.5
Last year	7.4	8.1	8.5	9.0

Table 4.19. Predictions for 1969-70

Hypothesis	Estimated real per capita agricultural production	95% confidence limits	
(a)	0.8541	0.5952	1.1311
(b)	0.9107	0.6347	1.1867
(c)	0.9712	0.6768	1.2656
(d)	1.0350	0.7212	1.3488
(e)	1.1040	0.7694	1.4386

Table 4.20. Real per capita agricultural production

Year	t	X_t real per capita agricultural production	G_t real per capita government expenditure on agriculture
1951-52	0	1.0347	0.0211
1952-53	1	1.2430	0.0278
1953-54	2	1.3063	0.0516
1954-55	3	1.4621	0.0516
1955-56	4	1.3870	0.0619
1956-57	5	1.2488	0.0360
1957-58	6	1.1347	0.0379
1958-59	7	1.1842	0.0405
1959-60	8	1.1076	0.0417
1960-61	9	1.0881	0.0437
1961-62	10	1.0647	0.0452
1962-63	11	1.000	0.0529
1963-64	12	0.9401	0.0548

agricultural production from 1963-64 in the year 1969-70. The lower
95 percent confidence limits indicate the great uncertainty of the effect
of agricultural policy measures in India.

A LOG-NORMAL DIFFUSION PROCESS APPLIED TO THE DEVELOPMENT OF INDIAN AGRICULTURE WITH SOME CONSIDERATIONS ON ECONOMIC POLICY[12]

Consider a stochastic variable (e.g., real agricultural production in
India per capita). Assume that real agricultural production per capita
in India follows a log-normal diffusion process: the logarithm of real
agricultural production in India is normally distributed, and the mathematical expectation of the logarithm and its variance are linear functions of time. Define a transition probability density as follows:

$$f(s,x; t,y) = \frac{\exp - [\log y - \log x - b(t-s)]^2/2c(t-s)}{y\sqrt{2\pi c(t-s)}}$$

This is the probability that real national agricultural production will
be y at time t if it was x at time ($<$t). We assume now that our random variable has with probability one the value x_0 at the point in time
t=0. Then the mathematical expectation of the random variable is

$$E[Y(t)] = x_0 \exp (b + 1/2c)t$$

and its variance is given by

$$\delta^2_{y(t)} = [Ey(t)]^2 [\exp (ct) - 1]$$

Hence the mathematical expectation and variance of our random variable are both exponential functions of time. Assume further that we
have n+1 observations and that our observations are evenly spaced from
X_0 to X_n. According to Fisz (20) we obtain the following maximum likelihood estimates of the parameters:

$$\hat{b} = (\sum_{t=1}^{n} \log X_t - \log X_{t-1})/n$$

$$\hat{c} = [\sum_{t=1}^{n} (\log x_t - \log x_{t-1})]^2/n - b^2$$

The asymptotic variances of the estimates are given by

$$\delta^2_{\hat{b}} = c/nt$$
$$\delta^2_{\hat{c}} = 2c^2/n$$

12. See Tintner and Patel (74). We are much obliged to C. H. Hanumanta Rao for providing
the data and to A. K. Banerjee for carrying out the computations. We are also obliged to
V. G. Panse and G. R. Seth for help and encouragement.

Table 4.21. Predicted real per capita
agricultural income

Year	t	X_t real per capita agricultural production
1964-65	13	0.9517
1965-66	14	0.9456
1966-67	15	0.9396
1967-68	16	0.9335
1968-69	17	0.9274
1969-70	18	0.9215

Since both variances tend to zero with increasing sample size (n+1),
we have obtained consistent estimates. Table 4.21 gives our predictions
for real per capita agricultural production in India. This table shows
that predicted real per capita agricultural production in India has a decreasing trend. It is also possible to compute confidence or fiducial
limits. For t=18, we predict a real per capita agricultural production of
only 0.9215. The 95 percent confidence or fiducial limits are 0.708 and
1.113. Now we consider also the influence of an exogenous factor on
real per capita agricultural production in India, namely real per capita
government expenditure on agriculture (G_t). Define

$$H_t = G_0 + G_1 + \ldots + G_t$$

as the cumulative real per capita government expenditure in India after t
years. Assume that the effect of expenditure will only be felt after p
years. The transition probability density becomes now

$$f(s,x; t,y) = \frac{\exp - [\log y - \log x - b_0 (t-s) - b_1 (H_{t-p} - H_{s-p})]^2/2c(t-s)}{y \sqrt{2\pi c(t-s)}}$$

This is the conditional probability that our random variable will have the
value y at time t if it had the value x at time s ($<$t) given the government expenditure between s-p and t-p. Assume now that our random
variable has the value x_p for t=p with probability one. Then its mean
value is given by

$$E[y(t)] = x_p \exp [(b_0 + (1/2)(c) (t-p) + b_1 H_{t-p}]$$

and its variance is given by

$$\delta^2_{y(t)} = E[y(t)]^2 [\exp (ct) - 1)]$$

Both mean and variance depend now on cumulative government expenditure (H_t).

Now we consider forecasts of the real per capita agricultural production in India under a variety of hypotheses for t=18 (1969-70):
(a) same real per capita government expenditure in the intervening years,
as in 1963-64; (b) an increase of expenditure by one half; (c) doubling
of expenditure; (d) two and a half times the 1964-65 expenditure; (e) three

Table 4.22. Forecast of real per capita production

Hypothesis	Estimated real per capita agricultural production, 1969-70	95% limits	
(a)	0.8541	0.5952	1.1130
(b)	0.9107	0.6347	1.1867
(c)	0.9712	0.6768	1.2656
(d)	1.0350	0.7212	1.3488
(e)	1.1040	0.7694	1.4386

times the expenditure of 1963-64. The resulting forecasts and their 95 percent confidence or fiducial limits are given in Table 4.22. This table shows that in the intervening years between 1964-65 and 1969-70 real per capita government expenditure on agriculture must be almost doubled (hypothesis c) in order to keep real per capita agricultural production at least on the level of 1964-65.

STOCHASTIC PROGRAMMING AND ECONOMIC DEVELOPMENT

A possible generalization of linear programming consists in the assumption that all parameters involved are random variables with a known joint probability distribution. The methods used in the following models are neither very realistic nor efficient. But they point to the need of taking the random influences in economic development into account as much as policy decisions are concerned. Abandoning the somewhat unreal but convenient assumption of single-valued anticipations, we have a case of risk. Here we have not a unique value of anticipated conditions (prices, etc.) but probability distributions. However the assumption is that at least these probability distributions are known with certainty. As an example, as illustrated by Tintner (69), consider the situation of an Iowa farm. We assume that the farmer uses only two factors of production, land and capital, since labor is abundant. Using data from the period 1938-52, we estimate the probability distribution of the input coefficients of land and capital in the production of corn and flax. We determine, by numerical methods, the approximate probability distribution of the net profit if certain proportions of the resources (capital, land) are used for the production of the two crops (corn, flax). This is a problem of stochastic programming. The input coefficients are assumed to be normally and independently distributed.

By numerical methods we might approximate the probability distribution of short-term profits (e.g., the mathematical expectation of profits is $11,081). This is called the passive approach. It might be used by comparing, for example, the probability distribution of profits for a farm in Iowa and a farm in California. More important perhaps is the active approach. Here the decision variables are the proportions of the factor of production (land and capital) assigned to growing various crops

Table 4.23. Arithmetic mean of profits

Proportion of capital used for:		Proportion of land used for:		
Corn	Flax	Corn: 0 1/2 Flax: 1 1/2		1 0
0	1	5704	5168	0
1/2	1/2	4082	7008	4945
1	0	0	5075	8472

(corn and flax). Table 4.23 shows the arithmetic mean of the estimated probability distribution of profits for various possible cases. The data in this table are interpreted in the following way. Assume that the farmer uses no land or capital for corn (hence all the land and capital for flax). Then, in the long run, his average profit will be $5704. But if he divides both land and capital evenly between the two commodities, he will receive on the average $7008, and so on. It is easily seen from this table that the best policy for the farmer is to devote all his land and capital to corn, none to flax. Then under our very simplified conditions his average profit in the long run will be $8472, which is the highest he can obtain. We should mention again that of course some very unrealistic assumptions underlie our analysis. The probability distribution is assumed known (actually estimated from past experience). Very crude numerical methods have been utilized in order to estimate the mean values of profits exhibited in the table. The enormous amount of computations involved, even for a simple example, makes this method of stochastic linear programming not yet practical for the study of important and realistic empirical problems.

APPLICATION OF STOCHASTIC PROGRAMMING TO THE UAR FIRST FIVE-YEAR PLAN [13]

The involvement of random variables, the distribution of which are approximated on the basis of samples from the past for use in future economic decisions, indicates that the anticipated economic performance of a policy is not a single sure value but rather a statistical distribution. That is what is identified as a situation of risk. Since the policy maker is always faced with sets of interdependent variables, targets, and conditions, his choice of future actions becomes a difficult and critical one. Nevertheless his task will be greatly facilitated if he can obtain more elaborate information, and if a set of rules for guiding choice can be set forth.

The present study, in its attempt to examine the complex situations that face the policy maker in a centrally planned system, benefits from previous work on the use of stochastic linear programming for economic

13. Based on Tintner and Farghali (71).

planning. It has been suggested that the treatment of technical coefficients of production as random variables is more realistic than the
fixed-coefficients approach. Our purpose here is twofold. We first aim
at applying the case of risk, along the same lines of previous works, to
the UAR's (Egypt's) experience of the First Five-Year Plan, trying to
obtain an objective measure for choice. We then attempt to evaluate the
role and significance of "risk" under conditions of central planning.
From the UAR's First Five-Year Plan (1960/61-1964/65), we select the
agricultural and industrial sectors where the problem is to determine
the "best" policy to maximize total output generated from both sectors
at the end of the plan; that is, to maximize $A_5 + S_5 = W_5$ where A_5 is the
value of agricultural output at the end of 1965, S_5 is the value of industrial output at the end of 1965, and W_5 is the value of total output of both
sectors at the end of 1965. We start with three basic assumptions:
(a) Only two factors of production are considered—total capital available
for investment for both sectors together over the plan period and total
labor force available for both sectors together over the plan period.
(b) The technical coefficients b_{11}, b_{12}, b_{21}, and b_{22} are independent normally distributed random variables with single known probability distributions (case of technical risk), where b_{11} and b_{12} are, respectively,
output/labor ratio and output/capital ratio in the agricultural sector, and
b_{21} and b_{22} are, respectively, output/labor ratio and output/capital ratio
in the industrial sector. (c) Sectoral allocation of factors of production
is determined a priori. Each decision policy, U_{ij}, represents a set of
arbitrarily selected values of u_{11}, u_{12}, u_{22}, and u_{22}, where u_{11} and u_{12} are,
respectively, the proportion of labor devoted to agriculture and that de-
voted to industry each year, such that $u_{11} + u_{12} = 1$; also u_{21} and u_{22} are,
respectively, the proportion of capital devoted to agriculture and that
devoted to industry each year, such that $u_{21} + u_{22} = 1$. We also have the
following data:

1. Estimates of the supply of capital available for both sectors together
   in each year of the plan, in millions of Egyptian pounds:[14] K_0 (1960/61)
   = 225.120, K_1 (1961/62) = 324.615, K_2 (1962/63) = 477.831, K_3 (1963/64)
   = 711.717, and K_4 (1964/65) = 1014.649, where t = 0, 1, 2, 3, 4 refers
   to capital supply at the beginning of each planning year.
2. Estimates of total labor force available to both sectors together for
   each year of the plan, in millions of workers.[15] $L_0 = 4.428$, $L_1 = 4.523$,
   $L_2 = 4.619$, $L_3 = 4.686$, $L_4 = 4.766$, where again t = 0, 1, 2, 3, 4 refers to
   labor supply at the beginning of each planning year.

14. The data used for the derivation of these estimates are obtained from Council of National
Planning, Outline of the General Plan for Economic and Social Development for the Five
Years—July 1960-June 1965 (1960, p. 18); UAR Ministry of Planning, Progress Under Plan-
ning (1964, p. 28); UAR, Institute of National Planning, A. H. Ahmed, Memo. No. 211,
Financing Capital Formation in UAR (August, 1962, p. 25); UAR, INP, M. M. El-Iman, Memo
No. 255, Models Used in Drafting the 20-year Plan (1959-78) (December 1962, p. 9).

15. The data used for the derivation of these estimates are obtained from Central Statistical
Committee, Basic Statistics (Jan. 1960, p. 38, and May 1963, p. 17); UAR, INP, M. Hamdy
(ed.), Memo No. 431, Manpower Requirements for UAR for the Period 1960-85 (May 1964,
p. 60).

3. The estimates of output-input coefficients are:[16]

	Agriculture			Industry	
	Mean	Standard Error		Mean	Standard Error
b_{11}	1.912	0.028	b_{21}	10.000	0.515
b_{12}	0.455	0.005	b_{22}	0.290	0.063

The mathematical model presented below is applied under five different allocational policies which we assume a priori. The final purpose is to compare results in order to select the "best" policy, and to select the one with the set of allocational proportions of the First Five-Year Plan.

The five policies are:

	u_{11}	u_{12}	u_{21}	u_{22}
Policy I	2/3	1/3	1/4	3/4
Policy II	2/3	1/3	1/3	2/3
Policy III	3/4	1/4	1/2	1/2
Policy IV	3/4	1/4	1/2	1/2
Policy V	1/2	1/2	1/2	1/2

Assuming that the above given technical coefficients, b_{ij}, are normally distributed random variables, our problem is to select a set of policy variables, U_{ij}, which maximizes the objective function. Since K_i's, L_i's, U_{ij}'s, A_0, and S_0 are knowns, the model is reduced to one of maximizing the objective function $W_5 = A_5 + S_5$ under the conditions that $A_1 \leq C_1$; $S_1 \leq C_2$; $-A_1 + A_2 \leq C_3$; $-S_1 + S_2 \leq C_4$; $-A_2 + A_3 \leq C_5$; $-S_2 + S_3 \leq C_6$; $-A_3 + A_4 \leq C_7$; $-S_3 + S_4 \leq C_8$; $-A_4 + A_5 \leq C_9$; and $-S_4 + S_5 \leq C_{10}$; where $C_1, C_2, C_3, \ldots, C_{10}$ are constants. With this very simple form, the maximization solution is obviously always obtained by a zero slack vector. To derive the approximate distribution of the objective function $W_5 = A_5 + S_5$ under different allocational policies, we assume that the coefficients $b_{11}, b_{12}, b_{21}, b_{22}$ have the following independent normal distributions which are derived from their means and standard errors:

$$p(b_{11}) = [\sqrt{2\pi(0.27,741)}]^{-1} e^{-(b_{11} - 1.912)^2 \cdot 2(0.028)^{-2}}$$

$$p(b_{12}) = [\sqrt{2\pi(0.005)}]^{-1} e^{-(b_{12} - 0.455)^2 \cdot 2(0.005)^{-2}}$$

16. From published figures of eighteen estimates of average capital/output and capital/labor ratios for each of the two sectors and for several industries independently (UAR, INP, M. M. El-Iman, Memo No. 225, Models Used in Drafting the 20-Year Plan, [1959-78], pp. 15-33), we estimated the corresponding output/labor and output/capital ratios. From these we picked population means in each sector. As for the standard errors of the means, we selected two samples from the eighteen values. By this arbitrary selection our aim was to obtain the suitable sample—from the point of view of factor proportions—for each sector. The samples were then used for the estimation of the standard errors.

$$p(b_{21}) = [\sqrt{2\pi(0.515)}]^{-1} e^{-(b_{21} - 10.000)^2 \cdot 2(0.515)^{-2}}$$

$$p(b_{22}) = [\sqrt{2\pi(0.063)}]^{-1} e^{-(b_{22} - 0.290)^2 \cdot 2(0.063)^{-2}}$$

For each coefficient we assume five standardized values; $0, \pm 1, \pm 2$, and calculate their corresponding values, cumulative probabilities, and probabilities. Thus for each policy we obtain a total of 20 values for the coefficients. These values give $5^4 = 625$ combinations, each of which is used for a linear programming problem whose optimum solution is W_5. To derive the distribution of the objective function W_5 under each of the five policies, we first estimate the probability of getting each value of W_5 (which equals the product of the probabilities of the relevant combination of coefficients). We then use the value of $P(W_5)$ to calculate the means and standard deviations under each policy. The following are the final results of the calculations. Policy I has a mean value of 1741.703, a standard deviation of 219.205, and a lower 5 percent probability level of 1724.518; the approximate distribution of the objective function W_5 is

$$f(x) = [\sqrt{2\pi(219.205)}]^{-1} e^{-(x - 1741.703)^2 \cdot 2(219.205)^{-2}}$$

Policy II has a mean value of 1974.526, a standard deviation of 120.551, and a lower 5 percent probability level of 1785.075; the approximate distribution of W_5 is

$$f(x) = [\sqrt{2\pi(120.552)}]^{-1} e^{-(x - 1794.53)^2 \cdot 2(120.1)^{-2}}$$

Policy III has a mean value of 1745.690, a standard deviation of 148.003, and a lower 5 percent probability level of 1734.087; the approximate distribution of W_5 is

$$f(x) = [\sqrt{2\pi(148.003)}]^{-1} e^{-(x - 1745.69)^2 \cdot 2(148.0)^{-2}}$$

Policy IV has a mean value of 1841.936306, a standard deviation of 77.433857, and a lower 5 percent probability level of 1835.865492; the approximate distribution of the function W_5 is

$$f(x) = [\sqrt{2\pi(77.433)}]^{-1} e^{-(x - 1841.93)^2 \cdot 2(77.4)^{-2}}$$

Policy V has a mean value of 1890.596, a standard deviation of 288.450, and a lower 5 percent probability level of 1872.686; the approximate distribution of W_5 is

$$f(x) = [\sqrt{2\pi(228.450)}]^{-1} e^{-(x - 1890.60)^2 \cdot 2(228.5)^{-2}}$$

Table 4.24 gives a brief comparison of the five policies.

We choose to select policy IV as the "best." It has the lowest risk and is among the highest in mean value. This policy is the closest, though not identical, to the actual one of the UAR First Five-Year Plan,

Table 4.24. Comparison of five policies

Policy	U_{11}	$\dot{U}_{12}$	U_{21}	U_{22}	Mean value	Standard error	Lower 50% limit	Absolute risk margin: (1) - (3)	Relative risk margin: % to (1)
I	0.67	0.33	0.75	0.75	1741.7	219.21	1724.51	17.19	0.99
II	0.67	0.33	0.33	0.67	1794.5	120.55	1785.08	9.45	0.53
III	0.75	0.25	0.25	0.75	1745.7	148.00	1734.09	11.60	0.67
IV	0.75	0.25	0.50	0.50	1841.9	77.43	1835.87	6.60	0.67
V	0.75	0.50	0.50	0.50	1890.6	228.45	1872.68	17.91	0.94

whose allocational propositions are estimated to be roughly as follows: U_{11} = 85 percent, U_{12} = 15 percent, U_{21} = 44 percent, and U_{22} = 56 percent. The approximate estimation of W_5 is 2489.120 L.E.M. It is important to note, however, that the big difference between the actual policy's estimated value of W_5 and the highest average value attained by any of the five policies (1890.6) would reasonably enough tempt us to attribute the major part of the explanation to data deficiencies. The figures obtained from various publications are unlikely to be accurate and the lack of very necessary information has often led us to carry out estimations that have always required simplifying and, at the same time, arbitrary and limiting assumptions. Thus one can only say that if our estimates of the actual allocational policy somewhat reflect the true picture, and if all the assumptions that we have had to make are not untrue or too limiting, then the estimated actual allocational policy is a proper one because of its relative closeness to policy IV, which we have chosen to be the "best."

STOCHASTIC LINEAR PROGRAMMING APPLIED TO A DYNAMIC PLANNING MODEL FOR INDIA [17]

We consider here a simple model taken from Mahalanobis (36) which refers to Indian planning. Let I_t be investment, C_t consumption, Y_t national income in year t, $(t = 0, 1, \ldots, T)$. Further, λ_i will be the proportion of investment devoted to new investments and λ_c the proportion devoted to consumption goods. Also let β_i be the marginal output coefficient in the investment sector, β_c the marginal output coefficient in the consumption sector. The dynamic models are then

$$I_t \leq I_{t-1} + \lambda_i \beta_i L_{t-1}$$
$$C_t \leq C_{t-1} + \lambda_c \beta_c L_{t-1}$$
$$Y_t = I_t + C_t, \ t = 1, 2, \ldots, T$$

17. Based on research in collaboration between Tintner and Narayanan (73).

We maximize the objective function Y_T and add additional restrictions, $I_t \geq 0$, $C_t \geq C_0 \geq 0$, and $\sum_{t=0}^{T} I_t \leq I_s$. Here C_0 is consumption in the period 0, and I_s is total investment available over the whole planning period $t = 0, 1, 2, \ldots, T$. This is a quite conventional planning model with the inequalities replacing the usual equalities.

Assume $t = 1, 2, 3, 4$, and maximize the objective function Y_4. The following data are taken from Indian economic statistics (1949-50): $I_0 = 14.40$, $C_0 = 121.70$, $I_s = 99.00$. All figures are in billions of rupees in constant prices of 1952-53. Further, $\lambda_i = 1/3$, $\lambda_c = 2/3$, $\beta_c = 0.706$ (average), $\beta_i = 0.335$ (average). Now in the deterministic case, our problem can be formulated as

$$Y_4 = C_4 + I_4 = MAX$$

The activities to be chosen are $I_1, I_2, I_3, I_4, C_1, C_2, C_3, C_4$; that is, investment and consumption in all four periods. Then we obtain by the simplex method the optimal solution for the activities. $I_1 = 16.01$, $C_1 = 128.48$, $I_2 = 17.81$, $C_2 = 136.02$, $I_3 = 19.80$, $C_3 = 144.40$, $I_4 = 22.02$, $C_4 = 153.72$. The optimal objective function is $Y_4 = 175.74$.

Stochastic Linear Programming

All the data in linear programming problems are given numbers. If this condition is abandoned, because it is unrealistic in practical applications, we obtain various problems.

Application of the passive approach to a dynamic planning model. Now we consider the two sector model of Mahalanobis (36) for India. From the data relating to marginal output/investment ratios, we derive the average values. The average value of β_i is given by $\bar{\beta}_i = 0.335$, and likewise $\bar{\beta}_c = 0.706$. Also the variances are given by $V_i = 0.031881$ and $V_c = 0.458160$. We have on the whole 16 observations on the marginal output/ investment ratios for each of the two sectors. We consider the passive approach according to which we fit an empirical probability distribution function to the random coefficients, which in our case are the output-investment coefficients, and then estimate the probability distribution of the objective function. We fit independent gamma distribution on the basis of the 16 values of $\bar{\beta}_i$ and $\bar{\beta}_c$. The coefficients β_i and β_c follow the distributions:

$$p(\beta_i) = \frac{\exp(-10.507825)\beta_i^{2.520121}}{(3.520121)(0.0951671)^{3.520121}}$$

$$p(\beta_c) = \frac{\exp(-1.540946)\beta_c^{0.087997}}{(1.087907)(0.748952)^{1.087907}}$$

It may be noted that the above distributions are derived from the empirical means and variances. We consider the passive approach to the above model (Tables 4.25 and 4.26). In the third five-year plan the

Table 4.25. Statistics for specified policies

No.	Policy[a] λ_i	λ_c	Mean value	Mode	5% (lower) probability level
1	1/3	2/3	196.632	192.381	159.591
2	1/2	1/2	187.672	185.594	101.067
3	2/3	1/3	176.351	169.727	164.724
4	1/3	2/5	192.436	190.010	159.405
5	1/3	1/4	204.733	199.834	175.201

a. i stands for the proportion of investment devoted to capital sector in the year t.

proportion of investment devoted to the investment sector is given by λ_i = 1/3, and therefore λ_c = 2/3. We use numerical methods to derive the approximate distribution of the objective function in the following way. The value of β_i and β_c for the 5 percent and the 95 percent levels of the cumulative probability distributions of both these coefficients are calculated. Now we consider the total range of the distribution except for the 5 percent upper and lower tails. This range is now divided into five equal parts. This gives six values of each coefficient spread over the respective range of distributions. Cumulative probabilities are then calculated for all these values. Since we have assumed that β_i and β_c have independent gamma distributions, we can derive an approximation of the joint probability distribution of β_i and β_c by 36 values. This can give us only crude approximation to the desired distribution of the objective function which is our aim.

On the basis of the 36 selected points in the parameter space, we finally derive 36 values of the objective function. The empirical distribution of the objective function can be fitted by the method of moments. It should be pointed out that the distribution thus obtained will only give a rough approximation of the true distribution.

$$f(Y_4) = 0.014801 \left(1 + \frac{Y_4}{63.440577}\right)^{3.254} \left(1 - \frac{Y_4}{85.089351}\right)^{4.364}$$

Table 4.26. Variance and coefficient of variation

No.	Policy λ_i	λ_c	Variance	Standard deviation	Coefficient of variation[a]
1	1/3	2/3	512.524	22.639	11.5
2	1/2	1/2	290.935	17.057	9.1
3	2/3	1/3	142.186	11.924	6.7
4	1/3	2/5	408.563	20.213	10.5
5	1/3	1/4	759.015	27.550	13.4

a. The coefficient of variation is defined by $100 \sqrt{V(Y_4)/E(Y_4)}$ where V denotes the variance and E stands for expectation.

From the fitted distribution we derive the mode and the lower 5 percent probability level. The mode is 192.381, the 5 percent probability level is 159.591, the mean is 196.632, and the variance is 512.524. The above passive approach could be used for comparing two methods of planning, depending upon the random distributions of λ_i and λ_c, or planning in two countries, say India and Israel.

The active approach in stochastic linear programming as illustrated by Tintner (69). The problem is again the derivation of the distribution of the objective function, say R(z,U). But now the distribution will depend upon the elements of U (allocation matrix). In economic planning we might consider the effect of the allocation of investment to various industries upon the probability distribution of the objective function of the planner. The active approach to a stochastic linear programming situation is adopted in our case when we take the proportion of the investment going to the capital sector as the policy variable or the decision variable, with the understanding, of course, that $\lambda_i + \lambda_c = 1$. We proceed with $\lambda_i = 1/2$. Our fitted distribution turns out to be

$$f(Y_4) = 0.20093 \left(1 + \frac{Y_4}{70.870301}\right)^{7.224} \left(1 - \frac{Y_4}{72.172997}\right)^{7.357}$$

The fitted distribution has for its mode 185.5925474 and for its lower 5 percent level 161.067458. Also, mean 187.67217, variance 290.935. Next we take up the case when $\lambda_i = 2/3$. Again using the same method and making use of the values of Table 4.25 we derive the various values of the optimal objective function. The fitted distribution is given by:

$$f(Y_4) = .002832 \left(1 + \frac{Y_4}{40.188226}\right)^{4.552} \left(1 - \frac{Y_4}{44.553304}\right)^{5.0449}$$

The distribution has mode 169.727, a 5 percent probability level of 164.724, a mean of 176.351, and variance of 142.186.

The problem of allocation of investment between different sectors discussed by Mahalanobis has led to some discussions in development planning. In this model the target is the desired increase in income. The instruments of adjustments are the allocational parameters, the proportions of investment in the two sectors. The main problem in our case is how to effect the allocation of investment funds available year after year between different sectors of a closed economy so as to reach a maximum national income at the end of a time horizon. From this point of view, even though we have considered in the active case only values of λ_i which are fixed through the planning period under consideration, we propose to vary the values of λ_i so as to allow for year-to-year variation in the proportion of investment used in the investment sector. We have two possible situations: (a) investment proportion increasing as we proceed from year to year up to the final year; (b) investment proportions decreasing as we proceed from the first year to the final year. The optimal values of the objective function Y_4 are given for the two different policies with regard to the proportion of investment going to the investment sector. The values of λ_{it} are as follows:

(a) $\qquad \lambda_{i_1} = 1/3; \; \lambda_{i_2} = 2/5; \; \lambda_{i_3} = 9/20; \; \lambda_{i_4} = 1/2$

(b) $\qquad \lambda_{i_1} = 1/3; \; \lambda_{i_2} = 1/4; \; \lambda_{i_3} = 1/5 \; ; \; \lambda_{i_4} = 1/10$

where λ_{i_t} is the proportion of investment going to investment sector in the year t. As in the previous cases, we use the same table and obtain approximations to the distributions for the two cases. The distribution function of Y_4 for case (a) is as follows:

$$f(Y_4) = 0.016226 \left[1 + \frac{Y_4}{57.373599}\right]^{2.679600} \left[1 - \frac{Y_4}{60.569992}\right]^{2.828993}$$

For case (a), we have the following moments on the basis of which the fitted distribution is obtained: mathematical expectation of 192.436, variance of 408.56300, third central moment of 201.500, fourth central moment of 405600.000, mode of 190.010 and a 5 percent level of 159.405. Finally, we derive the moments of the distribution of Y_4 for case (b) as mathematical expectation of 204.733, variance of 408.653, third central moment of 201.500 and fourth central moment of 405600.000.

The fitted distribution of Y_4 is given by

$$f(Y_4) = 0.064208 \left[1 + \frac{Y_4}{62.542955}\right]^{2.0603615} \left[1 - \frac{Y_4}{98.292474}\right]^{3.238063}$$

From the fitted distribution, we have a mode of 199.8343470 and a 5 percent level of 175.201.

We have tried to give a rough approximation to the actual distributions and we have made some assumptions which are not true in reality. Hence the policy suggestions given below are based on our approximate results. In Table 4.25 we have given the mean, mode, and the lower 5 percent level for each policy. Also, for the purposes of comparison, we have given in Table 4.26 the mean value, variance, and the coefficient of variation, so that we can use the criterion of minimum variability as measured by the coefficients of variation.

Analysis of the Results

It appears that the optimum mean value of the objective function is obtained by the policy of decreasing the value of λ_i each year as we move from the first year to the final year. Therefore it appears on the basis of the magnitude of the means that a policy of $\lambda_{i_1} = 1/3$, $\lambda_{i_2} = 1/4$, $\lambda_{i_3} = 1/5$, and $\lambda_{i_4} = 1/10$ gives rise to the highest average national income in the last year over a period of five years. But it is seen that the variance is also the greatest. If we consider only the policies of keeping the proportion of the investment devoted to the capital sector fixed throughout the five-year period of study, then the results indicate that we produce the highest mathematical expectation of national income in the last year. The reverse allocation of two-thirds of investment to the capital sector and one-third to the consumer goods sector gives a lower mathematical expectation, but the lower 5 percent probability level of the distribution is higher. In the former case, therefore, the average returns are greater but the risk is higher; in the latter case the average returns are lower while the risk is lower. Therefore the policy of two-thirds of investment to the capital sector appears preferable if the government wants to be on the safe side in its adoption of proper policy. But if we take into consideration year-to-year variation in the proportion of investment going to the capital sector, then the policy of decreasing the proportion of investment devoted to the capital sector as we proceed from the initial to the final year of a five-year period seems to be better than the policy of two-thirds of investment at the lower 5 percent probability level. Hence, if we choose the mean or the mode or even the 5 percent level, the policy $\lambda_{i_1} = 1/3$, $\lambda_{i_2} = 1/4$, $\lambda_{i_3} = 1/5$, and $\lambda_{i_4} = 1/10$

appears preferable. If the criterion of minimum variability (as measured by the coefficient of variation) is followed, then the policy of $\lambda_i = 2/3$ and $\lambda_c = 1/3$ is better than the policy in our list. The next best policy is $\lambda_i = 1/2$ and $\lambda_c = 1/2$. The policy $\lambda_{i_1} = 1/3$, $\lambda_{i_2} = 2/5$, $\lambda_{i_3} = 9.20$, $\lambda_{i_4} = 1/2$ occupies the third place.

REFERENCES

1. Aitcheson, J., and J. A. C. Brown. The Log-normal Distribution. Cambridge: Cambridge Univ. Press, 1957.
2. Albert, A. In *Social Science and Moral Philosophy*, ed. M. Bunge, pp. 385-409. New York: Macmillan, 1964.
3. Allen, R. G. D. *Mathematical Economics*. 2nd ed. New York: Macmillan, 1960.
4. Arrow, K. J. *Social Choice and Individual Values*. 2nd ed. New York: Wiley, 1963.
5. Babbar, M. M. Distribution of Solutions of a Set of Linear Equations. *J. Amer. Stat. Assoc.*, vol. 50.
6. Barone, E. The Ministry of Production in a Collective Economy. In *Collectivist Economic Planning*, ed. F. A. von Hayek. London: Routledge and Kegan Paul, 1956.
7. Bellman, R. E. *Dynamic Programming*. Princeton, N.J.: Princeton Univ. Press, 1957.
8. Bellman, R. E., and S. E. Dreyfus. *Applied Dynamic Programming*. Princeton, N.J.: Princeton Univ. Press, 1962.
9. Bergson, A. On the Concept of Social Welfare. *Quart. J. Econ.*, vol. 58.
10. Bernoulli, D. Exposition of the New Theory in the Measurement of Risk. *Econometrica*, vol. 22.
11. Blackwell, D., and M. A. Girshick. *Theory of Games and Statistical Decisions*. New York: Wiley, 1954.
12. Burger, E. *Einfuehrung in die Theorie der Spiele*. Berlin: de Gruyter, 1959.
13. Carnap, R. *Logical Foundations of Probability*. Chicago: Univ. Chicago Press, 1950.
14. ———. *The Continuum of Inductive Methods*. Chicago: Univ. Chicago Press, 1952.

15. Carnap, R., and W. Stegmueller. *Induktive Logik und Wahrscheinlichkeit.* Vienna: Springer, 1958.
16. Charnes, A., and W. W. Cooper. Chance Constrained Programming. *Management Sci.*, vol. 6.
17. Chernoff, H., and L. E. Moses. *Elementary Decision Theory.* New York: Wiley, 1959.
18. Chipman, J. A. The Foundations of Utility. *Econometrica*, vol. 28.
19. Davis, H. T. *Theory of Econometrics.* Bloomington, Ind.: Principia Press, 1941.
20. Fisz, M. *Probability Theory and Mathematical Statistics.* 3rd ed. New York: Wiley, 1963.
21. Fox, K. *Economic Analysis for Public Policy.* Ames: Iowa State Univ. Press, 1958.
22. Frisch, R. The Mathematical Structure of a Decision Model. *Metroeconomica*, vol. 7.
23. Georgescu-Roegen, N. ˙Choice, Expectations and Measurability. *Quart. J. Econ.*, vol. 68.
24. Gibrat, R. Les Inegalites Economiques. Paris, 1931.
25. Graaff, J. de V. *Theoretical Welfare Economics.* Cambridge: Cambridge Univ. Press, 1957.
26. Hadley, G. *Nonlinear and Dynamic Programming.* Reading, Mass.: Addison-Wesley, 1964.
27. Heady, Earl O., and Wilfred Candler. *Linear Programming Methods.* Ames: Iowa State Univ. Press, 1958.
28. Hicks, J. R. *Value and Capital.* 2nd ed. Oxford: Clarendon, 1946.
29. Holt, C. C., F. Modigliani, J. R. Muth, and H. A. Simon. *Planning, Production, Inventories and Work Force.* Englewood Cliffs, N.J.: Prentice Hall, 1968.
30. Koopmans, T. C., ed. *Activity Analysis of Production and Allocation.* New York: Wiley, 1951.
31. Kuenzi, H. P., and W. Krelle. *Nichtlineare Programmierung.* Berlin: Springer, 1962.
32. Lange, O. *On the Economic Theory of Socialism.* New York: Lippincott, 1948, pp. 55-141.
33. Lerner, A. P. *The Economics of Control.* New York: Macmillan, 1944.
34. Luce, R. D., and H. Raiffa. *Games and Decision.* New York: Wiley, 1957.
35. Madansky, A. Inequalities for Stochastic Programming Problems. *Management Sci.*, vol. 6.
36. Mahalanobis, P. C. The Approach of Operational Research to Planning. *Sankhya*, vol. 16.
37. Mandelbrot, B. The Pareto-Levy Law and the Distribution of Income. *Intern. Econ. Rev.*, vol. 1.
38. Marschak, J. Rational Behavior, Uncertain Prospects and Measurable Utility. *Econometrica*, vol. 18.
39. ——. Scaling of Utility and Probability. In *Game Theory and Related Approaches to Social Behavior*, ed. M. Shubik. New York: Wiley, 1964.
40. Marshall, A. *Principles of Economics.* 8th ed. New York: Macmillan, 1948.
41. Meade, J. E. External Economies and Diseconomies in a Competitive Situation. *Econ. J.*, vol. 62.
42. Mishan, E. J. A Survey of Welfare Economics 1939-1959. *Econ. J.*, vol. 70.
43. Morishima, M. *Equilibrium, Stability and Growth.* Oxford: Clarendon, 1954.
44. Morishima, M., and G. L. Thompson. Balanced Growth of Forms in a Competitive Situation with External Economies. *Intern. Econ. Rev.*, vol. 1.
45. Myrdal, G. *Das Politische Element in der Nationaloekonomischen Doktrinbildung.* Berlin: Springer, 1932.
46. Neumann, J. von, and O. Morgenstern. *Theory of Games and Economic Behavior.* Princeton, N.J.: Princeton Univ. Press, 1944.

47. Pareto, V. *Manuel d'Economie Politique*. Paris: Giard and Briere, 1909.
48. Phillips, A. W. La Cybernetique et le Controle des Systemes Economiques. *Cahiers de l'Inst. Sci. Econ. Appl.*, ser. N, no. 2.
49. Pugachev, V. F. On an Optimization Criterion for the Economy. In A. L. Vainstein, ed. pp. 63-106.
50. Ramsey, F. P. A Mathematical Theory of Saving. *Econ. J.*, vol. 36.
51. Rothenberg, J. *The Measurement of Social Value*. Englewood Cliffs, N.J.: Prentice Hall, 1961.
52. Savage, L. J. *Foundations of Statistics*. New York: Wiley, 1954.
53. Schultz, T. W. *Transforming Traditional Agriculture*. New Haven, Conn.: Yale Univ. Press, 1964.
54. Schumpeter, J. A. *Capitalism, Socialism and Democracy*. 3rd ed. New York: Harper, 1950.
55. Shubik, M. *Strategy and Market Structure*. New York: Wiley, 1959.
56. Simon, H. A. *Models of Man*. New York: Wiley, 1957.
57. Steindl, J. Random Processes and Growth of the Firm. New York: Hafner, 1965.
58. Stoleru, L. G. An Optimal Policy for Economic Growth. *Econometrica*, vol. 33.
59. Stone, R. Three Models of Economic Growth. In *Logic, Methodology and Philosophy of Science*, ed. Ernest Nagel et al., pp. 494-506. Stanford, Calif.: Stanford Univ. Press, 1962.
60. Strotz, R. H. Empirical Implications of a Utility Tree. *Econometrica*, vol. 25.
61. Sweezy, P. M. *The Theory of Capitalist Development*. New York: Oxford, 1942.
62. Theil, H. *Studies in Mathematical and Managerial Economics*. Amsterdam: North-Holland, 1964.
63. Thrall, R. M. Applications of Multidimensional Utility Theory. In *Decision Processes*, ed. R. M. Thrall et al. New York: Wiley, 1954.
64. Tinbergen, J. *Selected Papers*. Amsterdam: North-Holland, 1959.
65. Tintner, G. The Application of Decision Theory to a Simple Inventory Problem. *Trabajos Estadist.*, vol. 10.
66. ———. *Econometrics*. New York: Wiley, 1952.
67. ———. Game Theory, Linear Programming and Input-output Analysis. *Z. Nationaloekon.*, vol. 17.
68. ———. A Note on Stochastic Linear Programming. *Econometrica*, vol. 28.
69. ———. The Use of Stochastic Linear Programming in Planning. *Indian Econ. Rev.*, vol. 5.
70. Tintner, G., and O. Davila. Applicaciones de la Econometria a la Planificacion. *Trimestre Econ.*, vol. 32.
71. Tintner, G., and S. A. F. Farghali. The Application of Stochastic Programming to the UAR First Five-Year Plan. *Kyklos*, vol. 20.
72. Tintner, G., and B. Murteira. Un Modelo Input-Output Simplificado para a Economia Portuguesa. *Colectanea Estudos*, no. 8, Lisbon.
73. Tintner, G., and R. Narayanan. A Multi-dimensional Stochastic Process for the Explanation of Economic Development. *Metrika*, vol. 11.
74. Tintner, G., and M. Patel. Evaluation of Indian Fertilizer Projects: An Application of Consumers' and Producers' Surplus. *J. Farm Econ.*, vol. 48.
75. Wald, A. *Statistical Decision Functions*. New York: Wiley, 1950.
76. Whittle, P. *Prediction and Regulation*. London: English Universities Press, 1963.
77. Winch, D. M. Consumer's Surplus and Compensation Principle. *Am. Econ. Rev.*, vol. 55.
78. Wold, H., and L. Jureen. *Demand Analysis*. New York: Wiley, 1953.

Chapter 4 ⬳ DISCUSSION

Luther G. Tweeten, *Oklahoma State University* (U.S.A.)

P ROFESSOR TINTNER was assigned a large task, and I commend
him for his able attempt to cover the subject of systematic planning
and decision procedures. His examples illustrate that much of the
refinements in statistical models are not yet operational, and much remains to be done before the sophisticated techniques generate results
that can be taken seriously as decision makers. My discussion contains
some brief comments on welfare economics, then illustrates two theoretical planning approaches, Bayesian analysis and systems analysis,
which Professor Tintner has given little attention in his paper.

Professor Tintner begins his paper with welfare economics, a very
useful point of departure. Welfare economics is intended to bridge the
gap between national welfare and economic planning. Welfare economic
theory has progressed from cardinal utility concepts to the ordinal concepts of Pareto, to the "new" welfare economics of Hicks, Kaldor, and
Scitovsky, and finally to the social welfare functions of Bergson and
Samuelson.

It is unfortunate that welfare economics has progressed little in the
past decade. Pareto welfare economics looks for deviation from optimal conditions *at the margin* for signs of inefficiency. But we need to
know whether these deviations constitute sufficient social cost to warrant ameliorative action. It is of considerable interest that Professor
Tintner and others, including myself (7) have "reverted" to cardinal utility in applied problems.

Policy decisions take place in a dynamic environment, and we yet
await a dynamic theory of the Pareto optimum. Externalities continue
to plague welfare economics. When these are recognized, it is difficult
to conceive of an economic policy that makes some better off without
making someone worse off. In addition to being an impotent guide to policy, the basic postulate of the Pareto optimum is in question when we see
individuals or groups (A) following the policy of making someone else (B)
worse off if that policy does not at the same time make A as bad off
as B. Meanwhile numerous policies go unpursued in international trade
and consolidation of fragmented and scattered landholdings that appear
to be obvious opportunities to make someone better off without making
others worse off. We still seem to be relegated to accept the judgment:
"Economic welfare is a subject in which rigor and refinement is probably worse than useless. Rough theory, or good common sense is, in
practice, what we require" (5, p. 272).

IMPROVED TOOLS

Our tools for systematic national planning and individual decision making form an impressive array. Positivistic approaches such as least squares have been improved with techniques to handle least-squares bias (simultaneous equations), autocorrelation (autoregressive schemes), lagged responses (distributed lags), structural changes (dummy variables), and laborious calculation (electronic computers). Normative approaches such as linear programming have been improved with techniques to handle linearity (quadratic programming), indivisibility (integer programming), timelessness (multiperiod dynamic programming, recursive programming), and fixed coefficients (stochastic programming). Decision theory has progressed from giving single-valued recommendations applicable only to an "economic man," to including allowance for alternative goals, decision making under uncertainty, and inclusion of emerging information into previous recommendations. Gaming and simulation techniques offer great flexibility for improving instruction and policy evaluation in economics.

Despite these and other formidable tools for economic planning, we must ask to what extent economic policy formulation has progressed from the qualitative to the quantitative basis. Have our efforts adequately provided the precise and relevant answers that are needed by firm managers and policy makers? Too often the answer is no, and our efforts are often concluded with the statement that the results are tentative or suggestive, the problem needs further research, or the results apply to specific conditions which lie outside the context of the policy decisions which must be made.

We can do better. It is usually not the techniques that are inadequate. Rather the shortcomings are the data and our inability to understand and integrate human behavior into the techniques. There is much lacking in the theory and development of tools for economic planning. But the development of tools is far ahead of our ability to apply these in the systematic way needed to make better planning decisions.

BAYESIAN AND SYSTEMS ANALYSIS

Two fairly recent developments which I would like to have seen given greater attention by Professor Tintner are Bayesian and systems analysis. Both are significant means to organize our planning tools and make them more relevant to those who make decisions. Bayesian methods are being used with some success to bring more information from research results and other experience to farm managers operating in a situation of risk and uncertainty [4]. Systems analysis is basically a systematic way of organizing research tools to encompass the totality of the problem, research resources, and goals to be reached [1]. It may be regarded as an application of organization theory, often focusing research resources on the micro-macro objectives of research.

Bayesian Analysis

The development of Bayesian strategies in this paper is taken from Eidman (3; see also 2). The treatment is intended to provide a basic understanding of the technique applied to farm management research.

The decision-making problem under risk of uncertainty can be conceptualized as a game against nature, where the decision maker has a set of n alternative actions, a_1, a_2, ..., a_j, ..., a_n, among which a choice is to be made, and nature has a set of m strategies, θ_1, θ_2, ..., θ_i, ..., θ_m. A gain (or loss) table (Table 4.27) can be constructed by

Table 4.27. Gains table for hypothetical decision problem

Value of random price variable	Nature's strategies	Grower's actions a_1	a_2	a_3	a priori probabilities
Low	θ_1	- 7,000	1,000	-1,000	0.3
Average	θ_2	6,000	2,000	2,000	0.4
High	θ_3	18,000	3,000	4,000	0.3
Expected value using a priori probabilities P(θ)		5,700	2,000	1,700	...

setting the actions against the states of nature and filling in the body of the table with the decision maker's gains (or losses) in taking each action. For purposes of illustration, assume the decision maker is a livestock producer with a set of fixed production facilities. Further assume the producer has three possible actions he can take in any given year—independent production (a_1), production under contract A (a_2), and production under contract B (a_3). Also assume the producer faces three states of nature—low prices (θ_1), average prices (θ_2), and high prices (θ_3). The outcomes presented in Table 4.27 are the returns to the producer's fixed resources. The entries indicate that if the producer uses strategy a_1, he will receive a return of -$7000 if low prices are experienced, $6000 if average prices result, and a return of $18,000 if high prices prevail. The decision maker is willing to utilize the gains table and any other relevant information to develop the optimal strategy, one that will maximize income.

There are several variations of the Bayesian approach which utilize the hypothetical gains presented in Table 4.27. The simplest case utilizes probabilities of the θ_i estimated either from empirical data or subjectively by the decision maker. Suppose the producer makes subjective estimates of the a priori probabilities of 0.3, 0.4, and 0.3 for θ_1, θ_2, and θ_3, respectively. Applying these a priori probabilities, he develops the expected net returns shown in the last row of Table 4.27 for each of the three actions. Action a_1 with an expected value of 5700 is optimum. Chernoff and Moses (2) refer to strategies developed using only a priori probabilities as the solution to the "no data" problem because they do not utilize a prediction of which θ_i will prevail in making the decision.

Another case of the Bayesian approach allows the use of outside information to determine the state of nature that is likely to prevail in the current production period. Assume the producer in the hypothetical example has access to price predictions such as those made by the extension service or a trade magazine. Let the observations of the price forecasts be represented by Z, where Z_1 is a forecast of a low price, Z_2 of an average price, and Z_3 of a high price. By utilizing a historic series of price predictions (Z) and the actual prices which occurred (θ), the decision maker can derive the a posteriori probability distribution $P(\theta \mid Z)$ through application of the Bayes formula,

$$P(\theta \mid Z) = \frac{P(\theta)\ P(Z \mid \theta)}{P(Z)}$$

The method of computation is shown for the hypothetical problem in Table 4.28. The first step is to use the historic forecasts (Z) and the

Table 4.28. Derivation of a posteriori probabilities $P(\theta\ Z)$

States of nature	Conditional probabilities $P(Z \mid \theta)$			a priori probabilities $P(\theta)$	Joint probabilities $P(\theta)\ P(Z \mid \theta)$		
	Z_1	Z_2	Z_3		Z_1	Z_2	Z_3
θ_1	0.8	0.2	0.0	0.3	0.24	0.06	0.00
θ_2	0.2	0.5	0.3	0.4	0.08	0.20	0.12
θ_3	0.0	0.4	0.6	0.3	0.00	0.12	0.18
				P(Z)	0.32	0.38	0.30

States of nature	a posteriori probabilities $P(\theta \mid Z) = \dfrac{P(\theta)\ P(Z \mid \theta)}{P(Z)}$		
	Z_1	Z_2	Z_3
θ_1	0.75	0.16	0.00
θ_2	0.25	0.52	0.40
θ_3	0.00	0.32	0.60

actual prices that occurred to compile the conditional probabilities $P(Z \mid \theta)$. Suppose, for instance, that θ_2 actually occurred in ten years of the historic period and that Z_1 was predicted in two of the years, Z_2 in five years, and Z_3 in the remaining three years. Using these data, the conditional probabilities, given the true underlying state of nature θ_2, are $P(Z_1 \mid \theta_2) = 0.2$, $P(Z_2 \mid \theta_2) = 0.5$, and $P(Z_3 \mid \theta_2) = 0.3$. The conditioned probabilities for θ_1 and θ_3 are developed in a similar manner. The a priori probability distribution is given by $P(\theta)$. The joint probability of observing a given value of Z, P(Z), is the sum of the joint probabilities over all θ for a particular Z. The a posteriori probabilities are obtained by applying the Bayes formula. That is, the joint probabilities, $P(\theta)$ $P(Z|\theta)$, are divided by the probability of observing the corresponding value of Z. The resulting a posteriori distribution is shown in Table 4.28.

The a posteriori probabilities are used to develop the expressed payoff for each action for a producer using the price predictions. The computations are shown in Table 4.29. The gains for each action and

Table 4.29. Hypothetical decision problem showing optimal strategies for the "no data" and "data" problem

Nature's strategies	Grower's actions a_1 a_2 a_3			a priori probabilities $P(\theta)$	a posteriori probabilities $P(\theta\|Z)$		
					$P(\theta_1\|Z_1)$	$P(\theta_2\|Z_2)$	$P(\theta_3\|Z_3)$
θ_1	-7,000	1,000	-1,000	0.3	0.75	0.16	0.00
θ_2	6,000	2,000	2,000	0.4	0.25	0.52	0.40
θ_3	18,000	3,000	4,000	0.3	0.00	0.32	0.60
Expected value using a priori probability $P(\theta)$	5,700	2,000	1,700	...	...	...	...

Expected value of action using a posteriori probabilities

Value observed				$P(Z)$
Z_1	-3,750	1,250	- 250	0.32
Z_2	7,760	2,160	2,160	0.38
Z_3	13,200	2,600	3,200	0.30

Expected value of optimum strategy = (0.32) (1250) + (0.38) (7760) + (0.30) (13,200) = 7308.80

Value of the predictor = 7308.80 - 5700 = 1608.80

Expected value with a perfect predictor = (0.3) (1000) + (0.4) (6000) + (0.3) (18,000) = 8100.00

Value of a perfect predictor = 8100 - 5700 = 2400

state of nature are shown in the upper left-hand portion of the table. Applying the a priori probabilities results in the expected value of each action using a priori probability $P(\theta_i)$. These results were shown in Table 4.27 and are included again for comparison. Applying the a posteriori probabilities to the gains results in the expected value of each action, given that Z_i has been observed. That is, the value of the expected outcome for the j-th action, having observed the i-th value of Z, is obtained by multiplying the a posteriori probabilities for Z_i times the outcome for the j-th action and summing over i. For instance, if low prices (Z_1) are predicted and the decision maker selects action a_1, the expected value of the outcome is $(0.75)(-7000) + (0.25)(6000)$ (C) $+ (0.0)(18,000) = 5250 + 1500 + 0 = -3750$. If Z_2 is observed and the

decision maker selects action a_1, the expected value of the outcome is
$(0.16)(-7000) + (0.52)(6000) + (0.32)(18,000) = -1120 + 3120 + 5760$
$+ 7760$. The other expected values of the actions using a posteriori
probabilities are computed in a similar manner. Considering the entries in the completed table, the decision maker can write the optimal
strategy (a_2, a_1, a_1), indicating that the optimal action is a_2 if Z_1 is observed, but is a_1 if either Z_2 or Z_3 is observed. A producer can utilize
the probability distribution of the predicted prices, $P(Z)$, to determine
the expected income of the optimal strategy (a_2, a_1, a_1). Given the $P(Z)$
of Table 4.29, the expected value of the optimal strategy is $(0.32)(1250)$
$+ (0.38)(7760) + (.30)(13,200) = 1608.80$. The expected value for the
"no data" solution using a priori probabilities is 5700. Hence the value
of "the data" (the predictor) is $7308.80 - 5700 = 1608.80$. If the producer could develop a perfect prediction model, the a posteriori probability distribution would have ones on the diagonal and zeroes elsewhere.
In this case the expected value of the action using a posteriori probabilities would be given by the following table.

Value observed	Producer's actions			
	a_1	a_2	a_3	$P(Z)$
Z_1	-7,000	1,000	-1,000	0.3
Z_2	6,000	2,000	2,000	0.4
Z_3	18,000	26,000	32,000	0.3

The probability of observing Z_i would be the same as the a priori probability of θ_i. Hence the expected value using a perfect predictor
$= (0.3)(1000) + (0.4)(6000) + (0.3)(18,000) = 8100$, and the value of "the
data" for a perfect predictor is $8100 - 5700$ or 2400. Hence an individual with a perfect predictor is in the certainty situation.

Systems Analysis

One example of systems analysis applied to economic problems is
the S-42 interregional study of the economics of cotton production (8).
A committee specified in advance the methodology and assumptions to
be used in the study. Procedures were carefully outlined so that the micro results, developed by individual farm management personnel working in the respective geographic areas, could be aggregated to answer
questions of national policy. Local researchers, who knew each resource situation well, constructed enterprise budgets and programmed
the optimum resource use and production of individual farms. Data from
these representative farms were "blown up" to depict the resource situation, and the data from the resource situations were aggregated to form
regional totals.

The aggregated results were used to generate aggregate supply estimates, which in turn were related to aggregate demand; which in turn

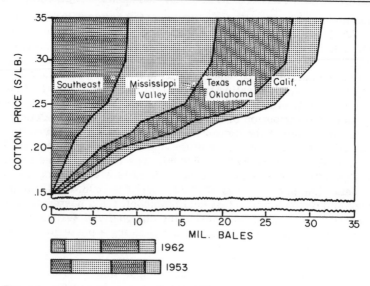

Fig. 4.1. Actual cotton production in 1953 and 1962, and estimated production at various prices in the absence of acreage controls or price supports, by major regions.

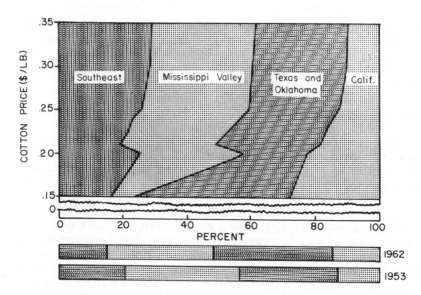

Fig. 4.2. Percentage shares of cotton production in 1953 and 1962, and estimated percentage shares of production at various prices in the absence of acreage controls or price supports, by major regions.

generated estimates of equilibrium prices, production, costs, and income. One interesting product of the research was estimates of interregional competition in cotton production, discussed below.

Figure 4.1 shows that the rise in cotton production, as the price is increased from $0.15 per pound to $0.35 per pound, is substantial in all areas (8). Production in the 17 study areas increased from 1.6 million bales to 31.2 million bales. The width of graphic areas for each region may be viewed as the supply curve. It is characterized by an inverted "lazy S." From low prices to $0.20 per pound, the supply curve rises steeply, because cotton is not then competitive with many crops for the use of resources. From $0.20 to $0.30 per pound, the historic range of prices, cotton becomes more profitable than alternatives, and acreage is expanded rapidly. Also yields rise as fertilizer and irrigation become more profitable. The result is a somewhat flat section of the supply curve for cotton in each area within this range of prices. Above $0.30 per pound, the supply curve is steep, as land suitable for cotton production is exhausted and the cost of greater production rises.

The average price for cotton in 1962 was $0.32 per pound. Production in that year in the four regions in Figure 4.1 was 12.6 million bales and in the United States was 16.5 million bales. Production in that year was restrained by allotments. Prices would have to fall to nearly $0.20 per pound, according to Figure 4.1, to reduce production to that level without production controls.

The line on the extreme right of Figure 4.1 that borders California is the normative *aggregate* supply curve for cotton. Anticipated production outside the study area was added to this supply curve to form the total supply. The aggregate domestic and foreign demand for cotton was also estimated. The two curves intersected at an equilibrium production of 17 million bales and equilibrium price of $0.21 per pound.

Figure 4.2 more clearly illustrates the comparative advantage of cotton production in the four regions. The share produced in the Mississippi Valley falls markedly as the price of cotton is reduced below $0.20 per pound. The Southeast maintains a somewhat stable share of output at all prices. At low prices, California and the Texas and Oklahoma region have a comparative edge in production. Their combined share is 78 percent of production at $0.15 per pound and only 38 percent at $0.35 per pound. Irrigation in the Texas High Plains and in California explains the ability of these areas to produce cotton at low prices. If the free market price were below $0.24 per pound, California would profitably have a larger share of production than in 1962; and above that price they would have a smaller share. Since the equilibrium market price without production controls was estimated to be $0.21 per pound, it appears that California would improve its market share under a free market. It does not follow, however, that income would increase—total farm income falls in all areas, including those that increase their market share, as the cotton price is lowered. At the equilibrium price the percentage shares of production in the Southeast, Mississippi Valley, Texas and Oklahoma, and California, respectively, would be an estimated 19, 30, 32, and 19 compared to 20, 36, 30, and 14 in 1962.

Research Complementarities

The analysis of interregional competition in cotton production was feasible only because it was complementary with other research goals. The linear programming analysis of profitable plans for representative farms was an excellent base for improving farm management decisions. The extension service and land grant universities utilized the results in classroom teaching of farm management and in extension programs to help farmers find the organization of crops and livestock that raise income on individual farms. This was the major contribution of the study.

In another phase of the study, researchers estimated the minimum size farm that will pay all real and opportunity costs of farming, including a $5000 income to the operator for his labor, management, and risk. The results were used for farm management planning. They also were used to compute the minimum number of farms possible in a given area if all farmers were to have a "parity" $5000 labor income. For example, the results indicated that the number of crop farms in Southwestern Oklahoma would need to decline by approximately 70 percent to assure at least $5000 operator labor income (8). These results of the adjusted farm structures were used to determine the farm population, and purchases of farm household supplies and production inputs associated with the adjusted structure through the use of income and population multipliers. The implications of this adjusted structure were determined for schools, machinery dealers, fertilizer dealers, grocery stores, and so on. A final phase of the study analyzed the implications for farm income of alternative cotton price supports and acreage allotments.

Systems Analysis—Where Do We Go from Here?

To avoid prohibitive research costs and at once achieve timeliness and accuracy, we must pursue complementarities in research. A significant development is record keeping by farmers utilizing high-speed computers. Some efforts are being made to combine modern planning approaches, including decision theory and programmed optimization, with data from farm records. In time there may be sufficient data and systematic analysis to use the results to answer questions of national policy. I can envision a time when the data from farm records (keeping the identity of individual farmers confidential, of course) will be fed into a national model of agriculture to provide timely information on past as well as prospective production and marketing plans. The data will also be utilized to analyze the implications of changes in commodity programs and other national policies.

The feedback from the national model to managers can be very useful. The proposed changes in national policy stemming from the aggregate farm decisions can provide timely guides to farm managers by incorporating changes in national programs into next year's production and marketing plans programmed by computer. This systems approach obviously offers real possibilities for coordinating the micro and macro aspects of farm planning.

SUMMARY AND CONCLUSIONS

In summary, the theory and tools for economic planning have progressed remarkably, and now outstrip our ability to provide data and coordination of the models to resolve micro-macro planning issues. Organization theory and the decision making in a stochastic environment need much additional attention. This discussion paper briefly examined Bayesian analysis and systems analysis as a step toward improving the organization of economic research.

Central planning has progressed rapidly, even in countries basically devoted to the enterprise system. In American agriculture, central planning is achieved through national production allotments and administered prices. Our farmers in time may be more receptive to annual variation in allotments and to government manipulation of carryover stocks, indispensable to enlightened central planning. Professor Y. C. Lu and I currently are developing a national inventory model at Oklahoma State, using a dynamic programming technique to form an inventory model, and simulation procedures to test the operation of optimizing and rule-of-thumb inventory decision guides. The inventory decision could be used in conjunction with projections of expected consumption to set production and hence acreage needs for crops next year. It is this combination of formal, sophisticated decision models with somewhat informal judgments that offers the greatest hope for systematic planning in the next few years in the United States. Ultimately we will work toward more rigorous, accurate, and complete models for practical applications, perhaps along the line suggested in the text of my discussion.

REFERENCES

1. Buckley, Walter, ed. *Modern Systems Research for the Behavioral Scientist.* Chicago: Aldine, 1968.
2. Chernoff, A., and L. E. Moses. *Elementary Decision Theory.* New York: Wiley, 1959.
3. Eidman, V. R. Bayesian Decision Models in Farm Management. Paper A.E. 6807, Dept. Agr. Econ., Oklahoma State Univ., 1968.
4. Eidman, V. R., G. W. Dean, and H. O. Carter. An Application of Statistical Decision Theory to Commercial Turkey Production. *J. Farm Econ.*, vol. 49.
5. Little, I. M. D. *A Critique of Welfare Economics.* Oxford: Clarendon Press, 1959.
6. Tweeten, Luther G., P. L. Strickland, and J. S. Plaxico. Interregional Competition in Cotton Production. *Agr. Econ. Res.*, vol. 20.
7. Tweeten, Luther G., and Fred H. Tyner. The Utility Concept of Net Social Cost—A Criterion for Public Policy. *Agr. Econ. Res.*, vol. 18.
8. Tweeten, Luther G., and Odell L. Walker. Estimating the Socioeconomic Effects of a Declining Farm Population in a Sparse Area. In Agricultural Policy Institute, Regional Development, North Carolina State Univ., 1963.

Chapter 5 ☙ SYSTEMIZATION OF AGRICULTURAL ECONOMIC-MATHEMATICAL MODELS

V. A. Edemsky, *Academy of Sciences* (U.S.S.R.)
V. N. Aidin, *Lenin Academy of Agricultural Sciences* (U.S.S.R.)

THE DEVELOPMENT of methods of planning in agricultural economics is linked with the introduction of mathematical methods and electronic computer techniques. In its course, this demands elaborating economic-mathematical models of the production processes of agriculture. The development of economic-mathematical models for the planning of agricultural production is extremely labor-intensive work, consuming much of the qualified specialist's time. However the work according to the composition of the models, with the consequent applications of them for the purposes of planning, has not come through in the quality of the plan. In this situation there is no possibility to compare the different variants of models and to choose the most appropriate of them.

Until now the construction of these models appears in some degree as a creation of scientists. At the present time there is an accumulation of a large quantity of models alone and of processes of working out all new variants. There arises a question of which of them are the best and which of them are ineffective or less preferable. From the ineffective models it is still possible to obtain promising experience or experiments. But what is to be obtained from the acceptable models? How can one choose the best models? With what stipulations should the choice comply? From our point of view the choice and construction of models from the existing large quantity of models should meet the following requirements, and these can be considered as restrictions in the choice of the economic-mathematical model.

1. The possibility of formulation of the economically arranged problems with the result that there is a list of technoeconomic indices (which characterize the considered object) and the interrelations of these indices. This is the necessary condition of building economic-mathematical models.
2. The economic formulation of problems should permit the possibility of a division of indices in the variables and constants and also permit the rejection of several interrelations between indices in relation to set objectives in research. This is the sufficient condition of developing acceptable economic-mathematical models.
3. The means of control in modifying the objectives and models to the necessary technoeconomic indices and obtaining them by acceptable methods for collecting information in a reasonable period of time.

4. The presence of methods for studying the attributes of the model. First of all, this indicates the means of deriving a solution of the mathematical models corresponding to the economic-mathematical models.
5. The possibility for the realization of the derived results in practice. The criteria for optimal choice of the best models from the admissible ones might be formulated in the following manner: starting from the above-mentioned conditions in order to receive maximum increase in the criteria which are used to evaluate the development of the field characterized by the model. Consequently the variant model is one of the measures for increasing the efficiency of agricultural production.

If the majority of us agree that there exists an optimal variant of the plan, which might be determined as a result of the construction of an economic-mathematical model, and that there exists an optimum economic-mathematical model in the multitude of possible models, then our task is a reasonable one. In Soviet and foreign technical papers there are several examples displaying that there is a choice of economic-mathematical models for the correctness of the conclusions in the objectives of planning. The present paper does not aim at formulating the exact criteria for the choice of an economic-mathematical model for computation, considering that before we do this it is necessary to show by what restrictions it is possible to formulize the economic-mathematical model. We propose to carry out the systemization of models on the basis of the specification of economic-mathematical model building. The first step is one of considering economically formulated questions — the relation of technoeconomic indices and their corresponding groups of constraints according to the problem of the model; secondly, with respect to the mathematical formulation of economic situations — the aggregation of these indices in terms of equalities and inequalities; and thirdly is the means of deriving models, that is, obtaining results by models with the help of algorithms and the solution to questions of linear programming.

Now we are considering the initial premises and assumptions which are necessary
1. As a result of economically formulated questions we get (a) selected technoeconomic indices according to the given economic problem; (b) economic, agronomic, and livestock data and other conditions according to the given economic problem with the indication that such technoeconomic indices enter into each condition; and (c) the economic formulation of a problem showing that for the given problem there might be a multitude or one solution and consequently that there ought to be guiding criteria for the optimum choice of the best solution (that is, formulizing this condition and controlling the indices that ought to enter into it).
2. As a result of mathematical formulization of economically stated problems, it is possible to get this or a different economic-mathematical

model. This signifies that (a) logical formulations in economically stated problems, economic, agronomic, and livestock conditions might be written through the given technoeconomic indices in view of the equalities and inequalities (groups of restrictions); (b) many or one possible solution-systems derived from equalities and inequalities corresponding to the multiple (or single) economic solution; and (c) criteria for optimization corresponding to conditions of the selection of the best economic solution might also be written in a mathematical form.

3. As an outcome of economically stated problems and the mathematical formulation of them we might get this or a different economic-mathematical model which would not offer any interest if it does not have the possibility of being organized in a solution of such mathematical questions. Today on a massive scale the majority of problems appear as problems of linear programming. At a lesser degree is the family of nonlinear problems. Therefore the systematization expediently covers, in the first stage, only economic-mathematical models. This brings us to the problems of linear programming and to a lesser degree to the problems of integral and nonlinear programming.

The conditions arrived at through economically stated problems and formulized in equations and inequalities can be expressed in terms of the "section" from which there is built a corresponding economic-mathematical model. The construction of such a section requires not only that such indices be taken in the capacity of variable quantities but also in the capacity of constant quantities. Each "section" of the model should be constructed in such a way so as to effect the best economically and technologically possible and practically expedited indices of the technoeconomic conditions. The diversity of possible economic-mathematical models depends on the following causes: (a) how many from the multitude of "sections" enter into the model; and (b) by how many methods it is possible to construct each "section."

The economic formulation depends first of all on the maximum number of "sections" of the model and for each "section" emphasizes these or different economic or technological and other special features of analyzing the problem. But with mathematical features in any given case there is the possibility for other preparations of the "formulized" schemes by standard methods for solving the problems of linear programming, depending upon the number of methods which might compose each "section." The mathematical side of economic-mathematical models can be taken narrowly with whatever indices would be considered as constants and whatever characteristics as variables.

We show how this is realized in the systemization of models in the example. We assume from the economically formulated problems the following.

Selected technoeconomic indices
1. X_j = size and j = branch.
2. Y_{kj} = output, k = production per unit size, and j = branch.
3. Z_{zj} = input, z = resources per unit size, and j = branch.

If the indices are given as constants they would be written as:

Selected groups of conditions

1. Of production, the j-th sort must not be less than a fixed quantity; to this group the restrictions enter the indices as X_j, Y_{kj}, C_k, where the quantity k is production according to the lower limits.
2. Of the resources, the sorts which can be expended ought not be larger than the fixed quantity; to this group the restrictions enter the indices as X_j, Z_{zj}, A_z — the quantity of resources according to upper limits.
3. The restrictions of the size of j for branches and quantities are Y_{kj}, Z_{zj}, according to the upper and lower limits. To this group the conditions enter the indices as X_j, A_j^{max}, and A_j^{min}. The size j enters according to the upper and lower limit as Y_{kj}, Z_{zj}, A_{kj}^{max}, A_{kj}^{min}, C_{zj}^{max}, C_{zj}^{min}. The possible size of quantities enters as Y_{kj} and Z_{zj}, according to the upper and lower limit.
4. We assume that the criterion of optimality is the maximum profit. The criterion enters the indices as X_j, Y_{kj}, Z_{zj}, C_k as the selling price per unit k of production; and S_z as inputs in terms of money per unit of the z-th resource. Normative fixed costs are estimated per unit of the j-th branch.

For greater clarity we shall use Table 5.1. We show how the range of possible models is formed and how it influences the range of mathematical and computed characteristics which it is necessary to take into consideration through systemization of the economic-mathematical models. In Table 5.1, according to the subject enumerated by name of the groups of indices and groups of conditions, the stated results bring us to the variants of the models. Each variant of the model is characterized: (a) by the indication of whatever groups of conditions (sections) are studied under the given variant and whatever groups not studied in the given variant; (b) by whatever correlation of variable indices in the model on the whole and according to the groups of conditions, provided the model can be brought into the problem of linear programming by simple substitutions of technoeconomic indices. For simplification the range of variants of the models in Table 5.1 is given only for cases in which all the groups are included in the variants.

In Table 5.1 are presented three variants of the possible models. In the first variant model, relatively simple in comparison with the others, are the variable indices only for the size of branches X_j. Of course, in this variant model, and as in all the models, there are the variables X_j. The conditions are according to the limitedness of the indices $\tilde{Y}_{kj}$, $\tilde{Z}_{zj}$. In the second variant of the model we take X_j and Y_{kj} variables as technoeconomic indices. Therefore, in order to solve corresponding mathematical problems of linear programming, we need in the model one of the following variants of variables: (a) X_j, $X_j Y_{kj}$; (b) $X_j Y_{kj}$, Y_{kj}; (c) X_j, x_j/Y_{kj}; and so forth. The conditions of our model can be realized by the first variant of the variable conditions.

Table 5.1. Example of systemization of linear economic-mathematical models

Variants of models	Characteristics		
	I	II	III
Groups of indices			
(a) Size of branches	X_j	X_j	X_j
(b) Amount of production	$\tilde{Y}_j$	Y_{kj}	Y_{kj}
(c) Amount of resources	$\tilde{Z}_{zj}$	$\tilde{Z}_{zj}$	Z_{zj}
Groups of conditions			
(a) Fulfillment of plan according to production	$\Sigma \tilde{Y}_{kj} X_j \geq C_k$	$\Sigma Y_{kj} X_j \geq C_k$	$\Sigma Y_{kj} X_j \geq C_k$
(b) Resource limitations	$\Sigma \tilde{Z}_{zj} X_j \leq A_z$	$\Sigma \tilde{Z}_{zj} X_j \leq A_z$	$\Sigma Z_{zj} X_j \leq A_j$
(c) Upper and lower limits	$A_j^{min} \leq X_j \leq A_j^{max}$	$A_{kj}^{min} \leq Y_{kj} \leq A_{kj}^{max}$ $A_j^{min} \leq X_j \leq A_j^{max}$	$C_{zj}^{min} \leq Z_{zj} \leq C_{zj}^{max}$ $A_j^{min} \leq X_j \leq A_j^{max}$ $A_{kj}^{min} \leq Y_{kj} \leq A_{kj}^{max}$
Criteria for optimization	$\Sigma S_k \tilde{Y}_{kj} X_j$ $- \Sigma S_z \tilde{Z}_{zj} X_j$ $- \Sigma e_j X_j$	$\Sigma S_k Y_{kj} X_j$ $- \Sigma S_z \tilde{Z}_{zj} X_j$ $- \Sigma e_j X_j$	$\Sigma S_k X_{kj} X_j$ $- \Sigma S_z Z_{zj} X_j$ $- \Sigma e_j X_j$
Methods of transformation linear programming models	$x_j = X_j$	$x_j = X_j$ $y_{kj} x_j = Y_{xj}$	$x_j = X_j, y_{kj} x_j = Y_{kj}, x_j = Y_{kj},$ $z_{zj} x_j = Z_{zj}$

After the solution of the corresponding problems of linear programming in the second variant model, in a way which is different from the first variant model, we obtain the "optimum" technoeconomic indices only as a result of the additional calculation $Y^*_{kj} = y^*_{kj}/x_j{}^*$. In the third variant model we get in terms of variable technoeconomic indices X_j, Y_{kj}, Z_{zj}. Therefore, in order to solve the corresponding mathematical problems of linear programming, we have to have in the model one of the following variants of variable combinations: (a) X_j, Y_{kj}, Z_{zj}; (b) X_j, $X_j Y_{kj}$, $X_j Z_{zj}$; and so forth. The conditions of our model can be realized by the second variant of the variable combinations. Also, as in the second variant model of "optimum" technoeconomic indices, we obtain by means of additional calculation: $y^*_{kj} = Y^*_{kj}/X_j$, $z^*_{zj} = Z^*_{zj}/X_j{}^*$.

We can estimate the total number of technomathematical models which can be constructed from the given groups of indices and groups of conditions. Let t be the number of groups of indices and p be the number of groups of conditions. The number of possible models is obtained from:

1. The number of methods by which it is possible to compose the model

from the available groups of indices (F_1); $F_1 = \sum\limits_{e=1}^{n} S^e_p$, where $S^e_p =$

$\dfrac{p!}{e!(p-e)!}$, and is the number of combinations without considering

the order $[e \le p;\ p! = 1 \cdot 2 \cdot 3 \ldots (p-1)p;\ e! = 1 \cdot 2 \cdot 3 \ldots (e-1)e;\ (p-e)! = 1 \cdot 2 \cdot 3 \ldots (p-e-1)\ (p-e)]$.

2. The number of methods by which it is possible to realize each group

of conditions (F_2). This quantity is the same $F_2 = \sum\limits_{k=1}^{t} S^k_t$, where

$S^k_t = \dfrac{t!}{k!(t-k)!}$, and is the number of combinations without considering

the sequence of calculation $[kSt,\ t! = 1 \cdot 2 \cdot 3 \ldots (t-1)t;\ k! = 1 \cdot 2 \cdot 3 \ldots (k-1)k;\ (t-k)! = 1 \cdot 2 \cdot 3 \ldots (t-k-1)\ (t-k)]$.

Consequently the total number of possible models by the calculation of the variety in the composition of sections and methods of realization of each section is the same $F = F_1 \cdot F_2$.

Of course such an estimated number of models is greatly conditional, but it permits us to evaluate the necessity of carrying out the systemization and the purposeful choice for the most appropriate model. In order to conduct such work it is necessary to conduct the systemization of construction of models by groups of economic problems in agriculture. There has to be an elaboration for the classification of all the technoeconomic indices by groups of conditions in forms of equalities and inequalities. The development and algorithmic construction of an economic-mathematical model proceeds from the classifications of indices and conditions and specific tasks of concrete research (what sorts

of indices are not necessary, what categories of indices are given, what
are variables, and so forth).

We are conducting studies of this kind in the field of the following
groups of economic problems: (a) long-run planning of agriculture and
related industrial sectors; (b) long-run planning of agriculture at the
following levels of branch, firm, and organizational units within farms;
(c) short-run planning of firm and subunits within farms; and (d) separate parts of the problem for allowances, structure of branches in the
firm, evaluation of technological variants, and so forth. The analysis
so far has demonstrated (a) the possibility of application of "traditional"
methods of solutions of economic problems and of the new economic-
mathematical methods; (b) the determination of the place and role of any
economic-mathematical model in the solution of a given economic problem; (c) the possibility of algorithmization and organization of machine
programs by the construction of economic-mathematical models in accordance with relevant problems, and (d) the ability to predict workable
economic-mathematical models and their characteristics and to plan
the development of economic-mathematical models.

Chapter 5 ❧ DISCUSSION

Danilo Pejin, *Agricultural University of Zemun* (Belgrade)
              (Yugoslavia)

THE DEVELOPMENT of technology and research work, as well as
specialization and intensification, is very characteristic for modern society. This progress and economic development has induced
the need for planning and for discovering methods which will coordinate
economic activities. This is a very complex and important task and,
because of difficulties involved in forecasting, also a very risky one.
This is also the reason why forecasting and planning of future development only slowly became part of economic science.

The systematizing of planning and decision procedures which are
discussed here should make it possible to express quantitative links and
the interdependence of economic factors, not only in the present period
but – even more important – in the future.

It has been said that the plan is a unique project of economic development, including all the aspects of increased reproduction (i.e.,
ratios in production, trade and consumption, repartition, and so on).
The production program is the basic element for planning and determines
all economic life (i.e., the size of investment, the level of employment,
the volume of trade, the proportion of individual economic branches,

and so on). The production program provides for enlargement of new
manpower and for training of personnel in order to increase their skills.
For this reason the production program is also concerned with productivity increases, which are of major importance in any attempt for expanding production and raising living standards.

YUGOSLAVIAN EXPERIENCE

In the West, as well as in the East, various methods of planning
are utilized. The underdeveloped countries also have some experience
in planning and in methods which they use. Yugoslavia is one of the
countries which has some experience in planning, which we shall illustrate briefly.

The Yugoslav economy is not a mixed economy as most of the economies in the West are, yet it has been planned in a very different way
from the socialist economies in Europe. Taking these facts into account,
Yugoslavia is really a specific case, with not much ground for generalization.

The characteristic features of the economic planning in Yugoslavia
are closely related to the whole socioeconomic setup. Several points
concerning the socioeconomic setup, relevant to the system of economic
planning developed in Yugoslavia are (a) to use in an efficient way the
means of all sectors of economic life; (b) the instruments of economic
policy; and (c) the workers' self-management of the enterprises, an
important feature of social ownership.

The Yugoslav economy is fully planned; consequently the economic
plans cover all economic and related social activities in the country.
According to the length of the period they cover, there are three types
of economic plans – annual plans, five-year-plans, and long-term plans.

We will describe briefly the main points concerning the five-year
economic planning. At first we shall see what methodology of planning
has been utilized in earlier times, and what methods have been applied
from our last five-year plan.

Since the war Yugoslavia has applied the method of balances, based
on determined theoretical assumptions. The starting point in the methodology of planning is Karl Marx's theoretical analysis of the reproduction process. This method consists in following the behavior of the most
indispensable quantitative ratios and links within individual branches
and sectors, as well as between branches and sectors, and in the social
reproduction as a whole (relationships in production, distribution, trade,
and consumption). The basic objective underlined by any five-year economic plan is the achievement of the highest possible rate of growth of
the economy as a whole, accompanied by the highest possible rate of
increase in the real level of living. The process of arriving at the
maximum possible rate of growth both of national income and level of
living implies, first of all, a careful study of the trends of economic
development in the past period.

In the balances method a system of proportions is very important.
A system of proportions and links for the distribution of the social
product, in material and money terms, has been expanded by Marx *(A
Critique of the Gotha Programme)*. Because Marx is based on a series
of abstractions, however, it was necessary to work at more concrete
schemes for the processes of production distribution, trade, and consumption, or briefly, for all stages of social reproduction.

An important field for which it was necessary to work out a concrete scheme is the social product. In this method the social product
has been taken as a fundamental analytical magnitude, indifferent to
Western planning methods where national income is treated as a fundamental analytical magnitude.

The social product consists of gross production from enterprises,
individual peasant small holdings, and artisan shops. After having computed the social product and other measures of economic life, we must
pay attention to the quantitative analyses of the factors that have influenced the course of development experienced in different economic sectors.

An important part of this analysis takes an appreciation of the
structural changes in the economy brought about by the past development, as well as the determination of sectors whose pace of growth
needs acceleration if the economy is to continue growing at a maximum
rate. In a similar way the relations between the rates of growth of the
total per capita national income and personal consumption, or the level
of living as a whole, are examined and conclusions about the future desirable relations are drawn.

The shares of consumption, and the level of living as a whole, in
the total of national income have the meaning of target variables. When
considering these target variables, the interdependence between national
income and level of living, as well as the complex role of the level of
living in the economy, have to be fully accounted for. The magnitude of
these target variables is determined on the basis of the following criteria: (a) the maximization of the level of living in the long run is conditioned by the maximization of per capita national income; (b) the rising
level of living of the people is to be accompanied by a growing market
for the increasing production; and (c) the upward tendency of the level
of living has to stimulate the productive efforts of the workers and thus
contribute to the raising of the overall economic productivity.

Finally, to complete this view, I would mention that the general
plan is based on the principle of basic balances which, apart from such
objectives of development policies as the raising of living standards
and of the country's economic potential, elaborates in detail and with
ample documentation the following proportions: basic relationships in
the distribution of national income; basic investment structure (namely
the general lines of development of economic and noneconomic activities), taking into account the essential structural problems, including
foreign trade; directions of integration into the international pattern of
the division of labor, and the methods by which integration should take

place; fundamental principles of the regional aspect of the country's development policies, more particularly of underdeveloped areas; and conditions of economic activities and the basic premises for changes in the mechanism of the economic system connected with plan implementation.

These and the other basic proportions of the plan had to be supplied with the documentation which contains a system of social accounts and a determined number of material balances and balances of intersectoral relations (input-output analyses). The balances upon which the plan is based are not only important as documents but serve as indicators for all the organs engaged in plan implementation, so that they can see the degree to which the target has been realized. The balances also serve in making analyses concerning further plan implementation.

From a methodological point of view the procedure of general balances goes from the general to the particular in the following way: general balance of the economy; balances of the material and social conditions of production, social product, and the balance of its distribution in value terms; balances of trade and consumption (including foreign trade); balance of investments; balance of revenues and expenditures of the social community; and balance of money revenues and expenditures of the population. From a purely methodological point of view, material and other balances play the same role as input-output tables used in the planning systems of Western countries. For instance we will give the scheme of material (Table 5.2) and money revenues balances (Table 5.3).

NEW ADMINISTRATIVE SYSTEM IN PLANNING

In the last few years the old administrative system of planning has gradually disappeared. In fact economic development plans continued to be passed by competent authorities; but being still burdened with the old methodology, they were increasingly at variance with the system of self-management and rights of enterprises to formulate independently their production, investment, income, and other policies. In practice, these plans remained more and more frequently a dead letter, especially as there was no more administrative coercion to enforce their implementation.

The introduction of the new planning system was thoroughly prepared in a series of discussions, which lasted several years, with the participation of a large number of experts and other persons interested in these matters. The entire work was accomplished within a certain number of committees especially set up for this purpose, but relevant discussions were also held within scientific institutions and social and political organizations. The results of these discussions were formulated in the thesis "fundamentals of the system of social planning."

The starting point in the endeavors to set up an elaborate planning system are the foundations of Yugoslavia's social and political system. According to the constitution of the Socialist Federal Republic of

Table 5.2. Scheme for a material balance of rolled steel products

Means	Distribution
Reserves at the beginning of the planned period	Production needs
	The needs of the basic branches (production of railway cars and locomotives, installations for metallurgical plants, tractors, automobiles, machine tools, electrical machinery, mining equipment, etc.)
Production according to branches	
Means (total)	
	The needs for repair and overhauling
	Needs for capital investments
	Increase of reserves
	Accumulation of state reserves

Table 5.3. Scheme for a balance of money revenues and of expenditures for the purchase of nonmaterial goods of the Yugoslav population, 1951

Revenues	Expenditure
Money revenues derived from employment in the socialist sector	Money expenditure in relation with the socialist sector
Wages	Taxes
Working days	on the income of peasant holdings
Rewards	on the income of artisanal trade
Travel allowances and allowances for removals	on the income of cooperative members
Allocations for invalid persons	on the income from other sources
Receipts from social security services	tax arrears
Social assistance	estate taxes
Scholarships	local taxes
Purchase of farm products	excise taxes
Artisanal trade	turnover tax on private transactions
Cottage industry	turnover tax on the sale of wine and brandy
Road haulage	Social contributions of private persons
Rents and leasehold dues	Contributions of social organizations
Receipts from the State Insurance Institute (DOZ)	Savings
Proceeds of loans	Loans
Receipts from abroad	Transportation and PTT
Compensation paid to households adhering to rural working cooperatives	Municipal services
	Rents and leasehold dues
	Cultural needs
Trade in privately owned goods	Medical services
	Artisanal trades
Export subsidies	Catering services (hotel rooms)
Various receipts	Various services provided to tourists
	Payments to the state
Total	Total

Yugoslavia, "The basis of the socioeconomic system of Yugoslavia is free, associated work with socially owned means of labor, and self-management of the working people in production and in distribution of the social products in the working organization and social community." Within this framework a special importance is attributed to self-management of workers, which is the very element through which the ownership of the major part of the means of production (social sector) becomes immediate social ownership, differing in quality from state ownership. Thus planning loses its former character of a state function and becomes one of the basic self-government rights of the citizen. It increasingly transforms itself into self-planning and self-organizing of workers in working organizations and sociopolitical communities, communes, component republics, and federations). Thus self-government is a function leading to a "decentralization" of planning and to an increasing socialization of this function.

Under a system based on self-management of workers, the working organizations have become relatively independent producers of commodities. But this system also involves some degree of coordination and direction of activities of independent producers of goods for market needs. This is why under a system of self-government all the main factors come to the fore which, at a given level of evolution of productive forces, direct the process of social reproduction: economic laws regulating the behavior of a market economy, and social planning.

Does it mean that an economy based on self-management can live without a definite planned policy? In fact practice has increasingly indicated a completely new experience — that social plans primarily constitute an obligation for government agencies and lay down economic policies for the planned periods, which should incorporate instruments and measures for the further perfection of the system of self-management. On the other hand, for enterprises and self-managing organizations in other activities, social plans provide guidelines for their general business orientation, so that the more the plans are adjusted to long-term programs the more efficiently they will be implemented. In this way the general interests of society and the individual interests of working collectives are increasingly able to be reconciled. On the one hand, social plans are based on the realistic programs of enterprises and their associations; on the other hand, individual interests are realistic only if they take into account the general principles of planned development stemming from the social plans of the community. It is obvious that this adjustment is more complete the closer the economy and other activities are internally integrated.

Hence the entire problem of planning presents itself now in a completely different light for government planners. They must in fact envisage as realistically as possible the future movement that will result from the logical behavior of enterprises and their associations, logical in the sense of an adequate understanding of their long-term interests. At the same time social plans should make it incumbent upon government agencies to pursue an economic policy and take other measures conducive to the development of the system of self-management that will economically encourage and even force enterprises to adjust their operations to the long-term development objectives of the community. Within such a framework it is really of no importance that in certain specific cases investment is administratively regulated and financed, since under this system of planning such administrative measures can always be said to be an expression of the most urgent economic needs which under given conditions can be most efficiently met in this way (for example the present policy of rapid construction of power generating plants, the solution of some other problems of infrastructure, and so on).

The successful implementation of the plans by which Yugoslavia has attained her level of economic and social development has accentuated even more the need for further work on the methodology of planning.

Measures intended to improve our planning methods through a wider use of mathematics and econometrics have been undertaken. For the first time electronics is used for complex mathematical operations. The computation of quantitative indicators, in order to show changes in an economy full of dynamism, has remained the first and the most important task of the methodology of planning.

The model which we used for a third five-year plan operates with the rate of accumulation and the capital coefficient. The rate of growth (tempo of economic development) is a function of two parameters: rate of accumulation and capital coefficient. The most general mathematical formula which can express this ratio is the following:

$$t = \frac{Npo + Ko}{K_1} \tag{1}$$

where

    t = tempo (rate) of growth of the economy
    Npo = rate of accumulation
    K = capital coefficient
    Ko = initial
    K_1 = capital coefficient for a certain period of time

This function shows that the tempo of economic growth is directly proportionate to the increase of accumulation earned in production, within a given period of time, and inversely proportionate to the tempo of time variations of the capital coefficient.

We can use a more simplified form of the formula which we express as

$$r = \frac{s}{k} \tag{2}$$

where

    r = rate of growth
    s = part of social product destined for investment
    k = capital coefficient (ratio between investment and the increase of production)

This formula shows that the magnitude of social product (d) depends on the amount of accumulated capital, or the magnitude of basic and turnover funds. In that case the social product is a function of capital accumulation: $D = f(K)$.

But we must bear in mind the fact that capital can be utilized more or less efficiently, so that the same amount of capital can produce various amounts of social product. If we designate by k the ratio between overall social capital in the function, on the one hand, and social production on the other, then k in reciprocal form will express the average efficiency of capital: $D = f(k)$. We may deduce from this that social product is a function of two independent variables, size of capital (K) and its efficiency (k): $D = f(K,k)$.

The opposite way of reasoning in model making is to abstain from considering the total size of capital and its average efficiency, and the total size of social capital. Instead functional relations are solely considered through rates of growth. For this reason we may assume that the rate of growth depends on the rate of investment (increase of capital) and on the efficiency of investment (i.e., on the capital coefficient).

Defined in this way the capital coefficient differs from the coefficient which would show the reciprocal value of total capital and of aggregate production. The difference resides in the fact that new capital may be more or less efficient than the existing one, a fact which contributes to reduce the average efficiency of total capital.

PRODUCTION-CAPITAL MODEL

I now give one example of the production-capital model.[1] Construction of the mathematical-econometrics model was realized by choosing a responsible system of differential equations which can be marked in this form:

$$\frac{dD(t)}{dt} = a\frac{d\,K(t)}{dt} \tag{3}$$

$$\frac{dK(t)}{dt} = I(t) \tag{4}$$

$$I(t) = f(t)\,D(t) + g(t) \tag{5}$$

where the endogenous variables are

D(t) = value of the gross national product
K(t) = average annual growth in fixed capital
I(t) = marginal average annual volume of new investment in fixed capital

---

1. J Cf. Nikolid, Daneika. Pavle Sicherl: Construction Production-Capital Econometrics Model for Economic Life in Yugoslavia.

and the exogenous variables are

f(t) = optional function of time
g(t) = optional function of time
a = marginal coefficient of effectivity of the fixed capital

If we solve these differential equations we get the mathematics (construction) production-capital model in the next form:

$$D(t) = \frac{D(0) - u(0)}{\lambda(0)} \, \lambda(t) + u(t) \qquad (6)$$

$$K(t) = K(0) + \int_0^t \left[\frac{D(P) - u(0)}{\lambda(0)} \, f(t) \, \lambda(t) + f(t) \, u(t) + g(t) \right] dt \qquad (7)$$

$$I(t) = \frac{D(0) - u(0)}{\lambda(0)} \, f(t) \, \lambda(t) + f(t) \, u(t) + g(t) \qquad (8)$$

The new symbol has the following mathematical sense:

$$\lambda(t) = e^a \int f(t) \, dt$$

$$u(t) = ae^a \int f(t) \, dt \int g(t) \, e^{-a} \int f(t) \, dt \qquad (9)$$

This form of equation system (7) which is solved is freed of differential elements, but it consists of the function which is expressed in the form of determined integrals. Nevertheless this functional form of integral can be deduced in the form of a common function when optional functions f(t) and g(t) are determined in mathematical forms.

The first analytical production-capital econometrics model for economic development of Yugoslavia for the period 1952-60 was constructed by using the methods of the smallest quadrant for the estimation of a parameter in a production-capital function as in an investment-production function, in which it is supposed that the instrumental optional function $f_1(t)$ and $g_1(t)$ are of constant value. Such a model has the following form:

$$D_1(t) = 3683.0 \, e^{0.0384t} - 2524.6$$
$$K_1(t) = 9446.6 \, e^{0.0384t} - 323.9 \qquad (10)$$
$$I_1(t) = 362.8 \, e^{0.0384t}$$

With different f(t) and g(t) parameters, a second analytical model, constructed in the same way, has the form:

$$D_2(t) = 2911.5 \, e^{0.0468t} - 1744.4$$
$$K_2(t) = 5398.0 \, e^{0.0468t} - 210.0 \qquad (11)$$
$$I_2(t) = 252.4 \, e^{0.0468t}$$

Chapter 6 ᑐᑐ PROBLEMS AND OBJECTIVES IN PLANNING AT
THE FARM OR MICRO LEVEL

Ulf Renborg, *Agricultural College of Sweden* (Sweden)

T HIS PAPER concerns itself with the management problems of
farm firms. Thus it does not cover problems of micro models or
plans of the farm as a part of a macro study. The objective of
planning is here looked upon as one of guiding decision making and action in a firm. Such a plan fulfills many roles. It is a goal or a target
to aim at. It is a schedule indicating the steps to be taken towards the
goal. It is a theory indicating criteria to be fulfilled to reach the goal.
It is a precedent representing the continuity over time of the firm's
activities (3, pp. 111-12). This is the notion of "plan" to be used in this
paper. The problems of this type of planning which will be discussed
are model of the firm, planning environment and the decision maker,
planning period and planning horizon, goals, expectations and forecasts,
and planning procedure or choice.

MODEL OF THE FIRM

As Milton Friedman has pointed out, the only crucial test of a theory is its predictive power, its realism per se (5). A model of the firm
suitable for decision making thus does not need to fulfill any specific
criterion in realism. The important question is its efficiency as a basis
for good management decisions, that is, decisions which fulfill the goals
of the entrepreneur. When defining the firm whose planning problems
we are discussing, I am inclined to follow Edith Penrose's (16) definition: The firm is an admistrative unit, subject to independent planning,
and a collection of physical and human resources.

In our case this firm is organized for agricultural production. It is
important to note that this production takes time and that the time dimension of production also is emphasized by the fact that part of the
physical resources are fixed and have a long lifetime.

In some cases the farm firm is administered by a manager who
at the same time is the owner of substantial parts of the physical resources. The traditional family farm in the West is of this type. In
other cases management is separated from the ownership of resources.
This is the case in Eastern European farming and in certain types of
large-scale farming in the West. The modern large-scale corporation
in industry as a rule is of this type. These two types of firms may well
require different theoretical images (11).

The traditional family farmer with no employed labor from outside the family is a typical representative of the classical "entrepreneur" of economic literature. Larger farms with a large managerial staff come closer to the administrative organization of modern business firms in industry and trade. In the latter case the models of how outputs act and react may be more adequate as starting points for firm models than the neoclassical theory of the firm (12).

Production and consumption is more closely connected in agricultural firms than in other firms, due partly to the fact that farm products are basic foodstuffs. In those cases when owners and managers are the same persons, the competition between saving and consumption enters very strongly into the decision-making process.

The economist's first attempt may very well be to use the "neoclassical theory of the firm" as the model of the firm when guiding the manager's decision making. This model is timeless and assumes that all parameters are known with certainty. Its basis is the existence of fixed and variable resources and of a number of continuous physical production functions relating inputs and outputs. The technological relationships between inputs and outputs is fixed. These inputs and outputs can be bought on markets at some prices. The goal of the firm is to maximize net revenue. This is the difference between outputs times prices and inputs times prices. Theory includes well-known rules for maximization of net revenue. These can be expressed compactly as

$$\left. \left(\frac{\partial y_i}{\partial x_j} P_{y_i} \middle/ P_{x_j} \right) \right| \quad \begin{array}{l} = 1 \text{ (without capital rationing)} \\ \geqq 1 \text{ (with capital rationing)} \end{array}$$

for all possible relationships between inputs, x, and outputs, y, and at the same time assuming being on the rational part of all production functions and substitution curves. The theory, indicating how the firm should react to changes in price relations, has been extended to cover imperfect input and output markets (monopolistic and oligopolistic competition).

As has been shown (4), linear programming in its standard profit-maximizing formulation is representative of this theory of the firm. However linear programming can include time. Further the linear programming formulation of the production function as a finite, discontinuous set of linear processes, and the availability of mathematical algorithms for solution of the optimization problem makes it more useful as a practical planning tool than the neoclassic theory of the firm. This theory of the firm has been criticized on some points of importance in this paper (3, pp. 8-16): (a) Profit maximization is either one of many goals of business firms or not a goal at all. (b) Neither certainty nor its more modern equivalent — knowledge of the probability distribution of future events — exists. (c) The "firm" of the theory of the firm has few characteristics of the modern business firm. "It has no complex organization, no problems of control, no standard operating procedures, no budget, no aspiring 'middle management,' no controller."

Cyert and March have developed a "behavioral theory of the firm" where the firm is viewed as an organization. This theory deals with the modern "large, multiproduct firm operating under uncertainty in an imperfect market" (3, p. 115). We have to assume that the model of the firm in this theory fulfills Penrose's definition of a firm. Within this firm the theory assumes that the decision-making process can be represented by three sets of variables and four sets of relations. The three sets of variables affect the goals, expectations, and choice of the organization.

The *organizational goals* are assumed to have both *dimensions* and *aspiration levels* on any particular dimension. The dimension of the goals is influenced by the composition of the members of the organization and by the subunits of the organization that make the decisions. They are evoked by the planning or decision problems that arise. The aspiration levels are some weighted functions of past goals, past performances of the organization, and past performances of other "comparable" organizations.

The *organizational expectations* are affected by the process of drawing inferences from available information and by factors influencing the search for problem solutions. In the *process of drawing inferences,* variables such as simple trend studies are recognized. The variable influencing the intensity and success of the search process is the extent to which goals are achieved; and the formation of new expectations is more intense the less goals are reached and the smaller the organizational slack is. Variables influencing the direction of search are the nature and location of the problem which stimulates the search.

The organizational choice takes place in response to a problem, uses standard operating rules, and involves identifying an alternative that is acceptable from the point of view of evoked goals. Variables affecting these three factors influence the choice of action. The four sets of relations are:

1. *Quasi resolution of conflict* between goals held by various members of the organization. The conflicts are solved by dividing its decision problems into subproblems and assigning them to subunits for solution (local rationality) by following acceptable-level goals instead of maximization type goals and by attending to different goals at different times (sequential attention to goals).
2. *Avoidance of uncertainty.* Organizations are assumed not to maximize expected values or to use decision criteria under uncertainty when planning their activities. Instead they are assumed to avoid uncertainty by avoiding planning where plans depend on predictions of uncertain future events and by emphasizing planning where the plans can be self-confirming through some control device (feedback-react decision procedures).
3. *Search for good alternatives is stimulated by problems* and directed towards finding solutions to the problems. This search process is stimulated by the problem and depressed by the solution of the problem. The search process proceeds on the basis of a simple model unless driven to more complex models by the seriousness of the

problem. Finally the search is biased, that is, influenced by the training, experience, and goals of the members of the organization.

4. *A learning process is continuously going on.* This process includes adaptation of the directions and aspiration levels of goals. It also includes changes in decision criteria and attention to different parts of the environment. Also search rules change.

The basic structure of the organizational decision-making process is given in Figure 6.1, which is an outline of the model of the firm in the behavioral theory of the firm. The language used to picture this model is the language of a computer program.

An alternative model of the firm is the *controlled system of production.* This model has its origin in Weiner's book on cybernetics (19).

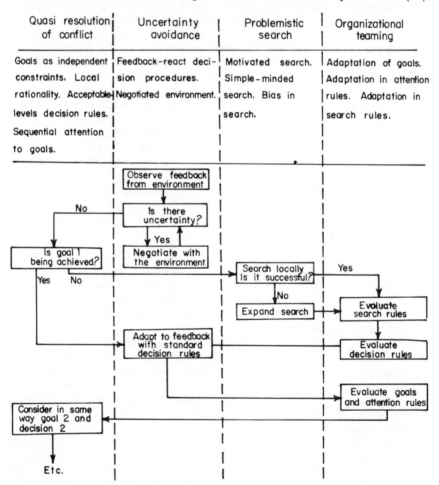

Fig. 6.1. Basis structure of the decision-making process in the behavioral firm model (3, p. 126).

It is more often used by engineers than by economists. The model assumes the existence of a controlled unit, for example for production, and another unit controlling the flow of inputs to and outputs from the controlled unit. The producing unit is influenced by an environment which creates disturbances in the production. The controlling unit receives information on these disturbances both ex ante and ex post. The ex ante information is received as forecasts of expected disturbances. The controlling unit compensates the controlled unit for these disturbances. Ex post, the controlling unit receives information on produced number of units through a feedback channel, compares it with the required number of units (i.e., with the goal), and if necessary orders supplementary production. The controlling unit also regulates the production according to received goals. A simple controlled system is given in Figure 6.2.

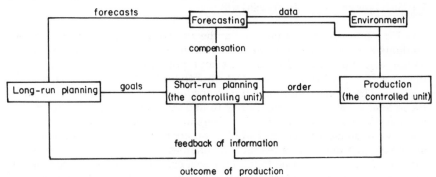

Fig. 6.2. The firm as a controlled system.

The flow of inputs and outputs within a firm is as a rule divided up into subsystems — for example acquisition of inputs; the technical flow of inputs, outputs and resources; the flow of labor services; the sales organization; and the economic control. Subsystems can also be plans covering different lengths of time. All these subsystems are parts of the total control system and connected via a flow of information between the systems. There can be many goals in this system — both economic and noneconomic and as a rule of the satisfying type. To function the goals have to be broken down into subgoals for the various parts of the system.

PLANNING ENVIRONMENT AND THE DECISION MAKER

Change is Normal[1]

Experiences from any country show that change is normal. Terms of trade between agriculture and other industries vary over time. Price

---

1. The subhead and part of the content is from (7).

relations between and within inputs and outputs in agriculture change as well as yields from crops and animals. Technology and institutional patterns — for example government programs — change, very often in unpredictable ways. Some variations can be illustrated with probability distributions, others not. Our planning environment may be a mixture of what Frank Knight (10) called risk and uncertainty. Georgesen-Roegen's (6) proposal that reality is not this but something in between seems to me to be a more appropriate description. Very few variations can be properly described with probability distributions, that is, very few situations are risk situations. On the other hand very few situations include the complete ignorance that Knight calls uncertainty. We have to accept that future events are uncertain and select our rules for choice of an optimal strategy according to this fact.

Partial Ignorance Is Universal (6)

Five broad areas of change can be recognized: prices; production methods and responses; prospective technological developments; behavior and capacities of people associated with farm businesses; and the economic, political, and social situations in which a farm firm operates. The farmer has imperfect knowledge for future events in all these areas. Moreover his ability to use the available information in computations is limited. His decisions are, as Simon says, characterized by "bounded rationality" (12). The consequences on his planning activities are that only a few of the possible alternatives and only a few influencing factors can be taken into account. It also means that simple rules of thumb are used as choice indicators and that satisfying replaces optimizing.

Managerial Functions and Manager's Knowledge Situations (8)

For discussion of the following papers it may be useful to recall the following five steps in the management process: observation, analysis, decision, action, and acceptance of responsibility.

It may be worthwhile to recall the following knowledge situations identified by the IMS to exist among farmers (8, pp. 44-53): (a) *Subjective certainty*, a situation in which a manager considers present knowledge adequate for either a positive or a negative decision. (b) *Risk action*, a situation in which a manager regards present knowledge as adequate for making a decision and in which the cost of additional knowledge is exactly equal to its value. Risk action may be either positive or negative. (c) *Voluntary learnings*, a situation in which a manager considers his present knowledge inadequate for action in the sense that he is subjectively unwilling to decide and take the consequences for the errors which he might make and in which the costs of acquiring more knowledge is less than its value. (d) *Involuntary learning*, a situation in which a manager is unwilling to learn more since the cost of additional information equals or exceeds its value to him, but in which some outside force makes it necessary to learn or for some learning to occur regardless of the volition of the manager. (e) *Inaction*, a situation in which a manager regards his present knowledge as inadequate for action and in which the cost of more knowledge exceeds its value. In this situation no action is taken and no learning occurs. (f) *Forced action*, a situation in which a manager's information is inadequate for him to be ready, willing, and able to make a decision subject to the errors involved but in which some outside force makes it necessary for him to act. Forced action decisions can be either positive or negative. The various knowledge situations require different types of plans for future action.

Problem Recognition and Values

Managers often have incomplete and inconsistent notions on the values to themselves of various goals. This makes the goal formulation of the firm unreliable and difficult. Even in cases where the goals are clearly perceived knowledge can be lacking as to the nature of the problem, which creates the gap between realized and aspired levels of various goals. Finally managers can fail to see profitable production possibilities (8). Planning procedures also should cover improvements in these areas. This, then, includes improvements of what Penrose (8) calls entrepreneurship (versatility, fund-raising ingenuity, ambition, and judgment). Cyert and March's (3, ch. 3) decision model includes the continuous adaptation of goals during the planning procedure. Planning and goal formulation interact in this model.

PLANNING PERIOD AND PLANNING HORIZON

Any planning faces the problem of determining the length of the *planning period*, that is, the time span from the planning moment to the latest time point in the future included in the plan. This latest future point in time is here called the planning horizon.

Each planning situation has its unique position of the planning horizon. This position is influenced by a number of factors. It is affected by the length of the production period of the goods to be produced. Some influences have the durability — or economic lifetime — of resources used in the production. The receding economic importance at the planning moment of economic events far in the future also has influence. This is also true of the subjective opinions of the entrepreneur or manager. In small farm firms also the anticipated future lifetime of the entrepreneur has some importance. A fruitful way of defining that part of the future which must necessarily be taken into account when making plans for the years ahead has been proposed by Modigliani and Cohen (14). They state that the most important thing is to determine the actions to be taken during the first of the future subperiods of the planning period. It is less important to specify exactly the actions to be taken during more remote subperiods. Increasing uncertainty over time is one reason for this. Another is the fact that the actions of the first time period are the only ones that really have to be put into effect. Modigliani and Cohen introduce the concepts of *relevant* and *irrelevant* future events and decisions to be able to judge which ones have to be taken into account to determine the first year's actions. A future event or decision is irrelevant at the planning moment if its anticipated value can assume any value and yet be of no importance for the determining of action during the first future subperiod of the planning period. Otherwise it is relevant. Irrelevance can be total, as was just mentioned, or conditional. An event or decision is conditionally irrelevant if its anticipated value has to fall within certain limits to be without influence of the first subperiod action.

By introducing these notions of relevant and irrelevant future events and decisions and by concentrating interest on plans for the first time period, Modigliani and Cohen make it possible to cut off that part of the future which is irrelevant to the planning of action during the first subperiod. This permits the establishment of the *relevant planning horizon*. This horizon indicates the latest future point in time which is necessary to include when planning the actions during the first time period.

It is possible to limit the time perspective ahead from other starting points than those of Modigliani and Cohen. One such approach was made by Svennilson as early as 1938 (18). He assumes that the length of time included in the perspectives of an entrepreneur is determined not only by the possible financial results of alternative plans but also by subjective judgments on the part of the entrepreneur. These last include not only his time but also his risk preferences and his confidence in his own ability to anticipate the outcome of future events. This makes it possible for him to introduce onto the future time axis a horizon determined in a way other than that of Modigliani and Cohen. A simple way of explaining the difference is to say that the definitions of relevance and irrelevance as given by Modigliani and Cohen are changed. Relevance and irrelevance become simply what is relevant and irrelevant for planning in the subjective judgment of the entrepreneur.

It seems possible to combine the views of Svennilson and Modigliani-Cohen. If so, the length of the planning period can be defined as the distance in time from the planning moment to the "relevant planning horizon" according to the subjective judgment of the entrepreneur, taking into account his knowledge of the relevant planning horizon as defined by Modigliani and Cohen.

GOALS

Without further discussion I should like to state that profit maximization as the only goal for a firm is not enough for planning on the farm level. A number of proposed substitutes or additions exist:

personal motives (9) of various types, maximization of utility, long-run
survival of the firm, maximization of sales (1), and satisfying a number
of goals of maximizing one goal subject to satisfying restrictions for
the other goals. It is necessary in farm planning to assume that a number of various goals exist. Alternatively it can be said that the goal
has many *dimensions* and each one is an *aspiration level*. The aspiration can be to satisfy or maximize.

Whether maximizing or satisfying is followed, these goals are all
of a *quantitative* type. In long-run planning there also exist *qualitative*
goals. They indicate the area within which the firm should work. In
the short run there exists as a rule very little choice as to change of
area of activity. The formulation of qualitative goals should preferably
cover a certain function (effective use of land and available human resources) or a specific need (production of foodstuffs) than a good just
now in demand (milk, beef, etc.). The classical example is the goal of
some U.S. railroads which assumed their goal to be to cover the need
for railroad transportation when a more imaginative goal would have
been to cover the need for transportation services in general (20). The
typical qualitative goal alternatives for the family farmer in Sweden is
the choice between full-time or part-time farming or leaving farming
altogether.

Many ways exist for treatment of goals in the planning procedure:
(a) Each aspiration level in every dimension can be fulfilled independently. In the satisfying procedure proposed by Simon, the first plan
that fulfills all given aspiration levels is accepted (12, p. 140). (b) The
various dimensions can be weighted together in one expression by establishing a preference function expressing total utility to the entrepreneur or organization as a weighted function of values in all given goal
dimensions. The utility function can be maximized or required to fulfill a given aspiration level of total utility. The well-known problem of
measuring utility makes this easier said than done. (c) It may be possible to indicate the most important goal dimension for the entrepreneur
or organization. A possible process is then to maximize along this
goal dimension and satisfy given aspiration levels in the rest of the
dimensions. This is a well-known procedure for planners using linear
programming where the goal consists of the objective function and a
number of restrictions. (d) By including the entrepreneur in the planning procedure, his preferences as to various goal dimensions can be
taken into account without establishing a formal preference function.
The general planning procedure is the one of satisfying, the first point
above. When a plan is reached that satisfies all given goal dimensions,
the entrepreneur can decide whether to raise one or many aspiration
levels. If the plan becomes unfeasible, planning can proceed in searching for a new acceptable plan. When such a plan is found, the procedure
can be repeated. This process can go on until the entrepreneur decides
that a "good enough" plan is reached.

Procedure (d) is useful when the goals cannot be clearly formulated
before the planning starts. The goals initially need not be exactly

established. The aim of the planning can, among other things, be to formulate acceptable goals. The initial aspiration levels for the planning procedure can be those reached earlier. During the planning process these goals will be continuously reconsidered.

EXPECTATIONS AND FORECASTS

Implicit in the neoclassical theory of the firm is a continuous gathering of information on performances within the firm and on changes in the environment to permit formulations of perfectly true expectations on the outcome of the planning parameters during the planning period. A continuous adjustment to these changes is also necessary to assume the firm will constantly stay at the optimal combination of available resources. The existence of uncertainty and the way in which entrepreneurs form their expectations is not consistent with this picture. Both studies on industrial (9) and agricultural (8, ch. 5) firms make it possible to formulate the following hypotheses as to the way in which expectations are drawn up: (a) Expectations are formulated discontinuously, as a reaction to the appearance of problems which are necessary for the entrepreneur to solve (11). (b) The search for more information (as a basis for formulating expectations) ceases when the costs for continuation of the search exceeds the expected advantage of more information or when the entrepreneur is satisfied with the gathered information (2). (c) The calculations used when formulating expectations are as a rule very simple (8, p. 78). (d) Expectations are influenced not only by observable facts but also by the entrepreneur's hopes, desire, and knowledge and by the way in which information is gathered and processed by him (9, pp. 81-82).

The standard procedure for formulating forecasts contains four steps: data gathering, model building, calculations (of expected values and variations), and control of the outcome of the forecasts.

The way in which expectations about future events are formulated by the entrepreneur has to be taken into consideration when carrying through this procedure. Assuming that the above-mentioned hypothesis describes the way in which expectations are formulated within the agricultural firm, the following can be noted about the forecasting procedure in these firms.

The data gathering covers information on performances within the firm (control and analysis) and on changes in its environment (variations in prices and technological change). This data gathering can very well be incomplete due to the discontinuity in the expectation-formulating process and incorrect due to personal biases in this process. This seems to require that a minimum of continuous data gathering is going on within the firm. This can mainly cover internal performances. A large part of the data gathering must be completed outside the firm as part of some consulting, cooperative, or advisory activity. The models used in forecasting are often grouped in the following categories (17): (a) subjective judgments based on guesswork or qualified anticipations by specialists; (b) analogies from earlier experiences with similar events; (c) simple intrinsic forecasts based on trend calculations; (d) extrinsic forecasts with regression and correlation analysis of time series; (e) supply and demand models based on basic economic theory; (f) introduction or innovation models for new products built on S-shaped acceptance curves; (g) alternative calculations, especially when large technological and other changes are expected.

For the choice of models, as well as for the calculations and the necessary ex post control of the outcome of the forecasts, it seems necessary to choose very simple methods, provided calculations will be going on within the firm. Many factors speak in favor of the use of more careful forecasting methods in the agricultural firm. This often means more sophisticated methods and a continuous improvement and control of these methods. Therefore an important part of the calculation activity has to be performed outside the agricultural firm in specialized units of a commercial or public service character.

PLANNING PROCEDURE OR CHOICE

After organizing all the basic information necessary, there are many possible methods to use to make the choice of future actions. First, it is possible to assume that future events are known with certainty, or at least with subjective certainty, and to use the neoclassical criteria for the choice between inputs and outputs within given resources. The operational tool is some variation of linear programming with the simplex criteria as the choice indicator. Secondly, it is possible to take the time dimension and noncertainty of future events seriously. If so, some possibilities are:

1. The well-known building of preference functions including both profit and its variance and maximizing it, for example, with a quadratic programming approach. Simpler approximations of this general approach also exist. This means that we assume that the variation in the planning environment can best be formalized as a risk situation.
2. If we assume that uncertainty or a mixture of risk and uncertainty is a better description of the planning environment, we may be inclined to use game theory or decision criteria under uncertainty. As we know, this requires among other things that all possible alternative actions and all possible future states of nature can be formalized in finite sets and expressed as a payoff matrix. Luce and Raiffa (11, ch. 13) have shown the properties of the various decision criteria under uncertainty and indicated that we by no means yet have a closed and self-contained body of decision rules in this area.
3. We can search for better production alternatives than the existing one and stop this search when the marginal cost of continued search equals the marginal expected return from it (3, p. 10).
4. We can choose more "behavioristic" approaches to the choice problem and assume (or accept) that alternatives are searched for

sequentially and that thus the theory of choice is closely connected with a theory of search (13).

In the latter case, the choice procedure can be formulated as by Cyert and March (3, ch. 5):

1. Multiple, changing, acceptable-level goals. The criterion of choice is that the alternative selected meet all the demands (goals) of the coalition.
2. An approximate sequential consideration of alternatives. The first satisfactory alternative evoked is accepted. Where an existing policy satisfies the goals, there is little search for alternatives. When failure occurs, search is intensified.
3. The organization seeks to avoid uncertainty by following regular procedures and a policy of reacting to feedback rather than forecasting the environment.
4. The organization uses standard operating procedures and rules of thumb to make and implement choices. In the short run these procedures dominate the decisions made.

An important problem is to choose between these procedures. The criterion for choice methods obviously is the one given by Friedman. Applied to this case, it means that the important question is how good the plan turns out to be, not how realistically the choice method pictures the firm and its environment and its decision procedure.

Close ties exist at any planning moment with the earlier history of the firm. These ties consist of available resources (physical and human), of various ages, and remaining economic lifetime. The existence of these ties and the uncertainty of the planning environment often make it preferable and necessary for the firm to work with a *system of plans* over various future time spans (18). These plans can be for example: (a) Executive plans, for the next year, strongly formalized and acting as immediate guidelines for action. (b) Plans for 3 to 7 years ahead, guiding the short-run development of the firm. The time span of these plans can for example be determined by the usual lifetime of machinery and by the period into the future for which detailed calculations of available resources and economic outcomes can be made. They can preferably be of the rolling plan type. (c) Perspective plans, for the long-run guidelines of the firm's development. These are rather loose plans with very little measuring of resources and economic outcomes. They can include the drawing up of alternative development directions and a systematization of the background material necessary to prepare the firm for an uncertain future.

The content and form of these various plans and the connections between them contain a number of important planning problems.

REFERENCES

1. Baumol, William J. *Economic Theory and Operations Analysis.* Englewood Cliffs, N.J.: Prentice-Hall, 1965.
2. Charnes, A., and W. W. Cooper. The Theory of Search. Optimum Distribution of Search Effort. In *A Behavioral Theory of the Firm,* ed. R. M. Cyert and J. G. March, p. 10. Englewood Cliffs, N.J.: Prentice-Hall, 1963.
3. Cyert, R. M., and J. G. March. *A Behavioral Theory of the Firm.* Englewood Cliffs, N.J.: Prentice-Hall, 1963.
4. Dorfman, R., P. A. Samuelson, and R. M. Solow. *Linear Programming and Economic Analysis.* New York: McGraw-Hill, 1958.
5. Friedman, M. *Essays in Positive Economics.* Chicago: Univ. Chicago Press, 1953.
6. Georgesen-Roegen, N. The Nature of Expectations and Uncertainty. In *Expectations, Uncertainty and Business Behavior,* ed. J. Bowman. Social Science Research Council, New York, 1958.
7. Johnson, G. L., and C. B. Haver. Decision-making Principles in Farm Management. Kentucky Agr. Exp. Sta. Bull. 593.
8. Johnson, G. L., et al. *A Study of Managerial Processes of Midwestern Farmers.* Ames: Iowa State Univ. Press, 1961.
9. Katona, George. *Psychological Analysis of Economic Behavior.* 1st ed. New York: McGraw-Hill, 1951.
10. Knight, F. H. *Risk, Uncertainty and Profit.* New York: Kelley, 1921.
11. Luce, R. D., and H. Raiffa. *Games and Decisions.* New York: Wiley, 1957.
12. March, J. G., and H. A. Simon. *Organizations.* New York: Wiley, 1958.
13. Marris, R. *The Economic Theory of "Managerial" Capitalism.* New York: Free Press, 1964.
14. Modigliani, F., and K. J. Cohen. The Role of Anticipation and Plans in Economic Behavior and Their Use in Economic Analysis and Forecasting. Univ. Illinois, 1961.
15. Partenheimer, E. J., and R. D. Bell. Managerial behavior of farmers. In *A Study of Managerial Processes of Midwestern Farmers,* G. L. Johnson et al. Ames: Iowa State Univ. Press, 1961.
16. Penrose, E. *The Theory of the Growth of the Firm.* New York: Wiley, 1959.
17. Trolle, V., and B. Sandkul. Foretaget och framtiden. Goeteborg, Sweden, 1963.
18. Svennilson, I. *Ekonomisk Planering.* Uppsala: Almquist & Wiksell, 1938.
19. Wiener, N. *Cybernetics.* 2nd ed. Cambridge, Mass.: M.I.T. Press, 1961.
20. Wilk, S., et al. Foretagets langsiktsplanering. Stockholm, 1964.

Chapter 6 ☙ DISCUSSION

Valerian Candela, *Research Institute of Agricultural Economics*
(Romania)

THE PAPER developed by Mr. Renborg deserves special attention
because it offers great significance in proceeding from the real
conditions of firms. That the question of planning and management in agriculture should stress the study of the economics of the firm
is a well-known fact. The processes are inherent not only in the firm's
development and progress but also in its relation to agriculture as a
whole and to other fields of economic activity. This condition clearly
promotes the designation of questions and research which are made in
the paper and which we are now exploring as contained in micro planning.

From here it is clear that the paper of Mr. Renborg, answering
the above-mentioned questions, is a great contribution to our fruitful
work. Although it does not exhaust the vast range of ideas, Mr. Renborg's paper has positive features. It is necessary to stress that the
paper encompasses a large range of questions about concrete planning
of firms and it is also necessary to stress the problems that are included in the paper that pertain to different periods of time, that is,
plans for discrete periods of time and stages of growth.

The basic consideration, according to developing models in order
to achieve stated goals, is the formulation of the relevant functions and
limitations of the possible solutions in relation to technology and so
forth.

Concerning these questions, permit me to briefly emphasize a few
ideas. We have to consider the concept of the firm in a profile of planning. These firms require a control system that enables them to select
an optimal strategy on the basis of accepted principles. Economic processes in large-scale firms and their relations with other branches become all the more complex. And for their management, the old methods are insufficient. It is necessary to apply a more sophisticated
method of calculation and analysis to the application of economic models
on the level of the firm. In the process of model construction and for
securing a high level of rentability of firms, it is necessary to take into
consideration a series of basic relationships and values. This problem
is quite extensively treated in the paper where they were listed. Treated
especially was the problem about which I have just spoken.

It is possible to come up with cybernetic models, which could be
employed after several adaptations on state farms as well as in the agricultural production of cooperatives. Schematic models are appropriate to describe the pattern of the increasing production on large farms.
Taking this into view it is important to consider the value indices,

namely, the dimension of gross product in money forms, the inputs
which include seeds, fertilizers, amortization (capital consumption allowance), and so forth, and also net product and another complex category, net income. On the basis of these categories we analyze the indices and their interrelationships in the process of constructing models.

If we are to speak about the programming of optimal economic
activity, then we consider the optimization of different value indices of
production. We shall take into consideration the computation of net
product. One could say that the firm would try to maximize the gross
production of the present year. The result would be the preferred
production involving too much material input and the deficient structure
of assortments. The consequent phase can be directed to the justification of the increased expenditures and wasteful use of labor.

We can take another element of the scheme which is presented in
the model. For example, if we estimate the results of production entirely within the realm of the application of human labor, it will slow
down the use of machines, fertilizers, and so forth. It can have a negative effect upon the increase of labor productivity. One can say, it
seems to me, that maximization of profits permits deficiencies; it can
understate the importance of gross product. This is true if we take into consideration the profit, that all efforts have to aim at the reduction
of labor and material input. The conventional maximization of profit
stands for the maximization of profits for one year. But maximization
of profit for one year can result in avoiding costs which are relevant to
the profits of the following period.

Besides this, if we take into consideration that modern technical
progress requires large investments that are almost always given as
the results after a longer continued period, then the maximization of
profit in one year only will lead inevitably to a slowing down of technical progress. Similar effects are obtained when the system of material
incentives is given to the workers and the peasants of the cooperatives.
The discussion continues in our country, concerned exclusively with one
of these indices and these profits linked with the maximization of one
factor. Therefore it is considered that whole systems of indices are
necessary with respect to the time factor.

Of course the systems of incentives are distinguished between state
farms and cooperative farms. On state farms the wage system is connected with the fulfillment of the production plan and assortments, as
well as with the productivity of labor and with the costs of production.
An increased material part of prime cost in relation to profit over and
above the plan relies upon the participating collective. On our cooperative farms material incentives and the whole system of indices is intended to provide the strengthening of the cooperative unit.

Taking into consideration all of this, naturally every system of incentives has its own deficiency; namely, for the exposure of the factors
which are inefficiently applied. In this respect, the Research Institute
of Agricultural Economics includes the theme of optimization of economic activity on state farms. The goal of this theme is to promote

modeling the economic activity of farms and to place the organization and management of farms on a scientific ground.

As was mentioned in the paper by Mr. Renborg, some very interesting examples result, it seems, to those who are now working on economic problems of agricultural firms. Large collectives of researchers are not only put to a task to solve the several questions of scientifically based management of farming units but also have to make more precise the concept of planning and management in agriculture.

Chapter 7 ✐ PROVEN TOOLS FOR MICRO PLANNING AND DECISIONS

Erwin M. Reisch, *University of Hohenheim* (German Federal Republic)

T HE PURPOSE of this paper is to show which new models and methods of farm planning have already proved to be applicable and can be recommended for a broader use. For this attempt it is important to stress the critical points and bottlenecks which are still left and which need to be perfected in further application of these models. Simultaneously background is given for the following chapter by Weinschenk, who deals with new and potential (prospective) models for application on the micro level.

The main starting points are the experiences which we have encountered in working with the modern methods. Importantly, these two papers show the stage of development of these methods in our country. The situation in the other countries, East and West, is incorporated as far as it is known from the literature and from personal information. Since the discussant is familiar with the situation in Eastern Europe (from his own work), I shall not go into details in this matter.

It is assumed further that the tools of planning and decision making can be considered as proven tools under two conditions. With their aid (a) it is possible to get more accurate, more detailed, and faster information through their use than was previously possible for the decision-making process at the farm level, and (b) a substantial increase in information is "produced" with a reasonable input, so that the utilization of modern tools is economical. The second condition depends to a high degree on the progress of computer techniques and the efficient organization of the planning and data processing systems and is subject to a rapid change. A tool which is not economical in today's use may very well be relevant under an advanced technological and economic stage. The emphasis in evaluating the methods therefore will be on the question of whether and how it is possible to supply relevant information with these methods for economic decisions of the farm firm. Also the question of the supply of data is to be discussed thoroughly. Since the micro decisions are finally made by the management of the firms, the practical value of the new tools can be determined by their contribution to the efficiency of the management and to the financial state of the firm.

EFFICIENT FARM MANAGEMENT

Farming was long considered to be kind of an "art" or even more a "way of life." Since the beginning of this century, mainly during the last two decades, effort has been toward diminishing the extent of the "art of farming" and widening the extent of "scientific management." The term "scientific" is defined as the process of acquiring knowledge and information to give the basis for a clearly formulated, successful management. The area of management, independently of whether it is for a one-man or a large collective firm, includes the following tasks: (a) formulating the frame of the firm, including decisions on goals and on the further development of the firm; resource, production, and marketing policy (decisions on goals); (b) setting up the production program which controls the program while the production is underway, optimizing the separate parts of the firm (for example the economics of labor use, forage growing, cropping patterns, resource budgeting, transportation activities), and selection of workers and inputs necessary for the production (decisions on production processes and operating procedures); (c) assigning and instructing workers and allocating inputs necessary for the production activities (decisions on instructions for realization); and (d) controlling the different parts of the firm and collecting information for the management (decisions on performance and control).

The four management functions mentioned above, according to our present opinion, are to be fulfilled on the basis of concrete internal and external information. Economic-oriented firms therefore cannot work without a good system of gaining information (collecting and processing data) and of transferring information (a system of communication). The importance of information-technique is increasing. It has the task to produce new knowledge and to bring it to those places that guide the production process by the help of this information. Figure 7.1 shows this process.

Figure 7.1 shows clearly the above-mentioned functions of management. The whole system is similar to a closed loop. If one transfers the functions of management into a system of functional responsibilities,

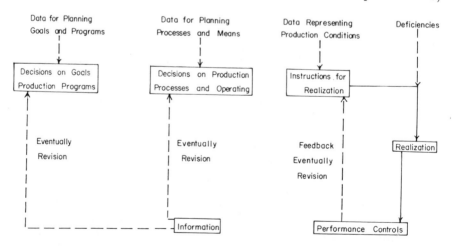

Fig. 7.1. Decisions and controls in the firm.

grouped according to the hierarchic levels, the closed loop of information flow is changed to a cybernetic system of official channels.

Figure 7.2 shows the upper, medium, and lower levels of decisions with their functions. For the purpose of demonstration, an example of the hierarchy of a large firm is added. The long-range planning of the firm and its strategy of development are indicated at the top level.

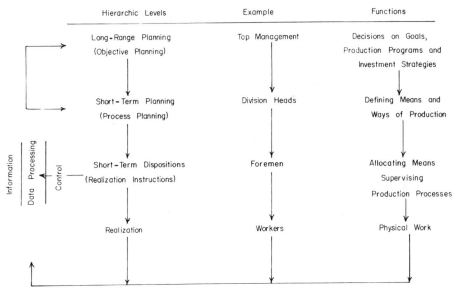

Fig. 7.2. Cybernetic scheme of hierarchic levels.

These are the principle decisions of the firm, to formulate the goals and the production program with the necessary investments and basic strategy measures. During a single production period this level of long-range decisions is touched only if by serious technical or economic difficulties the performance of the previously determined program is questioned and eventually a new plan is necessary.

On the second level the optimal solution for fulfilling the program has to be determined. This again includes planning, but for a shorter period and mainly with regard to particular sections of the firm. Therefore it can be considered as short-run and partial planning. This level also includes emphasis on data processing in order to determine if in performing the program the projected outputs and productivities have been reached or considerable deficiencies have arisen. It is closely connected with the third level where short-term dispositions are being made, the inputs are being allocated, the stocks are being managed, and the elements of the production process are being prepared.

In the specific case of an existing farm firm the different levels of the cybernetic scheme correspond to the following functions:

1. long-range planning — formulating the objectives; computing the

optimal organization for several periods of production; determining
the program for investments; determining an optimal strategy with
regard to the technological and economic development; supplying the
data for evaluating the production program and for optimizing it for
the next period.
2. short-run planning — budgeting the cropping, fertilizing, forage-
growing system; preparing the labor budget; determining working
procedures, and breeding and testing schemes; scheduling repair
and transport jobs; balancing requirements and stocks of inputs and
so on; further on, supplying data for controlling the technological
production process (measures of productivity).
3. short-term dispositions — splitting up the workers in groups; assigning and instructing workers and allocating machinery to the work
that has to be done; curing of deficiencies (by weather, breakdown of
machines, deficiencies of inputs); determining the order of jobs, recording the results of the work, of the supply of inputs, etc.
4. Work performance — performance of the work procedures; handling
tools and machines; taking care of the animals (doing the chores);
performance of manual work, etc.

All the levels are closely connected by a system to control the operation and to collect information data. It is obvious that different tools
are required for the different functions. To choose them correctly is a
primary function of those who have to work with them. The problem of
selecting the method to be used, however, is only one of the difficulties
on the way toward better information for micro decisions. Not less important is the problem of supplying the data. Further, as a third problem, the question of the efficient organization and costs of the information and decision-making system involved must not be overlooked. With
regard to the selection of the planning methods, a rather small discrepancy between the model used and reality must be reached. In other
words, a high degree of accuracy of isomorphy (9) is necessary. The
difficulties of an ideal accommodation are very important in agriculture
with its large risks in the natural production process and in the market.
Basically they are caused by the imperfect knowledge about the relevant
conditions of reality, the action alternatives, the value concepts, the
probability distributions of the data needed for planning, and by the difficulty of considering complex situations by operational model.

The same problems arise in trying to represent the complex reality
by figures. Therefore the problem of supplying data is closely connected
with the problem of selecting the methods. Without a corresponding data
setup the best methods are without practical value. On the other hand,
it is a matter of fact that more sophisticated planning methods can stimulate considerably the improvement of the data. They have caused many
discussions and reflections on how to meet the data needs and to set up
a modern economical system of information and decision making.

In countries with mainly large industry-like farm firms, this task
may seem easier than in countries where family farms prevail. However it has to be shown that it is not at all necessary in these countries

to forego the modern tools of microeconomic planning and decisions. Of course, one has to be aware of the fact that family farms are under the pressure of a rapid adjustment to dynamic technical and economic development. Therefore detailed long-run plans for individual farms which go beyond a period of five years are not very meaningful.

DISCUSSION OF PLANNING METHODS

The basic questions are: At the present state of methods and computers, which methods are suitable for practical use on the microeconomic level of agriculture? What information can they give and where are their gaps and weaknesses?

Methods for Long-Range Planning and Decisions

During the last decade, in the agricultural economics institutes of all developed countries, a vast amount of time and capital was invested in developing suitable planning methods for the optimal allocation of available resources to a set of production activities and for calculating the optimal expansion path of the capacities of land, labor, capital, and other factors that are to be used for several periods. A large number of models and algorithms were proposed. However, so far only a few have reached or gone beyond the stage of practical application. Linear programming, network planning, and simulation belong to these, the latter one with *cum grano salis*. In this paper, therefore, we are going to deal with these methods only and look forward to Weinschenk's presentation on new and potential models and tools for micro planning and decision making.

Nonlinear, integer, dynamic linear, and dynamic programming as well as stochastic programming have not proved to be applicable thus far. At least they are not yet in the stage for solving real problems of farm management. Certainly the theoretical and mathematical models for these methods have been defined and the application for agricultural problems has been demonstrated with simple examples; but the practical application of the results as information and "new knowledge" for more efficient management of farms has failed so far. The main reasons are (a) necessary data cannot be supplied; (b) setting up the models takes too much preparation time; (c) requirements of computer time and storage capacity for realistic models are still too high; and (d) inputs that go beyond the requirements necessary for standard programming are not within a reasonable relation to the value of the additional information gained by those more sophisticated methods.

In addition, the advanced methods may reduce the great importance of predecisions compared with standard linear programming. However they simultaneously create new problems which cannot be solved by the new methods, but only by a predecision of the man doing the planning. Examples are the assumption of an income and consumption function, replacement routines, and management strategies in dynamic linear programming models and the underlying shape of price and cost functions with varying amounts of outputs or the income-risk relation for quadratic and stochastic programming. Similar difficulties are encountered in integer programming if one takes care of the fact that the mechanization in modern agriculture is characterized by machinery chains rather than by single machines and implements.

The same is true for the concepts in the theory of the games. Of course any intelligent farm manager will agree that his activities can be optimal only if they are determined within a larger context. And since the behavior of his partners is unknown, he has to look for an optimal strategy under these conditions. But according to which one of the proposed criteria (the Wald, Savage, Laplace, or Hurwitz optimism-pessimism index) will he make his decisions? So far it has not been determined which one under which conditions gives the best result. Probably the statement of Dillon (2) is still valid today, that aside from games against the uncertainty of the weather, the game theory so far cannot be applied successfully.

Perhaps more positive, but we feel not yet apt for reality, are the replacement models with initial theoretical formulations by Taylor and Hotelling. The number of models has increased permanently since new algorithms (for example dynamic programming) provided new possibilities for quantitative treatment. Agreeing with Eisgruber (4), one can state that "all examples of applications are to be considered as illustrations of the models for academic and educational purposes and not for solving practical problems."

The application of production function analysis to management problems of whole farms also has proved to be unsuitable (8). From such structure these models are not capable of answering questions of the optimal production program. But also the information concerning the use of inputs is weak and practically valueless since the assumption of an overall farm production function is unrealistic. (The situations in the single farms are too different, even if the material is carefully stratified.) In addition, the problems of intercorrelation, of necessary aggregation of variables, and the influence of unconsidered variables cause many problems in deriving these functions. Compared with the production function analysis, linear programming gives a much more accurate description of the situation of the firm and of its different alternatives.

Opposite to this, the statistical analysis by mathematical-statistical methods (regression analysis, analysis of variance, factor analysis) to get technical information and coefficients can be evaluated positively. Estimating partial production functions out of deeply disaggregated farm records or experimental data can give a better basis for evaluating the efficiency and optimality of factor use than can a simple comparison of characteristic figures on the basis of classifying the farms into above-average, average, and below-average strata.

Summing up, in the review of planning methods in agriculture today, only linear programming can be considered as a widely accepted and used planning method. During the last ten years it was applied on thousands of farms. The models of standard programming and parametric programming belong to the readily available tools of an agricultural economist when he receives his academic degree. Starting from the short-run model under conditions of certainty and complete information, operational methods and computer programs were developed which extend the rather rigid and narrow validity of the optimal solution. It became a matter of course that for a single farm not only one solution but a multitude of solutions was calculated. This has been done by two means: not only the optimal solution but also the solutions of the last interactions which gave "almost" optimal solutions were considered. This approach arose through the experience that in many problems the last interactions increased the value of the objective function only by a small amount. Taking into account the uncertainty and inaccuracy of the coefficients and capacities used, they also could be considered "optimal," especially if one tried to incorporate the effect of likes and dislikes of the farmer. It was also recognized that the optimal solution in many cases is only the highest point of a rather flat hill — rather than a real peak. So the surrounding of the optimal solution, using the shadow prices as information, was tested by limited changes of the coefficients and/or capacities to gain information on the shape of the hill. Simultaneously one could get the stability of the optimal solution with regard to changes in the a_{ij}, b_i, and c_j values and/or the structure of the model. From the viewpoint of the method these analyses are mainly optima for a large number of single programs which can be printed out by high-speed computers within a few minutes after the first optimal solution is reached. These are readily attained if the relevant alternatives, represented by additional objective functions, capacity vectors, and activities, are fed into the computer with the matrix.

Programming with variable prices and variable resources gives similar results. In comparison to the techniques just mentioned, alternative values for certain vector elements are not put into the model, but one tests (a) the requirements of certain optimal solutions with variable resources or (b) the validity of the production programs with regard to price variations (5). This last question also can be analyzed by parametric variation of the relevant vector coefficients. In order to give a better basis to investment decisions it is possible to compute alternative programs for different technological procedures and to test future influences by sequential programming.

Two examples are given for indicating the kind of application of linear programming now widely done. The example in Figure 7.3 from Brandes (1) has an unusual objective function. The total labor input is to be minimized while parametrically raising the total net revenue with fixed land and capital capacity held constant. This analysis can be more appropriate than maximizing profit in farms with hired labor which is becoming more and more expensive. The curve of decreasing marginal productivity of labor gives a valuable indication of how far to go in building the production program.

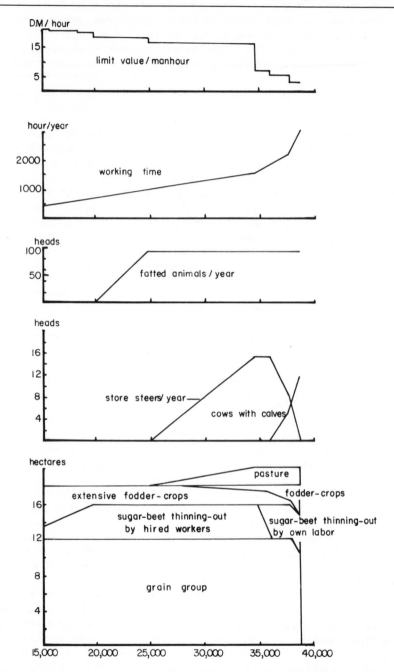

Fig. 7.3. Decrease of labor input as a factor of increasing total net income.

The other example in Table 7.1 (3) is one out of a total of 200 farms which we calculated at Hohenheim for studying (a) the income reserves and (b) the optimal farm organization under various basic assumptions. These assumptions included the possibility of varying the surface cultivated or of renting out land and investing capital in dairy barns and

Table 7.1. Optimum solutions under various basic assumptions

Item	Unit	Solution[a]					
		0	1	2	3	4	5
Total net revenue (000)	DM	20.9	25.4	25.7	30.0	28.8	26.5
Total gross income (000)	DM	16.8	21.3	21.7	23.1	22.9	21.3
Total gross income EEC prices (000)	DM	14.7	18.4	18.6	19.4	19.5	19.4
Land cultivated	ha	21.3	21.3	23.5	18.8	20.7	24.9
Land rented or rented out	ha	...	...	+ 2.2	- 2.5	- 0.6	+ 3.6
Labor	hours	3,400	3,400	3,400	3,400	3,400	3,400
Capital investments	DM	...	...	...	44,000	30,000	...
Rent to capital invested	%	...	...	...	6.1	6.9	...
Shadow prices							
cropland	DM/ha	...	+ 892	+ 500	+ 349	+ 340	+ 349
grassland	DM/ha	...	+ 650	+ 230	+ 2.4	+ 0.5	+ 2.5
dairy cow	DM/cow	...	...	...	-39.0	...	...
Production program							
grain	ha	8.0	11.6	17.0	11.6	11.6	12.6
potatoes	ha	2.7	2.1	2.7	2.2	2.1	2.4
beets	ha	0.7	1.0	0.3	...	0.2	0.4
forage	ha	3.7	2.6	3.4	3.4	3.4	3.9
grassland	ha	6.2	4.0	4.0	1.5	3.4	5.6
dairy cows	St/p	110.0	10.5	9.3	...	2.9	9.0
young cattle	St/p	9.0	9.4	9.3	...	2.5	8.3
sows	St/p	6.0	9.0	8.0	42.0	32.2	9.0
pigs	St/p	60.0	53.0	60.0	50.0	47.0	53.0
grain production	1000 kg	31.2	45.1	66.2	45.1	45.1	49.0
potatoes sold	1000 kg	40.5	42.2	40.5	42.2	42.2	42.2
milk sold	1000 kg	40.0	42.0	37.2	...	11.6	36.0
cattle sold	1000 kg	3.4	1.9	1.7	...	1.1	3.3
pigs sold	1000 kg	7.0	6.5	7.3	8.9	6.6	6.5
piglets sold	St/p	46	106	81	690	519	106
Gross revenue (000)	DM	56.1	57.7	60.0	76.1	70.4	64.1
Total costs (000)	DM	39.6	36.1	38.1	52.9	47.4	41.4
Feeds balance concentrates	1000 kg	+ 2.4	+15.6	+37.7	-20.3	- 1.8	+17.4
Labor budget							
labor unused total	hours	...	129	272	120	78	120
time span: grain harvest	hours	...	7	0	0	0	0
unused labor shadow price	hours	...	0	16.5	14.3	14.4	14.3

a. The symbol 0 refers to the existing farm plan, while plans 1-5 are optimal farm plans where 1 refers to existing farm; 2 allows land rental but no added capital; 3 has unrestricted capital investment; 4 is same as 3 except for EEC prices; 5 is same as 3 but is for minimal capital investment to attain 15000 DM gross income per man unit.

swine houses. Furthermore the minimum capital investment for a
given income level was sought. Finally, since EEC prices of several
farm products fell far below previous levels, optimal new farm organizations were sought. While other alternatives were calculated, they
are not of special interest in this context. But it may be worthwhile
mentioning that the printout of the results was arranged in a way as is
shown in Table 7.1. From these even farmers can read the figures and
understand their meaning. Since these planning methods cause a considerable increase in the preparation phase (setting up the model, providing the data) and in costs of the computer, the gain of these extended
calculations has to be checked critically.

Certainly the quantity of information is increased by these extensively applied techniques. The question remains whether the quality of
information also is improved relative to the long-run goals and programs of the firm. Is it possible with these methods to overcome the
uncertainty in input-output relations and the imperfect knowledge about
technological and economic development? Is it possible by this means
to eliminate the lack of accuracy in the basic data and the difficulties
in formulating the goals and restrictions? The answer is no to both
questions.

These manipulations and calculations cannot really overcome the
problems of optimizing over several periods under conditions of risk
and uncertainty — important elements involved in any long-run planning.
The linear programming model used remains a static one; and all calculated alternative production programs are restricted to the ceteris
paribus condition, which means that the information value of the results
is correspondingly limited. Nevertheless these calculations are valuable tools for decision making. Applied intelligently, they bring the
first optimal solution, by relaxing the initial restrictions step by step,
closer to reality. They also give information on which program is the
optimal one if this or that endogenous or exogenous factor changes.
But in evaluating and using the results, one has to be aware that nearly
all data used are prospective values that can be predicted only with a
certain (mostly unknown) probability and that the respective decisions
based on these results will include a considerable degree of uncertainty.

Summarizing, we can state that the modifications of linear programming, mentioned above and practiced widely, prepare for decisions
by supplying a set of solutions. But the decisions themselves are not
made easier by a number of alternatives. And one will be restricted to
these procedures for long-range decisions as long as there are no operational methods of dynamic (including risk) planning. How many solutions in this state of development are to be computed in a given case
has to be decided finally according to the situation in question. Simultaneously, the costs of calculations involved should be taken into consideration.

In this context a new method of calculation, farm simulation, should
be mentioned. In our country this method is presently on the way toward
practical application since Hesselbach and Eisgruber (7) developed a

simulator suited for German conditions. Simulation as a technique for farm planning is still a young tool, although any planning procedure is simulation since this method basically can be defined as making models of the real world. For the area of economics, however, one has to restrict this definition since simulation is a kind of "drawing samples with the possibility to evaluate the results." In this approach, simulation includes the whole farm. It starts from the question: "What is the result if... ? This means that, as opposed to a programming model, the farm manager is selecting preliminarily a number of organization plans, essentially on the basis of L.P. analysis previously done, which he feels should be worth treatment. Then, by way of a programmed budgeting procedure, this question is answered: What are the results of these plans with regard to work distribution, forage growing, investment plans, and net farm income when the plans are to be put into effect? It is easy to extend the calculations over a period of 10 to 12 years to take care of price trends and other factors as replacement of machinery and animals. Consideration of several production periods and integer figures does not cause real difficulties.

If one were to include all possibilities of combining variables similar to the "complete description method," simulation, like L.P., should show the optimal solution. This procedure is known as "kombinatoric simulation." But already with few variables at several levels the number of alternatives to be tested is so high[1] that the procedure is unrealistic for finding the optimal plan for practical problems. But since it is known in reality that the optimal solution does not exist and that there are a number of solutions "close to being optimal," it is possible to calculate a limited number of randomly selected solutions. One can expect with a certain degree of probability (depending on the number of selected plans) that the sample will contain such near-optimal solutions which can serve as a basis for management decisions. This approach is called statistical simulation or Monte Carlo technique.

From the methodological point of view, farm simulation is nothing but a highly mechanized budgeting procedure. The principle of marginal costs and marginal revenue is missing. Viewed from the theory of the firm this is a relevant shortcoming. Therefore the efficiency of its application as a decision-making tool lies in situations with a rather restricted number of alternatives. In addition, this method can improve the basis for decisions in connection with linear programming by simulating those optimal solutions that are of most interest with integer, dynamic, stochastic, or random data and by bringing deeper insights into the implications of the optimal solutions calculated. Certainly a broader application of this method will be hindered by the fact that the farm simulator has to be adapted to the different economic and technological conditions of various countries.

---

1. The number of alternative plans (possibilities of combining the variables) is $Ko = \sum_{j=1}^{n} m_j$, where n_j stands for the variables and m_j for different levels of variables; for example, 6 variables with 10 levels give 1 million possible combinations.

Methods for Short-Run Planning

Calculations with the purpose of finding the best way to determine the overall production program are to be considered short-run planning methods. The general frame of this program is given by the long-range plan. Now the gap has to be bridged between this plan and its realization. This is the "middle level" of management. Below it we find the lowest level of management, the area of short-term dispositions. It is useful to discuss it separately.

The classical tool of short-run planning was budgeting for the different parts of the farm: crops, fertilizers, livestock, forage, labor, money, and so on. If the objective is to determine the requirement, the stocks, and the additional amount of an input needed, this simple technique is still sufficient. When using a farm simulator these budgetary calculations can be worked out in a few minutes. In addition, for simple production planning, program planning is used to a certain extent, but not to analyze an optimal solution. If the optimal organization of forage growing, for example, is to be worked out with regard to growing, conserving, and feeding the forage, more efficient methods have to be employed. The same is true for fertilizer budgeting if buying in low or high seasons causes price differences to be considered or the quantity, types, form (solid, liquid, or gaseous), and the specific influence of different fertilizers on certain plants is to be considered. Finding the optimal organization for the use of labor and machinery normally is even more difficult. The acreage that can be covered with a machine varies with the weather condition, and the costs are decreased by increasing employment. Furthermore sequence problems and others are rather complicated matters to be handled with calculation techniques.

During the last decades a specific area of research, operations research, grew up for solving those complicated technical and organizational problems. The number of tools that are supplied and tested by research workers is large and still increasing, especially since rapidly progressing computer techniques allow more complex problems and models to be treated in a shorter time.

Following the classification of operations research (11) within a firm, the following problems can be dealt with: allocation, mixing, replacement, inventory, time-selecting, and waiting lines. In addition, transportation and work sequence problems can be handled. Planning techniques for these techniques can be used for many kinds of problems but partly are limited to specific problems. So far in agriculture only the more general methods are being used: linear programming, transportation models, network planning, and the recent farm simulation methods. Some economists will object to optimal solutions for parts of a farm since they are happy with L.P. as a method that enables them to handle all the relations within a farm simultaneously and to end up with definite solutions. But since we know how heavily the optimal solutions depend on the assumptions made and that any farm is part of an overall totality, one cannot object in principle to the analysis of certain parts of

a farm. Furthermore the production, of which we think almost exclusively in optimizing farms, is itself only a part of the total firm which
consists still of other (perhaps even more important) sections (buying,
selling, personnel, public relations, and others). Up to now haven't we
been inclined to overemphasize the production phase of farms?

In addition, using linear programming for such partial planning has
an advantage since the large number of events required in using the theory of risk can be more easily fulfilled (then it is the case for planning
the whole farm where uncertainty is the prevailing situation). Through
linear programming one has great flexibility in analyzing a wide range
of alternative procedures in growing, harvesting, conserving, buying, and
allocating homegrown forage and concentrates. Rather disaggregated
models with numerous transfer activities are being used for this purpose. In order to consider simultaneously problems of investment,
they have to be supplemented with such activities as constructing additional silo capacity and enlarging the barn. It is advisable to aggregate
the other parts of the farm strongly to be sure that the matrix does not
get too large; this, however, is an economical question rather than a
methodological one. The same is true for the planning of buying, mixing, and applying fertilizers. These questions can be connected with a
scheduling problem regarding the use of storage capacity and the date
of buying and spreading if one selects a corresponding model. In this
case the total costs of fertilizing a farm with a given cropping system
have to be minimized.

The problems of using labor and machinery are of a very different
type. For straight allocation problems linear programming can be employed usefully; often, however, a transportation model is the more adequate procedure. The condition of integer values can be fulfilled easily
and simple problems are solved with paper and pencil. Transportation
models have the same shortcomings as linear programming since constant costs per unit are implied. But not even network planning (PERT)
overcomes this difficulty. Nevertheless, for analyzing labor requirement
and work sequences, it gives much more information than the traditional
labor budget for the following reasons: (a) it separates clearly the com-
peting procedures; (b) it takes into account the different working conditions (for example during the row-crop-cultivating and hay-harvesting
period); and (c) it guarantees that the number of workers necessary for
a certain procedure are really allocated to this procedure.

Organizational problems of a similar kind arise in central processing plants and repair shops, in large livestock operations, and the like.
As workers become more scarce, machinery outfits become more expensive, and costs of maintaining service stations (or similar institutions) rise, the more useful it is to know the critical path for perfect
realization of a plan.

An example of a network analysis is given in Figure 7.4. This and
similar studies (6) bring two types of information of practical value:
the critical path through the working year and an accurate representation of the labor situation in separate time spans.

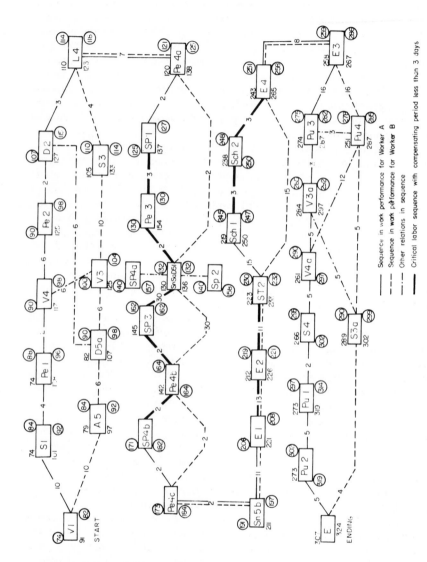

Fig. 7.4. Sequence in the work performance of 2 laborers on a 40-hectare farm.

Tools for Short-Term Dispositions

Some authors call the manager "the dispositive factor." On the lowest level of management, little time is left for real planning. Here the short-term dispositions, the decisions for realization, are dominant. The basis for optimal decisions in this area is given (a) by the "know-how" about the technical procedures involved and (b) by being informed permanently about the state of the processes and activities in the farm. The better and the more perfect the information is, the more rational can we expect the decisions of managers to be. The know-how mentioned under point (a) is a question of the state of scientific knowledge and training of the farmer and does not warrant further discussion here. The problem of being well informed about the state production processes, however, is closely related to the problem (already mentioned) of getting data. It is discussed more intensively in the following section. In this context it is sufficient to state that on this lowest level of decisions, there exist less methodological than organizational problems, which is true for an agriculture of decentralized family farms as well as for a centralized industry-like agriculture.

THE PROBLEM OF DATA FOR MICROECONOMIC PLANNING AND DECISIONS

The problem of data has two aspects: (a) how many data are needed and (b) how accurate do they have to be. It is somewhat trivial to state that artistry in formulating models is of rather little value without the availability of adequate data and that no results of planning can be better than the quality of the information used for the model. Therefore methods and models can prove to be applicable only if the problem of data has been solved. Hence one should strive for an optimal relation between the efforts for developing methods and those to improve the set of data. I feel that during the past decade, which was characterized by the rapid spread of mathematical tools for planning, the efforts were mainly on the side of the methods.

This bias is inevitable and the problem of collecting data is of secondary order as long as the efforts in research have to be directed toward finding and improving the methods and the methods have to be applied to show their possibilities. But as soon as a tool reaches the state of practical application, the problem of data claims priority. Very frequently one is forced to adapt the model to the data available in such a way that the result is an optimal accommodation of the decision model for a given level of information. There can be no doubt that the planning methods and models already available will be of much higher value for farms when the supply of data has been improved. Presently large efforts in this direction are being made and certain progress is evident.

Need for Data

Data requirements by quantity and quality are determined in the model selected for solving a specific problem. Generally the size of the model, and consequently the data requirements, increase progressively when striving for a higher degree of isomorphy, especially for the typically used matrix models. Therefore it is advisable to restrict the size of the model, and thus the data requirements, to the definite needs of the problems involved. Reducing or restricting the model can be done in different ways (13): (a) by ignoring less important facts, as for example when assuming that the farmer only wants to maximize profits; (b) by eliminating the implications of exogenous factors, for example when assuming prices to be constant, or starting out from given capacities of labor (afterwards, however, data eliminated before can be brought into consideration by parametric variation); (c) by summing up independent data that have the same effect on the result, for example the variable costs of machinery; and (d) by aggregating those activities which have complementary relations, for example several crops in one crop rotation activity.

It is left to the decision of the person doing the planning how far the limitation of the model with regard to the problem in question should be carried (in other words, to determine the optimal combination of the availability of data and of the size of the model). For this important predecision one should be aware that the availability and quality of the data may differ considerably between groups of data. For example in a farm with records over several years, very detailed figures on costs may exist but technical coefficients of the production activities may not be available. In these cases it would not be wise, especially when considering simultaneously technological progress, to strive for an exaggerated accuracy in other data.

Most calculations have led to the result that only in two cases is it necessary to look for a high degree of accuracy: (a) in the important activities and inputs and (b) in those coefficients that draw from scarce factors. In the results from planning 312 farms in a cash crop area by L.P., we found that in certain periods of the year the data for the labor organization have a rather large influence on the optimal solution (Table 7.2), and even small input and capacity variations cause considerable changes in the optimal solution; in other periods the labor coefficients have almost no influence on optimum programs. The same argument is true for some cost figures. From our experience it is not meaningful to spend much effort on a detailed supply of different small cost figures (e.g., machines and other production inputs) if their inaccuracy has fewer implications than a small change in outputs or product price.

By the extensive application of L.P. for planning farm organization, certain routines for providing data have been developed. However, with the application of mathematical models for partial and sequential planning, the demand for technical data is increasing beyond these collections. Since they apply specifically to individual farms, these planning

Table 7.2. Working time span acting as relevant
restrictions in linear programming

Activity	Number of cases	Percentage
Spring cultivation	2	0.6
Beets singling and hoeing and fodder harvesting	312	100.0
Early grain harvesting	307	98.0
Main grain harvesting	305	97.8
Potato harvesting	265	84.9
Sugar beet harvesting	120	38.5
Fall plowing	31	9.9

procedures require farm-specific data. Therefore there can be no
doubt that a special demand for internal farm data will arise.

Sources of Data

For farm planning, there are three main sources of data: (a) data
from the farm in question supplied by complete records (bookkeeping), by
surveys, or by interviews according to the need; (b) data taken from the
neighboring farm or farms that operate under similar conditions (book-
keeping-statistics belong in this category also); and (c) data taken from
scientific experiments and studies that have been done to analyze special problems and are normally used as normative coefficients (2).
Usually the data from these sources have to be supplemented by information about prices and costs (supply and demand). During the last
years the data from farm records, as well as those from other studies,
have been compiled in extensive data collections (10) in many countries.
In some cases they are extended toward formulating production processes and activities. They can be stored on discs or tapes and can be
taken directly from there into the programming tableau.

These efforts in the field of data supply already have resulted in a
quantitatively considerable data collection which permits us to perform
standard planning procedures fast and without difficulties. Nevertheless
we are still far from having reached a satisfying level for three major
reasons.

1. The supply of reliable data for the farm in question causes difficulties on all farms without records. It is especially impossible to get
information in these farms on the year-to-year input and output variations. Even for the year analyzed, exact input-output relations are seldom available. Data of other farms and normative figures must be used
very carefully. In any case, it is desirable to have records as a basis
for a farm planning service. The financial result, the net income, and
the degree of overall profitability are of smaller interest than the technical coefficients and yields and their range of variation. Since the
number of events will seldom be sufficient for a mathematical-statistical
analysis, the information on the variation of the results of several years
can improve the selection of accurate data. The main point, however,

is that those records can indicate, by comparison with normative figures, the level of management regarding the production techniques.

2. When normative data from scientific studies, data from farms, and (eventually) supplementary data from catalogs are available, the question will then arise of which data to use in the real planning situation. Should we use the data of the past, the farm data, or normative data? And which data ought to be chosen if new technologies or alternatives have to be taken into consideration? Programs that have been planned with normative data may give a wrong set of solution activities defined too favorably. In the planned farm this may cause activities with low output to be overestimated in the optimal solution. On the other hand, unfavorably defined activities may lead to profit chances not fully utilized. Therefore it is important to find those data that actually can be realized in the future.

This aspect of the data problem can be illustrated by the following result of *Schweinemastkontrollringen* (hog fattening circles) in our country. From scientific experiments it is known that 650 grams weight gain per day is a good normative figure. The results of 3888 fattening groups controlled (Fig. 7.5) show that less than one-fourth of all groups reached this standard. Although some farms had excellent results, other farms had extremely bad results. If only the groups on slatted floors were considered, the distribution was changed towards a higher

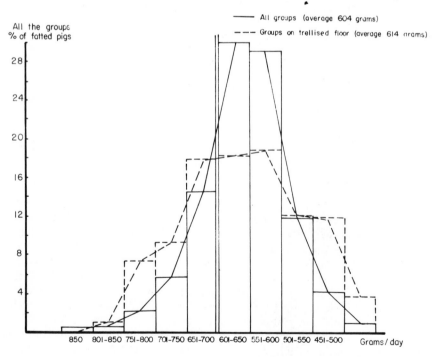

Fig. 7.5. Average daily gain of weight in pig fattening.

standard deviation, certainly indicating higher requirements of management. If the costs of feeds per 1 kilogram weight gain are analyzed (Fig. 7.6), large differences in costs are revealed. About 75 percent of all farms had higher costs than the generally accepted normative figure of 1.50 Deutsche Mark per kilogram weight gain.

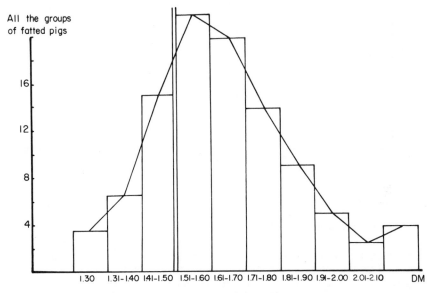

Fig. 7.6. Fodder costs of 1 kg (2.204 lb) gain in weight.

From these figures the difficulty in making "accurate" decisions for the level of costs and the production coefficients is easily imagined.

As a further illustration, the result of a study on the repair costs of tractors is shown (Fig. 7.7). Calculating the arithmetic mean for periods of 500 working hours gives the jagged, upwards sloped curve, a. A formula for calculation adapted to this shape results in the smooth curve, b. In reality, however, individual data are widely scattered on both sides of the calculated curve. Certainly these single points cannot be used for planning a farm, but one ought to be aware how inexact the calculated cost figures are. This is especially true for the number of years for which the machine can be used and for the replacement rate.

3. For long-range planning and decisions on the microeconomic level, the exogenous factors are of increasing importance. On the other hand, the accuracy of today's farm data will become less important than the knowledge about the areas of uncertainty and the degree of risk in the trend of yields, inputs, prices, costs, technology, and so on. Such information for practical farm planning is not yet readily available. In the single planning case they have to be computed in a troublesome manner by analyzing statistical data and trend calculations. But there is no argument why, as with bookkeeping systems being adapted to the

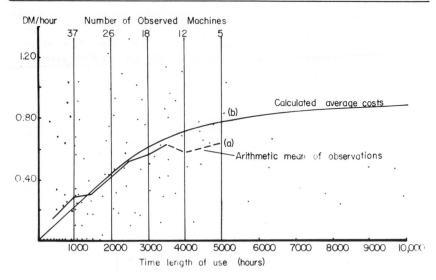

Fig. 7.7. Comparison of repair costs of 30-hp tractors.

needs of farm planning, the supply of data from the exogenous area of
the market could not be improved in a similar way. Further, it should
be possible for the results of experiments in the different fields of production techniques to be provided as continuous functions (yield and cost
functions) and with the standard deviation rather than as discrete figures. Even if the method is not yet suited to handle this information
explicitly, the planning itself will be improved considerably in the state
of the predecisions and hence in the results too.

ORGANIZATION OF DATA COLLECTION AND PLANNING SERVICES

There is no need for special proof that the modern tools for micro
planning and decisions can prove of economic importance in the real
world if they are based on good information with reasonable costs. This
means that efficient organization and performance in supplying data and
in the actual planning is as important as in farm production itself. In
fact, this is the same "production of knowledge" which we recognized
previously as an important prerequisite of good management.

The organization of a system has to be adapted to the structural
frame in which the system has to work. In this context it may be sufficient to distinguish in agriculture two principally different economic
structures: (a) the centralized industry-like farm structure and (b) the
decentralized family farm structure.

The industry-like farms are characterized by the following: (a)
high turnover in the total farm as well as in the different enterprises
(therefore large economic weight of the decisions); (b) hierarchic

decision-making systems with central authorities (by this means exists a short connection between planning and decision making and realization); and (c) data supply and planning which can be integrated directly into the single firm (an easier system to install and to carry on).

In a family farm structure we have these characteristics: (a) the sales of the individual farms are rather small, and thereby only limited costs for information services can be borne; (b) the firms represent individual planning and independent decision objects, which implies that numerous managerial abilities and operating conditions have to be considered and only recommendations but no orders can be given; and (c) the data for planning have to be collected in scattered farms of different types, and later on information has to be returned to them, thus causing higher costs.

Viewed together from the standpoint of technique and organization, heavily decentralized family farm structures are less open for the use of modern data supply and planning services than structures consisting of centralized big farms. But (as is true for the whole economy) this statement must not be overemphasized since on the way from planning to the financial success of the firm, at the beginning of two important phases, stands a human being as the determining factor: (a) when transporting the results of planning into a decision of realization and (b) when carrying out this decision in the firm. Probably in both positions the decisive role of men cannot be eliminated—at best changed.

Central Data Collecting and Planning Systems for Big Farms

An outline of an economical organization of a data collecting and planning system for large farms was given in Figure 7.2. Little has to be added to this scheme. It is only a question of the input and costs one is willing to spend for this service. For finding the optimal solution, following the principle of marginal costs and marginal revenue, the costs should be charged according to the contribution to the financial result. This procedure, however, is hindered since it is impossible to measure the contribution of such a service in monetary terms; not the least because planning can have an effect only if the results go forward through the phases of decision and realization. Shortcomings in these phases can reduce the value of planning to zero. In addition, the management of large farms needs an extensive data collecting and processing system for the control of the firm, for price calculations for determining fees and taxes, for decisions about credits, and for others. In many industrial firms these jobs already have been transferred to a computer. Therefore the problem left is to get the planning and improved information for decisions with as few as possible additional devices and with low costs. For this a corresponding programming of the total data processing of the firm is necessary, an activity for which large efforts are being made presently in industry. And it seems that the speed of the progress depends mainly on the number of adequately trained programmers available and on the supply of the computer industry.

Data Collecting and Planning Systems for Family Farms

In the family farm structured agriculture, the situations are different. The individual farm generally is too small to do data processing and to plan independently as do the large farms. In this regard they have to be organized according to the principle of labor division where frequently the extension service serves as an agent between the farmer and the planning service. Therefore a question arises on how to split up the functions between the farmer, the planning service, and the extension service in order to (a) keep the costs as low as possible and (b) find a solution that is as efficient as possible.

In two studies (4, 13) we have discussed these problems. The result may be demonstrated as an example, although it is obvious that for the organization in any other country the prevailing institutional arrangements have to be considered.

The proposal starts from the fact that the records of the individual farms must be definitely adapted to the purposes they serve, namely financial analyses for taxes and other purposes and data collection for micro planning and decisions. These two goals have to be combined in an optimal way even though there can be no doubt that the requirements of data supply go further.

For the financial analysis, the money spent on materials and services and the money received from sales and other sources must be noted and the result of the year supplemented with the balance of the stocks. All monetary transactions are either done through an account or are recorded with checks, money order, and credit slip, all with copies. The farmer has to fill in only the date, the object, the weight, the amount of money, and the receiver. These records are given through the bank or directly to the bookkeeping office that codes any transaction and charges the accounts of different production activities as far as possible. To lessen the burden and to hasten the booking, experiments are being made to do the coding with about 1000-1200 code words mechanically.

The bookkeeping for buying and selling already gives the frame for the data supply. The variable costs of the production activities, as well as important technical coefficients, can be taken from it. However they have to be supplemented by a register of the farm's internal events: (a) report on the use of inputs—seeds, fertilizers, animals for replacement (in the single production activities-enterprises); (b) report on the yields of the crops, the yields of the animals (number of pigs per sow, production of milk per cow); and (c) report on the allocation of workers and machinery.

The question is whether this procedure is meaningful. We are inclined to say that it is more useful to organize the calculations of the different management levels as a separate service and complete them only for the special problems discussed above, although it seems to be reasonable to have those planning services done by the bookkeeping station if there are trained persons and sufficient storage capacity with the computers and ready access to them. In order to guarantee economical use, high-speed computers always will have to be installed on a regional basis.

We have stated that problems are involved in using farm data directly for planning purposes and that the optimal solution requires data that are relevant for the future. In many cases one will wish to use a slightly higher level of productivity than is true for the present farm organization. This means that a competent evaluation of the internal farm data is necessary and eventually new alternatives should be added. For this task, the assistance of an experienced extension worker can be of great advantage. He should take the results of the farm records, go to the farmer, find his main problems, propose suitable planning, and perhaps determine the model. The question of who will do the planning itself is of secondary order. But it can be taken for granted that it is again the farm management expert who is to explain the results of the plannings to the farmer and to aid his decisions.

In such a cooperative system for a family farm structured agriculture, a management service of high quality can be offered with reasonable costs. Of course the partners of such a system can make use of it to an extent that changes from one year to another as is required by the situation of the farm. In the reports we also discussed the question of how such a system, depending on the number of participating farms, can be organized in the most efficient way. But to give the results in detail here would go beyond the scope of this paper.

The previously mentioned information is mailed in on adequate forms for certain periods, together with the records of monetary transactions, and does not cause any major difficulties. If the records are kept thoroughly, the reports mentioned under point (b) are not necessary since the outputs are completely determined by buying and selling. The coefficients for workers, machines for custom work, and seasonal workers are recorded with the monetary transactions. More detailed records are very hard to get in the family farms. Therefore one is heavily restricted to normative data, especially in the field of labor data.

The result of such bookkeeping is at first a regular monthly report on the financial state of the farm. At the end of the year a final balance of profits and losses is given. This is supplemented by an income calculation for tax purposes. For economic purposes the net revenue of the farm enterprises and also the technical coefficients (as far as they are included in the reports of the farmer) are computed.

This procedure, which in the main parts corresponds with proven practices in the United States, makes it possible to collect all important data in the farm which a bookkeeping routine can supply with a minimum of time-input of the farmer and of processing costs. Today it is rather a problem of organization and training.

As already mentioned, certain recent efforts were made to link directly this bookkeeping routine with a programming routine. From the standpoint of methods, this does not cause a problem if the storage capacity is sufficient for an extensive standard program.

We shall confine ourselves to indicating the underlying overall and

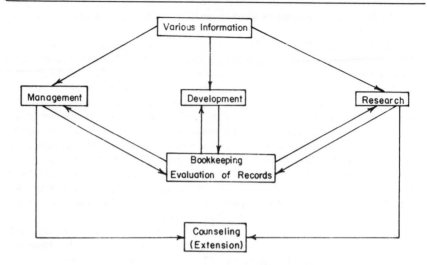

Fig. 7.8. Comprehensive system of agricultural information.

farm information system (Figs. 7.8, 7.9). They might show the functional organization of activities and the flow of information as well as the institutions involved. Figure 7.8 illustrates the general framework and puts the cooperating partners in the right position. Figure 7.9 may be looked at from the standpoint of a farm manager, an advisory man, or a bookkeeping institution. It gives each the task to be done for better management of a farm firm.

SUMMARY

This chapter has analyzed the question of which of the new mathematical methods and models of microeconomic planning and decision making can be considered as proven tools. The evaluation was oriented towards the gain of information about which of the methods mentioned could provide for a more efficient management of agricultural firms. Since the experiences of the last year's work show that only relatively uncomplicated methods have gained a broad use, effort was not spent on explaining their model structures.

On the background of the different levels of decisions which are to be made in the hierarchy of management, it was found that linear programming became the method with the widest field of application and the only one with which we have become fully acquainted. The standard model with L.P. can be modified in many ways to give necessary answers to different farm management questions. However the deficiencies of the static and linear versions of L.P. cannot be overcome by those manipulations.

Regarding the direct application of the optimal programs as a

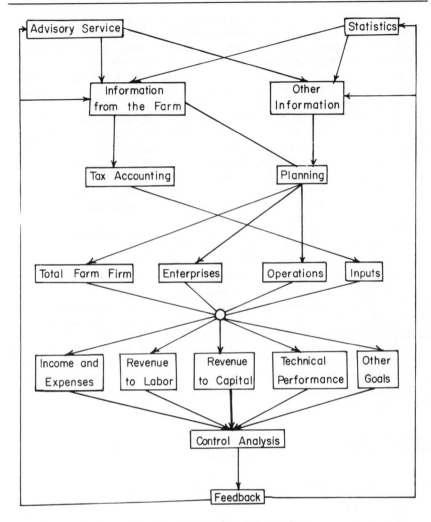

Fig. 7.9. Farm information system.

decision-making tool in setting up production and investment strategies, the information value of calculations is restricted by the uncertainty of the data on the real situation, technological progress, and economic conditions of the future.

Within the given resources and capacities for short-run planning, one encounters serious difficulties in taking into account the "real world" facets of risk in production, the nonlinearity of production and cost functions, integer values, and the complex relationships among many production processes. Nevertheless, in solving real farm problems, it is necessary to strive for a high degree of isomorphy in the model used. Of equal importance is the accuracy of data. Therefore, of the difficulties mentioned, not the least are data problems.

Some of the management problems can be treated with a farm simulator or with the network planning technique. However the application of the latter procedure still is and will remain rather restricted in agriculture. Much handwork and computer time is consumed in using it. A broader application of a farm simulator encounters the fact that the internal computing program has to be adjusted to the technical and economic situation of the individual country.

The application of the modern planning procedures has shown clearly that the availability of data in general still is unsatisfactory. Modern tools are of real value only as far as adequate data can be provided. It seems from our experiences today that the utilization of L.P. and other methods in practice is bounded more by the lack of data than by the deficiencies of methods. In a special section of this paper, therefore, the need for proper data is emphasized with indication of difficulties that may arise from their lack.

Finally an organizational scheme to demonstrate the position of data processing and planning work within the frame of a farm information system was presented. It becomes clear from this figure that planning is an important part of an overall task, but not more than a part. Planning finds its final evaluation only in the decision process which should be based on sound information. For purposes of management, methods and models are not valuable per se; they may become that if proper use is made of them. This is true since first their information must be transformed into knowledge, and second it must be put into a decision framework. Information never must be taken as decision; it can only lighten the "decision environment" and show the results of possible alternative decisions. The decision itself is up to the man in charge of the management.

REFERENCES

1. Brandes, W. Special Problems of Linear Programming. In *Quantitative Methods in Economic and Social Sciences of Agriculture*, ed. E. Reisch. Munich: BLV, 1967.
2. Dillon, J. L. Applications of Game Theory in Agricultural Economics: Review and Requiem. *Australian J. Agr. Econ.*, vol. 6, no. 2.
3. Egloff, K. Report on Application of Optimum Calculations on 200 Farms of Baden-Wurttemberg. Stuttgart-Hohenheim, 1968.
4. Eisgruber, L. M. Selected Techniques and Outlook for the Future. IBM-Symposium, 1966.
5. Heady, E. O., and Wilfred Candler. *Linear Programming Methods.* Ames: Iowa State Univ. Press, 1958.
6. Heiland, H. W., A. Jandl, and W. Kastner. Application of Web Planning Technique in Farm Business Research. *Agrarwirtschaft*, vol. 15.
7. Hesselbach, J., and L. M. Eisgruber. *Farm Decisions by Means of Simulation.* Hamburg-Berlin: Parey, 1967.
8. Kastner, W. Experience in Estimation of Production Function from Bookkeeping Data at Farm Level. In *Quantitative Methods in Economic and Social Sciences of Agriculture*, ed. E. Reisch. Munich: BLV, 1967.

9. Koller, H. Simulation as Method in Farm Management. *Z. Betriebswirtsch.*, vol. 36, no. 2.
10. Kreher, G., R. Adelhelm, et al. *Calculation Documents for Farm Management.* Vols. I and II. Frankfurt, 1964.
11. Lesourne, J. Farm Management and Farm Business Research. Deutsche Ausgabe. Munich-Vienna, 1964.
12. Skomroch, W. Modelbuilding as a Function of Data Accuracy. In *Papers of Association for Economic and Social Sciences.* Vol. 4. ed. E. Reisch. Munich: BLV, 1967.
13. Skomroch, W., and J. Hesselbach. *A Sketch Plan for Organization and Management of a Calculation Center in Agriculture.* Stuttgart-Hohenheim, 1966.

Chapter 7 ☙ DISCUSSION

Zoltan Bacskay, *Keszthely College of Agriculture* (Hungary)

IN HIS EXCELLENT REPORT, Professor Reisch has given us such a detailed and circumspect account of the well-proved means of planning and decision making in farm planning that I have very little to add.

Since I have made models for farm production and feeding, and have had some programs computed, I can only support the statement of Professor Reisch and all of us that the application of mathematical methods on a farm level depends on three factors: (a) on people who can inform practical specialists about these methods in a palatable way and in compliance with the level of their knowledge; (b) the supply of data depends on the practical specialists if they accept these mathematical methods; and finally (c) on the data supplied.

Professor Reisch has spoken of the problem of data, telling us that in many countries technical-technological coefficients fill bulky tomes. One such volume, for instance, contains the technical-technological coefficients of plowland plant production on 216 state farms of Hungary. These are arithmetical means. Scatters are not included in this volume. The data given in it are guide numbers or normative coefficients. They lend themselves very well to be compared with farm data, sparing us from groping in the dark.

Experience has taught us that the relative scatter of the technical-technological coefficients of agricultural products may be 10, 20, or even 40 percent. Therefore it is advisable to work with interval data in our computations. Since it is impossible to set all data parametrically into a starting linear program, the best practice is to calculate three programs: one for the lower effect of interval data, another for the upper effect, and a third for the middle of the interval. In this case we must account for the goal function: if the lower effect of technical coefficients is taken and in the goal function is the maximized output, in the goal function we have to count on the upper limits of the net output falling to unit product or unit territory.

In the foregoing, I mentioned the reliability of data in the third place, although what we primarily need in our calculations are good data. I did not do it unintentionally. If the second condition mentioned above is met, which means that if there are practical specialists who understand the necessity of this method and accept the approximately optimum solution while guiding their activity according to the results of mathematical programming, data in the next and over-next period will be more detailed and more reliable. If the practical specialist or the farm manager sees, through results, that the approximate optimum solution is really useful to him and that better data give better approximate solutions, he will do his best to supply more reliable and more detailed data. It follows from the above that the quality of data supply is a function of the experience of the farm manager based on improvement in results or farm engineering. For example, for the dairy herd of 600 cows on one of our state farms, a feeding project had been prepared with linear programming. When the manager of animal breeding had realized that this program would supply him with starch values, digestable raw protein values, and other quantities indispensable in calculating subsistence, milk yield, and the like, and that overfeeding by 20, 30, or 40 percent of unnecessary proteins could be avoided, he undertook a content analysis of feeds. A correction of output resulted. In other words, the manager of animal breeding realized that it is necessary for us to know the nutritive values of feed produced and purchased by the farm. Since the goal function included the reducing of the feed growing area of the farm to a minimum, the manager undertook to have the corrected output figures of fodders made out for the previous ten years.

I think that we have been supplied better data for linear programming because we succeeded in making it understood, to some extent, that with the kinds of fodder named by the farm manager it is impossible with traditional methods to make a feed composition meet biological and production demands alike at the lowest input cost or the smallest possible territory. If he succeeds in doing so, it is only by good luck. Data may improve if the manager of the farm realizes that they allow methods giving better solutions and may prove more economical for him. However we cannot talk to every manager. This is why we are in need of the condition mentioned first, of people who can convince the specialist of the merits of modern methods. I think and have also experienced that between the scientist versed in model calculations and the farm manager an intermediary is needed — a role that might be taken by our students — to act as a connecting link and propagator between us and the farm manager. It is possible that with some managers well-organized information may substitute for this role while others may need contact by word or mouth.

Let me repeat important statements made by Professor Reisch: "Methods are not useful in themselves but only if they are applied in the right way.... The right of decision making will always rest with the specialist responsible for management."

Chapter 8 ◌ RECENT DEVELOPMENTS IN QUANTITATIVE ANALYSIS AT THE MICRO LEVEL

Gunther Weinschenk, *University of Hohenheim*
(German Federal Republic)

THE RECENT DEVELOPMENT of quantitative research in microeconomics is characterized by a rapid adoption of mathematical research methods. In mathematics, linear optimizing is considered an almost classical theory, in spite of new and interesting contributions (like the theory of large systems) which have been handled successfully by the decomposition principle. Within the theory of linear optimizing the simplex algorithm has become the most common calculation procedure. Following this development the standard linear programming model has become the most common and almost classical calculation procedure for the solution of optimum problems. The mathematical structure of the standard linear programming model corresponds exactly to the structure of the linear production model. Hence the application of the standard linear programming model is based on the same assumptions as the linear production model. These assumptions refer to the production technique as well as to the environment of the firm. Let us consider the production technique first.

ASSUMPTIONS WITH RESPECT TO PRODUCTION TECHNIQUE AND REALITY

With respect to the production technique, the following assumptions are made: (a) all production functions are linear, and (b) all goods and all factors are infinitely divisible, or at least the inputs gained from the factors are infinitely divisible.

The shortcomings of the linear model with respect to production techniques in agriculture are due to the fact that these assumptions are not always in accordance with reality because (a) production functions are nonlinear in many cases, and (b) many factors and products cannot be divided infinitely. Economists have of course become aware of these shortcomings; and there have been a large number of effective and noneffective proposals to overcome them.

I owe special thanks to Ehrhart Hanf and Fritz Aldinger, both working at the Institute of Agricultural Economics, University of Hohenheim, who helped me in formulating sections 3 and 4.

Nonlinear Production Functions

The classical distinction between a convex production function (a maximum problem of decreasing returns per unit of input with increasing inputs) and a concave production function (a maximum problem of increasing returns per unit of input with increasing inputs) is useful here too. Both functions can be considered in two ways: (a) by linear approximation into a corresponding formulation of the linear model and by using the familiar simplex algorithm and (b) by using another algorithm which has been developed in the field of nonlinear programming.

Linear approximation of convex production functions. The linear approximation is very simple in the case of production functions with decreasing returns per unit of input. The production function is broken into linear segments. The more segments one uses the more precise is the result. If for instance the production function has the following form:

$$y = 125,875 + 21,361\ H - 1201\ H^2 + 71,710\ W - 10,900\ W^2 + 0145\ HW \quad (1)$$

where y = output of early potatoes in dz/ha, H = fertilizer input in dz/ha, and W = water input in 100 mm (100 mm = 1000 m^3 per ha), then the linear approximation can be written in vector form as shown in Table 8.1.

Table 8.1. Activities derived from production function 1

Inputs and outputs	I	II	III	IV	V	VI	VII	VIII	IX
Land	1.0	1.0	1.0	1.0	1.0	1.0	1.0	1.0	1.0
Fertilizer	8.0	9.0	10.0	8.0	9.0	10.0	8.0	9.0	10.0
Water	200.0	200.0	200.0	300.0	300.0	300.0	400.0	400.0	400.0
Output dz/ha	322.0	323.3	322.1	340.4	341.8	340.8	336.9	338.5	337.6

Linear approximation of concave production functions. Nonlinear production functions with increasing output per unit of input are handled according to similar principles. The nonlinear production function is approximated by a number of activities of which each represents a point on the function. However the logical sequence of the activities, which represent the points on the functions, is not satisfied automatically because the returns per resource unit increase with increasing output. In order to satisfy the requirements of a logic sequence, additional conditions have to be introduced. A simple example may illustrate the problem. Figure 8.1 shows total and average labor input and net returns with an increasing number of cows. The corresponding figures are given in Table 8.2. There are two ways to handle the sequence problem:

One uses the average values per cow as a basis and considers only two points of the curve, the estimated minimum number of cows which is expected to enter the solution and the estimated maximum number of

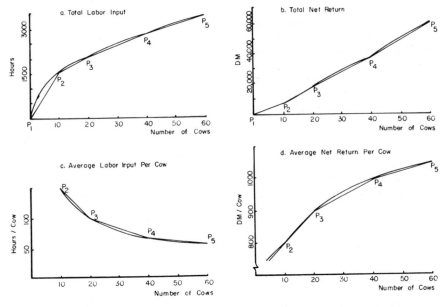

Fig. 8.1. Curve of labor input and net return with increasing number of cows.

cows (40). An additional equation requires that either the minimum or the maximum number of cows or any combination on the line P_1-P_2, P_2-P_3, and so on, must enter the solution.

In our example the equations have the following form:

$$1 - 1 P_1 - 0.1 P_2 = 0 \tag{2}$$

$$1 - 0.1 P_2 - 0.05 P_3 = 0 \tag{3}$$

$$1 - 0.05 P_3 - 0.025 P_4 = 0 \tag{4}$$

$$1 - 0.025 P_4 - 0.017 P_5 = 0 \tag{5}$$

Table 8.2. Net return and labor input per cow with increasing number of cows

Item	Activity and number of cows				
	P_1 0	P_2 10	P_3 20	P_4 40	P_5 60
Total labor input in hours	0	1500	2,000	2,800	3,300
Average increase of labor input h per cow between points	150		50	40	25
Labor input per cow		150	100	70	55
Total net return, DM		8000	18,000	40,000	63,000
Average increase of net return, DM, per cow between points	800		1000	1100	1150
Net return, DM, per cow		800	900	1,000	1,050

The equations are introduced alternatively. That means the quality of the results depends on the distance of the minimum and maximum point, which have to be predetermined, and on the "grade of nonlinearity" of the curve. The longer the distance of the predetermined point and the less the cost or input curve approximates a straight line, the less precise are the results. The quality of results can be improved by repeating the calculation using the first results for a better estimate of the minimum and maximum point.

The second method uses the total labor input curve and the total net return curve as a basis (18). The coefficients of the activities are given by the average marginal increase of labor input and net return input per cow. Geometrically the coefficients are given by the slope of the segments P_1-P_2 or P_2-P_3, and so on. The logical sequence is satisfied by the introduction of additional activities which must have integer values. The corresponding tableau has the form demonstrated in Table 8.3. The activities P_1, P_2, P_3 represent the average production unit between P_1 and P_2 or P_2 and P_3, and so on. That means the inputs

Table 8.3. Nonlinear convex functions (formulation with average values)

	Basis		P_1 0	P_2 10	P_3 20	P_4 40	P_5 60
			\multicolumn{5}{c}{Activity and cow numbers}			
Net return per unit			0	800	900	1,000	1,050
I	1	=	1	0.1			
II	1	=		0.1	0.05		
III	1	=			0.05	0.025	
IV	1	=				0.025	0.017
Labor available	0	≤		150	100	70	55
Number of cows	0	≤		-1	-1	-1	-1

and the returns are "average marginal values" on the corresponding part of the curve; while in the formulation in Table 8.3 average values per unit have been used. The activities V_{12}, V_{23}, V_{34} are transfer activities which have to be integers (have values of zero or one).

There are at least two other less known possibilities of solving the problem of linear approximation of digressive input functions. At least one is not very elegant but is attractive from the practical point of view if there are only one or a few digressive input functions. The first is apparent from the procedure described in Table 8.4. Instead of introducing integer transfer activities, one can define the variable P_2 (10 cows), P_3 (20 cows), and so on, as integer activities. The more activities one defines the better will be the approach to the real nature of the curve. The method of handling digressive cost curves by integer programming looks a bit artificial in our example. It is specially adapted

Table 8.4. Nonlinear concave production functions with "average marginal values"

Activities	Basis	0-10 cows P_1	V_{12}	10-20 cows P_2	V_{23}	20-40 cows P_3	V_{34}	40-60 cows P_4
Net return per cow		800	0	1000	0	1100	0	1150
Labor input per cow	0 $\geq$	150		50		40		25
I	10 $\geq$	1						
II	0	-1	10					
III	0 $\geq$	-10		1				
IV	0 $\geq$			2	20			
V	0 $\geq$			-20		1		
	0 $\geq$					-1	20	
	0 $\geq$						-20	1
Number of cows		-1		-1		-1		-1

to problems in which the digressive cost function results from the indivisibility of factor inputs (e.g., machinery).

The second method is to approach the curve by parametric programming using variable coefficients and/or variable restrictions, depending on the end of the curve from which one begins. In the first case, one estimates the possible maximum number of cows (or the estimated number of cows in the first solution) and introduces the corresponding input coefficient which is the lowest possible. If the number of cows is lower than estimated, one increases the input coefficient systematically until the number of cows and input coefficients coincide with the values of the real input function. The convergence of the estimated input coefficient and the "real input" coefficients, and thus the number of iterations, depends on the slope of the input function and on the feasibility of final solution. Usually the final result is gained after very few iterations, following the optimum calculation with the first estimate. Starting the other way around, one defines the activities as in Table 8.3 and introduces an additional condition which restricts the number of cows to 10 in the first approach in the example and blocks all activities but P_2. The optimal solution is found by parametric increasing of the restrictions to 20, 40, and 60 and allowing P_2, P_4, and P_6 to enter the solution.

Admittedly none of these methods is very elegant or satisfying from the viewpoint of mathematical preciseness, with the exception of the method of "average marginal values" which has not been applied until now.

Nonlinear Programming and Nonlinear Production Functions

A number of calculation procedures have been developed in nonlinear optimization to allow handling of the problem of nonlinear production functions (19). The existing applications in agriculture show that at least static optimization problems can be handled in principle. But the existing possibilities have been hardly used except in some more or less academic experiments with farm models (34). The reason for the limited application of nonlinear programming methods in this field seems to be the following: (a) The size of problems which can be handled in nonlinear optimization models with reasonable calculations is still rather small. (b) Computer programs are not available, or the available programs are not known. Therefore if one is ready to use a greater calculation input, one prefers to use the methods of linear approximation, thus avoiding the trouble with the computer program. At least some of the programs do not result in a unique solution. For instance, applying Rosen's gradient method and using the available computer program, the results depend on the choice of the first basic solution, the number of steps, and the tolerance of the gradients. All these factors have to be chosen more or less arbitrarily — hence simulated to arrive at an optimum solution. For instance, Seuster (34), who applied the gradient method to a simple problem optimizing the use of land, (Table 8.5), found the change of the optimum solution depending on the choice of these factors. The problem was to find the optimum solution (static) for a 40-hectare farm, with given labor capacity, given buildings for cattle and hogs, and quadratic return functions of the different activities which have the general form $r = a + bx - cx^2$. (c) The true nature of the production function is not known in most cases. Planners

Table 8.5. Influence of the predetermined tolerance of gradients (parameter) on the results of an optimum calculation

Activity	Unit	Level of the most important activities at different parameters			
		c_1 0.0005	c_1 0.01	c_1 0.1	c_1 0.5
Winter-grain	ha	12.04	12.00	15.0	15.0
Rape	ha	5.0	5.0	2.42	2.42
Cattle	no	62.9	62.9	66.2	66.2
Net return per farm	DM	43,345.0	43,721.0	44,082.0	44,082.0
Iterations		8.0	8.0	13.0	13.0

Influence of different basic solution

Activity	Unit	I[a]	II[a]	III[a]
Winter-grain	no	15.0	15.0	12.0
Rape	ha	2.42	2.36	5.00
Cattle	ha	66.2	66.0	65.0
Net return per farm	DM	44,082.0	44,041.0	43,719.0

Source: Seuster (34).

a. c = 0.1; I = basic solution near optimum solution; II = basic solution all production activities $\geq$ 0; III = all activities, which enter the final solution = 1, all other activities = 0.

know or estimate more or less roughly one or a few points on the production functions.

The methods of linear approximation of nonlinear functions are not very precise. In all cases the calculations input increases considerably. In order to keep it in reasonable limits, an estimation of the "optimal region" is necessary in all cases except in the method described in Table 8.4, in which, however, the standard L.P. procedure is not applicable. In spite of these shortcomings, the methods of linear approximation are almost exclusively used in agriculture. Lack of precise knowledge of the real nature of the production function, complicated calculation procedures, and a very limited number of computer programs with sufficient capacity are the factors which hinder the application of nonlinear programming methods better adapted to the nature of many production functions.

Integer Programming

All methods which have been developed to solve problems with some (all) integer variables use a more or less modified version of the simplex method. The basic approach common to most methods is the introduction of new constraints which satisfy the integer requirements. The integer requirements are introduced either after a noninteger solution or at the very beginning by selecting an integer point within the polyhedron. The different methods are distinguished by the way in which the constraints are introduced (7). There are mainly three ways which are described geometrically in Figures 8.2-8.5.

1. The cutting plane method (Fig. 8.2). A noninteger optimal solution is computed and additional constraints are introduced (A, B, C in Fig. 8.2) until the integer requirements are satisfied. The existing experience with the use of the cutting plane method shows that the convergence of the solution is very sensitive to the range of choice of the row from which to generate new constraints. Since there is no criteria for the sequence of the selection of rows, the calculation procedure may become very laborious.

2. The Branch and Bound method starting from a noninteger optimal solution (Fig. 8.3). The general approach is to start out as though to enumerate all feasible integer solutions (21). First a noninteger optimal solution is computed. If it does not satisfy the integer conditions for the x_i, one of the x_i of the objective function has to be forced to take an integer value, hence it either is increased or decreased by the corresponding fraction. After all possible integer values of x_i ($i = 1$) have been computed, the procedure starts again by calculating another set of solutions for another variable x_i ($i \neq 1$) which has to be an integer and the computed integer solutions of x_i ($i = 1$). Thus a tree of solutions is computed which satisfies the integer condition. The Land and Doig (20) procedure involves this enumeration, but it attempts to search only a subset of the tree in which the optimal solution is situated. This

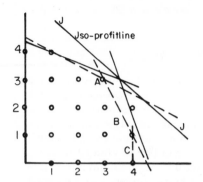

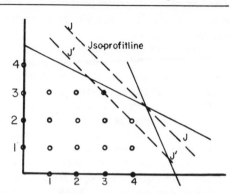

Fig. 8.2. Cutting plane methods.

Fig. 8.3. Branch and bound method
starting from a noninteger optimal solution.

is done by constructing a special graph (Fig. 8.4). The noninteger optimal solution is shown by A. In the first step, all integer optimal solutions for x_i are computed, one of which results in the highest profit
(solution next to A). This is used as a "preliminary basis" for the
computation of integer results for x_2 (step 2). The solutions gained
from the node B are clearly better than the solutions D, E, F. Hence
the calculation procedure has to be repeated only for the node C($x_1 = 3$).

3. The Branch and Bound method starting with an integer variable
inside the polyhedron. As a first step an optimal solution for a maximum value of one of the integer variables is computed (e.g., $x_1 = 4$ in
Figure 8.3), setting the other integer variables at either zero or a relatively low value. Then the level of the first integer variable x_3 in Figure 8.5 is decreased by one unit and the second integer variable is
increased again. If the integer variables are not subject to special restrictions and therefore can be increased as long as it is profitable
(e.g., labor or machinery in a static long-run optimum solution), one
starts at a relatively low level or at an estimated level, which is as
close to the optimum as possible. This method, which is somewhat

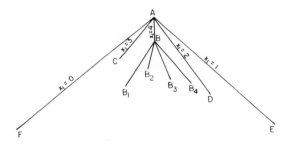

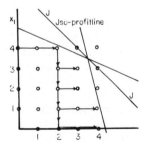

Fig. 8.4. Directing tree for the Land and Doig
method.

Fig. 8.5. Brand and
Bound method starting
from an integer nonopti-
mal solution.

similar to the RHS method by Maruyama and Fuller (25), is certainly
not very elegant since it comes very close to a full enumeration of all
possible solutions. However it is specially adapted to the technical
conditions.

One can look on the indivisible production factors like labor, tractors, and other machinery as a stock of inputs which are ready to use
in small quantities (labor, machine, tractor hours). The increase (decrease) of the stocks is possible only in given units. It results in an
increase (decrease) of capacities (available working hours) which can
be used in infinitely small units. Hence the problem of integer units
can be solved by a systematical (mostly parametrical) increase of the
respective capacity. One begins at a given amount of land, with the
possible maximum labor input if this is restricted, and increases the
capacities resulting from the equipment (machine hours, tractor hours)
stepwise as long as it is possible or profitable. Then one decreases
the labor capacities by one worker and continues the increase of equipment stepwise. If the labor input is not directly restricted, one can
start with a relatively low labor input and calculate optimal solutions
for the corresponding capacities of the integer equipment variables.
This method has the advantage that one can start with an estimated optimal level of the integer variables though it lacks the mathematical
glamour of the previously mentioned methods. Practical application is
more or less limited to static optimum solutions. Under static conditions where capital is not a restricting factor, the integer problem
which results from the indivisibility of equipment can be transformed
into a nonlinear problem and handled in one of the ways mentioned in
the previous chapter.

The practical importance of indivisibility of goods and factors depends on the grade of indivisibility in relation to the number of smallest
possible units used or produced in the optimum solution on the one hand
and on the strictness of the restrictions on the other hand. The bigger
the number of "smallest possible" units (used or produced) is and the
less severe are the restrictions, the less important is the question of
limited divisibility. In agriculture the problem of indivisibility is usually not important with respect to goods since the number of smallest
possible units is relatively great in general and at least some of the
restrictions (labor, some capital restrictions) are not severe with respect to the amount of rounding which is necessary to arrive at integer
solutions on the production side. Only on very small farms do some
difficulties occur with respect to the number of cows and cattle.

Lack of computational experience and lack of computer programs
are the main reasons for the "not very elegant" and "not very satisfying"
handling of integer problems. Furthermore the existing experience
with all methods shows that the calculation input in integer problems is
very sensitive to the range of choice, either for the row from which a
new constraint is generated or for the variables which are forced to be
integers directly. The guidance for the sequence of solutions, which is
given with the simplex method, is lost if integer variables are considered.

Table 8.6. Basic types of decision models on the micro level

	Consideration of uncertainty			Inter-dependence	Given are	Asked for	Analytical tool
	Time	Space	Risk				
Static point models:							
(a) Determined	no	no	no	no	Complete information about: 1. production functions 2. prices for products 3. variable means of production 4. available quantities of fixed resources 5. preference function of the owner or manager	Production of corresponding goods. Use of means of production grade of satisfaction of goals (profit, etc.).	Linear and nonlinear programming program planning. Modified versions of the simplex method. Considering integer variables and nonlinear functions.
(b) Stochastic	no	no	yes	no	Incomplete information of the data mentioned under 1a.	like 1a.	Quadratic programming. Combination of simulation and linear programming.
Dynamic point models:							
(a) Determined	yes	no	no	no	1-3 like 1a but for several points in time—in place of 4 production capacities available capital in time t_c and conditions of loaning and repaying capital.	Like 1 but for several points in time $t_1, t_2, \ldots, t_n$ and resulting from the determination of an optimal growth path.	Dynamic linear programming, dynamic programming.
(b) Stochastic	yes	no	yes	no	Incomplete information of the data mentioned under 2.	Like 2 but an optimal growth tree is determined in place of an optimal growth path.	
Space models:							
(a) Static determined	no	yes	yes	in many cases	Like 1-2 and transportation costs demand functions in most cases.	As in the corresponding models 1 and 2 and in addition location of production or firm size of firm.	Depending on assumptions usually rather pragmatic approach.
(b) Static stochastic	no	yes	yes				
(c) Dynamic determined	yes	yes	no				
(d) Dynamic stochastic	yes	yes	yes				

Hence the possibilities of an extensive use of integer programming methods depend widely on the finding of efficient criteria for the guidance of the trial and error process. Such criteria are much more important in dynamic integer solutions in which probably none of the methods mentioned is applicable because of the size of the problem, except one which uses the aggregation method described later.

ASSUMPTIONS WITH RESPECT TO ENVIRONMENT AND REALITY

The simplification of the real world is one of the most common, most effective, and most dangerous methods of economic analysis. A classification of economic models according to the neglect or consideration of the most important factors of the environment of the firm is given in Table 8.6. Recently the consideration of time and incomplete information have become the frontline of research. Dynamics and growth have been the most fashionable fields of research in recent years in microeconomics. Space and interdependency might become important again with the rapid increase of farm size in some countries.

The Consideration of Time

Consideration of time in microeconomic decision theory means usually that a sequence of production periods each of which is considered a point in time is analyzed simultaneously. Among the dynamic models we distinguish between determined and undetermined or stochastic models analogous to the distinction made in static analysis. We call a model determined if the decisions in period t depend in a unique way on the decisions in periods t-1, t-2, ..., . We call a model undetermined or stochastic if the decisions in period t are determined by the decisions in period t-1 (t+2) only by a probability distribution. In a dynamic planning situation we usually deal with situations which correspond to the assumptions of stochastic dynamic models; but we use determined models to handle them. That means we assume (a) that the decisions in period t depend in a unique way on the decisions in period t-1 and (b) that we have perfect information over the whole period under consideration.

The mathematic structure of a determined dynamic situation may be described as follows:

P_{1t} = production of good 1 at t
P_{2t} = production of good 2 at t
C_{1t} = capacity of resource 1 at t
C_{2t} = capacity of resource 2 at t
I_{1t} = investment of C_1 at t
I_{2t} = investment of C_2 at t

E_t = expenditure for investments at t
M_t = total expenditure
k_t = credit at t
L_t = maximum credit available
R_t = gross return at t

The technical conditions of the productive process are

$$a_{11}P_{1t} + a_{21}P_{2t} \leqq C_{1t}$$

and

$$a_{12}P_{1t} + a_{22}P_{2t} \leqq C_{2t} \tag{6}$$

The capacity in t+1 is equal to the capacity of period t plus investment in t:

$$C_{1t+1} = C_{1t} + I_{1t} \tag{7}$$

$$C_{2t+1} = C_{2t} + I_{2t} \tag{8}$$

Hence

$$C_{1t} = C_{11} + \sum_{t=1}^{t=t-1} I_{1t} \tag{9}$$

$$C_{2t} = C_{21} + \sum_{t=1}^{t=t-1} I_{2t} \tag{10}$$

The selling price of good one is 100 money units, and of good two 200 money units; then

$$R_t = 100\ P_{1t} + 200\ P_{2t} \tag{11}$$

The costs are divided into three groups:

1. Costs which are proportional to the capacities:

$$A_t = 20\ C_{1t} + 50\ C_{2t} \tag{12}$$

2. Costs which are proportional to the output:

$$K_t = 10\ P_{1t} + 15\ P_{2t} \tag{13}$$

3. Costs which are independent of output and capacity:

$$U_t = 10{,}000 \tag{14}$$

All figures are money units. The interest for credit is 10 percent. Hence the expenditure for interest is $0.1\ k_t$. Total expenditure in period t is given by

$$M_t = A_t + K_t + U_t + 0.1\ k_t + E_t \tag{15}$$

where

$$E_t = 30 \ C_{1t} + 70 \ C_{2t} \tag{16}$$

Credits are available for up to 50 percent of the acquisition value of investments plus basic amount of 50,000 money units:

$$L_t = 50,000 + 15 \ C_{1t} + 35 \ C_{2t} \tag{17}$$

with

$$k_t \leq L_t \tag{18}$$

At the beginning of the first period, 20,000 money units of own capital is available. Restriction for liquidity reasons is given by

$$20,000 + k_t + \sum_{t=1}^{t=n} R_t - \sum_{t=1}^{t=n} M_t \geq 0 \tag{19}$$

The criteria function is

$$G = \sum_{t=1}^{t=n} R_t - \sum_{t=1}^{t=n} M_t + \sum_{t=1}^{t=n} E_t = \text{max} \tag{20}$$

subject to equations 6, 7, 18, and 19. This means that the owner's capital is to be maximized. Problems of this kind can be handled in linear programming models in two ways: (a) one can transform the dynamic problem into a static one and solve it by parametric programming; and (b) one can solve the dynamic problem by a multiperiod model considering all periods simultaneously.

The Static Approach

Let us assume that we have to determine the optimal growth path of a new farm when given at point t_0. Is the land available, the labor force available, the initial capital of the farmer, and the credit available? The net return of all possible activities shall be equal during all time periods under consideration. In this case, we can transform the expenses for investments by the familiar formula for computation of annual costs in equal costs for all time periods under consideration:

$$K = A \ \frac{i \ (1+i)^n}{(1+i)^n - 1} \tag{21}$$

where K = annual costs, A = purchase (acquisition) value, and i = interest rate.

Using the annual costs, we can transform the problem into a static model using the familiar L.P. approach for determining the optimum: $Z_i = px = \text{max}$, subject to $Bx \leq c$; where p is the row vector of net returns per unit of output of the corresponding activities, B is the matrix of technical coefficients, and c is the vector of available capacities including capital restrictions. We solve the problem for the initial capital available in the first step. In the next step a sequence of solutions is computed, increasing the capital parametrically until capital is not a restrictive factor.

Having determined the expansion path of production with increasing capital, it is easy to determine the time path of growth. We start with the first feasible solution calculated with the capital which is available at the beginning of the planning period and determine the additional capital which is required for the second step. The number of periods during which the farmer has to follow the first solution is determined by the additional investment capital for step 2, the annual return in step 1, the consumption, and the repayment of credits in the following way:

$$t = \frac{I_{12}}{P_1 + A_1 - (C_1 + D_1)} \tag{22}$$

where

I_{12} = additional investment from step 1 to step 2
P_1 = profit at step 1
A_1 = annual capital costs at step 1 (depreciation)
C_1 = consumption during step 1
D_1 = repayment of credits

Certainly this procedure is missing elegance from the mathematical point of view. From the practical point of view, its application has one important advantage. It allows us to handle the problem of integer variables in time. Since all steps except step 1 can by chosen arbitrarily, it is always possible to select them in a way that the whole stable for the final number of animals is built in one investment period. The most important disadvantages are: (a) The optimal financing has to be considered separately. Specifically, one has to observe the risk of illiquidity if one is going to reinvest the amount of annual depreciation. (b) Disinvestment of selling at the time of consideration. The optimal time of the use of capital goods has to be determined in advance. (c) If only integer solutions are taken into account, the advantage of waiting for an integer solution which requires a higher amount of investment capital is not taken into account. (d) The range of application is limited to the following three conditions: returns per unit of output must be equal over the whole period under consideration; labor and land restrictions must also be equal over the whole period of consideration which means either the amount of land or labor is fixed for the whole period; and land and labor can be purchased or sold in limited or unlimited amounts per period at equal costs during the whole period under consideration. If these conditions are not given (e.g., if we have to assume increasing yields or changing real prices for the period under consideration), one has to use the multiperiod approach.

The Multiperiod Approach

The multiperiod approach may be roughly described as follows. For each period we formulate the familiar static model with the technical matrix, the column vector of constraints, and the row vector of net returns per unit. The periods are linked together by three kinds of transfer activities: (a) activities which transfer the real investment (the real capital like buildings, machines, etc.) from period t to period t+1; (b) activities which transfer the money capital from period t to period t-1; and (c) activities which transfer the obligations which arise from credit in period t to the following period. For each period a minimum consumption is required. The income at the end of the period under consideration is to be maximized.

The same problem can be solved in principle by the application of dynamic programming. The model structure of dynamic programming can be described according to Bellman (1) as follows: We assume 2y and $(z)[y + (x-y)] \leq x_0$. We write $x - y = z$. The profit function has the simple form:

$$G (x,y) = g(y) + h(z) \tag{23}$$

For the basic period we get

$$G_0 (z_0,y_0) = g(y_0) + h(z_0) \tag{24}$$

We assume that at the end of period t_0, the amount of y existing at the beginning of the period has been reduced to ay_0; the amount z_0 has been reduced to $b(z_0)$. Hence at the beginning of the second period is available

$$ay_0 + b(z_0) = g(y_1) + h(z_1) \tag{25}$$

Repeating this process of production, one gets at the end of period 2

$$G_1 [g(y_1) + h(z_1)] \tag{26}$$

The profit function of a 2-period process is given by

$$G_{s2} (x_0,y_0,y_1) = g(y_0) + h(z_0) + g(y_1) + h(z_1) \tag{27}$$

If we take an n period process instead of a 2-period process, we get the profit function

$$G_{sn} (x_0,y_0,y_1, ..., y_{n-1}) = g(y_0) + h(z_0) + g(y_1) + \tag{28}$$
$$h(z_1) + ... + g(y_{n-1}) + h(z_{n-1})$$

The available amount of x for the future periods is given by

$$x_1 = ay_0 + b(z_0)$$
$$x_2 = ay_1 + b(z_1)$$

.
.
.

$$x_{n-1} = a(y_{n-2}) + b(z_{n-2})$$

subject to

$$0 \leqq y_i \leqq x_i$$

The goal is to find a maximum for function 28. The difficulty is to find an effective algorithm for a large problem with the structure of equation 28. Almost no progress has been made to solve this problem; therefore only decisions of a relatively simple structure can be solved using the Bellman approach of dynamic programming. Hence dynamic linear programming has to be applied in investment planning if the static approach does not give satisfying results. The advantages of the application of dynamic linear programming are (a) growth, investment, and financing are considered simultaneously, and (b) since all periods are considered simultaneously, the returns per period may or may not change during the time under consideration. However the application of linear programming includes the assumption of infinite divisibility. Hence, a continuous optimal growth path is determined, which indicates in many cases that it would be optimal to increase the level of certain activities (e.g., cows, hogs, etc.) gradually from period to period. This is unrealistic if investment activities, like the building of stables or the buying of machinery, are involved. There are two different ways to solve the problem of integer variables in time: (a) By formulating a parametric dynamic model. In each of the alternatives each of the investment activities is considered in one period only. The number of alternatives depends on the possible combinations and sequences of investment alternatives in time. It is increasing rapidly with the number of investment alternatives and the number of periods included. (b) By using the dynamic linear programming model and treating the indivisible investment activities as integer variables. Since some of the investment activities like buildings are only indivisible with respect to the points in time, one has either to determine — more or less intuitively — the optimum solution or the "acceptable" units as a "smallest possible" investment activity.

After what has been said on the possibilities of considering integer variables, one can assume that there is not much difference with respect to calculation input between both alternatives. In both cases the calculation input is likely to be so high that it becomes a limiting factor. One therefore has to look for possible simplification.

Solution for Integer Investment Activities in Dynamic Problems by Aggregation

Dynamic solutions are distinguished from static solutions by the determination of an optimal growth path if capital is one of the limiting factors or if other factors such as land can be increased at a rate which is determined by exogenous factors. If all factors are available at

practically unlimited amounts, there is no difference between the static
and the dynamic solution. The optimum solution will be realized in the
first period.[1] Hence one can determine a sequence of feasible optimum
solutions with respect to different capital input or different input of other
factors by parametric static or by linear dynamic programming. Each
of these solutions can be considered as one activity. A new dynamic
problem can be formulated in which each of these aggregated activities
is considered as an integer variable. Since it has already been proved
in the first step that the solutions are feasible with respect to the production factors which remain unchanged in the time under consideration, only capital and those factors which change exogenously during
the time under consideration have to be included. Thus the size of the
problem can be reduced so much in most cases that it is easy to use
either the dynamic or the linear dynamic approach to solve the problem.

Table 8.7 shows an example. The optimal land use has been taken
into account but is not considered explicitly in this tableau. From the
parametric static solutions, five activities are selected:

P_1 = 170 hogs
P_2 = 10 cows
P_3 = 170 hogs + 10 cows
P_4 = 360 hogs
P_5 = 360 hogs + 10 cows

The dynamic linear programming problem is formulated in Table 8.7.
Calculation proceeds as follows:

Step 1. Select the feasible solutions for the first period t_0. (If no solutions have been calculated, only m solutions are feasible at
point t_0 $1 \leqq m \leqq n$ [if m = n, no dynamic problem exists]).

Step 2. Calculate a noninteger dynamic linear solution for the whole
period under consideration and consider only the feasible solutions determined by step 1 at t_0. If more than one activity enters the solution at t_0, repeat the calculation considering one of
the activities alternatively. In the example P_1 and P_2 are feasible; P_1 is selected.

Step 3. Determine the feasible solution for t_1 and proceed as in step 2.
In the example P_1 is repeated. Proceed until all periods are
considered. P_1 and P_2 are the only possible integer solutions
until period 8. In period 8, P_3 ($P_1 + P_2$) becomes possible.
However realization of P_3 in period 8 would postpone the possible realization of P_4 in period 4. Hence both alternatives
have to be computed. Calculation shows that it is profitable to
wait until period 9 and see that $P_4 + P_5$ is realized in period 12
in which the long-run optimal solution under the given conditions is realized.

---

1. Differences will occur only if it is profitable to use the existing equipment for part of the
time under consideration.

Table 8.7. Aggregated dynamic model

Restraint	No.	RHS	Rel.	1 P₁	2 P₂	3 P₃	4 P₄	5 P₅	6 Stable for hogs	7 Stable for cows	8 Credit	9 Saving	10 P₁	11 P₂	12 P₃	13 P₄	14 P₅	15 Selling hog stable	16 Selling cattle stable	17 Stable for hogs	18 Stable for cows	19 Credit	20 Saving	n Credit	n Saving
Period 1																								
Credit	101	+25,000									+1													+1	
Stable for hogs	102			+170		+170	+360	+360	−1																
Stable for cows	103				+10	+10	+10	+10		−1															
Money	104	+10,000		−17,000	−10,000	−26,000	−30,000	−38,000	+310	+4700	−1	+1													−1
		1	≧	1	1	1	1	1																	
Period 2																								
Credit	105	+25,000																				+1		
Stable for hogs	106												+170		+170	+360	+360	+1		−1				
Stable for cows	107													+10	+10	+10	+10		+1		−1			
Disinvestment	108								−1	−1								+1	+1					
Money	109	−10,000									+1.04	−1.03	−17,000	−10,000	−26,000	−30,000	−38,000	−1	−1	+310	+4700	−1	+1	−1	+1
		1	≧										1	1	1	1	1								

It is obvious that the applicability of this procedure in practice depends on the number of restrictions which change during the whole period under consideration. The greater the number of restrictions in addition to capital (which have to be considered in the aggregate dynamic model because the supply conditions of the corresponding factors change exogenously), the greater is the calculation input required and the less practical is the procedure. However in most practical cases to be solved at the farm level it would be possible to arrive at an aggregation level which permits the application of this procedure. The main advantages of this method are (a) the problem of considering integer variables in time can be solved with reasonable calculation input; and (b) no information is lost by the aggregation, which usually is necessary over activities and restrictions within the periods as well as over periods, in order to reduce the size of the problem. The parametric static calculation which precedes the aggregate dynamic calculation makes it possible to consider each organization as detailed as necessary.

Recursive Programming

Recursive programming has been applied to growth problems (9) and compared with the results gained by parametric static and by dynamic models (2). Recursive programming can be defined as a sequence of mathematical programming in which the parameters of a given problem are functionally related to the optimal variables of preceding problems of the sequences. Unlike the multiperiod model, it uses sequential optimizing to explain behavior and does not attempt to devise optimal decision rules which lead to optimal policies over the time period considered. These features make it applicable to describe an actual growth path rather than to show an optimal path. The growth path is described under the assumption of a given and defined behavior which deviates from the assumption of "classical decision models" mainly in the following points: (a) Investment and borrowing activities and sometimes changes of output between periods underlie certain behavior restrictions. (b) Farmers decide on investments according to the assumptions of the static theory. That means they calculate the annual costs of investment projects and confront them with the returns on the basis of present prices or of prices expected at the time of planning.

While the recursive approach is attractive for predictive purposes, it is equally senseless in application as a decision model. If the farmer has all the information for the whole time which is necessary to set up a recursive model, consisting of let us say 10 periods, then a model which considers periods simultaneously should be applied (if a static parametric solution is not applicable) as a guide for his decisions. Or if the farmer has only sufficient information to plan for the next period, then a simple static model can serve as a guide.

Consideration of Incomplete Information

The consideration of incomplete information has been more or less based on Knight's (16) distinction of risk and uncertainty in the past. The practical difference between two categories is that in the former the distribution of the outcome in a group of instances is known (either through calculation, a priori, or from statistics of past experiences), while in the case of uncertainty this is not true. The reason is that generally it is impossible to form a group of instances because the situation dealt with is in a high degree unique. In short, risk is used for the measurable noncertainty; uncertainty is defined as nonmeasurable noncertainty. The optimal decision in risk and uncertainty situations is governed by the subjective attitude to risk or uncertainty. A rational decision in risk and uncertainty situations therefore can be determined only under the assumption of a given attitude to risk. A number of decision rules have been developed by the theory of choice which considers different attitudes to risk or uncertainty (8, 13, 10, 26, 29, 31, 38).

These rules are based on the assumption of a given (equal in most cases) probability of events within a given range of uncertainty which is separated from the range of ignorance usually by subjective judgment based on the available information. This shows that rational decision on a given attitude to incomplete information cannot be based on a given attitude only but has to be based on a subjective or objective probability of the outcome of relevant events as well (30). Therefore if an objective function cannot be determined, modern decision theory introduces a subjective probability function (30). Hence risk and uncertainty have to be defined as follows. In a risk situation the distribution of the outcome in a group of instances can be described by an objective probability function, which is derived a priori or from statistics of past experience. In an uncertainty situation the distribution of the outcome of events can be described by a subjective probability function only. Risk and uncertainty situations can be handled in the same way as readily in decision theory as in calculations on the basis of this definition. They are handled in two different ways.

First, one can give simultaneous consideration to the variance of events and the corresponding variance of income. Quadratic (stochastic) programming is applied on the basis of the variance and covariance of the relevant events (4, 5, 7, 25, 35, 36). For each possible income situation the corresponding minimum risk organization is computed. The minimum risk organization is defined as the organization with the minimum variance of income which satisfies a given income goal. Hence variances of events which result in an increase of profit are considered equivalent to variances which result in a decrease of profit, certainly the most serious shortcoming of this approach.

Secondly, one can separate the determination of events and corresponding optimal solutions from the problem of variance and choice of a strategy. Renborg has put forward this approach by the distinction between stable and unstable elements of the farm plan. The stable

elements are defined as the activities, or more precisely, as the levels
of activities which remain in the optimal plan over the whole range of
expected variance of relevant events. The unstable elements are the
activities or the level of activities which are included in the optimum
plan only if certain constellations of the uncertain numerical values occur. Of course there is no clear objective distinction between the two
kinds of elements since any level of stability is possible. However the
inquiry for stable elements, which usually is done by changing the relevant events (prices, yields, etc.) parametrically, within the range of
subjective or objective uncertainty indicates whether there is information enough for rational decision. If all elements of the organization
are stable — there is only one optimal organization for the existing
range of uncertainty — no further information is needed. If there are no
stable elements, further information is needed.

Skomroch (32), who investigated the interdependencies of the problem, the corresponding optimal model formulation, and the optimal
grade of information, has extended this approach. He considers the
whole range of objective or subjective uncertainty by introducing the
probability function (more precisely discrete points from a probability
function) directly in the objective function and changing the distribution
of the outcome of events parametrically. This procedure becomes very
laborious if it is extended to coefficients and capacities as he proposes.
However it might be possible to simplify the procedure by parametric
consideration of the events, based on probability functions in place of
the parametric considering of the probability functions themselves.
Anyway, it indicates one direction of research: not to strive for complete information but to establish optimal relations among the grade
of information, the costs to get it, and the decision based on it.

It is obvious the marginal value principle is valid here too. The
optimal grade of information, given the marginal costs of getting it,
is equal to the possible increase of profit which results from decision
based on it.

Even if research in this field is only beginning, it is very likely
that we will remain confronted with the problem of incomplete information. The consideration of risk situations has been almost exclusively
limited to the variance of value in the objective function. Evers (4) recently has proposed a method of considering random variation of coefficients and constraints based on the work of Madansky (23). Evers
separates the matrix of the technical coefficients in a determined and
a stochastic part and considers the costs of infeasibility in the stochastic part of the matrix. He arrives at the objective function

$$\max = p'x = k'g(x) - M(1 - \gamma) \tag{29}$$

subject to

$$A_2 x \leq b_2 \geq 0 \tag{30}$$

in which P_x is the familiar vector of net returns, $k'y(x)$ are the costs of
infeasibilities weighted with the probability of occurrence, and M is

the "overhead costs" of an infeasibility which arises from any infeasibility again weighted with the probability of occurrence.

The objective function can be calculated only for a given x since at least M, and in a more general case even k, depends on x. (k may be a stochastic variable of which the variance may be dependent or independent of the variance of the restrictions.) Hence one has to calculate the x' vector separately, either by applying the Monte-Carlo method as Evers proposes or by linear programming calculating a number of solutions in the neighborhood of the optimum.

There is only little experience in the application of larger models which consider the grade of information and a rational attitude to risk and uncertainty, but it seems certain that investigation in this field will become increasingly more important after the application of determined models has been well established. Perhaps the practical application will be simpler than indicated by the models available at present. But certainly we are confronted with the fact that any decision, however carefully planned, has uncertain consequences.

CONSIDERATION OF SPACE

The introduction of space adds two questions to the optimum problem. Where should a given product be produced? What is the optimal size of the producing firm? Since land is an immobile factor, in agriculture the question of what to produce at a given location is approached and answered by simultaneous interregional considerations (including all farms of a region) rather than by microanalysis. Within the single agricultural firm the question of where to produce has lost importance. With modern production techniques it is relevant only in very big farms. Its consideration causes no principal difficulties since we can consider production of a given product in a given field as separate activity: introducing the corresponding restrictions and considering transportation costs explicitly.

Explicit consideration of transportation costs is also necessary if one considers the problem of the optimal size of the firm. Though not difficult in principle, only little work has been done in this field since Tschajanow (37) published his basic theoretical considerations in 1930, probably because the problem of the optimal size of the farm firm has been considered a political question rather than an economic problem. The problems of size and location are more important in the agricultural processing industry. The optimal location of such industries is governed by the principle of cost minimization, which includes the problem of the optimum size.

Neglecting the different changes of realization between processes which are directed by a central planning board and processes which are directed by the market mechanism, one can say the principle of cost minimization is realized (a) if the costs cannot be decreased by changing the locations of the processing firm; (b) if the cost cannot be decreased by changing the number of firms; (c) if the costs cannot be decreased by changing the supply area of a given optimal number of firms; and (d) if the costs cannot be decreased by changing the market outlet of a given number of firms. All conditions depend on each other and have to be considered simultaneously. The difficulties of doing this are increased by the necessity of taking into account the different possibilities of price differentiation in market societies. The simplest case is given if one can assume that it is possible to restrict consideration on one side of the market and to find a function in which production volume, market area, and transportation costs are related to each other (27, 39). In this case

$$A_c = \frac{P_c + T_c}{V} \tag{31}$$

where

A_c = average costs of production
P_c = total production costs
T_c = total transportation costs

Therefore one can determine from the cost function (substituted for P_c in equation 31) and from the function of transportation costs (substituted for T_c in equation 31) the volume with lowest average costs by taking the first derivative of equation 31, setting it to zero, and solving for V. The optimum number of firms is computed by dividing the total market output by V. Since only the distance between firms is determined, one has to select the location of one firm arbitrarily in order to determine the location of all other firms.

Practical application of this model is restricted by the difficulties of the determination of a transportation function for a given (continuous) area and by neglect of one side of the market (either supply for raw materials or selling of final products).

The Stollsteimer model (12, 33) and its possible extensions remove some of these difficulties, although they present difficulties in practical computation. It may be described as follows. Given $i = 1, ..., I$ supply points at which a given quantity M_i is produced at L different locations for processing industries, the number, size, and location of processing industries for the minimum costs of processing the raw material are to be ascertained. The problem has the following mathematical structure:

Minimize

$$TC = \sum_{j=1}^{J} P_j \cdot m_j \Big| L_k + \sum_{i=1}^{I} \sum_{j=1}^{J} C_{ij} \cdot m_{ij} \Big| L_k \tag{32}$$

with respect to the number and location of firms subject to

Table 8.8. Structure of a transportation model for simultaneous consideration of raw material and final products (2 processing locations; $P_1 \ldots P_n$ raw material markets; and $P_{n+1} \ldots P_m$ final product markets)

		t_{11}	t_{12}	$\cdots$	t_{1n-1}	t_{1n}	t_{21}	t_{22}	$\cdots$	t_{2n-1}	t_{2n}	t_{1n+1}	t_{1n+2}	$\cdots$	t_{1n-1}	t_{1n}	t_{2n+1}	t_{2n+2}	$\cdots$	t_{2m-1}	t_{2m}
P_1	$m_1 =$	+1																			
P_2	$m_2 =$		+1																		
.	.			.					.					.					.		
P_{n-1}	$m_{n-1} =$				+1					+1											
P_n	$m_n =$					+1					+1										
L_1	$0 =$	+1	+1	$\cdots$	+1	+1						−1	−1	$\cdots$	−1	−1					
L_2	$0 =$						+1	+1	$\cdots$	+1	+1						−1	−1	$\cdots$	−1	−1
P_{n+1}	$m_{n+1} =$											+1					+1				
P_{n+2}	$m_{n+2} =$												+1					+1			
.	.													.					.		
P_{m-1}	$m_{m-1} =$														+1					+1	
P_m	$m_n =$															+1					+1

$$\sum_{j=1}^{J} m_j = \sum_{i=1}^{I} \sum_{j=1}^{J} m_{ij} \qquad (33)$$

where

TC = total processing and assembly costs

P_j = unit processing costs in plant j located at L_j (j = 1, ..., I, whereby I ≤ L)

m_j = quantity of raw material processed at plant j per production period

m_{ij} = quantity of raw material shipped from origin i to plant j located at L_j

C_{ij} = unit costs of shipping material from origin located with respect to L_j

L_k = one locational pattern for J plants among the $\binom{L}{I}$ possible combinations of locations for I plants given L possible locations

L_j = a specific location for an individual plant (j = 1, ..., J)

The problem can be solved by a simple transportation model, calculating the minimum of transportation costs for each possible number of firms and the corresponding number of locations. The minimum cost solution is achieved by adding the sum of the corresponding processing costs to each of the alternatives and comparing results. Stollsteimer's approach is restricted to the consideration of the raw material side, but it can easily be extended to the final product side by using a more complex transportation matrix (Table 8.8). The calculation input increases rapidly if supply and demand functions are taken into account either by an iteration process described by Henrichsmeyer (11) or by using a nonlinear model if one has to consider multiproduction firms. Hence the proposal seems not very operational if larger problems have to be considered. Therefore Manne (23) has proposed a calculation procedure which he calls SAOPMA (steepest ascent one point move algorithm) which is a procedure to dynamic programming problems. Little is known about the efficiency of this procedure. Certainly it does not necessarily determine the absolute cost minimum.

Another way to reduce the calculation input might be described as follows. One estimates the minimum number of firms by taking into account only the cost function as a first step and determines the number of firms for which production costs have their minimum. Since transportation costs are above the minimum possible transportation costs, one begins the computation of the matrix listed in Table 8.8 with this number and increases the number of firms stepwise until total costs per unit begin to increase. Little practical experience exists (15, 17) with the calculation of optimal location models for processing industries, so further development has to show the direction in which research will move. The indicated way to calculate the number of optimal-sized firms, dependent (as in model 1) or independent from location and transportation costs, seems one possibility for finding an efficient starting point in the trial and error process of calculation. Even if we become able to determine the optimal location of processing industries with respect to cost minimization, it is by no means clear that the number of locations of firms at cost minimum is equal to the number of firms at the equilibrium of the market. Much research has to be done to understand this relation and to establish the "policy" conditions under which both points of equilibrium coincide.

SUMMARY

Standard linear programming procedures have become classical procedures in microeconomics. Recent research has been concerned with the attempt to overcome the shortcomings of the static "standard model" with respect to the reality of production technique and environment. Methods of linear approximation and integer programming are used to overcome these shortcomings with respect to the assumptions of production functions and divisibility. The methods of linear approximation of nonlinear functions are not very precise. In all cases the calculation input increases considerably. In order to keep it reasonable, limits on estimation of the "optimal region" are necessary in all cases except in the method described in Table 8.4, where the standard L.P. procedure is not applicable. In spite of these faults, the methods of linear approximation are almost exclusively used in agriculture. Lack of precise knowledge of the real nature of the production function, complicated calculation procedures, and a very limited number of computer programs with sufficient capacity are the factors which hinder the application of nonlinear programming methods better adapted to the nature of many production functions.

In agriculture the problem of indivisibility is usually not important with respect to goods, since the number of smallest possible units is generally relatively great; and at least some of the restrictions (labor, some capital restrictions) are not severe with respect to the amount of rounding which is necessary to arrive at integer solutions on the production side. Only on very small farms do difficulties occur with respect to the number of cows and cattle.

Lack of computational experience and lack of computer programs are the main reason for the "not very elegant" and "not very satisfying handling" of integer problems. Furthermore the existing experience with all methods shows that the calculation input in integer problems is very sensitive to the range of choice, either to the row from which a new constraint is generated or to the variables which are forced to be integers directly. The guidance for the sequence of solutions, which is given with the simplex method, is lost if integer variables are considered. Hence the possibilities of an extensive use of integer programming methods depend widely on the finding of efficient criteria for the guidance of the trial and error process.

With respect to the environment, research has been directed to overcome the shortcomings which arise from assumptions for time, uncertainty, and space. Time has been considered in two ways in decision models: (a) by a static approach considering the change of organization with respect to increasing capital separately from the time path and the financing and (b) by using dynamic or dynamic linear approximation. Both possibilities have their limits, either with respect to changes of returns over time or with respect to indivisibility over time. Therefore a new approach is developed combining a parametric static capital model with an aggregated dynamic model and considering alternative organization as integer variables.

The definition of risk and uncertainty has been changed in modern decision theory. According to the introduction of a subjective probability function, risk and uncertainty have to be defined as follows. In a risk situation the distribution of the outcome in a group of instances can be described by an objective probability function which is derived a priori or from statistics of past experience. In an uncertainty situation, the distribution of the outcome of events can be described by a subjective probability function only. Using this definition, risk and uncertainty can be handled by the same methods.

REFERENCES

1. Bellman, R. *Dynamic Programming.* Princeton, N.J.: Princeton Univ. Press, 1957.
2. Brandes, W. Special Problems of Linear Programming. In *Quantitative Methods in Economic and Social Science of Agriculture*, ed. E. Reisch. Munich: BLV, 1967.
3. Camm, B. M. Risk in Vegetable Production on a Fen Farm. *Farm Economist*, vol. 1.
4. Evers, W. H. A New Model for Stochastic Linear Programming. *Management Sci.*, vol. 13.
5. Freund, R. J. The Introduction of Risk into a Linear Programming Model. Mimeo. North Carolina State Coll., 1955.
6. ——. The Introduction of Risk into a Programming Model. *Econometrica*, vol. 24.
7. Gomory, R. E. An Algorithm for Integer Solutions to Linear Programs. In *Recent Advance in Mathematical Programming*, ed. R. L. Graves and P. Wolfe. New York: McGraw-Hill, 1963.
8. Heady, Earl O., and Wilfred Candler. *Linear Programming Methods.* Ames: Iowa State Univ. Press, 1958.
9. Heady, Earl O., and John Dillon. Theories of Choice in Relation to Farmer Decisions. Iowa State Univ. Agr. and Home Econ. Exp. Sta. Res. Bull. 485.
10. Heidhues, T. A Recursive Programming Model of Farm Growth in Northern Germany. *J. Farm Econ.*, vol. 48.
11. Henrichsmeyer, W. *The Sectoral and Regional Equilibrium of Agriculture.* Hamburg-Berlin, 1966.
12. Henry, W. R., and G. A. Seograues. Economic Aspects of Broiler Production Density. *J. Farm Econ.*, vol. 42.
13. Hoch, I. Transfer Cost Concavity in Stollsteimer's Plant Location Model. *J. Farm Econ.*, vol. 47.

14. Hurwicz, L. Optimality Criteria for Decision Making under Ignorance. Mimeo. Cowles Commission Paper No. 355. Chicago, 1951.
15. King, A., and S. H. Logan. Optimum Location, Number and Size of Processing Plants with Raw Product and Final Product Shipments. *J. Farm Econ.*, vol. 46.
16. Knight, F. H. *Risk, Uncertainty and Profit.* New York: Kelley, 1921.
17. Koch, A. R., and M. M. Snodgrass. Linear Programming Applied to Location and Product Flow Determination in the Tomato Processing Industry. *Proc. Reg. Sci. Assoc.*, vol. 5.
18. Kohne, M. First Steps of Considering Nonlinear Relationships in Linear Programming. *Agrarwirtschaft,* 1965, pp. 453-58.
19. Kunzi, H. P., and W. Krelle. *Nonlinear Programming.* Berlin-Gottingen-Heidelberg, 1962.
20. Land, A. H., and A. G. Doig. An Automatic Method of Solving Discrete Programming Problems. *Econometrica,* vol. 28.
21. Little, J. D. C., et al. An Algorithm for the Traveling Salesman Problem. *Operations Res.,* vol. 11.
22. McFarquhar, A. M. M. Rational Decision Making and Risk in Farm Planning. *J. Agr. Econ.,* vol. 14.
23. Madansky, A. Inequalities for Stochastic Linear Programming Problems. *Management Sci.,* vol. 6.
24. Manne, A. S. Plant Location Under Economies of Scale, Decentralization and Computation. *Management Sci.,* vol. 11.
25. Maruyama, Y., and E. I. Fuller. Alternative Solution Procedures for Mixed Integer Programming Problems. *J. Farm Econ.,* vol. 46.
26. Niehans, J. Pricing Under Uncertain Expectations. *Volkswirtscha. Statist.* 1948, pp. 433f.
27. Olson, F. L. Location Theory as Applied to Milk Processing Plants. *J. Farm Econ.,* vol. 41.
28. Raiffa, H., and R. Schlaifer. *Applied Statistical Decision Theory.* Cambridge, Mass.: Harvard Univ. Press, 1961.
29. Savage, L. J. The Theory of Statistical Decisions (a review). *J. Am. Stat. Assoc.,* vol. 46.
30. Schneeweib, H. *Decision Criteria at Risk.* Berlin: Springer, 1967.
31. Simon, H. A. *Models of Man.* New York: Wiley, 1957.
32. Skomroch, W. Optimal Start from Linear Decision Models. Diss., Stuttgart-Hohenheim, 1967.
33. Stollsteimer, J. F. A Working Model for Plant Numbers and Locations. *J. Farm Econ.,* vol. 45.
34. Seuster, H. Programming with Nonlinear Objective Function. In *Quantitative Methods in Economic and Social Science of Agriculture.* Munich-Basel-Vienna, 1967, pp. 121-43.
35. Tintner, G. Stochastic Linear Programming with Application to Agriculture. Second Symposium in Linear Programming. Proc. I, 1955.
36. Tintner, G., C. Millhalm, and J. K. Sengupta. A Weak Duality Theorem for Stochastic Linear Programming. *Unternehmensforschung,* vol. 12.
37. Tschajanow, A. Optimum Farm Size. Berlin, 1930.
38. Wald, A. *Statistical Decision Functions.* New York: Wiley, 1950.
39. Williamson, J. C., Jr. The Equilibrium Size of Marketing Plants in a Spatial Market. *J. Farm Econ.,* vol. 44.
40. Zapf, R. Application of Linear Optimization in Farm Planning. *Ber. Landwirtsch.,* vol. 179.

Chapter 8 ☜☞ DISCUSSION

Stanka R. Miric, *Agricultural University of Zemun* (Yugoslavia)

I T IS REALLY a very difficult problem to discuss new and potential tools and models in a period when even many standard tools and models are still not used enough in many countries. Not only is there enough space for enlarging the application of many tools and methods already mentioned by many authors but the application of many methods is a very important and good basis for further development of tools and methods. From science to application and from application to science, the continual way of progress is well known.

Each science emerges from a convergence of an increased interest in some class of problems and from the development of scientific methods, techniques, and tools which are adequate to solve these problems. The roots of many methods, techniques, and tools are as old as science and the management function. Many methods are well-developed in other organized activities. When a scientist is confronted by a new type of problem, he can inquire as to whether or not the methods he would use on the analogous problem in his own field are applicable to the new problem with which he is faced. In this way he becomes familiar with new problem methods which might not otherwise be thought of in this connection.

As certain classes of problems appear more and more frequently, it is only natural that for many types of repetitive problems new methods or modifications of old ones have been developed. The body of methods, techniques, and tools developed or adopted has grown to the point where it is extremely difficult for one person to keep well informed on all of these developments. Seminars like this one have the advantages of making a review not only of the methods, techniques, and tools well adapted to its special subject matter but also of the methods and models which have little application but which have potential for the future in decision problems.

In the very instructive paper of Professor Weinschenk we find many interesting ideas, principles, and applications, especially for linear approximation, nonlinear programming and nonlinear production functions, integer programming, and dynamic (determined and undetermined or stochastic) models. With similar impressions, like sensitivity to the range of choice in the input calculation for integer problems, we find in the paper of Professor Weinschenk some corroboration of our experiences.

In our research work we are very often in a situation that makes possible a comparison between farms grouped among the conditions realized on certain levels of organization, or on farm size and efficiency of agricultural production as a result of those in better conditions. After the use of direct comparison and many other well-known methods, we tried to use the method of discrimination analysis, especially after the improvement with the I-distance, which was made by our mathematician and statistician, Professor Branislav Ivanovic.

For n characteristics of the level of organization and efficiency, distance is an expression of all discrimination effects in one synthetic number. For the determination of distance we can use the following:

1. Pearson's coefficient:

$$CRL = \frac{1}{n} \frac{N_r \cdot N_k}{N_r + N_k} \sum_{i=1}^{n} \frac{d_i^2}{\sigma_i^2}$$

where N_r and N_k are values for farm groups r and k.

2. Frechet's distance:

$$F = \sum_{i=1}^{n} \frac{d_i}{\sigma_i}$$

3. Mahanalobi's generalized distance:

$$D^2 = \sum_{i=1}^{n} \sum_{j=1}^{n} W^{ij} d_i d_j$$

where W^{ij} are elements of a reciprocal matrix.

4. Ivanovic's I-distance:

$$D = \sum_{i=1}^{n} \frac{d_i}{\sigma_i} \begin{matrix} i = 1 \\ j = 1 \end{matrix} (1 - r_{ij})$$

"Distance" as a synthetic number (D) for all discrimination effects must satisfy the following conditions:

1. Distance between farm groups r and k must be

$$D(r,k) = D(k,r)$$

2. Distance cannot be negative, i.e.,

$$D(r,k) \geq 0$$

3. Distance as a numerical representative of all discrimination effects must be homogeneous functions d_1, d_2, ..., d_n and equal to 0; that is

$$D(r,k) = 0$$

4. For the farm groups r, k, and s must be satisfied:

$$D(r,k) + D(k,s) \geq D(r,s)$$

5. Distance must be increasing if d_i is increasing, or

$$\frac{\delta D}{\delta d_1} \geq 0$$

6. Conditions of an asymmetry. Since all characteristics are not of the same importance, it is necessary to make a rank list of X_1, X_2, ..., X_n, and distance must decrease with the decrease of rank of characteristics.

7. Condition of variability. Importance of difference must be in the opposite proportion to its variability; that is

$$\frac{d_i}{\sigma_i} \quad or \quad \frac{d_i{}^2}{\sigma_i{}^2}$$

8. Condition of stochastic dependence. If between characteristics observed there is stochastic dependence, or if it is

$$0 < r_{ij} < 1$$

I-difference must decrease for the amount of discrimination effects of characteristic i, and earlier $j(j < i)$.

9. If all characteristics are independent, that is, if

$$r_{ij} = 0$$

distance must be expressed in one of these two ways:

$$D = \sum_{i=1}^{n} \frac{d_i}{\sigma_i} \quad or \quad D^2 = \sum_{i=1}^{n} \frac{d_i{}^2}{\sigma_i{}^2}$$

10. If the dependence between all characteristics is functional; that is, if

$$r_{ij} = 1$$

the differences d_2, d_3, ..., d_n are consequences of the difference d_1, in which case the distance has only these two expressions:

$$D = \frac{d_1}{\sigma_1} \quad or \quad D^2 = \frac{d_1{}^2}{\sigma_1{}^2}$$

11. If two groups of characteristics are independent; that is, if

$$r_{ij} = 0$$

the distance for all characteristics (D_n) is

$$D_n = D_k + D_{n-k}$$

12. If for any two farm groups F^+ and F^- are taken, the characteristics for each farm group must be

$$X_i^- \leqq X_{ir} \leqq X_i^+$$

for each r = 1, 2, ..., m and i = 1, 2, ..., n. For the farm subgroups k and r must be

$$D_-^k - D_-^r = D_+^k - D_+^r$$

13. If additional characteristics are given, the distance D_n for two farm groups on the basis of n characteristics must be

$$D_{n+1} = D_n + E_{n+1}$$

(E_{n+1} is an addition from the new characteristic.)

The choice as to which method will be used to solve certain problems depends on the conditions which must be satisfied. In Table 8.9 all corresponding methods are compared (besides Pearson's, which is similar to Frechet's).

Table 8.9. The satisfied conditions by different methods
(+ satisfactory; - unsatisfactory)

Condition	I	F	M
1	+	+	+
2	+	+	+
3	+	+	+
4	+	+	-
5	+	+	-
6	+	-	-
7	+	+	+
8	+	-	-
9	+	+	+
10	+	-	+
11	+	+	+
12	+	+	-

Condition of an asymmetry is satisfactory only by I-distance. However important this condition is, it is very clear from the statement that all characteristics are not of the same importance, since between them there is a certain dependence. The result can be changed by splitting and joining the characteristics.

Repeated influence is avoided only in the case of I-distance. An important disadvantage is the unsatisfying of the condition number 12 by Mahanalobi's generalized distance. With the use of this distance all decisions are dependent on which farm group is basic (all decisions do not have the same basic farm group).

From the comparison of advantages and disadvantages of different methods, it is very clear why in our research work we used I-distance. On the basis of about 250 characteristics for each year during six years (1955-60) for 428,145 social farms (decreasing number is a result of continual integration) with total area 248,000-318,000 hectares (620,000-795,000 acres) we tried to find the rank of farm groups by level of organization and efficiency. In order to fulfill the condition of an asymmetry it was necessary to make a rank of characteristics of organization and efficiency. We used the result of our earlier research (about 670 correlation coefficients were used) to make the rank of characteristics.

The characteristics of the level of organization were fixed capital per land unit, buildings and land improvement capital per land unit, area per agronomist, number of tractors per 100 hectares of arable land, actual value of machinery and equipment in percent of the new

value, number of tractor plows per 100 hectares of arable land, combines (for small grain) per 100 hectares of arable land, number of animal units per 100 hectares of agricultural land, number of cattle per
100 hectares of agricultural land, and actual value of fixed capital in
percent of starting (new) value.

The characteristics of efficiency were cash receipts per 100
dinars of total capital, cash receipts per 100 dinars of total expenses,
cash receipts per 100 dinars of personal income, cash receipts per unit
of reduced land, income per unit of reduced land, yield of wheat per
land unit, yield of corn per land unit, milk per cow, meat production
per animal unit, and yield of sugar beets per land unit.

Enlarged forms of the earlier expression for the I-distance can be
attained in this way:

$$D = \frac{d_1}{\sigma_1} + \frac{d_2}{\sigma_2} (1-r_{21}) + \frac{d_3}{\sigma_3} (1-r_{31}) (1-r_{32})$$

$$+ \frac{d_4}{\sigma_4} (1-r_{41}) (1-r_{42}) (1-r_{43}) + \ldots$$

$$+ \frac{d_n}{\sigma_n} (1-r_{n1}) (1-r_{n2}) \ldots (1-r_n, n-1)$$

For the practical work, stochastic dependence can be expressed by
sign a_i.

$$D = \frac{d_1}{\sigma_1} + \frac{d_2}{\sigma_2} a_1 + \frac{d_3}{\sigma_3} a_2 + \frac{d_4}{\sigma_4} a_3 + \ldots + \frac{d_n}{\sigma_n} a_{n-1}$$

$$a_1 = (1-r_{21})$$

$$a_2 = (1-r_{31})(1-r_{32})$$

$$a_3 = (1-r_{41})(1-r_{42})(1-r_{43})$$

$$a_n = (1-r_{n1})(1-r_{n2}) \ldots (1-r_{n,n-1})$$

The results of our experimentation are in Table 8.10.

From the correlation analysis it is necessary to mention only a
few items: The multiple correlation coefficient between fixed capital
per land unit and all other nine organization characteristics is 0.94 for
the farms grouped on the basis of intensity level. Between the profitability and all other characteristics of efficiency, the multiple coefficient
of correlation is 0.999 for the farms grouped according to intensity
level, and 0.994 in the grouping according to total land. The multiple
correlation coefficient between efficiency (output per 100 dinars of input), and characteristics of organization level for the province of Ko-
sovo and Metohija is 0.87 for the farms grouped according to intensity
level, 0.79 in grouping according to cash receipts, and 0.78 in the grouping according to total land.

Similar investigations were made to find the rank for the groups of

Table 8.10. Rank of social farms in Yugoslavia

N°	Groups	1955-57		1958-60	
		I-distance	Rank	I-distance	Rank
1	2	3	4	5	6
	Cash receipt in millions (Old dinars)	Efficiency		Level of organization	
1	to 4	...	...	6.19	VI
2	5-8	7.13	IX	4.23	IX
3	9-13	7.91	VIII	5.25	VIII
4	14-20	8.87	VII	3.28	X
5	21-30	9.11	VI	6.97	V
6	31-50	10.41	V	5.29	VII
7	51-100	11.12	IV	7.53	IV
8	101-150	11.85	II	7.72	III
9	151-200	11.40	III	8.66	II
10	over 200	13.23	I	10.37	I
	Level of intensity (number of units)	Level of organization			
1	to 30	2.58	IX	6.84	VIII
2	31-40	12.41	VI	9.84	VI
3	41-50	11.27	VIII	9.93	V
4	51-60	11.66	VII	9.54	VII
5	61-70	13.64	V	14.02	II
6	71-80	14.10	IV	12.02	IV
7	81-90	15.23	III	12.93	III
8	91-100	17.19	II	...	...
9	over 100	21.51	I	14.86	I
	Level of intensity (number of units)	Efficiency			
1	to 30	6.40	VI	13.44	VIII
2	31-40	5.44	VIII	15.44	VI
3	41-50	5.79	VII	15.07	VII
4	51-60	5.58	V	16.01	V
5	61-70	9.87	II	16.64	III
6	71-80	9.53	III	17.22	II
7	81-90	8.23	IV	18.30	I
8	over 100	13.84	I	16.01	IV

the farm organization units separately for the size and efficiency characteristics (Table 8.11).

New investigations are in progress on an extensive basis to find the most efficient size of organization units on our big (social) farms. We expect to use discrimination analysis as a basic method.

SUMMARY

On the basis of our investigations, we find that discrimination analysis by the calculation of I-distance and ranking the farms according to

Table 8.11. Rank of organization units in the cropland

Size of organization units according to new value of fixed capital per land unit	Rank according to Conditions	Efficiency
1750-2750	2	2
2750-3000	6	7
3000-3250	1	3
3250-3500	3	1
3500-3750	7	5
3750-4000	5	4
4000-4250	4	6

the level of organization, size, and similar characteristics as to conditions and efficiency can be used successfully for the decision in similar investigations. When it is not a basic method, the discrimination analysis can be used as an additional method.

Very often it is enough to find the main tendency. On the basis of our investigation, we may say that better conditions and success of the farm business are realized in the bigger farm groups according to cash receipts and in the farm groups with a higher intensity level. Very often four or five groups of the biggest farms or with the highest level of intensity (number of units by the use of conversion coefficients) are in the first half of the total number of farm groups. In some cases there is a full tendency of the decreasing rank of farm groups according to level of organization, efficiency, farm size, and intensity level.

During the last few years, combined firms in Yugoslavia achieved much better conditions for successful agricultural production. Their processing, preservation, and selling exceeded the results attained by other social farms. With further development in horizontal and vertical integration, there will be a big change in farm organization and management. The whole situation of the farm will be changed. The discussion on farm size is less important than the detailed investigations of rationalizing the organizational unit along different lines of production. It will be a big problem to find the best possible and most efficient size of organizational units for given economic, soil, climate, and other conditions. Several methods can and must be used to solve this problem. Many of them are important in the first stage — to find the main input/output ratios, main characteristics of the earlier period — but some of them must be used for programming, projecting, and comparing the different projects for different sizes of organizational units in different lines of production on big farms.

Chapter 9 ⊙↜⊙ ECONOMETRIC MODELS FOR FARM
MANAGEMENT PLANNING

Rostislav G. Kravtchenko, *All-Union Scientific Research Institute for
Agricultural Economics* (U.S.S.R.)

A GRICULTURAL PRODUCTION in the Soviet Union is primarily
concentrated in collective and state farms which are large-scale
Socialist enterprises based on public property or land. In 1966
the Soviet collective and state farms averaged 216,500,000 hectares of
arable land which amounts to 96.6 percent of its total area. The collective and state farms fully provide the state purchases of grain, raw
cotton, and sugar beets. They produce 96 percent of milk, 96 percent
of beef, and 77 percent of eggs in the total volume of output purchased
by the state.

The historical process of transition from small individual peasant
farming to cooperatives, as well as the development of the national
form of property in agriculture, has led to the organization of large-
scale Socialist enterprises. Now the number of collective farms in the
country is 37,100 and that of state farms is 12,200. Their sizes can be
judged by the volume of land resources per farm, number of cattle, agricultural machinery, and by total production assets. Consideration
must be given to the fact that in many regions of the country the size of
farms is far in excess of the given parameters: collective farms have
10,000 to 15,000 hectares of agricultural lands, and state farms have
30,000 to 40,000 hectares.

The size of land utilization usually depends on farm specialization.
In recent years the process of specialization of agricultural production
in progress has resulted in the most intensive development of one or
two leading branches in each farm. In addition to these branches, there
are as a rule 10 to 15 branches necessary for the development of the
main branches or the utilization of their waste or by-products and for
ensuring a more complete use of resources. This complexity of the production structure of large-scale Socialist farms gives rise to a multi-
version opportunity of their development even within the bounds of one
production line. The complexity of production structure and large sizes
of enterprises require conforming types of management. Management
in the broad sense means determination of the objectives of production,
the ways and methods of their achievement (i.e., planning), as well as
realization of these ways and methods in the course of fulfilling the
plans (control proper). The multistage framework of interfarm management corresponds to the general principles of control of large-scale
systems. As a rule, agricultural enterprises of the Soviet Union are
characterized by a three- to four-stage organizational structure (i.e.,

groups of workers make up teams which form brigades, several brigades form a department, and all departments are subordinated to the central agency of farm management). In collective farms, brigades are usually subordinated directly to the board. The improvement of the management system is the most important prerequisite for increasing the efficiency of agricultural production.

The economic reform which now affects all branches of the national economy introduces significant changes in the planning and management principles of agriculture. The expansion of the autonomy of enterprises, self-supporting principles in the organization of production, submitting fixed procurement plans for a number of years to farms — all of these have modified the farm planning operations. But new forms and methods of planning must correspond to the new content. Unfortunately the process of modernization of planning techniques goes on very slowly. Therefore grave shortcomings connected with the use of old methods and primitive techniques for calculations still remain. It might be well to point out here the most important methods.

1. The current practice of planning includes the drawing up of four types of plans: (a) long-term plan of organization and economic structure (let us call it plan M); (b) medium-range plan of development covering 5 years (plan P); (c) current annual production and financial plan for the whole enterprise and production plans for its individual self-supporting branches and departments (plan D); and (d) working plans covering separate agricultural periods (plan O).

Plans D and O are to a certain extent linked numerically, whereas between plans D and P and P and M such coordination is expressed but very slightly or is practically nonexistent. This results in violation of the systems approach to the organization of planning.

2. Plan M characterizes the production structure of the farm, the utilization of its resources, the organization of territory, and so on, for a rather long period. The period of achieving the designed capacity will be different for farms with a different level of development.

Therefore it is next to impossible to forecast the state of agriculture for a long period by integrating these plans. On the other hand, the information of the state planning agencies on the development of separate regions along the desired line is not adequate and is received with delay. Therefore it is little used by the farms when drawing up plans of organization and economic structure. As a result of this, the forecasts of demand for farm produce and of the volume of its output will inevitably vary.

In other words, if the plan of agricultural development (N) stipulates the production of j kinds of produce in volumes A_j for a long-term period with allowance made for farm produce requirements, and each enterprise z draws up its own plan M_z with volumes of output A_{jz}, then $\Sigma_z A_{jz} \lessgtr A_j$. Thus the agreement between Σ_z, A_{jz}, and A_j can be obtained as a special case.

Consequently $N \lessgtr \Sigma_z M_z$, as well, while the iterative linking of plans on all levels along the entire vertical (using ordinary computing methods and techniques) is physically impracticable in acceptable periods of time.

3. Plan P is usually drawn up for 5 years. To achieve the level stipulated by plan M, t years are required (where t = 1, 2, ..., T). For different farms, T can assume any reasonable value. In the course of the established 5 years, the "drawn up" plan P remains practically unchanged since the correction procedure involves labor-consuming calculations. This decreases the reliability and soundness of the plan due to the fact that it will inevitably deviate from the actual production process. In addition, the absence of forecasting of objective conditions of carrying on business in each future year impels the expert on planning to determine the possible changes in yield and productivity on the basis of subjective estimates supported by elementary calculations by specialists. Consequently it is not infrequent that the plans of output increase for each forecast year are of a uniform character — i.e., $A_{j(t+1)} = A_{jt+\Delta}$, where $\Delta = (A_{js} - A_{ji})/5$.

With this approach the use of traditional methods of calculations results in rough planning.

4. Plan P drawn up per annum for 5-year intervals is not of a continuous character. The perspective to be planned decreases with each coming year, which is at variance with the very nature of planning the process of reproduction as a continuous process. This circumstance is responsible, among other things, for the disturbance of the M-P-D link which is natural for realistic reproduction. Such a shortcoming is unlikely to be eliminated with the existing planning methods and techniques.

5. All the plans of agricultural enterprises are drawn up in one, and rarely in two, variants due to the labor-consuming character of calculations and the difficulty of balancing each of them. It is clear that the only drawn-up variant will hardly prove to be optimum. Therefore potential production losses related to the nonoptimal utilization of resources are stipulated by the plan itself. This shortcoming is a natural effect of the traditional planning methods and techniques.

Large-scale Socialist agricultural enterprises cannot develop without plans linked and balanced both externally and internally. But at the same time the existing techniques and methods of counting have considerable shortcomings of methodical character which affect the rates of production growth. These shortcomings can be eliminated with the use of econometric methods and computers. Research into development of automatized management control systems in agriculture provides for the elaboration of an optimum planning system on all coordinative levels of farm production management. Intensive studies are now in progress on problems of theory, methodology, and methods of optimum planning for the branch as a whole, separate regions, and agricultural enterprises. The pivotal problem in these studies is the development of a system of models providing for optimum planning on all levels. Principles of development of such a system, its block diagram, content, and direction of intermodel information flow have been worked out in the

Department of Economic Cybernetics of the All-Union Research Institute of Agricultural Economics. Discussed here is a subsystem of models of interfarm planning, some of its most important elements, and individual problems of modeling reproduction in agricultural enterprises. The system of models for interfarm planning comprises four large units varying in time aspect of planning: long-term forecasting, perspective planning, current planning, and operation planning. This grouping agrees with the existing types of plans.

The *unit of long-term forecasting* includes (a) the whole complex of production functions for forecasting yield, productivity, and specific production costs; (b) a model for determining the optimum production pattern and enterprise economic capacities; (c) a model of interfarm distribution of production for principal items; and (d) a model of interfarm layout and distribution of stationary production units.

The *unit of perspective planning* includes (e) the whole complex of production functions for forming norms and forecasting yield, productivity, specific production costs; (f) a dynamic model of production development; (g) a model of interfarm distribution and specialization for subdivisions; (h) a model for choosing line, sequence, and units of capital investments; (i) a model of optimization of machine and tractor fleet composition; and (j) a model for choosing variants of production buildings.

The *unit of current annual planning* includes (k) the whole complex of production functions to analyze business activity for the previous year; (l) model of production and financial activities; (m) model for working out production programs of self-supporting subdivisions; (n) model of fertilizer distribution on farm fields; (o) model for optimization of herd turnover; and (p) model of freight traffic optimization.

The *unit of operation planning* includes (q) models of field work optimization in peak periods; (r) models for calculation of rations fed to all groups of cattle by periods; (s) a model of freight traffic optimization in peak periods; (t) models to control progress of large farm construction; and (u) models for resources control.

The above-mentioned models form the foundation of the future system of production optimum planning in agricultural enterprises.

The dynamic model of production development (f) is considered to be one of the most important models of the suggested system. This model makes it possible to reflect the progress of the farm from the starting level to the production level contemplated by the plan (b). Therefore it serves as a connecting link between the current planning and the long-term forecast of farm development. This is, on the one hand, accomplished by supplying to the dynamic model certain limitations ensuring outcome to the production parameters (b), and on the other hand, by using solution results obtained in the first unit of the dynamic problem to render concrete the current year plans (l). If it is remembered that models (b), (f), and (l) are the most important in their units, the information link between them provides a means for linking all the other models into an integral system.

To determine the perspectives of the enterprise development, several methods of modeling reproduction on an expanded scale are available in the Soviet Union. Discussed here is the method of approach which is being drawn up in the department of Economic Cybernetics. The essence of this method of approach consists in utilizing the linear programming apparatus for the purpose of realization of the unit dynamic model. The interrelated units of the model represent the plans of respective years of the perspective.

Formulation of the problem is exercised to determine the optimum structure and volume of output for each year of the perspective and to determine the accumulation volume and rates of production expansion which will make it possible to fully use the designed capacity over period T with constant improvement of the well-being of workers. The *criterion of optimality* takes into consideration the fact that the net return of the enterprise is the source of production expansion — the material stimulation of workers — and that the maximum of net returns should be considered as a criterion which best meets the formulation of the problem discussed above. Among other criteria worthy of attention are also the maximum of gross returns and the maximum of profitability.

The maximization of gross returns to a large extent meets the requirements of reproduction in farms with excessive labor. The solution of problems with such a criterion ensures the choice of a production structure capable of increasing employment during the whole period. This criterion, however, does not give any idea of possible volumes of additional investments and of rates of production expansion. The maximization of profit conforms to the peculiarities of farms with an inadequate level of development. To increase the possibilities of additional investments in production, it is very essential for these farms to provide the highest returns from fixed assets and current expenses. Such a criterion, however, does not stimulate complete utilization of available funds and does not define the absolute volume of accumulation. Thus in choosing the criterion of optimality it is important to give due consideration to concrete peculiarities of farms and if necessary to solve problems with several permissible criteria.

Each unit comprises several groups of *unknown variables*. Given below are the most important ones:

$x_j^{(t)}$ = agricultural branches (output volume or area under crops and cattle number)

$x_u^{(t)}$ = size of possible transformation of agricultural lands

$x_e^{(t)}$ = fixed production assets of kind 1 additionally obtained

$x_i^{(t)}$ = circulating assets of kind i additionally obtained

$y^{(t)}$ = gross agricultural output

$\bar{y}^{(t)}$ = total sum of production expenses

$z^{(t)}$ = net return volume

$\bar{z}^{(t)}$ = volume of long-term credit obtained

The modeling of reproduction offers means for determining the list of main and additional limitations. The most important *problem limitations* available in each unit are (a) limitations on the use of agricultural lands of kind i in volume $R_i^{(t)}$; (b) limitations on the use of labor resources $A_i^{(t)}$ in the peak period i of the year; (c) limitations on the use of kind 1 of fixed assets in volume $G_1^{(t)}$; (d) limitations on the use of circulating assets of kind i in volume $E_i^{(t)}$; (e) limitations on the guaranteed production of produce in volume $Q_i^{(t)}$; (f) limitations on the distribution of capital investments; (g) a group of limitations on the distribution of gross agricultural output and net returns; and (h) limitations of agrobiological nature.

The sown area of year t is provided with desired predecessors of year t-1 by connecting limitations of two adjacent units. The second group of connecting limitations provides the linking of additional investments in year t with net returns and part of amortization of year t-1.

Then a simplified model of reproduction of a farm on an expanded scale can be expressed as follows:

Determine

$$X \left[x_j^{(t)}, x_u^{(t)}, x_\epsilon^{(t)}, x_i^{(t)} \right]$$
$$Y \left[y^{(t)}, \bar{y}^{(t)} \right]$$
$$Z \left[\bar{z}^{(t)} \right]$$

where the objective function is

$$\max F(X,Y,Z) = \sum_{t \epsilon T} z^{(t)}$$

and T = number of years of planned perspective. The conditions of the problem are

$$\sum_{j \epsilon f} b_{ij}^{(t)} x^{(t)} + \sum_{u \epsilon U} b_{iu}^{(t)} x_u \leq B_i^{(t)} \tag{1}$$

where $b_{ij}^{(t)}$ = expenses of kind i of land resources per unit of branch j in year (t); and $b_{iu}^{(t)}$ = the variation factor of kind i of agricultural lands transformed with the use of method u; and

$$\sum_{j \epsilon J} a_{ij}^{(t)} x_j^{(t)} + \sum_{i \epsilon J} a_{il}^{(t)} x_1^{(t)} - x_i^{(t)} \leq A_i^{(t)} \tag{2}$$

where $a_{ij}^{(t)}$ = labor inputs in period i of year (t) per unit of branch j and a_{il} = labor input variation when using kind 1 of additional fixed means;

$$\sum_{j \epsilon f} g_{je}^{(t)} x_j^{(t)} + \sum_{v \epsilon u} g_{ul}^{(t)} x_u^{(t)} - x_1^{(t)} \leq G_1^{(t)} \tag{3}$$

where $g_{il}^{(t)}$ = fund capacity of produce j in kind 1 of funds and $g_{ul}^{(t)}$ = expenses of kind 1 of fund for kind U of agricultural lands to be transformed;

$$\sum_{j \in f} e_{ij}^{(t)} x_j^{(t)} + \sum_{l \in \alpha} e_{il}^{(t)} x_l^{(t)} - x_i^{(t)} \leqq E_i^{(t)} \qquad (4)$$

where $e_{ij}^{(t)}$ = expenses of kind i of circulating assets per unit of branch j and $e_{il}^{(t)}$ = expenses variations of kind i of circulating assets when using kind l of additional fixed assets;

$$\sum_{j \in f_1} d_{ij}^{(t)} x_j^{(t)} + \sum_{j \in f_2} e_{ij}^{(t)} x_j^{(t)} - x_i^{(t)} \leqq 0 \qquad (5)$$

where $d_{ij}^{(t)}$ = feed output of kind i per unit of branch j of plant growing;

$$\sum_{j \in f} q_{ij}^{(t)} x_j^{(t)} \geqq Q_i^{(t)} \qquad (6)$$

where $q_{ij}^{(t)}$ = output of kind i of marketable surplus per unit of branch j;

$$\sum_{j \in f} c_j^{(t)} x_j^{(t)} - y^{(t)} = 0 \qquad (7)$$

$$\sum_{j \in \alpha} s_j^{(t)} x_j^{(t)} + \sum_{l \in \alpha} s_l^{(t)} x_l^{(t)} - y^{(t)} = 0$$

$$y^{(t)} - \bar{y}^{(t)} - z^{(t)} = 0$$

where c_j and s_j = costs of produce and production expenses per unit of branch and s_1 = variation of production costs when using additional fixed assets;

$$\gamma_z + \tilde{z}^{(t+1)} \geqq \sum_{l \in \alpha} v_l x_l^{(t+1)} - \sum_{i \in j} v_i x_i^{(t+1)} \qquad (8)$$

where γ = assignment from net returns of year (t) for expansion of production and $v_l^{(t+1)}$ and $v_i^{(t+1)}$ = cost of unit of additionally obtained fixed and circulating means in year (t+1).

The last limitation makes it possible to link the funds set aside from net returns of year (t) for additional investments into fixed and circulating assets of year (t+1). Connected in a similar manner is year t with year (t-1). The whole combination of technical and economic factors of the problem and information on the farm resources are formed on the basis of branch technological charts, yield, and productivity forecasts, as well as on the basis of estimates of the state of production assets, labor resources, and lands by the beginning of the planned year. To determine factors a_{ie}, l_{i1}, S_1, it is necessary to recalculate technology with due allowance made for the variation of the mechanization level.

The application of the model to materials of concrete farms has confirmed its efficiency. For example, in calculations made for the twenty-first Party Congress, state farms located in the Moscow region have shown expansion of vegetable-milk specialization of the farm over the three years covered by the development plan drawn up with the use of the model discussed above. The results of calculations can be judged

Table 9.1. Descriptive statistics of soviet state and collective farms

Item	Unit of measurement	Farm average	
		Collective farm	State farm
Agricultural land	1000 hectares	6.1	25.7
Arable land	same	3.1	8.7
Sown area	same	2.8	7.3
Cattle number	head	1072.0	2071.0
(including cows)	same	378.0	742.0
Number of pigs	same	667.0	1049.0
Tractors (in terms of 15-HP units)	PCS	41.0	114.0
Fixed production assets	1000 rubles	784.4	2500.0

Source: Calculated from data of statistical collection, "Soviet country for 50 years" (Strana Sovietov za 50 let), Moscow: Statistica Publishers, 1967. Pp. 117, 118, 120, 127.

by the data in Table 9.2. The average annual rates of production expansion amount to 11 percent and annual increase of net returns to 18 percent. The additional investments are effected at the expense of the farm's own returns.

The linear-dynamic model makes it possible to obtain a series of transient plans bringing to full use the farm's designed capacity. The problem of development of a model for the calculation of the designed capacity of the enterprise is a very important and complicated one. In solving this problem, consideration must be given to the fact that since any farm belongs to a definite type of enterprise, this imposes limits on the variety of, and relation among different kinds of produce. In addition, in calculating the designed capacity of the enterprise, provision should be made for the possibility of a wide variation in yield levels due to the changes of weather conditions which affect the level of utilization of production resources. In other words the production structure and volume of resources should as much as possible reduce the risk of the farm under stochastically changing conditions. Studies on developing such a model are underway in a number of research institutions of the country.

Table 9.2. Summary of results in application of model

Item	Unit of measurement	Year under review	Plan		
			1st year	2nd year	3rd year
Gross output	1000 rubles	1959	2145	2380	2649
	%	100	110	122	135
Production expenses	1000 rubles	1106	1066	1172	1324
	%	100	96	106	120
Net returns	1000 rubles	853	1079	1207	1325
	%	100	126	141	155
Accumulation fund to expand production in the following year	1000 rubles	580	771	861	944
Capital investments in the given year	1000 rubles	300	580	771	861

Scientists of the Institute of Mathematics of the Siberian Branch of the U.S.S.R. Academy of Sciences suggest a model having a unit structure. The units are distinguished by the level of technical and economic factors intended for yields in favorable, medium, and unfavorable conditions of production. For this a fairly large row of yields for each crop is analyzed for 15 to 20 years; probability (P) of recurrence of its different values and relative frequency of these values (W_n) are determined. Then calculated for years with different results is the mathematical expectation $[M(\xi)]$ of yield. It is on the basis of this yield that all technical and economic factors are calculated. Used in the objective function is $C'_j = C_j \cdot P_1$. Equivalence of similar variables in all the three units is determined with the help of special limitations. The production structure determined in such a manner is considered to be fairly stable in all possible changes of objective conditions.

The model enables one to determine the farm commodity potential, volume, and structure of production assets and intensity of the development of branches (i.e., parameters characterizing the designed capacity of the enterprise). These and many other studies aimed at perfection of separate components of the system of models, their internal correlation, and linking will create the necessary prerequisites for a wide use of mathematical methods and computing machines in planning operations of agricultural enterprises.

Chapter 9 ☙ DISCUSSION

A. M. McFarquhar, *Cambridge University* (U.K.)

MAY I on behalf of the seminar thank Professor Kravtchenko for his paper. He is speaking of an organized economy in which planners really have an opportunity to apply the results of sophisticated techniques. There is also better opportunity than in the West for control of factors which tend to inhibit accurate planning. The paper has been especially interesting for those of us who are not well informed about the nature of economic organization and planning in the U.S.S.R. He has provided opportunity for questions on matters of importance to planners in both capitalist and socialist economies.

The first general point I would like to raise concerns the difference between planners in an academic environment and planners in the real environment. This difference seems relevant not only to the paper but to the discussion of the seminar. It is difficult to tell from the paper how far the plans and planning techniques discussed in the paper are actually applied in practice and how far they are simply models worked out by academic experts and which could be applied in practice. In a real situation it is difficult to test the effectivity of a plan since of course it is very hard to say what would have happened without the plan. This may be less true in rigidly controlled economies, but it would be interesting to know more about this problem. Assessing the usefulness of an academic exercise in planning is even more difficult, but the results of academic plans must be compared with the results which are obtained in practice in the planned situation. I would like to ask the author of the paper, if indeed any such comparisons have been made, for more information on the administrative link between desk planning, whether it be in the academic cloister or in the planning bureau, and what actually happens on the ground, especially at the nerve endings of the administrative heirarchy.

The second general issue concerns prices. It seems to me that socialist and capitalist economies are both in difficulties over prices. Increasingly the West appreciates that market prices do not determine or reflect the optimum allocation of resources, and there is an increasing move towards the use of social prices to reflect opportunity costs of resources in the use of investment criteria in planning. In the economies of the East there seems to be a move towards the increasing use of prices as a determinant of resource allocation and so on. However prices are still fixed exogenously; in addition, capital and materials inputs made available to business enterprises, for example state farms, are also controlled. Even in this situation it is interesting to plan for optimization of the microeconomic unit given controlled prices and materials. But with controlled prices, rigid control of material inputs, and a large part of output predesignated as part of an overall plan, the scope for variation in product-mix may be rather limited.

It is much more interesting to consider how the level of prices is fixed and how critical resource inputs are determined for state enterprises. If prices are arbitrary or irrational, how can "profits" determine planning decisions, especially on the scale involved in state farm planning? It is in this wider context of price determination and resource allocation or control that the application of planning techniques becomes really vital in rigidly controlled economies; I would like Professor Kravtchenko to say more about this and in particular about the relevance of the plan for the microeconomic unit in this situation.

The next critical problem I would like to raise is that of discounting in long-term planning. Professor Kravtchenko talks about long-term plans which involve a stream of inputs and outputs over a period of years. Presumably before a plan is chosen, alternative plans are considered. In order to consider the relative benefits of streams of costs and returns associated with different plans over a period of time, it is necessary to use some discounting technique or to calculate the internal rate of return for each project.

Now the author of the paper does not mention the application of discounting techniques in long-term planning, and I wonder if the technique does not exist in the U.S.S.R.; if not, what replaces it? How are future profits balanced against present profits, and how are two schemes (for example with different distributions of profits over time but perhaps approximately the same total annual profit summed) compared?

It seems to me that in the two problems of the determination of socially efficient prices and in discounting techniques, the economic criteria of the East and the West will come slowly together. I do not believe it is possible to overestimate the importance of this consideration. Both the East and the West seem to be stumbling towards the application of social prices in planning investment criteria which avoid the weaknesses of short-term market prices on the one hand and arbitrarily fixed institutional prices on the other as measures of the social opportunity cost of resources and output. In the long run it may not be exaggerating to suggest that the concept of opportunity cost as it is applied through the technique of social pricing will bring the socialist and capitalist economies into line with one another.

May I now turn to a number of minor points in the paper? At one point, the author talks of estimating a whole complex of production functions for forecasting yield, productivity, and production costs in various activities. I would like to ask how many production functions would be calculated for one crop such as wheat. What do these production functions mean in a situation where prices are fixed and some resource inputs, such as fertilizer, for example, are also controlled? Does this raise special problems, and how is the rate of technological change projected using these production functions in a situation where prices and material inputs are determined by control planning?

Also I am not clear about the difference between long-term forecasting and perspective planning, and I wonder if the results of either are compared with what happens in practice and if there is any evidence available of this comparison to show how near the perspective planning or long-term forecasting is to actual behavior? Or are the results of plans enforced in practice?

The author states that a complex of production functions are used to analyze business activity for the previous year. We all know of the problems of production functions derived from time series or cross-section data, and I wonder precisely what these yearly functions are, how seasonal effects are taken into account, and what the relevance is for future years of a production function based on activity input-output relationships for one year only.

The criterion of optimality is discussed, but no explanation is given of how this criterion is defined. Net returns along with other useful criteria, namely gross returns and "maximum of profitability," are mentioned, but no definition is given of these items. It is important to know what costs are in fact deducted in calculating net returns to the activity, what prices are used in calculating gross returns, and what these gross returns mean in a situation where prices are fixed exogenously from year to year. How is the influence of locality taken into account in determining prices, the costs of inputs, and so on? The "maximum of profitability" is mentioned as a criterion, but no definition

is given of how this is calculated. I should perhaps add that the term
is not known to me or I suspect to many of my colleagues here at the
seminar.

Later it is said that using this criterion makes it possible to ensure a production structure which increases employment during the
whole year. This raises a serious point regarding the use of more than
one criterion of optimality in investment planning. For example, in un-
developed countries plans often attempt not only to increase net return
but also to increase the level of employment. It may be, for example, that
one criterion of profit is return on capital, or return to labor. However to increase employment the appropriate criterion is the number
of men employed per unit of capital input, which is the reversal of a
labor productivity criterion. I venture to say that it is not possible to
find a single criterion which takes account of several objectives of
planning; thus one is left with a number of criteria and the problem of
weighing their relative value in determining an optimum. I would
therefore like to ask Professor Kravtchenko how this problem of giving
relative weights to criteria, some of which are mutually conflicting, is
dealt with in the planning methods he is using.

Although he states a general objective function, it is not possible
to see precisely what has been maximized; further the word "expenses"
is used, but no definition is given of what constitutes "expenses." In
this connection it seems vital to know what is included and what is left
out.

It is difficult to know what Table 9.2 is intended to show, apart
from purely hypothetical calculation of projected output measures. Are
the years in the plan past and future? Are the results for the year under review a measure of what has occurred without a plan in that year
or what has occurred under a different plan? If the latter, how does
the past plan compare with actual reviewed results, and what attempt
is made to compare results of plans with what occurs in practice?

I trust the number of general and detailed questions I have put to
Professor Kravtchenko will emphasize how very stimulating and valuable his paper has been in initiating constructive dialogue between
planners of the East and West.

Part III ⟊ REGIONAL MODELS OF PLANNING
AND DEVELOPMENT

Chapter 10 ᎒᙮ PROGRAMMED NORMATIVE AGRICULTURAL SUPPLY RESPONSE: ESTABLISHING FARM-REGIONAL LINKS

Earl R. Swanson, *University of Illinois* (U.S.A.)

MY ASSIGNMENT calls for an examination of the links between planning at the individual farm level and optimal supply response at the regional level. The analytical problem of coordinating plans on individual farms with those made at the regional level is parallel to the problem of linking regional plans with national plans or linking national plans with supranational plans. However the use of the region as a unit of analysis requires a few preliminary comments on the institutional context of planning, and hence the purpose for construction of formal optimization models which explicitly treat relationships between individual farms and the region.

The comments of C. B. Baker (1) on the purposes for regional adjustment research suggest the following observations. If the planning of the region's agriculture is centralized at the regional level, it would appear that formal optimization models for the region would be of importance to regional planners in indicating desirable resource use within the region. To accompany such a regional model, regional planners need information on how individual farmers respond to those elements of the regional plan which alter the decision-making environment of the farmers. This need at the regional level implies use of a predictive model rather than an optimizing model to characterize the behavior of individual farmers. Even if optimal plans for each individual farm are derived simultaneously with the optimal regional plan, these plans, unless modified, may not serve the regional planners well for predicting the production response at the regional level. The nature of the actual constraints on optimization at the farm level are difficult to determine empirically and to integrate into a comprehensive planning model. This reduces the value of many regional optimization models for prediction of firm behavior. Nevertheless such models should indicate the production potentials of a region and should provide guides for resource allocation within the region.

In contrast, consider the decentralized or "invisible-hand" type of organization of a region's agriculture in which deliberate planning does not occur at the regional level. Individual farmers in this situation would be interested in optimizing models which indicate choices in resource use. However in order for these farmers to use such models effectively for planning over a period of time, information is needed on the collective results at the regional level of the many individual-farm decisions. In a market economy these implications need to be traced through the product and factor markets. This indicates that a predictive type of regional model is needed by the individual farmer for making estimates of the impact of the aggregate effects of the actions of other farmers in the region on his own market situation.

Thus a comprehensive optimization model, such as the linear programming model presented later in this paper, does not appear to meet adequately the needs of either the regional planner under a centralized system or the individual farmer under a completely decentralized system. Cocks and Carter (5) have pointed out that a part of the problem of linking micro and macro planning is the lack of positive or explanatory types of models at either the micro or macro level which adequately recognize the existence of the other level. However modifications can be introduced into optimization models to increase their usefulness in the simultaneous planning of farms and the region.

INTERDEPENDENCE OF FARMS WITHIN A REGION

Placing the boundaries on the unit of analysis is a necessary part of economic planning. In this paper we consider only the agricultural sector of a region and the individual farms within the region. Chapters on interregional models by Harry Hall and Earl Heady, and on the relation of the agricultural sector of a region to its nonagricultural sectors by Vladimir A. Mash, are included in this book.

One special problem of regional analysis is that regional economies are usually more open than national economies in the sense that there is greater reliance on external trade. Indeed, the problem of defining a region on other than political grounds is that of defining which economic variables should be considered as exogenous.

In any formal optimizing model the results are the logical consequences of the data and the assumptions. An important set of assumptions for the topic under discussion deals with the interfarm relationships. In a market economy the connections between an economic unit and any other economic unit or group of units occur through the product and factor markets. The assumptions about the exact nature of these relationships in a planning model are a part of what may be called the specification procedure in building the model. For example, a simple assumption about the individual farm may be that it buys some resources in a competitive market, in which price is independent of quantity. The farm may also have, for example, a fixed supply of certain other resources. A third possibility is the purchase of additional resources at increasing costs per unit, perhaps with absolute upper limits. Parallel assumptions need to be made about the demand for the production of the farm. Again the possibilities may include the fulfillment of certain fixed requirements, sales of total production at constant prices, or a demand schedule with price being dependent on quantity sold. At the regional level similar assumptions must be made concerning the factor and product markets in order to specify the connection between the agricultural sector and the nonagricultural sector of the region. The specification of the nature of factor and product markets for the individual farms and for the region lies at the heart of an analysis of the simultaneous determination of optimal regional and farm plans. Consequently reliable estimates of these relationships are an important prerequisite to the use of optimizing models for a region's agriculture. Further discussion of the specification procedure and other empirical procedures will be facilitated by presentation of a simple linear programming model for a region.

REGIONAL LINEAR PROGRAMMING MODEL

It is hoped that the model presented in Table 10.1 contains the essential features needed for discussion of the problem of linking optimal individual-farm resource allocation and production with optimal resource allocation and production within the agricultural sector of the region. The following notation is used to indicate the requirements, activities, and objective function for the model presented in Table 10.1. Because regional development is normally considered over several periods of time, the model is multiperiod; in this example, three one-year periods. Each symbol in the model is either a vector or a matrix, with the elements denoting individual farms within the region.

Table 10.1. A three-period regional model with one mobile resource, one immobile resource, one product, and n farms

			X_1	X_2	Z	H	S	X_1	X_2	Z	H	S	X_1	X_2	Z	S
Period 1	Resource mobile	$B(1) \geq$	M_1	M_2	T											
	immobile	$F(1) \geq$	L_1	L_2												
	Product	$W(1) \leq$	A_1	A_2		-I	-I									
Period 2	Resource mobile	$B(2) \geq$						M_1	M_2	T						
	immobile	$F(2) \geq$						L_1	L_2							
	Product	$W(2) \leq$					I	A_1	A_2		-I	-I				
Period 3	Resource mobile	$B(3) \geq$											M_1	M_2	T	
	immobile	$F(3) \geq$											L_1	L_2		
	Product	$W(3) \leq$										I	A_1	A_2		-I

Maximize present value of product:

$$V = \frac{P(1)}{(1+r)} \sum_{i=1}^{n} S_i(1) + \frac{P(2)}{(1+r)^2} \sum_{i=1}^{n} S_i(2) + \frac{P(3)}{(1+r)^3} \sum_{i=1}^{n} S_i(3)$$

Requirements:

$$B(t) = \begin{bmatrix} B_1(t) \\ B_2(t) \\ \cdot \\ \cdot \\ \cdot \\ B_n(t) \end{bmatrix}$$ is the amount of mobile resource at beginning of period t on farms 1, 2, ..., n.

$$F(t) = \begin{bmatrix} F_1(t) \\ F_2(t) \\ \cdot \\ \cdot \\ \cdot \\ F_n(t) \end{bmatrix}$$ is the amount of immobile resource at beginning of period t on farms 1, 2, ..., n.

$$W(t) = \begin{bmatrix} W_1(t) \\ W_2(t) \\ \cdot \\ \cdot \\ \cdot \\ W_n(t) \end{bmatrix}$$ is the amount of withdrawal of final product for consumption during period t by farms 1, 2, ..., n.

Activities:

Production

$X_k(t) = [X_{k1}(t), X_{k2}(t), ..., X_{kn}(t)]$
is the level of production activity k at time t on each farm 1, 2, ..., n.

Interfarm transfer

$Z(t) = [Z_{11}(t), Z_{12}(t), ..., Z_{1n}(t), Z_{21}(t), Z_{22}(t), ..., Z_{2n}(t),$
$..., Z_{n1}(t), Z_{n2}(t), ..., Z_{nn}(t)]$
is the level of interfarm transfers of the mobile resource (only one such resource considered in Table 10.1) from farm i to farm j at time t. i, j = 1, 2, ..., n.

$H(t) = [H_1(t), H_2(t), ..., H_n(t)]$ is the level of interperiod transfer of the product from time period t to t+1 on farms 1, 2, ..., n.

$S(t) = [S_1(t), S_2(t), ..., S_n(t)]$ is the physical quantity of product sold at end of period t by farms 1, 2, ..., n.

Coefficient submatrices:

$$M_k(t) = \begin{bmatrix} M_{k1}(t) & & & & \\ & M_{k2}(t) & & & \\ & & \cdot & & \\ & & & \cdot & \\ & & & & M_{kn}(t) \end{bmatrix}$$

is a diagonal matrix of mobile resource requirements indicating quantities of the mobile resource required per unit level of production activity k during period t on each farm 1, 2, ..., n.

$$L_k(t) = \begin{bmatrix} L_{k1}(t) & & & & \\ & L_{k2}(t) & & & \\ & & \cdot & & \\ & & & \cdot & \\ & & & & L_{kn}(t) \end{bmatrix}$$

is a diagonal matrix of immobile resource requirements indicating quantities of the immobile resource required per unit level of production activity k during period t on each farm 1, 2, ..., n.

$$A_k(t) = \begin{bmatrix} A_{k1}(t) & & & & \\ & A_{k2}(t) & & & \\ & & \cdot & & \\ & & & \cdot & \\ & & & & A_{kn}(t) \end{bmatrix}$$

is a diagonal matrix denoting quantity of product produced per unit level of activity k during period t on each farm 1, 2, ..., n.

From farm   1   2   n

to farm 1 2 3 . . . n 1 2 3 . . . n . . . 1 2 3 . . . n

$$
T = \begin{bmatrix}
0 & -1 & -1 & \ldots & -1 & 1 & & & & \ldots & & 1 & & & & & 1 \\
 & 1 & & & & -1 & 0 & -1 & \ldots & -1 & & & 1 & & & & 2 \\
 & & 1 & & & & 1 & & & & & & & 1 & & & 3 \\
 & & & \cdot & & & & \cdot & & & & & & & \cdot & & \cdot \\
 & & & & \cdot & & & & \cdot & & & & & & & \cdot & \cdot \\
 & & & & & \cdot & & & & \cdot & & & & & & \cdot & \cdot \\
 & & & & & 1 & & & & 1 & \ldots & -1 & -1 & -1 & \ldots & 0 & n
\end{bmatrix}
$$

    Each of the farms in the model has two resources, one mobile among farms in the region and the other immobile among farms. The initial supplies and uses of these two resources are indicated in the first two rows of each period. There are no opportunities in this model to acquire these two resources outside the region. A predetermined amount of each of these resources, $B(t)$ and $F(t)$, is made available for each farm in each period. These simplifying assumptions may be modified to approximate the empirical situation.

    The model has a single product which requires these two resources for production. The production and use of this product appear in the third row in each period. A predetermined amount of product $W(t)$ is withdrawn in each period for consumption. Again, these assumptions may be modified to provide a better approximation of the planning environment.

    Two production activities are present on each farm in each period. In Table 10.1 these are the first two processes, X_1 and X_2, in each period. Provision is made for interfarm transfers of the mobile resource during each period by the process denoted $Z(t)$. The production of each farm during each of the first two periods may be stored until the succeeding period. The amounts stored by each farm are indicated by the levels of $H(t)$. The product may be sold at the end of each of the three periods by use of the process $S(t)$.

    The criterion for choosing the process levels is maximization of the present value of production. For convenience, the costs associated with interfarm transfers of the mobile resource and the storage costs are ignored. The price of the product is assumed to be independent of quantity sold.

EMPIRICAL PROCEDURES

    The specification of the various parts of a model, such as the one presented, determines the kinds of data required to develop optimal regional and farm plans. Thus the choice of constraints, activities, and objective function reflects what the model builder believes to be most relevant in characterizing the planning environment.

The data requirements for the linear programming model presented in Table 10.1 fall into three classes: the constraints, B(t), F(t), and W(t); the coefficients, M_k (t), L_k (t), and A_k(t); and the weights P(t) in the objective function.

Constraints

Complete information on the constraints in this model would include the quantities of the mobile and immobile resource available on each farm in each period. Even with only a single mobile resource and a single immobile resource, obtaining such information is not likely to be within the usual budget allocated to this type of project. Consequently there will be a need to obtain a sample of farms, not only for the constraints but also for the coefficients and price expectations. Within a given research budget a trade-off should be recognized between the number of representative farms used and the depth of detail as reflected in the number of constraints and the number of production alternatives.

If the entire population of n farms is included in a model such as the one in Table 10.1, there would be no problem of aggregating the production and resource use of individual farms. Since interdependence among farms is taken into account by the model, regional production is the sum of the production of individual farms. Similarly regional resource use is the sum of the resources used by individual farms. The problems of aggregation of individual farm plans developed with no regional resource constraints or interfarm resource transfer possibilities are discussed in a later section of this paper.

Since sampling is usually necessary for cost reasons, the farms represented by the constraints need to be classified and a typical or representative farm selected from each class. If the results are to be used primarily at the regional level, class averages of constraints levels may be used. If the results are also to serve individual farmers rather directly, it is better to choose typical or representative farms. Many resources, such as tractors, may appear as fractional quantities rather than integers if average resource quantities are used.

In a study which emphasizes supply response the ideal criterion for classification is the nature of the supply response. The ideal information necessary for such a classification is usually not available. Many studies in the United States have used size and type of farm as a basis for classification. Use of such criteria has the advantage of readily available data, but other factors such as age of farmer, equity position, and tenure status may be more important in determining supply response than farm size and present production. As our knowledge of the critical factors influencing supply response increases, we should be better able to classify farms for purposes of sampling. The

consumption of the final product by each farm, W(t), must also be estimated. If this is to be used for household consumption, estimates
might be based on family size and income. Modifications to introduce
cash flows and to permit investment are suggested in the final section
of this paper.

In the model presented in Table 10.1, the B(t), F(t), and W(t) for
each period are predetermined. The estimates of these future constraints may be based on surveys of farmers regarding their own estimates of resource availabilities and consumption requirements, or
estimates may be based on secondary data projected to reflect the development goals of the region. In practice, census data may not be
available in the detail required to provide a good basis for making projections. Over a long planning period, account must be taken of change
in quality of resources and perhaps introduction of new types of resources.

Coefficients

The estimates of coefficients for the production activities, $X_1(t)$
$X_2(t)$, may be made from observation of commercial farms (ideally, on
each of the n farms), from experimental data, or from the judgments of
technical experts. Estimates of coefficients with the detail needed to
be useful for individual farm planning are not usually available from a
large sample of commercial farms. Further, the use of only the production activities presently found on commercial farms may prevent
consideration of improved techniques which are available but not yet
adopted. Consequently in most empirical applications where some type
of optimization is desired, at least some reliance is placed on experimental data, perhaps adjusted to reflect what is possible under commercial farm conditions. For periods very far in the future it is
desirable to consult with technical experts in order to arrive at satisfactory estimates of coefficients. Of course a more comprehensive
model would include the generation of the new coefficients by the research sector of the economy and would also have the rate of adoption
of new techniques determined within the model.

Objective Function

If particular regional goals are to be attained, they may be incorporated into the constraints of the model, or the weights P(t) in the objective function may be altered, or these methods may be combined.
For example, the levels and rates of growth of the consumption goals
W(t) may be an explicit part of the model. If output above these requirements is to be determined by the price mechanism, the P(t) may
be varied over a range in order to obtain estimates of the price relationships most likely to generate the desired rate of growth and composition of production.

In such a model as the one in Table 10.1 in which there are only a few constraints and one product, it is likely that production would not be very sensitive to changes in the time pattern of P(t) outside a rather narrow critical range. In more complex models with many products and restraints, changes in growth and composition of output are more likely to occur in response to changes in the price regime. Exploring the dual solution aids in obtaining information about which resources are critical and may serve to aid in developing policies to attain desired goals (4, 13, 38).

The provision in the model in Table 10.1 for interfarm transfers of the mobile resource implies that we have information by which resources may be classified as mobile or immobile. Information on these interfarm transfers may be obtained by interviews of farmers to determine the extent of actual transfers and the conditions under which the limits on transfers may change. Because transfers are assumed to be costless in the present model, the distance among farms is assumed to be negligible. Transport costs are a part of the mobile factor supply function and would need to be included in a more realistic model.

In a situation where farm size is changing and where such changes are associated with changes in composition of output, it is very important to have a model which permits land to be "mobile" among farm units and that the appropriate specification of costs of transfer be included.

EMPIRICAL STUDIES

A number of studies have recognized, in some way, the interdependencies among farms within a regional planning model. Some of these will be cited; they are too numerous to review in detail. These studies fit into three broad classes. First, there have been attempts to aggregate optimal plans for representative farms under varying assumed price regimes (2, 6, 10, 22, 27, 28, 31). These studies have usually assumed a competitive market for the products and also for some of the resources and a fixed supply, at the farm level, of other resources.

A second type of study has taken into account the fact that certain resources are fixed at the regional level and that individual-farm plans must be developed with certain regional constraints (39, 41, 46). Algorithms for solutions have been developed for those cases in which these constraints take the form of price-dependent functions, representing product demands or factor supplies (35, 36, 43, 46). A simple means by which these price-dependent functions may be approximated in a standard linear programming model is by use of a step function (1).

Finally, less formal techniques have been suggested. For example, Malassis (19) has indicated the importance of individual-farm data in developing regional plans for agriculture, and Schickele (26) has suggested a method for harmonizing a national agricultural production development plan with individual-farm plans.

AGGREGATION PROBLEM

In those studies in which optimal plans for representative farms are developed without regional constraints on resources or production, either as absolute quantities or price-dependent functions, a question arises about how the individual results are to be combined into regional totals. This problem has received much attention in the United States (2, 3, 7, 8, 10, 18, 21, 24, 27, 28, 29, 31). Aggregation error is said to exist when the weighted sum of production of representative farms does not equal the total production on all farms in the region.

Day (8) has defined the sufficient conditions for exact aggregation as (a) all farms have identical coefficient matrices, (b) only proportional variation in net return expectations held by farmers, and (c) only proportional variation in the constraint vectors among farms.

Yaron (44) has pointed out that in a model in which all producers are treated as an aggregate that no aggregation error will occur if the farms have (a) identical proportions between the limiting resource levels and (b) sets of activities with identical or proportional input and net income coefficients.

Miller (21) has indicated that the sufficient conditions for exact aggregation are somewhat less restrictive than those proposed by Day and Yaron. Miller has shown that only the following conditions need to be met: (a) that all farms have identical coefficient matrices and (b) that all farms have the same activities included in the solution vector. Lee (18) has shown that the dual solution can be used to determine the range over which resource ratios may vary without causing aggregation error.

This view of the aggregation problem is somewhat limited and from an empirical standpoint may not be as important as the specification of appropriate regional constraints on resource use and product requirements, either as absolute quantities or price-dependent functions. Further, the specification of interfarm resource transfer relationships in a model such as the one presented in Table 10.1 may be more important in influencing total regional production than the usual range of alternative weighting systems of representative farms which might be used (10). This is of course an empirical question. In summation, the aggregation problem appears to be more in the nature of the high cost of a comprehensive model than a conceptual problem (11).

SOME POSSIBLE MODIFICATIONS OF THE LINEAR PROGRAMMING MODEL

Many modifications of the model presented in Table 10.1 are theoretically possible. The nature of the modifications depends on the purpose of constructing the model and the funds available for the study.

The goals of national development policy in a formal model are discussed in other papers at this seminar, and in a number of other places; for example, see Chenery (4) and Reiner (23); and for a discussion at the regional level, see Isard (16) and Meyer (20), who has reviewed various approaches to regional economic analysis. A book edited by Isard and Chamberlain (17) contains a number of papers on regional planning experience in less-developed areas.

The consistency between regional goals and individual-farmer goals may be studied by systematically modifying the constraints and objective function. Although this is theoretically possible, the technical problem of developing explicit statements of regional and individual-farmer goals is enormous at any particular point in time. Further, these goals are apt to change through time because expectations and desires are, in part, functions of current output and consumption. Thus the results of a multiperiod model may need to be revised annually. In addition to the changes in goals mentioned, there also may be unpredictable changes in the technical coefficients, especially if the model has a long planning horizon. Van Brabant (40) has reported that a common thread in Soviet multiperiod planning models is the idea of continuous planning with new data leading to new plans before the terminal date of the initial plan is reached. Chenery (4) has discussed the relationship between long-term programs and short-run directives.

While the individual-farm goals may be primarily profit oriented, the regional goals are more apt to be consumption oriented, if not in the short run, at least in the long run. However the overlapping of interests can clearly be seen in the questions of valuation of capital assets at the end of the planning period. The relative weight placed on terminal capital stock reflects the concern of both farmers and regional planners for the periods beyond the horizon of the plan. Vietorisz (42) uses a criterion of maximizing terminal wealth, which in effect is a proxy for post-terminal consumption.

Certain regional policy goals can be introduced by choice of the constraints, B(t), F(t), and W(t). For example, policies designed to improve equity may alter the distribution of the resources among farms. Regional policy goals regarding consumption levels may be introduced by the W(t) assumed for each period. Of course, this simple model abstracts from problems of implementation of such a policy.

The use of a multiperiod model in planning forces the model builder to explicitly consider the problems of capital formation and rate of growth (14, 32, 42). Rather than having the resources B(t) and F(t) predetermined, a more realistic model would provide for their acquisition either from individual-farm savings or with funds from other sources, within or outside the agricultural sector of the region. Heidhues (14) has provided an example of an individual-farm model which explicitly includes investment and disinvestment for durable assets and cash. Introduction of cash flows into the model, with withdrawals for consumption being based in part on level of income, represents a possible modification (33). This requires estimates of the propensity to consume out of current income.

The need for modifications to take into account interfarm resource mobility has been mentioned earlier in this paper. Appropriate characterization of the factor market is a difficult empirical problem, but one which is worth more effort than it has received. This need for more information on the factor market is not unique to the kind of model which emphasizes farm-regional links; it is a problem at other levels of planning and analysis. Among others, Strohbehn (30) has discussed the importance of specifying the form of the regional factor supply functions in the context of an analysis of income distribution in a region.

At the beginning of this paper I mentioned that the needs of regional planners using a comprehensive optimization model might require that the individual-farm models be more predictive of farmers' behavior than is usually characteristic of the results of optimizing models. Modifications in this direction may be accomplished by introduction of flexibility constraints (9, 14, 15, 25, 34). These constraints may be based on historical adjustments and observation of selected physical characteristics which restrict adjustment. Although these behavioral constraints are usually estimated rather arbitrarily, at least in the initial period, their use will usually provide a greater accuracy in predicting the actual behavior of farmers. A recursive analysis will generate the constraints for later periods. However discussion of this type of a model would lead us away from the assigned topic of "programmed normative response." The same is true of simulation methods, which may also have application at the regional level (12).

In summary, an adequate characterization of the farm-regional links in a formal optimization model is essential if the results are to be taken seriously by either regional planners or individual farmers. Our present techniques of analysis permit considerably more realism than is presently found in our primarily illustrative models. As our stock of technical data increases and our knowledge of individual and group goals improves, we may expect to advance from illustration to bona fide application.

REFERENCES

1. Baker, C. B. Evaluation of Economic Models Used in Regional Aggregate Studies. In Price and Income Policies, Agr. Policy Institute Series 17, North Carolina State Univ., April 1965.
2. Barker, Randolph, and Bernard F. Stanton. Estimation and Aggregation of Firm Supply Functions. *J. Farm Econ.*, vol. 47.
3. Berry, John H., and Gaylord E. Worden. An Alternative Approach in Production Adjustment Models and Complementary Research Methods. Ditto. ERS, USDA, March 1968.
4. Chenery, Hollis B. Development Policies and Programs. *Econ. Bull. Latin America*, March 1958.
5. Cocks, K. D., and H. O. Carter. Micro Goal Functions and Economic Planning. *Am. J. Agr. Econ.*, vol. 50.
6. Colyer, Dale, and George D. Irwin. Beef, Pork, and Feed Grains in the Corn Belt: Supply Response and Resource Adjustments. North Central Reg. Res. Publ. 178, Missouri Agr. Exp. Sta. Bull. 921.

7. Day, Lee M. Use of Representative Farms in Studies of Interregional Competition and Production Response. *J. Farm Econ.*, vol. 45.
8. Day, Richard H. On Aggregating Linear Programming Models of Production. *J. Farm Econ.*, vol. 45.
9. ———. *Recursive Programming and Production Response.* Amsterdam: North-Holland, 1963.
10. Green, H. A. J. *Aggregation in Economic Analysis: An Introductory Survey.* Princeton, N.J.: Princeton Univ. Press, 1964.
11. Grick, George E., and Richard A. Andrews. Aggregation Bias and Four Methods of Summing Farm Supply Functions. *J. Farm Econ.*, vol. 47.
12. Hartman, L. M. Simulating a Regional Economy. In Regional Studies of Income Distribution, ed. W. B. Back and John E. Waldorp, Jr. Dept. Agr. Econ., Louisiana State Univ. and ERS, USDA, March 1966.
13. Heady, Earl O., and Alvin C. Egbert. Programming Regional Adjustments in Grain Production to Eliminate Surpluses. *J. Farm Econ.*, vol. 41.
14. Heidhues, Theodor. A Recursive Programming Model of Farm Growth in Northern Germany. *J. Farm Econ.*, vol. 48.
15. Henderson, James M. The Utilization of Agricultural Land: A Theoretical and Empirical Inquiry. *Rev. Econ. and Stat.*, vol. 41.
16. Isard, Walter. *Methods of Regional Analysis: An Introduction to Regional Analysis.* New York: Wiley, 1960.
17. Isard, Walter, and John H. Chamberlain, eds. *Regional Economic Planning Techniques of Analysis for Less-Developed Areas.* Paris: O.E.C.D., 1961.
18. Lee, John E., Jr. Exact Aggregation—A Discussion of Miller's Theorem. *Agr. Econ. Res.*, vol. 18.
19. Malassis, L. The Relationship Between Farm Analysis and Regional Economic Studies. In *Regional Economic Planning: Techniques of Analysis*, ed. Walter Isard and John H. Chamberlain. Paris: O.E.C.D., 1961.
20. Meyer, J. R. Regional Economics—A Survey. *Am. Econ. Rev.*, vol. 53.
21. Miller, Thomas A. Sufficient Conditions for Exact Aggregation in Linear Programming Models. *Agr. Econ. Res.*, vol. 18.
22. O.E.C.D. Economic Planning Research in Agriculture: Optimal Location Models in O.E.C.D. Member Countries. O.E.C.D. Directorate for Agriculture and Food, Paris, 1967.
23. Reiner, Thomas A. Sub-national and National Planning: Decision Criteria. *Proc. Reg. Sci. Assoc., 14th Ghent Congress*, 1964.
24. Schaller, W. Neill. Estimating Aggregate Product Supply Functions with Firm-leveling Observations. In Production Economics in Agricultural Research. Dept. Agr. Econ., AE-4108, Univ. Illinois, 1966.
25. Schaller, Neill W., and Gerald W. Dean. Predicting Regional Crop Production—An Application of Recursive Programming. USDA Tech. Bull. 1329, April, 1965.
26. Schickele, Rainer. Farm Management Research for Planning Agricultural Development. *Indian J. Agr. Econ.*, vol. 11.
27. Sharples, Jerry A., Thomas A. Miller, and Lee M. Day. Evaluation of a Firm Model in Estimating Aggregate Supply Response. North Central Reg. Publ. 179, Iowa Agr. Exp. Sta. Res. Bull. 558.
28. Sheehy, Seamus J., and R. H. McAlexander. Selection of Representative Benchmark Farms and Supply Estimation. *J. Farm Econ.*, vol. 47.
29. Stovall, John G. Sources of Error in Aggregate Supply Estimates. *J. Farm Econ.*, vol. 48.
30. Strohbehn, Roger W. Relevance of Resource Supply Functions in Regional Analysis. In Regional Studies of Income Distribution, ed. W. B. Back and John E. Waldorp, Jr. Dept. Agr. Econ., Louisiana State Univ. and ERS, USDA, March 1966.

31. Sundquist, W. B., et al. Equilibrium Analysis of Income-Improving Adjust-
    ments on Farms in the Lakes States Dairy Region. Minnesota Agr. Exp. Sta.
    Tech. Bull. 246.
32. Swanson, Earl R. Integrating Crop and Livestock Activities in Farm Manage-
    ment Activity Analysis. *J. Farm Econ.*, vol. 37.
33. ———. Selecting Fertilizer Programs by Activity Analysis. In *Methodological
    Procedures in the Economic Analysis of Fertilizer Use Data*, ed. E. L. Baum
    et al. Ames: Iowa State Univ. Press, 1956.
34. ———. Short-run Crop Acreage Adjustments in Illinois. *Illinois Agr. Econ.*,
    vol. 1.
35. Takayama, T., and G. G. Judge. Spatial Equilibrium and Quadratic Program-
    ming. *J. Farm Econ.*, vol. 46.
36. ———. An Interregional Activity Analysis Model for the Agricultural Sector.
    J. Farm Econ., vol. 46.
37. Theil, H. *Linear Aggregation of Economic Relations.* Amsterdam: North-
    Holland, 1954.
38. Tucker, Albert W. Combinational Theory Underlying Linear Programs. In
    Recent Advances in Mathematical Programming, ed. Robert L. Graves and
    Philip Wolfe. New York: McGraw Hill, 1963.
39. Ueno, Fukuo, and Kazuo Muto. Study on the Methods of Regional Planning for
    Agriculture in Suburban Rural Area. Misc. Publ. Ser. H., no. 12., Nat. Inst.
    Agr. Sci., Tokyo, 1967.
40. Van Brabant, Josef M. Reflections on Soviet Attempts Toward the Construc-
    tion of an Objective Function for Multi-Period Planning. *Tijdschr. Econ.*,
    vol. 12.
41. Varley, A. P., and G. S. Tolley. Simultaneous Target Planning for Farms
    and the Area. *J. Farm Econ.*, vol. 44.
42. Vietorisz, Thomas. Locational Choices in Planning. In *National Economic
    Planning*, ed. Max F. Millikan. New York: Columbia Univ. Press, 1967.
43. Wolfe, Philip. Methods of Non-Linear Programming. In *Recent Advances in
    Mathematical Programming*, ed. Robert L. Graves and Philip Wolfe. New
    York: McGraw Hill, 1963.
44. Yaron, Dan. Application of Mathematical Programming to National Planning
    in Agriculture. *Farm Economist*, vol. 10.
45. ———. Empirical Analysis of the Demand for Water by Israeli Agriculture.
    J. Farm Econ., vol. 49.
46. Yaron, D., Y. Plessner, and Earl O. Heady. Competitive Equilibrium—
    Application of Mathematical Programming. *Canadian J. Agr. Econ.*, vol. 13.

Chapter 10 ☞ DISCUSSION

Gyorgy Szakolczai, *Central Bureau of Statistics*
(Hungary)

M AY I FIRST express my thanks to the organizing committee of this international conference for the invitation to make a contribution to the debate. I am honored by the fact that without being an agricultural economist I am allowed to join in this discussion. Of course, in my remarks I shall try to remain within the scope of my own *metier:* the mathematical theory of national economic planning.

While reading Professor Swanson's paper I was impressed by the striking similarity of the problems and approaches of American agricultural economists and Hungarian experts of national economic planning. This similarity is made even more pronounced by the introduction of the so-called new economic mechanism here giving much more freedom of action to the individual enterprise — state and cooperative farms in this case — and thus increasing the possibility of collision between the interests of the enterprises and of the national economy as a whole. My contribution will be devoted to these similarities. First, I shall briefly review Professor Swanson's paper; later I shall deal with our attempts and experiments concerning the problem set forth in the paper.

The problem submitted in the introductory part of his paper may be summarized as follows. The comprehensive optimization models generally used, such as the well-known linear programming models, do not seem to fit the needs of the regional planners (in the U.S. case), of the central planning authorities (in the Hungarian case), or the needs of the individual producing units (farms in the U.S. case and enterprises including cooperative farms in the Hungarian case).

On the one hand, planners are not only interested in the regional and national optimum but also in the ways and means to obtain it. Considering that no detailed directives may be given to the individual producing units either in the United States or — according to the new regulations here — in Hungary, production can mainly be influenced by indirect methods, such as subsidies in the United States and dictated prices, taxes, and similar methods in Hungary. These variables, however, are not included in the comprehensive optimization models, and predictive or behavioristic models are therefore needed to determine the reaction pattern of the producers to changes of subsidies, prices, and so on. No methods are available, however, to link up these two kinds of models and to provide the optimum and the means to obtain the optimum at the same time.

The problem is quite similar from the point of view of the individual producing units. They are interested in profit, in growth and market share, or in simple subsistence — but not in regional or national optima. Such results of the calculations that the regional optima requires the transfer of labor resources from the less efficient farms to the more efficient ones would hardly induce these farmers to abandon their plots and apply for farmhands' jobs on the more efficient farms for instance. They would rather press for optimal solutions on the farm level, even if these are clearly suboptimal from the regional or national point of view. In the socialist countries, for instance in Hungary, the problem is quite similar, or even more pronounced, considering that the Hungarian government deliberately aims at preserving the regional balance of the country and attempts to support the development of the less developed areas or less productive agricultural cooperative farms.

Professor Swanson illustrates the problem by a very ingenious linear programming model. To summarize shortly the features of this model, it (a) starts from a closed region; (b) attempts to optimize only the agricultural sector; (c) assumes a one-product, two-resources, two-technologies production structure; (d) considers the matrices $B(t)$, $F(t)$, and $B(t)$, and so on, (i.e., the constraints) as predetermined; (e) assumes that the matrices $M_k(t)$, $L_k(t)$, and $A_k(t)$ (i.e., the matrices of technological coefficients) are given and may be determined independently from the production structure resulting from the calculations; (f) assumes further fixed prices, fixed again independently of the results, as well as fixed discount rates; (g) introduces interfarm and interperiod transfers; and finally (h) maximizes present value of the output of all farms taken together.

This model clearly illustrates the basic problems set out in the introductory part of the paper and also in my comments. There are of course some further grave problems. I would only mention (a) the interdependence of prices, quantities, and technologies; and (b) the force of vested interests preventing the transformation of the regional or national economy and the shaping of a more rational economic structure.

The paper offers three possible solutions to these problems and gives a further discussion on some possible modifications of the linear programming model presented here. The three solutions are the following: (a) to determine optimal plans for the representative farms under various price regimes, to add up the solutions, and to determine their outcome on the macroeconomic level; (b) to represent the constraints as price dependent functions, and to imitate the working of the "invisible hand" market mechanism in such a manner; and (c) to apply less formal techniques, such as simulation. Finally, the greatest part of the discussion on further modifications of the model concentrates upon the problem of conflicting aims.

May I suppose that Professor Swanson will fully agree with my opinion that the above method and the later discussion do not give any final answer to the problems set forth by him, and also mentioned in these comments. I would point to the following questions:

1. The problem of conflicting aims seems to be as intractable as ever. (a) On the one hand, I do not see how this problem can be

solved by modifying systematically the constraints and the objective function. Constraints must be considered as given, while by modifying the objectives we may assume away our problem. (b) On the other hand, the proposal of maximal terminal wealth set forth by my fellow Hungarian economist Vietorisz seems to be inadvisable both in poor and rich countries, as it may be contrary to optimal macroeconomic investment policy. I suppose it is needless to emphasize in the presence of American agricultural economists the possibility of overinvestment in the farming of a rich country. This is, however, a real possibility — at least in comparison with other uses of investible funds — even in poor countries. (c) Third, it is also very difficult to introduce regional or national aims as constraints if there is no real possibility to assert these theoretical constraints against the actual ones.

2. The problem of interdependency of prices, quantities, and technologies seems to be equally intractable. The author introduces the very interesting proposal to consider these constraints as price dependent functions, but I would be very grateful for some further details on this subject. This proposal means the determination of the supply elasticities of the productive consumption of final resources and intermediate products. To preserve the logical unity of the model, price elasticities of final consumption are equally needed. These elasticities may be built in the model in their original form or in the form of giving different values to some variables within different intervals. The theoretical merits of this solution are evident, but there are enormous practical difficulties. Although some studies are available as to the price elasticities of final demand, we have very scanty knowledge as to the price elasticities of productive consumption and as to the supply of basic resources. Considering that I am working on similar projects, I would be very grateful even personally if Professor Swanson were kind enough to point to any empirical results on this line.

3. The same problem arises in connection with multiperiod models. If the computations lead to results not especially different from past values or from values obtained from simple extrapolations, the technical coefficients obtained by statistical methods, thus determined independently of these optimizing models, may be used in the subsequent period without any further modifications. In case of large-scale structural changes, however, a modification of the technical coefficients is to be expected, and the existence of predetermined technological matrices for future time periods cannot be assumed. I would again be very grateful to Professor Swanson if he were kind enough to point to any attempt at modifying later period technological coefficients on the basis of the results obtained from calculations relating to the first periods studied. Of course the same holds not only for technological coefficients but also for constraints.

4. The last problem I would like to mention is the limited capacity of any community to absorb technical and social changes. Even the most beneficent and necessary reforms meet with social and political resistance, and the speed by which changes — even the most necessary

changes — diffuse may be very limited indeed. I would now put the
question whether in Professor Swanson's opinion this intricate problem may be dealt with satisfactorily by introducing fixed constraints.

Let us now turn to some recent Hungarian attempts to deal with
these problems. I must emphasize that I am speaking only of attempts
and not of results, because we were clearly unable to arrive at methods
that could satisfactorily solve these problems. I shall shortly deal with
two attempts, the model developed in the Ministry of Finances and the
model prepared for the Price Office. The aim of the Ministry of Finances model is to determine the reaction pattern of the enterprise to
the financial measures introduced by January 1 of this year. I must
admit now that the econometric studies preceding the introduction of
the new system of economic administration were not particularly extended, so that there is some uncertainty as to the reaction of the enterprises to the new prices, tax rates, and other financial measures
introduced now. It is therefore excessively important to determine the
most probable income, at least now, after the inauguration of the reforms. No classical predictive model, however, can be built for this
purpose, because we have no empirical evidence as to the reaction patterns of the enterprises, considering that there were very few price
changes in the past, and enterprises had a very limited interest in the
financial results of their activities. Another approach therefore had to
be worked out.

The method applied was to select a sample of enterprises and to
solve for each element of the sample a linear programming model
where the objective function is profit maximization (or rather some
slightly modified form of profit maximization) and where price regimes, tax rates, and so on, are taken as determined by the planning
authorities. Individual results are then summed up, and after solving
the problem of aggregation some conclusions may be obtained as to
possible disproportions in the national economy. It is also possible to
collate the results with the outcome of some planning models for the
national economy as a whole. It may also be attempted to introduce
several different price regimes and to determine the price structure
leading to the smallest disproportions and to the best allocation of resources.

It is clear that this attempt is the exact counterpart of that mentioned in the paper (the section on empirical studies, first paragraph).
It is equally clear that the method has some serious shortcomings. To
mention only the most important ones: (a) the problems of sampling
and aggregation, as well as the problems connected with providing the
data are very difficult; (b) the assumed reaction pattern of the enterprises is exceedingly simple, as profit maximization is an especially
simple objective particularly under conditions here; and (c) the connection of the economy-level and enterprise-level models is not satisfactorily solved even from the theoretical point of view.

In spite of these obvious shortcomings the model presents a great
step toward bringing simple linear models closer to reality. No em-

pirical results, however, are available up to now, and therefore no further remarks seem appropriate.

The Price Office model too departs from the decentralized decision structure of the economy. It considers the objectives concerning the most important macroeconomic variables (set up by the central planning authorities) and the most important industry-wide variables (set up by the individual industries and enterprises). It aims at a solution where the weighted sum of squared differences between the value system of original objectives — which may be conflicting or even contradictory — and the system of consistent, computed values is minimal. Constraints are dealt with in this approach in the same way as objectives, and the consistency of the computed values is ensured using extrapolated input-output technological coefficients, capital and labor coefficients computed from industry-wide CES production functions, and so on. The whole system is solved by a generalized method of the Theil-Boot quadratic programming procedure.

The model allows two variants. The simpler one deals only with quantities, while in the more elaborate one the interdependence of quantities, prices, and technologies is also built in. It is easy to see that this approach has much in common with the second type of empirical studies mentioned in the paper (section on empirical studies, second paragraph). Further, this model attempts to keep computed values in the neighborhood of the original independent extrapolations in order to provide solutions avoiding excessive social and economic changes.

As to the merits of this approach, I wish to emphasize the following. (a) Although it is true that the model tries to deal with conflicting aims, it is unable to solve this problem in a satisfactory manner. The consistency is assured, but the content of this optimal solution is highly problematic. The solution may be optimal only from a purely technical point of view, and the system of weights used in weighing the different aims set up by the different authorities may be in no direct connection with the inherent importance of the different objectives. (b) Although the interdependence of prices, quantities, and technologies is introduced in the more elaborate model, the empirical basis of the determination of the parameters describing this interdependence is extremely scanty.

We have already obtained some empirical results using the simpler model. These results show that the lack of technological alternatives (this is a basic feature of the model) may lead to serious distortions, because the consistency of the system may be assured in some cases only at the price of extremely big differences in the growth rates of the individual industries.

Chapter 11 ⟨⟩ SUPPLY ESTIMATION AND PREDICTIONS BY REGRESSION AND RELATED METHODS

Bernard Oury, *International Bank for Reconstruction and Development* (France)

REVIEW OF REGRESSION, SIMULATION, AND OTHER STATISTICAL MODELS

Regression Models

 TYPICAL REPRESENTATION of the classical linear regression model would be as follows:

$$Y_0 = \alpha_0 + \alpha_1 X_{1t} + \alpha_2 X_{2t} + \ldots + \alpha_n X_{nt} + \epsilon_t$$

where ϵ_t is a random variable (residual) with a mean of zero and a fixed variance. Y_t is the dependent variable to be explained and possibly predicted. The X's are the variables which are taken as given, independent or exogenous.

Autoregressive models look like classical regression models except that only lagged values of the dependent variables appear as explanatory variables. This type of model is attractive for predictive purposes, though it should be borne in mind that predictions may also be derived from a classical regression equation using time as an independent variable. The attractiveness of autoregressive models is slightly diminished by the fact that there are still gaps in our knowledge about the properties of estimators of their parameters (28).

Single-equation regression models are easy to estimate. In practice, however, much of the theory of economics is cast in the form of a system of simultaneous relationships. Such models usually involve endogenous variables, exogenous variables, and possibly lagged values of the endogenous variables. Each one of the equations of the model is introduced as representing a particular category of relationship. They are called structural equations which have to be resolved into as many reduced form equations as there are endogenous variables, each expressing an endogenous variable as a function of the exogenous or predetermined variables and error terms. Estimation of the reduced form equations proceeds from the same principles as for multiple regression and autoregression. But the existence of restriction on the coefficients complicates the problem considerably since the coefficients of the structural form of the model are sometimes more numerous than those in the reduced form. A useful procedure when estimating each structural equation in a simultaneous equation model is to ignore the restrictions affecting the coefficients of the other equations. The model is not then estimated en bloc, but each of its structural relations is considered in succession according to the principle of limited information-maximum likelihood. Also used is the ordinary least-squares method. The two-stage least-squares method devised by Theil constitutes the best estimation method for overidentified models. It involves relatively light computation and its results have a fairly good degree of precision (23).

Regression analysis, especially in the form of time series analysis, was the first to come into use in the early days of quantitative research in agricultural economics. A large number of time series models have since been developed both on the supply and the demand sides, generally around national or regional aggregates, by areas or by commodities, both for crops and for livestock products. The regression method is also the usual tool for the analysis of cross-sectional data derived from interfarm or interarea surveys. It has many advantages; it is a versatile and flexible approach. Provided we are concerned with linear and nonlinear phenomena, properly specified regression models are fairly realistic and computations are easily handled. From a practical point of view, however, the introduction of a large number of exogenous variables ought to be avoided. Theoretically there are no limitations to the number of variables to be included on the right side of the single regression equation, other than those imposed upon us by the size of the sample, in compliance with the proper performance of the various statistical tests required. Hence the number of variables associated in a given equation will be generally small in time series analysis where consistent historical series of data are usually short. By contrast a large number of variables can be dealt with in a single equation in cross-sectional analysis of individual farm surveys generally covering several hundreds of farms.

Another recognized advantage of single-equation regression models is that the parameter estimates which are usually obtained through least-squares regression have a certain "robustness." That is, the performance of the statistical tests associated with the method, which are valid only on the assumption that the samples are drawn from a normal population, give good results even when the parent populations are not normal. However, other tests involving the comparison of sample variances are very sensitive to the relaxation of the assumption of normality (40).

Difficulties would arise in interpreting the results of the regression analysis depending upon whether we focus on the coefficient of determination or on the parameter estimates and their standard errors. In current practice the fit of the time series equations may be improved when we use a time variable. We then get some measurement of how the dependent variable has been behaving over time. But we do not know why. Agricultural economists have a tendency to put more emphasis upon the goodness of fit (high R^2) than is usually the case in engineering and other experimental sciences, rather than focusing primarily on making a diagnosis of the relative roles of the various exogenous factors associated with supply. Hence there is a frequent reliance upon auto-regressive models to predict crop yields solely on the basis of previous performance or upon recursive regression equations with a lagged value of the dependent variable being included among the predetermined variables. In other single-equation supply models the output of a crop is, among other things, either a function of the number of acres planted the previous year or a function of yield obtained the previous year or even a function of the production of the previous year; whereas acreage, yield, or production of the previous year are left unexplained. Although a model can be a good forecasting model even if it does not really explain the underlying structural relationships, we must be aware that the better the diagnosis, the better the prescription and the more adequate the model for planning purposes.

Because economic theory is not explicit about the mathematical nature of most relationships among specified variables and because there are no general rules for interpreting regression models, regression analysis generally takes the form of empirical fitting of alternative algebraic functions to various combinations of variables through trial and error and then trying to decide which is the best as measured by the value of the coefficient of determination, sometimes with little concern for the ultimate implications of the properties of the algebraic model fitted to the data. It is often overlooked, for instance, that the signs and significant levels of the parameter estimates as well as the value of the test (Durbin-Watson or some variant) for autocorrelation among residuals in time series analysis are of primary importance. This is often underscored in supply analysis where the parameter estimates of the price variables may yield different signs and be more or less significantly different from zero, depending on the interplay of other exogenous factors associated with the price variable in the supply equation. I have in mind, for instance, the so-called "perversity" of the price response. Most analysts are explicit in noting that in traditional agriculture farmers do respond to changes in relative prices of products and factors. Some negative price parameter estimates may have been observed in modern and heavily technological agriculture, but they are generally associated with strong asset fixities and lack of immediate substitutes for short-run adjustment. In addition deflators which are used to make allowance for inflation generally are far from being fully satisfactory.

Least-squares regression models are technically derived around a structure defined by the means of the variables involved. Hence projections derived from such models are valid only within the structural framework prevailing "at the means" within the sample period for which the model is derived. One realizes immediately that there would be no major problems regarding cross-sectional models. Things are different, however, in time series analysis. Forecasts beyond the sample period derived from the model are valid only in relation to the prevailing structure underlying the model. Samples of 20, 25, or 30 years may appear reasonable when dealing with an agriculture where structural changes are relatively slow and significant only from one generation to the next. Changes may be even slower in traditional agriculture of the developing countries. By contrast, they have been much faster in recent years in the developed countries. The size of the time series is therefore of major importance in time series analysis of agriculture supply. A regression model, whether time series or cross-sectional, may be primarily useful for short-run forecasting. It may be useless for long-run forecasting exceeding, say, five years (i.e., the time horizon most used in economic planning).

As discussed by Fisher (12), the primary device for estimation of short-run reactions from regression models would be the use of first differences of the data. The use of absolutes for estimation purposes must necessarily involve a complete specification of the time structure of the model and of the variables thereof, including long-run as well as short-run elements. The use of first differences, however, enables us approximately to isolate short-run elements since we may often assume the long-run components of the equation to be relatively constant during the interval over which first differences are taken. This is frequently of considerable advantage since we need not specify the precise form that the long-run elements take.

Clearly, however, the purpose of agricultural development being one of bringing new technologies to bear, and thus disturbing the equilibrium of traditional agriculture, makes it rather irrelevant to use regression models derived around past observations for long-range forecasting in developing areas.

There are indications that cross-sectional analysis will be more promising for operational purposes in regional agricultural development planning, especially for project appraisal, provided adequate samples of observations are available. While time series analysis is usually applied to aggregate data, the cross-sectional approach would allow us to derive estimates from a microeconomic data base or from an interregional data base, and thus bring the analysis to bear on factors generally left outside the more limited time series framework with no time interference. In addition, cross-sectional analysis does not raise some of the complex problems of statistical estimation encountered in time series analysis, notably the problems of collinearity and serial correlation among error terms. Finally, both time series and cross-sectional data may also be pooled (generally over a limited number of years) for the purpose of the analysis.

Simulation Models

With the advent of large-capacity high-speed computers, simulation has emerged as a practical means of solving models of microeconomic and macroeconomic behavior. Simulation is a word used quite freely among economists. In its broad meaning it is essentially a technique that involves setting up a model of a real-world system of phenomena and then experimenting on the model through manipulation of variables regarded as instrumental reaching certain targets. A mathematical model of decision rules, information sources, and other interactions among the components of a system is formulated. The validity of the model is tested by comparing computer results with all pertinent available knowledge about the actual system under analysis. The model is then revised until it is an acceptable representation of the real system. When an acceptable representation of the real system is achieved, those organizational relationships and decision rules which are feasibly altered in the actual system are redesigned. The behavior of the redesigned system is tested by simulation on the computer. Comparison of new results with the former will provide a simulated test of recommended improvements in the system (15). Simulation does not include the restrictive assumption of an optimum solution. Hence improvements are made through successive *tâtonnements*, and simulation may perhaps be viewed as the most effective method of dealing with decision making under certainty.

There are a number of basic techniques and many variations which might be applicable in searching for optimum values of the decision variables in simulation studies. The majority may be classified as either (a) techniques in which the analyst predetermines the pattern of search before the simulation runs begin or (b) techniques in which the analyst determines the method of search (or set of decision rules to be used in the search), and the computer carries out the search guided by the decision rules and results up to that point. Relatively little use of the latter type of technique in which the computer itself is used to guide the search has been reported in the literature (24). However techniques of the latter type which generally have been termed "optimum seeking" methods have been discussed extensively by Wilde (46).

In a more restrictive sense, simulation is a numerical technique for conducting experiments on a digital computer which involves certain types of mathematical and logical models that describe the behavior of a microeconomic or macroeconomic system (or some component thereof) over some extended period of real time (25). Two variants of the simulation approach are operating games, now popular in microeconomics, and Monte Carlo analysis, which is a simulation technique for problems having a stochastic or probabilistic basis. The Monte Carlo method capitalizes on the two basic facts: (a) that it is possible to empirically approximate a probability distribution as closely as desired on the basis of an adequate number of random drawings from the distribution and (b) that it frequently is a great deal easier to obtain random drawings from a distribution than it is to analytically deduce the form of the distribution (28). Monte Carlo methods have been developed for simulating most types of probability distributions, and computer subroutines are usually available to handle this part of the job. They can also be used to obtain approximate solutions to strictly deterministic models by simulating a stochastic process whose moments, density function, or cumulative distribution function satisfy the functional relationships or the solution requirements of deterministic problems.

In addition to exogenous and endogenous variables, simulation
models include status variables. As in regression models, the exogenous variables are the independent variables of the simulation model.
They are assumed to have been predetermined and given independently
of the system. They are classified as controllable by the policy makers
(or instrumental) and noncontrollable when generated by the environment. Exogenous variables may be used in two different ways in simulation experiments. They may be given parameters determined by either the environment or the decision makers, which have to be estimated
first and read into the computer as input data, or they are stochastic
variables generated by computer subroutines.

Status variables describe the state of the system or one of its components either at the beginning of a time period, at the end of a time
period, or during a time period. These variables interact with both the
exogenous and endogenous variables of the system according to the assumed functional relationship of the system under analysis. The value
of a status variable during a particular period may depend not only on
the values of one or more exogenous variables for some preceding period but also on the value of certain output variables for some preceding period.

Endogenous variables are the dependent or output variables of the
system and are generated from the interaction of the system's exogenous and status variables.

Basically a simulation model includes two types of functional relationships, namely identities and operating characteristics which are
used to describe and generate the behavior of the system under analysis.
Identities take the form of either definitions or tautological statements
about components of the model. An operating characteristic is a hypothesis, usually a deterministic relationship relating the simulator's
endogenous and status variables to its exogenous variables.

A computer simulation experiment therefore consists in a series
of computer runs in which we test empirically, using simulation data,
the sensitivity of the endogenous variables to alternative factor levels.
And as in regression analysis the accuracy of the results of a simulation depends to a great extent on the accuracy of the estimates of the
parameters of operating characteristics.

Besides farm management games (11), applications of the simulation approach are still few in agricultural economics where they are
primarily related to the livestock sector (15, 21), to water resources
development (16), and to the appraising of farm programs (44). Since
simulation is aimed at representing what happens in a system by trac-
ing simulated transactions and events, it may also be a useful tool to
generate missing data (1).

Other Statistical Models

Attempts have been made to use the transitional matrix approach
in supply analysis notably to forecast the components of output, namely

yield and acreage, showing how crop yield and crop acreage adjustments take place over time. A Markov chain process requires the definition of a given set of states. The process can be in one and only one of these states at a given time, and it "jumps" successively from one stage to another. Each move is called a step, and the probability that the process moves from state S_i to state S_j depends only on the state S_i that it occupied before the move. The transition probability matrix P_{ij} is given for every pair of states. Also required is the definition of an initial starting state at which the process is assumed to begin. The transitional matrix is a matrix which, when multiplied by the vector of frequencies representing the state of the process at any time t, yields the vector of frequencies specifying the state of the process at time t+1. In the simplest case the model specifies that the transition probabilities remain constant from period to period, and each of the transitional probabilities is estimated directly on the basis of some available body of data. When feasible this particular approach is highly attractive.

Difficulties relating to the use of this method to forecast yield and acreage changes relate in part to the terms of reference used for the definition of starting states. In the case of crop yields, they were defined by Bostwick (7) according to the level of income they would produce in relation to partial or total coverage of costs. In the case of acreage distribution among crops an optimal acreage distribution can be given as a function of current prices (37). The optimal distribution of land among crops is a function of prices prevailing in the market and the expected change in total cropland available. A change in the market prices of crops changes the optimal acreage distribution, making it necessary for farmers to rearrange their acreage distribution. Transition probabilities giving the probability of switching land from each crop in period t to any crop in period t+1 describe in probability terms the particular switching of land among crops. The acreage adjustment model could perhaps be better estimated with the current return from each crop (yield per acre times price) individually entering the transition probability function as an independent variable. This would require an advance knowledge of yields expected per acre.

The model can be reduced to a two-crop process. Take for example the empirical analysis of wheat and feedgrain supply. The acreage distribution among wheat, barley, corn, and oats can involve four separate crops, or it can be collapsed into only two crops — wheat and feedgrains. The price structure may then be collapsed into a single price variable defined as the difference between the return of crop i (wheat) and an index of return on the other three crops.

The application of the transitional probability approach may also be combined with linear programming (9, 22). The transition probabilities from one optimal crop distribution in one period to a new optimal crop distribution in the next period can be affected by the policy decision which dictates the action to be taken in every period. An optimal crop distribution will be the distribution under which total expected profit from the process is maximized. In this framework, for each

period of the process an optimal choice from a given set of alternative resource contributions can be made efficiently by programming
methods.

Agricultural adjustments at the regional level lead to, or result
from, changes at the farm level. The effects of any change initiated
either at the micro or the macro level on the other level may be accentuated or diminished by different directional changes in the number
of farms (43). Cohort analysis is a relatively simple technique often
used to estimate changes in the numbers of farms and farm operators
(5).

ECONOMIC AND DATA ENVIRONMENT WHERE THESE
MODELS ARE APPLICABLE

Economic Environment

There are several aspects to be considered with respect to the
economic and data environment where these models are applicable. A
first one is related to the stage of economic development. Obviously
these statistical techniques have grown not only with the data in advanced countries but also where the computing facilities were first developed, notably in the United States. The first known empirical studies
of agricultural producers' response in developing countries were, however, made in India as early as in 1934 (39). Attempts to estimate supply models in the developing countries have been relatively few in numbers until the last few years, although many studies have commented on
certain basic relationships which form the foundations for such models
for some commodities: coffee, cocoa, tobacco, cotton, rice, and jute.
The momentum has now been picking up while a genuine interest in applying modern techniques of analysis was developing in several international agencies.

A first characteristic of traditional agriculture is that the state-
of-the-arts is viewed as constant — there are no structural changes.
Expected crop yield per acre may then be hypothesized to be constant
in the long run. Hence yield may be regarded as predetermined. A
second characteristic is that changes in acreage may be little instrumental in explaining year-to-year changes in total production. A third
characteristic is that the considerable importance of the agricultural
sector in the whole economy implies a considerable on-farm consumption of unmarked agricultural products, thus making it difficult to estimate farmers' price responses satisfactorily. Attempts have been
made to estimate supply models restricted to the market surplus (4).
A fourth characteristic is a frequent lack of an adequate data base.
Experience would suggest that cross-sectional regression analysis may
therefore be more promising for regional planning purposes in developing countries as sample survey techniques and data gathering are
improving. Cross-sectional data often may be obtained for recent

years; as mentioned earlier, both time series and cross-sectional data may also be pooled (generally over a limited number of years) for the purpose of the analysis.

Differences in emphasis may exist between centrally planned economies and market economies, with perhaps more emphasis being put on the role of structural shifters and technical coefficients in the former rather than on the role of supply shifters proper and on farmers' price responsiveness as in the latter. This seminar may indeed throw more light on possible contrasts and similarities in application of quantitative methods between the two major types of economies, eastern and western, which otherwise seem more and more engaged in tackling problems of similar nature.

Another important aspect of the applicability of these models is concerned with the level of aggregation at which they may be used. Most regression models of supply response have so far been developed for individual commodities providing little basis for inference about the aggregate agricultural output. Griliches (14) has made some tentative estimates of the aggregate output agricultural function for the United States by expressing output as a function of relative price, weather, trend, and lagged output. The price variable was specified as the ratio of prices received by farmers to prices paid by farmers for input factors, including interest, taxes, and wage rates. Heady and Tweeten (19) have proposed a different aggregate supply model in which total current output entering the market system is predetermined by the ratio of past prices received by farmers and past prices paid, durable input levels, government programs, weather, and trend.

Agricultural economists have nevertheless gradually become aware of the problems associated with the analysis of highly aggregative time series data, including problems associated with errors of observation. No method of analysis is a substitute for evidence that has not been generated or that has been lost in aggregation.

A gradual realization of the inadequacy of aggregate data for predicting the effect of government policy measures has been developing over the last decade. This has been coupled in time with three major developments which are bringing about substantial changes in economic research and which now make the microanalytic approach feasible. The first of these developments is the emergence of improved sample survey techniques and instruments. The second is the development of computational facilities considerably more powerful than anything previously available. The third is the realization that even in a market economy the optimization of the behavior of each individual or sectoral unit does not necessarily coincide with the optimal behavior of the whole economy. It is ultimately a matter of how to reconcile the individual or sectoral interest (and for that matter the regional interest) with the general interest. As Béssière (6) pointed out, "Peripheral interest and general interest are not immediately compatible, but they should be rendered so as to allow the economy to function well. This is a problem which involves the structuring of economic systems, that is, the removal therefrom of agents which one would like to be able to leave as autonomous as possible." Hence, the notion of separability in economics.

A microanalytic approach aimed at deriving individual farm models would be attractive to analyze the implications of alternative developmental strategies at farm level, to derive estimates of regional production capacity and commodity supply, and to evaluate the sensitivity of farmers' response to price changes as well as to other variables instrumental in reaching planned targets. A large number of farms could be surveyed and one may conceive of specific types of models for every category of farms. Parameters of such models may be estimated from large samples and the number of variables associated with the process of agricultural production and supply that may be investigated may then be quite large. The approach does not appear feasible yet as it would remain expensive for some time. It would also raise organizational and coordination problems, and difficulties would still arise in the interpretation and the statistical aggregation of the results. A middle ground may exist between these two extremes which would deal with groups of farms having similar behavioral characteristics.

The principle of separability might also be called upon in support of the study of individual commodity supply model on a regional basis. Opportunities for substituting one commodity for another are theoretically great on farms because the same resources can be used to produce any one of several products. In practice, however, producers have only a few alternatives for short-run adjustments to price changes because of specialization and asset-fixities brought about by structural changes. In advanced countries supply analysts have learned from experience that prices have only a limited role in determining the volume of agricultural production. The supply function of a certain number of individual agricultural commodities therefore may be relatively autonomous at a regional level.

Data Environment

The factors affecting agricultural output can be classified as (a) ecological (soil and climate), (b) economic (cost and price relationships), (c) technological (the processes and methods of production involved), and (d) institutional (tradition, law, and government policy).

In deriving regional models of agricultural supply, variables have to be specified in such a way that in addition to being manageable the number of explanatory variables involved in the equations remains within the limits imposed by statistical theory. Time series data may be unavailable for some factors over periods of similar time spans. The size of the time series is therefore a major limiting constraint in regression analysis of time series. The difficulty may sometimes be obviated. On the one hand, it may be assumed that no significant change has taken place in land quality distribution among crops from one year to another. Weather would then be the only ecological factor of primary importance in agricultural supply time series models. On the other hand, in some cases data which are actually available may for some categories of factors be transformed into composite indexes (weather, technology, prices), which would help save degrees of freedom.

As pointed out earlier, the weather factor is especially important as a supply shifter, and it may overshadow the response to economic variables such as prices and even cancel out the effects of technological inputs. The concept of "normal" weather conditions and "normal" yields are at the heart of the problem of agricultural commodity supply analysis. Normal weather conditions at any location in the world are defined by the International Weather Convention on the basis of the averages of observed weather data calculated over a period of 30 years. Consequently the "normal" agricultural yield of any crop with regard to weather at any site would conceivably be that yield that is obtained under "normal" weather conditions. Departure from "normal" weather conditions would result in departures from "normal" yields.

Economic activity outside agriculture is generally much more subject to managerial control because of its nonbiological production processes and also because of the short period (sometimes very short) and fully controlled amplitude of the cycle of production. Since agricultural production takes time, producers cannot quickly adjust to prevailing market prices. On the other hand, individual farmers have almost no control over the market. The adjustment becomes perceptible only after a period of time depending on biological cycles and asset-fixities. The specification of farmers' price expectations is a difficult task. Price variables to be considered as supply shifters are usually the prices of the commodity under study and those of its most direct substitutes. Generally the number of such substitutes is rather limited and not as large as theoreticians sometimes like to assume. Generally the lag in the reactions of all farm operators will be distributed over a period of time. It will be a distributed response — the mathematical formulation of which has been attempted by Nerlove (26) and recently reviewed by Griliches (13). A major additional difficulty regarding the price response is related to the inflationary process which should be adequately allowed for. In time series models of agricultural supply, producers' price expectations are generally formulated on the basis of past prices deflated by some price index. Realism would indeed suggest that in producers' minds, year t-1 should weight relatively more than year t-2 which in turn should weight relatively more than year t-3 and so on down to year t-m. This view is close to Koych's formulation (23) that the coefficients of the price lag equation should be decreasing in a constant proportion with increasing lags. Alternatively some moving average pattern distributing the lag equally over preceding years may prevail in producers' minds, depending on the characteristics of the crop.

Because of the difficulties encountered in dealing with technological

changes, the time trend variable, t, has been the proxy generally used
in time series analysis of agricultural supply to allow for structural
changes. Observation of the real-world situation suggests, however,
the need for distinguishing among several dominant technologies at play
in agriculture and combining their effects in view of their complementary nature. Though the importance of current input factors such as
fertilizer is paramount, fertilizers are not very effective where there
is no adequate moisture (i.e., no water supply) available to the crop.
The water technology (irrigation, drainage) and the biochemical technology (fertilizer, pesticides) by their very nature are basically different and complementary.

Similarly we may also distinguish two more types of technology:
the mechanical technology (tractors, implements) and the biological
technology or genetic improvements (new varieties such as hybrids).
Depending on the stage of agricultural development, a crop supply model
would therefore include one or several structural shifters, namely irrigated acreage as percentage of total acreage or (better) acre-inches
of irrigation actually applied; draft power (i.e., tractor-cultivated acreage as percent of total acreage); hybrid (new varieties) planted acreage
as percent of total planted acreage; fertilizer consumption per acre or
fertilizer acreage as percent of total crop acreage; percentage acreage
treated to pesticides.

Observation also suggests that although the law of diminishing returns applies to a frozen technology, the underlying dynamic tendency
of each input category is one of technological progress. Hence the
marginal efficiency of technology in total should not be expected to di-
minish.

Factors having long-run effects would introduce rigidities in the
production apparatus. Others being short run are more likely to be
subjected to year-to-year variations. It should also be noted that any
one of these forms of technology has individually marked a historical
milestone in agricultural development. The age of irrigation, for instance, has been long lost in history, and the technique has been known
for centuries in many developing countries. By contrast, the age of
mechanical power and the age of artificial fertilizer go back a few decades only. And it may be observed that the use of fertilizer on a significant scale in Western Europe (an area with a low land-population
ratio) generally preceded the age of mechanical power, whereas it has
been the opposite in North America (an area with a high land-population
ratio), where the use of fertilizer on a significant scale has developed
only after the second World War. The relative, or the joint, importance
of the biochemical and the mechanical technology in the supply model
therefore will depend on the economic environment.

Should the data environment allow us to differentiate among current and long-run input factors, it might in some cases be possible to
substitute a two-variable technological matrix for the larger matrix
previously described. In such a case the main difficulty would arise
from the need for units of measurement which would allow us to collapse

several current inputs into a single variable and several long-run inputs into another single variable. A possible solution might be found in the use of production expenses data for current inputs along with production expenses data for long-run inputs — both adequately deflated — or in the use of current input expenses as percentage of total farm operating expenses. One advantage of including input quantities or percentage variables rather than input prices in the model is that it may be done both in market economies and in centrally planned economies. Since a major target of regional agricultural development is one of increasing agricultural output through planned implementation of modern technology, derived factor demand schedules may accompany the supply model to help in pricing the cost per unit of implementing necessary input factors and in estimating the proportion thereof that would be desirable for the government to subsidize in order to achieve a suitable rate of adoption of the various forms of technology by producers.

Depending upon the economic and data environment, the supply models would therefore include relevant weather variables, relevant supply shifters, and relevant structural shifters. It may also be possible to allow in the model for government policy including such devices as acreage allotments, production quota, carry-over in public storage (i.e., in government hands, such as C.C.C. in the United States or O.N.I.C. for grains in France), percentage of crop under loan, and so forth. A percentage-wise specification of such institutional shifters may also be possible (30). The ultimate formulation which the general approach would assume in an advanced economic environment cannot be ignored while attempting to construct simplified models for less developed regions where serious limitations arise. Sophisticated agricultural supply models may not yet be wholly appropriate for less developed areas; there should be, at least for the moment, a rather pragmatic approach to model construction in such environments where cross-sectional analysis and simulation techniques may in cases prove more relevant.

COMPARISONS OF REGRESSION MODELS WITH NORMATIVE MODELS IN REALISM AND APPLICABILITY

I will use the term development as being synonymous with economic policy. It requires an explicit formulation of the ends and means of regional development policy. Tinbergen (42) specified the theory of economic policy in terms of target variables (intended effects or goals of economic policy), instrumental variables (or causal factors that can be used to influence the target variables in the desired direction), and irrelevant variables (or negligible factors with respect to a given problem). Though Tinbergen was primarily concerned with the development of consistent economic policies at the national level, the same concepts appear applicable to regional development.

Areas in the process of economic development are essentially agricultural, and the major problems of agricultural development rest on supply response or output quantities and their inseparable relationships with resource inputs prices and ecological conditions. What is primarily needed for development is usually change in the structure of agriculture and supply (17).

I do not know of attempts to test a normative model against "conventional" regression analysis other than those of Schaller and Dean (38) in their study of agricultural production in Fresno County, California, and my (30) cotton regression model for the Mississippi Delta (1946-62), estimating acreage as well as yield per acre for comparison with Day's (8) recursive programming model for the same area. My remarks regarding the comparison of regression models with normative models with reference to supply prediction therefore are only tentative.

Normative models are essentially prescriptive. Linear programming models have been largely used by agricultural economists to specify the optimum organization of resources and activities on farms, to suggest desirable adjustments, to specify profit-maximizing mixes as well as cost-minimizing methods, to indicate interregional patterns of resource use and product specialization in agriculture, and to solve related types of problems (18). During the last few years a number of alternatives to the simple linear programming models have been proposed, which in some way take into account the elements of risk in the decision-making environment. Multiperiod or so-called "dynamic" programming models have been used to take into account the fact that production decisions require a certain period of time to complete and that investment decisions result in stocks of land and equipment that will last for several production periods (25).

Recursive programming is a synthesis of time series and linear programming. It uses linear programming to make year-to-year sequential predictions of output, prices, and incomes over a period of years. The theory underlying recursive analysis (48), is that current production depends upon past prices, while current prices depend upon current production in a cobweb pattern. Thus if we know prices and production prior to year t, we can predict the probable production in year t; thus probable prices in year t; and then probable production in year t+1; and so on. Regional recursive programming models of agricultural production have been developed notably by Day (8), Schaller and Dean (38), and Heidhues (20); my experience with the approach is only indirect and derived from my exposure to their works. Among Day's contributions is the basic idea that programming restraints can be generated in a recursive manner, thus giving the usual linear programming model a dynamic property. The essential difference between dynamic programming and recursive programming is that in the former, planning is subjected to a single optimizing decision, whereas in the latter it is subjected to a sequence of optimizing decisions.

A recursive programming "problem" can be defined for each year based on data for the preceding year. Farmers' decisions are assumed to be independent in the short run. It is assumed that these decisions are based on farmers' "expected" profits from production alternatives and on their available resources. Next year's plan is viewed as a deviation from the current cropping distribution. Accordingly the data used in the recursive programming model are "expected" values. For example, actual prices received in year t-1 may be defined on the expected prices for year t. Similarly, model restraints depend on the previous level or previous use of resources.

Restrictions in the model include, in addition to the resource constraints commonly specified in linear programming, "flexibility" and "technological capacity" restraints on the maximum allowable year-to-year changes in the solution from the preceding year. Estimation of the allowable rates of changes is based on time series data of past changes. Consequently, although the solution to the model is "optimum," it is a highly restrained optimum in conformity with farmers' past actual behavior, thus approximating a more predictive solution.

Apart from an explicit treatment of time and the addition of recursive restraints, the recursive programming model is quite similar to conventional linear programming. The basic unit of analysis may be a single farm, a group of homogeneous farms, or a geographic region. The activities in the model are the production alternatives or other choices open to the unit. The objective of the model is to maximize total net returns or profit to the unit, subject of course to the restraints estimated recursively for the particular year. These restraints are perhaps the most critical component of the model.

The flexibility restraints are simply upper and lower bounds on the allowable year-to-year change in the average solution for each crop entering the model. Their role is to account inasmuch as possible for the forces of various nature causing lags in adjustment. In a sense the flexibility restraints can be viewed as naïve forecasts of future production under "favorable" (upper bound) and "unfavorable" (lower bound) conditions. The recursive programming model then refines the forecasts by taking into account all the additional explicit information available. If this "refinement" did not take place, there would be no advantage (and probably a disadvantage) to the recursive programming method as compared to conventional regression analysis on a crop-by-crop basis.

Like the upper and lower crop bounds, the technological capacity restraints are determined from past year-to-year changes in the actual acreage or production associated with that technology. This procedure assumes that the rate of adoption of technology is limited less by factors such as lack of knowledge and limited supplies. It assumes that the demand for the asset equals or exceeds the supply. The resulting restraint on the expansion of a profitable technology indirectly restricts the abandonment rate of other less profitable techniques. Thus the technological capacity restraints isolate certain of the forces accounted for indirectly by upper and lower acreage bounds.

As in other programming models, physical resource restraints

such as available land, labor, fertilizer, and irrigation water are also
included. Often the restraint magnitude is known in advance, like the
total land area. However future resource restraints are often unknown
and must be estimated from data on past rates of change and resource
levels.

Schaller and Dean (38) tested the recursive programming model
against conventional regression analysis of time series data, using
three single equations, least-squares models fitted independently. For
each crop the regression model which gives the "best fit" (high R^2) is
selected for the comparison.

The alternate regression models used by Schaller and Dean for the
comparison were as follows:

$$X_t = a + bX_{t-1} + cP_t^* + dT + e_t \tag{1}$$

$$X_t = a' + b'X_{t-1} + c'R_t^* + d'A_t + e_t' \tag{2}$$

$$X_t = a'' + b''X_{t-1} + c''R_t^* + d''G_t + e_t'' \tag{3}$$

where the variables are defined as follows:

X_t = actual planted acreage of a given crop in year t (or harvested acreage if planted data are not available)

X_{t-1} = acreage planted (or harvested) in year t-1

R_t^* = "expected" gross per acre returns, year t (yield per harvested acre, year t-1, times P_t^*)

P_t^* = "expected" price per unit of output, year $t = P_{t-1}$, the price actually received in year t-1, or the support price for year t, whichever is higher

A_t = total country acreage available to "included" crops, year t, equals the recursive programming model's total land restraint

G_t = a shift variable representing acreage controls on other crops or the diverted acreage effect; $G_t = 0$ when no control; $G_t = 1$ when control

T = a trend or time variable representing the effects of changes in technology

Like the recursive programming model, these equations express
the hypothesis that the acreage of a crop depends on its acreage in the
preceeding year and on other variables such as expected price, expected
gross returns, total resource in land, and the presence or absence of
government programs. Both the recursive programming and the regression model are recursive, meaning that acreage in year t can be
predicted in year t-1 from known values.

In the recursive programming model the historical relation between X_t and X_{t-1} is used to estimate crop bounds and P_t^* or R_t^* are
used to compute expected net returns. The variable A_t is broken down
into subregion and soil types that serve as restraints. The government
allotment variable is also handled as a restraint of the recursive programming model.

To obtain estimates of crop output as well as acreage from regression analysis, the acreage estimates from the most acceptable of the regression equations were multiplied by "expected" yield taken as the three-year moving average of actual yields over the past three years.

In the recursive programming model, acreage and yield are predicted simultaneously, whereas in the regression analysis model, the yields are predetermined. The comparison of output results should therefore provide insight into the effect of treating the two components of output endogenously.

From the explanatory point of view, Schaller and Dean observed that regression analysis would provide better estimates during periods of smaller changes and relatively stable structure and that the recursive programming model would be more effective for prediction purposes under situations of sharp changes in structure.

Although they are an attractive feature of the recursive programming approach, one may question the importance of the flexibility constraints, and Schaller and Dean do. If the upper and lower bounds were indeed always effective, the upper bounds would always be predicted acreages of the most profitable crops and lower bounds the predicted acreages of the least profitable ones. Conclusions based on predictive tests indicated that neither model does a particularly outstanding job of real prediction as opposed to explanation, though the regression analysis would still appear slightly superior. As to projections, it is difficult to draw any definite conclusions since actual data are unavailable for reference.

Schaller's and Dean's arguments are (a) that errors in yield estimates also occur because of weather variations and like other predictive techniques the recursive programming model does not attempt to account for these factors and (b) that it is generally difficult to allow for government policy variables, namely acreage allotments in regression analysis (where they use dummy variables; acreage allotments are used as the upper acreage bound in the recursive programming model, and government payments are included).

I find it difficult to agree with them at this moment on these points. There still are open questions. Nevertheless I have some hunches that there might be better regression equations of crop acreage than those proposed by Schaller and Dean to perform their test, where, incidentally, the parameter estimates of the expected return variable are generally found nonsignificant. First, one may say that there are alternative algebraic formulations which could have been used, such as the log linear of semilog ones. In addition, although it seems logical to use recursive regression models for the sake of comparison, it does not mean necessarily that the recursive acreage regression model provides the best acreage regression equation. Second, the specification of the exogenous variables entering the acreage regression equations might also be different. Third, instead of using dummy variables to allow for acreage allotments, one might think of introducing this institutional factor either as percentage of total cropland or as percentage of the acreage grown to the crop the previous year. I have used such a specification in my cotton model for the Mississippi Delta with satisfactory results. Fourth, allowing for weather variations is undoubtedly a most difficult problem in regression analysis. Nevertheless many composite weather indexes of broad meaning have been proposed. Ambitious formulas have been calculated which were recently reviewed by O.E.C.D. experts (27). These generally focus on the importance of precipitation and of evaporation from the soil surface and transpiration from plants called "evapotranspiration," as those of Thornwaite (41) and Penman (36). Unfortunately time series of the data required for these types of indexes are not generally available everywhere, least of all in the developing areas. Hence these more complex formulas cannot meet current needs.

A relatively simple approach to the problem of allowing for weather influence upon crops in agricultural production analysis has been tried (29) by using de Martonne's (10) and Angström's (2) aridity or humidity indexes. The main advantages of the method are simplicity and consistency in definition over long periods of time. These indexes are easily computed provided basic weather data, namely precipitation and temperature, are available. They may provide for various types of analysis of agricultural production, especially in time series analysis, an acceptable alternative to more elaborate and expensive estimations.

In many respects, then, regression analysis would appear more directly useful for predicting farmers' response than conventional linear programming. Because regression results are based on actual past changes in production, they are more likely to take into account farmers' likes and dislikes and other considerations which are omitted in the usual programming model. Further advantages of regression are (a) the relative accessibility of aggregative data compared with the difficulty of obtaining more detailed input, output, and resource data required in linear programming, (b) relatively low cost and quick aggregative results, and (c) the ability, given the satisfaction of certain statistical assumptions underlying the model, to make probability and confidence statements about the results.

Despite these advantages the regression techniques cannot account for the effects of changes in the decision-making environment with the same degree of realism as is possible with linear programming. Estimated coefficients reflect only a historical structure. Thus sharp changes in structure, due to forces such as technological change and government programs, make it exceedingly difficult to use regression analysis for direct prediction. Purely statistical problems also occur when the number of past observations is limited or when the intercorrelation among "independent" variables is high.

Therefore the comparison would rather suggest the complementary or supplementary roles of programming and regression for predicting farmers' supply response.

APPROPRIATE REGRESSION MODELS

Adequacy of Regression Models in Supply Analysis

Much has been written about the adequacy or inadequacy of regression models and their suitability or unsuitability for supply analysis; yet most of the work in supply analysis has been in the form of regression analysis of time series or cross-sectional data (17). Alternative supply regression models need to be evaluated with reference to the purpose of the analysis and the pertinent answers needed by policy makers.

Should the criterion be only one of how the equations meet various statistical tests, then we may be content with high coefficients of determination and high levels of significance of the parameter estimates.

Should the criterion be also how well the model fits into the whole conceptual framework upon which it is built, then we should be aware of Wold's (48) warning that "in regression analysis of nonexperimental data the formal tests of significance, however refined, carry little weight as compared with the nonformal and nonquantitative significance that is embodied in results derived from independent sources, provided these results support one another and form an organic whole."

Should the criterion be one of timeliness and flexibility, regression models should not be regarded as once-for-all constructions. They should be updated and if necessary reformulated as time passes in order to improve their validity and derive better explanation and new projections for the years ahead.

Supply models needed in regional agricultural development must have a twofold purpose. On the one hand, they are needed to assist economists in formulating a diagnosis to support a judgment. On the other hand, they are intended to be prescriptive and predictive by throwing some light upon the consequences of future changes in the variables involved in their construction and instrumental in achieving certain desired targets. In attempting to derive such models we always work in two stages. First we have to specify a structure and estimate its parameters. Second we go on to use the structure as a basis for prescription and prediction. Regression models therefore may be appropriate or inappropriate as to the mathematical formulation of the theory of the phenomenon, as to the availability of the data, and as to the statistical estimation of the parameters. A model should nevertheless be sufficiently bold to ask for the data. Data collection is difficult — a time-consuming job which may take as much as 90 percent of the time required for its construction. Assuming that there are four to five dominant factors in every one of the categories described earlier, the theoretical supply model would ultimately involve about 16 to 20 explanatory variables. The size of the sample jointly with the availability of the data is therefore likely to be one of the major constraints as to the adequacy of supply regression models, although each category of factors may also be dealt with separately through stratification of the sample observations.

In discussing the adequacy of regression models we must also be aware of the limitations of the technique itself despite its advantages and its near universal application. Frequently the econometric approach will itself be able to produce no more than crude and unreliable estimates of the supply relationships. As recently recalled by White (45), experience in countries where the regression approach has been used intensively suggests that, for some reason, "reliable" findings frequently are not trustworthy. Three major criticisms are often made.

First, the criterion of reliability most used currently, while seeming to be a very rigorous one, is actually somewhat lax, for it accepts as "significant" or "reliable" any estimate of causal relationships which is very unlikely to be in error by as much as 100 percent.

Secondly, the improved efficiency of electronic computers has made it easy, and customary, to try out many alternative sets of plausible causal factors which might influence the dependent variable. This greatly increases the likelihood that the movement of the set of independent factors selected conformed to the movements of the dependent variable by pure chance.

Thirdly, where the estimated relationship can be used to make a successful forecast of next year's value of the dependent variable, the reliability of the relationship is considered to be very greatly increased. But the improvement of reliability is likely to be made inadequate by allowance for several factors of particular interest to policy makers. The fact that the econometric evidence provided by regression analysis is often much less reliable than usually admitted does not mean, however, that it should be discarded without discernment. Careful regression analysis may still be superior to any other means of obtaining estimates of the needed supply relationships. Models may be formulated and reformulated again and again until more reliable evidence is obtained. When he does use the findings, the policy maker must know how trustworthy they really are because policy measures will be influenced by the degree of confidence that can be placed in the regression estimates of expected results. Even when regression models succeed in deriving the influence of particular causal variables with a sufficient degree of reliability, it still may be necessary to place some reliance on other guides to policy making, such as the survey method.

Much of the skepticism as to the validity of supply regression models can be ascribed to the misspecification of the mathematical form of the regression as well as to the improper specification of the explanatory variables. In addition, a misuse of statistical tests of reliability consists in their application to series of data which have been "purified" of so-called "non-sense" observations. While the exclusion of years in which the dependent variable was affected by important external "disturbances" may be justified in some cases, it is an objectionable practice as to the adequacy of a regression equation for diagnosis as well as forecasting purposes.

Tentative Supply Model of General Applicability (31)

As previously described, changes in agricultural supply may be influenced by changes in the number of producing units and/or by changes in output per producing unit.[1] These changes may be transitory and attributable to supply shifters and/or lasting and associated with structural changes. It is often argued that the acreage and yield components of agricultural output are generally influenced by different factors. Proponents of this hypothesis suggest that if a model is intended to explain both acreage and yield, respective equations considered in reduced form would involve two different sets of exogenous variables. Pursuant to the same reasoning, however, it may be quickly realized that the argument amounts to saying that a certain factor influencing significantly one component of output, say acreage, does not influence significantly the other yield or vice versa. Therefore one may as well regard acreage and yield as being determined by a single set of exogenous factors. And when the hypothesis is statistically tested on the data, some of the factors in the set will turn out to be statistically significant about yield or vice versa.

Hence we may hypothesize that should it be possible to "explain" output Q independently from a certain equation in reduced form, the "explanation" thus obtained should be consistent with the "explanation" of Q derived indirectly from the combination of concomitant "explanations" derived from acreage and yield respectively. In the generalized model, visualized factors which would give parameter estimates with the same sign in both the acreage and yield equations would be expected to end up adding up their effects in the reduced form equation of Q. Factors which would give parameter estimates with opposite signs in both the acreage and yield equations would be expected to balance out and would ultimately be expected to yield nonsignificant parameter estimates in the reduced form equation of Q.

At this point a choice has to be made about the possible mathematical formulation of the model in reduced form equations. The algebraic formulation selected must be coherent with observable facts. It must be based on available statistical data and policy information and solvable at reasonable cost.

Alternative mathematical formulations may reflect alternative conceptions. In addition, the quality of the data is such that we are rarely in a position to quantify successfully the theoretical relationships. Whereas natural scientists work on controlled experiments and let experimental data define the law of the phenomenon, economists have generally to work the other way around trying to fit their own

---

1. This section deals only with nonperennial crops. Specific problems arise when dealing with perennial ones, especially tree crops.

mental conceptions of the possible law of the phenomenon to observed
and usually short and incomplete data series.

As the following relationship stands by definition as a mathematical indentiy:

$$Q = N \cdot Y \tag{4}$$

it is clear that the "explanations" of Q, N, and Y should be consistent
with one another in the sense that their estimated values should verify
equation (4).

The symbols used in this section are as follows:

Q = total domestic production or supply
N = number of producing units (i.e., acreage)
Y = average yield per producing unit (i.e., per acre)

X_i are the n predetermined variables allowing for the various factors determining Q, N, and Y, respectively (i = 1, ..., n)

a_0, b_0, c_0 are the constant terms in the respective equations of Q,
N, and Y

a_i, b_i, c_i are the parameter estimates corresponding to variables
X_i in the respective equations of Q, N, and Y

u_Q, u_N, u_Y are residual terms in the respective equations of Q,
N, and Y.

As yield appears generally strategic in supply analysis, the form
of the yield equation may be regarded as the cornerstone of the supply
model. Should the yield equation have the linear form

$$Y = c_0 + \sum_{i=1}^{n} c_i X_i + u_Y \tag{5}$$

we could not take the logarithm of the estimated polynomial on the right
side. Many yield regression equations have nevertheless been estimated in this form or merely in the form of a linear trend equation. In
this linear formulation, all other independent variables being at constant levels, the rate of change of Y with respect to any X_i is constant.
The inadequacy of the linear yield equation formulation has long been
recognized and would appear to have prompted Barton (3) to report in
1961 that in the United States "with few exceptions (yield) projections
failed to anticipate the rapidity of the changes in farming" and that evidence indicated "a tendency toward conservatism in gauging production
potential and to underestimate potential increases in crop yields."

Other possible formulations of the yield equation are log-log and
exponential or semilog. The generalized log-log yield model may be
formulated as

$$Y = c_0 \prod_{i=1}^{n} X_i^{c_i} u_y \tag{6}$$

It has constant elasticities of changes in the dependent variable with

respect to any of the independent variables, all others being held constant; if either factor is zero, the dependent variable is zero. On the
other hand, all other independent variables being at constant levels, the
rate of change with respect to any X_i decreases at high levels of X_i.

The generalized exponential or semilog yield model may be formulated as

$$Y = e^{(c_0 + \sum\limits_{i=1}^{n} c_i X_i + y_Y)} \qquad (7)$$

It does eliminate some of the inconveniences of the linear and log-log
models previously described. As in the linear equation, the dependent
variable is not zero when either factor is zero, in contrast to the log-
log equation. On the other hand, all other independent variables being
at constant levels, the rate of change with respect to any X_i increases
at high levels of X_i. This property might be viewed by some as a draw-
back of this formulation.

Nevertheless plotted crop yield data generally suggests some exponential or semiexponential secular trend. And we may indeed assume
that the yield of a crop has never been actually zero. In addition, although the law of diminishing rates of increase, a saturation phenomenon, suggests that in some future time a crop yield may stop increasing
after having perhaps reached a still unknown ceiling level, nothing suggests that the point of inflexion has yet been reached or that it is foreseeable in a relatively near future for most crops except perhaps in
some areas of extremely intensive farming. Therefore we may generally assume that the point of inflexion of the yield curve is still relatively ahead in time. The secular yield trend therefore could be deemed
in first approximation to exhibit some semiexponential pattern; the horizontal no-trend line encountered in traditional agriculture is only incidentally a particular case of the exponential or semiexponential curve.

In other words, and as stated before, observation of the real world
situation suggests that though the law of diminishing rates of increase
applies at a given time to a frozen level of technology, the underlying
dynamic tendency for each input category is one of technological progress. The exponential or semilog formulation of the yield estimation
may therefore be plausible, permissible, and convenient.

Should we abide by the general hypothesis made earlier, we may
also for the sake of coherence formulate the acreage model through a
similar equation. In reduced form the unrestricted exponential or
semilog supply model may therefore be formulated as follows and all
equations estimated independently through the least-squares method.

Direct formulation:

$$Q = e^{(a_0 + \sum\limits_{i=1}^{n} a_i X_i + u_Q)} \qquad (8)$$

Indirect formulation:

$$N = e^{(b_0 + \sum_{i=1}^{n} b_i X_i + u_N)} \tag{9}$$

$$Y = e^{(c_0 + \sum_{i=1}^{n} c_i X_i + u_Y)} \tag{10}$$

(i = 1, ..., n explanatory variables)

The model being linear in logarithm form:

$$\log_e Q = a_0 + \sum_{i=1}^{n} a_i X_i + u_Q \tag{11}$$

$$\log_e N = b_0 + \sum_{i=1}^{n} b_i X_i + u_N \tag{12}$$

$$\log_e Y = c_0 + \sum_{i=1}^{n} c_i X_i + u_Y \tag{13}$$

One sees immediately that the requirement of consistency between the direct and the indirect formulations is automatically met by the coefficient estimates and the residuals of the equations as:

$$a_0 = b_0 + c_0$$
$$a_i = b_i + c_i$$
$$u_Q = u_N + u_Y$$

In this model all elasticities are equal to the corresponding coefficient weighted by the level of the factor investigated as

$$e_i(Q) = a_i X_i$$
$$e_i(N) = b_i X_i$$
$$e_i(Y) = c_i X_i$$

Another formulation of the supply model favored by agricultural economists is the log-log formulation. Returning to yield equation (6), we may again formulate the acreage model through a similar log-log equation. In reduced form the unrestricted log-log supply model may then be formulated as follows and all equations again estimated independently through the least-squares method.

Direct formulation:

$$Q = a_0 \prod_{i=1}^{n} X_i^{a_i} u_Q \tag{14}$$

Indirect formulation:

$$N = b_0 \prod_{i=1}^{n} X_i^{b_i} u_N \qquad (15)$$

$$Y = c_0 \prod_{i=1}^{n} X_i^{c_i} u_Y$$

($i = 1, ..., n$ predetermined variables)

with the similar requirement of consistency among coefficients and residuals:

$$\log a_0 = \log b_0 + \log c_0$$

$$a_i = b_i + c_i$$

$$\log u_Q = u_N + u_Y$$

In this formulation the elasticities are equal to the corresponding coefficient estimates. In addition, the dependent variable is zero if any factor is zero in the relevant equation. This last property might make the log-linear formulation appear less realistic than the exponential or semilog.

Supply models of the exponential or semilog types have been tried for milk in Wisconsin (1946-62) (33) and for cotton in the Mississippi Delta (1946-62) (30) with interesting results, yielding high coefficients of determination along with little evidence of serial correlation among the residuals for all equations. Lower coefficients of determination were obtained in less advanced agriculture where the specification of the variables appears to be more difficult, as suggested by wheat and feedgrains for France (1946-61) (32) which, I feel, could be made more realistic through reformulation in semilog form. In developing countries the empirical equations are still less sophisticated; and as their goodness of fit is usually lower, they might not be as helpful. Typically, however, a traditional agriculture being a particular type of equilibrium where the state-of-the-arts remains constant and where the yield trend equation therefore is that of a horizontal line, the expected yield may be derived from the past yield distribution and a reasonably good forecasting equation may then be estimated for log Q (total output) which would include expected yield in log among the predetermined variables. Presumably the inclusion of the yield variable in the acreage equation would also considerably improve its fit. Hence we would end up with a relatively simple model for a traditional agriculture (35). In addition, both the log-log and semilog formulations have been tested comparatively in partial analysis of cross-sectional data (34); a better fit was obtained with the semilog model for both the acreage (log N) and the total output (log Q) equations along with similar R^2's for the yield (log Y) equations.

CONCLUSION

This expository discussion of possible appropriate regression models in agricultural supply analysis leads me to stress again that there is an urgent need for improving the comparability of agricultural supply models. To attain this comparability there is a need for a consensus over a few conceptual models; over the size of the sample to be used in the various types of analysis; over the general type of model to be used in time series analysis, including the major variable to be included; and over a systematic production of models both micro and macro, sectoral and regional, of the types agreed upon in order to generate comparative information useful to the policy makers.

As to forecasting from regression models, caution is required. If the problem is one of short-run analysis, one year ahead, regression equations exhibiting a good fit may provide estimates which would usefully assist our judgment. If the problem is one of intermediate-run analysis, more than a year and up to five years (the usual time horizon in planning), extrapolation of the parameters of the supply equations may be possible in an environment where structural changes are relatively slow, as is often the case in agriculture. The equations should nevertheless be updated and reformulated in order to adjust the estimates on the basis of more recent information as time passes. Clearly, however, if the problem is one of longer-run analysis, the very purpose of agricultural development, which is one of bringing new technologies to bear and thus disturbing the prevailing structure, makes it generally rather irrelevant to use regression models derived from past observations for long-range forecasting.

Structural changes of a permanent nature may follow some deterministic paths in the long run and their analysis might then, in some cases, usefully draw on methods used by physical scientists for dealing with "les systemes asservis."

Physics provides me with another remark. There have been suggestions that the response of acreage, yield, and total output to upward changes in various factors involved in agricultural supply models (including weather as well as prices) and to downward changes might not necessarily be of the same magnitudes. Therefore we may need to estimate separate upward and downward response models. The case may again be illustrated through an analogy with physics and the so-called "hysteresis" phenomenon (47). When producers receive higher prices, they are willing to increase their production as they expect to increase their returns, and thereby their standard of living. If prices decrease, there may be a natural reluctance to see a decrease in their standard of living and thereby to reduce their production. There may be a phenomenon of "hysteresis" familiar in textbooks of physics and representing the relationship between the intensity of electric current and induced magnetism. Hence supply relationships may not be independent of the direction of the movements of the independent variables.

REFERENCES

1. Aldabe, H., and W. Van Rijckeghem. The Use of Simulation for Forecasting Changes in the Argentine Cattle Stock. D.A.S. Harvard Univ. Paper presented to Bellagio Conference, June 1966.
2. Angstrom, Anders. A Coefficient of Humidity of General Applicability. *Geograph. Ann.*, vol. 18.
3. Barton, G. T. Projecting Crop Yields for the United States. Paper presented at Second Consultation of Experts on Problems of Methodology of Agricultural Production Projections, Geneva, 1961.
4. Behrman, J. R. Supply Response in Underdeveloped Agriculture: A Case Study of Four Annual Crops in Thailand 1937-1963. Ph.D. Diss., Massachusetts Institute of Technology, 1966.
5. Berry, J. E., B. Oury, and A. W. Khan. Changes in the Numbers of Farms and Farmers in the United States, 1950-1959. A.E. Inform. Ser. no. 127. Dept. Econ., North Carolina State Univ., 1966.
6. Bessiere, Fr. De l'Importance du Concept de 'Separabilite' en Economie. *Rev. Econ. Politique*, Nov. 1967.
7. Bostwick, Don. Yield Probabilities as a Markov Process. *Agr. Econ. Res.*, vol. 14.
8. Day, R. H. *Recursive Programming and Production Response*. Amsterdam: North-Holland, 1963.
9. Dean, G. W., S. E. Johnson, and H. O. Carter. Supply Functions for Cotton in Imperial Valley, California. *Agr. Econ. Res.*, vol. 25.
10. de Martonne, Emmanuel. Une Nouvelle Fonction Climatologique: l'Indice d'Aridite. *Meteorologie*, Paris, 1926.
11. Eisgruber, L. Farm Operation Simulator and Farm Management Decision Exercise. Program 10.2010, IBM 1620 General Program Library, May 1964.
12. Fisher, R. M. *A Priori Information and Time Series Analysis: Essays in Economic Theory and Measurement, Contributions to Economic Analysis*. Amsterdam: North-Holland, 1962.
13. Griliches, Zvi. Distributed Lags: A Survey. *Econometrica*, vol. 35.
14. ———. The Aggregate U.S. Farm Supply Function. *J. Farm Econ.*, vol. 42.
15. Halter, A. N., and G. W. Dean. Use of Simulation in Evaluating Management Policies under Uncertainty: Application to a Large Scale Range. *J. Farm Econ.*, vol. 47.
16. Halter, A. N., and S. F. Miller. Simulation Systems in Making Water Resources Decisions. Paper presented to WAECR Water Committee, San Francisco, 1964.
17. Heady, Earl O., et al. *Agricultural Supply Functions*. Ames: Iowa State Univ. Press, 1961.
18. Heady, Earl O., and Wilfred Candler. *Linear Programming Methods*. Ames: Iowa State Univ. Press, 1958.
19. Heady, Earl O., and L. G. Tweeten. *Resource Demand and Structure of the Agricultural Industry*. Ames: Iowa State Univ. Press, 1963.
20. Heidhues, Th. A Recursive Programming Model of Farm Growth in Northern Germany. *J. Farm Econ.*, vol. 48.
21. Hutton, R. F. A Simulation Technique for Making Management Decision in Dairy Farming. USDA Agr. Econ. Rept. 87, Feb. 1966.
22. Kislev, Y., and A. Amiad. Linear and Dynamic Programming in Markov Chains. *J. Farm Econ.*, vol. 50
23. Malinvaud, E. *Statistical Methods of Econometrics*. Chicago: Rand McNally, 1966.
24. Meier, R. C. The Application of Optimum Seeking Techniques to Simulation

Studies: A Preliminary Evaluation. *J. Financial and Quantitative Anal.*, March 1967.
25. Naylor, T. H., et al. *Computer Simulation Techniques.* New York: Wiley, 1966.
26. Nerlove, Marc. Time Series Analysis of the Supply of Agricultural Products. In *Agricultural Supply Functions*, ed. Earl O. Heady et al. Ames: Iowa State Univ. Press, 1961.
27. O.E.C.D. Cooperative Research on Input/Output Relationships in Use of Fertilizers in Crop Production. Paris, 1966. Pp. 42-45 (which give the latest review of major research works on weather-crop output relationships).
28. Orcutt, G. H. Statistical Models. *Proc. NATO-Gulbenkian Foundation Summer Inst. on Forecasting on a Scientific Basis*, Curia, Portugal, 1966.
29. Oury, Bernard. Allowing for Weather in Crop Production Model Building. *J. Farm Econ.*, vol. 47.
30. ———. A Cotton Supply Model for the Mississippi Delta (1946-1962). Unpubl. computer result, Dept. Econ., North Carolina State Univ., 1966.
31. ———. How Successful are Alternative Research Methodologies for Predicting the Effects of Price and Income Policies? *Proc. Workshop on Price and Income Policies.* Agr. Policy Inst., North Carolina State Univ., 1965.
32. ———. *A Wheat and Feedgrains Production Model in France* (1946-1962). Amsterdam: North-Holland, 1966.
33. ———. A Milk Supply Model for Wisconsin 1946-1962. Unpubl. paper, Dept. Econ., North Carolina State Univ., 1965.
34. Oury, Bernard, and H. M. Kim. Some Factors Influencing Wheat Production in West Punjab: Cross-Sectional Analysis of West Punjab Watercourses Wheat Production Data (1964/65). Unpubl. paper, Econ. Dept., International Bank for Reconstruction and Development, Washington, 1968.
35. ———. Time Series Analysis of West Punjab District Wheat Production Data: Lahore District (1920/21-1945/46). Econ. Dept., International Bank for Reconstruction and Development, Washington, 1968.
36. Penman, H. L. Estimating Evapotranspiration. *Am. Geophys. Union Trans.*, vol. 37.
37. Russell, W., R. H. Day, and B. Oury. Informal Discussion of the Possibilities of Adapting Russell's "Commercial Bank Portfolio Adjustment Model" to Commercial Farm Crop Acreage Distribution Adjustments. Social Systems Res. Inst., Univ. Wisconsin, Madison, 1964.
38. Schaller, W. N., and G. W. Dean. Predicting Regional Crop Production, An Application of Recursive Programming. ERS, USDA Tech. Bull. 1329, 1965.
39. Sinha, A. R., H. C. Sinha, and J. R. C. Thakurta. Indian Cultivators Response to Prices. *Sankhya*, 1934.
40. Thomas, J. J. Notes on the Theory of Multiple Regression Analysis. Center Econ. Res., Athens, 1964.
41. Thornwaite, C. W. An Approach Toward a Rational Classification of Climate. *Geograph. Rev.*, vol. 38.
42. Tinbergen, J. *On the Theory of Economic Policy.* 2nd ed. Amsterdam: North-Holland, 1955.
43. Tolley, G. S., and R. A. Schrimper. Feasible Ways for Relating the Micro and Macro. *Proc. Workshop on Price and Income Policies.* Agr. Policy Inst., North Carolina State Univ., 1965.
44. Tyner, F. H., and L. G. Tweeten. Simulation as a Method of Appraising Farm Programs. *J. Farm Econ.*, vol. 50.
45. White, W. W. The Trustworthiness of "Reliable" Econometric Evidence. *Z. Nationaloekon.*, vol. 27.
46. Wilde, D. J. *Optimum Seeking Methods.* Englewood Cliffs, N.J.: Prentice Hall, 1964.

47. Wold, Herman. Model Building and Scientific Method. Lecture, C.E.I.R. Symposium on Model Building, London, 1967.
48. Wold, Herman, and Lars Jureen. *Demand Analysis.* New York: Wiley, 1953.

Chapter 11 ☙ DISCUSSION

Luther G. Tweeten, *Oklahoma State University* (U.S.A.)

D R. OURY gives a lucid account of some problems in supply estimation, and some advantages and disadvantages of regression and related models. I wish to supplement his remarks in these specific areas: (a) use of autoregressive least squares, (b) alternative ways to estimate positivistic supply functions, and (c) some weaknesses and suggested changes in methodology.

AUTOREGRESSIVE LEAST SQUARES AND RELATED ISSUES

Provided the other customary assumptions of the least-squares statistical models hold, autocorrelation in the residuals results in loss of efficiency but the parameter estimates remain unbiased and consistent. Autocorrelation becomes particularly troublesome because it results in biased coefficients when there is correlation between the residuals and an explanatory (independent) variable. Since the error residual is generally associated with the dependent variable Y_t, the use of lagged values of Y as an independent variable is likely to entail a correlation between Y_{t-1} and the residuals. If residuals are uncorrelated, estimates derived from the distributed lag model yield consistent though possibly biased (small sample) parameter estimates. If errors are autocorrelated, however, serious bias may result. Unfortunately tests for autocorrelation such as the Durbin-Watson or the von Neumann ratio are inadequate and tend not to detect autocorrelation in residuals when in fact it is present. Methods such as use of first differences have been suggested to treat the problem of autocorrelation — a troublesome problem with the growing use of distributed lag models. The following equations help to clarify the issues.

Assume that the residuals e_t follow a first-order autoregressive scheme as in (1)

$$e_t = \beta e_{t-1} + \mu \tag{1}$$

where β is the first-order autoregressive coefficient and μ is a random element, independently distributed. The use of first differences or other means to eliminate autocorrelation in the regression residuals can be illustrated by the statistical model in (2)

$$Y_t = \alpha_0 + \alpha_1 T_t + \sum_{i=2}^{m} \alpha_i X_{it} + e_t \tag{2}$$

where Y_t is the dependent variable, T_t is a linear time trend, X_i are the remaining independent variables, and α_i are the coefficients. Lagging equation (2) one year and multiplying by β, the result is (3). Subtracting (3) from (2) the result is (4).

$$\beta Y_{t-1} = \beta \alpha_0 + \alpha_1 \beta T_{t-1} + \sum_{i=2}^{m} \alpha_i \beta X_{it-1} + \beta e_{t-1} \tag{3}$$

$$Y_t - \beta Y_{t-1} = (1-\beta)\alpha_0 + \alpha_1 (T_t - \beta T_{t-1})$$

$$+ \sum_{i=2}^{m} \alpha_i (X_{it} - \beta X_{it-1}) + (e_t - \beta e_{t-1}) \tag{4}$$

Now if the residuals have no first-order autocorrelation, i.e., $\beta = 0$, then ordinary least squares can be used to estimate directly equation (2). If $\beta = 1$, then from (1) $\mu_t = e_t - e_{t-1}$ and (4) becomes (5).

$$Y_t - Y_{t-1} = \alpha_1 + \sum_{i=2}^{m} \alpha_i (X_{it} - X_{it-1}) + e_t - e_{t-1} \tag{5}$$

The residual is randomly distributed as μ_t; the first differences eliminate the autocorrelation in the residuals. It is apparent that the constant α_1 in the first difference equation (5) is the time trend coefficient in (2).

In short, ordinary least squares are appropriate when $\beta = 0$, and first differences when $\beta = 1$. But what do we do in cases where $0 < \beta < 1$? One approach is to use a computer program for least squares which estimates β, where the estimate is unrestricted, allowed to take any value. At Oklahoma State we make frequent use of a computer program for autoregressive least squares written by Martin (6). The program also computes the standard error of the estimated first-order autoregressive coefficient. Another approach for those who lack such a program is apparent in equation (4). The procedure is to estimate least-squares equation (4) under several hypotheses about the magnitude of β. It is only necessary to use transformed variables such as $X_{it} - bX_{it-1}$ where b is an estimate of β. By observing the R^2 and Durbin-Watson tests with various values of b, the best estimate of β can be found.

Hierarchial Regression

It seems to be fashionable these days to belittle high R^2's and the use of lagged values of the dependent variable. Other things equal, a high R^2 minimizes many of the statistical problems that plague estimates. As the R^2 approaches 1.0, least-squares bias approaches zero, and the precision of t-tests and prediction increases. Autocorrelation is likely to be less serious also. Then what is wrong with a high R^2? The complication is that other things are usually not equal. High R^2's are often associated with time series which are intercorrelated and serially correlated, making estimation hazardous. Also the high R^2's may arise because the researcher has experimented with a large number of independent variables until he finds the subset that most nearly "explains" the dependent variable. If so, this reduces the validity of the test of significance and gives misguided confidence in the ability (measured by the standard error) of the equation to predict.

It is incumbent on the researcher to retain structural validity in equations. Statisticians tell us to pick say four independent variables based on theory, and stick with these. Our theory is seldom precise enough to select four variables in advance which not only are structurally sound but also adequately explain the dependent variable. Hence a common practice is to let the equation generate theory, judging the relevance of that theory on the performance of variables in the equation. Stepwise regression is an example. I have used hierarchial regression to experiment at once with alternate variables and still preserve some structural validity and meaning for statistical tests. The procedure is to group variables into hierarchies. The variables within a group (hierarchy) are alternative, equally acceptable expressions of a given economic phenomenon; each hierarchy represents different economic phenomena of expected declining influence on the dependent variable. In an equation explaining land prices the first hierarchy might be several variables that measure the earning power of land, such as ratio of prices received to prices paid by farmers, gross farm income per acre, and net farm income per acre. Theory says this earnings hierarchy is important, but it is unable to tell which variable within the group best represents this economic effect. The second hierarchy might be composed of structural variables such as farm size, investment in machinery, and the like. The next hierarchy is composed of variables representing the direct effect of government programs. Additions hierarchies are not specified until the complete economic model is formed. The regression procedure is to select the "best" variable from the first hierarchy, then leave it in the equation when choosing the best variable from the second hierarchy, and so on until the equation is complete.

Distributed Lags

A great many economic phenomena are characterized by lags in response to stimuli because expectations are being formed or because of other barriers to immediate adjustments. One way to accommodate this lagged adjustment is to include all relevant past values of explanations variables in the equation. But this procedure quickly leads to overwhelming problems of multicollinearity as more variables are added. The shortcut is to use the lagged value of the dependent variable as an independent variable. This does not destroy the integrity of the equations by implying that the dependent variable becomes a function only of itself; it merely expresses the functionally valid argument that the dependent variable is a weighted function of all past values of the independent variables other than the lagged dependent variable. The procedure does introduce messy statistical problems. But because nearly all economic phenomena entail lags, the only thing worse than using a distributed lag model seems to be to not use it.

USE OF POSITIVISTIC AND NORMATIVE MODELS

Dr. Oury and others have discussed advantages and disadvantages of normative models such as linear programming and positivistic models such as least squares for economic planning and analysis. The choice of models is not clear-cut and definitely depends on the nature of the data and objectives of the research.

Regression models are often inappropriate. An example is the misuse of cross-sectional data to estimate a production function, then the use of that function to test the economic efficiency of the parent population. If one wishes to test the hypothesis that farmers in LDC's are efficient, he has gone a long way toward confirming that hypothesis by selecting the least-squares production function technique. If one samples from a population where all farmers are inefficient, the resulting estimate of the production function will contain this inefficiency built into the coefficients. The results may show that the marginal value products are equal to factor prices, hence indicate economic efficiency. But a true production function, showing the response that efficient farmers would get from application of inputs, may look very different from the estimated function. The marginal value products of the *true* function, at the input levels at which farmers are operating, may bear little resemblance to factor prices. Furthermore the production function estimated from farm data tells us nothing about inputs and practices which may be of proven value, based on experimental results and farm trials. Finally, the usual procedure is to aggregate inputs into perhaps four categories. The resulting production functions and tests of efficiency then can tell us little of the optimality of the output (or input) mix within the aggregates, though this can be a major component of efficiency.

For these and other reasons, linear programming, which can handle numerous resources, products, and production processes, some of which may be very relevant alternatives but not yet used on farms, offers major advantages in flexibility and reliability for testing whether farmers are efficient, and for helping them to improve their efficiency.

The mix of agricultural economics research resources in the United States may be weighted too heavily toward firm studies and not enough toward macroeconomic (policy) studies. From spending some time in developing countries and from reading the literature, I judge that the opposite situation prevails in most developing countries. A national plan based on aggregative models may prescribe a given amount of investment to raise national income a certain amount. But the national plan is likely to go awry when inadequate attention is paid to what specific input forms that national investment should take, the rate of return on alternative inputs, the efficiency with which farmers will use the inputs, the rate of adoption of the new inputs, the complementary inputs required, and the changes in sectors supplying inputs and marketing products to accommodate the changes in farming investment.

ESTIMATING THE ELASTICITY OF SUPPLY

Since Dr. Oury focused much of his discussion on the estimation of supply by regression models, I will present some promising additional approaches to estimate supply response in U.S. agriculture.

The elasticity of supply is closely related to the level and productivity of farm resources. The supply elasticity shows the speed and magnitude of output adjustments in response to changes in product price. The parameter is especially important for public policy because it measures the ability of farmers to adjust production to changing economic conditions that continually confront them in a dynamic economy.

Positivistic Supply Elasticity Estimates for Individual Commodities

The elasticity of supply tends to be highest for commodities that comprise a small part of farm production, can be produced under a wide range of resource conditions, have alternatives that are readily substitutable in production, and have a short production period.

Output of eggs and poultry meat, which have a short production period, is considerably more responsive to price than is milk production (Table 11.1). The components of any one category in Table 11.1 tend to have a higher elasticity than the total. Because milk can be used for many purposes, the supply elasticity for fresh fluid milk may be 0.6 while the total milk supply elasticity is 0.3.

Although the supply elasticity for fruits in total is only 0.2, Brandow's (1) estimate places the elasticity for fresh apples at 13.

Normative Supply Elasticity Estimate for Cotton

Dr. Oury compared estimates of supply from normative and posi-

Table 11.1 Estimated short-run elasticities of supply for
selected U.S. agricultural products[a]

	Elasticity	Livestock products	Elasticity
Potatoes	0.8	Eggs	1.2
Soybeans	0.5	Poultry meat	0.9
Feed grains	0.4	Hogs	0.6
Cotton	0.4	Beef	0.5
Tobacco	0.4	Milk	0.3
Vegetables	0.4		
Wheat	0.3		
Fruits	0.2		

a. Data interpreted from numerous estimates found in Cochrane (3), Heady (4), Buchholz et al. (2). Estimates are for an adjustment period of approximately two years.

tivistic models. The cotton supply elasticity for the United States, taken from a normative supply schedule computed by linear programming is shown in Table 11.2. The normative supply elasticities are several times as large as the positivistic estimate, 0.3, of the elasticity of cotton supply in Table 11.1. The normative estimates are unrealistically large as a predictor of the short-run response, but they may have relevance as a long-run predictor of supply response.

Positivistic Supply Elasticity Estimates for U.S.
Farm Output in Aggregate

Farmers have considerable latitude to substitute one commodity for another in production over a long period. Eventually this should lead to adjustments among commodities until each is earning a somewhat comparable profit. Public policies concerned with the earnings of all farm products and total farm income must consider the aggregate response of farm output to changing economic conditions. The aggregate response of output to price depends on total resource adjustments in

Table 11.2. Estimated cotton supply elasticities from
an aggregate normative cotton supply schedule
computed by linear programming[a]

Cotton price range ($/lb lint)	Average elasticity of cotton supply (production)
0.00-0.15	1.00
0.15-0.20	5.04
0.20-0.21	8.79
0.21-0.22	3.32
0.22-0.23	2.29
0.23-0.24	4.47
0.24-0.25	2.24
0.25-0.30	0.93
0.30-0.35	0.12

a. For source of data see Tweeten et al. (8).

agriculture. Because farm resources can be adjusted much more easily among farm commodities than between farm and nonfarm commodities, it follows that the aggregate supply response, which tends to determine total resource earnings in agriculture, will be less than the
supply response for the individual commodities shown in Table 11.1.

Three approaches are used to estimate the aggregate supply elasticity. The first is a direct least-squares estimate of the supply function with total farm output a function of prices, technology, and other
variables. This gives a supply elasticity of 0.1 in 1-2 years, 0.2 in
3-4 years, and 0.6 in many years, as estimated by Heady and Tweeten
(5, ch. 16).

The second approach is to separate supply into its yield and basic
production unit components. For all crops the acreage response to
price is quite low in both the short and long run (Table 11.3). The yield
response is considerable in the long run, however. The total elasticity
of supply of farm crop production with respect to prices received by
farmers is the acreage elasticity plus the yield elasticity corrected for
the negative effect of higher acreage on yields as production moves to
lower yielding land.

Table 11.3. Estimated aggregate supply elasticity of U.S. farm output,
with crop and livestock components[a]

| | Elasticities | |
	Short-run (2 years)	Long-run (Many years)
Crops[b] E_{CP}	0.17	1.56
acreage E_{AP}	0.04	0.10
yield per acre E_{YP}	0.15	1.50
Livestock[c] E_{LP}	0.38	2.90
animal units (stock) E_{AP}	0.12	1.80
yield per animal unit E_{YP}	0.26	1.10
Aggregate supply elasticity[d]	0.25	1.79

a. Data interpreted from Heady and Tweeten (5, ch. 16), Buchholz et al. (2).
b. The elasticity of crop production C with respect to farm price P is E_{CP}. Given
the elasticity of acreage with respect to price E_{AP}, the elasticity of yield with respect
to price E_{YP}, and the elasticity of yield with respect to acreage $E_{YA} = -0.4$, then

$$E_{CP} = E_{YP} + E_{AP} (1 + E_{YA})$$

c. Computed as in above footnote, with the elasticity of livestock yield with respect to
animal units E_{YA} equal to zero.
d. Computed by the formula:

$$E_{OP} = E_{CP} \frac{C}{O} + E_{LP} \frac{L}{O} + E_{LC} E_{CP} \frac{L}{O}$$

where O is total farm output, C is crop output, L is livestock output, and P is the index of prices received by farmers. E_{OP} is the supply elasticity of O with respect
to P. Other elasticities E_{ij} are interpreted accordingly. E_{LC} is assumed to be -0.4
in the short run and -0.6 in the long run.

The production period for livestock such as poultry and hogs is comparatively short; hence animal units of livestock show a greater response than acreage to higher farm prices (Table 11.3). While output per animal unit is more responsive to price than is the number of animal units in the short run, the reverse is true in the long run. That is, there is greater potential for expanding livestock production by increasing the number of animal units than by increasing the yield per unit over an extended period. My empirical results do not show that increasing the number of animal units depresses the yield per unit. Hence the supply elasticity of total livestock output is the simple sum of the unit and yield components.

The total elasticity of farm output with respect to product price is a weighted sum of the livestock and crop components. There are opportunities to substitute livestock for crops by feeding. This interaction is at least partially included by a term E_{LC} which is the elasticity of livestock output with respect to crop output (footnote d, Table 11.3). With a given supply of crops, an increase of livestock means less crops for final sales to consumers — hence E_{LC} is negative. The elasticity of total supply computed from data in Table 11.3 is 0.25 in approximately two years and is 1.79 in many years. This implies that a sustained 10 percent increase in prices received by farmers raises farm output 2.5 percent in two years and 17.9 percent in many years.

The final estimate of the elasticity of aggregate supply is determined from the elasticities of production and the elasticities of input demand with respect to prices received by farmers. In other words, output is a function of the productivity of an input and its level of use. And the level of use is a function of farm product prices.

Policy research has been plagued by inability to develop a good estimate of the aggregate production function. Direct least-squares estimates were hampered by multicollinearity; factor shares estimates of production parameters were hampered by the assumption of equilibrium; and all estimates were hampered by data problems. To circumvent some of these problems, Fred Tyner and I (9) developed an indirect estimation procedure. It is well known that in equilibrium the marginal product of output O with respect to a factor quantity X_i is equal to the factor-product price ratio P_i / P as in equation (6). Multiplying both sides of (6)

$$\frac{\partial O}{\partial X_i} = \frac{P_i}{P} \tag{6}$$

by X_i / O, and defining the elasticity of production E_i and the factor share F_i as indicated, the result is (7). The advantage of (7)

$$E_i = F_i \qquad E_i = \frac{\partial O}{\partial X_i} \frac{X_i}{O} \quad \text{and} \quad F_i = \frac{P_i X_i}{O\, O} \tag{7}$$

is that F_i can readily be computed from costs and income data, which are usually more reliable than are data on O or X_i.

While the factor share can be observed and used as an estimate of the elasticity of production in a Cobb-Douglas type production function in a dynamic environment, there is no reason to believe the $E_i = F_i$. But if farm decisions trend toward equilibrium, we can estimate the unknown E_i by making an assumption about how resources adjust. One assumption is that the E_i adjusts to F_i with a Koyck-Nerlove type of distributed lag as in (8).

$$F_{it} - F_{i\ t-1} = g(E_{it} - F_{i\ t-1}) \qquad (8)$$

That is, the actual adjustment in the year t in observed factor shares is some proportion g of the equilibrium adjustment. It is apparent that simple least squares provide a ready estimate of g and E_{it}. The least-squares form is (9)

$$\Delta F_{it} - A - gF_{i\ t-1} \qquad (9)$$

where the first difference ΔF_{it} is the dependent variable and $F_{i\ t-1}$ is the independent variable. The estimated coefficient of $F_{i\ t-1}$ is the adjustment rate g, and the least-squares constant A is gE_{it}. Hence the elasticity of production can be computed as $E_{it} = A/g$. E_{it} can also be computed by solving for E_{it} in (8), to form (10).

$$E_{it} = \frac{F_{it}}{g} + \frac{g-1}{g} F_{i\ t-1} \qquad (10)$$

Then with known values of g from (9) and of F_i, the elasticity of production can be computed for specific years. With numerous modifications, including alternative algebraic forms, dummy variables, first-order autoregressive schemes, and other devices to obtain a realistic model, the basic model (9) provided the framework to estimate a production function. This function in turn was used in a simulation study by Tyner and me (10), a resource efficiency study by us (9), and to derive the elasticities of production used to estimate the aggregate supply elasticity in Table 11.4.

A 1 percent increase in use of fertilizer increases farm output 0.06 percent, whereas a 1 percent increase in farm real estate increases farm output 0.28 percent (Table 11.4). Because farm real estate tends to be quite fixed, its large impact on output is offset by its low response to farm product prices — hence fertilizer contributes more to the aggregate supply elasticity than does farm real estate.

The total elasticity of supply is 0.26 in two years and 1.52 in many years, according to results in Table 11.4. The three approaches used to compute the elasticity of farm output with respect to prices indicate that the supply elasticity is low but is decidedly positive. An interpretation from the above three estimates of supply elasticities is that a sustained 10 percent increase in prices received by farmers would be likely to increase farm output approximately 1 percent in one year, 3 percent in three years, and about 15 percent in many years.

These results primarily apply when farm prices are increased. Fixity of assets tends to reduce the supply elasticity applicable to falling farm prices. If only operating inputs in Table 11.4 are variable when prices fall, then the short-run elasticity is reduced from 0.26 to

Table 11.4. Estimated elasticities of production, input demand, and
product supply for U.S. agriculture[a]

Input	Elasticity of production	Elasticity of demand				Contribution to aggregate supply elasticity	
		Own price		Product price			
		SR[b]	LR[b]	SR	LR	SR	LR
Fertilizer and lime	0.06	-0.6	-1.8	0.5	2.4	0.030	0.144
Machinery operating expenses	0.11	-1.0	-1.5	0.5	2.5	0.055	0.275
Feed, seed, and livestock	0.09	-0.8	-1.5	0.7	2.0	0.063	0.180
Miscellaneous current operating expenses	0.09	-0.3	-0.5	0.3	2.5	0.027	0.225
Crop and livestock inventories	0.04	-0.2	-1.0	0.2	2.5	0.008	0.100
Machinery inventory	0.10	-0.2	-1.0	0.2	2.6	0.020	0.260
Labor	0.25	-0.1	-0.5	0.1	1.0	0.025	0.250
Real estate	0.28	c	c	0.1	0.3	0.028	0.084
Total elasticity	1.02					0.256[d]	1.518[d]

a. Data based on Heady and Tweeten (5), Tweeten and Nelson (7), Tyner and Tweeten (9), and Tyner and Tweeten (10).
b. SR refers to a short run of two years; LR refers to a long run of many years.
c. Nearly zero.
d. The total price elasticity of supply of farm output E_{OP} is

$$E_{OP} = \sum_i E_{Oi} \, E_{iP}$$

where E_{Oi} is the production elasticity of the farm output O with respect to input quantity X_i, and E_{iP} is the demand elasticity of input X_i with respect to product price P.

0.18, and the long-run elasticity is reduced from 1.52 to 0.82 in Table 11.4. If product prices fall sufficiently low, some of the fixed resources would be abandoned, and the supply elasticity would be raised accordingly.

CONCLUSIONS

There is little point in contending that either normative or positivistic models are appropriate alone for national planning and individual decision making. The relevant methodology depends on the nature of the data and the economic questions to be answered. Often the various approaches can be combined, and there appears to be no substitute for eclecticism.

There has been considerable criticism of distributed lag models, the associated high R^2, and statistical problems generated by introduction of the lagged dependent variable as an explanatory variable. Recognizing that a large number of economic phenomena do entail adjustments and expectations, the use of distributed lag models is essential. It is also recognized that autocorrelation is frequently present in regression residuals because of errors in data or omitted variables.

Autocorrelated residuals may lead to serious bias in the estimated co-efficients in distributed lag models. A common practice is to use au-toregressive least squares or other methods discussed in the text to deal with such problems. Hierarchical regression was suggested to deal with another common regression problem, selecting the best set of explanatory variables from a larger set of admissible variables.

Some approaches to estimation of the elasticity of supply were il-lustrated. Two suggested approaches which provide useful information about the components of aggregate supply response are (a) to estimate supply individually for crops and livestock, then combine the estimates with proper accounting for interactions, and (b) to compute the aggre-gate supply elasticity from estimates of production elasticities and in-put demand elasticities, the latter computed from positivistic (least-squares) input demand functions.

REFERENCES

1. Brandow, George. A Statistical Analysis of Apply Supply and Demand. A.E. and R.S. No. 2, Pennsylvania Agr. Exp. Sta., 1956.
2. Buchholz, H. E., G. G. Judge, and V. I. West. A Summary of Selected Behavioral Relationships for Agricultural Products in the United States. Dept. Agr. Econ., AERR-57, Univ. Illinois, 1962.
3. Cochrane, Willard W. Conceptualizing the Supply Relation in Agriculture. *J. Farm Econ.*, vol. 37.
4. Heady, Earl O., et al. *Agricultural Supply Functions.* Ames: Iowa State Univ. Press, 1961.
5. Heady, Earl O., and Luther G. Tweeten. *Resource Demand and Structure of the Agricultural Industry.* Ames: Iowa State Univ. Press, 1963.
6. Martin, James E. Computer Programs for Estimating Certain Classes of Non-Linear Distributed Lag Models. Dept. Agr. Econ., Misc. Publ. 546, Univ. Maryland, 1965.
7. Tweeten, Luther G., and Ted R. Nelson. Sources and Repercussions of Changing U.S. Farm Real Estate Values. Oklahoma Agr. Exp. Sta. Tech. Bull. T-120, 1966.
8. Tweeten, L. G., P. L. Strickland, and J. S. Plaxico. Interregional Competition in Cotton Production. *Agr. Econ. Res.,* vol. 20.
9. Tyner, Fred H., and Luther G. Tweeten. A Methodology for Estimating Production Parameters. *J. Farm Econ.*, vol. 47.
10. ———. Simulation as a Method of Appraising Farm Programs. *Am. J. Agr. Econ.,* vol. 50.
11. ———. Optimum Resource Allocation in U.S. Agriculture. *J. Farm Econ.,* vol. 48.

Chapter 12 ᏫᎧᎩ MODELS FOR THE ANALYSIS OF
INTERREGIONAL COMPETITION, PRODUCT ALLOCATION,
LAND USE, AND SPATIAL EQUILIBRIUM

Harry H. Hall, *University of Kentucky*
Earl O. Heady, *Iowa State University* (U.S.A.)

S PATIAL ECONOMICS has long been of prime interest to economists. Work on the theory of international trade and on location theory are but two examples of this interest. Among agricultural economists the delineation of type-of-farming areas, the studies of interregional competition, and the analysis of the differential effects of various combinations of soil, climate, and location are all expressions of a similar interest. Until the advent of modern computers, however, these interests were largely confined to qualitative and descriptive analyses. To be sure, some early studies did attempt to analyze interregional competition by means of farm budgeting and planning techniques.[1] The sheer volume of arithmetical manipulations associated with these techniques precluded their use for the comprehensive analysis of interregional problems. To an increasing degree, data availability and not computational capacity sets the limits on quantitative studies. In the future, empirical analysis will likely advance as rapidly as the appropriate kinds and quantities of data can be generated.

ALTERNATIVE TYPES OF MODELS

Although several different models are available for interregional competition studies, they all can be roughly classified in one of two categories: (a) regression type models and (b) activity analysis or mathematical programming models. For regression type models, regional supply and demand equations are first estimated (typically from time series data) using regression techniques. Adding appropriate transportation linkages between regions completes the model. In our opinion, regression techniques will find only limited use in interregional studies. Certainly regression methods will continue to be used to estimate demand functions (both national and regional), and they may also

Walter Haessel read an early draft of this paper and suggested several changes. Since we reserved the right to accept or reject his suggestions, he is not responsible for the final product.

1. An example is Mighell and Black (22). The historic planning activities in the U.S.S.R. necessarily involved problems of interregional competition in the allocation of food targets over the nation. We are not acquainted with the Russian literature on these problems, however.

prove to be useful for characterizing the short-run supply structure
(past or future). However supply relationships estimated from time
series data cannot adequately reflect those "shifters" which result in a
complete restructuring of the industry. Moreover countries are often
more interested in production potentials and optimum allocations of
planned output goals than in patterns of the past. For these reasons we
will emphasize models of the activity analysis type.

   Among activity analysis models several alternatives are possible
with the choice depending on data, time, and funds available, computer
capacity, and the kinds of computer programs obtainable, among other
things. One of the more useful alternatives, especially if optimal output allocation among regions is of prime interest, is what might be
called the "interregional linear programming model." We have used
such a model to analyze U.S. crop and livestock production, delineating
as many as 150 producing regions and 31 consuming regions. Production restraints (typically land) and crop-producing activities are defined
for each producing region. Demand restraints consisting of fixed quantities of each final commodity are designated for each consuming region.
Each producing region is completely contained in a consuming region,
and production in the producing region contributes to supply in that
consuming region. Transportation activities permit movement of commodities from consuming regions with excess supply to those with excess demand. Conceptually each farm can be regarded as a distinct
producing region with its own production restraints. Of course the
more detailed the disaggregation, the greater the data requirements
are and the more involved the computations. In a Swedish study (3)
each producing region was divided into two land classes with two farm-
size groups in each class. In a study in progress, we partition each
producing region into three subregions on the basis of farm size.

   A second alternative among activity analysis models is the representative-farm model. The procedure is to classify all the farms in a
region into one of several farm-type groups and to designate a representative (typical) farm for each group. Production restraints and activities are specified for each representative farm, and an optimal production plan estimated by linear programming. An optimal plan for the
group is obtained by multiplying the optimal representative-farm plan
by the number of farms in the group (or some other appropriate weighting factor). Finally, the regional totals are the sums of the group totals.
The process is repeated for each region. This type of model has been
used extensively in the United States to analyze regional supply-response
potentials; we are cooperating with several other states in such analysis
(1, 18, 28). To date the representative-farm approach has not been used
to analyze interregional competition, at least not in the usual sense of
jointly determining production levels in many interdependent regions.
Conceivably the principal characteristics of the interregional linear
programming model and the representative-farm model could be incorporated in a single model, and each farm could be treated as a region with its own restraints and production activities. Once again, data
and computer requirements would be massive.

Models with dynamic, recursive, or other time-oriented character-istics provide a third alternative. However these models, like the rep-resentative-farm models, pose massive and perhaps prohibitive data problems if the number of regions is large. Some of their character-istics are appealing, and data availability and computer capacities may eventually permit their large-scale application. In our estimation, single-period models are more promising for practical applications, and we restrict our comments to this type for the remainder of the paper.

Finally, nonlinear formulations of single-period, regional alloca-tion models are now possible. We recently completed work on a model which includes 144 producing regions and 9 consuming regions, each with a set of linear demand functions. The objective function is quad-ratic, but the restraints are linear just as in the linear programming models. Prices and quantities, as well as production and transportation patterns, are determined endogenously. As of now it is not possible to deal with nonlinear restraints though it probably will be in the future.

Despite some pronounced limitations, the models now available of-fer a wide range of flexibility for dealing with interregional allocation problems. We move now to a more detailed discussion, including spe-cific applications, of some of these models.

LINEAR ACTIVITY ANALYSIS MODELS

For interregional linear programming models, the producing re-gion is the basic producing unit, and resource restraints and producing activities are defined for each such region. Production contributes to supply in the consuming region in which the producing region is located. A set of demands is defined for each consuming region, and these de-mands, along with crop yields in the producing regions, are assumed to be fixed and known quantities. The objective is to find the regional allo-cation of production which minimizes the cost (production plus trans-portation) of satisfying the given demands. Other methods of analysis used for the "national agricultural planning" of many countries require similar assumptions but may be less effective than linear programming. Heady, Skold, and Randhawa (20), for example, found that for a given set of resources, food output from a linear programming allocation exceeded that from another type of allocation by 12.5 percent. Models of this type have the capacity for a high degree of realism despite their rela-tive simplicity. We regard them as a logical first step in the analysis of regional comparative advantage.

Let us move now to the discussion of a specific model, chosen from one of our own studies. This is one of roughly 15 U.S. interregional models we have completed (7-9, 16-20, 28, 33).

The Specific Model

For this model we partitioned the continental United States into 144

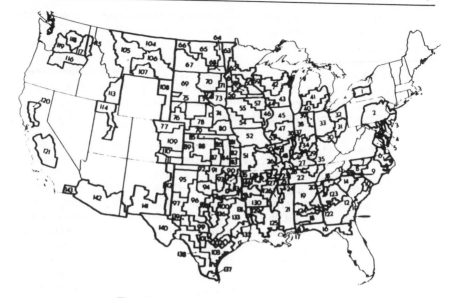

Fig. 12.1. Location of producing regions.

producing regions and 31 consuming regions (Figs. 12.1, 12.2). We were
interested in the major field crops: wheat, corn, oats, barley, grain
sorghum, soybeans, and cotton. Historically the 144 producing regions
have accounted for approximately 95, 97, 93, 84, 99, 99, and 99 percent,

Fig. 12.2. Location of consuming regions.

respectively, of the U.S. production of these seven crops. The objective of the study was fourfold: (a) to determine the optimal distribution of crop production among the 144 producing regions; (b) to determine the acreage required to satisfy the nation's food and fiber requirements; (c) to determine the quantity and location of land which could or should be shifted from crop production to other uses; and (d) to determine the transportation patterns between the 31 consuming regions.

In the interest of homogeneous producing regions, a state (sometimes a county) was first partitioned into contiguous areas which were economically uniform. These areas were partitioned into producing regions on the basis of (a) similar numbers of tractors, combines, and corn pickers per thousand acres, (b) similar proportions of cropland planted to particular crops, (c) similar yields of the 7 field crops, and (d) similar soil classes or types. Five production activities were possible in each producing region: wheat, feed grain rotation, feed grain-soybean rotation, soybeans, and cotton. A production activity was included in a producing region only if there was a historical record of the crop in that region. Cotton is not produced in the state of Minnesota, for example, so we did not allow that and other similar possibilities. A land restraint, which reflects the total amount of land available for the 5 crop activities, was defined for each producing region. The soybean activity was limited to no more than 50 percent of the total land available for crops.

Consuming region boundaries coincide with state boundaries, and each region includes at least one state. If a region includes more than one state, those states adjoin and are economically similar. For each region three commodity demands were defined: wheat, feed grains, and oilmeals. A single, national demand for cotton lint was defined. Each region has a wheat-to-feed transfer activity which permits the use of wheat as feed if wheat is the least cost source of nutrients. Transportation activities permit the movement of commodities between consuming regions. Potentially, there are 930 (31 x 30) transportation activities for each commodity, or 2,790 for the three commodities. All can be included, or those with no historical basis can be eliminated in order to reduce the size of the model. Using the second alternative, we reduced the number of transportation activities to 1,376. In regions from which foreign shipments are usually made, demand includes a portion of the estimated U.S. exports.

The year 1975 was chosen as the base year for this model. Using a future date necessitated projections for much of the data. A population of 222 million was projected; real per capita income was projected to be 150 percent of that in 1955, and per capita consumption of farm products was projected to increase accordingly; livestock feed-conversion ratios were projected linearly from the 1940-60 period; exports of wheat, feed grains, and oilmeals were projected to follow the 1956-64 trends; crop yields were projected linearly using 1940-64 as the base period.

It will be evident that a model of this kind requires a very large quantity of data. As outlined, the model has a coefficient matrix of order

402 x 1923, excluding slack vectors. (By contrast, the model which includes three farm types per producing region has a coefficient matrix of order 4,000 x 37,000, excluding slacks.) Roughly 5 man-years were required to collect and reformulate data for the several models now in use. The more detailed the model, the greater are the data requirements and the more complex the computations. It finally becomes necessary to strike some kind of balance between the number of regions and restraints and the amount of time or computation funds available.

Mathematical Structure

First, let us define the symbols we will use.

x_{ki} = acres of the k-th crop activity in the i-th producing region, k = 1, ..., 5; i = 1, ..., 144. (k=1 refers to wheat, k=2 to feed grains, k=3 to feed grain-soybean rotation, k=4 to soybeans, k=5 to cotton)

c_{ki} = cost per acre of the k-th crop activity in the i-th producing region

L_{Ti} = total land available for crop production in the i-th producing region

L_{Si} = amount of land available for soybean production in the i-th producing region

L_{Ci} = amount of land available for cotton production in the i-th producing region

y_m = quantity of wheat transferred into feed grains in the m-th consuming region; m = 1, ..., 31

d_m = cost per unit of transferring wheat into feed grains in the m-th consuming region

h_m = quantity of feed grains per unit of wheat in the m-th consuming region

D_{gm} = demand for the g-th product in the m-th consuming region; g = 1, 2, 3. (g=1 refers to wheat, g=2 to feed grains, g=3 to oilmeals)

D_c = national demand for cotton lint

a_{gki} = yield of the g-th product per acre of the k-th crop activity in the i-th producing region (e.g., a_{231} = yield of feed grains per acre of the feed grain-soybean rotation in producing region 1)

z_{gmn} = quantity of the g-th product transported from the m-th to the n-th consuming region; m, n = 1, ..., 31

b_{gmn} = cost per unit of transporting the g-th product from the m-th to the n-th consuming region

r_m = number of producing regions in the m-th consuming region

The problem is to minimize the objective function, equation (1), subject to the restraints, expressions (2)-(9).

$$\min f(x_{ki}, y_m, z_{gmn}) = \sum_{i=1}^{144} \sum_{k=1}^{5} c_{ki} x_{ki} + \sum_{m=1}^{31} d_m y_m \tag{1}$$

$$+ \sum_{g=i}^{3} \sum_{m \neq n} b_{gmn} z_{gmn}$$

subject to:

$$\sum_{i=1}^{r_m} a_{11i} x_{1i} - y_m + \sum_{n \neq m} (z_{1nm} - z_{1mn}) \geq D_{1m} \tag{2}$$

$$\sum_{i=1}^{r_m} a_{22i} x_{2i} + \sum_{i=1}^{r_m} a_{23i} x_{3i} + h_m y_m + \sum_{n \neq m} (z_{2nm} - z_{2mn}) \geq D_{2m} \tag{3}$$

$$\sum_{i=1}^{r_m} a_{33i} x_{3i} + \sum_{i=1}^{r_m} a_{34i} x_{4i} + \sum_{i=1}^{r_m} a_{35i} x_{5i} + \sum_{n \neq m} (z_{3nm} - z_{3mn}) \geq D_{3m} \tag{4}$$

$$\sum_{i=1}^{144} a_{c5i} x_{5i} \geq D_c \tag{5}$$

$$\sum_{k=1}^{5} x_{ki} \leq L_{Ti} \tag{6}$$

$$x_{4i} \leq L_{Si} \tag{7}$$

$$x_{5i} \leq L_{Ci} \tag{8}$$

$$x_{ki}, y_m, z_{gmn} \geq 0 \tag{9}$$

The objective function (1) is the linear sum of production costs, wheat-to-feed grain transfer costs, and transportation costs, and we want to find values for the variables that minimize this sum without violating any of the restraints. Restraints (2)-(5) require that production, plus net imports, plus adjustments for wheat-to-feed grain transfer (if any), be at least as great as demand for every product in every consuming region. Restraints (6)-(8) require that land use not exceed availability for every producing region. Restraint (9) requires simply that all the variables be nonnegative.

Since the objective function and all the restraints are linear, we have a bona fide linear programming problem. A word of caution may be in order, however. In some countries there may be no feasible solution to a problem of this kind unless the possibility for foreign imports is explicitly included in the model. The difficulty is illustrated for two products (say soybeans and feed grains) in Figure 12.3 where the area OABC is the feasible region defined by the land restraints. Without foreign imports, it is impossible to satisfy, simultaneously, the demand for D_{2m} of feed grain and D_{3m} of oilmeals. In the United

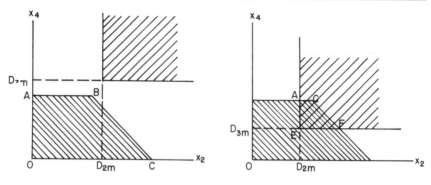

Fig. 12.3. No feasible solution.   Fig. 12.4. Many feasible solutions.

States and many other countries, this difficulty does not arise. Figure 12.4, where any point in the area ACEF satisfies demand and the land restraints simultaneously, illustrates this case.

Summary of Results

Regional crop production patterns are illustrated in Figure 12.5. The principal change from present patterns of production is for cotton.

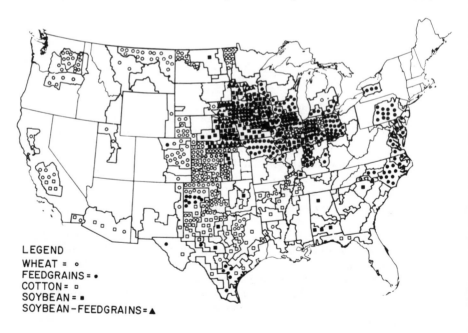

LEGEND
WHEAT = ○
FEEDGRAINS = ●
COTTON = ▫
SOYBEAN = ◼
SOYBEAN-FEEDGRAINS = ▲

Fig. 12.5. Regional production pattern for programming model. (Each dot represents 200,000 acres.)

Under the 1975 pattern most of the cotton is produced in Texas, Arizona, and California. These states produce large acreages of cotton now, but in addition there are large acreages in the southeastern states of Mississippi, Alabama, and Georgia. For the other crops there is relatively little change. Most of the wheat is produced in the Great Plains states and most of the feed grains and soybeans in the Corn Belt states, much as they are now. Approximately 153 million acres of cropland are used for crop production, leaving roughly 71 million acres which could be shifted to pasture or forest production or to recreational uses. Increased pasture production would permit increased beef production which is consistent with the relatively high income-elasticity of beef demand.

Interregional flows of oilmeals are shown in Figure 12.6. Transportation patterns for the other commodities as well as a detailed listing and discussion of other results are available in Heady and Skold (18).

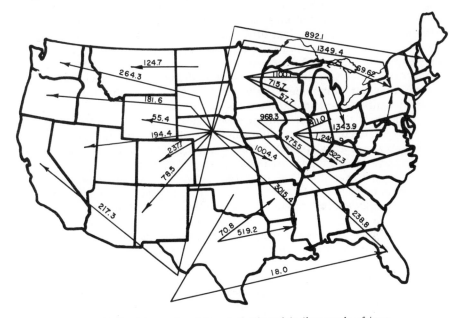

Fig. 12.6. Interregional flows of oilmeal in thousands of tons.

Common Difficulties

Several interrelated problems are associated with choosing the number of regions, defining the restraints, and developing the necessary technical coefficients. Using producing regions as the basic producing unit presumes constant returns to scale over all land in the region. It further presumes that every farm in the region has the same production function. Thus the necessity for the maximum possible homogeneity among soils, climatic conditions, crop yields, and technology within a producing region becomes evident. This necessity operates in favor of small regions. We have already seen the conflict between larger numbers of regions on one hand and data and computational requirements on the other. To add to the complications, the smallest political subdivision for which data are available is often the county, district, township, Olekminsk, or other comparatively large unit. Regions of smaller size can be defined only at the expense of greatly increased data collection efforts. In most countries the potential number of regions will be large, but the number finally defined will be limited by computational capacities and the purposes of the study.

Criteria for defining consuming regions are even less precise than those for producing regions. As with producing regions, the range of choice may be limited by the size and nature of civil units for which data are available. Population concentrations, ports, and usual directions of commodity flows provide some basis for defining consuming regions. If transportation costs are important in the interregional allocation of outputs, there must not be too few consuming regions. We have found, for example, that different regions, separated by as much as 800 kilometers, may have similar production patterns. However they export to quite different markets. Hence if we are interested in transportation flows, we cannot include both such areas in a single region. For nonlinear models the regions must be such that we can estimate or synthesize demand functions for them.

In general the fewer the number of restraints, the more specialization of regional production the solutions will exhibit. Including only land restraints, as we have, assumes that all other resources are variable and available in unlimited quantities. Thus solutions to problems with only land restraints are long-run in nature; they may also exhibit a high degree of specialization. Overspecialization can be avoided to some extent by adding maximum and minimum restraints on crop acreages or upper and lower bounds on the variables themselves. Such restraints or bounds should be based on agronomic or engineering knowledge. (We used historical production patterns in the case of soybeans and cotton.) If short-run allocation is the primary interest, it may be necessary to include restraints on resources other than land (on labor, machinery, and capital, for example) and to consider separate restraints for different seasons of the year. In one study (3) restraints were defined for labor, capital, and buildings. The interregional linear programming model we have underway, which has three subregions in each producing region, includes restraints on labor, capital, and land for each subregion.

In general we must have input-output coefficients (some of which may be zero) which reflect the requirement of each product for each resource. It follows that the quantity of data required will be proportional to the number of restraints, other things equal. If the interest is in potential production using new technologies (or even known technologies not widely used), yield and cost coefficients must reflect such technologies. If present technology is of prime interest, yield and cost estimates will be some kind of average of present yields and costs. In some countries, a "stock" of data sufficient to estimate the necessary coefficients may be available already. If not, a sample survey is probably the best source of the needed data. In view of the potential value of models such as these, governmental statistical agencies should be persuaded, if possible, to collect the required data. Transportation cost data are often more readily available than farm data. In some countries several modes of transportation (e.g., truck, rail, water) are available. If transportation problems are a major interest and computer capacity permits, all types of transportation can be included, and the optimal mode will be selected endogenously. Otherwise a single mode (the least cost or most used one) can be arbitrarily selected in advance.

A More Detailed Model

It is at least conceptually possible to include almost any desired amount of detail in linear activity analysis models. Limited data or restrictive computer capacity may limit the amount of detail but not the conceptual model. To illustrate, let us formulate a model in which m farm products can be transformed into u intermediate commodities, which in turn can be processed into w final goods. Suppose that there are n producing regions, each with s resource restraints and r consuming regions (markets). Define the following symbols:

b_{gj} = cost per unit of producing the g-th farm product in the j-th producing region, $g = 1, ..., m; j = 1, ..., n$

x_{gj} = output of the g-th farm product in the j-th producing region

t_{gjk} = cost per unit of transporting the g-th farm product from the j-th to the k-th producing region, $j \neq k$

x_{gjk} = quantity of the g-th farm product transported from the j-th to the k-th producing region, $j \neq k$

c_{hj} = cost per unit of producing the h-th intermediate commodity in the j-th producing region, $h = 1, ..., u; j = 1, ..., n$

y_{hj} = quantity of the h-th intermediate commodity produced in the j-th producing region

t'_{hjk} = cost per unit of transporting the h-th intermediate commodity from the j-th to the k-th producing region, $j \neq k$

y_{hjk} = quantity of the h-th intermediate commodity transported from the j-th to the k-th producing region, $j \neq k$

d_{ij} = cost per unit of producing the i-th final good in the j-th producing region, $i = 1, ..., w; j = 1, ..., n$

z_{ij} = quantity of the i-th final good produced in the j-th producing region

t''_{ijp} = cost per unit of transporting the i-th final good from the j-th producing region to the p-th consuming region, $j = 1, ..., n; p = 1, ..., r$

z_{ijp} = quantity of the i-th final good transported from the j-th producing region to the p-th consuming region

The objective is to minimize the aggregate cost of satisfying the given (fixed) demands in the consuming regions without violating any of the restrictions on resource availability or processing capacity. The objective function is given by (10),

$$\text{Min } F = \sum_g \sum_j b_{gj} \, x_{gj} + \sum_g \sum_j \sum_k t_{gjk} \, x_{gjk}$$

$$+ \sum_h \sum_j c_{hj} \, y_{hj} + \sum_h \sum_j \sum_k t'_{hjk} \, y_{hjk}$$

$$+ \sum_i \sum_j d_{ij} \, z_{ij} + \sum_i \sum_j \sum_p t''_{ijp} \, z_{ijp} \tag{10}$$

subject to the restraints described below. There are r·w demands for final goods (11), where D_{ip} is the quantity of the i-th good consumed in the p-th market and this demand is satisfied by imports from the n producing regions.

$$D_{ip} \le \sum_{j=1}^{n} z_{ijp}; \quad i = 1, ..., w; \quad j = 1, ..., n; \quad p = 1, ..., r \tag{11}$$

If some producing region is contained in a consuming region, the transportation activity between the two regions may be only a formality with no associated cost.

There are n·s restraints (12)

$$S_{fj} \ge \sum_{g=1}^{m} a_{fgj} \, x_{gj} + \sum_{h=1}^{u} a'_{fhj} \, y_{hj} + \sum_{i=1}^{w} a''_{fij} \, z_{ij};$$

$$f = 1, ..., s; \quad j = 1, ..., n \tag{12}$$

on the availability of basic resources. For the j-th producing region, S_{fj} is the quantity of the f-th resource available; a_{fgj} is the quantity of the f-th resource required per unit of the g-th farm product; a'_{fij} is the quantity required per unit of the h-th intermediate commodity; and a'' is the quantity required for the i-th final good. If the situation demands it, any of these resource availabilities or requirements can be zero. The model does not allow for the interregional movement of basic resources. Resources must be used, if at all, in the region where they are available.

The following accounting rows are required; m·n of the form (13), u·n of the form (14), and w·n of the form (15). Formulation of the accounting rows as inequalities permits surpluses, which are possible in the case of joint production (e.g., oil and oilmeal from soybeans). In (13)

$$T_{gj} \le x_{gj} + \sum_{k \ne j} (x_{gkj} - x_{gjk}) - \sum_{h=1}^{u} b_{ghj} \, y_{hj};$$

$$g = 1, ..., m; \quad j = 1, ..., n \tag{13}$$

x_{gj} is the quantity of the g-th farm product produced in the j-th producing region; $\sum\limits_{k \neq j} (x_{gkj} - x_{gjk})$ represents net imports (exports if

negative); $\sum\limits_{h=1}^{u} b_{ghj} y_{hj}$ is the quantity used in the production of the u

intermediate commodities; b_{ghj} is the quantity of the g-th farm product required per unit of the h-th intermediate commodity in producing region j. In (14)

$$T'_{hj} \leq y_{hj} + \sum_{k \neq j} (y_{hkj} - y_{hjk}) - \sum_{i=1}^{w} d_{hij} z_{ij};$$

$$h = 1, ..., u; \qquad j = 1, ..., n \tag{14}$$

y_{hj} is the quantity of the h-th intermediate commodity produced in the j-th producing region; $\sum\limits_{k \neq j} (y_{hkj} - y_{hjk})$ represents net imports (exports if negative); $\sum\limits_{i=1}^{w} d_{hij} z_{ij}$ is the quantity used in the production of the w final goods; d_{hij} is the quantity of the h-th intermediate commodity required per unit of the i-th final good in producing region j. In (15),

$$T''_{ij} \leq z_{ij} - \sum_{p=1}^{r} z_{ijp}; \qquad i = 1, ..., w; \qquad j = 1, ..., n \tag{15}$$

z_{ij} is the quantity of the i-th final good produced in the j-th producing region and $\sum\limits_{p=1}^{r} z_{ijp}$ is the quantity exported to the r consuming regions.

Restraints, if any, on the capacity to produce intermediate commodities from farm products and final goods from intermediate commodities take the forms (16) and (17), respectively.

$$S'_{hj} \geq y_{hj}; \qquad h = 1, ..., u; \qquad j = 1, ..., n \tag{16}$$

$$S''_{ij} \geq z_{ij}; \qquad i = 1, ..., w; \qquad j = 1, ..., n \tag{17}$$

For the j-th producing region, S'_{hj} is the maximum quantity of the h-th intermediate commodity and S''_{ij} is the maximum quantity of the i-th final good that can be produced in a given time period. These capacity restraints could be formulated in terms of input capacity rather than output capacity if they were more meaningful that way.

Finally, we require that all the variables be nonnegative (18).

$$x_{gj}, x_{gjk}, y_{hj}, y_{hjk}, z_{ij}, z_{ijp} \geq 0 \tag{18}$$

In terms of economic relationships the model is a simple one. It supposes fixed demands and preassigned weights (costs) in the objective function for all the variables. The objective is to find the production, processing, and transportation patterns which minimize the cost of satisfying the given, fixed demands, subject to the restraints on basic resource availabilities and processing capacities. In terms of data requirements, however, the model is a complicated one. Permitting more than one level of technology (method of producing or processing a given product, commodity, or good) would increase the data requirements even further.

REPRESENTATIVE-FARM MODELS

To date the principal use of representative-farm models has been in estimating regional, aggregate-supply responses.[2] No attempts have been made to include demand restraints, interregional transportation activities, or other characteristics which permit the endogenous determination of equilibrium as in the interregional linear programming model. Nevertheless representative-farm models have the potential for such applications, and they have some distinct advantages over interregional linear programming models. The individual farm rather than a producing region is the basic producing unit, and that is the principal advantage. Because of it, short-run resource immobilities can be reflected more accurately. To illustrate, suppose that a farm has two limiting resources, land and labor, and that land is more limiting. The excess labor will not be used, at least not on the farm. However if all farms were combined into a single producing unit (as in the interregional model), the excess labor on one farm could in effect be used on another farm with excess land.

For large multiregional models advantage turns to disadvantage. If data is required for every farm (or even a substantial proportion of farms) in every region, the data collection task will be a large one indeed. Regional models with subregions can be regarded as compromises between interregional models and representative-farm models. They capture some of the realism of representative-farm models but only a portion of the data problems.

Formulation Process

The following steps are typical (2): (a) define the commodity and population for which regional supply or production estimates are to be made; (b) draw a sample of farms and obtain data on the resources, costs, and production alternatives for each farm in the sample; (c) stratify the sample into groups and define a representative farm for each group; (d) using variable-price programming, as outlined by Heady and Candler (14), estimate a supply function for each representative farm; (e) expand the supply function of the representative farm to obtain a supply function for the group it represents; (f) sum, horizontally, the group supply functions to obtain an estimated supply function for the sample; and (g) expand the sample estimates to obtain the desired population estimates.

---

2. A series of articles on the uses of representative-farm models, including the use for interregional competition analysis, appears in *J. Farm Econ.*, 45:1438-68.

Sources of Error

Representative-farm models are not error-free, just as the purely interregional models are not. Stovall (29) discusses three sources of error in representative-farm models. (a) Specification error arises because the programming model does not accurately reflect the conditions actually facing the farm firm. It may include errors in the technical coefficients, the resource restraints, or the prices (product or input).[3] (b) Sampling error arises because the parameters which characterize the population of farms are estimated from a sample. (c) Aggregation error is the difference between the estimated area supply functions and the actual ones, where the actual supply function is the summation of the individual supply functions of all farms in the area. The three types of error are not independent. Specification error, for example, may result in part from sampling error. Either sampling or specification errors may lead to aggregation error, though there may be still other sources of aggregation error which are independent of both.

Problems of specification arise in every phase of formulating a linear programming problem and must be dealt with where they occur. Sampling error is a statistical problem, and its elimination lies in improved samples — larger sample size and more effective stratification, for example (5). There seem to be no simple corrections for aggregation error. Hartley indicates that aggregation error will be serious if stratification is based on two resources, say land and buildings, and the estimated supply functions are based on a third resource, labor (13). Using the duality theorem of linear programming, Day shows that under certain conditions the aggregate supply function for a group of farms is equivalent to the sum of the individual supply functions (6). The conditions are that resource restraints, technical coefficients, and prices be proportional among all farms. Day defines these conditions as "proportional heterogeneity."

Nature of the Aggregation Problem

Consider the linear programming model for the g-th farm from a set of n farms. The problem is to find a vector of production levels, X_g, which maximizes profits subject to the resource restrictions. We have

$$\max \ \pi_g = C'_g X_g \tag{19}$$

subject to

$$A_g X_g = S_g \tag{20}$$

---

3. This definition does not agree exactly with the usual concept of specification error. Failure to incorporate appropriate activities, restraints, and objective function coefficients are obviously specification errors. Errors in technical coefficients and prices, on the other hand, appear to be more in the realm of sampling error.

$$X_g \geq 0 \tag{21}$$

where π_g is total net returns, C_g is a vector of net returns per unit of output, X_g is the output vector (including slacks), A_g is the matrix of input-output coefficients, and S_g is the vector of available resources.

Total output for the n farms is given by $\sum_{g=1}^{n} X_g$. This sum is not subject to aggregation error because it includes the output from every farm. Hence it is the logical benchmark with which all other estimates should be compared.

The magnitude of n is usually so large that it is impractical to obtain a solution for every farm. Instead it is common to define a representative farm and to determine its optimal output level. Total production for the n farms is estimated by appropriately weighting the results for the representative farm. If the representative farm is, in some sense, an average farm (total resources for all farms divided by n), then n is the appropriate weighting factor. A representative farm which includes the resources of all n farms (i.e., a purely regional formulation) will give the same results. The programming model for the region as a whole might be as follows:

$$\max \pi = C'X \tag{22}$$

subject to

$$AX = S \tag{23}$$

$$X \geq 0 \tag{24}$$

where C, X, A, and S represent per unit net returns, output, input-output matrix, and resource restraints, respectively. If $X \neq \sum_{g=1}^{n} X_g$, there is some aggregation error.

Day's "proportional heterogeneity" requirements for exact aggregation are

$$A_1 = A_2 = \ldots = A_n = A \tag{25}$$

$$C_g = \delta_g C, \ \delta_g \geq 0, \ \text{a scalar} \tag{26}$$

$$S_g = \lambda_g S, \ 0 \leq \lambda_g \leq 1 \tag{27}$$

By (25) the input-output matrices for the n farms are identical. By (26) and (27) net returns and resource levels, respectively, are proportional between farms. If (25) to (27) are satisfied, a representative-farm solution, multiplied by n, will exactly equal the sum of solutions for all n farms. It is evident that "proportional heterogeneity" is a very exacting requirement, one that is unlikely to be satisfied completely, especially if n is large.

Other, purportedly less restrictive, conditions for exact aggregation have been proposed by Miller (23). He argues that if a set of farms have (a) identical coefficient matrices and (b) qualitatively homogeneous output vectors (QHOV), then exact aggregation is possible. For each

farm in a set of farms the QHOV condition is that the same activities
be optimal, despite any differences in resource levels and net-return
vectors. These requirements appear to be rather exacting also. To
use the QHOV criterion, it would be necessary to obtain a programming
solution for each farm before stratifying the farms into groups — not an
inviting prospect.

Common Problems

Since the requirements for exact aggregation are so stringent, it
is probably unrealistic to expect to eliminate all aggregation error.
However, large samples and relatively detailed stratification should
make it possible to reduce aggregation error to tolerable levels. For
analyses of a long-run nature, interregional linear programming models appear to be at least as appropriate as representative-farm models
and they are less demanding of data and computer capacity. As computer capacities increase and decomposition algorithms reach greater
perfection, the outstanding characteristics of both models may be combined in a single model.

In some applications in the United States, representative-farm
models and, to a lesser extent, recursive models have been used in attempts to simulate farmers' decisions. Optimal solutions are compared with actual production patterns of farmers, and further restrictions are added, if needed, to approximate more closely observed production patterns. Generally programming models are not designed to
simulate or predict farmers' behavior, although such flexibility would
certainly be helpful. For simulative and predictive purposes, regression models are more appropriate than normative programming models.

NONLINEAR ACTIVITY ANALYSIS MODELS

There are many potential sources of nonlinearity in interregional
competition models. Until recently, however, it was necessary to make
assumptions which eliminated most nonlinearities before empirical applications could proceed. We may still choose to ignore nonlinearities
if they are not crucial to the results. We now have tools for handling
at least some nonlinearities. One of the more obvious sources of nonlinearity is the treatment of both prices and quantities as endogenous
variables. In this section, we will discuss some of the characteristics
of nonlinear models and summarize an application we have recently
completed which deals with prices and quantities endogenously.

Most countries or research workers just beginning the study of interregional allocation will probably still be well advised to begin with
linear models. For a given computer capacity, linear models permit
greater detail (e.g., more regions, more restraints) than do nonlinear
ones. Given the number of regions, linear models have substantially
smaller data requirements. Moreover, depending on the purpose of the

analysis, linear models may provide information more efficiently than nonlinear ones do. Even so, many researchers will eventually turn to nonlinear models, and when they do, previous experience with linear models will be invaluable.

Brief Review of Nonlinear Models

In the most general case of nonlinear, interregional competition problems, regional supply and regional demand are functions of factor and product prices. We cannot as yet handle all problems of this nature. However Takayama and Judge have shown that it is possible to formulate the interregional problem in a quadratic programming format which does have a solution, if appropriate dependencies exist between regional supply, demand, and price (32). At the other extreme, if both supply and demand are known, the problem is simply finding the optimal distribution pattern. This is the familiar transportation problem which Koopmans and Reiter, among others, have shown how to solve (21). There are of course all combinations of linearities and nonlinearities between the two extremes.

Early attempts at solving nonlinear problems used iterative applications of linear programming (26). Iterative procedures are very laborious under any circumstances; where large numbers of regions are involved, they are also very impractical. Takayama and Judge formulated an activity analysis model which could be solved as a quadratic programming problem (31). They showed that their model was general enough to allow interregional transportation of factors of production, final products, or both. Plessner and Heady also developed an activity analysis model which could be solved as a quadratic programming problem (24). Their model is also general enough to permit interregional shipment of either products or factors or both. In addition, they demonstrated that a solution to their model is consistent with a competitive equilibrium.

In the remainder of this section we will discuss the characteristics of, and the results from, a specialization of the Plessner-Heady model. The specialized model permits interregional transportation of final products but not factors of production.

Mathematical Model

Suppose there are K consuming regions, each subdivided into H producing regions. We define the following symbols:

b^{hk} = an m-vector of primary resources (land) for producing region h in consuming region k, h = 1, ..., H; k = 1, ..., K

x^{hk} = an n-vector of output levels for producing region h in consuming region k

A^{hk} = a technology matrix relating b^{hk} to a unit of x^{hk}

p^k = an n-vector of prices for the elements of x^{hk}

c^{hk} = an n-vector of costs associated with x^{hk}

u^{hk} = an m-vector of imputed values of the primary resources, b^{hk}

s^{jk} = an n-vector of shipments from market j to market k, $j \neq k$

t^{jk} = an n-vector of costs associated with s^{jk}

The variables are x^{hk}, p^k, u^{hk}, and s^{jk}. Finally, we assume a linear demand system given by (28).

$$d^k = d_0^k + D^k p^k, \quad k = 1, \ldots, K \tag{28}$$

where

d^k = an n-vector of quantities demanded

d_0^k = an n-vector of constants

D^k = a negative semidefinite matrix of constants

The programming problem we want to consider is the following one:

$$\max f(x^{hk}, p^k, u^{hk}, s^{jk}) = \sum_{k=1}^{K} [(d_0^k + D^k p^k)' p^k -$$

$$\sum_{h=1}^{H} c^{hk} x^{hk} - \sum_{h=1}^{H} u^{hk} b^{hk}] - \sum_{j \neq k} t^{jk} s^{jk} \tag{29}$$

subject to:

$$A^{hk} x^{hk} \leq b^{hk} \tag{30}$$

$$p^k - (A^{hk})' u^{hk} \leq c^{hk} \tag{31}$$

$$D^k p^k - \sum_{j \neq k} (s^{jk} - s^{kj}) - \sum_{h=1}^{H} x^{hk} \leq -d_0^k \tag{32}$$

$$p^j - p^k \leq t^{kj} \tag{33}$$

$$p^k - p^j \leq t^{jk} = t^{kj} \tag{34}$$

$$x^{hk}, p^k, u^{hk}, s^{jk} \geq 0 \tag{35}$$

The objective function (29) is a net profit function because it consists of total revenue, minus production costs, minus land rents, minus transportation costs. Constraint (30) prevents land use from exceeding availability. Constraint (31) requires that marginal returns from an activity be no greater than marginal cost (c^{hk}, a constant). Constraint (32) requires that supply (production plus net imports) be at least as great as demand. Constraints (33) and (34) are Samuelson's conditions for equilibrium in trade (25).

Suppose that $\bar{f} = f(\bar{x}^{hk}, \bar{p}^k, \bar{u}^{hk}, \bar{s}^{jk})$ is the optimal value of the objective function, and $\bar{x}^{hk}$, $\bar{p}^k$, $\bar{u}^{hk}$, and $\bar{s}^{jk}$ are the optimal values of the variables. Plessner and Heady have shown that this solution has the following characteristics: (a) $\bar{f} = 0$, that is aggregate net profits are zero; (b) if all H producing regions in the k-th consuming region face the prices $\bar{p}^k$, net profits for each producing region are also maximum and zero; (c) for every product with positive output, marginal cost will equal price; (d) for every product with positive price, supply will equal demand; (e) the trade equilibrium conditions will be satisfied as equalities for every product actually traded (24).

Plessner and Heady discuss the general model in detail; the specialized model is discussed in more detail in Hall, Heady, and Plessner (12).

A Specific Problem

For this problem we partitioned the United States into 9 consuming regions (Fig. 12.7). For each region we defined a system of 6 linear demand equations in the form of (28), one each for wheat, corn, oats, and barley for food use, one for feed grains, and one for oilmeals. The year 1965 was taken as the base year, and we apportioned 1965 commercial exports among those consuming regions from which foreign shipments are made. These exports were added to the demand intercepts (d_0^k). A set of 79 transportation activities permitted movement of the 6 commodities from regions with excess supply to those with excess demand.

We used the 144 producing regions shown in Figure 12.1. Each producing region is completely contained in a consuming region, and production in the producing region contributes to supply in the consuming region. There were seven potential crop activities in each producing

Fig. 12.7. Location of consuming regions.

region: wheat, corn, oats, and barley for food use, feed grains, wheat-for-feed use, and soybeans. After deleting crops unlikely to be grown in some regions, we were left with 927 crop-producing activities.

In Table 12.1 we compare estimated national-average prices and quantities with actual 1965 prices and quantities. Estimated prices are substantially lower than market prices, as we expected. Only three of the six estimated quantities are greater than market quantities, however. Notably, actual quantities of corn and oats for food uses are greater than the estimated quantities. A partial explanation for the discrepancy is that since 1955-57 the base period for the demand data, actual rates of increase in the food uses of corn and oats have been greater than the rate of increase indicated by the trend terms in the demand equations.

Table 12.1. Estimated U.S. demands and prices compared
with actual 1965 usage and prices

	Projected		Actual	
	Price[a] (dol.)	Quantity[b] (mil.)	Price[c] (dol.)	Quantity[b] (mil.)
Wheat, food (bu)	0.74	798.74	1.35[d]	796.50[e]
Corn, food (bu)	0.63	285.86	1.16	332.00[f]
Oats, food (bu)	0.33	43.22	0.62	47.00[g]
Barley, food (bu)	0.57	5.96	1.02	6.00[h]
Feed grains (ton)	22.49	172.27	40.62[i]	148.77
Soybean oilmeal (ton)	43.98	21.42	65.41[j]	13.45

a. Weighted average of estimated regional prices with estimated regional production as weights.
b. Includes commercial exports.
c. Seasonal average price received by farmers.
d. Participants in the government wheat program received an average additional $0.44 in the form of wheat certificate payment.
e. Includes food and industrial uses.
f. Includes breakfast foods, cornmeal and grits, and wet process products.
g. Includes domestic use for food.
h. Includes barley equivalent use of malt for food. Does not include uses of malt for alcohol and alcohol beverages (98.35 million bu.)
i. Weighted average of the prices of corn, oats, barley, grain sorghum, and wheat. Weights were the quantities fed plus commercial export of the first 4 grains and quantity of wheat fed.
j. Assumes (a) 0.0233 tons meal/bu soybeans, (b) meal constitutes 60 percent of the value of soybeans, (c) price $2.54/bu soybeans.

Figure 12.8 shows the interregional flow patterns for one of the commodities, feed grains. In general, regions of excess supply are in the Corn Belt and Great Plains; regions of excess demand are on the two coasts. Such patterns are very similar to observed patterns in the United States.

This discussion of results is only intended to give a sample of the kinds of results which can be expected from this kind of model. A more complete discussion of the results and of the derivation of the

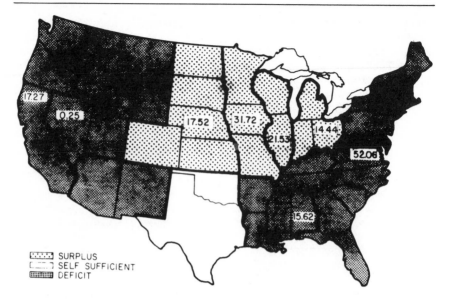

Fig. 12.8. Interregional flows of feed grains (including feed wheat and food uses of corn, oats, and barley) in millions of tons.

data is available in Hall, Heady, and Plessner (12). A reasonably self-contained discussion of quadratic programming is in Hadley (11).

Problem in Progress

In a problem now underway we are attempting to incorporate livestock as well as crops. According to plans, there will be 157 crop-producing regions and 10 consuming regions, which will also serve as livestock producing regions. Each consuming region will have farm-level food demand equations for cattle, calves, hogs, fluid milk, manufacturing milk, vegetable oils, wheat, corn, oats, and barley. Thus the model will require, among other things, a system of 100 demand equations.

Special Difficulties

In nonlinear activity analysis models of the type we have discussed, production data requirements are no greater than for linear models. The producing sector is characterized by a set of activities, and so far as production is concerned, it is immaterial whether the consuming sector is described by demand functions or fixed quantities demanded. Representing the producing sector by supply functions would increase production data requirements. However such a formulation is no longer an activity analysis model.

In the area of demand data, nonlinear models are much more

demanding than linear ones. For a nonlinear model we must have a linear demand function for every final product in every consuming region. A linear model, as we have seen, requires only discrete quantity estimates. Ignoring questions about the relevance of linear (as opposed to nonlinear) demand functions, there is still the problem of finding functions which fit the data well. Estimating such functions is a major undertaking in itself. Consequently, if "reasonable" demand functions are not already available, this may be sufficient reason to begin the study of interregional competition with a linear model.

Present computational algorithms present difficulties also. The one we used, for example, requires that every basic equation be entered twice. Although this does not increase data requirements, it means that the largest nonlinear problem which can be handled is, at most, one-half the size of the largest linear problem. Since decomposition algorithms are available for linear (but not nonlinear) problems, the actual size difference is much greater. No doubt decomposition algorithms will eventually be available for quadratic programming also. This will certainly increase the usefulness of nonlinear models.

REFERENCES

1. Anderson, Jay C., and Earl O. Heady. Normative Supply Functions and Optimum Farm Plans for Northeastern Iowa. Iowa Agr. Exp. Sta. Bull. 537.
2. Barker, R., and B. F. Stanton. Estimation and Aggregation of Firm Supply Functions. *J. Farm Econ.*, vol. 47.
3. Birowo, A. T. Interregional Competition in Agricultural Production in Sweden. *Ann. Agr. Coll. of Sweden*, vol. 31.
4. Brokken, Ray C., and Earl O. Heady. Interregional Adjustments in Crop and Livestock Production in the United States. USDA Tech. Bull. 1396.
5. Cochrane, W. G. *Sampling Techniques.* 2nd ed. New York: Wiley, 1963.
6. Day, Richard. On Aggregating Linear Programming Models of Production. *J. Farm Econ.*, vol. 45.
7. Egbert, Alvin C., and Earl O. Heady. Regional Adjustments in Grain Production, A Linear Programming Analysis. USDA Tech. Bull. 1241.
8. ———. Regional Changes in Grain Production, An Application of Spatial Programming. CAED Rept. 14T. Center for Agr. and Econ. Adjustment, Iowa State Univ.
9. ———. Regional Changes in Grain Production, An Application of Spatial Linear Programming. Iowa Agr. Exp. Sta. Bull. 521.
10. Judge, George. Interregional Price and Allocation Models of Agriculture. Interregional Competition in Agriculture. Agr. Policy Inst., North Carolina State Univ., 1966. Ch. 7.
11. Hadley, G. *Nonlinear and Dynamic Programming.* New York: Addison-Wesley, 1964.
12. Hall, Harry H., Earl O. Heady, and Y. Plessner. Quadratic Programming Solution of Competitive Equilibrium for U.S. Agriculture. *Am. J. Agr. Econ.*, vol. 50.
13. Hartley, H. O. Total Supply Functions Estimated from Farm Samples. Unpubl. paper, Dept. Stat., Iowa State Univ., 1962.
14. Heady, Earl O., and Wilfred Candler. *Linear Programming Methods.* Ames: Iowa State Univ. Press, 1958. Ch. 8.

15. Heady, Earl O., and Alvin C. Egbert. Activity Analysis in Allocation of Crops in Agriculture. In *Studies in Process Analysis*, ed. A. S. Manne and H. M. Markowitz. New York: Wiley, 1963.

16. ———. Efficient Regional Allocation of Farm Products and Programmed Supply Prices. *Agr. Econ. Res.*, vol. 16.

17. ———. Programming Regional Adjustments in Grain Production to Eliminate Surpluses. *J. Farm Econ.*, vol. 41.

18. Heady, Earl O., and Melvin Skold. Projections of U.S. Agricultural Capacity and Interregional Adjustments in Production and Land Use with Spatial Programming Models. Iowa Agr. and Home Econ. Exp. Sta. Res. Bull. 539.

19. Heady, Earl O., and Norman K. Whittlesey. A Programming Analysis of Interregional Competition and Surplus Capacity of American Agriculture. Iowa Agr. and Home Econ. Exp. Sta. Res. Bull. 538.

20. Heady, Earl O., M. D. Skold, and N. S. Randhawa. Programming Models of Interregional Efficiency and Land Use in Agriculture. In *Activity Analysis in the Theory of Growth and Planning*, ed. E. Malinvoud and M. O. L. Bacharach. New York: Macmillan, 1967. Pp. 245-69.

21. Koopmans, T. C., and Stanley Reiter. In *A Model of Transportation in Activity Analysis of Production and Allocation*, ed. T. C. Koopmans. New York: Wiley, 1951.

22. Mighell, R. L., and J. D. Black. *Interregional Competition in Agriculture.* Cambridge, Mass.: Harvard Univ. Press, 1951.

23. Miller, Thomas A. Sufficient Conditions for Exact Aggregation in Programming Models. *Agr. Econ. Res.*, vol. 18; and Lee, John E. Exact Aggregation: A Discussion of Miller's Theorem. *Agr. Econ. Res.*, vol. 18.

24. Plessner, Y., and Earl O. Heady. Competitive Equilibrium Solutions with Quadratic Programming. *Metroeconomica*, vol. 17.

25. Samuelson, P. A. Spatial Price Equilibrium and Linear Programming. *Am. Econ. Rev.*, vol. 42.

26. Schrader, L. F., and G. A. King. Regional Location of Beef Cattle Feeding. *J. Farm Econ.*, vol. 44.

27. Sharples, Jerry A., and Earl O. Heady. Potential Agricultural Production and Resource Use in Iowa. Iowa Agr. Exp. Sta. Bull. 429.

28. Skold, Melvin D., and Earl O. Heady. Regional Location of Production of Major Field Crops at Alternative Demand and Price Levels, 1975. USDA Tech. Bull. 1354.

29. Stovall, J. C. Sources of Error in Aggregate Supply Estimates. *J. Farm Econ.*, vol. 48.

30. Sundquist, W. B., et al. Equilibrium Analysis of Income-Improving Adjustments on Farms in the Lake States Dairy Region. USDA Tech. Bull. 246.

31. Takayama, T., and G. G. Judge. An Interregional Activity Analysis Model for the Agricultural Sector. *J. Farm Econ.*, vol. 44.

32. ———. Spatial Equilibrium and Quadratic Programming. *J. Farm Econ.*, vol. 46.

33. Whittlesey, Norman K., and Earl O. Heady. Aggregate Economic Effects of Alternative Land Retirement Programs: A Linear Programming Analysis. USDA Tech. Bull. 1351.

Chapter 12 ✑ DISCUSSION

Max Borlin, *Center for Research* (Switzerland)

T HE SEMINAR PROGRAM makes a distinction between models at
the micro level, regional models, and national models. In the
sections about regional models a paper will be presented concerning the relations, in the models, of the agricultural sectors and the
other sectors. It therefore can be taken for granted that the difference
between interregional and national models is not at the level of space
but at the level of the sectors considered. With the authors, we are
therefore talking of interregional models of agriculture. In their paper
about interregional models of agriculture, the authors probably considered two possibilities, (a) to write a review article on the subject or
(b) to present new outstanding developments in the field. It is quite
clear that a choice had to be made, since time would not have allowed
for treating both aspects of the problem in an extensive way. I should
like to present some comments considering the coauthors' paper a
broad review article, and then considering the paper limited to an extensive treatment of latest achievements. However I am aware of the
fact that for every one of the topics I shall discuss there is in this
room at least one person much more competent than me to handle it;
I would like that they consider the present discussion as an invitation
to go themselves deeper into the subject and communicate their findings to us.

THE PAPER AS A BROAD REVIEW ARTICLE

Looking at the coauthors' paper in this way, we note that not all non-
static and all single-product or few-product models (e.g., 2, 11, 12) have
been mentioned; the limitation to the static case has been acknowledged.

It is quite obvious that just reviewing the models existing in the
United States is a time-consuming task. However it is my feeling that
such a review would show that the corn sector, the livestock-beef sector, and the hog-pork sector have been treated by independent researchers. If this is true, one might wonder if a comparison of the results
would not help to evaluate the different models.

This question of testing the models and comparing different methods has already been brought up in connection with regression analysis
and recursive programming. The same analyst involved in this comparison, Professor Dean, is also coauthor of the study on world trade
in fresh oranges (3) and has tried to check the predictive power of his
transportation model comparing actual with predicted results for some
past time period. These efforts of checking the results of models are

very necessary and if a broad review article would include the topic it would be very valuable.

Moreover, such a broad review article should also point to the fact that the regions treated in an interregional competition model might be different nations. In this case, spatial equilibrium models would represent a contribution to international trade theory, as publications by Bawden (1) and Dean-Collins (3) show.

THE PAPER LIMITED TO AN EXTENSIVE TREATMENT OF LATEST ACHIEVEMENTS

The outstanding information Mr. Hall and Professor Heady gave us was the presentation of the large numerical Plessner-Heady quadratic programming model for a quadratic objective function and linear constraints. Just in passing we may mention two more articles on this model by Plessner (9) and Yaron-Plessner-Heady (13). Up to now, activity analysis models had to be solved by laborious iterations. One of them asks for the parametrization of a given output mix and the following steps: (a) estimate regional price-quantity demand schedules; (b) select a particular level of output for each commodity required in each region; (c) minimize total costs subject to this given output mix; (d) compare the dual prices of the output restriction with the demand prices corresponding to the given output mix; (e) if the two prices are practically equal, the equilibrium solution is obtained; and (f) if there is a discrepancy, new supply levels would be selected that are in the direction of equilibrium. Such a procedure would be followed until all markets are in balance (i.e., all price-quantities have converged).

This procedure is explained in Egbert-Heady (4, pp. 215f.). A second iterative approach consists of simultaneous parametric changes of the prices for all products: (a) Estimate regional price-quantity demand schedules, each curve having a limited number of points, at which the price and quantity data are specified, and the demand curves are downward sloping; (b) For each set of prices corresponding to one of the n points a maximum profit model is solved. The results consist of a series of n solutions — one for each price level. As prices increase, a stepped supply function is generated; and (c) The quantities obtained in the solution are compared with the demand schedules; the market-clearing equilibrium prices are found where the requirements within each consumption region are just met.

This approach is explained in Egbert-Heady (4, p. 216) and applied in Heady-Skold (5) and in Skold-Heady (10).

Onigkeit (8, pp. 152f.) suggests an elaboration of the latter approach in which the stepped supply functions are gained changing iteratively from a maximum to a minimum problem, and regression analysis is applied to translate the stepped into a continuous supply function. These refinements are particularly useful for dealing with aggregation errors.

Finally, Henrichsmeyer (6, pp. 193f.) developed an iterative procedure based on the idea of solving the problem of spatial equilibrium separating the production equilibrium from the spatial equilibrium of interregional trade.

These time-consuming iterative search methods for equilibrium solutions can now be substituted for by the more efficient Plessner-Heady (13) quadratic programming model as long as the constraints remain linear. It would be very useful if in the discussion this breakthrough could be compared with previous procedures and further developments could be sketched.

REFERENCES

1. Bawden, D. L. A Spatial Price Equilibrium Model of International Trade. *J. Farm Econ.*, vol. 48.
2. Bawden, D. L., H. O. Carter, and G. W. Dean. Interregional Competition in the United States Turkey Industry. *Hilgardia*, vol. 37.
3. Dean, G. W., and N. R. Collins. World Trade in Fresh Oranges: An Analysis of the Effect of European Economic Community Tariff Policies. Univ. California, Div. Agr. Sci. a Giannini. Foundation monogr. 18, 1 (1967).
4. Egbert, A. C., and E. O. Heady. Interregional Competition or Spatial Equilibrium Models in Farm Supply Analysis. In *Agricultural Supply Functions*, ed. Earl O. Heady et al. Ames: Iowa State Univ. Press, 1961. Pp. 203-30.
5. Heady, E. O., and M. Skold. Projections of U.S. Agricultural Capacity and Interregional Adjustments in Production and Land Use With Spatial Programming Models. Iowa Agr. and Home Econ. Exp. Sta. Res. Bull. 539, 1965.
6. Henrichsmeyer, W. *Das Sektorale und Regionale Gleichgewicht der Landwirtschaftlichen Produktion.* Hamburg-Berlin, 1966.
7. O.E.C.D. Interregional Competition In Agriculture: Problems of Methodology. AGR/T (65) 1, Paris, 1965.
8. Onigkeit, D. *Zur Anwendung der Mathematischen Programmierung bei der Losung Interregionaler Strukturprobleme der Landwirtschaft.* Zurich, 1967.
9. Plessner, Y. Activity Analysis, Quadratic Programming and General Equilibrium. *Intern. Econ. Rev.*, vol. 8.
10. Skold, M. D., and E. O. Heady. Regional Location of Production of Major Field Crops at Alternative Demand and Price Levels, 1975. USDA Tech. Bull. 1354.
11. Williams, W. F., and R. A. Dietrich. An Interregional Analysis of the Feed Beef Economy. ERS, USDA and Oklahoma and Texas Agr. Exp. Sta. Agr. Econ. Rept. 88, April 1966.
12. Williams, W. F., and T. T. Stout. *Economics of the Livestock-Meat Industry.* New York: Prentice Hall, 1964.
13. Yaron, D., Y. Plessner, and E. O. Heady. Competitive Equilibrium-Application of Mathematical Programming. *Canadian J. Agr. Econ.*, vol. 13.

Chapter 13 ⬿ OPTIMIZATION OF AGRICULTURAL
DEVELOPMENT OF A REGION IN RELATION TO
FOOD PROCESSING AND CONSUMPTION

Vladimar A. Mash and V. I. Kiselev,
Central Economic-Mathematical Institute (U.S.S.R.)

THIS PAPER deals with the coordination of the optimum development of agriculture in a region with the development of other economic branches — both in the same region and in other regions of the country. Planning for such a coordination is essentially nothing else than planning for a multibranch system which is a component part of the national economy. It appears reasonable, therefore, to preface the analysis of the particular problem and its specifics with a brief discussion of some theoretical aspects of optimum planning for the national economy and its component blocks.

OVERALL CONSIDERATIONS

The development of a national economy may be considered as a process which is optimal with respect to a certain goal and carried out under a set of limiting conditions, such as the level of scientific and technological development achieved, the availability of resources, and the social system. Hence the best alternative to the economic development in principle can be obtained by solving an extremum problem — the the problem of temporal and spatial development of the national economy.

Needless to say, the complexity and dimensions of such a problem are tremendous. In stating and solving it, serious difficulties will have to be faced that concern methodology, information, and computations. In particular, the difficulties with information are bound to arise in describing the expected future conditions of the economic activity, on the one hand, and in stating the optimum criterion (the goal of development) and the corresponding objective function of the extremum problem on the other. The former sort of difficulties springs from the involved nature of the present-day production technology, multiple relations between the units, and the like, and above all from the uncertainty of information about the future. The latter kind of difficulties are due to the fact that the goal of the economy ought to be formulated in quantitative terms. In actual fact, however, it often happens that it is not stated clearly and has not been defined even in words (in a program or a statement of the basic principles). Moreover it is not always obvious that such formulation is possible in principle, especially in countries with an unplanned economy. Nevertheless it certainly can always be defined. Let us examine this point a little closer.

As with any other system contained in a system of a higher level, that is, possessing a "super-system," the goal of the national economic development is set before it from outside, from the standpoint of the exogenous super-system placing the "social orders" of the economy. This goal may lie, for instance, in growth of population welfare while meeting the given relationships between the levels of personal and social consumption of the different segments of population in various regions; or in reclaiming uncultivated areas; or in creating or increasing a production and defense potential. The economic development goal for the socialist countries can be set in keeping with the fundamental law of socialism — the maximum satisfaction of the constantly growing needs of the community.

However the goal of development, as mentioned above, is to be stated in quantitative terms, which may be done in a variety of manners. For illustration we shall consider one possible approach — defining the goal of development over a past period and extrapolating it to the future.

The goal of development in a past period can be, in principle, defined on the basis of the results produced, solving what looks like a "reciprocal problem" for that period. The initial and the final states of the economy (the results achieved) and the prevailing conditions and limitations are to be known to solve this problem, and what is sought is the criterion under which the actual final state achieved will be considered as the optimum. Having found that criterion (or a family of criteria) for the past, we shall extrapolate it into the future, taking into account the adjustments known since, the emerging trends, programs envisaged, and so on.

We should like to emphasize that this by no means implies that, say, the spontaneous process of market economy development actually leads to results optimal for the whole community. This process may be described as "optimizing" but nominally, since its criterion in point of fact reflects mostly the purposes and strivings of the ruling groups. Obviously such a criterion may be absolutely unsuitable for the community as a whole, widening the gap between the wealthy and the indigent and leading to unemployment, devastation of the natural resources, propagation of products harmful to the community, and overpopulation of some areas. In adjusting the criterion during the extrapolation, its deficiences can be set right to an extent depending on the virtual capability of the state (or, say, the regional planning body) to interfere in the process of development.

Since a solution of the extremum overall problem for the national economy makes it possible to formulate the optimum plan of economic development, a uniform approach to the partial problems becomes possible; that is, to the problems of planning the development and location of production for the individual units of the economy. The optimum variant for a unit will be nothing else than a detailed description of the respective part of the solution of the economic development problem. Consequently to find this variant one should proceed from the plan adopted for the whole economy and use the corresponding information.

Different methods can be employed to coordinate the overall (for the whole economy) problem and the partial problems. These methods will lay specific requirements for information about the overall plan. However, independent of the method, the indispensable and most essential part of such information will be the shadow prices of products and resources as specified in the optimum plan of the overall problem. These values characterize the variation of the extreme value of the objective function under minor changes of the limitations relating to the resources and products available. Thus the shadow prices map the objective function of the overall problem in the context of conditions this problem takes into account.

The shadow prices of the optimum plan of the overall problem must be used in constructing the objective functions of the partial problems. These should provide that the implementation of the resulting partial plans leads to a state of the economy which would be balanced but shifted towards meeting the social assignment and the development goal it defines.

These are some of the theoretical conclusions flowing from considering the development of the national economy as an optimization process liable to be formally described by an extremum problem. The practical implications are evident. A great number of partial problems of long-run optimum planning are being solved in the U.S.S.R., mostly for the individual branches of industry. However, in the absence of an optimum development plan of the whole economy, we realize well the inadequacies of such problems and try to apply them in such spheres where their place within the general system can be grasped, so that the resulting solutions should fall in the proximity of the expected national optimum. At the same time we try to adjust the existing economic parameters as much as possible in order to come closer to the probable shadow prices of the optimum plan. Thus the shadow prices of fuel have been already elaborated and attempts are being made to evaluate the arable land and the water resources.

Qualitative conclusions are most likely to be expected in the short run; some interesting findings have been made already. These results in particular refer to decision theory, and they have been obtained by combining the existing methods of decision making with techniques based on mathematical optimization algorithms.

Since planning for a real economy consists in choosing among variants of a development pattern lying within the set of feasible plans, analogous algorithms are of a prime interest for us. Three main types of such algorithms with proven convergence are known: the simplex method, the decomposition method, and some game methods. All the algorithms proceed from a centralized planning and use a criterion of the best production methods which can be interpreted as maximizing the total profits (in this or that modification) in reference to the prices obtained at the preceding iteration.

Similarly it is possible to make decisions in the individual units of the economy, proceeding from the criterion of maximized total profit in fixed prices.

In formulating the problem in terms of maximized profit, the prospective activity level of the whole economy unit concerned is not fixed in advance. Conversely it is necessary to find the justified upper limit for the output of the unit by comparing the benefits to be gained for the national economy by the increased output and selling of this or that product, on the one hand, and the losses due to the utilization of more valuable resources for that purpose, on the other. Such comparison in respect to profits will make it possible to confront the variants of the unit's production development and location, in particular those differing in respect to the output level, product mix, and production dynamics.

In case identical output, product mix, and dynamics of production have been set a priori for all the variants compared, so that the returns from selling the product are equal in all the cases, the effectiveness of each variant is evaluated in terms of costs. The cost minimization criterion may be regarded as a specific case of the maximum profit criterion applicable under certain conditions.

However the process of decision making in a real world essentially depends on the type of control over the individual units of economy and it is sometimes based on different principles. In particular, the decision-making mechanism in a market economy is especially interesting, for the market availability is to a certain extent a necessary, although by no means a sufficient, condition of an optimum development.

This mechanism (at any rate, some of its modifications) resembles an algorithm lying somewhere in between such finite methods as the simplex or decomposition methods and game methods. The algorithm makes use of demand and supply curves.

Certainly it would be more correct to speak of curved surfaces in an n+1 dimensional space, rather than of two-dimensional curves, for example, to consider the surface corresponding to the dependence of the selling price of every i-th product on the sales volume of all n products circulating in the national economy. However in practice we operate with the section of this surface obtained on the basis of the past development of the economy, and extrapolate the resulting curve into the conditions of activity expected in the future. Decisions are made on the basis of the extrapolated curve, which is adjusted as the corrected data flow in. Sometimes the cross-elasticities coefficients are also taken into account; that is, a surface is constructed instead of a curve. But generally these are tens or hundreds of times less than the direct elasticity coefficients and therefore are negligible.

It appears reasonable to suppose the existence of an optimization algorithm, thus far unknown, which is based on analogous principles. We are currently engaged in an attempt to find it; the results achieved are quite hopeful. If we shall be able to prove that it is possible to build such an algorithm which we have for convenience labelled the "long-stride decomposition method," it will not be difficult then to elaborate in detail the corresponding decision-making procedures. It should be emphasized that even in this algorithm the relations between economic units belonging to the same level will be planned by the central bodies. We hold that such bodies are always necessary, since horizontal relations alone are insufficient. The planning bodies of a superior hierarchical level are needed to establish the rent payments for resources and to supply the lower levels with other data which will promote the drifting of the economy in the required direction with the aid of economic levers.

The observed extension of the scope of planning in market economies seems to corroborate the above assumption, this extension taking place not only within individual companies but manifesting itself in the governmental programs of economic development as well.

Investigations into optimization algorithms thus facilitate the search for a scientific system of combining centralization and decentralization in planning and controlling an economy. Much remains to be done along these lines, but the direction of research and its likely qualitative conclusions are apparent even now.

After these general considerations, we should like now to turn to the specific problem, namely the problem of optimum development of agriculture and food processing in the Moldavian Republic.

MODEL OF AGRICULTURE AND FOOD PROCESSING

Agricultural output is largely destined for the manufacturing of products whose volume and product mix of consumption cannot be reliably predicted on the basis of partial calculations isolated from the model of agricultural development. In particular, this is the case when the volume of consumption essentially depends on possible selling prices while the lowest feasible level of these is determined by the costs of the agricultural system at hand.

In addition, one must take into account the seasonal variation in the deliveries of agricultural stuffs and the capacities of the processing mills and refrigerators which set restraints on the utilization of those stuffs.

This means that in long-run optimum planning for the agricultural process, one often is to include in the optimized system the industry processing agricultural outputs and the end consumers of this industry. Over and above such typical "agricultural" factors and conditions as soils, average annual yields of perennial plants weighted to accommodate the varying values of output in the different years of the planning period, and so on, one must take into account (a) capacities of the existing and projected processing mills and seasonal variation of their loading with various raw agricultural products (in particular, the availability of refrigerators for storing raw and finished products to level out seasonal peaks); (b) seasonal availability of labor, both in farming proper and in the processing industry; and (c) seasonal dependence of the possible sales volume on the production costs level, etc.

For the formulation of and experimentation with extremum problems of large dimensions that arise in such conditions, the Moldavian

Republic, where farming and the food industry play major roles in the economy, was chosen.

In order to simplify the problem and reduce its dimensions, only the most probable lines of future development of Moldavian agriculture were considered: viticulture, horticulture, market gardening, tobacco, and oil-bearing crops. In order to improve the product mix, some limited possibility was allowed for decreasing plantation areas of perennial cultures. Corn, sugar beet, and live farming were assumed to be fixed at their present levels, and correspondingly the resources consumed by these lines (land, labor, refrigerator capacities, etc.) were left out of consideration.

There were some other simplifications as well. In particular, it was assumed that during 1975-80 Moldavia will continue to sell farming products in her traditional markets: within the republic, in the northern and central regions of European Russia, in Siberia, and in the Far East. Naturally it would be better to consider the distribution of selling markets proceeding from the optimum economic plan; however the present assumptions also have a realistic basis.

On the other hand, the complete flow of the farming product through all stages, including its processing and end consumption is comprised in the problem formulation. The model incorporates such processing branches as fresh and frozen vegetables and fruit, wine, tinned food, jams and juices, tobacco, and oil-milling. The necessary and appropriate capacities of the processing plants, refrigerators, and transport vehicles to be put into operation are determined accordingly.

As for the end consumption, the market capacities of each product are generally assumed to be limited and rising with decreasing selling price (the assumptions of virtually unlimited market capacities of certain individual products do not impinge on the model's generality, corresponding to a specific case of the infinite price elasticity of demand). The influence of prices on market capacities varies for the different seasons of the year.

Since the end demand cannot be strictly fixed in the problem under consideration, the costs minimization approach would be insufficient. Therefore the formulation in terms of the maximum economic effect criterion was used (1, 2), otherwise called the consumer surplus criterion (3, 4). This means maximizing the overall effect of the system "agriculture-processing industry." This approach determines the production output and the products mix in the course of solving the problem, rather than setting the values a priori. The output of every product is brought up to a level at which marginal per unit costs are equal to marginal selling prices, i.e., the maximum possible volume of break-even selling. This formulation, strictly speaking, more correctly belongs in the procedure of the iterative optimum planning for the whole economy, but it is used here because it provides for the maximum feasible satisfaction of the population needs and for the corresponding activation of the productive potential. Such an approach is justified by peculiarities of Moldavia. This region has excellent possibilities for growing such valuable cultures as grapes and different fruits, or to some degree a "tropical rent" which we ought to realize in the best possible way. It means that apparently we do not have to decide whether the Moldavian agricultural growth possibilities should be fully utilized, but the problem is for what crops such possibilities are to be used. Accordingly the Moldavian agriculture and food-processing industry development is the most natural way of increasing employment. A reduction of agricultural population was neither stipulated nor envisaged while formulating the optimum problem described here. We ought to mention that the solutions and results obtained fully correspond to our anticipations and preliminary assumptions. For instance, available development possibilities were in fact fully utilized in the problem solutions. It turned out that restrictions of the market capacities and allowed investment played the major role in this problem.

Extremely large dimensions of the problem suggest a two-stage approach, analyzing and optimizing the system under consideration as the totality of interrelated subsystems. Accordingly an aggregated coordinating problem is constructed (the model of the first stage) as well as a number of problems for isolated subsystems (for models of the second stage), for example, farming and the canned food industry. The coordinating problem seeks the optimum outputs of various products in an aggregated product mix, disregarding the space distribution, that is, leaving out of consideration the problems of location of farming and food industry. The coordinating problem, therefore, does not consider individual plants and enterprises. Conversely the second-level problems assume the activity level of an individual subsystem as expressed in terms of the aggregated product mix to be known as well as the resources allocated to that system. Proceeding from these data one seeks here a more detailed statement of the product mix of the subsystem at hand, its optimum location, plant sizes, and so on. An iterative procedure is envisaged for reciprocal coordination of the solutions to the problems of the first and of the second level.

The following discussion is concerned with the coordinating problem. Let us specify some of its features that have not been mentioned above.

The maximum effect (or consumer surplus) formulation gives rise to an extremum problem with a nonlinear (convex) objective function relating to the product selling. In order to keep within the scope of linear programming and utilize the available computer programs for solving this problem, a piece-wise linear approximation of the curves showing the dependence of demand on prices is used; for this a number of discrete selling prices are fixed and the potential market size range is determined for each of them. This assumption means but a minor increase of the problem's dimensions. As for the nonlinear nature of expenditure relating to the economies of scale, it is inessential and hence negligible for the aggregated problem which does not consider individual plants. Thus the coordinating problem is a problem of linear programming.

As mentioned above, the means of transportation are included in the optimized system. Naturally the transportation of raw materials to the processing factories is not considered in the aggregated problem. As concerns the conveyance of the end product to consumers, the model described herein, for the sake of simplicity, includes but one kind of vehicle — refrigerator lorries. For each product its spatially separated selling markets are aggregated into a single market and the weighted average distance is computed.

Presently the coordinating problem is posed in a static formulation. In constructing the objective function, the per unit costs and selling prices were computed as weighted annual average values (5), that is using expression (1):

$$Z_i = \frac{\sum\limits_{t=1}^{T_{p,i}} (K_{ti} + C_{ti}) B_t}{\sum\limits_{t=1}^{T_{p,i}} X_{ti} B_t} \tag{1}$$

where

$\quad$ i $\quad$ = plant or a variant of its development
$\quad$ Z_i $\quad$ = weighted average per product unit expenditure at the i-th plant, equal for all the years of the period of calculation
$\quad$ K_{ti} $\quad$ = lump sum investment in the t-th year at the i-th plant
$\quad$ C_{ti} $\quad$ = operational expenditure in the t-th year at the i-th plant
$\quad$ X_{ti} $\quad$ = output in the t-th year at the i-th plant
$\quad$ $T_{c,i}$ = the calculation period for the i-th plant
$\quad$ B_t $\quad$ = the remoteness factor (the discounting rate) computed from (2):

$$B_t = (1 + E)^{-i} \tag{2}$$

where

$\quad$ t $\quad$ = serial number of the year in the period under consideration
$\quad$ E = the rate of efficiency, which was taken equal to 0.15

The discounting rates here roughly express the uneven economic significance of the inflow and expenditure of resources at different time points; the value of the efficiency rate adopted may be approximately interpreted as fixing the recovery period at seven years.

The activities of identical units (for example, similar tinned food plants) were represented in the model by two variables: the first described the activity of the existing plants and the second that of the newly built ones.

In this paper the model has been somewhat reduced and modified for the sake of clarity. The two variables describing the activities of identical existing and new plants have been replaced by a single variable;

accordingly, lump sum investment and operational costs and selling prices are included in a simplified form (expression 3).

The costs of processing and storage of products at refrigerators and dispatching them to the consumer have been taken into account in the following fashion. A typified annual operation pattern had been established for a unit of the j-th equipment (including the production and selling of refrigerators and vehicles), and the operational costs of this unit were computed in conformity with that pattern. The operational costs and lump sum investment involved in the creation of new equipment are not a priori distributed among the kinds of product which are processed, stored, or transported using the equipment concerned; this distribution is to be determined from the solution of the problem. Thus it suffices to include in the model conditions 9-12, checking the sufficiency of all the kinds of equipment required and determining how many new units of every kind are to be introduced into the system.

The relationships between the sales volume and the selling price were obtained as suggested by an analysis of data on price dynamics and the growth of the sales volume as observed for the various products during the last 15 years. As mentioned, the selling price-sales volume correspondences were considered for the traditional Moldavian markets. The calculations took into account the expected population incomes increase and eliminated the influence of partially uncovered demand for certain products as well as of the variation of prices of interchangeable products. These calculations were carried out in accordance with the method of Shvirkov (6), based on the assumption of linear relationship between selling price and sales volume. The demand curves for fresh vegetables and fruit were constructed on a monthly basis. In reference to the demand curves, some five to eight discrete selling price levels were chosen and the corresponding piecewise linear relationships constructed.

Finally, we shall mention that the problem took into account possible restraints of funds allocated to the optimized system for capital investment during the planning period. The investments proceeding from the profits of the optimized system during the planning period have been included in these funds too.

The model of the problem of optimum development of Moldavian agriculture and the related processing industry uses the following notation of parameters:

s   = symbol of a cultivated crop
S   = number of crops
p   = symbol of a group of crops characterized by a common category of suitable land plots
P   = number of p-th groups of crops
i   = symbol of product kind
m   = number of products
τ = symbol of month
j   = symbol of a productive capacity (where j=n-2 refers to

refrigerator lorries, j=n-1 to the refrigerators used in the industry, and j=n to refrigerators used in selling)

n = number of kinds of productive capacity

I_j = group of products manufactured using the j-th capacity

$f_{s\tau}$ = yield of s-th crop in τ-th month

a_{is} = input of s-th raw product per unit of i-th end product

N_j = monthly capacity of j-th equipment available at the moment of planning

β_{ij} = relative ratio of j-th capacity usage when manufacturing the i-th product

g_s = refrigerator capacity necessary for storing a unit of the s-th crop

θ_i = time spent by refrigerator lorry on transportation of a unit of i-th product to the market

$\tilde{\theta}_\tau$ = time resources of one refrigerator lorry in τ-th month

$\gamma_{s\tau}$ = labor input into harvesting of s-th crop in τ-th month per area unit

γ_i = labor input per unit of i-th product

Γ_τ = availability of labor in τ-th month

L_s = area under s-th crop at the beginning of the planning period

$\underline{L}_s$ = the lower permissible limit of area under s-th crop $(L_s \geq \underline{L}_s \geq 0)$

L_p = total area of land plot usable for p-th group of crops

k_s = per unit investment into expansion of area under s-th crop

k_j = per unit investment into construction of j-th equipment

K = total investment allocated to the optimized system for the planning period

C_s = annual operational expenditure on tillage, harvesting, and transportation to processing mills per unit of area under s-th crop

$C_{i\tau}$ = per unit operational costs of manufacturing i-th product in τ-th month (taking into account seasonal overtime and night shift wage increases during the periods of intensive inflow of raw product)

C_j = per unit annual operational expenditure on maintenance of j-th equipment, not included in $C_{i\tau}$

r = symbol of discrete level of selling price

R_i = number of selling price levels for i-th product

V_i^r = price of i-th product at r-th discrete level

$V_{i\tau}^r$ = the same for τ-th month, for products with seasonal variation of price

D_i^r = the maximum possible demand for i-th product at selling price V_i^r (an increase of V_i^r does not lead to an increase of D_i^r)

$D_{i\tau}^r$ = the same for τ-th month, for products with seasonal variation of price

For variables, the following notation is used:

X_s = area under s-th crop

X_{sT} = deliveries of s-th raw product flowing directly from the field in τ-th month into the output of products

X^*_{sT} = the same, but delivered from production refrigerators

$\overline{X}^*_{sT}$ = the same, but delivered from "selling" refrigerators (for manufacturing of cooled or frozen product)

$_sX^*_T$ = s-th raw product delivered in τ-th month to production refrigerators

$_s\overline{X}^*_T$ = the same, delivered to "selling" refrigerators (for subsequent selling as cooled or frozen product)

X^0_{sT} = stock of s-th raw product in production refrigerator as per beginning of τ-th month (in the real problem a condition was included that stock left of preceding harvest would be equal to zero at the moment of new harvest beginning. In the described model this condition for clarity is not included explicitly.)

$\overline{X}^0_{sT}$ = same as above, but for "selling" refrigerator

X_{iT} = output of i-th product in τ-th month

Y_j = increase of j-th capacity during the planning period

Y_s = expansion of area under s-th crop

Z^r_i = annual increase of the volume of selling of i-th product following transition from (r-1)-th price level to r-th level

Z^r_{iT} = same as above, for products with seasonal variation of price

The mathematical model of the problem of optimum development of Moldavian agriculture and the related processing industry is formulated as follows: find the plan which maximizes the value of W.

$$W = \sum_{i=1}^{m} \sum_{r=1}^{R_i} (V^r_i Z^r_i + \sum_{T=1}^{12} V^r_{iT} Z^r_{iT}) - E(\sum_{s=1}^{s} k_s Y_s + \sum_{j=1}^{n} k_j Y_j)$$

$$- [\sum_{s=1}^{s} C_s X_s = \sum_{i=1}^{m} \sum_{T=1}^{12} C_{iT} X_{iT} + \sum_{j=1}^{n} C_j (N_j = Y_j)] \qquad (3)$$

where E = 0.15 and satisfies the conditions (a) through (p).

(a) Sufficiency of land plots for the p-th group of crops:

$$\sum_{s\epsilon p} X_s \le L_p; \qquad p = 1, 2, ..., P \qquad (4)$$

(b) Monthly deliveries of s-th raw product to production and refrigerator storage do not exceed the possible total yield of s-th crop for the given month:

$$X_{sT} + {_sX^*_T} + {_s\overline{X}^*_T} \le f_{sT} X_s; \qquad s = 1, 2, ..., S; \tau = 1, 2, ..., 12 \qquad (5)$$

(c) Balance between the input and output of raw product in the refrigerators and its stock in the adjacent months:

$$X^0_{s\tau} + {}_sX^*_\tau - X^*_{s\tau} = X^0_{s,\tau+1}; \quad s = 1, 2, ..., S; \ \tau = 1, 2, ..., 11 \quad (6)$$

$$\overline{X}^0_{s\tau} + {}_s\overline{X}^*_\tau - \overline{X}^*_{s\tau} = X^0_{s,\tau+1}; \quad s = 1, 2, ..., S; \ \tau = 1, 2, ..., 11 \quad (7)$$

(d) Sufficiency of raw product resources for the output of end product in every month:

$$\sum_{i=1}^{m} a_{is} X_{i\tau} \le X_{s\tau} + X^*_{s\tau} + \overline{X}^*_{s\tau}; \quad s = 1, 2, ..., S; \ \tau = 1, 2, ..., 12 \quad (8)$$

(e) Sufficiency of j-th capacities for product output in τ-th month:

$$\sum_{i \in I_j} \beta_{ij} X_{i\tau} \le N_j + Y_j; \quad j = 1, 2, ..., n-3; \ \tau = 1, 2, ..., 12 \quad (9)$$

(f) Sufficiency of refrigerator capacities for storing the stock of raw product:

$$\sum_{s=1}^{S} g_s X^0_{s\tau} \le N_{n-1} + Y_{n-1}; \quad \tau = 1, 2, ..., 12 \quad (10)$$

$$\sum_{s=1}^{S} g_s \overline{X}^0_{s\tau} \le N_n + Y_n; \quad \tau = 1, 2, ..., 12 \quad (11)$$

(g) Sufficiency of vehicles for transportation of product:

$$\sum_{i=1}^{m} \Theta_i X_i \le \tilde{\Theta}_\tau (N_{n-2} + Y_{n-2}); \quad \tau = 1, 2, ..., 12 \quad (12)$$

(h) Sufficiency of labor:

$$\sum_{s=1}^{S} \gamma_{s\tau} X_s + \sum_{i=1}^{m} \gamma_i X_{i\tau} \le \Gamma_\tau; \quad \tau = 1, 2, ..., 12 \quad (13)$$

(i) Sufficiency of investment:

$$\sum_{s=1}^{S} k_s (X_s - L_s) + \sum_{j=1}^{n} K_j Y_j \le K \quad (14)$$

(j) Balance between output and sales volume:

$$\sum_{\tau=1}^{12} X_{i\tau} = \sum_{r=1}^{R_i} Z_i^r; \quad i = 1, 2, ..., m \quad (15)$$

(k) Same as above, but accounting for seasonal price variation:

$$X_{i\tau} = \sum_{r=1}^{R_i} Z_{i\tau}^r \cdot \qquad i = 1, 2, \ldots, m; \ \tau = 1, 2, \ldots, 12 \qquad (16)$$

(l) Limiting of possible increase of sales volume following a price reduction:

$$Z_i^1 \leq D_i^1; \qquad i = 1, 2, \ldots, m \qquad (17)$$

$$Z_i^r \leq D_i^r - D_i^{r-1}; \qquad i = 1, 2, \ldots, m; \ r = 2, 3, \ldots, R_i \qquad (18)$$

(m) Same as above, but for product with seasonal price variation:

$$Z_{i\tau}^1 \leq D_{i\tau}^1; \qquad i = 1, 2, \ldots, m; \ \tau = 1, 2, \ldots, 12 \qquad (19)$$

$$Z_{i\tau}^r \leq D_{i\tau}^r - D_{i\tau}^{r-1};$$

$$i = 1, 2, \ldots, m; \ r = 2, 3, \ldots, R_i; \ \tau = 1, 2, \ldots, 12 \qquad (20)$$

(n) Limited possibility of decreasing area under s-th crop:

$$X_s \geq L_s; \qquad s = 1, 2, \ldots, S \qquad (21)$$

(o) Equality of total area under s-th crop to the sum of existing and new areas:

$$X_s \leq L_s + Y_s; \qquad s = 1, 2, \ldots, S$$

(p) Nonnegativeness of all the above variables

As it was mentioned, first solutions of the coordinating problem have been obtained by now. They testify that the formulation of the problem presented above is well grounded and produces realistic results. On the other hand, it has become clear that more precise data are needed; specifically, that it is necessary to replace the linear form of expression of the dependence of demand on price by a more sophisticated relationship.

REFERENCES

1. Abraham, C., and A. Thomas. *Microeconomics*. Paris: France Publ., 1966.
2. Mash, V. A. Survey of Research in the Field of Long-Term Branch Planning and Basic Directives for Further Work. All-Union Sci. Res. Inst. Econ., Moscow, 1966.
3. Masse, P. *The Choice of Investments*. Paris: France Publ., 1959.
4. The Basic Principles of Optimal Planning of Development and Allocation of Production. *Science*, vol. 10.
5. Pugachev, V. F. Local Criterion and Stimulization of Workers in an Optimum Economic System. *Econ. Math. Methods*, vol. 2.
6. Shvirkov, V. V. *An Economic-Mathematical Analysis of Consumer Demand*. Moscow: Moscow Univ. Press, 1966.

Chapter 13   ⌒   DISCUSSION

Theodor Heidhues, *Georg-August University*
(German Federal Republic)

THE MODEL DESCRIBED in this paper calls for a long-run optimal plan for part of the agricultural industry and the corresponding food processing industry. Both are connected through their
product and input markets, and through predetermined capital and labor
allotments. The authors propose a two-stage iterative approach with a
feedback mechanism between them. The aggregated model is based on
the assumption of complete mobility of resources between firms within
sectors and between sectors. The subordinated branch problems serve
to determine the detailed product mix, firm size, and location.

    The objective of the plan is to obtain a competitive solution to the
allocation problem with given demand functions. The *objective function*
is defined to approximately maximize the area under the demand curve
less total cost

        W = sales revenue - 0.15 investment expenditure

             - variable costs - maintenance

    The behavioral assumption for the planning authority must be that
of a discriminating monopolist (Fig. 13.1), charging each potential buyer
the price he is just willing to pay.

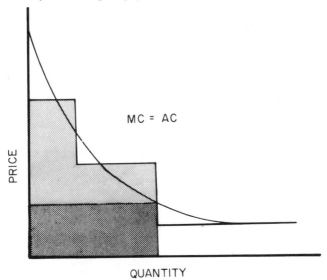

Fig. 13.1. Discriminating monopoly.

The *activities* include production of different commodities, various storage activities, processing of agricultural commodities, sale of final commodities, investment in permanent crops, investment in durable equipment, variable cost in production, processing and storage, and maintenance of equipment.

The *constraints* include land for particular groups of crops, balances for various quantities (crops, monthly refrigerator stocks, intermediate products, final products, and sales), capacities of durable assets (equipment allowing for investment, refrigerator facilities, transportation system), labor investment capital, and linear demand approximation balances.

DISCUSSION OF THE MODEL

The objective function of this problem can be interpreted in two ways which depend on the pricing policy of the planning authority. One interpretation would be to use this formulation merely as a device to obtain the competitive solution of the problem in quantities and prices. In other words, the marginal price obtained in the solution is charged for the total output such that consumer surplus would actually accrue to consumers. In this case, it is important to recognize that the optimal value of the objective function has no meaning; in particular it could not be used as an indicator of profits available for further investment.

The second possible policy of the planning authority would be to actually differentiate prices and have the area under the demand curve accrue to the industry or the government. This would be a progressive tax system.

A formal structure of using a linear approximation with corresponding activity constraints will solve the problem as long as no cross-elasticities are introduced. The introduction of cross-elasticities will require a more elaborate formulation, perhaps even including integer constraints.

The variables X_{isT}, X^*_{isT}, X^*_{sT}, X^0_{sT}, X^{0*}_{sT} appear in the constraints, but not in the objective function. Presumably the variable cost coefficients C_{sT} for final products X_{sT} are defined so as to include all variable costs contained in the product, i.e., costs of growing, storing, and processing. This reduces the size of the model in case only one storing and processing alternative is permitted. It considerably increases the size if alternative ways of storing and processing a particular commodity are taken into account. In this latter case it might be desirable to include storage and processing activities with variable costs in the objective function.

At this point I should like to ask Mr. Mash to explain in some detail the definition of the objective function coefficients. The revenue enters through sales activities. But how do you treat activity costs? Perhaps you could indicate in the following diagram which lines are entered.

	Unit	Quantity	Price/Unit	Cost

Variable inputs for:
 	
    Production (i.e., fertilizer)
    Storage (operating costs)
    Processing (operating costs)
Labor
Capital
Land				

Total objective function coefficient

Of particular interest is the treatment of labor, capital, and land in this context. Secondly, for investment activities the coefficient E=0.15 is entered. How do you arrive at this coefficient? Does it relfect the requirements of the payback period (i.e., between 6 and 7 years), or is it periodized costs consisting of depreciation and interest? If it is the latter, which interest rate was used?

The formulation of crop expansion activities, $(X_s - L_s)$, where X_s is the area of crop "s" and L_s is the area of crop s at the beginning of the planning period, will lead to difficulties. Either a reduction of crop area is not permitted for any of the "s" crops which would require additional constraints of the form $X_s \geq L_s$ or the implicit assumption is made that disinvestments in crop area will bring 15 percent of the investment cost. In actual practice the abandonment of special crop areas like vineyards will probably *incur* costs.

DEMAND FUNCTIONS

As to the estimation of demand functions, I should like to ask whether in your experience the price variances are sufficient for statistical estimation of demand functions. Of particular interest would be a methodological expansion on the problem of taking into account "partially uncovered demand."

Turning to a more general problem, this seems to be an appropriate opportunity to discuss briefly the problem of functional forms used in the estimation of demand functions. In econometric forecasting work we are normally concerned with a very narrow part of the total demand curve. Therefore the choice of an appropriate functional form, though important, is not absolutely decisive for the working of a system. This problem acquires high priority, however, when demand functions are introduced into optimizing models where the endogenous determination of quantities and prices may easily take us out of the range relevant in econometric forecasting. The total revenue function will look completely different for different parameters of a particular function and

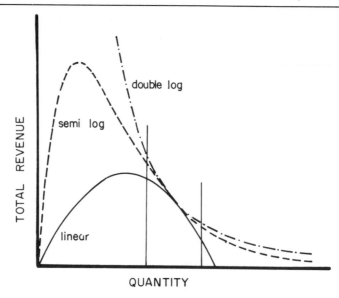

Fig. 13.2. Total revenue for different functions.

for different functions, as in Figure 13.2. Therefore it would be interesting to know which functional forms were used by Mr. Mash.

THE PROBLEM OF COORDINATING SECTORAL MODELS

The real problem which lies behind the model discussed here is of course the general problem of long-run planning. A static long-run equilibrium solution is very often obtained on the assumption that most resources are variable in the long run. In this particular problem the total land, labor, and investment capital capacities are given in fixed quantities; everything else is variable. This implies not only complete mobility of resources within, but also between, firms and even sectors. Moreover firm size is variable. Such a set of assumptions raises a number of serious questions. These are hardly less important for a centrally planned economy as compared to a market economy.

In particular I believe that we are *not* justified to assume complete mobility of durable assets within firms, between firms, and especially between regions. It is certainly true that over a sufficiently long period all assets are variable at some point in time; but any asset is embedded in a complicated structure of assets which together form the productive capacity. The growth of this capacity and its changes — taking into account technological innovations — proceeds slowly over time, with different speed in different lines of production. Not all assets are economically variable at the same time.

Moreover, what is the meaning of a capital constraint in such a model? Does it refer to the total capital requirements of the planning period, in this case until 1980? If yes, the capital accumulation within firms in the intermediate period — certainly not a minor variable — is disregarded or must be determined beforehand. Thus I believe that it is imperative to include the time structure of production if one wants to obtain results.

This may be done in two ways. The first approach would be along the line of dynamic linear programming to obtain what is sometimes called a normative optimum. Given this optimum one could devise policies to reach it. Such norms, based on parameter projections far into the future, may be questioned, however. The first problem arises in the definition of the objective function, whether this should be maximization of consumption with constraints on capital stock or vice versa. The second problem of course is that such a plan is strictly optimal for one period only, given parameter changes not anticipated at the time of planning.

The most serious problem, however, is the disregard for the social, institutional, and political mechanisms of change. Practically all developed economies attempt to create these mechanisms, and it is in this sphere that quantitatively oriented economists should not deny their aid. A call for an increasingly efficient agriculture with rapid outmigration of farm labor in the face of insufficient demand for these types of skills may engender social costs far outweighing the benefits from a more efficient agricultural sector. We do not have to search very hard for examples of such situations, I believe. Therefore the term normative, in my opinion, should be replaced by nontestable in this context.

The second approach would proceed from a basically different point of view in that the question is asked, "How can we explain the decisions of a large number of individual decision units deciding within a particular environment?" The corresponding policy problem would be to test the response of decision making units to various policies. In this case we could incorporate the flow of information between firms within a sector and between different sectors by a feedback process which links various submodels in a dynamic way. Examples of this model type for individual sectors are the recursive programming studies in agriculture and in various other industries. Here we can adapt the choice of the objective function to the structure of the industry. I should like to mention a model of the U.S. steel industry where R. H. Day geared the model to an oligopolistic organization of the industry. This approach is more rigid in that it can be tested against events in the real world. It is more realistic in that it recognizes explicitly the limited amount of usable information available to the decision units. It is more practical in that the economy can be broken down into a number of interdependent segments each with its own decision structure. A combination of multiperiod and recursive systems is possible.

Chapter 14 挒 BRANCH AND REGIONAL MODELS FOR
OPTIMAL PLANNING OF AGRICULTURE IN THE U.S.S.R.

V. V. Miloserdov, *All-Union Scientific Institute for Agricultural
Economics* (U.S.S.R.)

D EVELOPMENT OF MODELS for planning on a countrywide scale
is of great importance in socialist agriculture. Social property
in the means of production requires the direction of all producers
to the national goal and provides opportunity for planned development of
all branches of the national economy.

One of the first major problems of national planning, using
economic-mathematical methods, was the problem of the distribution
and specialization of agricultural production over the country's territory. First attempts at solving this problem by the Soviet scientists
were in the early 1960s. The purpose of these economic-mathematical
models was a rational specialization of agriculture in the entire country on the basis of centralized planning and principles of material incentive in expansion of the production by enterprises.

Economic-mathematical objectives of models of this kind are used
with the following aims for evaluating the optimality of the variant obtained: (a) to minimize the total labor consumption for production of
the projected volume of produce; and (b) to maximize production in a
set structure with available production resources and consideration of
their dynamic changes.

The structure of an economic-mathematical model for a long-term
distribution and specialization of agricultural production with the objective function to minimize total labor consumption can be presented
in the following somewhat simplified form:

$$C_{min} = \sum_{k=1}^{z} \sum_{j=1}^{e'} c_{jk} x_{jk} \tag{1}$$

The obtained meanings of the variables x_{jk} ($x_{jk} \geq 0$) (production of the
j-th product in the k-th zone) should meet the economic, technological,
biological, and other conditions which determine the distribution and
specialization of agricultural production. Such conditions are incorporated into the general system in the form of the following linear relations:

$$\sum_{j=1}^{e'} a_{ijk} x_{jk} \leq b_{ik} + \bar{x}_{juk} \tag{2}$$

This linear inequality formulates the condition that $\sum_{j=1}^{e'} a_{ijk} x_{jk}$, the total area of the i-th cultivated lands in the k-th zone occupied for growing of the j-th crop, should not exceed the area of cultivated lands of this kind available in this zone (b_{ik}) and the area of additional lands brought under cultivation ($\bar{x}_{juk}$, the amount of the j-th resource related to the u-th branch group in the k-th zone; in this case the agricultural lands transformed into cultivated ones, $\bar{x}_{jik} \geq a$); i means cultivated lands of different fertility and dry or irrigated lands; and e' is the total number of agricultural crops.

$$\sum_{j=e'+1}^{e''} a_{ijk}x_{jk} + \bar{x}_{juk} \leq b_{ik} \tag{3}$$

This inequality formulates the conditions of using the natural agricultural lands (i denotes restraints related to natural hay lands, pastures, and other lands of the total acreage equal to e"; j is the ordinal number of farm lands). In the k-th zone b_{ik} lands can be used, except for the transformed lands.

$$\sum_{i=1}^{e''} a_{ijk}x_{jk} + \sum_{j=e''+1}^{e} a_{ijk}x_{jk} - \bar{x}_{juk} = b_{ik} \tag{4}$$

Here $(\sum_{j=1}^{e''} a_{ijk}x_{jk})$ is the use of production resources in plant husbandry, and $(\sum_{j=e''+1}^{e} a_{ijk}x_{jk})$ in animal husbandry.

$$\sum_{j=1}^{e''} a_{ijk}x_{jk} \leq \sum_{j=e''+1}^{e} p_{ijk}x_{jk} + y_k + y_{ik} + D_{ik} \tag{5}$$

This formulation gives the conditions for the balance of fertilizers. In the inequalities are shown the sources of the i-th fertilizers (i is the active substance NPK, manure, peat, and manure composts) produced as by-products of animal husbandry $(\sum_{j=e''+1}^{e} p_{ijk}x_{jk})$, contained in the soil as a residual nitrogen (y_k), the active substance in peat ($\bar{y}_{ik}$), and allocated mineral fertilizers (D_{ik}). The object for fertilizer disposal (farm crops) is shown in the left part of the relation $\sum_{j=1}^{e''} a_{ijk}x_{jk}$.

$$\sum_{j=1}^{e''} V_{hjk}x_{jk} \geq \sum_{j=e''+1}^{e} a_{hjk}x_{jk} + \sum_{j=e''+1}^{e} s_{hjk} \tag{6}$$

This linear relation formulates the balance of production and consumption of feedstuffs, and also the conditions for making optimal rations for feeding animals. The production of the h-th kind of feedstuffs (by groups of stuffs and kinds of nutrients) is provided in cropping branches ($\sum\limits_{j=1}^{e''} v_{hjk} x_{jk}$, where $v_{hjk} = d_{jk} q_{hj}$; d_{jk} is the share of the product in the j-th branch detailed for animal feeding in the k-th region; and q_{hj} is the content of the h-th feedstuffs in a production unit of the j-th branch of plant husbandry). The feedstuff consumption in animal husbandry is equal to $\sum\limits_{j=e''+1}^{e} a_{hjk} x_{jk} + \sum\limits_{j=e''+1}^{e} s_{hjk}$.

In this case a_{hjk} is the norm of the h-th feedstuff consumption for the j-th animal husbandry branch in the k-th region. For nutrients the full norm is given, and for individual stuffs the minimal permissible norm in the total ration is given. The optimal quantity of the given forage (concentrates, roughage, succulent forage, roots, green forage) in the ration is obtained by adding s_{hjk}, which means an increase of the h-th feedstuff in the ration for the j-th animals in the k-th region, where $p_{hik} \leq n_{hjk}$, and n_{hjk} means the difference between the maximum permissible content of the h-th feed in the ration for the j-th animals in the k-th region.

$$\sum\limits_{j=1}^{e} a_{jk} \bar{x}_{juk} \leq D_{ik} \qquad (7)$$

This relation formulates the condition of capital investment distribution among the u-th branch groups in the k-th region, D_{ik}. In this case D_{ik} is the total amount of capital investment for the i-th restraint in the k-th region, and a_{jk} is the norm of capital investments, insuring an increase of the amount of the j-th resource in the k-th region in terms of the adopted measuring units.

Other linear relations of the problem's mathematical model assume that the per unit input for the j-th branch in the k-th region (x_{jk}) is restrained by the possibilities for development of the branch, and that the total sum of capital investment in the whole region cannot exceed the sum of capital investment allocated for the whole of agricultural production (B_p):

$$\sum\limits_{k=1}^{r} D_{ik} \leq B_p$$

(r is the number of agricultural regions.)

A similar formulation is used for requirements related to distribution of mineral fertilizers among the regions. In this case B_p denotes the amount of allocated fertilizers and D_{ik} has the meaning above.

Biological peculiarities of production of individual crops in each region are taken into account in a group of linear inequalities, which are formulated as follows:

$$\sum_{j=1}^{v} V_{ijk} a_{ijk} x_{jk} \leq \sum_{j=1}^{e'-v} a_{ijk} x_{jk} \tag{8a}$$

$$\sum_{j=1}^{v} a_{ijk} x_{jk} \leq V_{ijk} x_{jk} \tag{8b}$$

Formulation (8a) denotes the development of a particular branch or of a group of plant husbandry branches (in the amount of v, where j = 1, 2, ..., v) in the k-th region should not exceed a certain percent relation (V_{ijk}) to the rest of the branches; (b) expresses the same condition, but is related to the whole cropland area, where

$$\bar{\bar{x}}_{jk} = \sum_{j=1}^{e'} a_{ijk} x_{jk} \tag{9}$$

These linear relations formulate the requirements which concern the preceding and subsequent crops, the requirements for individual crops interrelated in competition for the land area, the suitability for cultivation of a given crop, and so on.

For each region there is fixed a guaranteed volume of produce to meet the intraregional needs. This condition is formulated as

$$\sum_{j=1}^{e} E_{pjk} x_{jk} \geq Q_{jk} \tag{10}$$

where Q_{jk} is the guaranteed volume of production for the j-th branch in the k-th region, and E_{pjk} is the amount of the p-th produce, obtained per unit of the j-th commercial branch in the k-th region.

$$\sum_{k=1}^{r} \sum_{j=1}^{e} E_{pjk} x_{jk} \geq H_p \tag{12}$$

These linear relations formulate the requirements which insure an optimal distribution of farm commodity production over the whole of agriculture, in the amount not less than has been set, h_p.

Such are conditions that must be considered to obtain an optimal meaning of the objective function of this model.

APPLICATIONS

Most of the similar economic-mathematical models devised and experimentally tested in the country are of regional character (used for distribution of production in individual republics or regions). At present the State Planning Committee has adopted the economic-mathematical model devised by R. Kravtchenko. This model is being used for estimations of agricultural production distribution on a national scale for

1980. The general problem of optimal agricultural production distribution over the country's territory for a long term should be solved in principle as a complex one with due consideration to all branches of plant and animal husbandry. But if an individual branch is relatively independent of others (itself determines the development of other branches) the formulation of a model of distribution of this production branch may have a self-contained importance. These conditions, significantly expanding the freedom of search for optimal solutions, are fully applicable for distribution of cereal crops over the country's territory.

Such a problem has been devised and solved for the U.S.S.R. Ministry of Agriculture for 1975 on the scale of republics and economic regions of the RSFSR. The objective function maximizes grain production with respect to fixed production resources, crop yields, and the need to guarantee the original structure of the grain balance. Estimations have shown that even with fairly rigid distribution areas of some crops, the agrotechnically allowable redistributions of production alone, the derived variants of the plan, make it possible to increase the gross output of grain to a considerable extent.

One of the most important problems of chemicalization of agriculture, for solution of which mathematical methods can be applied, is that of the distribution of mineral fertilizers over the country's territory. At present, several models for distribution of mineral fertilizers have been devised. Some of them have been tested experimentally. For instance, the model devised at the All-Union Research Institute for Agricultural Economics has been tested on farms of the Lipetsk and Belgorod regions. This model can be used for distribution of fertilizers at any degree of detailing (over agricultural zones of the country, regions, districts, farms, or individual plots). The authors, when devising this model, proceeded with consideration of the efficiency of fertilizer application for different crops on different farms (and even plots differing by soil characteristics).

By using mathematical methods, computers, and models for the interbranch balance in agriculture, the selection of optimal types of agricultural machinery for agricultural zones of the country, and so on is also proceeding in the country. Development of economic-mathematical models for distribution of purchases of farm products according to the state plan commenced in 1963. The importance of a scientifically based solution of this problem consists in the fact that at present centralized planning of agriculture in our country is carried out principally through planning of state purchases. Since about 80 percent of the total farmland area is used for production of the total volume of state purchases, the government controls the agricultural production through the plans of purchases.

GENERAL FORMULATION OF PURCHASE MODEL

The economic-mathematical model for distribution of state plans of purchases is based on the following main principles: (a) attaining a rational specialization and concentration of agricultural production on a national scale; and (b) insuring proper relations between the state and intrafarm interests. In the model, the sought values of variables for each block constitute volumes of procurements of basic kinds of agricultural products. The number of products procured does not exceed 26.

Besides basic variables, other variables indicating the volumes of produce exportation are introduced. Restrictions in the problem are conditioned (a) *in blocks (objects)* with specialization of agricultural production, area involved in the production of the total volume of procurements, separate types of agricultural machines (if funds are simultaneously recorded); (b) *in the coupling block,* with planned volumes of procurements as a whole, area involved for the total volume of procurements, internal requirements of objects in separate kinds of produce; and by (c) *conditions of transportation.*

The assortment of produce subjected to transportation is defined. Available variants of transportation of separate kinds of agricultural produce are also known. The solution of the problem allows obtaining the following data: (a) planned volumes of procurements of agricultural produce per objects; (b) the degree of utilization of labor resources and mechanized labor in objects; (c) the total area expended on the production of all procurements volume per object and the country as a whole; and (d) the volumes of commodity products expedient to be produced for meeting the requirements of other objects.

Proceeding from a general statement of the problem, the system of restrictions, and the variables, the structural economic and mathematical model follows where we first introduce conventional notation.

Indices:

I_{1r} = ensemble, the elements of which are numbers of restrictions per volume of produce procured in an object

I_{2r} = ensemble, the elements of which are numbers of restrictions per the area expended

I_{3r} = ensemble, the elements of which are numbers of restrictions per separate types of production resources

I_{4r} = ensemble, the elements of which are numbers of restrictions for satisfying the requirements of objects in separate products

I_{5r} = ensemble, the elements of which are numbers of restrictions for sums of planned volumes of procurements not subjected to transportation outside the objects

r = numbers of objects in which the plan of procurements is placed; $(r = 1, 2, ..., R)$

i = numbers of restrictions

J_{1r} = ensemble, the elements of which are numbers of variables per kinds of products

J_{2r} = ensemble, the elements of which are numbers of groups of j-type products transported from the object Z for meeting the requirements of the object r (Z = r, from where the product is transported)

j   = number of a kind of products procured (j = 1, 2, ..., n)

j_k = number of a kind of procured products transported; outside according to the k-type variant (k = 1, 2, ..., K)

l   = number of variables groups indicating the volumes of transportation of the j-type products according to the k-type variants (l = 1, 2, ..., L)

Variables:

X_{jr} = sought volumes of the j-type product procured in the object r for its own consumption

X_{jkr} = sought volumes of the j-type product procured in the object r and transported according to the k-type variant

Known values:

P_{jr} = the area expended on the production of the j-type product in the object r

t_{jr} = required production funds per unit of the j-type product in the object r

b_{ijr} = the low limit of the possible volume of procurements of the j-type product in the object r

B_{ir} = minimum permissible expenditure of area in the object r on the production of total volume of procurements

B_{ir} = maximum permissible expenditure of area in the object r on the production of total volume of procurements

T_{ir} = the presence of labor resources in the object r for the production of planned volumes of procurements

E_{ir} = the existence of basic production funds in the object r for the production of planned volumes of procurements

q_{ijr} = the need of the object r in the j-type product

Q_{ij} = planned volume of procurements of the j-type product as a whole per the sum of objects

C_{jr} = social necessary expenditure on the production of the j-type product in the object r

L_{jzk} = transport expenditure on the delivery of the j-type product per unit from the object z according to the k-type transportation variant

It is required to determine the plan $X = X_{jr}, X_{jkr}$ — by means of which the minimum of the sum of necessary social expenditure on production and delivery of products to the places of consumption is obtained:

$$C_{min} = \sum_{r=1}^{R} \left[\sum_{j=1}^{n} C_{jr} X_{jr} + \sum_{l=1}^{L} \sum_{j=1}^{n} (C_{jr} + L_{jzk}) X_{jrk} \right] \quad (12)$$

under the conditions that:

$$b_{ijr} \leq (x_{jr} + \sum_{k=1}^{K} x_{jrk}) \leq b_{ijr} \quad (13)$$

(restrictions on specialization)

$$B_{ir} \leq (\sum_{j=1}^{n} P_{ijr} X_{jr} + \sum_{l=1}^{L} \sum_{k=1}^{K} P_{ijr} X_{jrk}) \leq \bar{B}_{ir} \quad (14)$$

(restrictions on the area expended)

$$\sum_{j=1}^{n} t_{ijr} X_{jr} + \sum_{l=1}^{L} \sum_{k=1}^{K} t_{ijr} X_{jrk} \leq T_{ir} \quad (15)$$

(restrictions on existing labor resources)

$$\sum_{j=1}^{n} l_{ijr} X_{jr} + \sum_{l=1}^{L} \sum_{k=1}^{K} l_{ijk} X_{jrn} \leq \Sigma_{ir} \quad (16)$$

(restrictions on production funds)

$$X_{jz} + \sum_{r=1}^{R-Z} \sum_{K \in J_{2r}} X_{jrk} = q_{ijr} \quad (17)$$

(restrictions on requirements of objects in the j-type products)

$$\sum_{r=1}^{R} X_{jr} = Q_{ij} \quad (18)$$

(restrictions on the total volume of procurement of the j-type)

$$X_{jr} \geq 0, X_{jkr} \geq 0 \quad (19)$$

(conditions of nonnegativeness of variables)

Alternative functions:

$$C_{min} = \sum_{r=1}^{R} (\sum_{j=1}^{n} C_{jr} X_{jr} + \sum_{l=1}^{L} \sum_{k=1}^{K} C_{jr} X_{jrk}) \quad (20)$$

where C_{jr} = expenditure of area on the production of the j-type product unit in the object r.

$$C_{min} = \sum_{r=1}^{R} (\sum_{j=1}^{n} C_{jr} X_{jr} + \sum_{l=1}^{L} \sum_{k=1}^{K} C_{jr} X_{jrk}) \quad (21)$$

where C_{jr} = purchase price on the j-type product unit in the object r.

$$C_{max} = \sum_{r=1}^{R} \left(\sum_{j=1}^{n} C_{jr}X_{jr} + \sum_{l=1}^{L} \sum_{k=1}^{K} C_{jr}X_{jrk} \right) \qquad (22)$$

where C_{jr} = net income from the sale of the j-type product unit to the state in the object r.

$$C_{max} = \sum_{r=1}^{R} \left(\sum_{j=1}^{n} C_{jr}X_{jr} + \sum_{l=1}^{L} \sum_{k=1}^{K} C_{jr}X_{jrk} \right) \qquad (23)$$

where C_{jr} = the sum-total index of economic effectiveness of production of the j-type product unit in the object r.

Thus application of mathematical methods for state planning of agriculture gives a rather high economic efficiency, even when applying for practice the models of local objects as parts of the economic system.

Planning of socialist agriculture includes quite a number of closely interconnected problems and presents a single system. Hence a functional approach to various economic problems, with solution of each economic planning problem in the interests of the single national economic aim or plan can produce far greater economic efficiency. In this connection we are working on systems of economic-mathematical models for planning agriculture with qualitatively new information facilities and systems of criteria and clearly defined demands on the original volumes and flows of information. In this case one of the important aspects of agricultural planning on a national scale (planning of the whole system) consists of a clear-cut determination of the local objectives of planning for individual subsystems, insuring a single direction for these objectives and for the general goal of branch planning.

Chapter 15   CZECHOSLOVAKIAN PLANNING MODEL

Jarimar Havlicek, *Research Institute for Economic Planning*
(Czechoslovakia)
Stanislav Hrabe, *Ministry for Economic Planning* (Czechoslovakia)

OVERALL NATURE[1]

THE SYSTEMATIC TREATMENT which until now has characterized the preparation and construction of plans in Czechoslovakia, and in other countries as well, relied heavily on the branches of techno-economical conceptions originating from the heavens, intuition, and similar foundations. If it were possible to construct mutually coordinate variants in the development of separate branches in such ways, then the influence of their formation on the complex conception of the development of the whole national economy would rightly always be a disproportionate system. Otherwise there seems to be a lack of coordination of the volume and structure of capital investment, working force, exports and imports, and so forth.

The instrument for overcoming such obstacles and for working out a mutually coordinate variant for the composite development of the national economy in its entirety is a model of the structurally dynamic type. Such a model was constructed by the researchers of the Ministry of Planning for the purpose of preparing for the Czechoslovaking national economy a plan. Mr. Hrabe is reporting this aspect.

One of the constructed parts of this macro model is also a model for the development of the agricultural economy. This model is of the implemented type: the precondition is in itself an object for analysis in the final definite direction for future agricultural development and for economic evaluation of the variants for the development of the economy. The variants themselves serve as initial functions for a working plan. The description of its construction and the test of its use in the preparations of a plan is contained in journals which were presented to parts of the seminar in a limited number of copies in English and Russian.

The model of the agricultural economy originates from the output (production) function. Within this context, there is determined the main indices for development of agricultural production, dependent on the degree of application of the most important methods for an increase in production (intensification of agricultural production) of fertilizer and crops, and from the basic funds for production. Changes entering into the production function of the model have much the same character as those of material factors; the choice of factor is representative, not

---

1. Presented by Jarimar Havlicek.

accidental. It is always a basic production factor, the increase of which can be relatively reliably quantified. The dependence between causes and effects in the model is not of the ordinary type.

The composite parts of the model, along with the output or production function, appear also to be a function of expenditure. This affords us the chance, with the help of a comparison of the variants of production and expenditures, to determine the volume and tendency of the future development of net production and of net profits and to obtain a more specific qualification of the contribution of the agricultural economy to general economic growth.

The model permits us to express all the parameters of several variants. First of all, the dependence on the type of applicable production function and function of expenditures, as a rule, were always defined as two projections of development, the base and the optimality. The so-called prognosis zone is found between these. This projection was brought up in the dependence on the initial data used for the calculation of the coefficients of the production function. For example, the base projection is described as originating from the statistical series of government data for a fifteen-year period. The optimal projection is described on the basis of multiyear experimental data and data of selected investigations.

Besides this, it follows that different variants are generated in consequence of the initially altered preconditions, which enter into the function of the model. We are referring here to the area of farmland, the amount of spread fertilizer, the specific weight of the feedstuffs in the gross production of plant growth, the labor force, livestock, and the use of computations of value indices. A number of these changes have the character of regulative factors on the economy so that the relationship of the cost of the political economy of the planning center can be expressed quantitatively and is to be included in the function of the model and described as unknown parameters.

The model for development of the agricultural economy in its present stage permits us to numerically describe the variants of the proposed agricultural economic production, work output, the output of production calculated in sectors of land, size of present expenditures, the fund capacity of gross and net production and its increase.

With the aid of the model, the goal of such calculations was obtained. Their results were compared, for example, with the concept of long-term development of the agricultural economy of Czechoslovakia which was worked out in a traditional method in the Ministry of Agriculture and Food. A comparison of the derived parameters was conducted with the help of this model inserted in the plan and with the calculations of the expected demand for agricultural production with consideration of (a) change in population, (b) consumer income and demand tendencies, and (c) their consequences in the sector of the main groups of agricultural products.

All these practical calculations helped us to display the complexity of future development and difficulties which are anticipated as originating from the present or ongoing unsatisfactory conditions of the agricultural economy. All these undoubtedly are shown to help in the formulation of the plan. However, for the preparation of a plan of long-term development of the agricultural economy, it is impossible to restrict significantly only the determination of the agricultural indices of a macroeconomic character. Therefore a following stage of our work in the construction and use of a model includes a structure for agricultural output. Its goal is the establishment of an optimal area of use of agricultural production for the natural and economic conditions in Czechoslovakia. It provides for separate growth in relation to resolved factors of growth, rational expectations of growth in the national economy, and international trade and division of labor. In this direction, we have already worked out a series of models for the separate branches of plant growth and stock raising which ought to enter into the basis of the general modular structure of the agricultural economy of Czechoslovakia.

DETAILED ASPECTS[2]

The scheme of the Czechoslovak agriculture forms a part of our dynamized, structural, overall model representing the long-term development of our productive forces. From the methodological as well as practical point of view it is a kind of a macroeconomic simulation model with an implementation flavor. It is decisively production oriented. In it the agriculture forms a sector in the same way as other industries.

Our model is constructed as a combination of classical forms of Leontief approaches and models of economic growth. In this respect it is in compliance with the trends of research which were proclaimed and accepted at the January conference on input-output models in Geneva. At present, after a ten-sectoral model had been constructed and computed, a new version with thirty sectors is being developed. This degree of disaggregation seems to be sufficient for practical analytical work in our new Ministry of National Economic Planning. For computational purposes, we are using the IBM-7040 type and hope to finish our work with the new version at the beginning of 1969.

A detailed description of the ten-sectoral version is contained in a study where more than 300 pages are devoted to the model and 30 pages concern a complete program written in FORTRAN IV.

In order to get an appropriate idea about the structure of our macroeconomic model we may point out that its backbone is formed by the most relevant sectors of our economy — production of machinery, construction, power, supply, transportation, and agriculture. The agricultural sector is divided, according to traditional patterns, into two parts. Consumer industries form the rest.

Besides the input-output matrix of the Leontief type, the following

2. Presented by Stanislav Hrabe.

relations are taken into account. More than 50 equations have a current econometric character, 175 equations formulate assumptions of economic decision making and trends of development. Within this number, 27 equations concern simulation of investment decision making. More than 50 equations have the definitional character; some are of the transformation type. On the whole our model contains 300 equations with 552 variables.

As to the detailed character of individual equation groups, the econometric relations are represented mainly by production functions and the distribution of factors of production, (i.e., labor force, capital funds, distribution of power supply). A behavioristic character is reflected in the transfer equations expressing the transformation of the level of some activities from the t-1 period to period t. Technical coefficients are projected over the period of 10 to 15 years on the basis of some special research and analytical work. In this way the technical coefficients applied in the input-output part of our model are dynamized. Some auxiliary and complementary computations are carried on besides. This part of our computational work is expected to be increased much more in the enlarged version of our model.

Now I will try to show you how the model works. First some assumptions are made as to the probable development of the labor force. The possibility to influence the distribution of the labor force by governmental measures is taken into account and can be expressed in the model. According to the assumption concerning the labor force and investment activity, a 15-year development of main elements of the production structure is computed. The results are obtained either in a report containing data about the development of various growth trajectories or in a form of an abbreviated survey. Both reports point out automatically the main features in every year which are relevant in a negative way; that is, signals for serious signs of disproportion automatically cause the computer to stop, and the results attained are printed. The purpose of experimentation of this type is threefold: to get a picture of possible development of national income, to get a picture of possible development of individual aggregated sectors or industries, and to be warned if the possible development shows some fundamental disproportions in the long run.

First, numerical experiments with our model already prove the real possibilities to compute many alternatives of possible development. As a basis for a detailed analysis, 250 alternatives were obtained.

Alternative results are obtained by changing basic data in the following way. First, so-called initial alternatives are given. Any initial alternative is then developed into various subtypes by changing some parameters whose impact we may think to be of interest. Thus a repetitive utilization of the same program is carried on.

Now what about the computation time needed for the purposes mentioned above? To obtain results concerning 50 or 100 variants printed in a survey form takes 40 or 60 minutes of computation time when the IBM-7040 is used. The preparation of necessary data for a group of variants takes 2 days and their transfer to computer media by means of punching takes another 2 days, or a little less. The next day is used for computation purposes, for repetitive computing, ordering, and printing results. Within 3 or 4 weeks, 5 initial alternatives with 300-500 variants can be analyzed. Thus the central planning authority has at its disposal quantitative analysis which is not attainable by other means.

J. C. Tirel, *Center for Rural Economic Study*
(France)

THE FRENCH EXPERIMENTAL MODEL for 1970 is constructed by the economic studies division of the Ministry of Agriculture, whose director is Mr. Morin. The central team (15 persons) is located in Paris, but at least one liaison officer has been appointed for each of the 21 Economic Programming Regions. These liaison officers work at a regional level in cooperation with farm management officers who are paid by Farmer Associations.

France has been divided into 100 regions according to physical and economic criteria, and 500 types of farms have been selected according to the size, land use, and sometimes the technological level of farmers. The selection of these benchmark farms has been made on the basis of a national survey dealing with one-tenth of French farms in 1962. (A similar survey has been undertaken again in 1967.) This survey has been used in addition to complementary information which describes French agriculture through aggregation of 7000 representative farm production plans.

The model is a static activity analysis model with separable demand relations; therefore it can be solved using conventional linear programming procedures. The main activities are farm production plans. For each benchmark farm, five to ten plans are considered as practicable. Theoretically these plans should be feasible solutions of benchmark farm models and the national model can be seen as the principal problem in a programming decomposition process. In fact, information about these plans has been supplied directly by regional farm management officers according to the selection of representative farms. All the farm programs do exist presently in some profitable farms of each region. More advanced plans also have been introduced in the model, but only a limited acreage can be allocated to them.

Other activities deal with quantities of product (or factor) which are supplied (or needed) according to the demand (or supply) relations and each level of price. A summary is given in Figure 16.1. The activities y_1^d, y_2^d, y_3^d refer to the same product d but to different levels of price p_1, p_2, p_3. We have of course: $y_1^d \leq Q_1$ and $y_2^d \leq Q_2 - Q_1$. The dual value u is the equilibrium price.

About twenty products or groups of products are considered. The demand relations have been specified at the national level, according to present E.E.C. policy. One labor supply relation is specified for each economical programming region. The model includes about 2500 activities. The constraints of the models refer to the following aspects at the representative farm level.

348

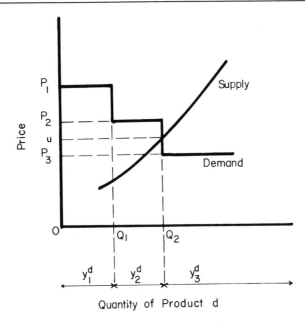

Fig. 16.1. Product supply and demand.

1. Some farm plans are bounded (minimum or maximum acreage)

$$X_{jk} \lessgtr S_j$$

The acreage allocated to the various plans of one given representative farm is limited by structural constraints

$$\sum_j X_{jk} \geq S_k$$

2. At the regional level, the sum of acreages allocated to the various types of farms is limited by available land in the region

$$\sum_k \sum_j X_{jk} \leq S_r$$

If $\sum_k S_k = S_r$, the structures are fixed; if $\sum_k S_k < S_r$, partial competition is allowed between types of farms.

3. At the economic programming regional level one constraint insures that labor used has to be supplied by the labor market. Other constraints insure that for each level of wages available the number of workers is limited; therefore the level of wages increases with increasing employment.

4. At the national level one constraint insures that any marketed quantity of each product has to be supplied by agriculture. Other constraints are introduced for each product in order to limit the additional demand at each level of price (as it is shown in the previous example).

Fig. 16.2. Regions used in French model.

The model includes about 650 restraints. Transportation and processing sectors are not explicitly included; the related costs are taken
into account at the producer level. The objective is maximizing net surplus for consumers and producers. The model has been progressively
adjusted through testing at regional, multiregional, and national levels
(Fig. 16.2). Each national solution requires about half an hour of IBM
360-75 computer time, using a starting feasible solution. Experimental
work is being done on this model in applying parametric programming
procedures to analyze effects of changes in structure and demand relations.

A new model is planned for 1975 using the principle of decomposition at the economic programming regional level. The regional submodels will be founded on the structure of the present national model.
The activities of the new national model will be alternative regional programs. The results of this study should be used to prepare the Sixth
National Plan.

Wilhelm Henrichsmeyer, *University of Hohenheim*
(German Federal Republic)

IN A RESEARCH GROUP of the Institute of Agricultural Economics
at the University of Hohenheim (under Professor G. Weinschenk)
work has been done for some years on problems of structural change
and regional specialization of agricultural production. The studies
cover both the testing and extension of the available methodological
tools and the formulation of empirical location models. The work is
supported financially by the German Society for the Promotion of Research, in the main program of "Econometrics." The model I will explain to you[1] belongs to the class of interregional activity analysis
models. It has the same formal mathematical structure as some of the
models which have been presented here during the last days, especially
the models of Heady and Hall and the French model. But I think our
approach is rather different as far as economic content and aims of research are concerned. In the following I will stress these differences
in approach.

In the short time which is available to me, I cannot give a broad
and detailed outline of the model and the concept of economic analysis
behind it. I will limit myself to the following three points: (a) a short
description of the economic structure of the model, (b) an explanation
of the general line of approach and aims of analysis, (c) and finally, in
response to many questions which have been directed to me during the
last days, I will make a few remarks on some technical and computational problems.

ECONOMIC STRUCTURE OF THE MODEL

This comprehensive model of agricultural production in Germany
is based on microeconomic decision units. The decision units consist
of aggregated groups of more or less homogeneous farms, which are
assumed to act like single farms and which compete for regional and
national factors of production and demand potentials. The economic
structure of a model of this kind depends upon data, research costs,
computation facilities, and mainly on the specific conditions of agricultural production in the country concerned and on the aims of the study.

Agricultural production in Germany can be characterized generally

1. Scientific co-research workers are F. Bauersachs and K. Welker.

and in short by the following points. (a) A diversity and close connection of different branches of production within single farms, resulting
from natural conditions and (small) farm size, requires the construction
of a comprehensive production model for each group of farms. Each
model contains the main production alternatives and quite a number of
constraints, especially for (seasonal differentiated) labor, crop rotation,
feed balances, and other intermediate products. Actually our production
model for each farm group contains about 30 to 50 production processes
(including different technical levels) and 20 to 25 group restraints. (b)
A mixture of farms of different sizes within the same region (small
farms constituting in most regions a large part of agricultural production) requires the distinction of different groups of farms within regions.
We have distinguished up to 4 groups according to farm size. (c) A
wide range of different natural conditions and a scattered distribution
of centers of industrial activity and consumption makes it necessary to
distinguish a rather large number of regions. We have 32 production
regions in our model.

So we arrive at a production model of about 32 regions, 4 groups of
farms within regions, 30 to 50 activities, and 20 to 25 restraints for
each model group. In addition, we have from 5 to 10 restraints for regionally fixed factors of production and intermediate products in each
region and corresponding regional transfer activities. Then the basic
production model ends up to have a size of about 3,500 restraints and
4,000 to 8,000 production activities. On the demand side we have distinguished 12 demand regions, demand functions being derived from national estimates and regional distribution of population and income.

The simultaneous solution of a comprehensive interregional competition model comparing production and interregional exchange is not
possible within given computer capacities. So we have developed an
iterative procedure, which Borlin mentioned in his paper, in which the
production part and the transportation part of the model are split up.
I cannot go into the details here of that iteration procedure. The rules
for the iterative steps, which have to be observed, are fairly complicated in the general case (especially the problem of self-sufficient regions). But for specific German conditions the procedure seems to be
rather efficient, because the directions of interregional exchange are
not very sensitive for most sets of assumptions. (For example trade of
feed grain is mainly determined by imports from the harbors of the
North Sea.) So much for the general structure of the basic model.
Some technical questions of model generation in the computer and computation will be summarized later.

OUTLINE OF THE RESEARCH PLAN

The strategy of our research work comprises four stages. In the
first step we tried to establish a regional input-output balancing system
within the framework of our model. The aim is to describe for a given

base period the existing patterns of factor use, production, and inter-regional exchange as close to reality as possible and especially to in-sure consistency of data.

In the second stage we tried to analyze the sensitivity of the model results for the base year. The starting point has been just an inversion of the input-output model for the base year, that means the solution of our spatial equilibrium model for actual capacities of resources and pro-duction patterns. The comparison of resulting dual values with actual product — and factor prices — not only allows a second check on the plausibility of assumptions on the data side but gives a good insight into the economic interdependencies of the model. Of the several runs we have done this way, the majority have produced rather reasonable re-sults. Equilibrium price levels approach actual prices within a range of 10 percent. (Notable exceptions are, for example, the prices of sugar beets, for which we have contingents and for which lower equilibrium prices are to be expected.)

Valuation of production factors and intermediate products has been more difficult to interpret because it is influenced by the simultaneous interplay of a large number of different factors. So we tried to analyze systematically the impact of single factors of location by isolating ab-straction, following Thunen's approach. Then starting from a rather abstract model which contained some basic regional differences only, we introduced step-by-step further differentiating factors. We have taken only first steps in this direction so far. It will be a continual task to improve information and to approach reality by the introduction of more and more special regional features.

In a third stage we use the model for comparative static analysis. Basis and point of reference for this analysis is the base-year model described above. Many possible questions which might be analyzed were mentioned in the report of Heady. The alternatives we have ana-lyzed so far are the consequences of demand increase, technical prog-ress and further mechanization on regional specialization, changes in farm structure, and the incidence of farm workers leaving agriculture.

To summarize the question of the economic meaning of model re-sults, which has been discussed widely during the last several days, I think the results of the static normative models can be interpreted in one of the two following ways. First, very unambitiously, just as the logical consequences of certain assumptions which cannot be overlooked without the help of a formal model. In this way, model calculations may help to make transparently possible consistent developments. Second, more ambitiously, as the description of an optimal structure which might be aimed at by means of agricultural policy. For the interpretation, I think it is necessary to check very carefully whether all restraints which are relevant for the planning situation are incorporated (under German conditions, especially financial restraints which might limit the process of structural change and mechanization). And further it is necessary to check whether the results are consistent with a more comprehensive system of goals of economic policy.

Finally, in a fourth stage, we plan to introduce elements of recursive programming. The starting point is the base year model mentioned above. The computed marginal values show the economic incentives to increase or decrease production and investment processes, labor migration, and so on. Using this information, as well as the knowledge of the development of variables in the past and different kinds of case studies (development models for samples of single farms, adaption studies, and so on), we try to develop some hypotheses on relations which might be incorporated in a recursive manner. In this way we hope to come to a framework for consistent forecasting and policy analysis.

I think there will be no chances for several years for a formalization of this more pragmatic approach in an explicit recursive programming model for Germany at the national level. For many important variables, we do not have sufficient regionally disaggregated time series to estimate the necessary behavior relations. Much empirical work is being done in several case studies, but we have a long way to go until the results of these studies can be generalized and introduced in a nationwide model.

SOME TECHNICAL REMARKS ON
DATA PROCESSING AND COMPUTATION

One should mention technical matters too at this meeting because there are quite a number of participants who work in this field empirically or plan to do so. Hence an exchange of experience might be of interest and save much time and money. If one is aiming at the kind of analysis proposed in this report, it is necessary to find a flexible way to generate the model from basic data and to analyze the results. We have developed programs to generate the L.P. matrix from original data. This method reduces mistakes in data processing, allows a fast incorporation of new information, and makes it possible to adjust the model in a very flexible way to different questions of agricultural policy. We have developed output programs[2] which transform the result of the model directly into tables and charts.

This technical work has consumed several man-years of time, but I think that only in this way can a program of the kind I have suggested be handled.

---

2. These programs are written for the Univac 1107. They have been developed by F. Bauersachs and G. Joch.

Chapter 18 ⌾ NATIONAL PLANNING MODELS FOR HUNGARIAN AGRICULTURE

J. Hoos, Karl Marx, *University of Economics* (Hungary)

MATHEMATICAL MODELS used in national economic planning and analysis in Hungary are aimed, by nature, at giving information on the economy as a whole. Thus they deal with agriculture as one of the sectors of the economy, pointing out first the interrelations between agriculture and the national economy as a whole and the role that agriculture plays in the total process of production and trade. This national economic view, at the same time, renders it possible to consider the inner relations of agriculture from a national economic aspect. Besides the models of nationa᠆ economic character, efforts have been made to elaborate models which quantify agriculture as a whole or its main economic relations to other branches of the national economy in a comparative way, thus giving possibilities of a more comprehensive evaluation.

Actual results concerning agriculture, as well as experiences promising such results on the basis of experimental calculations made so far, have been obtained by the following mathematical methods and models: (a) branch-relational balance sheets based on the input-output technique; (b) experimental national economic programming; (c) the so-called M.I. and M.II. statistical macroeconomic models; and (d) production functions.

In Hungary, since the 1950s, balance sheets of branch relations have regularly been elaborated on the basis of planning and factual data (input-output balance sheets). These balance sheets, besides presenting in detail the direct relations of agriculture to the major sectors of the national economy and the direct cost structure of agricultural production, give also possibilities to determine (with the aid of the matrix of total input coefficients) the national economic cost structures of agriculture and other branches of the national economy. That is, the balance sheets determine the inputs required for a final issue of unit value as accumulated from the various elements of additional values (wages, net income, and so on).[1]

On the basis of the national economic cost structure, new ways have been opened to evaluate the national economic role of agriculture. Thus, owing to the present price system, the direct net income per unit production value is very low in agriculture. The cumulative net revenue of agricultural products also is behind that of other sectors to a much lower

---

1. Debate on the New System of Economic Management in Hungary, Budapest: Közgazdasági és Jogi Könyvkiadó, 1966. Pp. 125-68.

extent than the direct net income, due to the relatively large amount of industrial products of high direct costs utilized in agriculture. These balance sheets render it possible also to analyze more intensively the export and import activities and capital and labor requirements of agriculture. Finally, on the basis of the plan balance sheets of branch relations, agricultural planning can be more adequately combined with the other targets of the national economic plan.

Analyses made with the balance sheets of branch relations give, however, the highest result under numerical determination of mathematical models of price types by which national economic proportions could be evaluated without the distortion of the present price system. The calculations were first made on the basis of the balance sheet of 1961. These and subsequent calculations have unanimously shown that in the present price system, with the fundamental indexes taken into consideration, industry has an extremely great importance in the national economy, due primarily to the very high level of net income realized in industry. On the other hand, the price system underestimates the national economic role of agriculture. (At prices effective in 1961 the share of the industry in the national income was 58.1 percent, while at prices expressing the produced value a mere 37.1 percent. Conversely agriculture had a share of 33.0 percent instead of 20.4 percent in the national income.)

These calculations called attention to the fact that the importance of agriculture in the national economy, as well as its role in solving the economic tasks and problems facing the country, are considerably greater than they seem to be as reflected by the present price system. As a consequence, in the present plans, development of agriculture is given a much greater part as compared to the earlier plans, and agriculture is considered to be one of the key activities.

In the course of national economic programming, experimental calculations are made concerning the mathematical programming of the long-range plan of 1966-70. Within the work of programming, models were first prepared for 48 branches of the national economy, aimed at determining the optimum production and foreign trade structures of the respective branches. By coordinating the programs of the individual branches, the calculation is given a national economic character when the national economic optimum is calculated. This work is presently in its final phase. One of the 48 sector models represents agriculture.[2]

Optimization in the agricultural sector was to attain a double aim: to help agricultural planning by optimally distributing the available resources between and within its branches, and to make calculations in order to provide agriculture with national economic resources to the extent it can utilize. Branch programming shows how effectively, under

2. National Economic Programming (1966-70). Bull. 26, Description and Analysis of Agricultural Calculations. National Planning Office, Institute of Planned Economy; Calculation of the Technical Center of the Hungarian Academy of Sciences, Research Institute of Agricultural Economics.

the given conditions and within their sphere of activity, the individual branches are able to utilize financial, labor, investment, and other resources available to the whole national economy, and how central resources can be regrouped accordingly.

In the course of the programming work agriculture was divided into six branches, and separate models were prepared for each branch. These models covered about 90 percent of all agricultural production. The models contained and represented plans previously elaborated with traditional methods. The optimum branch program, determined by calculations at a sector level, was required to contain no major index worse than those in the starting official program. These requirements were included in the restrictive conditions of the models. Besides, further restrictions insured that the branch program took into consideration the actual conditions, possibilities, and limitations of economic life and other relations (such as the upper limits of exportation, the technical conditions of product utilization within the branch, and dry matter and starch content of feeds). Under the given conditions, the agricultural branch models were expected to improve the capitalist balance of payment as compared to the traditional plan; that is, the maximization of the capitalist balance of payment was the content of the target function.

The calculations were completed with tests which calculated the sensitivity of the optimal program to the change in one or another of the limits. Such calculations concerning export possibilities and the narrow increase of certain resources have been completed.

Calculations for the models were made with linear assumptions, with both restrictive conditions and the target function being determined in the form of linear equations. Consequently cost and price changes depending on the volumes of production or marketing could not generally be taken into consideration.

Calculations made so far produced many interesting correlations and numerical results. If done carefully, however, results obtained can be applied in practice only to a small extent. One of the reasons is that this work is of experimental character aimed at testing modern mathematical methods. Another reason is that the sphere of programming (covered by the calculations) is narrower than that of planning. The agricultural model does not encompass the total agricultural calculation material of the plan and uses a number of simplifying assumptions; a proportion of the fundamental data used has been estimated at a high margin of error. In addition, calculations have been made for such a long time that most of the results are no longer current.

National economic programming, however, even in a case where calculations are completed in due time, cannot replace comprehensive national economic and branch planning, including the permanent elements of traditional methods. This naturally follows from the main characteristics mentioned above. Even in the case of adequate preparation and the availability of organizational, personal, and financial conditions, it is only able to help, complete, and improve the traditional methods of planning. The main result of the experimental calculations made so far is that they confirmed these expectations and provided concrete experiences by which programming of this kind can be carried out more efficiently in the future.

In Hungary experiments on constructing and practically applying statistical macroeconomic models have been performed for several years. In the course of this work in the laboratory for Economic Application of Statistical and Mathematical Methods of the Central Statistical Office, the M.I. statistical macro model of the Hungarian People's Republic has been completed. An improved form of this model, the model M.II. is at present under process.[3] The models are constructed — beyond the aim of obtaining methodological experiences — to find out whether certain stable relations existing in the Hungarian economy can be reckoned with, since they are indispensable from the point of view of applying the statistical macro models in practice.

The models are descriptive and statistical. That is, by determining and describing certain national economic correlations and indicating the close or less close statistical (stochastical) relations of their variables, they describe the major characteristics of national economy. In one point, however, they are also of dynamic character since among their variables the trend and direction of permanent progress also can be found. Further, they include delayed variables. Due to their parameters indicating stable correlations, they are suitable for certain projection purposes as well.

Both model M.I. and model M.II. deal with agriculture separately by the equation of the national income of agricultural origin. At the same time major parameters relative to agriculture are found in more than one equation of the model. Model M.I. tries to determine the changes in agricultural production as the function of labor force employed in the agricultural sector, investments made by agriculture and the trend of agriculture, as well as of a factor reflecting the improved technology of agricultural production. Changes in the unfertilized area were taken for this latter factor, considering that fertilization is one of the most important indices of a developed agriculture. The climatic factor has not yet been taken into consideration in model M.I.

The equation of national income production of agricultural origin in this construction has not given any significant result concerning the parameters. (The nonagricultural part of the model at the same time gave realistic, acceptable values.) Variables employed in the equation proved neither sufficient nor suitable to explain the trend of the national income of agricultural origin. The decisive reason for this (besides the high degree of aggregation in the equation) was that in the period covered by the time series used, the structure of agriculture changed considerably and weather conditions, which have a great influence on agricultural production trends in Hungary, were not taken into consideration.

---

3. The M.I. Statistical Macro Model. Nemzetkozi Modszertani Fuzetek, vol. 7, 1965. The M.II. model has not yet been published.

Model M.II., presently under process, mostly eliminates the deficiencies of model M.I. In this respect the climatic factor included in the equation of agricultural production as well as a wider range of appropriate features of agricultural activity taken into consideration are especially important (e.g., in the equation of foreign trade agricultural export is dealt with separately).

Hungarian calculations based so far on production functions, similarly to foreign calculations, in fact endeavored to determine to what extent and in what proportion the various factors promoted the increase of production. Thus mainly the numerical effect of technical development on the increase of labor force and capital was emphasized. Within known possibilities given by these functions, the volume output and the marginal proportion and elasticity of replacement were determined in relation to examined growth factors. The calculations were made, however, mostly for the whole of the national economy and the most important branches of Hungarian industry. The agriculture production function, on the basis of time series between 1950 and 1967, was calculated only by the Department of National Economic Planning of the University for Economic Sciences. This function was to determine the role played by the labor force and capital employed in agriculture during the period examined in the increase of production in this period. Calculation results obtained gave acceptable values (e.g., in the period examined, agriculture was characterized by an increasing output; the elasticity of capital was 0.42 while that of the labor force 0.71).

Concrete results obtained so far have unanimously shown that production functions can be used and results obtained by this method can be utilized respectively not only in analyses but also in overall planning. Utilization can take place either independently or in combination with other methods and models. In case of an independent utilization, fixed capital and labor force requirements of various development plans, and possible production increasing effects of various investment plans, can be determined. Besides, information can be obtained on prospective changes in the cost levels of the individual branches. In case of utilization in combination with other methods, certain parameters determined by these functions may form part of the parameters of other models. At present, intensive work is completed to exploit these possibilities. During the work, however, abstractions, consequences, and reality of results obtained by these functions are always taken into consideration and emphasized.

We have summarized above the experiences and results obtained so far in Hungary concerning agriculture in the course of elaborating national economic models. We should like to emphasize that only experimentation has taken place in most cases. Thus concrete practical results, except for those given by the balance sheets of branch relations, are poor. However experiences obtained are promising for the future, and the optimism of model builders and practical planners in this respect is wholly justified.

Chapter 19 ✑ U.S. NATIONAL AGRICULTURAL MODELS CONDUCTED AT IOWA STATE UNIVERSITY

Earl O. Heady, *Iowa State University* (U.S.A.)
Harry H. Hall, *University of Kentucky* (U.S.A.)

WORK ON NATIONAL MODELS of agriculture has been underway at Iowa State University since 1956. Initially the models started in two directions: models based on samples of typical farms with their aggregation to regional totals and models based on regions as the producing units. Major emphasis shortly turned to the later type of models, although we have continued to participate in individual farm models in cooperation with regional research groups and the U.S. Department of Agriculture. We have made many applications of these models, and they have been used for planning and policy purposes. They allow interdependencies among producing regions of the United States and allow production of the various commodities within regions and flows among regions to be determined within each model. Around 40 models have had solutions made for them.

The models started out rather modestly at the outset because of restraints in data and computer capacity. They have, however, grown each year in scope and coverage. Our initial model included only wheat, corn, oats, barley, and sorghum. Since, however, soybeans, cotton, and livestock products have been added. The first model included a coefficient matrix of 225 x 430 order. The most recent one underway has a coefficient matrix of 4,000 x 37,000. More recently models have shifted from the linear format of earlier ones to a quadratic form and include demand functions so that market prices and quantities are both determined endogenously.

Our main purpose has been to analyze national policy or planning programs, to determine the optimal allocation of production and land use, to analyze facets of interregional competition, and to examine the structure of agriculture among about 150 producing regions and 31 major consuming regions of the nation. (The exact number of each varies with the specification of each model.) We now review some of the evaluation involved in the models.

The initial models had equations representing fixed demand restraints in each consuming region, the land and other cropping restraints in each producing region, and equations to allow grain conversion, transportation, and so on. Now, however, demand functions have been added to the models to allow examination of equilibrium prices and quantities. All models are normative relative to a given objective function.

EVALUATION OF MODELS

In 1961 Egbert and Heady (2, 8) reported the results from the first U.S. national agricultural model formulated at Iowa State University. This model was initiated in 1956. The United States was partitioned into 104 producing regions and a set of crop-producing activities (food wheat, feed wheat, feed grains) were defined for each region. The 104 regions accounted for roughly 90 percent of U.S. wheat and feed grains production in 1954. We attributed normal (average) production to the excluded area. Next we established gross national requirements (domestic plus export demands) for food wheat and feed grains. Deducting normal excluded area production from gross national requirements left net national requirements to be supplied by the 104 producing regions. Finally, the distribution of production among producing regions which minimized production costs incurred in satisfying net requirements was determined. Transportation costs were ignored, the implicit assumption being that commodities could be shipped at no cost from producing areas to final consumption points.

Subsequently numerous additional models have been formulated, each adding refinements or expanding the scope of its predecessors. Heady and Egbert (3, 7) added a second model incorporating 122 producing regions and including soybeans and cotton as well as wheat and feed grains. Heady and Whittlesey (10, 12) and Heady and Skold (9, 11) formulated models with 144 producing regions and 31 consuming (demand regions). These two models are distinct from the earlier ones since wheat, feed grain, and oilmeal requirements are specified for each of the 31 consuming regions, and interregional shipments are permitted. A national demand for cotton lint is retained. Whittlesey and Heady used 1965 as a base year; Skold and Heady used 1975 with projections made accordingly. Heady and Mayer (8) made projections to 1980 for 150 regions, analyzing optimal production location, national production potential, the effects of alternative programs of policies, and the requirements for labor and capital in each producing region. Brokken and Heady formulated a model including livestock as well as crops. This model incorporated 157 producing regions and 20 consuming regions. Requirements were specified on a regional basis and interregional commodity shipments were permitted. In a model similar in many respects to the Heady-Whittlesey model, Hall, Heady, and Plessner (5) used linear regional demand functions to reflect regional requirements. Prices and quantities demanded, as well as production, are determined endogenously in this model. Some characteristics of a few of these models are summarized in Table 19.1.

In the models that feature consuming regions, each producing region is completely contained in a consuming region. Production in the producing region contributes to a central supply in the consuming region. Transportation activities then permit commodity shipments from regions with excess supply to those with excess demand. Typically a

Table 19.1. Characteristics of some national agricultural models formulated at Iowa State University

Model	Consuming regions	Producing regions	Commodity demands	Base year	Reference
Egbert-Heady #1	0	104	food wheat feed grains	1954	(2)
Heady-Egbert #2	0	122	food wheat feed grains soybean oilmeal cotton lint	1954 1965	(3)
Heady-Whittlesey	31	144	food wheat feed grains soybean oilmeal cotton lint[a]	1965	(10, 12)
Heady-Skold	31	144	food wheat feed grains soybean oilmeal cotton lint[a]	1975	(9, 11)
Brokken-Heady	20	157	beef (2 grades) pork milk (fluid, manu- factured) food wheat feed grains (food uses) cotton lint[a]	1965	(1)
Hall-Heady-Plessner	9	144	wheat for food corn for food oats for food barley for food feed grains, oil-meals	1965	(5)

a. National demand only.

nonzero cost is associated with a transportation activity. The usual objective in this type of model is to find the production-transportation pattern which minimizes the aggregate cost (production cost plus transportation cost) of satisfying all the regional demands.

In Tables 19.2 through 19.5 we summarize the optimal distribution of production in the various models for wheat, feed grains, soybeans, and cotton, respectively. Except for the Whittlesey-Heady model, all the distributions are of actual production as distinct from acreage. For comparison purposes, the actual 1965 distributions are also listed. Generally speaking, the models indicate at least as much (and often more) regional specialization than is actually the case. To a large degree some tendency toward overspecialization is characteristic of programming models of this type. This tendency is due in part to the usual assumption that crop yields are uniform over an entire producing region. Producing regions are delineated so that crop yields are as uniform as

Table 19.2. Distribution of U.S. wheat production by regions, percent of total

Region	Actual 1965	Egbert-Heady #1[a] (solution A)	Heady-Egbert #2[a] (model B.1)	Heady-Whittlesey[b] (solution 43)	Heady-Skold (model I)	Brokken-Heady (solution 1)	Hall-Heady-Plessner
Northeast	2.08	...	2.00	1.99	...	...	...
Appalachian	1.49	...	...	0.83	0.97	1.15	...
Southeast	0.42	...	9.27	0.55	...	...	0.86
Delta	1.10	...	...	0.20	2.80	3.47	5.74
Corn Belt	12.67	...	9.06	8.70	14.37	9.54	4.21
Lake States	3.86	4.45	4.42	4.95	5.57	4.27	8.54
N. Plains	38.44	41.48	54.89	39.76	33.42	38.73	25.55
S. Plains	15.91	13.77	15.17	17.50	15.80	14.46	23.60
Mountain	14.41	21.50	3.27	17.79	12.96	15.45	17.95
Pacific	9.62	18.81	1.69	7.73	14.02	12.93	13.55

a. Includes only wheat for food.
b. Percent of total acreage.

Table 19.3. Distribution of U.S. feed grain production by regions, percent of total

Region	Actual 1965	Egbert-Heady #1[a] (solution A)	Heady-Egbert #2[a] (model B.1)	Heady-Whittlesey[b] (solution 43)	Heady-Skold (model I)	Brokken-Heady (solution 1)	Hall-Heady-Plessner
Northeast	2.94	1.01	3.14	2.55	5.01	4.32	2.58
Appalachian	4.64	...	2.89	5.46	5.57	4.40	5.28
Southeast	2.60	...	5.18	1.89	0.21	...	0.21
Delta	0.63	...	...	0.16	...	0.22	...
Corn Belt	49.02	62.48	55.52	43.27	63.85	60.73	61.22
Lake States	11.99	7.84	8.67	17.03	13.67	15.56	13.44
N. Plains	16.41	24.81	14.29	19.62	7.45	7.79	11.08
S. Plains	6.42	2.99	3.78	7.55	3.80	5.32	5.84
Mountain	2.92	...	3.53	0.59	0.42	0.63	0.35
Pacific	2.43	0.86	3.01	1.87	...	1.03	...

a. Includes wheat for food.
b. Percent of total acreage.

Table 19.4. Distribution of U.S. soybean production by regions, percent of total

Region	Actual 1965	Egbert-Heady #1[a] (solution A)	Heady-Egbert #2[a] (model B.1)	Heady-Whittlesey[b] (solution 43)	Heady-Skold (model I)	Brokken-Heady (solution 1)	Hall-Heady-Plessner
Northeast	1.21	...	...	1.87	...	...	...
Appalachian	6.00	...	6.40	1.53	...	1.71	3.36
Southeast	3.34	...	...	1.60	6.05	...	4.69
Delta	14.49	...	15.11	2.07	...	13.40	3.39
Corn Belt	60.73	...	72.63	62.24	36.20	81.16	51.80
Lake States	8.43	...	4.56	4.05	14.60	3.28	4.29
N. Plains	5.25	...	1.30	24.97	40.57	0.45	28.05
S. Plains	0.55	...	...	1.67	2.58	...	4.42
Mountain	...	...	...	...	...	...	...
Pacific	...	...	...	...	...	...	...

a. Soybeans not included in this model.
b. Percent of total acreage.

Table 19.5. Distribution of U.S. cotton production by regions, percent total

Region	Actual 1965	Egbert-Heady #1[a] (solution A)	Heady-Egbert #2[a] (model B.1)	Heady-Whittlesey[b] (solution 43)	Heady-Skold (model I)	Brokken-Heady (solution 1)	Hall-Heady-Plessner
Northeast	...	...	...	...	...	...	...
Appalachian	5.74	...	...	6.17	6.57	...	...
Southeast	12.64	...	9.24	7.13	0.41	...	...
Delta	28.20	...	14.69	21.46	10.66	0.03	...
Corn Belt	2.57	...	...	2.81	0.22	...	...
Lake States	...	...	...	...	...	...	...
N. Plains	...	...	...	...	...	...	...
S. Plains	33.04	...	38.45	55.99	60.09	58.20	...
Mountain	6.72	...	13.80	0.33	10.07	10.21	...
Pacific	11.09	...	23.82	6.12	11.98	31.57	...

a. Cotton not included in this model.
b. Percent of total acreage.

possible, but in fact they are never completely uniform. Specialization is more pronounced in the models that ignore transportation. The tendency in such models is for production to be located where production costs are minimum, regardless of the distance from the point of consumption.

None of the models uses all the land available. Table 19.6 shows the distribution of idle land in the various models.

Table 19.6. Distribution of unused cropland by regions, million acres

Region	Egbert-Heady #1[a] (solution A)	Heady-Egbert #2[a] (model B.1)	Heady-Whittlesey (solution 43)	Heady-Skold (model I)	Brokken-Heady (solution 1)	Hall-Heady-Plessner
Northeast	2.99	...	0.04	...	2.95	...
Appalachian	5.51	2.88	1.53	3.10	6.27	2.05
Southeast	6.78	4.21	8.30	10.63	5.05	9.08
Delta	1.23	2.40	5.55	7.09	...	5.98
Corn Belt	3.46	0.29	1.02	10.43	14.34	2.84
Lake States	4.96	...	1.65	5.92	9.73	4.29
N. Plains	1.55	...	14.50	26.44	25.55	20.97
S. Plains	1.80	1.42	1.81	4.44	...	1.45
Mountain	3.67	2.41	6.03	5.93	3.38	3.53
Pacific	...	...	0.08	...	...	...
United States	31.95	13.61	40.51	73.98	67.27	50.19

a. Grainland.

Egbert and Heady #1

Five different models, A-E, were included in this set. A, B, C, and D were minimum cost models; E was a maximum profit model. For A, B, C, and E, production possibilities were food wheat, feed wheat, and feed grain rotation; for D, they were food wheat, feed wheat, corn, oats, barley, and grain sorghum. In model B, land rent was included in activity costs; it was not included for the other models. The authors regarded the results from models A, B, and E as more realistic than those from models C and D. Only the results from model A are summarized.

Compared with 1965 results, wheat production is more concentrated in the Mountain and Pacific regions, and feed grain production is more concentrated in the Corn Belt and Northern Plains. There is no feed grain production in the Appalachian, Southeast, and Mountain regions. The absence of wheat in the Corn Belt is probably the result of the overspecialization which flows from ignoring transportation costs. There are nearly 32 million acres of unused cropland. The amount of unused cropland ranges from 22.96 million acres in model C to 62.39 million acres in model D.

The addition of land rents to activity costs (model B) led to only minor changes from the distribution of production in model A.

Heady and Egbert #2

Six models were included in this set. A.1, A.2, and A.3 used 1954 as a base year; B.1, B.2, and B.3 used 1965. Yields and demands for 1965 were based on projections of the 1940-54 trends. The 1954 models were maximum profit models; the 1965 models were minimum cost models. Production possibilities for all six models included food wheat, feed wheat, feed grain rotation, feed grain-soybean rotation, and cotton. Only the results for model B.1 are summarized in Tables 19.2-19.6.

There are several changes from model A of the previous set. Cotton replaces much of the wheat in the Mountain and Pacific regions, and there are additional amounts of cotton in the Southern Plains, Delta, and Southeast. Wheat production shifts to the Northern Plains, Corn Belt, and Southeast. Soybeans replace some feed grains in the Corn Belt; much of the remaining soybean production is in the Delta. Feed grain displaced in the Northern Plains by wheat and in the Corn Belt by wheat and soybeans moves to the Northeast, Applachian, and Southeast regions. The amount of unused cropland ranges from 13.61 million acres in model B.1 to 31.7 million acres in model A.3. In model B.1, most of the unused land is in the Appalachian, Delta, and Southeast regions.

Heady and Whittlesey

There were three different models in this set. Model I featured a two-price plan for wheat; model II had a one-price plan for wheat; model III had three qualities of land in each producing region. There were 17 different solutions: 10 for model I, 2 for model II, and 5 for model III. Each solution represents a different combination of prices (consequently demands) and land constraints (more or less limiting). Solution 43 was the benchmark to which the other 16 solutions were compared; it is summarized in Tables 19.2-19.6.

Compared with 1965: (a) wheat production is more concentrated in the Northern Plains, Southern Plains, and Mountain States and less concentrated in the Corn Belt; (b) feed grain production is more concentrated in the Lake States and Northern Plains and less concentrated in the Corn Belt; (c) soybean production is more concentrated in the Corn Belt and Northern Plains and less concentrated in the Delta and Lake

States; (d) a smaller percentage of cotton is produced in the Southeast and Delta and a substantially higher percentage in the Southern Plains.

The amount of unused cropland ranges from 24.6 million acres in solution 41 to 52.4 million acres in 1955 solution 513. The 40.5 million acres in solution 43 are concentrated in the Southeast, the Delta, the Northern Plains, and the Mountain states.

Heady and Skold

The authors formulated two sets of models for 1975: a set of 10 profit maximization models and a set of 14 cost minimization models. Each profit maximization model represents a particular level of product prices and consequently a particular level of demand (requirements). The authors attempted to derive aggregate commodity supply curves using this set of models. Each cost minimization model represents a particular combination of assumptions about population, per capita income, export levels, and crop yields. Population estimates for 1975 ranged from 222 to 244 million, per capita income ranged from 150 percent to 165 percent of the 1955 level, exports ranged from 100 percent to 200 percent of the 1956-61 average, and crop yields were based on either the 1940-60 trends or the 1950-62 trends. Despite some success in deriving supply curves, the authors regarded results from the cost minimization models as more reasonable than those from the profit maximization models. Model I was a cost minimization model.

For model I the projected 1975 population was 222 million, per capita income was 150 percent of the 1955 level, exports were at the 1956-61 levels, and crop yields were projected from 1940-60 trends. Compared with 1965 results: (a) higher percentage of wheat is produced in the Corn Belt, the Lake States, and the Pacific region and a lower percentage in the Northeast, the Northern Plains, and the Mountain region; (b) a higher percentage of feed grains is produced in the Corn Belt and less in the Northern Plains; (c) more soybeans are produced in the Lake States and Northern Plains and fewer in the Corn Belt; (d) cotton production is more concentrated in the Southern Plains and less concentrated in the Delta and Southeast. Model I has 74.12 million acres of unused cropland with substantial amounts in all except the Northeast and Pacific regions. For other cost minimization models the amount of unused cropland ranges from 42.2 million acres in model IV-F to 98.9 million acres in model VI-A.

Brokken and Heady

Brokken and Heady developed three models, a 1954 model, a 1965 model, and an efficient management (EM) model. Livestock output coefficients in the EM model are those attained by the more efficient producers; otherwise the 1965 and EM models are the same. There were 5 solutions for the 1954 model and 26 each for the 1965 and EM models. Each solution reflects a particular set of assumptions about demand levels and livestock capacities. If we take 1.0 as the index of demand and livestock capacity in the base period, the index of demand ranges from 1.0 to 1.22 and the index of livestock capacity ranges from 1.0 to 3.0 for the different solutions. Solution 1 is a 1965 model with an index of 1.0 for both demand and livestock capacity.

Comparing the results from solution 1 with the 1965 results: (a) there are minor increases of wheat production in the Delta and Pacific regions and minor decreases in the Corn Belt and Northeast; (b) feed grain production increases substantially in the Corn Belt and decreases substantially in the Northern Plains; (c) soybean production increases in the Corn Belt and decreases in the Appalachian, the Lake States, and the Northern Plains regions; (d) cotton production shifts from the Appalachian, Southeast, and Delta regions to the Southern Plains and Pacific regions. There are 67.27 million acres of unused cropland (i.e., land which could be shifted to other uses) with some in most regions but with the largest amounts in the Northern Plains and Corn Belt.

Hall, Heady, and Plessner

The use of regional linear demand functions in this model leads to a quadratic programming problem. By contrast, all the models described previously use linear programming. Product prices (consequently quantities demanded) as well as production and transportation patterns are determined endogenously in this model. The optimal solution conforms with a competitive equilibrium in the agricultural industry.

Comparing with actual 1965 results once more: (a) wheat production is more concentrated in the Southern Plains, the Mountain States, the Pacific States, the Lake States, and the Delta and less concentrated in the Corn Belt; (b) feed grain production is more heavily concentrated in the Corn Belt; (c) more soybeans are produced in the Northern Plains and the Southern Plains and less in the Corn Belt and the Delta. Cotton was not included in this model. In general the equilibrium quantities produced in this model are larger than the actual 1965 quantities. Even so, there are roughly 50 million acres of unused cropland in the model. Nearly 21 million acres of these are in the Northern Plains, but sizable amounts are in other regions. Only the Northeast and the Pacific States have no unused cropland.

Eyvindson-Heady

Currently underway also is a linear model which incorporates restraints of individual farms, along with the restraints of regions. The current model requires 4000 equations and 37,000 real equations. This model is just ready for solution.

Results from these various models lead to the conclusion that for any kind of "reasonable" level of demand (domestic plus export) there is excess capacity in U.S. agriculture. That is, there is more than enough capacity to satisfy current demand. Moreover, as the Heady

and Skold results indicate, this overcapacity is not only likely to per-
sist into the foreseeable future; it is likely to increase. Heady and
Mayer found that U.S. agriculture could increase its exports by three
times and still have 50 million excess acres for crops in 1980 if agricultural production were allocated optimally among regions. Most of
the reports described here at least touch on the problems to which this
overcapacity leads. Whittlesey and Heady (10, 12) estimate the government costs associated with various agricultural programs designed to
solve, or at least relieve, some of these problems. The regional formulation used in all the models gives some indication, however imperfect, as to where problems of overcapacity are likely to be most severe.
The models developed already have had wide use in planning and policy
recommendations and they generate large amounts of data for the large
number of producing and consuming regions.

REFERENCES

1. Brokken, R. F., and Earl O. Heady. Interregional Adjustments in Crop and
   Livestock Production: A Linear Programming Analysis. USDA Technical
   Bulletin 1396, July 1968.
2. Egbert, A. C., and Earl O. Heady. Regional Adjustments in Grain Production:
   A Linear Programming Analysis. USDA Tech. Bull. 1241, June 1961.
3. ——. Regional Analysis of Production Adjustments in the Major Field Crops:
   Historical and Prospective. USDA Tech. Bull. 1294, Nov. 1963.
4. Egbert, A. C., Earl O. Heady, and R. F. Brokken. Regional Changes in Grain
   Production: An Application of Spatial Linear Programming. Iowa Agr. and
   Home Econ. Exp. Sta. Res. Bull. 521, Jan. 1964.
5. Hall, H. H., Earl O. Heady, and Y. Plessner. Quadratic Programming Solution of Competitive Equilibrium for U.S. Agriculture. Am. J. Agr. Econ., vol.
   50.
6. Heady, Earl O. Iowa Linear Programming Models for Interregional Competition and Other Analysis. O.E.C.D. Publ. AGR 65-1, 1965. Pp. 79-65.
7. Heady, Earl O., and A. C. Egbert. Programming Models of Interdependence
   Among Agricultural Sectors. J. Reg. Sci., vol. 4.
8. Heady, Earl O., and Leo V. Mayer. Food Needs and U.S. Agriculture in 1980.
   Technical Papers. Vol. 1. National Advisory Commission on Food and Fiber, 1967.
9. Heady, Earl O., and M. Skold. Projections of U.S. Agricultural Capacity and
   Interregional Adjustments in Production and Land Use with Spatial Programming Models. Iowa Agr. and Home Econ. Exp. Sta. Res. Bull. 539, Aug. 1965.
10. Heady, Earl O., and N. Whittlesey. A Programming Analysis of Interregional
    Competition and Surplus Capacity of American Agriculture. Iowa Agr. and
    Home Econ. Exp. Sta. Res. Bull. 538, July 1965.
11. Skold, M., and E. O. Heady. Regional Location of Production of Major Field
    Crops at Alternative Demand and Price Levels, 1975. USDA Agr. Bull. 1345,
    April 1966.
12. Whittlesey, N., and Earl O. Heady. Aggregate Economic Effect of Alternative
    Land Retirement Programs. USDA Tech. Bull. 1351, August 1966.

Chapter 20 ☜☞ USDA NATIONAL MODEL FOR THE U.S.A.

C. B. Baker and Earl R. Swanson, *University of Illinois* (U.S.A.)

THE NATIONAL MODEL PROJECT was initiated in 1964 with the objective of providing a systematic quantitative framework for estimating aggregate changes in acreage, production, resource use, and implied farm income changes associated with a variety of factors. These factors include prices paid and received by farmers, resource supplies, technological changes, and government programs. The analysis was to emphasize timely short-run (one to three years) estimates of the effects of varying these factors.

The nature of the objective required a reliable depiction of the current national agricultural production plant and production processes, and these data need frequent updating to remain relevant. To meet this objective, the major crop-producing sections of the country were divided into about 50 geographic areas, defined along county lines. Some areas were further broken down into aggregate resource situations. A resource situation is an aggregate of farms (not necessarily contiguous farms) having similar production alternatives, costs, returns, resource combinations, and other characteristics. The idea is to group together the farms that are likely to respond in a similar manner to important stimuli. There are about 90 resource situations in the model.

An aggregate linear programming submodel is constructed for each resource situation. In some areas where there are two or more resource situations, the L.P. matrices are combined into a single model for the area. The resource situations in this case compete for some resources restricted only at the area level. The L.P. matrix for any area is independent of the L.P. matrix of any other area. Aggregate estimates are obtained by simply adding up the area results and adjusting for areas outside the model.

The national model uses the technique called recursive programming. Each year is regarded as a different profit-maximizing decision problem for farmers, hence a different programming problem. When making plans for next year, the farmer knows that he cannot influence the prices he pays and receives. He does not know what yields he will obtain. He must formulate his expectations largely on the basis of recent experience. Accordingly, the price and yield data in the programming problem for each year — the data we assume to represent farmers' expectations — are based on data for the preceding year(s).

This is a summary of a paper presented by Gaylord Worden and Fred Abel, "A National Model of Agricultural Production Response," presented to the North Central Farm Management Research Committee, Chicago, March 1968.

369

For example, the expected price of a given commodity may be the price received in the previous year. Expected yields are derived from simple trend analysis, taking account of abnormal weather years.

L.P. MATRICES

As one might expect, there is great variation in the L.P. matrices used to represent the various resource situations. However some common characteristics will be discussed.

The approximate size of the matrix for each resource situation in the North Central Region is 80 rows and 55 real activities. About one-third of the rows are physical and institutional restraints, one-third are flexibility restraints, and one-third are transfer rows and accounting rows.

ACTIVITIES

Separate activities depicting the alternatives of government programs are included in the model. Where an individual farm may have only one of these alternatives, any or all of the alternatives may appear in the solution of an aggregate model of this type. Any linear combination of the government program alternatives is feasible in the aggregate. Activities are included for most major crops and by most major practices. Livestock activities also are included in many areas to account for the resource supplies and intermediate products required by livestock and to provide an internal feed price for feed grains and forages.

PHYSICAL RESTRAINTS

Acres of cropland and hours of labor are the principal physical restraints used in the model. Some attempt was made to include livestock facility restraints, but estimation of these quantities is difficult. Cropland restraints were estimated on an included activity basis; that is, the final estimate of acres of cropland was based on the total acres of cropland used by the *included* crop activities. The estimate may have been a simple average of several recent years, a projection of any trend in this average, or a subjectively adjusted average of a few recent years.

INSTITUTIONAL AND FLEXIBILITY RESTRAINTS

Current and probable government programs require the inclusion of several institutional restraints.

It is obvious that the behavioral or flexibility restraints play a

major role in a model of this type. Numerous methods of constructing
these restraints were tried. However one principal method was used
in most regions. For each commodity in each area, year-to-year percentage changes in acreage are calculated for the past ten years. A
simple average of the percentage changes in years of decrease and an
average of percentage changes for years of increase are then calculated.
These averages are used as the flexibility coefficients.

THE NATIONAL MODEL TODAY

Our immediate goal is to become timelier so that we have an operational model and some analytical results *before* the questions are
asked. We also need to develop a procedure that will enable us to
shorten the time that it takes us to develop estimates for specific policy questions. In view of these needs, our 1969 analysis is well underway. We are several months ahead of the 1968 timetable and will be
able to begin looking at programming solutions this spring instead of
early next fall. Since current farm program legislation remains in effect through 1969, no major changes in model structure are necessary
for the 1969 analysis. All key variables such as cost, yields, and product prices are being updated and restraints are being reestimated. We
should have sufficient time to take a close look at questions that appear
relevant for 1969.

Chapter 20 ✑ DISCUSSION of All National Models

Vladimar Stipetic, *University of Zagreb* (Yugoslavia)

A S A DISCUSSANT I am in a very unpleasant position. I received
only one of the presented papers at home. A second paper arrived only two days ago. So I was faced with a dilemma: Should
I write another paper, regardless of the qualities of those prepared, or
should I give a discussion of the papers on a very superfluous first-
listening basis? I have decided that as a discussant I am obliged to
choose the second solution, despite all dangers involved. I would appreciate it if you keep these things in mind as you listen to my comments.
    I think that we are dealing today with a very recent acquisition of
methods for the agricultural economy. The very first start on those
methods began in the United States in 1956 at Iowa State University by
Heady, but the results of these investigations were published only in
1961. In the Soviet Union the early sixties were witnessing the beginning

of work on econometric models for agriculture. In many other countries, as we were able to see, the start came even later and still is in an
experimental phase, as was pointed out by the French, Czech, Hungarian, and other delegates. As often happens with new developments, the
continuity brought improvement to the methods in use, and efficiency in
solutions became more and more evident. We were able to realize how
enormous was the progress made. However I ought to mention that the
majority of the papers presented did not mention errors and pitfalls
encountered or avoided. The cheapest way of learning is to know the
faults on your own. In that respect, I would have appreciated it if the
papers spoke more about weaknesses than about results obtained. For
many nations which will use these methods tomorrow, it would be extremely useful if those aspects were mentioned more elaborately.

At the beginning all models started with some oversimplified assumptions, those being replaced by the more refined models of today.
Instead of linear programs, more quadratic functions and regressions
models are being used. Coefficient matrices in the United States
reached the volume of 4,000 x 37,000. In this way, today's models are
in the position of corresponding to the complicated nature of the agricultural economy.

However, in spite of the enlargement of the matrices, many theoretical aspects are still left aside. I recall the statement made a
couple of days ago by T. W. Schultz in which he mentioned the absence
of rent for land, nonexistence of coherent wage policy, pricing in models, and so on. We still do not include in the model the optimum size
of the holdings and so on. I am not surprised that these factors are absent in American models; only twenty years ago a leading theoretician,
Hayes, accused all who were dealing with planning that they were preparing the road to serfdom. It seems to be a natural response of planners to discard such a theory or proposition. It is much more difficult
to understand why in the papers of our Soviet colleagues the underlying
theory is missing too.

With all those and similar weaknesses, the econometric models
are still very useful tools. Miloserdovs' paper provides a useful measure of economies obtained by solving the transport model for fertilizers. They were able to save 606.9 million metric tons of transportation, with the total effect of 1.7 million rubles saved annually. Region-
alization of production gave 5 million metric tons of additional grain
output. This is approximately 3 percent of the future grain production
of the Soviet Union obtained by better planning.

Finally I should mention that some production functions used still
oversimplify the actual problems. Let me take the model of Havlicek-
Jenicek concerned with the long-term development of Czechoslovakian
agriculture. In this model we can see that the results expect the wors-
ening of the capital/output ratio from 1.7 in 1970 to 2.1 in 1980 (total
productive and circulating productive funds divided by the value of gross
production). Could we expect such tendency if it is known that all developed agriculture is witnessing the improvement of the capital/output

ratio? Or, in the same model, an assumption has been made about the relationship between the amount of disposable forage and animal production on the basis of statistical data for 1950-64. Is such a production function a valid one for projection in the period when technological progress permanently brings an improvement in feed-conversion rates?

By picking those two examples only I am unfair to my Czech colleagues, who gave me their paper in advance. I hope that they won't mind, since only the critical efforts and perpetual improvements of the methods used can bring the fastest rate of growth to the welfare of the people in whom we are so interested.

Part V ✑ FORMULATION OF NATIONAL MODELS

Kalman Kazareczki, *Ministry of Agriculture and Food* (Hungary)
Joseph Sebestyen, *Research Institute for Agricultural Economics*
(Hungary)

T HE ELABORATION of any plan, even for that of the smallest unit, requires a careful preparation and deep and many-sided consider- ations. Of particular importance is the formulation of the basic goals and decision principles. From this formulation follows to a great extent the kinds of problems which emerge in the course of the planning process and the methods by which they must be treated. The compli- cated internal and external relationships of an industry require even more watchful work in the determination of the goals, conditions, and decision criteria because they have important direct and indirect influ- ence upon the well-being of many people.

In the United Nations report entitled "Economic Planning in Europe" (22), planning in a predominately market economy was defined as a proc- ess involving serious attempts at the following:

1. Determination of the major economic goals and their relative prior- ities.
2. Expressing these goals in a complex of explicit, consistent, and quantified targets for a specified period by (a) an assessment of re- sources, analysis of relevant interdependencies between the variables, and a survey of possible effects of acceptable policy alternatives and (b) quantitative analysis and projection of the actual and possible fu- ture forms and rates of development.
3. Choosing and applying the measures which, according to the analyses, offer the possibility of realization of the targets and goals.

NATURE OF GOALS

The goals for a whole economy, as well as for any industry includ- ing agriculture, can also have a rather general first formulation. These general goals are very similar in most countries. They refer to the improvement of living standards, to productivity growth, to balanced growth or to the improvement of the actual structure, to employment, and to the requirement of an improvement or even equilibrium of the balance of payments. These general goals get a more concrete shape in the course of the elaboration of the plan. The goal for the living stan- dards may involve targets relative to nutrition, housing, supplies of du- rable goods, and further steps toward social justice as far as levels and distribution of incomes are concerned. As to economic development, the

377

targets may be expressed in either indexes or average rates of growth for national income or for gross output in a certain sector or in the whole national economy. Volume of exports in most cases may be found among the targets as a means for improving the balance of payments, for earning foreign exchange for necessary imports, and for development, particularly in countries with a more open economy.

Until we have a uniform terminology, misunderstanding and arguments may surround the distinction between targets and goals and between plans and policies. The above-mentioned United Nations report qualified categories of goals such as economic growth, industrialization, full employment, and so on. Others such as output, growth in various sectors, changes in productivity, and investment were classified as targets.

Despite a high degree of similarity, there are considerable differences in goals of various countries according to the social system and stage of development. As to the latter, growth may be emphasized in highly developed market economies while the goals referring to structural changes may come into the foreground in less-developed countries. The plans of socialist countries embrace as a single complex the economic, political, and social goals relative to growth and structural changes and the strategies for realization of development.

However a proper formulation of basic goals and targets is not sufficient. Special attention must be paid to systematically making them valid in the course of the elaboration of the plan, particularly in the interdependence between goals. Professor Currie found a number of mistakes in this field when he analyzed the plans of developing countries (4). Some of them should be emphasized to warn us that we find them not alone in plans of the above-mentioned countries. Mistakes belonging to this collection are identifying social well-being with national income, neglecting the relationships between improvement in the distribution of incomes and economic growth, and further neglecting the positive indirect effects of investments in housing and other communal development projects.

PERSPECTIVES

The reality of the basic goals and the quantified targets derived from them depends to a great extent on the assessment of the perspectives and their evaluation. This no doubt is a difficult task. It requires a combination of judgments of political, economic, and technological (technical progress) character about an uncertain future. A great difficulty is the evaluation of future developments in the world market. The conclusions imply that investments costing many billions of dollars in the development plans of a country must be drawn from them relative to directions and volumes of production.

The analysis of research results, directions of development of industries in known stages, character and expected rate of technical progress, and so on, must lead to plans which are sufficiently flexible to allow relatively quick adjustments without incurring great losses. One must assess such flexibility in terms of technical facilities, skill of workers and managers, and the professional elasticity of the educational capacity. One must estimate the possible changes in the structure of production and their costs, particularly in terms of past unused investments and the volume of national income to be consumed by the changes. All must be considered in a cumulative manner, that is, not only in the sector in question but also in its interdependent interrelationships with other sectors. Because much depends on the assessment and evaluation of these perspectives, a detailed elaboration and standing refinement of these methods must be considered to be a first-order task of scientific research.

In the course of the assessment and analysis of the perspectives, one must take into account indirect effects linked with the possible changes as far as their acceptability is concerned from both a professional and political point of view. This means running risks of course. The test of a politician is in his ability to make a good estimate of the bounds for this risk: the lower one that must be borne for the sake of the successful economic development and the upper one that must not be trespassed in the interest of the country. (However we should not leave out of consideration the fact that setting these upper and lower bounds also depends on the personality of the politicians.)

GOALS AND PLANNING PERIOD

Foresight is limited with respect to both the world market situation and technical progress. Equally important are the difficulties with estimates about the political situation. Thus for a period longer than 10 to 15 years one cannot estimate future developments with the seriousness required by considerations for a plan of economic development. However realistic goals can even be set for a much longer period in certain fields of the plan. Examples are nutrition, housing, urbanization, living standards in general, further development of the energy basis, and water resources.

The goals for the medium-term plans can be formulated in a much more concrete and detailed form, and a given group of goals is admitted to characterize a certain (feasible) policy. The traditional method of planning in the socialist countries used to accept, in most cases, a single policy (and a single group of goals). It has been rather recently that one has elaborated several variants of the plan. The situation also may be similar in the capitalist countries making use of some type of planning. The plans elaborated by traditional means and methods are sometimes problematic: some of the goals may be discovered, after the plan is underway, not to belong to the set of feasible solutions.

An important guarantee for the realization of medium-term plans is that system of measures which, adjusted to the timing of the interdependent targets, appears as the set of short-run policies to be carried out in the various phases of the plan.

The plans developed in the traditional way in the socialist countries as a rule contain not only the terminal state but also a detailed (yearly) timing of the targets. This is true for only a part of the plans set up by mathematical methods (not true for most of programming calculations), although the primary condition for the realization of the goals expressed as the terminal state is, according to our experience, the appropriate planning of steps leading to it.

QUANTIFICATION OF GOALS

Depending on the requirements to be met by the plan, one can quantify the goals to be fulfilled by the terminal state or by the intermediate states (the stations on the road to the terminal state) in various ways. The policy makers may sometimes be content with the projection of past trends. But this may only serve for the immediate future since simple projections of the past can be accepted only as an element for comparison of the calculations in developing a plan. One can of course extrapolate the volume of social product, the national income, the consumption, and so on, for periods of medium or longer length. However the formulas used for these projections must then involve variables which policy makers can use in terms of technical, economic, and political considerations.

Common forms of quantifying targets are basis indexes and average rates of growth which express complicated technical-economic relationships, the details of which are generally not included in the official documents of the plan. The upper bound for the growth rate may be set, for example, by a certain proportion between consumption and investment. Or in some cases it may be set by the balance of payments and other considerations. Different levels may be set as a lower bound for the national income. To each level a certain complex of welfare, development, and production policies may be assigned. While employment generally appears among the quantified targets, it seems more reasonable to substitute for it the levels of income or real consumption for various groups of the population to be attained. Or all of them can be included in one group of targets.

GOALS FOR AGRICULTURE

Building up a specialized, commercial agriculture flexible enough to quickly adjust to the changing conditions may be a realistic goal for many countries. In a number of them, in which the smaller family farms constitute the majority, this means to a great extent the problem of transformation of the agrarian structure. The changes in number of farms in different size groups, as they are and as they should be, has been the concern of many calculations and different policies aimed at stepping up or slowing down this process.

A goal, too, may be building up a productive potential (knowledge and material resources) which can meet sudden changes in demand. According to Black, this is a societal obligation (3). Of course this obligation may also exist for supply and processing industries. This goal should refer not only to establishing capacity by the producers but also to creation of the conditions under which it may be reasonable to maintain this capacity.

The greater flexibility of agriculture requires that some elements of the goals should be aimed not only at the material resources but also at influencing the thinking of producers and administrators. Further, this influence should be extended over the industries linked with agriculture. As an example of the latter, we may mention the thought emerging from preparatory work for the fourth Hungarian Five-Year Plan: The incoordination between agriculture and food industry (due possibly to inaccurate survey of the domestic and foreign markets) and the difference in the speed of reactions (inherent in the character of these sectors) should be counterbalanced not only by piling up buffer stocks but also by economic incentives which induce the food industry to adjust to agriculture as well as to consumer markets.

A specific group of major goals may be regarded as steps towards making social justice valid. Some such goals are intended to decrease the disadvantages of rural life, create conditions for rural youth equal to those of urban youth in education, and so on. The realization of such goals can considerably influence the development of agriculture. In most cases it is generally within the frames of regional development programs that such goals can be set and realized. Their effect then can be felt directly in the field of agricultural plans, as they affect the productive agents of agriculture, the efficiency of their use, the production and use of income, and other targets.

Among the targets that can be specified for agriculture, the best-known ones are those relative to supplies of food and raw materials for industry, exports, and those relative to the technical conditions of production. These targets may be specified as absolute quantities, basis indexes, or growth rates. Owing to the importance of food supplies, it is useful to deal with the manner of establishing the targets. In countries where explicit target setting is in use (as in socialist countries) or where improvement of nutrition is a major factor of development (in some developing countries facing serious nutritional problems), the targets in the medium-term plans usually express a quantified compromise for components such as the scientific norms of nutrition (rather than such petrified habits which change slowly) and more or less realistically assessed possibilities. Demand analysis in these cases has a supplementary role but will gain much in importance over the near future.

In one type of calculation for planning in capitalist countries, quantities representing selected points on demand curves are used as requirements (16). In another type, only the producers' prices derived from demand functions, as the major factor influencing supply, are used (21, 22). Both types of studies have a deep analysis of consumers' demand in the background. The national targets of course have not been projected into the plans of the various administrative units or even firms, although one should not categorically exclude this case. On the other hand, the consistency of the plan in terms of the space-time relationships of national goals and their components (the local targets) is an essential requirement.

SOME PROBLEMS OF PLANNING DECISIONS

The Model

In agriculture, just as in any other sector of the economy, goals may be rather complex. Some of the constraints representing the boundaries of the set of feasible solutions may refer to very scarce resources while others seem to be less binding. A considerable part of the targets and facilities show interdependence. On the one hand they are targets while on the other hand they are facilities-constraints.

The traditional method of planning in the socialist countries guarantees a certain degree of perspicuity and consistency of the targets and facilities through an extensive system of balances wherein the authorities accept or modify this plan on the basis of political and technoeconomic considerations. The literature of the traditional way of planning claimed optimality for the decisions but also accepted decisions of the above type to be optimal without specifying a criterion of optimality. By coincidence, of course, of plans developed by the traditional methods the one accepted by the government may constitute not only a feasible one but also one of optimum solution.

A national plan may be fixed in such a way that the government or another authority accepts one of the solutions generated by the econometric model for the national economy or for a certain sector. These solutions may serve as a basis for financial measures, welfare, production policies, and so on, elaborated by the different authorities and organizations. The detailed elaboration of these action programs also may be chosen from the solutions.

Mathematical programming may be used to optimize a relatively detailed national plan. If this is a terminal state program, a problem still exists: how to optimize the measures and action programs for the various phases of the plan. If the computer facilities available permit the use of dynamic linear programming, an optimum for the entire period can be obtained with a year-by-year timing. In review of the development of the planning methods in the socialist countries, we can state that the role of mathematical methods as organic, built-in elements of the traditional methods is growing. As examples, we can point to input-output models and to the process underway which leads to building mathematical programming into the continuously changing traditional system of planning by sheer force of habit.

Goals, Targets, and Criterion of Optimum

A plan that claims to be optimal may be elaborated from different points of view. The choice from these points of view, or from plans maximizing their prevalence, is the task of the politician helped by the judgment of the economist and sociologist. As mentioned earlier, these goals and targets may cover for example the output, the national income, consumption, social net income, investment, the state of the balance of payments, and social cost measured in terms of labor. In some cases we find the volume of production to be maximized as the criterion of optimum. However this criterion may be justified only in special cases for specified groups of agricultural commodities (in war or under embargo, in a densely populated, less-developed country struggling with a food shortage). Even if a policy considers agriculture to be the only or main source of capital formation for industrialization without foreign aid or loans, it is not reasonable to simply enforce increases in the volume of output; the appropriate goal is more nearly a program of production which maximizes net income channeled to the state without unnecessary harm to the basic interests of farmers.

In connection with increased output as a highest-order target, we may mention a standpoint already passed away but which even in recent years one had still to oppose vigorously. According to this standpoint, plans—even for farms—ought to be aimed at maximization of gross output. But if any economic unit were to "optimize" its plan according to this criterion, the worse the transformation ratio for intermediate products, the more beautiful would be the picture on the paper.

National income represents a far better goal as the basis for development and increases in living standards. However our earlier investigations (10) showed that by maximizing net farm income we can generally get a national income greater in volume and different—more advantageous for development purposes—in composition. (The objective function looks for savings in both labor and other costs if it refers to net income, while it is indifferent to labor inputs if it refers to national income.)

Capital formation as the central goal of a planning period may serve for acceleration of development, particularly in the case of built-in positive and negative incentives (assistance from the state in proportion of the capital formation on the one hand, a progressive income tax on the other). If capital formation is used for a criterion of optimization, the model must have equations as built-in guarantees concerning the living standards of the producers. These guarantees assure that they can accept and realize such a plan without any harm to their own interests.

To increase consumption is a far-looking goal, but pursuing it may be subject to relatively tight constraints in many countries. This is due to the changes in the structure of the consumption necessarily associated with the increases in volume. In connection with this, it is worth reviewing two Soviet models. One was developed by Kantorovich and Makarov (7). The goal set is to meet a demand of given volume and structure in the shortest time. The other model published in the same volume (by Gavrilets, Mihalevsky, and Leibkind) specifies one part of the population's consumption as a lower bound, while the other part of consumption and investment is maximized.

The net receipts from foreign trade, if not referring to a specific variant, should be a constraint rather than the objective function in optimization for either a sector or for the national economy. If taken as the optimum criterion, maximizing foreign trade would cause the economy to serve the comfort of the foreign trade agencies rather than the realization of important national goals.

The minimization of the volume of social labor, or the maximization of its productivity, may yield optima of special importance. Objective functions representing the volume or the productivity of social labor may be preferred if one wants to have optima independent of money effects (11) or if one has to select from a set of optimum programs. An example of the latter case may be the integration of optimum regional plans (each region having a set of optimum programs) into a national optimum plan (12).

The planners are often in trouble with the objectives. Each objective ought to be effective by necessity. On the other hand, they are not only interrelated but also contradictory; thus their simultaneous extremization is impossible. In such cases a useful way to solve this problem is the optimization in different variants: one of the targets will be the criterion, the others will appear as side conditions. This procedure yields a series of optima of which the politicians can select one for implementation. With respect to the above-mentioned problem, one can expect that a certain type of model will afford a satisfactory treatment of the various objectives and will come into the foreground. Such a model must have, among others, constraints reflecting the increasing volume, changing structure, and appropriate timing of consumption, while the source of development—the social net product—is maximized.

Activities and Technologies

After having chosen the goals and the criterion of optimization, the next task for the planners is selection of the system of activities. This becomes a problem of professional judgment. We must decide upon activities which can reasonably (or necessarily) apply in a certain region or soil type and the rational system of technologies that can be assigned to the set of activities. When selecting the technologies, one must take a stand in connection with technical development: the experts must judge which of the technologies now in use should be considered for the next planning period and the kinds and extent of new technologies which will be available for producers at the beginning or in a later phase. These judgments must consider the general conception for development of the national economy and specific components of it (e.g., programs for in-

dustrial production and development, foreign trade, etc.). If requirements for consistency of the system of planning are to be met, variants
of plans for industry and foreign trade can be regarded as optimal only
if they conform with the variant accepted as the optimal plan for agriculture.

As far as optimum solutions for Hungarian agriculture are concerned, one must reckon with heavy costs (in terms of research and
computer hours). This is due to the fact that our former system of planning preserved the high degree of diversification characteristic of the
predominantly autarchic small family farms, and inherited by the cooperatives formed from their fusion, while the selective effect of the market could not exert any serious influence. In order to show with a high
degree of probability which activities can be regarded as components of
optimum programs for a region, we must compute a good number of optima with models of which we know only that a small fraction of the many
variables may be included in the optimal solution. We cannot guess, even
after an analysis for dominance, which subset of the variables will probably constitute this fraction. This outcome may seem to be dictated by
overcaution. However our experience provides its justification. (It may
be supposed that this situation is not specific to Hungary only because
the system of economic planning and direction was highly similar in all
socialist countries.)

The variables must reflect the differences in ownership too (e.g.,
cows with a milk yield of 3600 liters on state farms, on cooperative
farms, or in the household), due partly to specific interrelationships and
partly to their different requirements on resources. This type of disaggregation enables the planners to build various policy alternatives into
the model (e.g., energetic development of production in cooperative animal husbandry and/or incentives for maintaining or increasing output of
animal products on household plots). The timing of the prevalence of
policy parameters is of course a matter of special consideration.

System of Constraints and Problems of Resource Assessment

If the planners desire optimality in their plans, one of the most important problems they face is building the system of constraints. In the
course of constructing this system, technological, economic, and political considerations take the form of boundary conditions or balance equations and some of their conflicts may have already come to light in this
phase. In the following, we try to review the problems that emerge, according to groups within the system of conditions.

Land. It is important to recognize its variability in both quantity and
quality. The quantity is decreasing in many countries (with us too) due
to compulsory purchases for nonagricultural use, while increases in
area and changes in quality have enormous costs to agriculture. Thus
government must set appropriate rules in diverting land from agriculture, in compensation for it. Further subventioning of land reclamation

and improvement also requires government decision. When assessing
land for purposes of resource constraints, differentiation according to
quality (soil types) must not be neglected, although this may lead to computational difficulties in countries such as Hungary with a wide variety
of soil types.

Labor. Unlike other sectors of the national economy, agricultural labor
should appear among the constraints in its distribution over the year
(i.e., as number of days generally suitable for field work in each month,
at least May through October). A differentiation for age and sex is suggested, or at least a constraint showing the proportion of labor capable
or incapable of doing certain jobs. (It is important especially for less
mechanized agriculture.) Neglecting the above-mentioned differentiation may almost certainly lead to infeasibility of the plan. It is very
difficult to estimate the supply of agricultural labor by youth. Under
conditions like ours, the rural exodus is only partly a consequence of the
comparative level of earnings in agriculture and its uncertainty, and un-
equal distribution over the year. Very important reasons for leaving agriculture are the working conditions and the conditions of rural life.
Further, society's poor evaluation of agriculture as an occupation generally is important. In such a case one cannot think of introducing a
labor supply function into the model as seen in the French model (21).
One can hardly estimate the parameters for factors like the above-
mentioned ones. On the other hand, the flow of labor from other sectors
to agriculture is almost negligible. However, in case of regional development models, a labor supply function might efficiently deal with
flows of labor between sectors, particularly if we could calculate marginal propensities to enter various jobs of both agricultural and nonagricultural nature according to wage rates, fringe benefits, employment
opportunity, working and housing conditions, urban and rural communal
services, and the like.
    The relationships between plans for agriculture and education also
should be mentioned; particularly in the necessary role of education in
guaranteeing that the supply of skilled workers needed for advanced technologies, and managers (with knowledge in technology, economics, and
farm organization) will be available. This requires, of course, an assessment of future demand in workers and managers (with respect to
quality too) and taking steps to enable the institutions of education to
furnish the desired type of knowledge.

Machinery. In the case of machinery, just as with labor, distribution of
capacity over the year must be taken into account. Among the factors
affecting capacity, of special importance is the policy of scrapping, which
may appear in the plan either as (a) a certain rate not necessarily constant over the planning period (11) or (b) as a decision variable. At
present, the first procedure seems to be applied. But for the future, the
second one may, in case of correct formulation, adjust the scrapping to
the requirements of efficiency in use. It also is hoped that such a treatment might relate to demand due to investment decisions and to supply

by industrial production or foreign trade in a more lively way. Transport policies also are a factor in this group of constraints. Transport costs may exert a heavy influence upon interfarm flows of agricultural commodities as intermediate products. In an unspecialized agriculture, high transport costs may strengthen tendencies for preserving autarchic farming and serve as obstacles to rational specialization. In our railway system, for example, there is a process of establishing district freight stations. This procedure influences farm decisions about the structure of production and encourages investment in the farm's own transport facilities. Adjustments to the market require investment in special transport facilities which the model should consider.

Buildings. Buildings present a problem in the fact that they represent huge amounts of capital made immobile and they restrain adjustment to new economic conditions. (One can often hear: the buildings must be used as they exist.) In Hungary, due to investment policies of the past system of planning, we have a building distribution over the country, mainly barns, that application of the profitability requirement probably will lead, in many cases, to decisions of leaving them idle. Their use may not be profitably reshaped except at considerable expense. In other parts of the country, the same profit principles may lead to decisions of increasing production and of erecting new buildings. With respect to this, the variables representing new technologies must refer to types of buildings which, if they are durable, can easily and at a low cost be reshaped to serve another purpose. Storage buildings and special structures like refrigerating plants also represent a group of constraints. Because the establishment of such special structures is closely connected with marketing policies, the variables associated with erecting these buildings may be regarded with a high probability as components-to-be of the optimum solution for a medium- or long-term plan.

Livestock. Here also emerges the problem of differentiation, although there is, at least in our country, no reliable information about the distribution according to potential productivity. Until now we have made guesses based upon information from competent persons for the various regions. But it has meant a rather mechanical way of estimation.

Balances of products. This group of the constraints was already, at least implicitly, referred to when goals and targets were discussed. Balances of animal nutrition constitute part of this group. In connection with the coefficients, we shall return to these kinds of balances.

Financial constraints. A most important part of the system of constraints, particularly from the point of view of economic policies, is the group of the balances of financial character. One of these balances has been referred to several times when the disposable income or the real consumption was mentioned in the discussion of goals.

In our traditional planning system, a separate chapter is devoted to questions of living standards. The problems of living standards for the agricultural population are also treated there. However, in case of a plan claiming to be optimal, this must be an element of the decision process in an interrelationship with other elements. Thus the personal disposable income of the agricultural population must appear, for each year, as a lower bound which provides a decent living standard even in a case where the optimum solution would mean equality for this constraint. The year-by-year timing must be emphasized. If we set the condition so that terminal wealth, or the total for the whole period, constitutes the lower bound, the plan may be optimum although the income oscillates between years with an inadmissible amplitude.

The balance of investment equates sources and requirements where sources are own capital formation, credit, and subventions from the social net income channeled to the state. For credits, a constraint alludes to central banking principles the variants of which, along with subventions, may be the source of variants for the optimum plan of agriculture.

Coefficients

As may be seen, the variables and the constraints give rise to a number of problems, but the planner may have even more trouble with the coefficients of the A matrix linking the variables and the constraints. According to the character of the variables, efficiency of a technology may be different, depending on managerial qualities. In such cases the planner must have recourse to assumptions not always justified but helpful in such difficult situations.

As mentioned in connection with the variables, a definite technology is assigned to each of them, with input-output coefficients relating to yields attainable by good farmers. Under such circumstances the coefficients relative to both yields and inputs can be regarded as realistic. The differences between coefficients of technological variants for a certain product always refer to the natural environment and technical progress, particularly in connection with investments. One must mention here that the coefficients of a variable (e.g., a machine bought in a certain year) must reflect the obsolescence relating to differences in their values in different years (11).

According to our experience, the coefficients relative to animal nutrition are more problematic than others. This is due partly to the absence of feeding response functions and partly to the wide variation in the nutrient content of fodder as a consequence of harvesting and storing conditions.

Some of the coefficients appearing in the financial constraints reflect principles of financial (banking) policies. Such coefficients are the interest rate and the amortization (with the timing of the beginning of repayment of the credit) which may vary according to different policy considerations. These coefficients may also be modified by special incentives which reflect preferences for the different variables.

Aggregation

Although the majority of the literature on the aggregation problem
has been produced in capitalist countries, it also has been a problem in
planning practice for the socialist countries. The methodologists of
planning in the Soviet Union and in other socialist countries have emphasized the importance of regional planning, not only because they considered it to be an efficient means in the struggle against the damaging
effects of overcentralization but also because they used it to decrease
the errors of planning due to oversimplifying aggregation. We must admit, however, that results of deep-digging research in our countries
have not been widely known, at least to the extent that the question has
been treated in American literature on agricultural economics.

Investigations in Western Europe known to us show aggregation over
farm size, commodity groups, and some sources (land and labor) without
distinction relative to quality (2). From the United States, we know about
the theories developed by Day (6), Miller (9), and Lee (8). Day's conditions would probably allow an even smaller number of farms to be aggregated into a group for us than in the United States. The interpretation
and extension by Lee of Miller's theorem seems to be worthwhile for us
also through a series of case studies. A first attempt just underway at
decreasing the aggregation error in mathematical analysis applied to
Hungarian agriculture has been the case of a Leontief analysis of a sample of farms. Starting from this, we intend to estimate Leontief coefficients for the whole sector of cooperative farms. A method in our reach
for aggregation is the analysis of the distribution of the whole population
and the sample according to the productivity of labor. Then we will use
the relative frequencies for the whole population as weights in the sets
of Leontief coefficients of the respective groups of farms in the sample.

We must be aware that the extensive use of mathematical methods
of planning has caused the profound problems of aggregation to become
a most urgent task for researchers engaged in both general and agricultural economics.

Data and Knowledge about Reality

To get a reliable set of basic data constitutes a first-class difficulty
for any planning. This difficulty is more acute in agriculture than in
other sectors of the economy. Among the many reasons, we may mention the influence of natural conditions and our inaccurate knowledge
about laws governing the functions of the living organism. Further is the
difficulty, in some cases even the impossibility, of measurements with
the needed accuracy on farms (for example the detailed analysis of the
nutrient content of the hay just consumed).

A careful analysis may eliminate part of the sources of bias as far
as the numerical values of the data are concerned. However we cannot
assert that our knowledge about a coefficient, certain upper or lower
bounds on prices not fixed in advance, or any other data is perfect.

Stochastic programming would be the appropriate method of optimizing a plan in these cases. Information about its theoretical foundations is available in literature (17, 18), but as far as practical application is concerned, we know only about cases of relatively small dimensions with heavy aggregation.

PRICES AND PRODUCERS' BEHAVIOR

Literature dealing with the influence of market mechanism upon the behavior and decisions of consumers and producers is large. Part of this literature asserts that prices have a central role while another part finds these hopes to be exaggerated. Among others, the U.N. report (22) points to the serious economic consequences of an unleashed price mechanism when it gives rise to the necessity for state intervention and to the expediency of economic planning.

In socialist countries the determination of prices and exchange of products has always been an important problem assigned mainly to the sphere of authority of state organs. Practice however, has not offered the results expected, and now the economic reform which reached different stages in the various socialist countries regards the market mechanism, under given conditions, to be one of the means of planned economic development. But the views characteristic to the economic reform do not by themselves guarantee that the different price authorities set correct prices and that the producers react to them in a most suitable way.

Mathematical programming affords, with shadow prices, useful information to both the central economic direction and to the producers. This has been widely treated by professional literature (7, 14, 15, 16, 21). If we want to attain a sufficiently detailed and reliable system of equilibrium prices, through converging shadow prices, we must state that the models now applied are still too highly aggregated ones. Their formulation is sometimes rather problematic and they require a broader system of computers than now available to use.

If we want to shape out a reasonable behavior of producers, we may be aided by the normative supply analysis known till now mainly from examples by American authors. If applied correctly, these analyses may become a most useful tool for planners of the central direction (1, 22). In order to detect the opportunities offered by normative supply analyses, we carried out a 1966-67 study about changes in the optimum structure of agriculture in a region for 125 different price settings. The experience gained in the course of this study was extensively used in developing a framework for a broader project just underway, the philosophy of which is summarized in the following section (13).

Multiregional Study of Normative Effects of Prices

The calculations made by the central direction and the decisions based upon them may become rather questionable if the people in the direction do not have enough information about the reactions of producers to prices. Knowing the present price levels, one can infer by logic the direction of the reactions. But as far as the extent of reactions is concerned, one has recourse only to guessing. A positive element not to be underated of such guesses is the generally justified belief in the caution of the producers.

The system of planning which prevailed in Hungary until recently did not allow producer reaction to prices to take a shape clear enough to afford useful information for the central direction. On the other hand, the producers also were unable to develop that routine of decision making which they would badly need after 1968. It will take several years before the thinking of the majority of the producers develops the type of judgment necessary to provide reactions for measurement to the central direction. Until then, even relying upon the caution of the producers, we can expect a great deal of random events, particularly if we regard the regional distribution of reactions or decisions made by the producers.

One of the methods of analyzing producers' reactions to prices is the empirical (positive) supply analysis based on time series of actual data. Our past planning system not only made no use of such analyses but there was no possibility for reliable calculations. Even now such analyses are hampered by the lack of data. It will be several years before we have a data base sufficient for research which can tell the central direction of probable producer reactions by time and space. Hence we must lean on normative analyses if we want information not about the true behavior of producers but about their most reasonable behavior if we assume that (a) they consider the system of constraints of the model to be the boundaries of their actions and (b) they serve as profit maximizers who decide according to the severe logic of the computer. After having received the primary solutions for each region, measurements of effects of price changes for various products by a series of parametric solutions may offer valuable information about optimum reactions under the conditions of the model. This information, after an aggregation to the national level, may show what price changes are necessary to meet the national demand in various commodities. They also could show in which region and by which technologies changes must be made to attain demand quantities. We are aware that the producers are still unable to behave in the optimizing way prescribed by the computer. We are also aware that even if they were able to do so, the results would be different from the normative optima; if not for any other reason, because they shape out the model somewhat differently, according to their own conceptions.

This project involves a series of optimizations for every region of the country starting with 1968 prices. Our intention with this project is to invite a discussion aimed at influencing to some extent the thinking of people in the central direction and that of the leaders of regional farmers' organizations. We think that through results to be gained from computations with eventually modified models (reflecting lessons from the discussion) we can exert conditioning on the thinking of producers by giving them a yardstick for this purpose. Consequently, we believe, the producers could develop for themselves a more efficient routine of decision making more quickly and without great zigzags connected with considerable losses. This routine of managerial decision making might soon be quantified as a system of supply response functions and contribute to more solid government measures in the field of price policies.

The results from the parametric solutions of the regional models may appear as variables of a central model. By solving this model we can get that national program of production and pricing which provides the national volume of products demanded with the smallest possible amount of price corrections from central sources. This solution can be reached by an optimum selection from the regional optima through integer programming of the zero-or-one type.

PROGRAMS OF AGRICULTURE WITHIN GENERAL REGIONAL DEVELOPMENT PLANS

The model described in the study under (12) can be used for the elaboration of plans that optimize agricultural development as an organic part of the economy of a region. The same model allows the integration of the regional optima into an optimal medium-term plan of the national economy.

An outline of the regional model may be given according to blocks embracing certain columns and rows. The first block of columns refers to agriculture; the second one to the existing industry and to that which might be established; the third one refers to communal services and other infrastructural elements; and the fourth block contains the variables for interregional relationships. When the model is segmented by groups of rows, the first block embraces the resources of production (labor differentiated according to mobility and employment opportunities), while the second one deals with the balances of products including interregional relationships. The third block refers to the financial balances. Here we find capital formation, credits, and the income of the population specified by years and by groups of population (at least for the agricultural population).

Two variants may be considered according to the objective function: one of them maximizes net income; the other is aimed at maximum capital formation.

The balance of investments contains the contribution from central sources to the funds of development of the region in a specific form: in proportion to the capital formation by the region itself. The value of this parameter may vary according to central considerations, and it may also be different in each year of the planning period. The maximization of net income is favorable for receiving central contributions to the funds of development in proportion to the region's own capital formation. However, if own capital formation is the criterion of optimization, the contribution from central sources will be a maximum, accelerating the development of the region.

In a similar manner, as was mentioned earlier, the central model embraces the optimum regional program belonging to the different values of the parameter relative to contribution from central sources. The system of variables of the central model consists of the various optima for each region and of the variables relative to interregional flows of commodities. The balances of products deal with national final demand and with intersectoral and interregional flows. The financial balances embrace income equations on the national level and those describing flows of credit and contributions to development of regions. The last block provides the coefficients for integrating the optima selected for each region into an optimum national plan. The productivity of social labor may serve here as the objective function.

The model described above may of course be extended by the inclusion of other variables and constraints relative to the balance of payments, to interregional flows of labor, and the like. Besides the productivity of social labor, national income or net income to be channeled to the state may also be considered as a potential objective function.

Integer solutions are even on the regional level, particularly because of indivisibilities connected with major investments. For the central model only integer solution of the zero-or-one type can be considered, according to the assumption about the indivisibility of any policy represented by the various optima computed for different regions.

REFERENCES

1. Andersen, J. C., and E. O. Heady. Normative Supply Functions and Optimum Farm Plans for Northeastern Iowa. Iowa Agr. and Home Econ. Exp. Sta. Res. Bull. 537.
2. Birow, A. T. Programming Models for Regional Planning: Approach to the Problem of Regional Specialization in Swedish Agriculture. Agricultural College of Sweden, 1963.
3. Black, J. D. Societal Obligations to and of Agriculture. In *Problems and Policies in American Agriculture*, ed. Earl O. Heady. Ames: Iowa State Univ. Press, 1959.
4. Currie, L. *Accelerating Development: The Necessity and the Means*. New York: McGraw-Hill, 1965.
5. Dantzig, G. B., and P. Wolfe. Decomposition Principle for Linear Programs. *Operations Res.*, vol. 8.
6. Day, R. H. On Aggregating Linear Programming Models of Production. *J. Farm Econ.*, vol. 47.
7. Kantorovich, L. V. *Ekonomichesky Raschet Nailuchshevo Ispolsovania Resursov* [Economic Analysis for Optimal Use of Resources]. Moscow: Izdatelstvo Akademii Nauk, 1960.
8. Lee, J. E. Exact Aggregation: A Discussion of Miller's Theorem. AER, USDA, April 1966.
9. Miller, T. A. Sufficient Conditions for Exact Aggregation in Linear Programming Models. AER, USDA, April 1966.
10. Sebestyen, J. Optimumszamitasok Alkalmazasa a Legkedvexobb Termelesi Szerkezet Meghatarozasara [Optimization of the Structure of Agricultural Production]. MTA Mezogazdasagi Uzemtani Intezet, vol. 19.
11. ――――. A Short Sketch of a Mathematical Method of Planning Agricultural Production. Inst. Farm Econ., Hungarian Acad. Sci. Bull. 2. Budapest, 1962.

12. ———. Some Thoughts on a Spatial Model for Development Purposes. *Proc. Reg. Sci. Assoc.*, vol. 13.

13. ———. Egy Teruleti Arhatasvizsgalat Mahany Eredmenye Kezirat [Some Results from A Normative Supply Analysis for a Region]. Unpubl. Ms., Inst. Agr. Econ., Hungarian Acad. Sci.

14. Simon, G. Trends and Stability of Economy-wide Shadow Prices. 4th Intern. Conf. on Input-Output Techniques. Geneva, 1968.

15. Simon, G., and G. Kendor. *Gazdasagi Hatekonysag es Arnyekarak* [Economic Efficiency and Shadow Prices]. Budapest: Kozgax-Dasagi es Jogi Konyvkiado, 1965.

16. Skold, M., and E. O. Heady. Regional Location of Production of Major Field Crops at Alternative Demand and Price Levels. USDA Tech. Bull. 1354, 1966.

17. Tintner, G. Stochastic Linear Programming with Applications to Agricultural Economics. *Proc. Second Symposium in Linear Programming.* Vol. 1. Washington: National Bureau of Standards, 1955.

18. ———. Game Theory, Linear Programming and Input-Output Analysis. *Z. Nationaloekon,* vol. 17.

19. Tintner, G., and S. A. S. Farghali. The Application of Stochastic Programming to the UAR First Five-Year Plan. Univ. Southern California, 1966.

20. Tintner, G., and N. S. Raghavan. Stochastic Linear Programming Applied to A Dynamic Planning Model for India. Univ. California, 1967.

21. Tirel, J. C. Programmation Interregional INRA. Grignon, 1966.

22. United Nations. Economic Planning in Europe. Geneva, 1965.

Chapter 21 ᔕ᠊ DISCUSSION

John Ashton, *University of Newcastle upon Tyne* (U.K.)

IT IS A DIFFICULT TASK to discuss briefly the large area Joseph Sebestyen summarized. I express first my appreciation to him and to Mr. Kazareczki for an important evaluation of some of the underlying conventional planning results and planning methodology. There were some significant remarks in Mr. Sebestyen's presentation which represent some important changes in standpoint. I will restrict my comments to two of the issues raised and make some remarks which, I hope, will contribute to the debate. We could, in fact, even restrict the debate to the very important issue of definition of goals and problems of attaining them.

I think that few politicians in any country would have difficulty in subscribing to certain of the goals that Sebestyen outlined. Economic goals are generally expressed in terms of increasing living standards. These and similar generalized goals are likely to be acceptable in most countries. But how they are attained, and what sectors are to be restrained while others thrust ahead more rapidly (thereby increasing the average attainment of the generalized goal), is not so easily resolved. It is at the administrative and policy implementation level where decisions have to be made as to which regions and groups will advance most rapidly, which will be allowed to lag or become obsolete, as well as the exact means of attainment.

These problems of attainment of goals emerge under every economic and social system, but little in the realm of the planning processes themselves and model building throws light on how to handle them. They are questions and problems which are not dealt with by the economist's caveat: "If the policy makers will give us the targets and their relative priorities, we will provide an efficient model for optimizing the goal set." Instead this broad complex of problems has to be solved largely through the interaction of public administrators, politicians, and the broad public whom they serve.

Goals themselves, in broad terms, abound. However a goal expressed in general terms has little meaning for the people who are not immediately concerned with reaching it. It only opens a broad perspective for them. In other words, the general public can be presented with a boundless agricultural policy, as for example in the preamble of the Agricultural Act in Britain, which can be interpreted in many ways.

The British government thought the goals outlined in its preamble would fit domestic production as near as possible to the nation's food needs (thereby diminishing imports), protect producers' interests, provide a reasonable standard of livelihood for farmers, and provide good living standards for agricultural workers and consumers with fairly priced food. But for all its many words and interpretations, achievement is extremely difficult.

Goals stated too broadly fail to allow any useful guides in determining priorities for the specific elements or subsets of policies which relate directly to different groups of people and their aspirations. Such goals do not provide any basis for formulating a reasonable or workable possible instrument for attaining the goals of optimization and reorganization. Profit seeking may get the economy close to its goals, but even be identified. Some papers and economic reforms mention profits as a possible instrument for attaining the goals of optimizing and reorganization. Profit seeking may get the economy close to its goals, but even more specific instruments such as market prices serving as weights which set the social ordering of goods and services may prove more successful. In those realms of economic activity where goods are produced and consumed outside the market (e.g., public services in some countries and as a large portion of the product mix in the planned economies), how do we get the "weights" or prices reflected back into the planning system or models with greater precision and urgency?

These are among the more profound problems in planning and the application of planning methods. It is an important task of policy administration to make planning methods less bureaucratic and more responsive to public needs. I spent quite a number of years in government service in my country, and I am sure that the problems are equal or greater in the government services of other countries. In this experience, I see the problem as one of feedback—the critical area of involving people in improving their own services as a result of a more responsive system of governmental machinery working on their behalf.

In this respect, I like Sebestyen's remark on the role of the politician. Apart from other services which he has to provide, he should now have the backing of computer services to concentrate on attainment of people's aspirations more rapidly. It is an especially able politician who, in addition to the personality, courage, and integrity appropriate to this profession, also has the ability to envisage those changes that are needed and then orient policy rapidly.

Some of our papers have emphasized the identification of a goal or direction, then the creation of models to attain it—as if the goals were never-changing. It seems to me that this presentation is grossly over-simplified. If we look at a relatively mature economy, like the United Kingdom with a long history and background in industrialization, we find that the most urgent British problem, in the long-range sense, is today's need for a very radical structural change in our units of production, our institutions, and our general arrangements. I live in the heavy industry area of the River Tyne, an area which was the center of a very early stage in the industrialization process in the United Kingdom. We already have widespread obsolescence in long-established industries which cannot be changed easily except over a long period of adaptation and adjustment.

And in the second stage of industrialization it is not only necessary to change the scale of operations but also the product mix necessary for the present and future balance. The needed commitment is larger than capital; it is the commitment to look for the need of change. It seems to be important to recognize, as perhaps one of the most basic issues confronting any country, that we spend very little time in dealing with this continuing problem in an explicit way. The realization needed is that the maturing of an economy is accompanied by not only obsolescence of its physical plant but also of its planning processes. One benefit of model building is in fact to help to become more systematic over those issues and thereby identify and generate new potential organization.

Finally I would like to say a word or two about the question of treating individual components of change which are so relevant in overall change. It is a special difficulty in agriculture. For instance, from a methodological point of view, you find interesting problems involved in productivity measurements. If you look underneath these processes, in a national or regional productivity context, you have a certain average increase in productivity whether measured in terms of one or more factors of production or the total input-output relations of the region or industry. What does this mean in terms of the units within industry? First, there are many units within the industry that make no progress in the measured periods. They are in positions of stagnation for the time being. On the other hand, a small number of individual units have shifted onto new supply functions because they have changed drastically their organization and use of their resources. The actual process, in fact, is a very large change in a small number of individual units.

Generally this change was effected through a considerable input of capital and new technology. Properly managed, an impressive collective thrust can be made if two factors are identified with clarity and their importance recognized. First, many broadly beneficial changes come about largely as a product of widespread intellectual investment. This is now recognized in the services to the agricultural industry in the form of extension, education, and research. The benefits of these services are now widely acknowledged and are being applied on a widespread scale.

Second, there also is a very important element of innovation at the farm level. It is unplanned innovation, occurring largely as the result of the unrestrained imagination of individuals. The individual on the farm itself can be a very important factor in change and improvement, and important national innovations in farm practice have in fact originated not in the research station but on the individual farm. In view of the potential and importance of these changes, capital and institutions should be created to foster this kind of innovation if the full utilization and realization of human intellect and imagination is to be developed.

Chapter 22   FORMALIZING NATIONAL PLANNING AND POLICY INTO SYSTEMATIC ECONOMIC MODELS

Wiktor Herer, *Institute of Planning* (Poland)
K. Porwit, *Institute of Planning* (Poland)

THE ROLE of comprehensive, economy-wide models must be considered against a background of a wider, multilevel system of plans. All particular plans included in such a system, which are different from the viewpoint of their scope and time horizon, are constructed according to a multistage procedure involving participation of numerous organizational units. Such a procedure allows us to take into consideration information available on various levels of management, as well as the constructive initiative of people working in particular sectors and links of the economy. The central level of planning has its specific tasks within this system. These tasks are mainly related to the choice of socioeconomic objectives and of corresponding proportions in allocation of resources, as well as the choice of policies aimed at implementation of such objectives. Decisions made at the central level in that respect form a basis for respective sectoral (branch and regional) programs, but they are also influenced by the information concerning feasible alternatives for choice, which information stems out of sectoral programs. Consequently it is obvious that the models employed at the central level of analysis must have specific features. They are not supposed to include details pertaining to the respective sectoral activities. On the contrary, they are used as instruments helping to assess relative merits of particular variants for basic proportions of growth, related to the rate of growth, structural and technical changes, as well as to the path of development over subsequent periods considered within a plan in question. Simultaneously it is necessary to take into consideration that such models include a number of exogenous variables and parameters which are subject to estimation with various degrees of uncertainty. In that respect the models help to find out how far particular patterns of development may be sensitive in response to possible deviations in the values of exogenous elements.

In this sense our main concern in this paper is with the mutual interconnections between agriculture and the rest of the economy as seen in the analysis of basic, economy-wide proportions. At the same time we are less interested in models and techniques serving the purpose of estimation of exogenous variables and parameters. We are dealing with a type of model which helps to systemize an analysis of interdependent factors influencing feasible development policies and to make relevant decisions within a wider framework of a multilevel planning system.

Part I of this paper, written by W. Herer, gives a description of the main interconnections between development patterns related to the economy as a whole and to agriculture. Particular attention is devoted to the impact of the latter on the former. This part is supplemented with an appendix which gives short characteristics of basic information and of analytical procedures employed in practice in order to study possible patterns of such interconnections for the future.

Part II, prepared by K. Porwit, presents an example of a comprehensive interbranch programming model. Special attention is being given to possibilities of analyzing the impact of agriculture on other relevant features of feasible development patterns.

Part I. AN ATTEMPT AT FORMULATING THE
OBJECTIVES OF AGRICULTURAL PLANNING

IN FORMULATING the objectives of agricultural planning, it is necessary to distinguish two groups of countries: developing and mid-developed countries and developed countries. The characteristic features of the first group are the following:

1. Low or medium level of nutrition, not exceeding 40 grams of daily protein content per head of population.
2. High proportion of population earning their living from agricultural production.
3. Large share of agriculture in the national income (over 15 percent).
4. Significant differences in nutrition between agricultural and nonagricultural population.
5. High income elasticity of the consumption of agricultural products.
6. Low price elasticity of the consumption of agricultural products.
7. Restricted possibility of substituting agricultural products by industrial goods in the pattern of consumption.
8. Limited possibilities of financing and subsidizing agricultural development through redistribution of the net product of the nonagricultural sector due to high share of agriculture in the national income.
9. Existence of manpower reserves in agriculture, with marginal productivity equal or close to zero.
10. Prevalence of labor-intensive rather than capital-intensive techniques in agricultural growth due to the availability of manpower reserves.
11. Small volume of industrial exports per head of population; hence no possibility of supplementing domestic food resources with food imports paid from industrial exports. High ratio of required imports of agricultural means of production[1] in relation to industrial exports.

1. Including the requirements of industries making means of production for agriculture.

The main features of the developed countries are the following:

1. High level of nutrition, exceeding 40 grams of protein content per head of population; complete elimination of malnutrition even in lowest-income groups.[2]
2. Low proportion of population earning their living from agricultural production.
3. Small share of agriculture in the national income (under 15 percent).
4. No difference in consumption of agricultural products between agricultural and nonagricultural population.[3]
5. Low income elasticity of consumption of agricultural products.
6. High price elasticity of consumption of agricultural products.
7. Possibility of replacing consumption of agricultural products by consumption of industrial goods.
8. Low share of agriculture in the national income, owing to which agricultural development can be financed and subsidized through redistribution of the net product of the nonagricultural sector.
9. Absence of manpower reserves in agriculture.
10. High capital/output ratio of agricultural growth in most countries.
11. High volume of industrial exports per head of population in relation to import intensity of agricultural production; hence a possibility of supplementing domestic food resources with imports if necessary.

Throughout the past two decades Poland's development has been marked by nearly all the features typical for a country at middle stage of development. During the last twenty years we have moved from a fairly low protein content to a figure close to the standards prevailing in developed countries (e.g., meat consumption per capita grew from 17 kilograms in 1934-38 to 51 kilograms in 1967).[4]

Essential changes have occurred in the cost of increasing agricultural production. Manpower reserves in agriculture were practically exhausted by the end of the 1950s. To obtain an increase in agricultural produce with dwindling manpower, resources require large investment outlays; the incremental capital/output ratio in agriculture thus increases (2).

Today Poland is in the final stage of transition from the middle stage to a high stage of development. In the early 1970s, it is expected to answer nearly all the criteria of a developed country. That is why the problem of adjusting the methods of agricultural planning to the level of economic development is of particular importance for Poland.

2. This condition is fulfilled in countries with a planned economy, highly equalized incomes, and well-developed social insurances. It is also fulfilled in some advanced countries having no planned economy (e.g., Sweden).

3. Elimination of differences in consumption of agricultural products need not necessarily imply the liquidation of differences in food consumption. Indeed, foodstuffs consumed by the nonagricultural population have a higher content of valuable components added to the agricultural products during industrial processing.

4. Note that malnutrition in lowest-income groups in Poland was eliminated by the end of the postwar reconstruction period, owing to far-reaching equalization of incomes in different groups of population.

SOME OBJECTIVES OF AGRICULTURAL PLANNING IN DEVELOPING AND MID-DEVELOPED COUNTRIES[5]

Given the rate of growth of national income and nonagricultural employment, the rate of growth of agricultural produce must reach a certain minimum[6] derived from the difference in the level of consumption of agricultural products between the agricultural and the nonagricultural sectors. The minimum level of agricultural production can be written as

$$P_a = LaC_{aa} + L(1-a)C_{ai} \qquad (1)$$

where

P_a = agricultural produce destined for domestic consumption
L = total population
a = ratio of agricultural to total population
C_{aa} = consumption of agricultural products per head of agricultural population
C_{ai} = consumption of agricultural products per head of nonagricultural population

According to this formula, given the values of C_{aa} and C_{ai} ($C_{aa} < C_{ai}$), the demand for agricultural products increases as the ratio of agricultural to total population (a) decreases.

Real wages in the nonagricultural sector must inevitably be reduced unless agricultural produce is kept at the minimum level expressed in the formula above. If this minimal condition is fulfilled, then a reduction in the ratio of agricultural to total population makes possible an increase in the consumption of agricultural products per head of population. Indeed, a developing country may live through periods in which the per capita consumption of agricultural products increases solely through changes in the structure of population (the division into agricultural and nonagricultural population), while the level of consumption of agricultural products within different groups remains unchanged.

The objective of agricultural planning is to achieve a given increase in the consumption of agricultural products in the nonagricultural and agricultural sectors. The volume of increase in the consumption of agricultural products is postulated to a certain degree independently of the effectiveness and cost of agricultural growth. The improvement of consumption standards has priority over the criteria of cost and effect. Consequently major importance is attached to quantitative targets for agriculture, set in terms of the number of tons of various products envisaged in the plan. The planned targets must be accomplished regardless of the cost.

Apart from attaining a given increase in per capita consumption, the

5. This paper is not concerned with the objectives of planning related to the transformation of the social structure of agriculture.

6. We are considering a closed economy, leaving aside foreign trade problems.

plan must be aimed at achieving a certain rise of real wages in the agricultural[7] and nonagricultural sectors. When the income elasticity of the consumption of agricultural products is high, and so is the share[8] of agricultural products in the individual consumption fund, then the rate of growth of agricultural produce has a decisive impact upon the rate of growth of real wages. An insufficient rate of growth of agricultural produce erects a barrier, as it were, which circumscribes the possibility of accelerating the rate of growth of real wages. Mutual substitution between consumption of agricultural products and consumption of industrial goods is thus restrained. Changes in the relationship of prices for industrial goods and agricultural products, which shape the structure of consumption in a developed country, cannot play the same role in a developing country.

The supply of agricultural products being inelastic and the demand for these products highly elastic, retail prices for agricultural products must rise in relation to prices for industrial goods. This relative rise of the prices of agricultural products, to be noticed in Poland and other countries overcoming their backwardness, brings demand in line with supply and creates the conditions for equilibrium on the food market.

In this sense prices are an instrument of equilibrium and not an instrument for shaping the structure of consumption. The instrument of prices can be used to ensure market equilibrium; it cannot act towards separating the dynamics of real wages from the dynamics of agricultural growth. High income elasticity of demand for agricultural products and limited possibilities of mutual substitution between industrial and agricultural consumption form an inseparable link between the rate of growth of real wages and the rate of growth of agricultural produce.

The role of prices as a regulator of market equilibrium is also subject to some constraints. In a planned economy, retail food prices are to a certain extent autonomous in relation to prices paid to the agricultural producer. This autonomy is the consequence of the monopoly for purchases of agricultural products being in the hands of state and cooperative trade organizations. On the other hand, it is only a limited autonomy because farm products are also sold directly by the producer to the consumer. There are certain limits to the process of restraining the growing demand for farm products by means of increasing the price of food. The gap between retail food prices and prices paid to the producer cannot be too big. In some conditions a rise in retail prices leads to a rise in the prices paid to the producer. Higher prices paid to the producer mean higher revenues for farmers; this in turn generates additional demand for foodstuffs on the part of the agricultural population. The double effect of the rise in prices for agricultural products (i.e., reduced demand on the one hand and revenues for farmers on the other)

7. Real wages in the peasant sector are considered here as income consumed per head of employee in agriculture.

8. The high proportion of agricultural products is due, among other things, to the low degree of food processing; this results in excessive content of agricultural raw materials in the value of consumed food.

represents one more element in the set of phenomena which we call the agricultural barrier to the growth of real wages.

SUPPLY FUNCTION OF AGRICULTURAL PRODUCTION IN A DEVELOPING COUNTRY

Transforming the Kalecki formula (3), this function can be written as

$$P_a = \frac{I_a}{m} + P_a \cdot u - P_a \cdot a$$

and

$$\frac{P_a}{P_a} = \frac{I_a}{P_a} \frac{1}{m} + u - a$$

where

P_a = final product of agriculture as a branch[9]

I_a = cumulated investment related to agricultural production increase[10]

m = capital/output ratio

u = increase in production resulting from factors not directly related to investment (e.g., progress in quality seeds or pedigree cattle)

a = amortization parameter

It is assumed that manpower resources in a developing country are practically unlimited.[11] These unlimited resources may exist in the following forms: (a) disguised unemployment in agriculture, revealed by zero or near-zero marginal productivity per employee, (b) underemployed manpower, revealed by low marginal productivity per employee, and (c) possibility of increasing agricultural produce without substantial investment as a substitute for labor by means of employing the natural increase of agricultural manpower with more working days per year and longer hours per day.

In the formula given above, unlimited manpower resources appear in an indirect way. The formula includes capital/output ratio. Owing to the existence of manpower reserves, labor-substituting investment can be reduced and capital/output ratio can be kept at a correspondingly low level.

The main constraint of the plan rests in the limited possibility of

9. The final product of agriculture as a branch is understood as the sum of products destined for natural consumption, for sale (commodity production), for stock increase, and for increase in current and capital assets produced in agriculture.

10. Cumulated investment includes investment in agriculture and in the industries which directly or indirectly supply agriculture with nonagricultural raw materials (e.g., investment in industries making fertilizers and in industries which supply fuel to the fertilizer industries).

11. The annual increase in the demand for agricultural labor is not sufficient to employ in full the growing manpower resources.

allocating investment outlays to agriculture. In those countries where the share of agriculture in the final product of the national economy is high, the volume of cumulated investment outlays in agriculture in relation to the output of the industrial sector is inevitably high. This can be presented as

$$I_a = P_a i$$
$$P_a i = P(1-a_a) - R$$

where

P   = overall final product of the national economy
a_a = the share of final agricultural product in overall final product[12]
i   = ratio of cumulated investment to final agricultural product
R   = final product of the nonagricultural sector, destined for consumption and investment in the nonagricultural sector

Given the values of P and R, the greater the value of a_a, representing the share of agriculture in the overall final product, the smaller is the value of cumulated investment destined for agricultural development.

The relation of cumulated investment in agriculture to the output of the nonagricultural sector, written as $\frac{I_a}{P(1-a_a)}$, is of great importance. In a developing country it may reach a very high value. The possibility of changing this relation in the sense of increasing the share of cumulated investment destined for agricultural development in the final product of the nonagricultural sector may prove very limited in view of the rigid needs represented by the symbol R.

It seems that the above constraints limiting the increase of investment outlays allocated for agricultural development are among the main features causing inelasticity of production.[13] Agricultural development requires various types of capital intensive investment. For example, greater use of mineral fertilizers implies highly capital-intensive investment in the chemical industry and in mining.[14] This proves to be a heavy burden for the developing country in view of its relatively small industrial potential.

In a developing country the relation between increase in fertilizing and increase in agricultural produce is very favorable. Fertilizer inputs

12. This share is considered in a different way than is traditionally the case. The whole agricultural product destined for food is assumed to be directly included in the overall final product. The output of the food industry is counted in the final product only to the extent of its processed value (final product of the food industry minus agricultural input).

13. Some authors (1) seem to be overoptimistic in estimating the prospects of growth of agricultural produce on the basis of the available resources of untilled farm land. Indeed, in many countries it is not the land shortage but the capital shortage that hampers agricultural development.

14. Nothing will change in our reasoning if we envisage that fertilizers can be purchased abroad. For instead of investing in the fertilizer industries, we shall have to invest in industries making export goods to finance imports of fertilizers.

are often made in the sphere of growing marginal effects; hence the increase in production is inexpensive from the point of view of allocations on the development of the fertilizer industry in relation to increases of the final agricultural product.

This leads to a reduction of the incremental cumulated capital/output ratio of the growth of agricultural produce $(I_a/\Delta P_a)$.

Technological progress not directly related to investment is an important factor contributing to agricultural growth, especially in view of the great disparity in economic effects obtained by individual farms. This form of technological progress operates through the extension of better agricultural techniques. Popularization of new agricultural techniques among millions of peasants is organically related to cultural and civilizational progress in the village. The process of acquiring new knowledge is part and parcel of the process of transformation of man. It must, therefore, take time and cannot be accelerated at will. In order to promote agricultural growth, it is necessary to couple development of investment with extension of agricultural knowledge. The two processes must be closely coordinated. If the knowledge of agricultural techniques lags behind the development of productive investment, then the effects of investment outlays in agriculture will be inevitably reduced.

FIXING TARGETS OF AGRICULTURAL GROWTH

By analyzing the supply function we obtain information on the possibilities of agricultural growth.

A comparison between possibilities and needs serves as a basis for fixing the targets of production increase. As a rule the needs of economic development exceed the possibilities of agricultural growth. In a developing country the rate of agricultural growth determines fairly uniquely the rate of growth of employment and real wages in the nonagricultural sector. Indicators of income elasticity are the exogenous indicators of the plan; they can be altered to a limited extent only as a result of price changes.

To make the plan consistent, the rate of growth of the wage fund in the nonagricultural sector must match the rate of agricultural growth. This may involve certain modifications of the structure of investment in the whole national economy such as would insure an accelerated rate of growth of agricultural produce. To do this, it may prove necessary in some cases to restrain the rate of employment increase in the nonagricultural sector (i.e., to adjust the planned rate of employment increase in the nonagricultural sector to the limited possibilities of agricultural growth).

"AGRICULTURAL BARRIER" TO ECONOMIC GROWTH

In a developing country, agricultural growth has a double impact upon the rate of growth of the national income. First, there is the direct impact, expressed in the share of agriculture in national income increase. If agriculture accounts for a large share in the formation of national income, then its share in the increase of national income is also relatively high.[15] Consequently the direct impact of agriculture upon the rate of national income increase in a developing country is always quite large. The fact that substantial investment outlays must be made in agriculture does not hinder the growth of national income because the difference in capital/output ratio between industry and agriculture is fairly small. Secondly, there is the indirect impact, expressed in the fact that the rate of agricultural growth largely determines the rate of income increase in the nonagricultural sector. Different variants of the rate of agricultural growth correspond to different variants of the rate of income increase in the nonagricultural sector.

Indirect Impact on Farm Income with Stable Nonfarm Investment Outlays (I_i)

Owing to the availability of manpower reserves in agriculture, it is possible to plan an accelerated rate of employment increase in the nonagricultural sector corresponding to the accelerated rate of agricultural growth. Nonagricultural employment, increased due to a higher rate of agricultural growth ($\Delta Z + \Delta Z'$), will reveal a lower capital/labor ratio at stable level of investment, I_i, and a correspondingly lower level of productivity, P_{i1}.

The indirect effect of additional increase in agricultural produce can be formulated as

$$\Delta D = (\Delta Z + \frac{\Delta P'_a}{C_{ai} - C_{aa}}) P_{i1}$$

where

ΔD = national income increase in the nonagricultural sector

ΔZ = manpower increase without additional increase in agricultural produce

$\Delta P'_a$ = additional increase in agricultural produce

C_{ai} = consumption of farm products per employee in the nonagricultural sector [16]

C_{aa} = consumption of farm products per employee in the agricultural sector

P_{i1} = productivity of new employees in the nonagricultural sector at capital/labor ratio equal to $J_i /(\Delta Z + \Delta Z')$ [17]

15. The share of agriculture in national income increase is nearly always smaller than its share in the formation of national income.

16. For the purpose of simplification, consumption of farm products by dependents is not considered here.

17. Higher manpower increase will be characterized by capital/labor ratio equal to $J_i/\Delta Z + \Delta Z'$. At a lower rate of growth of agricultural produce and employment (ΔZ), the manpower increase will be characterized by a higher capital/labor ratio $J_i /\Delta Z$. Additional increase in employment will lead to increased production if the rate of productivity decrease is smaller than the rate of decrease in capital/labor ratio.

It is easy to see that if the whole additional increase in agricultural produce is destined to be consumed by the additionally employed manpower, then the quotient $\Delta P_a' /(C_{ai} - C_{aa}) = \Delta Z'$ will determine the additional increase in manpower ($\Delta Z'$).

The problem will be illustrated by the following example. Let us consider two variants of a five-year plan. [18]

Variant 1:

$$C_{ai} - C_{aa} = 1000 \text{ zloty}$$
$$\Delta P_a = 2 \text{ milliard zloty}$$
$$\Delta Z = 400,000 \text{ persons}$$

Variant 2:

The plan envisages an additional increase in agricultural produce $\Delta P_a' = 0.1$ milliard zloty (total increase in agricultural produce under this variant will equal $\Delta P_a + \Delta P_a' = 2.1$ milliard zloty).

If the additional increase in agricultural produce $\Delta P_a'$, worth 0.1 milliard zloty, is destined for consumption by the additional increment of manpower employed in the nonagricultural sector, then it will be possible to employ additionally $\Delta Z' = \Delta P_a /(C_{ai} - C_{aa}) = 100,000$ persons. Total employment increase under this variant will thus be $\Delta Z + \Delta Z' = 500,000$ persons.

Indirect Impact on Nonfarm Income with Growing Nonfarm Investment Outlays $(I_i + I_i')$

An accelerated rate of agricultural growth renders it possible to increase employment in the nonagricultural sector and raise investment outlays at the same time.

Assuming that acceleration of the rate of growth of nonagricultural employment does not lead to a reduced capital/labor ratio, the effect of additional increase in agricultural produce can be written as

$$D = (Z + \frac{P_a}{C_{ai} - C_{aa}})P_{i2}$$

where P_{i2} stands for productivity of new employees in the nonagricultural sector, at capital/labor ratio equal to $(I_i + I_i')/(Z + Z')$.

To sum up our remarks on the "agricultural barrier" to economic growth, let us note that the rate of growth of agricultural produce largely determines the feasible rate of growth of national income; and the inelasticity of supply of agricultural products is an important factor restraining the possibility of accelerating the rate of economic growth.

The choice of investment structure (division into agricultural and nonagricultural investment) is limited. The given rate of growth of real wages and nonagricultural employment determines the necessary rate of

18. The order of magnitude corresponds to 1950-55 figures.

growth of agricultural produce and the necessary level of agricultural investment. Any additional increase of agricultural production automatically finds a market; hence it cannot bring down the prices paid to farmers.

SOME CONDITIONS OF AGRICULTURAL PLANNING IN A DEVELOPED COUNTRY[19]

Once the consumption of agricultural products has achieved a sufficiently high level and significant disproportions in the level of incomes of different groups of population have disappeared, new conditions are created for agricultural planning.

The central planner can now choose between different patterns of consumption, specifically between giving preference to the rate of growth of food consumption or that of factory-made goods and services.

It is thus possible to substitute consumption of industrial goods for that of agricultural products. The rate of growth of national income becomes largely independent of the rate of growth of agricultural production. The given rate of growth of national income and nonagricultural employment can be achieved at various rates of growth of agricultural production. Manpower reserves in agriculture are absent. Consumption of the agricultural product in the agricultural sector equals that in the nonagricultural sector. The problem of the agricultural barrier no longer exists.

The Supply Function in a Developed Country

The supply function changes its nature: (a) Manpower resources turn out to be a factor restraining agricultural growth. The social cost of agricultural labor can be calculated according to the additional increase in national income that might be obtained by transferring labor from the agricultural to the nonagricultural sector.[20] (As a rule, net product per employee in the nonagricultural sector is much greater while capital/labor ratio is often smaller). In Poland and in many other countries the rate of growth of productivity in the nonagricultural sector is higher than in the agricultural; hence the difference in productivity between the two sectors keeps growing and so does the social cost of labor in agriculture. In Poland distribution of incomes between industrial workers and peasants is guided by social criteria. Despite the lower

19. This paper omits foreign trade problems, confining itself to a closed economy.

20. An additional increase in national income, resulting from transfers of labor from the agricultural to the nonagricultural sector, is actually obtainable, for example, when choosing between two variants of consumption increase (either an increase in the consumption of agricultural products or in that of industrial goods). If, say, the second variant is chosen, then it may predetermine the choice of allocations of capital assets and labor. Allocation of capital assets and labor to the industrial sector will result in greater productivity of the labor transferred from the agricultural sector.

rate of growth of productivity in agriculture, remuneration of labor in this sector is growing at the same rate as in the nonagricultural sector. Consequently the relation between the rate of productivity increase and the rate of labor remuneration increase is less favorable in the agricultural than in the nonagricultural sector; and the social cost of agricultural production keeps growing in relation to the social cost of production in the nonagricultural sector.[21] (b) Since agricultural produce must be increased while manpower reserves get continuously smaller, large outlays have to be made to substitute labor—hence the climbing incremental capital/output ratio of agricultural production. Many other factors contribute to the increase of capital/output ratio. For example, mineral fertilizers must be used in the sphere of diminishing effects which leads to a rise of the cumulated capital/output ratio in agriculture. This is caused by a substantial increase in investment outlays in industries supplying agriculture with fertilizers calculated per unit of agricultural produce. The increase of agricultural produce is thus becoming more and more expensive. At the same time, with a growing elasticity of supply of agricultural products and with reduced ratio of cumulated investment outlays in agriculture in relation to the output of the industrial sector, investment outlays in agriculture become highly elastic.

The central planner has much more freedom in fixing the volume of cumulated investment outlays destined for agricultural development. Owing to the reduced share of agriculture in the national income, agriculture can be subsidized.

To sum up, agricultural planning in a developed country takes place in the following conditions: (a) an increase in the consumption of agricultural products is no longer the main objective of the program of consumption increase; (b) the social cost of agricultural production becomes increasingly higher in relation to consumption of industrial goods; (c) the planner has much more freedom in fixing the rate of growth of agricultural produce.

Some Objectives of Agricultural Planning in a Developed Country

It is now possible to optimize the structure of consumption. Optimization of the structure of consumption consists of dividing the increase in the consumption fund into agricultural and industrial consumption in such a way as to minimize outlays per zloty-worth of consumption. (The value of consumption increase can be calculated in prices of the base year.)

Outlays can be written as (4):

$$E = IT^{-1} + K$$

---

21. I have in view the increased cost of agricultural produce related to higher dual pricing of labor. As productivity increases the per unit cost of agricultural production, in terms of labor priced according to stable remuneration standards, becomes smaller.

where

I = cumulated investment

K = cumulated cost

T = marginal recoupment period (in Poland, the rate of interest, T^{-1}, is 16 percent)

The above formula covers all investment outlays involved in obtaining the production increase and all current costs incurred at various stages of agricultural and industrial growth (indirect costs in branches producing nonagricultural raw materials plus indirect costs in agriculture).[22]

The gap between outlays on foodstuffs and outlays on industrial goods is very great. It is estimated that within the five years between 1966 and 1970, the cost of every zloty-worth of increase in the output of foodstuffs (excluding stimulants) is twice as high as that of every zloty-worth of increase in the output of industrial consumer goods.[23] (The striking difference in costs is explained mainly by the high cost of production of the agricultural input: outlays per zloty-worth of agricultural input are twice higher than outlays per zloty-worth of processed foodstuffs.)

Owing to the great difference in costs between agricultural consumption and industrial consumption, it is possible to reduce social outlays on consumption by shifting the proportions of agricultural consumption and industrial consumption. Optimization of the structure of consumption becomes all the more important in view of the fact that the disparity in intensity of outlays between agricultural products and industrial goods has grown a great deal in the last decade. This is caused by two factors: (a) the growing difference between incremental capital/output ratio of industrial goods and agricultural products destined for consumption, and (b) the growing difference in productivity between the agricultural and industrial sectors, resulting from a higher rate of productivity increase in the industrial sector.

Any program of optimization of the structure of consumption must take into account not only the outlay/effect ratio as it is today but also its estimated changes in the future. It is to be expected that the rate of productivity increase, the rate of cost reduction, and the rate of technological progress in the industrial sector will continue to be higher than in the agricultural sector (and in practically all the other branches producing raw materials). Consequently optimization of the structure of consumption may lead to spectacular effects from the point of view of the future outlay/effect ratio. The structure of consumption must be optimized not only from the point of view of the proportions of food consump-

22. Direct cost of labor is priced according to the value of the consumption fund of the population employed in the peasant sector.

23. The figures are valid for prices ensuring market equilibrium, given the demand and the volume of agricultural produce. Unfavorable indices of the cost of agricultural produce cannot be improved by raising the price of foodstuffs. A rise of these prices would reduce the market for agricultural products.

tion and industrial consumption but also from the point of view of the share of unprocessed agricultural products in the value of food. Outlays per unit of agricultural input contained in food are far higher than outlays per unit of food (agricultural raw materials plus value added in food processing). Consequently improvement of food-processing techniques (i.e., an increase of the value added in food-processing industries in relation to the total value of consumed food) is an additional important factor contributing to optimization of the structure of consumption.

To sum up, let us note that in a developed country a given rate of income growth can be obtained at various rates of agricultural growth. The rate of agricultural growth should be determined with a view to optimizing the structure of consumption, subject to certain constraints.

CONSTRAINTS TO THE PROGRAM OF OPTIMIZING THE STRUCTURE OF CONSUMPTION

The program of optimization of the structure of consumption must be carried into effect by means of a price policy encouraging increased consumption of factory-made goods, in view of their favorable outlay/effect ratio. But the program for optimization of consumption is subject to several constraints. Here are the most important ones: (a) Consumption of agricultural products must increase at a rate at least as high as the rate of population increase. (b) The optimization program must take into consideration the interests of lowest-income groups of population. Price policies encouraging substitution of industrial for agricultural consumption must consider the interests of those groups; among other things, nominal prices of food must grow at a slower rate than nominal incomes of the lowest-paid categories of employees. It is necessary to collect information on income elasticity in the lowest-paid categories of employees so as to take all the indispensable measures in respect to wages and prices, conducive to accelerated increase of food consumption by the lowest paid groups. (c) Constraints generated by the foreign trade balance must also be taken into account in the program.

To sum up, let us note that the cost of consumption increase should be minimized subject to the condition that food consumption by lowest-income groups of population must increase.

Increasing Agricultural Incomes While
Attaining Consumption Objectives

Let us see whether optimization of the structure of consumption, which requires a shift in outlays in favor of the nonagricultural sector, is in conflict with the interests of peasants. Such a conflict does not seem to occur in a planned economy. All social classes are interested in arriving at a structure of investment and labor outlays that is conducive to maximizing the rate of growth of the consumed portion of the national income. In a planned economy the criteria of distribution of the increase in national income are fairly independent of the rates of productivity increase in the agricultural and the nonagricultural sectors.

Maximized income can be distributed between the agricultural and nonagricultural sectors according to the criteria of social justice without relation to the rate of productivity increase. In a planned economy the state has at its disposal a variety of tools to control the dynamics of peasant incomes and to adjust the rate of increase in incomes to the objectives of social policy. These tools include the policy of prices, the fiscal policy, and the credit policy.

In Poland the rate of productivity increase during the past ten years has been much higher in industry than in agriculture, as shown in the figures below:

	1955/60	1960/65
Industry	6.7	5.4
Agriculture	3.1	2.7

But in spite of these differences, the rate of increase in labor remuneration in the two sectors has been equalized.[24]

Poland's example demonstrates that application of the criterion of optimization of the structure of consumption and the principle that outlays are distributed between agriculture and industry according to the expected effect does not run counter to farmers' interests in a planned economy.

CONSTRUCTION OF FIVE-YEAR PLANS
OF AGRICULTURAL DEVELOPMENT

For the time being, in view of scanty information[25] on the parameters of agricultural development on a macroscale, econometric models cannot be applied in the practice of plan construction. Present plans are built on the basis of statistical analyses by applying various types of balances.

Following is a brief review of the whole process of plan construction.[26]

24. This equalization incurs a certain annual cost (C_e) for the national economy. Its formula can be written as:

$$C_e = Z \cdot W (\alpha_w - \beta)$$

where
    Z = agricultural employment in the base year
    W = labor remuneration in agriculture per employee in the base year
    α_w = rate of growth of labor remuneration in agriculture
    β = rate of growth of productivity in agriculture

The lower the proportion of agricultural employment in total employment, the smaller is the impact of the cost of equalization upon the dynamics of real wages in the nonagricultural sector.

25. The types of information available are listed in the appendix.

26. It will be remembered that this is an agricultural plan in a country where 90 percent of land belongs to individual peasants.

Fixing the Planned Targets for Agriculture

Social demand for agricultural produce is based on an analysis of the degree to which the requirements of the population in regard to agricultural products are satisfied today, taking into account rational nutrition standards, the rate of increase of the population's incomes, and indices of income elasticity. Requirements related to foreign trade balance are also taken into account in fixing the planned targets.

The planner finds out what volume of investment outlays can be allocated to meet the cumulated needs of agriculture and how much hard currency can be obtained to pay for imports of capital goods needed in agriculture. (In Poland's planning practice throughout the past twenty years, the requirements in regard to the increased supply of agricultural products have invariably surpassed actual possibilities of agricultural growth, the latter having been always restrained by the limited investment outlays and hard-currency resources.) The targets of agricultural production increase are finally fixed as a compromise between the estimated needs and the potential possibilities of agricultural growth, subject to the limited resources. In some cases the demand must be adjusted to the limited possibilities of agricultural growth by means of diminishing the planned rate of increase of the wage fund in the nonagricultural sector.

The Supply Function of Agricultural Products

In constructing the supply function, we depart from forecasts of crop increase as a function of the increase in investment outlays, fertilizing, and technological progress. Accurate forecasting of crop increase is by no means an easy job, if only because of significant nonlinearity of the relationship between increased fertilizing and investment and increased crops. The ratio of marginal increase in fertilizing to marginal increase in crops rises steeply when the rate of increase in fertilizing becomes very high.

In spite of the difficulties, our forecasts of crop increase within the successive five-year periods have proved fairly accurate as shown in the data below:

	1960 Planned	1959/62 Accomplished	1965 Planned	1964/67 Accomplished
Grain crops (in q/ha)	16.0	16.4	17.6	18.3

The planner proceeds to draw balances of vegetable products based on the forecasts of crop increase. Once these balances are prepared, it is possible to estimate the volume of vegetable products to be earmarked for fodder. Given the standards of fodder input per kilogram of different types of animal products, and given also the initial cattle population, the planner can build a plan of increase in animal production.

Thus we can say that in order to construct a plan it is necessary to have accurate forecasts of crop increase and to be well oriented in fodder input standards. Knowing these standards, it is possible to adequately relate the plan of increase in vegetable production to the plan of increase in animal production. To estimate fodder input standards seems to be an easier task than to forecast grain crops since the standards of fodder input are rather stable. Given the information on cattle population and fodder input, one can build a feasible plan of increase in animal production so as to adjust the structure of supply to the demand.

Transmission of Planned Targets to Individual Peasant Farms

Owing to socialization of industry and commerce, the planned targets can be transmitted to individual farms by means of fixing prices of the means of production to safeguard their sale on the peasant market. A large portion of the investment plan, destined to boost production in peasant farms, is executed by state or cooperative organizations. These organizations have their own plans which are part and parcel of the national plan. For example, they may be plans of state constructing enterprises engaged in land amelioration and electrification projects, or plans of Agricultural Circles (cooperative organizations of peasants) set up for the purpose of joint purchase of machines and tractors. Since the credit system has been socialized and subordinated to the planned tasks, it can be used to finance increased purchases of means of production by peasant farms. Since purchases of farm products are exclusively in the hands of state and cooperative organizations, it is possible to fix the purchase price paid to agricultural producers in such a way as to adjust the structure of production to the structure of demand.

Special plans control the rate of employment increase in the nonagricultural sector. This has an impact upon the dynamics of migration from the agricultural sector, hence upon the dynamics of agricultural employment. It should be noted, however, that the impact of planning in this field is rather limited because of the indivisibility and uneven distribution of manpower in peasant farms. Even if the distribution of manpower in agriculture is well balanced on a national scale, it does not mean that there is no shortage or surplus of labor in some individual farms.

We have briefly described how five-year plans of agricultural development have been constructed in the planning practice of the past decade. Since Poland is now passing on to a new and higher development stage, agricultural planning is facing new tasks and some new methods of plan construction will have to be devised.

Part II. AN EXAMPLE OF A COMPREHENSIVE
ECONOMY-WIDE MODEL

THE MODEL presented here belongs to a class of models applied at the central level for an analysis of general interbranch proportions of development. It has to be considered as one of the tools of analysis within a wider system of multilevel planning. It assumes a relatively high level of aggregation and consequently does not allow us to consider more detailed patterns of development in the field of quantitative and qualitative changes of demand and production techniques. Furthermore it must be based on a wide range of studies related to respective exogenous variables and parameters which have to be determined autonomously (i.e., outside the model itself).

The aim of this model is to show the impact of variables related to agriculture (the volume of output, intensity of outlays, the level of agricultural incomes, and the pattern of consumption of rural population) on the overall path of economic development as expressed by the rate of growth and structural interbranch proportions.

The model is based on the following assumptions:[27]

1. The national economy is subdivided into n sectors $(i, j = 1, 2, \ldots, n)$, one of which is agriculture.
2. The variables are considered separately for particular subperiods of a multiperiod plan $(t = 1, 2, \ldots, T)$.
3. Intermediate demand is determined by intersectoral input-output coefficients a_{ij}^t which are exogenously set separately for all the subperiods; these coefficients express inputs from internal production and imports.
4. Intermediate imports are treated as linearly dependent on the volume of internal gross output; this relationship is expressed by respective coefficients m_i^{rt} determined separately for foreign markets $(r = 1, 2, \ldots, R)$.
5. Investment demand is explained in a twofold manner: partly as a linear function of the net increase in capital stock and partly as a linear function of replacement needs. Initial capital stock, for $t=1$, is given; for $t = 2, 3, \ldots, T$ it is a linear function of gross output with capital-output coefficients of the type b_{ij}^t; replacement demand is a linear function of initial stock in the period in question.
6. Personal consumption demand is treated as a linear function of consumers' incomes; its sectoral pattern is determined by varying structural coefficients which are set separately for several groups of income earners (farmers and agricultural workers are one

---

27. A complete list of variables and parameters is given in the appendix.

group); consumers' incomes are considered as linearly dependent on the respective volumes of gross outputs (with predetermined wage-intensity coefficients).

7. Export demand (on respective foreign markets) is determined in a twofold manner: its total volume by exogenously assumed maximal feasible rate of growth, its sectoral pattern by exogenously set structural coefficients (which are introduced in some variants).

8. Remaining domestic final demand volumes (collective consumption, nonproductive investment, changes in inventories) are treated as exogenous variables.

9. Final imports are taken as linear functions of foreign exchange surplus, which results from export earnings and intermediate import outlays.

10. The demand for labor, dependent on the volume of output, must be smaller than (or equal to) a predetermined quota of supply.

11. An annual rate of growth of real consumers' incomes (corresponding to consumption, as explained in 6) must not be smaller than a predetermined postulated rate.

With these assumptions the model is formulated as a linear programming model with an objective function which postulates maximization of the sum total of consumers' real income (over all the subperiods considered in the plan) and a set of constraints which express (a) output balances for respective sectors and subperiods, (b) labor balances for a number of labor categories in each subperiod, and (c) postulated rate of growth of consumers' real income.

Taking into consideration assumed equality of consumers' income with the volume of personal consumption, it may be stated that the model postulates maximization of GNP as investments are functionally dependent on consumption and the remaining items of domestic final demand are exogenously given.

Using the notations presented in the appendix, we have the following formulation of the model:

Objective function, F:

$$F = \sum_{t=1}^{T} \sum_{w=1}^{W} \left(\sum_{i=1}^{n} P_i^{wt} P_i^t + J^{wt} \right) \quad \text{(a maximum)} \quad (1)$$

Constraints:

$$P_i^t + \sum_{r=1}^{R} m_i^{rt} P_i^t - \sum_{j=1}^{n} a_{ij}^t P_j^t - C_i^t \left(\sum_{j=1}^{n} b_{ij}^{t+1} P_j^{t+1} - \sum_{j=1}^{n} b_{ij}^t P_j^t \right) \quad (2)$$

$$- \sum_{j=1}^{n} V_{ij}^t b_{ij}^t P_{ij}^t - \sum_{w=1}^{W} f_i^{wt} \left(\sum_{j=1}^{n} P_j^{wt} P_j^t + J^{wt} \right)$$

$$- \sum_{r=1}^{R} \sum_{g=1}^{G} h_i^{ergt} E^{rgt}$$

$$+ \sum_{r=1}^{R} \frac{h_i^{mrt}}{D^{mrt}} \left(\sum_{g=1}^{G} D^{ergt} E^{rgt} - H^{rt} - \sum_{j=1}^{n} d^{mrt} m_j^{rt} P_j^t \right) = F_i^t$$

Constraints (2) express the necessity of internal consistency in the form of output balances. They are formulated for each sector and time period (i.e., assuming a classification of 10 sectors and 5 subperiods). We have 50 constraints of this type. They read as follows: output + intermediate imports - intermediate demand - investment demand for net increase of stocks - investment replacement demand - personal consumption demand - export + final imports = remaining domestic demand. Investment demand elements are formulated in a different way for t=1 and t=T because for the first subperiod exogenous estimates of initial stock must be introduced instead of $\sum_j b_{ij} P_j$, whereas for the last subperiod it is necessary to introduce an exogenous "terminal condition" for the rate of increase of stocks beyond the plan horizon.

Further on we assume that output of the agricultural sector is exogenously determined for the consecutive subperiods, which also means that (a) demand related to agricultural output (i.e., material inputs from other sectors, investment demand, and personal consumption demand related to agricultural income) will be exogenously determined and their level will depend on the respective coefficients; (b) exports as well as both categories of imports (intermediate and final) will be treated as separate endogenous variables (i.e., they will be excluded from the elements of equation 2 determined by coefficients m_i^{rt}, E^{rgt} and the last item pertaining to final imports, and they will be introduced as separate items into equation 2); and (c) demand for agricultural labor will be exogenous, depending on the level of assumed labor inputs intensity.

Consequently the next type of constraints (labor balances) can be formulated as follows:

$$\sum_{j=1}^{n-1} z_{kj}^t P_j^t < L_k^t - z_{kn}^t P_n^t \tag{3}$$

which pertain to the respective labor categories. We assume here that for agriculture j = n.

For exports:

$$\sum_{g=1}^{G} E^{rgt} < E^{ro} (1+i_r)^t \tag{4}$$

which depends on the estimates of external demand (as expressed with the feasible rates of growth i_r).

For consumers' real income:

$$\sum_{w=1}^{W} \left(\sum_{i=1}^{n} P_i^{wt} P_i^t + J^{wt} \right) \geq S^o (1+i)^t \tag{5}$$

in which parts of income related to agriculture (i.e., for i=n) as well as secondary incomes (J^{wt}) will be exogenous depending on the assumptions concerning income distribution policy.

This model is of a size feasible from the computational point of view.

With an assumption of 10 sectors, 5 subperiods, 3 categories of labor, 3 foreign markets, and 3 variants of export structure we have the following number of constraints and variables.

Constraints:

> 50 output balances (type 2 constraints)
> 15 labor balances (type 3 constraints)
> 10 export demand constraints (type 4 constraints)
> <u>5</u> income rate of growth constraints (type 5 constraints)

Total <u>80</u>

Variables (endogenous):

> 45 sectoral outputs
> 45 export levels (except agriculture)
> 5 agricultural net exports
> <u>5</u> agricultural net imports

Total <u>100</u>

The number of endogenous variables can be increased by means of introducing additional variants of export patterns and separate variants of output variables differing from the point of view of production techniques (i.e., input coefficients) as well as input-output relations. In addition, personal consumption demand can be expressed in this model not only by means of structural coefficients related to various groups of consumers but two or three variants of such structural coefficients can be introduced. Such variants would correspond to a range of feasible changes in consumption patterns which could result from specific policies pertaining to market prices.[28]

It is necessary to point out that this model is not supposed to give an ultimate and final solution which would be considered as the optimal one. One of its main advantages seems to lie in the possibilities to study possible consequences of various assumptions related to (a) feasible rate of growth of agricultural output, (b) outlays considered as necessary in order to have this output, and (c) estimated shifts in employment and income distribution between agriculture and other sectors. Using a comprehensive but highly aggregated model, it is possible to trace down such consequences to all respective sectors and subperiods considered in the model.

It can be intuitively felt that the feasible maximal rate of growth of national income will depend, among others, on the feasible rate of growth of agricultural output and on the amount of outlays necessary for that purpose in relation to the elasticity of demand for agricultural products and to the balance of payments constraints. By means of this model it is possible, however, to get approximate quantitative characteristics of such interdependencies.

---

28. Experiments are made with a similar model, which also takes into consideration some variants of market pricing policies. This direction of work is not directly related to the main subject of this note.

The relevance of such an analysis will depend very much on the quality of all exogenous variables and parameters. At the same time it is hardly possible to make meaningful estimates of these variables and parameters without going into more detailed specification of sectors. Consequently other and simpler models are used at earlier stages of analysis in which a more detailed specification of variables is introduced at the cost of limiting their scope only to the terminal year with a comparison with the base year (or to the increments of some variables over the five-year period). The estimates of exogenous variables and of various coefficients are made within this approach on the basis of input-output statistics and of the information included in sectoral programs and other studies which are prepared according to a multilevel planning procedure.

APPENDIX 1

Symbols used in the model have the following meanings.

Variables (all superscripts t refer to a respective time period):

P_i^t = gross output of sector i (for $i, j, = 1, 2, \ldots, n$)

E^{rgt} = total volume of exports (in internal prices) for the foreign market r with a variant of structure g (this variable does not include agricultural exports)

J^{wt} = net amount of secondary incomes for a group of consumers w

H^{rt} = net exports (at foreign exchange prices) on the market r

F_i^t = remaining domestic final demand items (including collective consumption, nonproductive investment, and change in inventories)

L_k^t = supply of labor in category k

E_n^{rt} = net exports of agricultural products for market r (this variable as well as the next one will appear only in the balance for the agricultural sector—it has been omitted in the general formulation of the model)

M_n^{rt} = net import of agricultural products from market r

Data:

E^{ro} = initial volume of export (in internal prices) in the base period (t=o)

S^o = volume of personal consumption in the base period

Parameters:

a_{ij}^t = input-output coefficients

m_i^{rt} = coefficients representing ratios of intermediate imports of i to gross output in the same sector

b_{ij}^{t} = capital-output coefficients related to capital stock of origin i

c_i^{t} = ratio of investment outlays to the increase of stocks

v_{ij}^{t} = ratio of replacement to the initial stock of capital

p_i^{wt} = ratio of personal income (in consumer group w) accrued in a sector i to the gross output in the same sector

f_i^{wt} = share of i in the consumption expenditure of group w

h_i^{ergt} = share of exports of i in the total volume of exports for market r within variant g

h_i^{mrt} = share of final imports of i from the market r in the total outlays determined by a surplus of exports over intermediate imports and postulated net earnings

D^{mrt} = average ratio of foreign exchange value to internal value of final imports from the market r

D^{ergt} = average ratio of foreign exchange to internal prices for exports to market r in variant g

d_j^{mrt} = ratio of foreign exchange to internal prices for intermediate imports of j from the market r

z_{kj}^{t} = labor-input coefficients related to labor category k

i_r = estimated feasible rate of increase for exports to the market r

i = postulated rate of growth of personal real income

APPENDIX 2

The stock of information may be characterized as follows.

1. *Agricultural area.* The annual inventories provide the information on the size and structure of agricultural area.
2. *Yields per hectare.* Public Crop Inspection (Panstwowa Inspekcja Plonow) through its net of informants has the possibility to estimate the level and dynamics of yields.
3. *Livestock.* The annual inventories of livestock give the information in this respect.
4. *Animal production.* Data concerning the unit livestock productivity are based on estimates. The bulk of these products are bought by the State and cooperatives and this facilitates the respective estimates. The fact that the state and cooperative organizations are buying up—in principle—the whole increment of animal production is of great importance. Thanks to that, comparatively accurate determination of the dynamics of animal production is possible.
5. *Supply of production means.* Production means are manufactured by the state industry and are sold by the state and cooperative trade organizations. This makes it possible to get an accurate picture of the magnitude of the supplies.
6. *Agricultural investments.* A great part of the investments in peasant

farms is realized by the state and cooperative organizations, and detailed statistics in this respect are available. Basing the information on the sale of building materials and machines makes it possible to determine the outlays of investments undertaken directly by the peasants.

7. *Technological progress.* The State Agricultural Service has detailed data on the realization of particular undertakings concerning the generalization of agricultural knowledge and technological changes.

Much less information is available on particular relations characterizing the effectiveness of techniques applied in agriculture, such as:

1. *Technical effectiveness of using fertilizers.* The institutes and interregional experiment stations have some information in this respect, but it is not sufficiently representative. Such data therefore cannot characterize the relations appearing in peasant agriculture at a macro scale.
2. *The effectiveness of feed consumption.* The macroeconomic relations between total consumption of feeds and the obtained animal production are known. The information at the disposal of the institutes and data derived from about 1,500 farms, keeping the agricultural accounts on the effectiveness of the consumption of particular sorts of feeds by particular animals, are representative of the agriculture as a whole only to a relatively small degree. The indices of the effectiveness of feeds used in planning therefore are based on estimates.
3. *Capital intensity of the development of production of particular agricultural products.* Studies in this field have only been initiated.
4. *The rates of crop substitution obtained with the change of agricultural pattern.* Since those relations vary in time and space, the possibility to get appropriate data is limited.

To construct a model for planning purposes at a macro scale requires a large stock of information. To collect such information is a task exceeding the capabilities of Public Statistic and Administrative Agencies. If adequately representative data are to be obtained, it is necessary to initiate studies on a large scale. Such studies cannot be limited to experimental fields of the research institutes. They have to take into consideration real conditions of peasant farms and the level of technical knowledge of farmers.

REFERENCES

1. Castro, Josue. The Geography of Hunger. Boston, 1952.
2. Herer, W. Coefficient de Capital et Croissance Economique. *Econ. Rur.*, vol. 72.
3. Kalecki, M. *Zarys Teorii Wzrostu Gospodarki Soczalistycznej* [An Outline of the Theory of Growth of the Socialist Economy]. Warsaw: Gospodarka Planowa, 1963. P. 18.
4. ———. *Zogadnienie Optynalnej Struktury Spozycia* [The Problem of Optimal Structure of Consumption]. Warsaw: Gospodarka Planowa, 1963.

Chapter 22 ☜☞ DISCUSSION

Gerald W. Dean, *University of California* (U.S.A.)

T HE PAPER by Herer and Porwit can be divided into three rather
distinct parts. Sections I through XI, part I, sketch a theory of
economic development under socialism, emphasizing the importance of the agricultural sector. Section XII, part I, contains a brief description of economic planning in the agricultural sector of Poland as it
is actually done at present (i.e., without use of formal mathematical
models). Part II describes a multisector, multiperiod linear programming model which apparently is a possible tool to be used in Polish
economy-wide planning in the future. The three parts of the paper appear to be rather independent. Specifically, it is not clear how the theoretical economic growth model in the first part of the paper guides the
actual and potential planning procedures described in the later portions
of the paper. Each of the three main sections will be discussed in turn.

The growth theory sketched in the first part of the paper is apparently inspired by the general theory of economic growth developed by
Kalecki. It is unfortunate that this theory does not appear to be available
in English, particularly in view of the assessment by Zauberman in his
review article (14, p. 411) that Kalecki's work represents the first systematic attempt at the formulation of a general theory of growth for a
Socialist economy. According to Zauberman, the Kalecki model is two-
sectoral, formed of an investment-goods sector and a noninvestment
goods sector. Each sector's growth rate follows a fundamental equation
of the form shown by Herer where the capital/output ratio (m) differs by
sector, but where the "independent improvement of the system" parameter (u) and the depreciation parameter (a) are constant for both sectors.
Herer appears to revise Kalecki's framework to a two-sector model of
"agriculture" and "nonagriculture" (although the "nonagriculture" equation does not appear explicitly), with the added refinement that the parameters u and a are specific to each sector.

To the extent possible, it is interesting to compare the assumptions
and policy conclusions of Herer's theory with two-sector models (agriculture, nonagriculture) more familiar to Western economists, such as
the well-known Ranis and Fei (11) theory. Starting from the policy conclusions, the Herer model seems to place greater importance on the necessity for rapid absolute growth of agricultural output, hence of heavy
agricultural investments during the "takeoff" period for a developing
country. While the Ranis-Fei model stresses "balanced" investment between agriculture and industry, the Herer model seems to imply emphasizing investment in agriculture since "the rate of growth of agricultural
produce largely determines the feasible rate of growth of national income.

This difference in emphasis can be traced primarily to some differences in basic assumptions. Both theories start from the assumption of "unlimited labor" in agriculture at a low stage of development; that is, a zero or near zero marginal productivity of labor in agriculture. However the Herer model adds three critical assumptions that are not contained in Ranis and Fei: (a) per capita consumption of agricultural products cannot decline during the development process, (b) per capita consumption of agricultural products is higher in industry than in agriculture $(C_{ai} > C_{aa})$, and (c) every worker shifted from agriculture to industry must be fed at the higher industry level.[29] Specifically, during Phase I of their model (marginal physical product of labor in agriculture = 0), Ranis and Fei can transfer workers from agriculture to industry and begin industrial growth without any increase in agricultural output, hence no new net investment or technological change in agriculture; unproductive agricultural workers shifted to industry are simply fed at the same rate as if they were still in agriculture. On the other hand, the Herer model requires an upward shift in the agricultural production function (upward shift in agricultural productivity per worker) to feed at a higher level the agricultural workers shifted to industry. This upward shift can be accomplished by more investment (I_a), by upward shifts in the independent improvement u factor, by depleting the capital stock in agriculture (reducing depreciation a), or by some combination of these. By implication, Herer assumes that new investment will carry an important load in this process.

At a certain point, sufficient labor will be withdrawn from agriculture to lower total agricultural product. That is, the MPP of labor in agriculture becomes positive and Ranis and Fei's Phase II of development begins. Obviously, if the agricultural production function is static and no agricultural products are imported (both Ranis and Fei and Herer use the closed economy assumption), average consumption of agricultural products must decline. Thus there is a substitution in consumption of industrial for agricultural goods. In the Herer model this is ruled out by assumption for a developing country, presumably because food consumption is already at an irreducible nutritional (or political) minimum. Once again, therefore, Herer finds it an absolute necessity to shift the agricultural production function through new agricultural capital investment. Of course Ranis and Fei also stress the necessity of agricultural investment if the rising relative prices of agricultural products due to falling agricultural output are not to bring the growth process to a premature halt. However the Herer requirement of an earlier and heavier agricultural investment seems clearly traceable to the food consumption assumption.

The consistency of Herer's food consumption assumption with planning practice can be questioned. Many countries, both socialist and

---

29. However at one point in Herer's paper this assumption appears to be violated; ΔZ is defined as manpower increase in industry without additional increase in agricultural produce. Only the "additional" amount of labor transferred from agriculture to industry $(\Delta Z')$ is required to be fed at the higher industrial rate (C_{ai}).

nonsocialist, have consciously taken the decision to sacrifice current consumption in agriculture (lower C_{aa}) in order to increase the amount of investment in industry at an early stage of development.

The ideal situation clearly would be one in which the agricultural production function could be shifted rapidly upward through independent technological progress (the u factor) with a minimum of new investment (I_a). Although these two factors appear as independent variables in the basic Kalecki growth equation, they are obviously highly related.[30] Herer recognizes this interdependence when he stresses that "it is necessary to couple development of investment with extension of agricultural knowledge. The two processes must be closely coordinated. If the knowledge of agricultural techniques lags behind the development of productive investment, then the effects of investment outlays in agriculture will be inevitably reduced." Perhaps even more emphasis should be placed on the importance of combining these u factors with investment in order to shift the agricultural production function. For example, Herer's statement of frequent increasing marginal returns from fertilizer investment mentions no other inputs; yet if this statement is to have widespread application, it certainly presupposes use of complementary inputs, including knowledge. Johnson (5), Moseman (9), Mosher (10), and others with widespread experience in developing countries repeatedly stress the importance of a "package program" of complementary inputs if investment in agriculture is to have a favorable capital/output ratio. The question might also be raised as to whether the u factor includes structural changes such as changes in farm sizes which would directly and perhaps drastically affect the capital/output ratio (m).

A further important difference between the Ranis-Fei and Herer models concerns the relationship of labor productivity and wages in agriculture at a later stage of development. At the "commercialization" point (start of Phase III) of the Ranis-Fei model, a sufficient number of workers have been shifted from agriculture to industry to raise the MPP of agricultural labor to the institutional wage. After this point, disguised unemployment in agriculture is eliminated and marginal productivity equals the real wage rate in agriculture. In these terms, Herer's developed countries never reach Phase III's "commercialized" agriculture. He stresses that agricultural productivity grows relatively slowly in the agricultural sector, but that wage rates tend to be equalized between agriculture and industry. Hence the marginal productivity of labor in agriculture appears to remain permanently less than the real wage rate paid: "Maximized income can be distributed between the agricultural and nonagricultural sectors according to the criteria of social justice, without relation to the rate of productivity increase." Obviously this difference in the two theories arises from the different form of economic system hypothesized (socialism versus capitalism).

However this "permanent" and apparently rising gap between agri-

---

30. Zauberman (14, p. 414) also stresses the probable positive correlation between net investment (I) and the depreciation parameter (a).

cultural labor productivity and wages raises several questions. Herer characterizes developed countries as those with an "absence of manpower reserves in agriculture," and whose goal is "maximizing the rate of growth of the consumed portion of the national income." These statements appear inconsistent with the gap between productivity and wages in agriculture. If productivity in agriculture is below wages paid, then an "absence of manpower reserves in agriculture" means only that unemployment is disguised rather than open.[31] Further, if the MPP in agriculture is lower than in industry, a shift of workers to industry could raise national income; therefore national income is not being maximized. Thus, as Herer recognizes elsewhere, there is a "cost" involved in the equalization of wage rate increases between agriculture and industry. Two other questions might be raised for further discussion: (a) With productivity independent of wages, what incentives or motivations do workers have to be efficient? (b) How are reallocations of labor effected between agriculture and industry? For example, may not workers with low productivity be content to remain in agriculture so long as wages are relatively high?

Finally, the role of prices in Herer's theory raises other questions: (a) If the state and cooperative trade monopolies maintain artificially low producer prices relative to retail prices, is there a negative supply response to price from peasant farms? If so, this would place ever greater pressure on technological change and agricultural investment outlays to maintain food supplies. (b) Since the idea of "optimization of the structure of consumption" requires relative prices of different categories of products, are market prices distorted by government policy used in this calculation, or are market prices replaced by some concept of shadow or accounting prices? (c) Is agricultural marginal value productivity computed using the artificially low agricultural prices received or using higher accounting prices? (Use of the former might explain part of the low productivity in agriculture.)

I hope the above comments may serve to initiate some further discussion of the interesting growth theory sketched out in the first part of the Herer-Porwit paper.

We turn now to the later two sections of the paper dealing with current agricultural five-year planning practice in Poland (section XII, part I) and with a proposed five-year mathematical programming model (part II). The first point to be recognized is that the latter is not a direct substitute for the former. The two planning schemes might be put in perspective by considering the following planning phases: I. Macroeconomic plans; II. Sector plans including intrasector plans and intersector plans; and III. Project (including firm plans) and regional plans.

Briefly, following Tinbergen (12), the function of step I is to determine politically the desired time paths of the key *macroeconomic* variables of savings and investment, and consequently, via the aggregate

---

31. Zauberman (14, p. 420) in discussing Kalecki's theory, states that "the position throughout the industrialization era could be described as in a sense one of successive disguised unemployment equilibria."

capital/output ratio, of national income. *Sector* planning might be usefully considered in two phases. First, an aggregate intrasector plan is
developed for each sector independently (such as for agriculture). Final
demands or desired output levels for the sector's products are determined, followed by estimates of the labor, investment, and intermediate
goods from other sectors required to support those levels of final products. Next, an intersector comparison is required to check the consistency of the independent sector plans. Consistency could be approximated by national aggregations and subsequent sector adjustments of the
major resources (including capital investment) and of the most important final and intermediate products. Or this phase could be done more
formally employing input-output analysis to estimate sector outputs consistent with a final bill of goods. The role of project planning involves
detailed technological and economic investigations to develop a stock of
relevant investment alternatives, formulated by *region* in cases where
specific regional as well as national objectives are included in the overall economic plan.

In terms of the above scheme, the five-year planning procedure described by Herer is primarily an aggregate intrasector plan for agriculture. The allocations of investment funds and foreign exchange for use
by the agricultural sector are apparently made at the level of the macroeconomic plan and handed down to the agricultural planners as constants.
Given this amount of investment and foreign exchange, aggregate demand
and supply balances are made for each agricultural product. There is
no discussion of how more detailed project and regional plans are used
in developing the aggregates for the agricultural sector. Furthermore
there is no indication of how consistency with other sectors is achieved.
While the paper claims to provide "a brief review of the whole process
of plan construction," it omits any discussion of feedback and successive
revision among planning levels. Suppose that detailed project evaluation
in the agriculture sector showed that extremely high returns on investment were being foregone because of a shortage of capital, while another
sector showed few favorable projects. Would not this information be
passed on to the macroeconomic planners, leading to an adjustment of
the original sectoral investment allocations and, in turn, requiring subsequent sector replanning?

Most planners stress the necessity of successive approximation of
iterative procedures among planning levels before a final consistent plan
is reached.[32] While a close interrelationship among planning levels is
implied in the introduction to the paper, there is little evidence of such
a process in the later description. This point might prove an interesting
focus for further clarification and discussion.

The discussion of "transmission of planned targets to individual peasant farms" raises other points. Although major capital investments are
under state control, the use of new inputs such as fertilizer is voluntary

---

32. For example, see the articles by Tinbergen (12), Chenery (3), Malinvaud (8), and
Kornai (7).

and must be induced by providing credit and fixing low purchase prices. Experience has shown that in some peasant economies fertilizer or other improved practices must promise an extremely high ratio (perhaps 2:1 to 4:1) of marginal return to marginal cost before farmers will adopt them. How does this compare with the experience in Poland, and do price and credit policies alone provide sufficient leverage to induce desired levels of fertilizer use? Second, given the importance of the transfer of labor from agriculture to industry implied by the growth theory in the first part of the paper, it is somewhat surprising to find that "the impact of planning in this field is rather limited." Since labor transfers from agriculture to industry are important for countries at all stages of development and under different economic systems, it would be interesting to hear more about Poland's programs and problems in this area.

Turning from actual planning techniques to the proposed linear programming model, it is clear that the latter is not a direct substitute for the former since it is primarily an intersector model which likely would be under the control of the macroeconomic planners. In terms of central planning it is a fairly elegant model, inasmuch as it simultaneously (a) guarantees intersector consistency and (b) optimizes, rather than takes as given, certain of the macroeconomic parameters such as savings, timing and sectoral distribution of investment, and growth of national income (subject to certain restraints, e.g., minimum levels and desired distributions of consumption). While the model is to be used to evaluate the impact of particular agricultural policies and parameters on the entire economic system, the model could be used for similar analyses emphasizing other sectors. Thus the scope of policy evaluations conceptually possible with such a model far exceeds those pertaining to agriculture alone.

Once again there is the question of how this intersectoral model is to be coordinated with more detailed project and regional plans within the agricultural sector. Will use of more formal tools of planning at the macro level be matched by similar tools at lower levels? It is easy to imagine, for example, a fairly disaggregated model of the agricultural sector, with regional and temporal (say five-year) subdivisions, designed to allocate investment, extension effort, fertilizer supplies, labor transfers, and so on, in an optimal way within agriculture. The aggregate results of this model could then be fed into the intersectoral model described in the paper. Are such ambitious models more than a glint in the planner's eye at this stage?

We consider now several technical aspects of the linear programming model proposed. The model maximizes the undiscounted total of consumers' real income over five periods, subject (in addition to technological restraints) to minimum consumption each year and an "exogenous 'terminal condition' for the rate of increase of stocks beyond the plan horizon." In view of the lack of agreement on appropriate preference functions in the literature on optimal growth models, it is surprising that there is no justification of the objective function selected. Since the time horizon for such models is logically infinite, the only practical approach is to employ a finite-horizon model with explicit stipulations on the terminal conditions. However within this category many alternatives remain. Chakravarty (1, p. 160-66) distinguishes two main categories of preference functions for finite-horizon models: (a) where all nonzero variables in the objective function pertain to the terminal situation (fifth year in our case), thus ignoring the attractiveness of the time path that leads to that end configuration; (b) where nonzero variables enter the objective function each year, permitting a scalar number to be assigned to each time profile of consumption so that the attractiveness of alternative time paths is considered.

I would agree with Porwit's choice of a model which falls in the second category. However the decision not to discount future consumption should be defended. There are at least two possible justifications for discounting consumption. First, assuming diminishing marginal utility of consumption, and growth in absolute consumption levels over time, marginal consumption increases in the future should receive less weight than marginal consumption increases at present. Second, a time discount could be applied to favor the current generation over a future generation, even if both generations should be consuming at equal levels. While some economists consider the second discount ethically indefensible, many would agree on some form of the first, even though it is not unambiguous in that utilities of different people at different times are being compared. Actually a case for Porwit's preference function could be made on three grounds: (a) the time horizon is short (five years), (b) a rising minimum consumption is specified each year, and (c) lower income classes are given special consideration. Presumably the latter two assumptions would be determined by planner's or political preferences. Selection of the minimum consumption levels each year appears critical, since it seems likely that without discounting the programming solution will show consumption equal to the minimum specified in every year except the last.

Chakravarty (1, p. 162) points out that there is nothing in the logic of economic analysis which dictates what the terminal conditions should be. However he proposes a simple method for working out, under specific assumptions, the levels of capital stocks required in the final year to insure output growth at chosen rates r_i for i sectors for period $t > T$, where T is the final year of the plan. It should be recognized that the minimum consumption levels and terminal conditions chosen may be inconsistent; that is, there may be no solution to the linear programming problem which satisfies both conditions. Thus preferences may need to be restated. Discussing the difficulty of selecting a single preference function, Koopmans (6, p. 10), quoting Malinvaud, suggests that "pertinent ethical judgments are perhaps more easily called forth by a comparison of the optimal growth paths implicit in alternative utility functions than by a direct and prioristic comparison of these utility functions." This would suggest solving aggregate programming models with several plausible alternative objective functions and terminal conditions and letting the final choice among such programs be made from direct study of the resulting growth paths. Cocks and Carter (4) have experimented with this idea for growth models at the micro level.

A final question regards the use of a completely deterministic model in the context of changing and highly uncertain economic relationships, particularly over a time period of several years. Because of the high degree of uncertainty, some economists (3, p. 410) have even expressed doubt about the wisdom of trying to make programming models more dynamic. However I am attracted by the various attempts to treat risk explicitly in dynamic linear programming problems. Ideally we would like to find the probability distribution of the objective function given probability distributions of the a_{ij}, b_i, and c_j coefficients. (Planner's subjective probabilities may be required where there are no objective data for estimating probability distributions of various coefficients.) Given these probabilities the probability distribution of the objective function can be approximated, perhaps using the methods of stochastic linear programming. Tintner and Raghavan (13) have demonstrated this approach using data for one of India's five-year plans.

For practical computational purposes, however, the use of stochastic programming appears to be limited to models with a much higher degree of aggregation than the one proposed by Porwit. This leads to a discussion of a number of halfway measures, none of which is completely satisfactory but which may be quite helpful in specific cases. Perhaps the best-known method for treating uncertainty is some form of sensitivity analysis. Porwit may have this type of approach in mind when he talks of testing out the effects of various values of exogenous variables. Other approaches involve reducing the probability that the programming solution will subsequently turn out to be infeasible, such as using "conservative" coefficients or, more formally, chance-constrained programming as suggested by Charnes and Cooper (2). Still another approach may be simulation, where deterministic linear programming solutions are used to suggest efficient decision rules for further testing by simulation. In some cases linear programming can be used to carry out various "runs" of the simulation process. A further discussion of experience with these and other methods of approaching risk and uncertainty would be useful.

My comments on this very stimulating paper are not intended as criticism; rather they are possible points for further clarification and discussion.

REFERENCES

1. Chakravarty, S. Alternative Preference Functions in Problems of Investment Planning on the National Level. In *Activity Analysis in the Theory of Growth and Planning*, ed. E. Malinvaud and M. O. L. Bacharach. New York: Macmillan, 1967. Ch. 6.
2. Charnes, A., and W. W. Cooper. Chance Constrained Programming. *Management Sci.*, vol. 6.

3. Chenery, Hollis B. Approaches to Development Planning. In *Problems in Economic Development*, ed. E. A. G. Robinson. New York: Macmillan, 1965. Ch. 23.

4. Cocks, K. D., and H. O. Carter. Micro Goal Functions and Economic Planning. *Am. J. Agr. Econ.*, vol. 50.

5. Johnson, Sherman E. Combining Knowledge, Incentives, and Means to Accelerate Agricultural Development. In *Economic Development of Agriculture*, Center Agr. Econ. Dev. Ames: Iowa State Univ. Press, 1965. Pp. 209-23.

6. Koopmans, Tjalling. Objectives, Constraints, and Outcomes in Optimal Growth Models. *Econometrica*, vol. 35.

7. Kornai, J. Mathematical Programming of Long-Term Plans in Hungary. In *Activity Analysis in the Theory of Growth and Planning*, ed. E. Malinvaud and M. O. L. Bacharach. New York: Macmillan, 1967. Ch. 8.

8. Malinvaud, E. Decentralized Procedures for Planning. In *Activity Analysis in the Theory of Growth and Planning*, ed. E. Malinvaud and M. O. L. Bacharach. New York: Macmillan, 1967. Ch. 7.

9. Moseman, Albert H. Research Needed for Technological Knowledge in Agricultural Development. In *Economic Development of Agriculture*, Center Agr. Econ. Dev. Ames: Iowa State Univ. Press, 1965. Pp. 224-37.

10. Mosher, A. T. Research Needed on the Development Process for Agriculture. In *Economic Development of Agriculture*, Center Agr. Econ. Dev. Ames: Iowa State Univ. Press, 1965. Pp. 238-45.

11. Ranis, G., and J. C. H. Fei. A Theory of Economic Development. *Am. Econ. Rev.*, vol. 51.

12. Tinbergen, J. Single Devices for Development Planning. In *Problems in Economic Development*, ed. E. A. G. Robinson. New York: Macmillan, 1965. Ch. 22.

13. Tintner, G., and N. S. Raghavan. Stochastic Linear Programming Applied to a Dynamic Planning Model for India. Unpubl. Ms., 1968.

14. Zauberman, A. A Few Remarks on Kalecki's Theory of Economic Growth Under Socialism. *Kyklos*, vol. 19.

J. C. Tirel, *Center for Rural Economic Study*
(France)

I DO NOT INTEND in this paper to give a perfect analysis of problems dealing with use of models for agriculture as a whole. More-. over I think that because of delay between research work and the disposal of printed matter, seminar meetings give us opportunities to complete this formation in an extensive way and to amend some provisional opinions. From another viewpoint, it seems unreasonable to me to give details in this paper on the mathematical structure of each model (deep analysis of them has been, or will be soon, published). Also, it has been planned that during this seminar various people will present national models. Hence I will limit my task by referring only to principles of alternative models and suggesting their possibilities and their limitations.

In planning economies at the national level in some countries, agriculture has always been treated in a rather superficial manner. In the economic growth process, agriculture has often been regarded as a residue, holding a potential supply of resources such as labor and thus enabling development of other industries. Only a few parameters dealing with agriculture have been introduced in intersectorial models. Through this approach it has not been possible to derive from such models the information needed by policy makers to set up reliable programs for agriculture. Of course, as Tinbergen (39) stressed, economic policy must apply to the economy as a whole; but the given characteristics of some sectors, and the peculiar nature of measures which can be used by policy makers, make sectorial policies necessary. A main difficulty lies in giving full importance to the links existing between the studies sector and the other sectors.

The nature of quantitative policy as a rule requires that a model supply a picture of the existing or predicted state of agriculture, allowing an answer to the following questions: What changes may occur concerning some variables which cannot be directly controlled? What will be the most likely results of those changes on economic variables?

Generally discrepancies exist between actual or predicted situations as described by model and the desirable situation of policy targets. Hence it becomes necessary to test potential efficiency of alternative measures in view of the task of policy makers. According to the type of models being used, "comparative static" or "comparative dynamic" approaches can supply needed information for decision making. Of course, problems for policy makers are numerous. Day and Judge (10) suggested the following list:

431

1. Optimum levels of production of final and intermediate products in each country or region.
2. Optimum flows of primary (e.g., labor), intermediate, and final mobile commodities between regions within a country and between countries.
3. Optimum number, size, and location of agriculturally related firms.
4. Levels of regional prices and rents.
5. Surplus and deficit position of each region for each commodity.
6. The extent these solutions are dependent upon the existing structure of the agriculture farms, processing firms, marketing institutions.
7. Potential effects of a policy directed to changes of this structure.
8. Potential effects of a policy of trade control and aids (quotas, subsidies).
9. Effects on the balance of payment of alternative situations.
10. Differences between short, intermediate, and long-run optimum situations.
11. Economic consequences of different phenomena such as economic integration of countries, changes in level and location of population, and changes in economic policy of other countries.

As we shall see, different models have been suggested and applied to provide some solutions to these problems. Some of these models are of course inadequate and unable to supply more than general guidance. Others are surely too ambitious according to the level of knowledge and available data.

Day (11) suggested that any model used to solve agricultural production problems has to take into account the following aspects: the *interdependence* of outputs using common inputs; adjustment over *time; technological* change; planned or projected *policy action;* changes in both the *acreage* and *yield* components of field crop production; *uncertainty* on physical and economic results; *demand, supply,* and *price* interactions; aggregate supply of production *inputs;* rates of *investment* in factors fixed in the shortrun; and regional *specialization* and *competition.* If a model is to fulfill these conditions, many parameters are needed and it is clear that the main difficulties of application lie in reconciling the informative value of this model with the *actual possibility* to use it. In this possibility, allowance must be made for available data and for means and delay in gathering and processing information. A few years ago the limiting factor was computing facilities. This seems no longer true today. Solving processes exist and high-speed computers can solve most current problems. Following such change, there is a tendency to give up conventional statistical models and replace them by mathematical programming methods. The latter supply more flexibility in both target specification and the possibilities of increasing the number of mathematical relations in the models.

SOME GENERALITIES ABOUT CONVENTIONAL
REGRESSION MODELS

From an historic point of view, and considering the lack of available data and computing facilities, economists naturally first tried to build up very simple and general models. The agricultural economy was pictured by means of a few relations dealing with very large aggregates. Generally no more than one or two aggregates were used for production: total gross product or crop production and livestock production (as, for instance, in the Brookings model). In most of these models we find (a) an *aggregate production function* giving the value of agricultural gross product, (b) *investment functions* both for durable production commodities and consumption goods, (c) *demand functions* for agricultural products, and (d) import-export relations. In such general models the most critical point is setting up the supply function. Many different approaches have been suggested. The simplest one, of course, uses trend methods to obtain direct estimates of aggregates. The most serious deficiency in this approach is the assumption that effects of each parameter are the same over time—an assumption inconsistent with high rates of change observed in agriculture. Moreover opportunities of substitution between factors (labor-capital) and between products and the discrete character of some technical changes do not fit in this assumption. While trend methods are probably the main tools of economists working in prediction fields, it seems difficult to rely on sectorial coefficient values derived from these extrapolations, except in peculiar conditions and for short-run purposes.

Estimation of supply-price functions also is limited by some overwhelming statistical difficulties. As a matter of fact, in a long-run view, agricultural product supply is connected with technological change, the effects of which have to be explained. In a short-run view, supply is connected with *random weather parameters* which have to be measured. Concerning the last point, we mention an application by Griliches (17) to give an estimate of agricultural supply for the United States through a regression model including (a) level of agricultural prices, (b) a trend variable, (c) previous year's physical production, and (d) a weather index. Another approach is to introduce factor costs in the production function; in fact supply response results from changes in factor allocation implied by changes in prices of inputs.

Generally aggregate functions for agriculture explain physical production by variables relating to the quantities of the major factors (land, labor, capital-purchased commodities) used during the investigated period. Large freedom is left in the choice of the alternative type of mathematical function according to the structure of model, the available data, and the planning horizon. We may consider for instance that one unit of aggregate production needs a fixed quantity of each factor. It is then difficult to account for possible alterations of coefficients over time as technical advance and factor substitution occurs. More sophisticated functions such as the Cobb-Douglas function provide possibility of substitution; but when estimated from time series, these functions also have problems created by technical advance (which may be introduced by means of a trend variable), especially the statistical problems of autocorrelation and multicollinearity.

To avoid some statistical difficulties, other approaches have been tested, for instance by Solow (35). The function he suggested allows direct derivation of an annual rate of technical change using annual rate of production growth and changes occurring in the weight of different inputs. Production functions of constant elasticity of substitution types allow any type of input substitution and return to scale (5). While these functions represent an advance in the descriptive value of models, their estimation requires that time series of more detailed information be available.

In addition to production functions, investment functions are generally used. These relations define investment as a function of different parameters such as profit, liquidity, depreciation, costs, and prices. The effect of these parameters can be time-lagged. Indeed, investment deals with many different concepts depending on the nature, field, and term of decisions. But available time series do not allow estimation of functions including a great number of explanatory variables. Given deep alterations of the economy over time, the time series we consider must be rather short and only a few regression coefficients can be tested by statistical procedures. Moreover variables are seldom independent, and as in production functions, they involve multicollinearity phenomena and inconsistent regression coefficients.

Estimation of aggregated functions in models based on cross-section data enables us to avoid some disadvantages of time series data. Methods such as *factorial analysis* can be used for preliminary studies directed to facilitate choice of explanatory variables. Nevertheless difficulties still exist because of various interdependencies between farms and also because of aggregation problems raised by nonhomogeneity of physical and economic environments and structural conditions. We also encounter aggregation problems in analyzing programming models.

Generally sectorial regression models include some agricultural product demand relations. These intend to describe supply-demand interdependency or in other cases are designed to enable derivation of demand functions for different commodities. Relations are estimated on the basis of time series data for such parameters as income, expense, and prices, or on the basis of family budget data.

Interdependency between farm and nonfarm product demands implies use of constraints conforming to consumer behavior theory. Estimation of such relations also involves difficulty. In a complete market model, particular estimation procedures must be used for time series data since the same endogenous variables—prices and quantities—exist both in supply and demand functions. Frequently, since the series are short, the number of explanatory variables must be limited. Market models also raise the difficulties in supply function estimation mentioned pre-

viously. Finally the different demand equations may be mutually inconsistent. Nevertheless this approach based on market processes may be
very useful for solving special policy problems such as price stabiliza-
tion programs to maintain farm income. Difficulties involved by simultaneous specification of supply and demand functions encouraged estimates of an islated demand function for each product from time series or
family budget data. Estimation from time series data allows introduction
of dynamic aspects of consumer behavior but gives rise to risk of errors
and mutual inconsistency of demand equations. Wealth of data is an advantage of estimation from family budget. However this method does
not allow analysis of dynamic aspects such as changes in expense patterns.

A comparative evaluation of regression models against the other
types of methods is difficult. Many of both use exogenous data or relations which are specified by means of the same statistical procedures
and have common deficiencies. However a main criticism can be formulated about the general structure of models consisting of only regression equations. First *spatial* and *structural* features are not considered
in these models. This deficiency is important because agricultural supply depends on a spatial environment with heterogeneity of production
factors. Neither do regression models supply information about discrepancies between farms and regions, and nothing is said about what
these differences could be if alternative agricultural policies were
applied. Moreover problems of product-product and factor-product interrelations are not readily expressed in these aggregate relations. Assumptions on continuity and reversibility of some relations also sometimes prove inconsistent with actual conditions. For instance certain
policy measures may have discrete effects; also, for an intermediate-
run analysis, decision-making processes used by managers can be
changed if investments are made. But we must credit these models because of their compact structure and possibility of quick solution. Also
they can indicate tendencies and outline the main economic features, allowing discussions to be focused and guidance to be supplied rapidly on
further analysis.

INPUT-OUTPUT MODELS

Recently Sebestyen (33) indicated that interindustry analysis had
become a tool of everyday use in studies dealing with the past or with
short-term forecasts at the national level. By nature interindustry tables are a powerful means of investigation in the field of interrelations
of various sectors within an economy, and also in the field of interconnections of different regions within a country. Input-output analysis is
simple and had first published applications by Leontief (25) as far back
as 1936. Considered as an analytical tool, an input-output table gives a
detailed description of the insertion of any given industry in the national
(or regional) economy. Numerous applications of this analysis have

been made in various countries, for instance in preliminary stages of forecasting studies (1). Several countries are using detailed tables for agriculture.

Such a table can be used as a prediction in addition to a national (or regional) demand vector, in order to specify activity levels of each industry. Computers easily calculate the inverse coefficient matrix required, but the basic assumptions of the model present some limitations. These are related to the concept of constant input-output coefficients and to the nature of assumed production functions. So-called input-output coefficients do not reflect pure technical relationships, especially when a high level of aggregation is used in specifying industries. These coefficients are usable only if the technological environment is assumed to be unchanged, a condition expected to hold true only in a short-run view. Moreover industries are seldom homogeneous; any change affecting the structure of one necessarily implies alterations of its relations with others and also modifies coefficient values. Since we have to assume that industry structures remain approximately constant, we must limit the use of this model to a short-run framework. Use of constant coefficients eliminates possibilities of substitution between products from different industries. For instance, corn and barley are assumed to be supplied by two different industries, and thus would be considered as complementary for the milk industry. Inputs of corn and barley are maintained in a constant ratio while these feeds actually do substitute for each other according to their prices. Accordingly, as far as possible substitute products should be aggregated in specifying industries. While products are assumed to substitute perfectly within an industry, we should avoid aggregation of complementary products. Unfortunately agricultural economics shows that complementarity and substitutability concepts are only meaningful for a given *allocation* of factors and for a given *level* of production; two factors may be complementary for one product but substitutable for another, or they may be first complementary then substitutable within the same production process.

The matrix coefficients do not account for return-to-scale effects. But industry growth is not a homogeneous process; it implies establishment of new firms where returns to scale may be important. For example, when the poultry industry raises output by 30 percent, labor consumption does not increase in the same proportion. This is another reason that only short-run predictions can be based on the coefficients. The underlying restrictive assumptions of an interindustry table also limit its use as a closed model. Therefore final demand is usually generated by other methods and introduced as an exogenous variable into input-output models.

The breaking down of the economy into industries may be followed by spatial division, so interregional interdependency may be shown in addition to interindustry relations. Isard (24) suggested use of the concept for this purpose in 1951, and regional applications have been undertaken in various countries (6) within a national accounts framework.

Lack of statistical information on interregional flows in several countries is a difficulty impeding this approach. The nature of the model makes it well suited to interregional complementarity analysis but less useful for analysis of competition. For instance, it is difficult to measure how changes in supply relations of one region affect the output of others.

At the agricultural policy level, input-output analysis presents some advantages in specifying some interrelations existing between agricultural industries and also interdependencies between agriculture and the other sectors. One possible procedure consists of breaking down the national agricultural table while the other sectors are highly aggregated. Some applications along this line have been undertaken by several countries including Hungary. During the initial shaping of the national plan, analysis of annual tables including only a few industries can be used. It seems that the degree of aggregation does not greatly influence the tendencies over time for the main coefficients. Breaking down the agricultural sector into 32 industries has allowed a better analysis of some agricultural policy decisions; in this table the interindustry relations within agriculture, the flow of commodities from and to nonagricultural industries, and labor consumption are simultaneously described. Such a model presents both direct and indirect consumption of commodities needed for a given demand of final product and can be derived from the various interindustry tables.

An interesting aspect of the Hungarian studies is the attempt to complete input-output analysis undertaken at the national level with input-output analysis made at the farm level. One objective is to draw up a detailed input-output table for the agricultural cooperative sector from an accounting reports sample. (This procedure gives rise to some problems of adjusting and harmonizing the accounting systems in use with the values for representative cooperative farms.) Use of such a detailed agriculture table, in addition to the general interindustry table, may supply policy makers with useful information and improve their decisions.

SPATIAL EQUILIBRIUM MODELS

Spatial models using mathematical programming methods are usually divided into equilibrium models and activity analysis models. The main difference concerns the supply definition. In equilibrium models, exogenous price-supply relations are introduced. In activity analysis models, supply is defined within the programming model; the nature and size of production and investment activities are given according to constraints of resources and various farm limitations. Indeed, no clear-cut division can be made between the two types of models; for instance, some equilibrium models are designed with supply functions obtained through aggregation of results from representative farm programming models.

Static Equilibrium Models

The simplest of these models can be summarized as follows. Supply functions for each production region, demand relations for each consuming region, and transportation costs for each commodity and each pair of regions being determined, what are the optimum location and levels of supply and demand, and the optimum interregional flows and regional prices of products? The basic model can be altered through many ways. A processing sector may be included, several transportation systems can compete with each other or different types of demand relations may be introduced. Derivation of equilibrium conditions, under perfect competition assumptions, is possible through maximizing net surplus. This concept, suggested by Samuelson (30), corresponds to the area between demand and supply curves, deduction being made for intermediary (transportation and processing) costs.

When supply and demand relations are linear, the problem can be solved by quadratic programming procedures as Takayama and Judge suggested (38). An attractive aspect of these models consists of the spatial characteristics of the different aggregates. But previous definition of regional supply and demand relations (which gives rise to well-known difficulties) must be assumed. A central part of these models is of course a transportation problem. Good knowledge of costs is required for its application. Also we must assume that transportation managers are rational and well informed. Indeed, use of transportation programs offers possibilities to describe influence of comparative spatial situations; but as Bawden (2) indicates, transportation results give only general guidance and cannot be used as a basis for decisions for several reasons: transportation costs constitute a small part of total costs; knowledge is necessary about the real costs structure and about decision-making processes of conveyors; and interregional flows are closely dependent on one another. Therefore one error may alter the whole transportation pattern. These remarks apply only to static equilibrium models or to any static or dynamic model including a transportation program.

These models have often been applied for a single product or a group of products. In this form they are not very useful for agricultural sector analysis. But they also are used, in addition to other models, in placing results in broader framework, as for example, in the U.S. Department of Agriculture project. It includes recursive programming features to specify agricultural product supply. In France it is planned to use equilibrium models for analysis of transportation and processing sectors wherein supply functions will be derived from a general activity analysis model and parametric programming procedures.

Intertemporal Equilibrium Models

It may be noted that Judge and Takayama (37) have given a broad scope to their model in order to introduce both space and time characteristics. Introducing the time factor does not raise peculiar mathematical problems. Economic relations connected with time have qualities in common with spatial relations. The time periods serve as do regions, and storage is no more than transportation between periods. Judge and Takayama's model includes supply and demand defined as functions of regional prices and fixed transportation and storage costs. If these relations are linear ones, the problem can be solved by quadratic programming procedures. This model may deal with price adjustments over time, according to possibilities of product storages and product substitutions at the consumer level. Expressed in this way, the problem assumes perfect knowledge of the future, a condition perhaps inconsistent with prevailing economic uncertainty. Moreover the problem is defined for a definite period, thus implying certain difficulties and possible testing of the influence of period length. Schrimper suggested some adjustments in this model: discounting of the objective function to account for the fact that the expected surplus for the last period has practically no influence on current decisions; the restraining of time transfers accordingly; specifying storage location and use of storage costs expressed as a product price function. Concerning this first point, it seems that the additional information would be useful for regional investment policy makers. But if we consider the limited reliability of transportation program results, it is doubtful whether such added information would be significant. Concerning the use of storage cost-price functions, attention must be paid to implications concerning the additional complexity of models.

ACTIVITY ANALYSIS MODELS

We limit our survey in this section to some static activity analysis models. The basic model can be summarized as follows. The agricultural sector is divided into producing, processing, and consuming regions. Each is represented by one geographical point to facilitate the definition of interregional flows. The producing regions in turn are divided into producing unit subsets; a subset is usually defined by available fixed resources or by a benchmark farm structure. Within one subset homogeneous producing conditions are assumed. Potential activities, technological level, and comparative situation with regard to factors and product markets are the same therein for all farms. Producing, transporting, and processing activities are limited by linear restraints, specified either at firm level (use of resources, producing, or processing capacities) or at regional or interregional level (markets and factories supplying, production quota). The proper nature of models depends on the way in which demand is incorporated and consequently on the choice of the relevant objective function.

Some Applied Models

I. Completely inelastic demand model. These are the most usual models. The first models set up by Heady's team (18, 20, 21, 22), the first Swedish models (15), and the German (22) and Spanish (28) projects belong in this group. A given demand of each final product must be satisfied in each consuming region; the objective is defined as the least overall cost (production, transportation, and processing costs). The problem can be solved by means of linear programming. The primal solution gives information on the optimal level and location of production, interregional flows of intermediate and final products, the regional pattern of intermediate product processing, and the needed investments for increasing processing capacities. The dual solution allows derivation of regional equilibrium prices at producer and consumer levels as minimum prices needed by managers to satisfy given demands. In addition, the model supplies marginal values of limiting resources in the different economic units (the rents for land processing capacity of each region, the marginal substitution costs which would occur if nonbasis activities were introduced in the optimal solution) as well as irrational transportation routes and unprofitable crops.

In this basic structure many adjustments have been made in order to analyze alternative paths of development or the effects of alternative policy measures. This approach, using comparisons of different solutions of static models related to alternative assumptions, is known as "comparative statics." While static models are not suited to describe technological advances, it is possible to introduce activities concerning improved practices of crop or livestock production. They then can be evaluated in their potential effect on the equilibrium solution for the planning period. In the Swedish model three technological levels are considered. A model used by Heady and Skold (20) is computed under assumption of extension of improved practices in several southern states.

Changes in structure, which are considered fixed in the short run, are limited for mobility of resources. When all resources are completely allocated to the various economic units and the structures are fixed in the model, their fixed costs have no influence on decision making. Producers then are reputed to make only short-run decisions. It may be considered that quasi-fixed factors can be purchased on markets and that some commodities (land) can be transferred among farm subsets. Discrete alternative solutions corresponding to different structures thus can be obtained. Finally the model can be adjusted to allow competition for mobile resources. This step may imply flexibility restraints to limit changes to a magnitude conforming with the planning horizon.

Policy targets can also be introduced explicitly in these models. The policy consequences then can be examined. The Swedish model quoted previously is based on the following policy constraints: physical agricultural production is limited to 80 percent of domestic needs; and agriculture must ensure a fixed minimum return for each of the various factors (land, labor, capital). Since the authors consider these factors to have opportunities outside agriculture, they also have opportunity costs which are to be paid when used in farm production. In this peculiar case the model specifies price levels needed to satisfy the whole set of constraints, including those related to policy targets. Another example can be found in the Randhawa and Heady study for India (19); a peculiar constraint ensures that the optimal solution must at least maintain the previous regional income level. Hence interregional competition is limited in order that no adjustment in one region occurs at the expense of income in another region. One of the usual policy measures concerns production quota, a limitation fitting well in linear programming models. But usefulness of a model must be evaluated according to reliability of results. Therefore the optimal program given by any model, including quota constraints, can be useful only if policy makers are able to carry it out; this can be done through an individual quota system, or through adoption of equilibrium prices given by the dual solution.

II. Perfectly elastic demand model. Several approaches are available for this model. If we consider fixed prices at the farm level, activity returns can be used in the objective function. Each producer increases his production until marginal return (product price) is equal to marginal opportunity cost (supply price), according to usual conditions of optimality in linear programming at the farm level. Individual farm supply is therefore independent of market equilibrium conditions. Moreover overall supply is not connected with transportation and processing activities. Production processes must be studied apart from other activities. Overall supply then results through aggregation of results for benchmark farms which have independent solutions.

Now let us consider the regional prices fixed at the consumer level. The basic model can be completed with additional activities giving the level of net demand in each consuming region (or export point); these activities give the value of the agricultural final product in the objective function. Regional prices at the farm level can be derived from the model according to interregional flows, transportation, and processing costs. Such a formulation of the problem can be given when the assumption is made that agriculture constitutes an open sector in which any demand could be met with imports and any surplus could be exported.

III. Fixed prices applying to demand intervals. In some models product prices are fixed but only for intervals of demand lying between specified minimum and maximum levels. According to the width of the different intervals, these models serve either as inelastic demand models or perfectly elastic demand models. For each product the initial price holds valid if supply falls just within the interval. If supply meets the minimum demand, equilibrium price derived from the dual solution will generally be higher than the initial price; if maximum demand is met, the equilibrium price will be lower. Use of this procedure can be justified in the difficulty of specifying one set of fixed demands. Under these conditions one set of prices is considered to be more reliable than others; whenever supply of a given product lies between minimum and maximum demand restraints, the interval limits constraints have no effect and the dual solution does not imply any change in initial price.

IV. Models including separable demand relations. This model assumes that for each consuming region and each product there is one relation between demand quantity and price. Moreover this relation is defined as *independent* of other products; implying that no substitution between products is possible at the consumer level. The demand curve may be replaced by an approximate step function. Demand is therefore divided artificially into portions which are connected with decreasing price levels. For each portion, one activity is introduced with an upper restraint at the level to which this part of the demand is met. Each activity is limited to the size of the concerned portion of the demand function. The objective function expresses the maximum net surplus for producers and consumers. An approximate solution of the problem can be given through usual linear programming procedures as suggested by Yaron and Heady (42). The dual solution allows direct derivation of regional equilibrium prices of products and supplies information needed to specify surplus distribution between producers and consumers. The model of the French Ministry of Agriculture belongs in this category (14, 41). Definition of separable demand functions maintains equilibrium prices of each product within a reasonable range. However such a model does not answer the theoretical question dealing with the possible mutual inconsistency of equilibrium prices at the consumer level due to product interdependency in quantity-price relations.

V. Nonseparable demand functions. Demand depends not only on the price of one product but also on the prices of other products. The functional nature of these relations is connected with complementarity or substitutability among the various products. Takayama and Judge (38) suggested that the problem can be solved using quadratic programming procedures when demand relations are linear. The objective is maximizing net total surplus; the model including production, processing, transportation, and consuming activities. Other linear relations can be introduced in the model to deal with factor markets; increased factor demand giving rise to substantial increase in prices (e.g., skilled labor). Special designs of model, taking both primal and dual problems into account, allow simultaneous derivation of information regarding production levels and equilibrium prices (26, 31).

Considering recent improvements in quadratic programming solutions, we can now consider these models as belonging to the most complete ones. (See Chapter 12.) The possibility of introducing interdependency relations between products at the consumer level is the important point in this approach. But establishing reliable demand functions is also the main source of difficulty.

Aggregation Problems

Activity analysis models give rise to important problems of aggregation bias. Regional and structural aspects give rise to problems in the large size of needed models. We discuss here the rules which can be used to reduce aggregation bias for reasonable-sized models.

It is unreasonable to introduce individual programming of each economic unit of national agriculture in the model. Hence, within each producing region, farms are grouped, each group being considered as homogeneous. This assumption means that perfect mobility of resources exists between farms within a given group. In some cases every farm of one region serves as a benchmark farm, or as identical in the subset. This does not mean that group behavior resulting in quasi-monopolistic decisions is assumed, but only that farmers' decisions are identical within the group.

Aggregation bias or error, measured for one given parameter, can be defined as follows. Bias is the difference existing between the sum of optimum values of this parameter as derived from the different individual farm programming models and the optimum value given for this parameter by the programming model established for the farm subset as a whole. Some authors have tried to measure and explain these errors (16, 34). Some have focused attention on sufficient conditions for perfect aggregation. Day (12) suggests very restrictive conditions: the technical coefficients matrices have to be identical, and the individual objective function coefficients and/or resources coefficient vectors have to be proportional. Miller and Heady (27) suggest less stringent rules: proportionality of vectors can be substituted for qualitative homogeneity of basis solutions. Hence, if all farmers belonging to a given subset obtain the maximum profit, use the same activities, and are limited by the same restraints, then aggregation of results will be free of bias.

Such theoretical considerations have no general practical value. They are only sufficient conditions and must not be used as necessary conditions. For Day's rules, we know that nonproportionality of nonlimiting factors does not imply any aggregation bias. Moreover the Miller and Heady conditions, as completed for the dual solution, show that somewhat heterogeneous differences concerning returns and available resources coefficients can be accepted without risk of aggregation error. Structural changes over time restrain possibilities of applying Day's conditions; the structural adjustments process does not fit the proportionality concept since a lack of resources balance exists on small farms and is gradually improved as farm size increases. Moreover, even if resources and consequently returns are proportional, investment capacity will *not* be so because farm household consumption is not a linear function of return. Then, because of investments, resource proportionality cannot be maintained over time.

The conditions suggested by Miller and Heady allow more flexibility, but have a disadvantage because they require economic results which are not available, until individual models are solved. Therefore it can be asked whether aggregation *does* reduce the burden of calculations. Furthermore the qualitative homogeneity of basis solutions has to be tested for each set of prices which may apply to the general model.

Other authors have suggested other practical rules which are able to improve the selection of representative farms. As an example, we can sort out farms according to the homogeneity of the limiting factor for one main product. This procedure gives rather good results when the regional level of specialization is high. Authors agree that previous statistical analysis of farms, or a good sample of them, is always useful. The first French model concerns about 500 subsets of farms, a farm sample including 10 percent of the total number of farms. Analysis and programming studies undertaken at both firm and regional levels allow a better specification of criteria which can be used to define types of farms. The most usual criteria are the nature of alternative activities (products and production processes), the homogeneity of technical coefficients, the behavior of managers, the level of economic results, the nature of available resources, and the balance of resources within the farms.

It seems difficult to me to suggest any general rule in this matter. Theoretical approaches are very useful in guidance for selection of criteria allowing definitions of farm subsets. However large flexibility must be maintained in relation to the nature of study aims, the available means of analysis, and the characteristics of the farms to be studied.

Model Size and Decomposition Principles

Every linear programming problem in which can be found one subset of constraints, S, referring to one subset of activities, J, can be solved by decomposition procedures (8). According to these procedures, the problem can be divided into several parts for computation. This overcomes difficulties relating to the large size of models. The method consists in replacing each submatrix, SJ, by one convex linear combination of vectors; each of them represents a feasible solution of the subproblem, SJ, which is solved separately. The size of the problem in its new form is reduced, as compared to the size of the starting one. This reduction is the consequence of the substitution of each set of constraints, S, for only one relation and insures the convex linear combination of vectors. The derivation of these solution-vectors implies the computation of the various subproblems, but these are generally very easy to solve. The optimal solution of the starting general problem is obtained through a sequence of steps. First the principal problem is solved for one set of solution-vectors which are obtained by solving the different subproblems according to arbitrary assumptions concerning regional prices. The dual solution given by this first computation is used to adjust prices which are introduced in the subproblems. These in turn supply new solution-vectors which are introduced in the principal problem. Following this procedure, the optimal solution for the starting general problem can be obtained through a finite number of steps.

The basic structure of interregional activity analysis models is well suited for such a procedure. For instance, the relations which concern the limitations and the use of resources of one subset of farms are only related to the potential activities of this type of farm. Therefore a decomposition at this level is possible; one subproblem is set up for each subset of farms (or for each benchmark farm). Then convex linear combinations of feasible solutions computed for each subset (or for each type of farm) are introduced in the principal problem.

The structure of the 1970 French model is similar to those of a principal problem which would be solved from decomposition at the farm level. The model has not been exactly computed according to the decomposition principle. For each farm type several feasible solutions have been first selected. Then the model has been completed in an empirical manner whenever the first computations at the regional level show some lack of flexibility in the adjustment process. The use of a predetermined set of feasible solutions without reference back to the subproblems may lead to a suboptimal solution. In addition, this procedure implies some difficulties of adjustment because of artificial interdependencies introduced between various activities.

If we consider the structure of interregional activity models, we see that decomposition at the regional level also is possible. According to this approach, the subproblems are regional models supplying feasible regional solutions which may be introduced in the national model. A main advantage is the small number of subproblems (only one for each region) and the possibility of the model in a decentralized structure of planning.

The French model for 1975 (41) was prepared for the Sixth Plan according to this design. The spatial model for development purposes suggested by Sebestyen (30) also includes a regional decomposition. When regional solutions are defined according to discrete assumptions (e.g., large investments), integer programming can be used; in the convex linear combinations of some variables (weighting coefficients) will be 0 or 1, insuring that the connected regional plans cannot be mixed.

Of course, in addition to aggregation problems and difficulties implied by large model size, activity analysis methods raise other problems. One is that of dealing with region delineation or heterogeneity of the data collected in the various regions. These models assume that the various agents have perfect knowledge of technological opportunities and of conditions which will prevail in markets over the planning horizon period. We must suppose that a path exists starting from the present situation of agriculture and reaching to the specified equilibrium situation. The length of the adjustment period is generally assumed to be 5 to 10 years—a delay long enough for allowing the economic agents to modify their behavior, adjust their decisions, and make needed changes in structures. The use for long-run purposes of such models seems difficult because of technological changes and modification in tastes and habits related to demand assumptions. Use of static models for short-run purposes also proves dangerous because of the normative aspects implied. If a very short delay is left to the agents for adjustments, it is necessary to introduce stringent constraints to bound the range of adjustments and maintain sufficient reliability of results. Recursive programming makes an extensive use of similar constraints.

These static models seem most suitable for intermediate-run studies. Their main deficiency still lies in their inability to describe the path leading from the existing situation to the equilibrium solution. Two difficulties prevail. If the equilibrium situation really exists, we are sure that it can be reached within the planning period. Moreover the exogenous data of models (as technical coefficients, structures, amount of available resources, demand) are separately predicted. Hence it is difficult to certify that each is consistent with others, and we are not sure that all the conditions specifying the equilibrium situation can ever occur simultaneously. Explicit use of a "time" factor in these models allows some of these gaps to be overcome, as we shall see in the last section.

DYNAMIC APPROACHES

Dynamic programming deals with many different problems and is not easy to define. Some authors consider dynamic programming as referring to every problem in which the objective function depends on an *orderly series of decisions* (29). Of course, problems including time structures belong to the dynamic programming field, the basic principles of which are given by Bellman (3). A policy may be considered optimal if, for any period, and whatever the previous decisions are, the other decisions constitute an optimal policy for the remaining periods according to the results of previous ones. Various applications of this principle can be given depending on selected assumptions of uncertainty about the future and the planning horizon of decision makers.

Multiperiod Models

Applications of such models have been suggested at the farm level for analysis of investment problems. Production and investment programs of the various time periods are linked by liquidity transfer activities. These models are generally large. As far back as 1957 Dantzig (9) suggested a solving procedure for this type of model using period decomposition. This approach is interesting because it demonstrates the dynamic programming approach. Let us consider a simple developmental model for n periods. The amount of liquidities available for the production plan of a given period depends on decisions made during previous periods and on direct and indirect consequences of them (capital expenditure and returns). If we focus first on the last period, we are able to specify a relation between the last period's contribution to the objective function and the amount of liquidity, n, which is available at the beginning of the last period; this can be done through parametric linear programming procedures. The convex and stepwise nature of this relation allows us to introduce it in the n-1th period program. Parametric programming is used to derive a relation between the last two periods' contribution to the objective function and the amount of liquidity, C_{n-1}, which is available at the beginning of the n-1th period. Following this process back to the first period (for which the amount of liquidity is known), the problem can be solved. From the first period solution we can then derive other period plans.

Such a simple design can only be used when a single resource is transferred between periods. We suggest it only for demonstration purposes. When computer facilities are sufficient, the problem can be solved directly without period decomposition. In fact the model is set up with assumption of a *perfect certainty* about the future, all the parameters needed for decision making being explicitly or implicitly introduced in the model. Hence the optimal sequence of decisions can be specified in one run.

Use of such models at the interregional level involves some difficulties. For a given period the investment level depends on the amount of liquidity (which is a function of returns in the previous period). But the derivation of equilibrium prices needed to estimate these returns requires that the problems be previously solved. Thus it is necessary to adapt the design of models to overcome this difficulty.

Henrichsmeyer and Weinschenk's model (23) allows use of information given by the dual solution. Simultaneous solution of primal and dual problems enables the connection of investment activities with the marginal return of resources where liquidity constraints are used. The model supplies information concerning variation over time of production, investment, capital use, and product and factor prices.

The normative character of such a model constitutes another point for discussion. The decisions of managers are specified on the assumption of perfect knowledge. For instance, first-period decisions are made in terms of the consequence they will have in following periods, according to conditions as predicted by the model but which cannot be known in fact by producers. By nature this model describes what should be and not what will be, according to the natural course of the development process. When such models are used for forecasting purposes, some authors suggest adding constraints to draw the solutions nearer to the actual behavior of farmers. These constraints can be simple relations limiting the range of adjustments between periods (a procedure very similar to recursive programming). To reduce the range of actual changes, Boussard (4) suggested introduction of constraints to describe producer behavior with respect to risk. Such relations give more reliability to the predicted adjustment pattern over time, but they do not modify the basic assumption of time reversibility in the decision–making process.

Another important problem concerns the number of periods. The number can be reduced by use of discounting methods since the expected returns for a remote future period have no practical influence on decisions of the first period. Furthermore, after a certain number of periods of transition, a development process follows a regular trend which has little influence on decisions to be made during the first periods. Nevertheless the minimum number of periods needed may be great and involve difficulties related to long-run analysis.

Recursive Programming Models

Recursive programming is designed to describe the variations of the parameters over periods (11). The basic structure of a linear programming problem for one period is used; additional relations are used to estimate coefficient values of this programming model starting from the observed values of the same coefficients in the previous period. These estimates concern, for instance, the return expectations for each activity, the level of available resources, and the intervals of variations allowed some variables or aggregates. The analysis of a development process over n periods implies the computation of n problems which have to be generated progressively.

This type of model has been used especially for supply analysis. Economic function coefficients are return expectations which are estimated assuming, for instance, that the expected prices of products and factors are equal to those paid or received during the previous period. The acreage of a given crop for the studied period is maintained within an interval whose bounds are specified according to the acreage value obtained for the previous period. The possible change is usually defined as a fraction of this past value. Finally, the spreading of an improved practice can also be limited by such constraints; the acreage of a given crop grown under an improved practice cannot increase more than a given proportion to its value in the previous period. Such mechanisms may be used to describe continuous phenomena such as population migration, farm consolidation, and so on.

The approach allows incorporation of important agricultural production dynamics. First, the decision of production, being anterior to the marketing process, cannot be made according to equilibrium prices but only in reference to *expectations*. Furthermore decision making for one period cannot be founded on equilibrium conditions for the next periods (as assumed in multiperiod models). The decisions predicted by recursive programming are a compromise between a "wish" for more profitable solutions and the effect of various factors which serve as a brake in this process. Some of these constraints refer to physical factors such as the needed delay for setting up new investments, the duration of production cycles, and the nonreversibility of supply functions when some production must be decreased. Others deal with producer behavior such as the attitude towards uncertainty and risk, the carefulness of farmers, and the passive resistance to change.

The model must be computed for each period, each period usually giving rise to a linear programming problem. The dual values supplied by the optimal solution can be explained as rents for the fixed resources and as quasi-rents for the constraints which limit technological change. Finally, they indicate risk-insurance premiums for the constraints which limit changes in the production pattern. The descriptive value of such models can be tested using time series. For this purpose, exogenous parameters have to be introduced in the model for definite time periods when discrete changes have occurred (innovation, policy measures, etc.)

and corrections have to be made for random effects (weather phenomena). Crom and Maki (7) suggested procedures to enable adjusting such models to improve their predictive ability.

Having been tested for a certain number of periods, such a model can be used for short-run or intermediate-run forecasting purposes and applied in a "comparative dynamics" framework. The adjustments resulting from alternative agricultural policies might be predicted for several years.

Application of recursive programming has numerous problems. Most important is the amount of needed data. In testing the model over time, one set of dated information is no more sufficient than it is for static models. For such purposes, time series of every needed nature are necessary. Another difficulty lies in the specification of coefficient values for flexibility constraints. While time series data can be used, this is a "tricky" job. The variations of each parameter are not explained only by farmer behavioral constraint but also by other limitations we intend to include in the model and by random events. Finally, if producer decisions are no longer explained by equilibrium market prices but are connected with expectations, separate treatment of production models theoretically is possible at the representative farm level. The results then can be aggregated to estimate supply. This procedure implies homogeneity of information used in the models computed for each region or each benchmark farm by different regional teams.

While recursive programming eliminates the perfect knowledge assumption implicitly used in multiperiod models, it gives rise to the opposite question. Is this method, stressing one-period decisions, well suited to describe the development process? As far as some types of investment are concerned, the one-period programming concept does not allow the introduction of all parameters needed to explain decision making. We can question too the behavior constraints which are used in recursive programming to supply sufficient reliability, considering the lack of knowledge existing in this field. It can be suggested that the value of flexibility-constraint bounds for each period should be related to several economic parameters and should not be fixed using only constant coefficients.

Some authors suggested defining each flexibility coefficient as a function of the dual value which supplied the corresponding flexibility constraint in the previous period. It then would be assumed that the extension of an improved practice is more rapid when it is more profitable. Through this approach predicted changes surely would be more realistic than the ones resulting from the use of prices of the last period, for return expectations may prove insufficient and more sophisticated price expectation models should be investigated.

Recursive programming may be introduced in more complete sectorial models considering transportation, processing, and marketing activities. The principle of dynamic-coupling suggested by Day (13) supplies an opportunity to consider both the intertemporal structure of production and supply-transportation-demand interdependence. The model includes (a) recursive programming submodels allowing supply analysis and (b) one temporary equilibrium model giving the needed information about interregional flows, supply-demand equilibrium, and regional prices. Some grounds exist to justify such a model. For supply, the intertemporal structure of the model is given by recursive programming analysis. We can assume that the farmer's objective consists of maximizing expected profit with respect to behavior constraints. The possibility of testing the models for past periods supplies an opportunity to check the reliability of this assumption. Considering the temporary equilibrium model, it can be said that a time lag does exist between the decision of production and the establishment of market price; logically, supply thus cannot be considered as a function of future price. In this design it becomes possible to take into account random weather effects which modify expected supply (aggregated results of submodels) to give effective supply   Therefore the temporary equilibrium model distributes a given supply between the various consuming regions and specifies the conditions of temporary market equilibrium and allows derivation of regional prices for the studied period. These prices can be used to estimate return expectations for the next period. The system operates according to "cobweb theorem" characteristics with possibilities of convergent, cyclic, or explosive phenomena.

The national model of the USDA presently worked up by Schaller's team, is founded on this principle. The objective of their model is to develop a quantitative framework for estimating (a) aggregate changes in the commercial acreage and production of major farm commodities and (b) resource use associated with changes in prices, technology, resource availability, and government programs. Separate recursive programming submodels are defined for 47 geographic regions and 91 aggregate resource situations within those regions. The objective criterion is short-run profit maximization subject to physical and institutional restraints as well as behavioral limitations. The programming submodels have been tested for 1960-64. The model is being operated for short-run forecasting purposes.

In the present state of the model, the main difficulty may be in reconciling (a) the wish of reducing aggregation bias and (b) the impossibility of dealing with a sufficient number of submodels. Other sources of difficulty are the model's simplification of the decision-making process and the missing or inadequate data needed to quantify submodel restraints. It is too early for us to give an evaluation of this approach for the actual analysis of possible effects of a given policy or for comparisons of alternative policies. Random weather effects present difficulties. One possibility here consists of predicting changes over time implied by each policy when mean statistical values (expected mean yields) are used. Another possibility is to consider, for each policy, different sequences of random events and to analyze the series of results. Whatever the case be, the calculation bulk implied by the recursive programming approach is always important since the model must be computed for each period and each set of general assumptions.

CONCLUSIONS

Recent advances in the field of information processing have supplied policy makers with new tools well-suited for analysis and forecasting purposes. Programming methods allow three very important aspects of agriculture to be taken into account, namely product-factor interdependence, spatial structure, and the intertemporal structure of the farm production process.

More conventional tools such as regression or input-output analysis are surely insufficient to answer all agricultural problems, but they are still essential. Complete programming methods incorporating interrelations between agriculture and the other sectors of the economy must be developed parallel to these conventional approaches.

Considerable work remains to be done in most countries. New advances are possible only if the models are set up in cooperation with users who, within both regional and national organizations, can supply sufficient means for gathering and processing appropriate information. However some national research teams have now left behind the exploratory stage. Useful results will be forthcoming if they really enter a new stage in application of models to actual regional and national planning.

REFERENCES

1. Agricultural Economics Institute. Supply and Demand, Imports and Exports of Selected Agricultural Products in the Netherlands for 1970 and 1975. The Hague, 1968.
2. Bawden, D. L. An Evaluation of Alternative Spatial Models. *J. Farm Econ.*, vol. 46.
3. Bellman, R. *Dynamic Programming*. Princeton, N.J.: Princeton Univ. Press, 1957.
4. Boussard, J. M. Un Modele pour l'Etude des Decisions a Long Terme des Agriculteurs. *Rev. Econ. Politique*, no. 6, 1967.
5. Brown, M. *On the Theory and Measurement of Technological Change*. Cambridge, Mass: Cambridge Univ. Press, 1966.
6. Carter, H. O., and Earl O. Heady. An Input-Output Analysis Emphasizing Regional and Commodity Sectors of Agriculture. Iowa Agr. and Home Econ. Exp. Sta. Bull. 469.
7. Crom, Richard, and W. R. Maki. Adjusting Dynamic Models to Improve their Predictive Ability. *J. Farm Econ.*, vol. 47.
8. Dantzig, G. B. *Linear Programming and Extensions*. Princeton, N.J.: Princeton Univ. Press, 1966.
9. ———. On the Status of Multistage Linear Programming Problems. *Intern. Inst. Bull.*, vol. 36.
10. Day, L. M., and G. Judge. Use of Interregional Competition Models for Studying Agricultural Adjustments. O.E.C.D. AGR/T (65) 29. Paris, 1966.
11. Day, R. *Recursive Programming and Production Response*. Amsterdam: North-Holland, 1963.

12. Day, R.H. On Aggregating Linear Programming Models of Production. *J. Farm Econ.*, vol. 45.
13. ———. Dynamic Coupling, Optimizing and Regional Interdependence. *J. Farm Econ.*, vol. 46.
14. Fahri, L., and J. Vercueil. Etudes Concertees pour la Definition d'un Programme Agricule: Le Modele de Prevision 1970. Roneo Sedes. Paris, 1967.
15. Folkesson, L. An Interregional Linear Programming Analysis of the Agricultural Sector in Sweden. Mimeo. Uppsala, 1967.
16. Frick, G. E., and R. A. Andrews. Aggregation Bias and Four Methods of Summing Farm Supply Functions. *J. Farm Econ.*, vol. 47.
17. Griliches, Z. Estimates of the Aggregate U.S. Farm Supply Function. *J. Farm Econ.*, vol. 42.
18. Heady, E. O., and A. C. Egbert. Programming Regional Adjustments in Grain Production to Eliminate Surpluses. *J. Farm Econ.*, vol. 41.
19. Heady, Earl O., and N. S. Randhawa. An Interregional Programming Model for Agricultural Planning in India. *J. Farm Econ.*, vol. 46.
20. Heady, Earl O., and M. Skold. Projections of U.S. Agricultural Capacity and Interregional Adjustments in Production and Land Use with Spatial Programming Models. Iowa Agr. and Home Econ. Exp. Sta. Res. Bull. 539.
21. Heady, E. O., and N. K. Whittlesey. A Programming Analysis of Interregional Competition and Surplus Capacity of American Agriculture. Iowa Agr. and Home Econ. Exp. Sta. Res. Bull. 538.
22. ———. Aggregate Economic Effects of Alternative Land Retirement Programs: A Linear Programming Analysis. USDA Tech. Bull. 1351.
23. Henrichsmeyer, W., and G. Weinschenk. Spatial Equilibrium and Prediction of Structural Change in Production. Paper for European Meetings of the Econometric Society, Warsaw, 1966.
24. Isard, Walter. Interregional and Regional Input-Output Analysis: A Model of a Space Economy. *Rev. Econ. and Stat.*, vol. 4.
25. Leontief, V. *Studies in the Structure of the American Economy.* New York: Oxford Univ. Press, 1953.
26. Maruyama, Y., and E. I. Fuller. An Interregional Quadratic Programming Model for Varying Degrees of Competition. Massachusetts Agr. Exp. Sta. Bull. 555.
27. Miller, T. A., and Earl O. Heady. Sufficient Conditions for Exact Aggregation in Linear Program Models. *Agr. Econ. Res.*, vol. 18.
28. Ministerio de Agricultural, Secretaria General Tecnica. Programacion Interregional de la Agricultura, Madrid, 1967.
29. Rosenstiehl, P., and A. Ghouila Houri. *Les Choix Economiques. Decisions Sequentielles et Simulation.* Paris: Dunod, 1960.
30. Samuelson, P. A. Spatial Price Equilibrium and Linear Programming. *Am. Econ. Rev.*, vol. 42.
31. Schrader, L., and G. A. King. Regional Location of Beef Feeding. *J. Farm Econ.*, vol. 46.
32. Sebestyen, J. Some Thoughts on a Spatial Model for Development Purposes. Reg. Sci. Assoc.: Lund Congress, 1963.
33. ———. On Structural Analysis in Agriculture. Res. Inst. Agr. Econ. Bull. 15. Budapest, 1967.
34. Sheehy, S. J., and R. H. McAlexander. Selection of Representative Benchmark Farms in Synthetic Supply Functions. *J. Farm Econ.*, vol. 47.
35. Solow, R. M. Technical Change and the Aggregate Production Function. *Rev. Econ. Stud.*, vol. 39.
36. Takayama, T., and G. G. Judge. An Interregional Activity Analysis Model for the Agricultural Sector. *J. Farm Econ.*, vol. 46.

37. Takayama, T., and G. G. Judge. An Intertemporal Price Equilibrium Model. *J. Farm Econ.*, vol. 46.
38. ———. Spatial Equilibrium and Quadratic Programming. *J. Farm Econ.*, vol. 46.
39. Tinbergen, J. *Economic Policy, Principles and Design.* Amsterdam: North-Holland, 1960.
40. Tirel, J. C. Programmation Interregionale—Decomposition des Programmes Lineaires. Roneo Laboratoire, INRA d'Economie. Grignon, 1967.
41. ———. Programmation Interregionale. La Structure de Modele Theorique Zidore. Roneo Laboratoire, INRA d'Economie. Grignon, 1966.
42. Yaron, Dan, and Earl O. Heady. Approximate and Exact Solution to Non-Linear Programming Problem with Separable Objective Function. *J. Farm Econ.*, vol. 43.

Part VI GAPS BETWEEN PLANS AND REALIZATION
AND PRACTICAL POSSIBILITIES FOR
IMPROVEMENT IN PERFORMANCE

Chapter 24   REASONS FOR DEVIATIONS FROM PLANS

Geza Kovacs, *Keszthely College of Agriculture* (Hungary)

T HE ANALYSIS of earlier development, the basis of this investigation, is an important part of planning. The importance of such investigations is given by the relation of the national economic plan to greater production. The plan contains the most important relations of the increased production in words and figures. The enlarged production is submitted to rules determined by the stage of development, productive forces, and production relations and — within the limits of these rules — by the policies of the government. Hence earlier development is the starting point of development to be realized in a later period: future development is based on the results of the past. As a consequence of the development of productive forces and social conditions, certain tendencies and trends of the progress fade or cease to exist, others become stronger, and new ones arise. Activity begun in the past often ends only in future periods of planning and thus effects of decisions concerning the fundamental questions can really be evaluated only in the future.

The role of the evaluation of earlier development depends on the length of the planning period and on the planning methodology applied. When elaborating a plan it can be laid down as a general rule that the longer the period the more we can render it independent from earlier development. The role of evaluation of the past and the utilization of the conclusions will be different also according to the method chosen to establish the targets of the new plan.

Within the framework of the basic investigation, we analyze the actual degree and rate of development in the past. Further, we analyze the course and degree of the structural changes to determine how far the actual development was in harmony with the schedules for that period. These two aspects of the basic investigation give answers to various questions and provide the reason why it should be conducted.

From the standpoint of the degree and rate of development, we can study the differences among countries, branches of the economy, and sectors: whether they increase or decrease; whether underdeveloped countries, branches, and sectors succeed in rising to the level of the more developed ones or whether their backwardness becomes even greater.

From the extent of deviations from the plan, we can infer the level of social consciousness. Closeness of planned and actual development indicates on the one hand that the possibilities of development have been gauged correctly. On the other hand, we can determine whether the means to realize the plans have been chosen well. Thus deviations from the plan indicate either the correctness or not of both planning and execution. When studying deviations from a plan, we must submit the plan to a given time and means of execution.

Targets and fulfillment of a plan do not necessarily agree. Ideal plans cannot be elaborated. Thus neither can the means for fulfilling them be chosen to result inevitably in 100 percent fulfillment. Since objective measures are lacking, it is unreasonable to claim that social consciousness can be claimed only in case of 100 percent fulfillment of a plan. However the targets of a plan can be formulated with different contents. For example there were confirmed plans in Hungary with indices establishing the minimum of the target. Their overfulfillment was considered as useful and was thus stimulated. On the other hand, indices of other targets represented maximum levels (the upper limits) so that an underfulfillment was considered favorable. As a consequence, 100 percent fulfillment of a plan must not be "fetishized." Not all overfulfillments are worthy of praise and not all underfulfillments must be condemned.

Acceptable conclusions can be drawn from an analysis of deviations from plans only over a relatively long period. From the trend we must determine whether the deviations are of increasing, decreasing, or alternating tendency and what their causes are. I studied deviations from the plan of Hungarian agriculture covering 15 years and compared them to deviations from plans of key figures in the development of the national economy. Within the period in question, the years 1950-54 were the period of the first five-year plan in Hungary. In 1951 the targets of the first five-year plan were raised. As a result of the stress caused by raising them too high after June 1953, the plan was much less a living guide to action. Between 1955 and 1957 only one-year plans were made. The period of 1958-60 was covered by a three-year plan while the second five-year plan was elaborated for 1961-65.

DEGREE OF DEVIATION FROM THE PLAN AND
DURATION OF THE PLANNING PERIOD

It was generally observed that deviations from the second three-year plan were less than the deviations from the five-year plans. A fundamental cause of this phenomenon is the fact that radical changes either in rate of growth or in structure cannot be accomplished in a short period. Development in a short period had been decisively determined by earlier measures and decisions; essentially it was decided in the past. Hence foresight was better here than for plans of a relatively long duration, where larger deviations are unevenly distributed over time and occur toward the end of the period. In the first years planners are rather influenced by previous decisions. Consequently creative imagination manifests itself rather in the targets of the second half-period of the plan.

There were essential differences in the degree of deviations between the first and second five-year plans. In the second five-year plan, deviations were of a much smaller degree. The actual increase of the national income fell behind the first (original) five-year plan by 13 points and behind the raised one by 80 points. The first four years of the second five-year plan was short only 5 points. However, during the period of the second five-year plan, deviation from the planned gross output of agriculture was larger than expected. The difference was due mainly to a temporary vacuum: the changes in ownership (i.e., the collectivization) took place more rapidly than the establishment of a modern technical basis for the new structure, although the government released more resources for this purpose than originally planned.

TENSIONS INSIDE PLANS

In most of the cases major deviations from the plan were underfulfillments. In the three-year plan not only was the degree of deviations smaller than in the five-year plan but also the overfulfillments were more frequent. Demands of different character can be regarded as the main source of tension in agricultural plans. A considerable part of them consisted of the consumers' demand, which was raised by the occupational regrouping of the population and by the accomplishment of a living standards program laid down in the national economic plan. Since an initial demand was one of the starting points in elaboration of agricultural plans, this change in demand caused a considerable upward shift of targets for agriculture.

Since demand relationships had been applied inconsistently, the supply of financial and technical means for agriculture was "underproportional" to the requirements in production to meet the increased demand. Due to this "underproportionality" in planning of factor demand, the deviations from the plan of agriculture appeared, particularly after 1957, mainly as underfulfillments in comparison with plan figures relating to supplies of machines and materials. Among them, the financial-technical factors, with an effect primarily in increasing production, played a considerable role. The problem arose from the fact (it is again a question of planning methodology) that certain peculiarities resulting from the reorganization of agriculture on a large scale were not sufficiently considered. A major proportion of financial-technical means put at the disposal of agriculture only replaced the means of peasant production eliminated by the reorganization. Transformation into large-scale farming is favorable from a perspectivic point of view because it clears the way for the development of productive forces. Consequently, as traditional means of peasant farm production, representing fundamentally backward technology, become useless, the loss can be considered as an element of the cost of socioeconomic transformation. However, in a given period, this loss requires additional investments; if this cannot be realized within a short time, the rate of growth of production and resources of agriculture may be considerably slowed even with a proper structure of current inputs.

A further result of these tensions in agricultural plans was that the equilibrium of the balances became formal in more than one case. To insure the various relationships of enlarged production, the plan serving as a program of action must be coordinated. Coordination postulates, at least within certain limits, the harmony of the indices and an equilibrium of the balance system. This equilibrium of balances was realized mostly by raising arbitrarily the targets for yields. Within certain limits, such increases were reasonable because average yields have fluctuated considerably from year to year. These fluctuations were due partly to the given stage of development of productive forces and partly to the climatic conditions of the country. For example, in 1965 the average yield of wheat was 12.5 quintal per cadestral yoke (one hectare equals 1.7 cadestral yoke). The probability of attaining it was estimated to be only 18 percent by previous experiences.

As suggested by these statistical data, targets exceeding the average of several years are justifiable especially when agriculture receives an increasing quantity of financial and technical means. But if agricultural targets are set too high and a considerable failure occurs in crops owing to bad weather, the deviations of the agricultural plan which present themselves as underfulfillments transfer their negative effects to other fields of the economy. Hence they disturb the balance at more than one place. The author of this paper compared the indices of the real wages of workers and employees to those of the real income of the agricultural population and to the trend of agricultural production between 1950 and 1965. The curves representing the development were rather similar. Agricultural production is a highly important factor in living standards as Hungarian consumers spend a considerable but decreasing proportion (about 50 percent) of their income on food. In Hungary tensions in living standards programs were in most cases connected with the unsatisfactory level of agricultural production.

DIFFERENCES IN DEVIATIONS FROM PLANS

Deviations from the plan were generally smaller for aggregate indices than for those relating to individual components. Planned figures for gross output differed from the actual figures by only 1 to 10 percent. On the other hand, we found deviations from the targets of the particular years amounting to 35 percent for cereals and up to 44 percent for potatoes. We pay more attention to the deviations of indices representing aggregate relationships not because they offer a more "flattering" picture but because it is the trend of comprehensive relationships that primarily casts light on the correctness or not of the economic and political conception of the plan and expresses its sound foundation or superficiality. Perspective plans, both those of medium and long duration, must possess a definite character and reflect a precise developmental conception. And the problems of conception are connected with the most comprehensive relationships of growth.

It was observed too that deviations from the plan were greater in the branches of agriculture treated as key sectors than in other branches. For example, deviations of indices pertaining to planned and actual acreage of wheat, considered to be a key sector of agriculture, gave a more unfavorable picture than those relating to sugar beets, though the latter was not considered to be a key sector. For acreage, the deviation was usually an underfulfillment by 3 to 12 percent for wheat, and an overfulfillment of 2 to 12 percent was characteristic for sugar beets. (One must add that great efforts were made to fulfill the targets for the acreage of wheat.) The development of certain branches of agriculture as key sectors was due to the importance of the role they played during a given period. In fact, the special role of the key sectors was more often emphasized by targets of production forced upward than as targets to meet the real demand in development.

The key sector principle of development has proved to be entirely correct, according to the experiences gained so far. Especially in small countries, a concentrated utilization of available resources is an indispensable requirement of growth. However, in order to apply the principle of key sectors in a proper way, we must pay more attention to their interdependence than we did in the past.

A study of the time span of development programs for various branches of agriculture also shows differences due only partly to biological characteristics of various sectors. Lessons from the past in this field are very important. Our experience shows that in case of radical changes in ownership, when the new social framework is still slowly getting consolidated while the old one fades away more quickly, one must pay special attention to the problems of sectors in which the unfavorable tendencies can be eliminated only in a relatively long period.

Chapter 25 ❦ EXTENT OF GAPS BETWEEN PLANS AND REALIZATION

Finn Reisegg, *Norwegian Institute of Agricultural Economics* (Norway)

THE FAMOUS Danish humorist Storm P. is frequently quoted when questions about plannings and forecasts are discussed. He says: "It is difficult to make forecasts, and particularly about the future." By this statement he has pointed out an important thing about planning. Frank Knight made a more scientific approach in his book *Risk, Uncertainty and Profit*.[1] He makes a distinction between risk and uncertainty. By definition, risk is possible to calculate. Uncertainty, however, is not possible to calculate, either for insurance companies or for agricultural economists. This is true even with the most advanced planning methods. Thus we may always expect a gap between plan and realized outcomes. To be 100 percent right in forecasting or planning would prove more about good luck than skill.

For several years agricultural economists in the Western world have engaged themselves in working out new planning methods. In recent years the move has been from farm business planning methods to regional and national planning methods. This is easily proved by the number of meetings organized by O.E.C.D. on different planning methods. The O.E.C.D. activities give an indication of fields of interest among specialists in member countries.

There are considerable practical experiences on farm business planning in most countries. The practical experiences in regional and national planning are rather limited. Before going into a discussion about the extent of gaps between plans and realized outcomes, I should like to make a rather important distinction between different types of planning activities, a distinction which is frequently ignored when people are discussing planning methods. I shall make a distinction between what I may call *planning for decision making* and *planning for action*. The first method is a tool for management and decision making at the administrative level. It should be used to decide the right approach for solving problems when several alternatives exist. It should be expected that the result may turn out somewhat different when compared to the plan. One should expect that the method should give the best approach in a certain situation. One would not have to include all sorts of details in such a plan. The alternative budgeting method has for several years been used in decision making. Today the simulation technique is a more sophisticated and better method for the same purpose. To argue against

1. New York: Kelley, 1921.

the usefulness of planning because of a difference between a plan and realized result may only prove that one does not understand the idea of planning as a tool for decision making. The second method, *action planning*, should give more details and should be decided in time. Such a plan is much more technical than a decision-making plan. A gap between a plan and realized result is not very acceptable even if it is in a positive direction. Problems solved by PERT is a typical example of such planning activities. One may say that decision-making planning is analytical, giving a direction for development rather than the exact result. Action planning is a program to be followed and fulfilled. Several wrong conclusions about planning methods may be made if one does not make this distinction.

There are three levels for planning activities: farm level (micro), regional level (semi-macro), and national level (macro).

PLANNING ON THE FARM LEVEL (MICRO LEVEL)

Farm business planning as known in the work of farm management experts is two-step planning. The first step is decision-making planning to decide the best possible alternative; the next step is the action planning to decide technical details such as a fertilizer program, feeding program, and so on.

I am going to discuss the extent of the gap between plan and realized result in micro planning on the basis of experiences from the pilot farm program in my country. To decide a long-run plan for a farm, one would have to work out several alternatives and, together with the farmer, decide the best possible plan. We do not expect to get a zero-difference between plan and realized result. Neither do we expect to be on schedule after six years of work (the pilot scheme is six years). It would be fantastic if everything turned out exactly as we expected according to the original plan.

I would like to give you an illustration of the extent Norwegian pilot farms have been able to realize their farm plan. It is a rather simple study based on 24 pilot farms with completed programs and where results have been published. To make the example simple and avoid the problem of reduced money-value due to inflation during the pilot farm period, I have used physical data only; all figures are relative figures. If the figure is less than 100, the realized result is below the original plan. The contrary condition holds true when the figure is above 100. One may see from Table 25.1 the extent that each pilot farm has realized the plan. The majority of pilot farms have more than completed their program, but there are also pilot farms which are below the goal set. For the main production the majority of farms have completed the program. The average realized plan for clearing new land and drainage is 4 percent above the original plan. It has been more difficult to reach the level of expected crop yield. This may be somewhat surprising since one would think it rather easy. It should also be

Table 25.1. Extent of gap between plan and results

Farm no.	Land drainage	Feed unit/decar.	Main production	Yield/ animal	Labor productivity
1	93	86	87	77	100
2	123	100	112	100	128
3	72	66	100	104	108
4	100	87	100	100	79
5	94	90	113	105	100
6	100	74	91	95	105
7	100	93	111	151	100
8	100	101	114	100	115
9	83	104	115	100	93
10	90	91	128	102	122
11	95	94	71	98	127
12	124	88	111	123	100
13	123	101	122	100	132
14	163	108	108	100	132
15	91	99	93	124	143
16	94	99	98	103	101
17	125	78	94	117	115
18	98	107	100	105	88
19	100	103	129	87	137
20	98	113	124	105	97
21	100	117	140	96	76
22	105	88	93	142	139
23	126	93	93	118	96
24	95	76	113	248	84
Ave.	104	94	107	112	109

noticed that the yield per animal is 12 percent above the plan. Also productivity of labor is higher than planned.

This rather simple study corresponds with a similar study made by Professor Westermark for pilot farms in Finland. He made a study to determine the extent that pilot farms had realized their pasture plan, forest business plan, cropping and fertilizer plan, and cattle feeding plan. The results are presented in Table 25.2.

Out of 59 finished pilot farms, 8 had completed their plan according to the program. Forty had a result which was satisfactory and 11 farms were far behind the schedule. Twenty-five pilot farms explained why they

Table 25.2. Changes in finished pilot farms; percent completing

Realization	Pasture plan[a]	Forest business plan[a]	Cropping fertilizing plan	Cattle feeding plan[a]
Fully	19	34	53	50
Fairly well	33	1	. . .	. . .
Partly	5	20	6	8

a. The number of responses is lower than the number of study farms for the reason that not all the section plans were set up for every farm. Concerning the forest business plan, it is to be noted that only the first five-year period is referred to here.

had not succeeded: 9 had an excuse because of bad weather conditions; 5 had a reduced number of working hours available and were behind schedule for this reason; 4 farmers had an excuse because of illness; 4 had increased their agriculture area more than originally decided; and 3 explained that they had engaged themselves in economical activity outside the farm.

The two studies indicate that there is nearly always a gap between plan and realized result. There are, of course, several reasons for this. Some reasons may be due to the farm management expert; other reasons may be due to the farmer himself or the farm. I shall discuss some of the important things.

DIFFERENCE IN PLAN AND REALIZED RESULTS
DUE TO THE FARM MANAGEMENT EXPERT

Today we are in a fortunate situation when it comes to the question of methods. We have a range of methods, and it should always be possible to select one that is suitable for the special situation. Personally I believe in rather simple methods for practical farm planning, because I do not think we may ever overcome the existence of uncertainty.

The main difficulty is, according to my opinion, the *data problem*. The two studies mentioned indicate that the farm management expert tends to overestimate the possibility of increasing crop yield, while he underestimates the possibilities of increasing milk yield. The reason for being too optimistic about crop yield may be explained by the fact that yield is frequently estimated on the basis of local research. The farm yield is decided by reducing research findings to a "practical farm level." It is obvious that this procedure tends to give a level which is too high. For milk yield, however, figures used frequently are based on actual milk testing records for the district. The increase in milk production has been more rapid than expectations by specialists due to improved breeding and feeding programs.

Data for labor productivity have also been too low for a great many pilot farms. There are, however, farms where labor productivity is not that expected. Productivity figures are strongly influenced by the human factor. The ability of farmers to organize labor varies considerably. Farmers also often believe that the way they do things is the best. They may resist change and do not believe it possible to expand production because they feel they are already too busy. I have heard many pilot farmers complain about plans for this reason. However, when things have been organized according to plan, they found to their surprise that they did have time enough.

Clearing and draining land is 4 percent above the plan in Table 25.1. There is, however, a substantial difference among farms; the figure varies from 63 percent higher on one farm to 28 percent lower on another farm compared to the original plan. The reason for the great variation is probably lack of technical data. I may mention one particular case

where the farmer finished in half the time a drainage program which
was doubled compared with the original program. In Table 25.1 two
farms are far behind schedule. One should notice that the same farms
are behind schedule in almost everything, indicating again the importance of the human factor. The majority of pilot farmers have more
than completed their original program for the main activities. This
again has something to do with the human factor. Many farmers were
afraid to go on with a program they thought they could not manage. A
typical example was a pilot farmer who refused to accept more than 80
ewes on his farm. After some years he agreed to increase to 100, and
after his pilot program was finished he went on by himself and increased
the number to 140 ewes.

For a pilot farm program to succeed, one thing is important: the
follow-up by extension specialists. Pilot farms frequently visited by
specialists generally do a much better job compared to those without
sufficient contact during the pilot farm period. When the specialists
fail, something nearly always went wrong. Most frequently this happens
when the new plan is very different from the old one. Not only must the
farmer be given a good plan, but also he needs the knowledge to succeed.

DIFFERENCES IN PLAN AND REALIZED PLAN
DUE TO THE FARMER HIMSELF

As already pointed out, the difference between a plan and realized
results depends to a great extent on the farmer himself. First, he
should be *motivated* for changes which are caused by the new plan. A
pilot farmer nearly always was motivated for the changes. The plan
had been explained to him and he accepted the plan. For this reason it
is not always an optimum farm plan from an economic point of view that
is chosen. The plan had to correspond with the special interest and
abilities of the farmer. Frequently I have seen the "best" plan refused
by the farmer because he disliked something in it. I remember one
farmer who refused to go into a rather profitable egg production because he disliked hens so much. This dislike, of course, had to be accepted by the farm management expert.

A study recently finished in Norway gives some rather interesting
information about motivation. Farmers who are rebuilding or building
new barns are granted a special building subsidy. To get a grant a
farm plan must also be worked out and put into practice to make sure
that there is a sound economic reason for making investments.

The extent to which the program for clearing new land was completed on farms getting a building grant is indicated in Table 25.3. Only
about 50 percent of the programs were completed. This is very low
compared to the pilot farms cited earlier which had an average of 104
percent completion. Milk yield per cow, however, increased more than
expected, just as for the pilot farms (Table 25.4) or farms getting a
building grant.

Table 25.3. Clearing new land (0.1 hectare); percent completed

	Before building	3 years after	5 years after	Plan	Increase	Increase according to plan
Region I	56.2	67.1	63.9	72.7	7.7	16.5
Region II	80.7	84.8	87.8	94.8	7.1	14.1
Region III	76.2	78.3	80.4	84.4	4.2	8.2

Table 25.4. Milk yield per kg per cow

	Building	3 years after	5 years after	Plan	Increase	According to plan	Increase compared to test group
Region I	2580	3240	3587	3146	1007	566	384
Region II	2939	3580	4021	3510	1082	571	448
Region III	3408	3776	3916	3439	508	31	58

Lack of motivation for changes introduced through the new farm plan was obvious in answers given by the farmers. When asked about the usefulness of the farm plan, 27 out of 82 farmers getting building subsidies said that the farm plan had little value for them, and 11 farmers said that they did not even know about a farm plan. Thus almost 50 percent were not at all motivated for changes introduced by a plan. They more or less accepted the farm plan as something they had to adopt in order to get the building grant.

The next thing I mention is the *possibilities of frustrations.* Many times the farm plan does not give the economic result expected. There are several reasons for this. A rather technical one which I will mention especially has to do with our planning methods. The economic optimum solution does not always give sufficient money income for the family. Too often we ignore the liquidity in farm planning. Liquidity is going to be even more important in the future when agriculture is more capital consuming and financing is based on loans. The study just mentioned gives support to this statement. The figures in Table 25.5 indicate how liquidity has changed from before to after a construction period on farms with barn subsidies. Each family had their budget reduced substantially in the immediate years after the construction period.

Table 25.5. Changes in private economy before and after construction; funds left for family living and debt repayment

	Before years		After years			
	1	2	2	3	4	5
Region I	9063	9459	5476	6868	3125	9725
Region II	5721	6638	2665	4025	4809	5108

It takes 5 to 6 years to get back to the family's previous fund level. Some farmers said that if they could do it all over again, they would not go into construction work.

I mention another example showing the problem of liquidity. For several years a family farm of good size had been in small grain production. The profitability, however, for several reasons was reduced to a low level, and the farmer decided that he would go into animal production. This would require a total investment of about 250,000 Norwegian kroner. The local extension specialist made a new plan, and capital and family-labor income were to be approximately 35,000 Norwegian kroner. The farmer and the local adviser found this quite satisfactory. They did not, however, realize that only 10,000 Norwegian kroner were left for the family budget because of down payment of mortgage loans and interest for money borrowed. It was quite obvious that the situation would give rise to frustration. Obviously the local adviser made a big mistake. He had never before worked out a plan under a condition where liquidity was so important. He used the traditional planning method for small farms where loans never went so high.

The interrelationship between farmer and farm management expert is close when planning is at the farm level. It is a short way from the farm management expert who is responsible for getting things started to the farmer himself. A capable farm management expert always finds the farm plan that would be the right one for the individual farmer. Thus the farmer may always be motivated for the changes. This may help to close the gap between plan and realized results.

PLANNING AT REGIONAL LEVEL

Planning at the regional level (semi-macro planning) may be an activity very different from micro planning. First, there is a very different relation between the farm management expert and the person who puts the plan into operation — the farmer himself. We have two different types of planning activity at the regional level. The planning activity may be directed to a group of farmers with no local government involved. In this case the planning activity and the problems involved are to a certain extent the same as for micro planning activities. More frequently regional planning is done at the request of a local government. In this case the farm management expert does not have a direct connection with the farmers. For example, a local government may ask for a plan to determine possibilities of improving the agricultural structure within an area. The result depends on the local government as well as on the farmers. The local government may wish a change; but if the farmers do not want to go into it, there will not be a change. Thus it is possible to have a zero result, and the gap between plan and realized result is wide open.

I would like to say a few words about a regional approach directed toward farmers and not including a local government. I give a few

references to the four pilot area programs which have been completed
in Norway. The methods used for working out regional plans have been
rather simple. The intention of the planning work is only to decide a
direction for development. The direction is decided by means of a set
of models for typical farms. For each pilot area several activities are
organized within the frame of the total plan for the area. Experiences
differed widely with respect to the results obtained. Some activities
were extremely successful. Other activities were almost complete
failures.

As for individual farm planning, the success of a pilot area depends
upon the motivation of farmers. In a pilot area (Uvdal pilot area) re-
markable progress was made in a very short time for some activities.
The main reason for progress was the fact that the farmers had been
thinking about a change for years, but they never made the final decision.
The only thing the farm management expert had to do was to work out a
few alternative plans which explained the situation. Other things in the
same pilot area were almost impossible to get started, even if the farm
management specialists spent much time in explaining why and how it
should be done and what the farmers would gain by accepting the changes.
A good example was a plan for using pasture land in the mountains on a
cooperative base. The project included the building of a rather expensive road and the building of two or three cooperative summer farms at
a relatively low cost. The road was built, but the summer farms were
not. The building of a road had been discussed for years in the pilot
area, but cooperative summer farming was something completely new
to the farmers.

In a pilot area a farm management specialist would help individual
farmers with farm planning and management advice. The planning activities were often based on a group approach including several farms.
But one always had the individual approach which is a necessity to get a
plan realized. The farm management expert in a pilot area would be
able to decide the best possible data and to decide the right assumptions.
This is possible when he knows the district and the conditions quite well.
In a pilot area the total plan is a guideline for the farm management expert when he is working out individual plans. A relationship exists between the farm management expert and the farmers very similar to a
situation where the farm management expert is working on the micro
level.

Regional planning activities where a local government is involved
may be something completely different from the planning activity just
described. Planning activity for a local government may be more analytical, and it may not even be the intention of the local government to
put a plan in operation. The local government may ask the farm management expert to decide different alternative solutions for structural
changes in agriculture and to determine the effect on the labor force. If
the effect is such that political trouble may be expected, the local government will not try to introduce the plan to the people. A regional plan,
good from an economist's point of view, may not be acceptable to the

politicians. There may be two reasons for this: one is the simple fact that what is good economy may not always correspond to what it is possible to get people to accept. If people do not accept the solution, they are not motivated for a change; and the politicians may only run into trouble if they introduce the plan. Second, it may be rather difficult to get the assumptions for the regional plan into specific terms. Thus local governments may be rather vague when giving assumptions. If the expert decides to give only one solution, he may put the local government in a "take it or leave it" position. Accordingly they may refuse the plan even if it is acceptable from a political point of view. What happens is that the expert places himself in the position of the administrator. The risk of the expert instead of the administrator deciding increases with the use of more sophisticated methods. Unless the local government is very specific about assumptions, a regional plan should be presented in terms of different alternatives so a choice is possible.

To obtain the best possible result in regional planning, it is important to know the function of each agency and to know the decision-making process. To succeed in regional planning where a local government is involved in the decision making, one should probably include the following steps:

1. The politicians decide what is a reasonable frame for change.
2. The local government asks a professional planning authority to work out a number of solutions. Political assumptions are fixed as decided by the politicians.
3. The planning authority works out alternative solutions as a base for a final decision by the local government (decision-making planning).
4. The planning authority and technical specialists work out an action plan with all necessary details.
5. Economical and technical help to producers will include action for motivations.

The time necessary to complete a program is nearly always underestimated, because farmers or others who are responsible for a final decision are not motivated for the changes. This was quite clear in the pilot areas. Considerable time had to be spent to explain to the farmers why they benefit from a change, and it was necessary to have several activities organized at the same time. We may better succeed if we try to decide what time is the best for a change. Changes which today cause resistance among people may be a natural thing in the future. Thus timing of a plan is important. This is particularly true when economic problems are involved. Young people are more easily motivated than older people for economic changes.

PLANNING AT THE NATIONAL LEVEL (MACRO PLANNING)

Agricultural economists in recent years have engaged themselves strongly in developing national models. I should like in particular to mention Professor Heady's pioneering work. Today several outstanding young agricultural economists work on his models.

Planning at a national level is much more complicated than planning at the farm level, or even at the regional level. The reason is due mainly to three things: the integration of problems between different economical activities; the difficulties in fixing right assumptions; and again the problem of data, particularly for prices. A true representation of a complex society is probably impossible even with the most advanced model and technique. I really think you cannot talk about the existence of a gap between plan and realized plan because it is nonsense to use a national plan for anything else than a rough tool in decision making.

I do not know to what extent national plans based on formal models are a reality. In 1966 at an O.E.C.D. meeting of experts in Paris to discuss regional and national models, no one present could really report great success in the use of national models. I think the situation may have changed somewhat since then, but I have a feeling that the only thing we have accomplished is to develop a simulation technique for simplified national models. Thus national models may be used for decision-making at a national level. One should not expect a plan to be realized, as in farm business planning. Unfortunately one has to oversimplify the model to make it workable, so a great risk is involved in using assumptions and data which are very realistic. I may give you a typical example which was discussed at a Scandinavian seminar last year. On the basis of different studies, it was found that the productivity of labor in agriculture was low compared to other economic activities. To increase economic growth, one could lower agricultural prices to reduce the number of marginal farms. In theory this would be a sensible thing to do. In real life, however, something else may happen. The farms located in the plains area near the big cities may go out of production, while the mountain farms may stay on. The reason is the fixity of labor. The mountain farmers have a very low alternative value of their labor, while the farmers in the plains region find themselves in a situation where labor has a rather high alternative value. If alternative values for labor were used, the model could of course be improved to give the right answer. But again, this is very difficult because alternative values of labor may change very much from district to district and from time to time. Several similar examples could be mentioned.

When using different sets of assumptions, lack of stability in solutions is a real problem in national planning. I know agricultural economists who fix assumption rather artificially to prevent nonsense results. At the Mexico conference of I.A.A.E., Professor Heady warned agricultural economists against careless use of complicated models and electronic computers. He said that agricultural economists in the future should spend considerably more time in deciding the model and the data to be used. And even more important, they should spend more time in interpreting the results.

Personally I believe in national models mainly as a means for decision making at an administrative level. One could also use them for a national business game. I do not believe that national models can do much more than give a rough idea of the situation in a very complicated world. The economic man is a superman which economists have created, but he does not really exist. As long as human factors always are involved when a plan is to be realized, we should never expect to close the gap between plan and realized result.

I conclude by saying that agricultural economists probably should use their economic principles to decide how to spend their own time. Too many economists are playing around with mathematics and principles instead of being engaged in the very practical work so important where rather rough methods may be as useful as highly sophisticated mathematical methods.

Chapter 24-25 ☞ DISCUSSION

Michele de Benedictis, *Center for Specialization in Agricultural Economic Research* (Italy)

IN DISCUSSING problems of "gaps" between plans and realizations at the micro level, I will direct my comments particularly to the paper by Dr. Reisegg.

First of all, I think we should thank Dr. Reisegg for calling to our attention most of the very few empirical studies that have attempted to measure and to interpret the differences between plans and realizations for specific farm situations. Thus a first, and not very encouraging, conclusion with respect to this area of investigation is that the number of studies dealing with the empirical evaluation of the way farm plans are implemented and of their final results is, in fact, quite meager. From a cursory survey of the Western literature one receives the impression that significant and systematic attention to this area of research has been given mainly, if not exclusively, in the Scandinavian countries.[1] Elsewhere there seems to be a sharp disproportion between the number of studies concerned with the various aspects of plan preparation and those aimed at an assessment of the effective results.

From this observation follows a first point of discussion which I would like to suggest to the group. Is this impression confirmed by experience in the individual countries? If so, how do we explain the limited attention received by this sector of research?

---

1. A bibliography of the most recent contributions to this area in the Scandinavian countries is contained in the paper by Isaksson (1).

The second direction which our discussion should logically take is to measure the size of the gap and to investigate the nature of the factors that create and explain the gap.

I suggest we define the "gap" as the difference between the farm organization adopted by the farmer and the one previously planned and that we use the difference in farm income in the two situations as a concise measure of the gap at the farm level. Such a simplification is necessary since the size of deviation between realized and original plan could vary considerably among the production branches inside the farm.

The data that Reisegg has brought to our attention confirm, as could be generally expected, the existence of a gap. It is, however, quite important and encouraging that the observed gap on the Norwegian pilot farms is not always negative: in several cases, and in more than one production sector, the realized plan achieves a figure higher than the one foreseen by the original plan. The data in Table 25.1 show that the farms with a positive gap in the series of data relative to main production, yield per animal, and labor productivity are more numerous than those which have barely achieved, or have remained below, the target set by the plan. We should not forget, however, that these data refer to pilot farms, that is, to situations where presumably all the necessary steps had been taken to prevent the emergence of negative gaps. On the other hand, it is reasonable to expect a considerably different situation in "nonpilot" farms (such as the Norwegian plans designed only to obtain a loan). Here the effort to control the factors that may engender negative deviations from the original plan is presumably smaller and less specifically applied.

Reisegg also reminds us that in practice there will always be a gap, caused by the stochastic nature of some of the technical and economic variables whose value cannot be accurately predicted with respect to one specific production period. In this connection it may be useful to specify a criterion for ascertaining the absence of a gap: we can speak of a perfect implementation of the plan when there is no difference between the results of the realized plan and the results of the original plan calculated ex post, using the values of the stochastic variables as occurred during the production period. (This assumes that the differences in coefficients used ex ante and realized ex post is due entirely to a stochastic element and not to error in, say, the mean value of a variable.)

Given the above definition of the gap, our main interest is directed to the identification of controllable variables which can be used to insure adoption of the plan. I believe that the major part of our discussion should be aimed at the identification and analysis of these variables.

In this connection Reisegg gives some examples of gaps due to the farm management expert and to the farmer. Undoubtedly most factors concurring to create the deviation of reality from the plan are associated with these two causes, as is documented by some of the interesting evidence mentioned by Reisegg in his paper. However I feel that our efforts should go somewhat deeper, attempting to identify and classify the specific "instrumental" variables on which we can act to eliminate or reduce the gap. I will try to suggest a tentative classification within whose boundaries I hope that a fruitful discussion will develop.

As a starting point, it is relevant to make a basic distinction. The gap may be due to the fact that the farmer does not adopt the plan or that the plan, once adopted, does not give the expected results.

A closer look at the first cause brings into evidence the underlying factors that may have inhibited adoption of the plan by the farmer. First of all, the decision maker may find the plan unsatisfactory because either it ignores some of his specific preferences or, in more general terms, the "behavioral theory" in the plan formulation is not an accurate representation of his preferences. Secondly, the results of the plan may be judged unrealistic by the farmer if he feels that some of the technical and economic assumptions used in constructing the plan do not apply to his own farm. Finally, the lack of adoption may lie not in the plan itself but in the professional ability of the decision maker and/or the way the advisory service has presented the problem to the farmer.

A similar distinction can be made with regard to the gap generated by the failure of the plan after it has been implemented. On one hand, the plan may reveal its defects by showing internal inconsistencies or a too loose adherence to the real conditions of the farm. On the other hand, the failure to achieve the targets set by the plan (aside from the purely stochastic elements mentioned previously) may be due to a poor execution of the plan, which in turn is again related to the professional ability of the manager and to the efficiency of the extension service.

These considerations are rather helpful in identifying what I believe are the main factors that contribute to establish the gap and which at the same time can be viewed as the instrumental variables on which we must operate to reduce the differences between the original and the realized plan. In synthesis the existence of the gap, coming both from lack of adoption and the failure after adoption, can be attributed to the following factors: (a) accuracy of the tools we are using to prepare the plan, (b) efficacy of the institution connecting the plan-making phase and the decision maker, and (c) professional competence of the decision maker. With the purpose of stimulating the discussion, I would like to make a few comments on each of these points.

DECISION-MAKING TOOLS

The arsenal of tools the economist has at his disposal to prepare plans at the micro level has been increasing steadily both in number and quality. However it must be recognized that a gap also exists between the level of sophistication and accuracy achieved by some tools as they appear from methodological applications in the literature, and the type of tools that are generally employed in elaborating the plans.

The size of this gap certainly varies considerably from country to country, and it may be interesting to hear the comments of the group on this point.

A critical evaluation of the tools which are commonly used in preparing the plans at the farm level — and which basically all belong to the budgeting-linear programming family — should begin by judging their adequacy with respect to (a) representation of the technical and economic relationships within the farm, (b) incorporation of a satisfactory "behavioral" theory of decision making, and (c) treatment of risk and uncertainty.

With regard to the first point, certainly great progress has been made in the degree of accuracy with which we can describe — and incorporate in the planning tool — the technical and economic interrelationships inside the farm. It is probably safe to assert that inadequacies in this direction stem more from lack of technical information than from incapacity of the tool to absorb and coordinate the available information. The *data problem*, mentioned by Reisegg, contributes greatly to impoverish the analytical capacity of the available tools. A greater effort should be devoted in the future to the improvement in the quantity and quality of the planning data. It is my impression that a considerable portion of the gap could be eliminated by working with more realistic planning data.

Another aspect which deserves to be mentioned in this connection is related to the way we have been using the tools. It is, in fact, important to recognize that the majority of plans prepared and applied have been constructed in a *static* or a *comparative static* framework. On the other hand, it should be clear that most long-term planning problems call for a *dynamic* analysis, since the knowledge of the expected changes of certain economic variables through time is essential for the life of the firm. For example, it is my impression that the case of a *possibility of frustration* of the farmer mentioned by Reisegg should be interpreted as a consequence of the fact that in preparing the plan the temporal aspect had been treated unsatisfactorily. This is obviously a consequence of the comparative neglect with which agricultural economists have treated so far the problems of firm growth. But also in this direction it should not be too difficult to overcome the present limitations: even though restricted to methodological applications, we are beginning to find in the literature examples of planning models in which the aspects of consumption and capital formation can be adequately treated in a temporal context.

The main limitations of our planning tools can be traced to the way we have been treating, or ignoring, the behavioral and the uncertainty aspects. With regard to the first aspect, specific attention should be given to ascertain the decision-maker attitude toward (a) short-run and long-run goals, (b) inclusion or exclusion of specific enterprises or production techniques in the plan, and (c) uncertainty elements in planning. The straightforward profit maximization framework, within which have been placed the majority of plans produced by research or extension

to help farmers, is certainly too rough an approximation of their preference system.

A careful specification of the goals pursued by the farmer is not an
easy task, particularly in a long-run perspective where the profit goal
must be combined with objectives related to capital accumulation and
level of liquidity. The "work sequence for practical long-run planning
for growth of the agricultural firm" adopted by Swedish researchers
looks like a promising approach (3). More experimentation in that direction should contribute greatly to reduce the gaps caused by plans
which look conventionally at the objectives pursued by the entrepreneur.

Our sins seem to be less serious and persistent with respect to the
preferences of the farmer toward the presence or absence in the plan
of specific enterprises. In preparing the plans for particular farms we
have become accustomed to attempt to incorporate restrictions reflecting this category of preferences.

Less satisfactory is the situation with respect to the problem of
uncertainty. However I do not think we should share Reisegg's pessimism and accept his conclusion that simple methods should be used for
practical farm planning because we shall never overcome the problem
of uncertainty.

There are several possibilities to improve the way we have so far
treated the problem. First of all we should make more serious attempts
toward the conversion of some categories of "uncertainty" to "risk" by
ascertaining the "objective" probabilities by past data. We may then be
able to present the planning results in terms of probability distributions
or outcomes rather than point estimates.

If no objective probabilities are available, there are at least two
possibilities. One is to conduct a "sensitivity analysis" with key parameters to find outcomes under various hypothesized values of the parameters. The results could then be presented in a type of "payoff" table
where planners' subjective probabilities could be used to select the plan
that maximizes expected value.

On the other hand, if the problem is such that the use of subjective
probabilities is excluded, a game against nature could be transformed
in the linear programming format and solved jointly with the standard
problem of optimum resource allocation within the farm (2).

INSTITUTION CONNECTING THE RESEARCH PHASE
WITH THE DECISION MAKER

The role of the intermediary institution — the extension service in
Western countries — is fundamental both before and after the adoption
of the plan. We can distinguish four essential phases in the contacts
with the farmer: (a) preliminary discussion, data gathering, and preparation of the plan; (b) discussion and evaluation of the plan with the
farmer; (c) periodical contacts during the implementation period; and
(d) evaluation of results. The first two are the most delicate, and on
them greatly depends the adoption and the final success of the plan.

The main danger lies in the conscious or subconscious attempt by the extension man to *change* the preference system of the farmer as such, instead of convincing him that the change established by the plan is one which will really satisfy his preferences, and that he will be inconsistent if he rejects the plan.

The four phases are certainly facilitated when we are dealing with pilot farms, where the involvement and the participation of the farmer are presumably assured from the beginning and where the contacts between the farmer and the extension worker are particularly intense and frequent. Matters become more complicated in the "normal" cases, that is, in the farms that are not the object of a specific program. The situation in which the extension worker operates may be quite different from case to case. He may have a blueprint computed with reference to a typical farm and he must perform the necessary adaptations, or he may have to start from scratch and go through all the phases needed for the preparation of the plan. Whatever the situation, it is in these conditions — in the majority of the cases — that the competence and the ability of the extension worker are called for. It is also here, I think, that the gap from the original to the realized plan may assume considerable magnitude. Unfortunately the empirical evidence on the size of the gap in farms where the extension "investment" has not been particularly intensive is, to my knowledge, very small or nonexistent. (One of the few exceptions is given by the recent work of Westermark, 4.) Considering the predominance of this situation, in the future more attention should be given to the measurement and analysis of the gap under "normal" conditions.

It is fairly reasonable to hypothesize that the amount and the success of farm planning vary largely in Western countries as a consequence of the different situations existing with respect to the quality and intensity of the extension work. Another consideration of some importance is the gap existing in many countries between the level of planning tools used in the research stage and the economic training of the extension workers. An improvement of the professional level of extension workers should contribute greatly to reduce the gap between plans and realization.

PROFESSIONAL ABILITY OF THE DECISION MAKER

Motivation, as pointed out by Reisegg, and professional competence of the decision maker are undoubtedly critical variables both for the adoption and the success of the plan. In a recent study Professor Westermark (4) has examined the existence of a possible connection between the entrepreneurial ability of farmers and their attitudes toward planning and other individual advisory activity. The variables under examination were the age of the entrepreneur, his theoretical vocational education, and his mental ability. The data have shown a strong relationship between the last two variables and the attitude and competence of the farmers toward economic planning.

The ability of the farmer may be particularly useful during the application phase of the plan in reducing the potential gap between effective and planned results. Considering that many decisions will be made during the production period, a capable entrepreneur may be able to assimilate new information and revise the expectation on yields and prices made at the time of planning, thereby introducing modifications in the original plan. This "intermediate replanning" may lead to better results than those which would have been achieved if the farmer had followed exactly the original plan. Following the criterion mentioned previously, we would have in this case a positive gap, since the realized results would be superior to the ex post evaluation of the original plan.

INSTITUTIONAL SETTING OF THE FARM

So far we have mentioned, as a possible framework within which to develop our discussion, factors related to the decision-making tool, to the organization assisting the farmers in adopting and implementing the plan, and to the professional ability of the farmer. However a final variable which is very likely to influence considerably the extent of the gap is the institutional setting within which the farm operates. We can distinguish two basic types of institutional situations. The first situation is characterized by a "stable" farm structure, in the sense that there have been no recent and drastic changes in the tenure system. The decision makers are accustomed to operate within a certain institutional and economic environment and have complete familiarity with the specific level of responsibility required by decision making. In situations of this kind, which correspond to those discussed by Reisegg and studies by the other Scandinavian researchers, one could hypothesize that a "good" extension service would eliminate major gaps between plans and realization.

On the contrary, we can think of the second situation as one where profound changes in the tenure and farm structure have recently taken place. In capitalist economies land reform interventions have usually brought about a transition from dependent farm workers to independent decision makers. In socialist economies the process of collectivization may induce the transition from independent and individual decision maker to dependent worker (state farms), or from a status of independent decisions to one of collective decisions (cooperative farms).

In all these cases the gap between plan and realization, especially in the first years following the tenure change, could be quite large. The professional ability of the farmer may not be adequate to understand and implement the plan, and because the farmer is facing new risks, it becomes more difficult to ascertain and incorporate in the planning tool the preferences and the "behavioral" theory of the decision makers. The problem may become quite dramatic when the plans at the farm levels are, in a sense, the disaggregation of national targets; the presence of a gap then becomes not only a question of efficiency of the individual farm but one involving the rate of agricultural and general economic growth.

REFERENCES

1. Isaksson, Nils I. Comparison in Retrospective in the Realization of Plans with Particular Interest in Rationalization Proposals. Economic Commission for Europe, Work Group on Rationalization. Sixth Session, Geneva, 1968.
2. McInerney, J. P. Maximum Programming—An Approach to Farm Planning Under Uncertainty. *J. Agr. Econ.*, vol. 66.
3. Renborg, V., B. Johnson, and E. Skolosa. Swedish Experiments in Planning for Growth of Agricultural Firms. South Dakota Agr. Exp. Sta. Bull. 541.
4. Westermark, Nils. Role of Planning and Management on Family Farms and Advisory Services on Economic Results. *Acta Agr. Scand.*, vol. 17.

Chapter 24-25 ෨ DISCUSSION

T. W. Schultz, *University of Chicago* (U.S.A.)

THESE TWO papers include some useful data that provide a simple and plausible way of evaluating the planning process. These papers raise a number of important points. Reisegg gives us some useful tables, and some pilot plans that can be understood by the uninitiated. He is troubled by the fact that so little is known about the economic value to farmers of any part of the farm planning "output." Eremias (see below) also is concerned about the economic value of these plans. Neither of these papers, however, is intended to solve this problem. Hence I shall stress the plan outputs to remind us that we do not know. They could be of zero value. Thus far we have been silent with regard to this matter. I offer five rather abrupt remarks.

First, the "macro" models presented at this conference, using Professor John Hick's expression, are like other metaphysical entities, boats that are loose from their moorings. They are detached from the economic domain. They are not tied to the capital market. Thus the heterogeneity of human capital and of nonhuman capital and the differences in the rates of return to the array of different forms of capital are not taken into account. Nor is the market for human effort that is determining wages an integral part of these models. No specifications are given for the network of the relative prices of factors (services) and products or for changes in these relative prices over time under dynamic economic growth conditions. For want of price theory, wage theory, and capital theory, the analytical battle is lost.

Secondly, in testing how satisfactorily a model performs, the USDA model described so ably by Baker and Swanson is in operation and it is testable each year. If its performances are weak, steps might be taken to strengthen it so that its maximum possibilities can be established. I wish the USDA model could be designed to forecast so far as it can the farm wages in the different parts of agriculture, preferably by age and education. I am sure that this could be achieved.

Thirdly, in a centralized economy, the gap between the national plan for agriculture and the realized agricultural production, leaving the level aside, is small for very strong reasons. Mr. Kovacs assures us that this is true in fact. The reasons for the small deviation are of two sorts. One is the fact that the important components in the planning models are controlled substantially. The input and output prices and goals of output, and the rates of change in the coefficients of production, are under control and the quality of the labor and its prices are established. Furthermore there is legal capacity to impose the production plan. Many of the planning models considered at this conference appeal to the control "advantages" of a centralized economy. It is true, however, that the criterion that this gap is small in a centralized economy is not a measure of the overall economic efficiency of agriculture. A small gap between planned and realized production does not mean that the country is performing well in overall efficiency.

Fourthly is the important issue of testing models. Certain normative efficiency models are not designed to serve as behavioral models (see Heady, Chapter 12). These normative efficiency models are not deficient in technical conception. They are very tight in formulation. I do not want to discuss these aspects, however. It is not my intention to repeat the critique made in these respects at an earlier meeting. The more important question I wish to pose is, How can the results of these models be tested? No test has been proposed. I respectfully submit the proposition that this is the important issue that is overlooked. The methods we propose must be consistent with the overall economic realities if we care to use the results to implement policy. So far it is impossible to test the results of certain of these models. The results might be perfectly consistent with economic efficiency, but to have confidence in them requires an appropriate test. Up to now, such a test is not forthcoming, and I doubt that the results as they now stand will ever be tested. In Table 25.2 the Northern Plains are shown as having produced 38 percent of U.S. wheat output. The Heady-Egbert model II-B allocated 55 percent of all U.S. wheat to this region whereas the Hall-Heady-Plessner model allocated only a little over 25 percent to this region. Surely both of them cannot be consistent with economic efficiency.

Consider also Table 25.5, in which the Delta accounts for 28 percent of all U.S. cotton in 1965. This was the actual production of U.S. cotton in the rich Delta of the southern U.S. in 1965. By the above models the efficient allocation of U.S. cotton, according to the solutions, would reduce the production in this rich Delta region to near zero. But there is no test of this implausible result, and consequently no basis for confidence. I am not opposed to the search for ways of determining economic efficiency, nor am I saying I can prove these results to be wrong. I am asking how one would proceed to test these results to determine whether or not they are consistent with economic efficiency? I tried yesterday to work out an analytical proof that might be valid, but it exploded. I submit that this is the stage of my limited thinking on the matter.

Lastly, I take it to be true that economic planning is a part of rational economic behavior. I want to go to my final proposition which relates to the role of data.

Advances in knowledge about planning are a joint product of data and analytical involvement. I underscore joint product because it does not come from the data and will not come solely from models. National planning is a part of macroeconomic thinking, as I specified on my first point. It is true that high precision can be attained in microeconomic studies. Parts of this seminar have shown this in no uncertain terms. But we have not been trying to close the gap between what the models are about and the real organization of resources and economic efficiency of agriculture. That is the heart of the matter. I am regretful we have not even tried to resolve this problem.

Vaclav Eremias, *Research Institute of Agricultural Economics*
(Czechoslovakia)

THE PRESENT SITUATION in the application of economic-mathematical methods and models in planning and decision making in Czechoslovakian agriculture is characterized to a certain extent by the extent and structure of the work performed by the automatic computer of the Research Institute of Agricultural Economics. In 1967 this automatic computer (Minsk 22) working in two shifts was employed 25 percent in doing calculations for agricultural enterprises and 10 percent for calculations of the central controlling economic body (the Ministry of Agriculture and Nutrition). The remaining capacity of the computer was used cooperatively in solving research tasks with various research institutes, agricultural supply and commercial organizations, colleges, and the like.

In overall calculations for agricultural enterprises, the optimalization of the plan of production predominated (optimum specialization of enterprises using 35 percent of computer time) and was followed by calculations of the propagation of herds (25 percent), the optimum structure of the fodder base and fodder rations (14 percent), calculations of the plan of seasonal work by means of the critical path method, and so on. In the calculations performed for the central controlling institute (the Ministry of Agriculture and Nutrition) in 1966 and 1967 there was a predominance of various calculations making possible a quantification of the different economic tools of the new system of management of agriculture (prices, grants, bonuses, agricultural tax) and a checking of their effect on agricultural enterprises under different natural and economic conditions. To a smaller extent, calculations for the proposed plan of the distribution of agricultural production over the different regions also were carried out. The calculations performed by means of the computer connected with the application of economic-mathematical methods of agricultural cooperatives and at state farms are subsidized by the state.

MODELS AND METHODS BEING APPLIED

The above mentioned is an enumeration of facts. However, this state of affairs does not fully conform to the established possibilities, in results to be obtained in research, for the application of economic-mathematical methods and models. This is true even though research has not had placed at its disposal the whole system of possible models, especially under the conditions of systematic control of the market, with optimum decisions at all levels of management. The problems of the utilization of economic-mathematical methods and models in planned agriculture can be divided according to the following: (a) Application of economic-mathematical methods in establishing the plan in the central sphere of management, that is, above all in determining the extent and structure of the needs of society regarding agricultural and foodstuff products. (b) Application of economic-mathematical methods in the optimum spatial (territorial) distribution of the determined needs of society in a way so that by means of an application of economic tools it should be possible to achieve an optimum distribution down to individual agricultural enterprises. (c) Application of economic-mathematical methods in the planning and making of decisions for an agricultural enterprise in a way making it possible to attain, under the given conditions, a maximum effect of the activity of the enterprise. This means that both in the central sphere of management and at the enterprise level it should be possible to make the most suitable decisions with the exclusion of administrative interference in the agricultural enterprise.

As regards the application of economic-mathematical methods and models in the forming of the plan at the center, research in this country is only at its beginning. In this direction there exist some research works (Research Institute of Planning of National Economy, Economic Institute of the Czechoslovak Academy of Sciences) which of course for the time being do not permit exact calculation of the needs of society as regards agricultural and foodstuff products in conformity with all factors that may, directly or indirectly, influence the extent and structure of this consumption. So if it is necessary to plan the extent and the structure of the demands of society without any application of exact methods, it is possible of course to perform a checking of the reality of the given need for agricultural and foodstuff products. It also should be possible to compare the existing need and supply sources on the one hand, relative to the consequences of changes that might occur in this need caused by changes in the linked branches of the national economy. In this regard, we see need for application of a structural model of the plan of agriculture and of the foodstuff industry. Work in this area is underway in the Central Research Institute of the Foodstuff Industry and in the Research Institute of Agricultural Economics. After working out a structural model of the plan for the whole complex of branches (agriculture and nutrition) attention will be paid also to the problems of an optimum plan (together with a simultaneous checking of the applied coefficients). When the reality of the central plan has been checked (with regard to its conformation with supplies) the further procedure is based on a most suitable spatial (territorial) assignment of this plan from the point of view of the best utilization of the different soil and climate conditions in the country. It also will balance the combination of branches (products) in the most effective manner in obtaining final products for consumers.

The low proportion of agricultural and arable land per inhabitant in Czechoslovakia requires the best possible utilization of the existing natural conditions. Therefore priority is given to the most suitable distribution of agricultural production. At the Research Institute of Agricultural Economics in Prague, the research task of the territorial distribution of agricultural production has been completed. The optimum distribution of agricultural production so determined is based on the simplex method of linear programming. It determines the most suitable structure of production in the individual microregions (defined according to the differences above all in the climatic and soil conditions) from the point of view of the desired effect, together with a full utilization of the given natural conditions. In this task, use has been made of the technoeconomic parameters forthcoming from systematic research of a sufficiently large number of agricultural enterprises under different natural conditions. Also there is a formulation of limitations resulting from the production characteristic of the given unit as a whole, together with a consideration of the different sources in the given microregion. As a criterion of the optimality of the planned distribution of production in these models, an objective function (or several functions) has been determined to express most precisely the maximization (minimization) of the desired goal (e.g., maximization of gross production, market production, gross income, minimization of per unit costs, etc.).

The successful functioning of this method depends on correctly arranged models for the different producing units and on appropriate technical coefficients conforming to reality. In the model, there is a combination of natural and value aspects in the search for the most suitable variant of the plan. In the territory of the whole country the number of microregions with equal natural conditions amounts to 142. To indicate the magnitude of the problem and needed models, the territory of the country contains approximately 7,000 socialist agricultural enterprises.

Two problems have emerged: (a) the optimum production structure in the microregion (according to natural conditions) is not identical with the optimum production structure of every agricultural enterprise in the individual microregion; and (b) the economic interest of the market partners of the agricultural enterprises — the purchase organizations and the processing industry — need not be identical with the interest incorporated in the solution of the optimum territorial distribution. It was assumed that for the purchase organization and for the processing industry, the optimum distribution of the plan of agricultural production would serve as information on the most suitable structure with regard to the utilization of natural conditions. The interest in a maximum approach to this optimum by the processing industry and purchasing organization would be stimulated by the state (with regard to the priority of the interest in a maximum utilization of natural conditions). The means used would be the economic tools of direct control in a way that the market partners of agriculture should be directed towards the concluding of contracts at localities for which, from the point of view of effectiveness of agricultural production, the most suitable extent of the production of the given product has been calculated. Thus by offering the conclusion of long-term contracts the purchasing organization and the processing industry would contribute significantly towards the most suitable specialization of every agricultural enterprise. Of course, the whole of this procedure is possible with a distribution of the needs of society for agricultural products determined for at least five years. Above all, there would be provided the possibility of a choice and the realization of an appropriate specialization of agricultural enterprises (including the establishment of the required cooperative relations).

From the point of view of the preparedness and elaboration of economic-mathematical methods and models, the best preconditions for their application exist in the planning and control directly at the agricultural enterprise level. Previous research has solved, and checked in practice, the following problems: determination of the optimum structure of production in agricultural enterprises; determination of the optimum structure of the fodder base; calculation of the enterprise plan; optimization of transport problems (transport to and from fields, placing of plants, etc.); optimization of livestock production with regard to a rational utilization of disposable feed supplies; compilation of plans of seasonal work; calculation of the optimum composition of feed mixtures; distribution of fertilizers and compilation of the plan of fertilizing; calculation of the propagation of herds of cattle and pigs; and machine and tractor pools. This list refers mostly to partial models. The aim is to establish a whole system of models and programs based on an optimization of the long-term plan of development of the agricultural enterprise to serve as an instrument for planning and management at an enterprise level. This procedure simultaneously assumes developing a system for the automatized flow of information indispensable in the development of the whole concept.

REASONS FOR INSUFFICIENT APPLICATIONS OF MODELS

If we are to evaluate the reasons why new and effective methods and models are not applied to a sufficient extent in practice, it is suitable to mention how this question is answered by the agricultural practice itself. We use the data obtained in an inquiry performed with a group of agricultural enterprises in Czechoslovakia (see K. Svoboda: A Retrospective Comparison of Plans and Results With Special Regard to the Reaction of the Human Factor to Suggestions of Rationalization). By means of questionnaires, the views of 18 percent of all agricultural enterprises regarding the application of various economic-mathematical methods and models were investigated. It was found that these methods were applied only by 14.4 percent of the examined agricultural enterprises.

In reply to the question why these methods are not applied, reasons were given in the following order: ignorance of the methods; distrust of these methods; and the complexity of the working out of original data for the application of economic-mathematical methods in connection with automatic computers. From the answers to the question of results that had been obtained by means of these progressive methods by agricultural enterprises that had applied them, it appeared that only in one case out of ten had these methods been applied on the initiative of the leading workers of the enterprise. In nine cases out of ten these methods had been suggested by the workers of the advisory service, research institutes, and colleges. Only in 12 percent of all cases had the agricultural enterprises themselves prepared the original data; in the remaining 88 percent of cases, the whole preparation of original data and the checking of calculations, as well as further alternative calculations, had been carried out by external advisers or with the participation of the leading workers of the enterprise. The fact must be added that of the total number of results only 59 percent of the plans were realized in practice — either wholly or partially. A major part of the realized results belonged to the sphere of optimum structures of the production of the enterprise, which, compared with the previous state, recorded a rise in gross production and gross income by up to 20 percent. Among the reasons why in 41 percent of cases the results had not been realized was that their application was contemplated only for a later time (or also after certain modifications).

If we are to evaluate the application of these modern methods in the central sphere of economic management (in the controlling activity of the Ministry), we must mention this fact: For the time being we are performing work of several types of mass data elaboration rather than an optimum planning on a national scale. For the time being, in connection with the automatic computer, these works are directed less towards saving central administrative work and more toward facilitating data processing to an extent that would be impossible without modern computing techniques. This increases the accuracy of the decision making. An example is the introduction of the economic reform in Czechoslovak agriculture from January 1, 1967. However, at present these modern methods of decision making are mastered by the expert apparatus of the central economic bodies only to a limited extent which, in this direction, requires the performance of services by the corresponding technical organizations and institutes.

It is worth mentioning that in Czechoslovakia — in conformity with the conception of the earlier central directive system in management of agriculture — the first experiments with the application of the methods of optimum planning of agricultural production were carried out not at the level of individual enterprises but at the level of a national distribution of agricultural production. In a majority of cases these models proved failures because of the lack of credible information on the diversity of the conditions of production in the territory of the country, because of the considerable aggregation of data, and because of the insufficient concordance of the central aims expressed in material balances with the economic tools of their realization.

OVERCOMING INADEQUATE PRACTICE

The notions of how to overcome the state of the present inadequate practical spreading of economic-mathematical methods and models in agricultural planning are simultaneously also an indication of the reasons why — at least under the conditions of this country — this has not yet been done.

First, what is to be achieved is above all the establishment of such an economic climate for the different stages of management that would make possible an adequate freedom for decisions and so also a choice of the optimum variant. Practically, this means a changeover from central orders contained in the plan for the regulation of the market mechanism on the basis of the plan. Under the conditions of this country, the first step in this direction was made by the application of the system of economic management of agriculture, which for the time being forms a temporary model of management in which the directivity of the central plan has been eliminated. However the form of its realization is still not a regulation of the market mechanism but mostly centrally determined economic tools (fixed prices, tax, bonuses, etc.).

Secondly, it is necessary that education and training of leading workers at all levels should be directed towards a deepening of economic thinking and towards an extending of knowledge of the substance and applicability of economic-mathematical methods and models in planning and controlling activity. Especially important is the application of exact methods in agricultural economy indicating the need for a much deeper knowledge of connections and relations in agricultural production, of the task of the human factor, of the position of the agricultural enterprise, and so on.

Furthermore it is necessary to work out and practically apply a whole system of information adequate to the needs of economic management with the application of exact methods. In Czechoslovakia the hitherto applied system of information conformed to the earlier demand of directive management with an orientation, above all, towards the checking of natural indices of the central plan rather than making possible a systematically deeper analysis of all connections of the reproduction process in agriculture.

A further reason for the inadequate models is that under the conditions of this country — with the existence of large, socialist agricultural enterprises with numerous collectives of agricultural workers — it is practically impossible to determine the optimum plan of the enterprise on an empirical basis alone. Besides, this has been confirmed by the existing practical comparison of the empirically determined production structure with the optimum plan. It is necessary to awaken the interest of the largest possible part of the collective members of agricultural cooperatives and of the workers of state farms in an application of modern methods of deciding production and maximum effects. This requires finding an effective means of transferring the effects of the economic conditions under which the enterprise operates to the smallest possible collectives or to groups of individual workers within the collective or farm. The aim must be a stimulation of their interest not only in the immediate remuneration for work performed but also in the long-term prosperity of the enterprise. With its consequences this requires agricultural cooperatives based on democratic principles of management— the determination of a suitable proportion between democratic decision making by the majority and the expert decisions in the choice of an optimum variant, for example, of the production structure.

As further important preconditions we consider the stability of external economic conditions under which the agricultural enterprise works. An optimum production structure means mostly a narrowing of the production program. Excessively frequent changes of prices, instability, and shortness of cooperative relations — all of these urge the enterprise to be careful with regard to a limiting of the production assortment and to act as a factor impeding specialization.

Finally, it is necessary to complete the establishment of an advisory service, which, as a service, would insure a higher standard of the processes of decision making, above all at the level of agricultural enterprises.

Jan de Veer, *Institute of Agricultural Economics* (Netherlands)

T HE REASONS why new and appropriate models and methods for
planning and projection, as developed by economists and econometricians, are not used widely and sufficiently in agriculture are
examined in this paper. These models could improve the functioning
and policies in agriculture.

The scope of this paper will be restricted to planning problems
with regard to resource allocation in agriculture and to supply and
marketing of agricultural products. Such planning problems as the
efficient organization of advisory services, agricultural research, agricultural statistics, and agricultural policy departments will not be
considered. Planning problems with regard to agricultural resource
allocation, production, and marketing exist at different levels. On the
national level all countries have fairly elaborate agricultural policies.
Also on the regional level are various types of development policies involving agricultural production and resource use. The planning problems in these fields vary among countries and among regions.

First, policy instruments differ depending on political, economic,
and social systems. Further, there are differences due to such factors
as the degree of economic development of the country or region, the
relative importance of the agricultural sector, the structure of agricultural production, the natural factors such as climate and soil, and the
marketing situation of agricultural products. The nature of the planning
problems and the appropriate planning methods on the farm level are
probably much more similar than those at the national and regional
level.

We will not go into details with respect to the nature of the planning
problems and the way to solve them. Instead we will focus attention on
general features in the application of the results of economic and econometric science in the planning process. Moreover we will not deal intensively with insufficiencies in the models and techniques themselves
and their possible improvement because these are the subject of previous papers.

DEFINITION OF PLANNING

Planning can be defined as the formulation of objectives to be
achieved in a more or less distant future, the analysis of possibilities
of achieving these objectives, and the determining and systematizing

as to functional and chronological order the actions which have to be taken. This definition indicates that planning is always aimed at the future and that it involves three elements: formulation of objectives, analysis of possibilities, and determination of a program of action.

ECONOMIC AND QUANTITATIVE METHODS IN DECISION MAKING AND PLANNING

From the viewpoint of planning, the contributions of quantitative models and methods can accomplish two things: an increase in knowledge about the planning situation and improvement of decision making on the basis of existing knowledge. This is not a sharp distinction in methods and models and of procedures. Application of models and methods aimed at choosing an optimal solution from a given set of alternatives will as a rule necessitate an increase in knowledge about the planning situation. An optimal plan also will provide, generally as a by-product, a better insight into the planning situation. This is often even the most valuable contribution. As a first attempt, a linear programming model for a farm, for example, rarely results in a workable farm plan; nevertheless it usually gives important indications about management problems. On the other hand, models and methods aimed at increasing knowledge can often, with slight modifications, be used for decision making. A forecasting model, for example, strictly speaking only gives information about future developments under certain conditions. However when these conditions can be influenced by policy interventions, such a model also might be used as a decision-making model by the introduction of an optimality criterion or simply by comparing consequences of alternative policies.

Most so-called plans at national and regional levels in Western countries are essentially forecasting models, but can be and are used as decision-making models. Therefore they often serve different purposes. For the planning represented by use of instruments to intervene in the structure of the model they can be used as decision models; at lower levels of planning they provide an increase in knowledge about the planning situation. These plans therefore also serve the purpose of improving coordination between various levels of planning. The composition of these plans, which necessitates a cooperative effort of experts of different branches and levels, consequently promotes coordination through an exchange of information.

The distinction we made at the beginning of this section between an increase in knowledge and improvement of decision making is useful in this respect. Increased knowledge as a rule has a wide field of application and can be used at various levels and places. In this regard we raise the questions if, at different planning levels, sufficient use is made of available results of quantitative economic research. Which factors prevent wider use of available knowledge and which methods exist to promote further increase and widen the application of useful knowledge? To be effective and useful, decision-making models have to be adapted to the particular planning situation and their results must have a specific and restricted meaning. The question is how a wider use and acceptance of decision-making models in practical planning can be acquired.

REASONS FOR THE SCANT USE OF QUANTITATIVE RESULTS

Before summarizing reasons why available knowledge acquired from quantitative economic research finds only limited use, we should recognize first that this branch of science is still young and developing. Its contribution is still more in the field of potential methods which are not yet in full stages of practical application, partly because practical applications are hampered by lack of data. In this section we shall not yet speak about the application of methods by decision makers at different levels, but only about the usable knowledge which they can derive from available results. This usable knowledge is to be found particularly in the forecasting of demand and market situations, and to a lesser degree in the projection of trends in agricultural population and farming structures.

If we attempt to sum up reasons why available results are not accepted or not used sufficiently, we come to the following: (a) lack of acquaintance with results, (b) lack of confidence in results, and (c) irrelevance of results to the planning situation. For lack of acquaintance with results, we can lay the blame on two sides.

On the one hand economic scientists often are primarily interested in publishing their results for a restricted circle of colleagues working in the same field. Moreover they are inclined to lay more stress on methodological aspects and the advance of science than on the practical application of results. They are not interested in, and often do not like to be bothered with, the clear and understandable presentation of their results and conclusions which is needed for practical purposes. An economic scientist may even fail to see fully the practical implications of his results. His scientific discipline makes him reluctant to draw conclusions or generalizations of a more speculative nature, although he usually is best qualified to do so and could provide information of value to decision makers. On the other hand, decision makers and their advisers often lack sufficient economic and mathematical schooling or sufficient time to study the results and follow the progress of quantitative economic research.

This void on the part of users may lead also to lack of confidence in results. It is human and sometimes justifiable that one mistrusts results and conclusions attained by methods he does not understand and is unable to evaluate. The contradiction in the results and conclusions with which outsiders often are confronted when studying the results and conclusions of various investigations and scientists is another factor. These contradictions are partly a consequence of the immaturity of our science wherein various methods and approaches, often still in the development stage, compete with each other. They arise also from differences in the premises. It is difficult for people who are not specialists to evaluate such results and translate them into usable knowledge for decision making. The economic scientists themselves are sometimes also responsible for the confusion by expressing among themselves opposing views on actual policy problems, based not on differences in opinion on the subject matter but on different premises with regard to policy aims. For the outsider this difference is not always clear. Although the economic scientist, like anyone else, is entitled to express his private views, he should be careful to make his premises clear and to indicate to what extent opposite views stem from different scientific insights or from another set of values.

Finally, the information may not be relevant to the planning situation of the decision maker either (a) because he lacks the instruments to intervene opportunely or (b) because the premises, and hence the results, of the model do not comply with the real situation in which he is placed. One may wonder, for example, why farmers do not make better use of market outlooks for the pig market which gives predictions for the next six or nine months. A farmer who has to decide when to start building a new shed however, needs a longer prediction period. Besides getting information which they cannot use, policy makers often do not get answers on questions which are of vital importance to them and which they expect can be answered best by economic scientists. An actual issue of Common Market agricultural policy is the butter surplus. A minister who asks the leading economic scientists of his country to indicate the effect of a lower milk price on national milk production would probably not even get unanimous answers about the direction of the supply response. This situation leads, of course, to much frustration on the side of policy makers and their advisers.

To improve this situation better communication and closer contact between decision makers and their advisers on the one hand and economic scientists involved in research on the other hand will be necessary. An obvious need exists for people who can act as intermediaries or liaison officers — people who will be able to evaluate and interpret results of quantitative economic research and to translate it into usable knowledge for decision making. At the same time, they should be able to identify at the right time the information needs of decision makers which might be met by research. Of course, these people already exist but their function is often not yet sufficiently recognized. The ultimate need is a better organized coordination between decision making and research.

SUPPLY OF INFORMATION FOR DECISION MAKING

To be useful for decision making, information has to be relevant for the planning situation of the decision makers. The information must relate to the policy instruments the decision maker is able and willing to use and the policy aims he pursues. The information also has to be timely enough to enable decision makers to adapt their policies. To realize this, it will be necessary and inevitable that decision makers have more control of the decisions concerning research projects. The supply of information from the side of research is, as far as I can see the situation, often a by-product of scientific development work or scientific training, even when the funds for a research project are provided largely by decision makers to meet their information needs. However, the better quantitative economic research is able to provide useful information for decision making, the bigger the need will be for a better adaptation to the needs of decision makers. This accomplishment could be attained, of course, by integrating research through creation of staff departments into policy-making agencies or advisory services. This would give the best guarantee that research is directed to the needs of decision makers or their advisers.

At the same time, however, it would lead to an inefficient organization of research. Concentration of quantitative economic research offers better opportunities for specialization, training, teamwork, data collection, development of methods and models, and so on. The information needs for different purposes and at different levels are, from the viewpoint of research, often closely related and can be covered by the same research projects. Fragmentation of research by spreading it over a large number of small research departments of limited scope would consequently lead also to inefficient duplications. Hence a better and wider use of methods and models of quantitative economic research requires specialized research institutes of a scale large enough to have a staff of specialized researchers and the necessary auxiliary services and research equipment. But such institutes can function well only if the research programs are geared to the needs of decision makers. This will not be attained sufficiently if the decision makers are represented only on the boards of these research institutes or act as sponsors for a research project. It will also be necessary to create committees or working groups to accompany the research projects in order to allow (a) a continuous exchange of ideas and (b) a continuous confrontation of researchers with the information needs of decision makers, and of the decision makers with the progress and results of research.

APPLICATION OF DECISION-MAKING MODELS AND METHODS AT THE NATIONAL AND REGIONAL LEVEL

On the national and regional level, a sharp distinction is not made between decision and forecasting models and methods. The application often will depend on the way in which models and methods are used. This is at least the case for models and methods which are based on the behavior of economic subjects with a high degree of independence and on which policy makers at the national and regional level can exert only limited direct influence on behavior. In Western countries these are the only realistic models for the prevailing economic and political systems. Normative models which rest on the assumption that the decision of economic subjects with regard to agricultural resource use and production are geared directly to policy aims on the national or regional level have only an indicative value. They may show deviations between an "ideal" world and reality and because of this may be helpful in the formulation of policy aims. But as a rule, because of lack of instrument variables, they will not provide a basis for intervention by policy makers.

The use of models and methods for decision making at the national and regional level of course requires a still greater cooperation between decision makers and scientists and a still greater influence of decision makers than research which is aimed only at the supply of information. As a rule these models will overlap the fields of different policy-making agencies. The building and operation of these models is itself an act of policy making since the integration of these decision models into practical planning requires a reorganization of the whole framework of decision making, if it is intended to be more than an intellectual exercise. These models will also be an instrument for the coordination of policies on different levels and in different fields. The task of building and operating these decision models can therefore only be assigned to institutes or departments working under the authority of decision makers at the highest level.

In the introductory information for this seminar, it was mentioned that national models up to this point of time have incorporated insufficient details of agriculture and that similarly agricultural planning and policy often are not sufficiently related to national economies and economic development. To this could be added that in economic science, agricultural economics also has a particular place as a specialized branch with specialized research institutes and, in many countries, even as specialized academic training. This situation prevails not because economic problems in agriculture differ essentially from those in other sectors. Its justification exists only in the fact that economic research for agriculture requires knowledge of technical relations and farm situations which is not readily accessible. As national econometric models are developed which allow integration of the development or structural adjustment of the agricultural sector with other sectors of the national economy, there will be an increasing need to incorporate the specialized knowledge of agricultural economics into these models and to coordinate research programs of agricultural economic research with the work on the development of national econometric models.

APPLICATION OF DECISION MODELS AT THE FARM LEVEL

At the farm level decision makers normally have much more control of human actions than at national and regional levels. Their decisions, consequently, will be based more directly and exclusively on technical input-output relations and prices. The modern mathematical models represented by linear programming have proved to be appropriate tools to tackle decision-making problems on the farm level. Although agricultural economists were fast in adopting these techniques for application to farm management problems and a great number of applications are described in the literature, the practical application has been developing more slowly than in most other industries. The small size of agricultural firms is the main reason for this retardation. In bigger firms the manager is assisted by a staff of experts, whereas the farmer not only stands alone for this task but generally has to perform other tasks as well. The gains to be earned by better decision making are, moreover, small because of the small scale of production, and they do not warrant high costs for decision aids.

The tasks in the field of research and management advice, which in a big firm are committed to specialized staff departments, are committed to external services in agriculture. Particularly the extension services existing in most countries have the task of assisting the farmer in the solution of his management problems. In these extension services, linear programming has not found wide application until now. The main reasons are (a) the management advisers lack sufficient mathematical schooling for application and interpretation, (b) the data concerning technical relations and restraints necessary for an effective use are not available or the collection of these data takes too much time, and (c) it is difficult to transfer results and conclusions to the farmer and to make farmers accept them.

Particularly the first and the last reason have been used as an argument for developing and using simpler methods which require less mathematical schooling and less complicated calculations. As such, program planning (which may be characterized as a crossing of simple budgeting and linear programming) has been introduced in the extension services of many West European countries. By this method calculations can be made by hand and the deduction of the farm plan from the data and assumptions can be explained to the farmer, which of course makes them more convincing to him. The deviations between farm plans calculated with help of this method and linear programming are small, as long as the models are not too complicated. In practice it appears, however, that one often needs complicated models, and program planning then does not yield satisfactory results or the calculations require too much time. The practical application of program planning therefore has not taken a great flight.

The data needed for program planning are the same as for linear programming. Therefore the introduction and promotion of program planning in extension work has had a favorable effect on the availability of data. Technical research institutes have paid more attention to the production of data needed for programming. Extension services and farmers also have gathered experience in the collection of these data and have acquired a better insight into the restraints of the farm. Computer costs are no longer a bottleneck for a wider application of linear programming. In fact they are lower than the calculation costs of simpler methods like program planning. The bottlenecks lie in data collection, the transformation of data into models, and the transfer of the results to the farmer. Experience has shown that it is possible to collect the data concerning the particular farm situation with a set of forms to be filled in by the farmer or the extension service. These data regarding acreage, geographical situation, implementation, buildings, yields, fertilizer inputs, and price expectations have to be combined with general knowledge concerning labor needs and periods, rotational restraints, and prices of various cost components which can be collected from other sources. With a good organization and a good design of forms and models, it is possible to cut down the costs of data collection and model building developing a system which can be operated by administrative personnel with only little intervention of experts. It also is possible to develop computer programming models in the form of a conventional budget which can be understood and checked by farmers and farm advisers.

The farm plans developed in a first attempt generally will not be satisfactory, as the planning situation of the particular farm probably will not yet be adequately covered by the model. As a rule, however, it will be sufficient for a check of the data and assumptions underlying the model. Hence farmers and advisers should then be able to provide the additional information necessary to adapt the model to the planning situation. A linear programming model, strictly speaking, is based on a certain fixed outfit. The farmer, however, often will be more interested in assistance for decision making with regard to changes in the fixed outfit than in optimal use of the existing outfit. Nevertheless it will be better to start with a model on the basis of an existing outfit, as this offers better opportunities for testing the assumptions and data, and identifying the bottlenecks. Too, the outcomes may yield valuable suggestions concerning most changes in the existing farm outfit to be incorporated in the model. Under a good organization with integrated data collection, model building, and presentation of results, it must be possible for farmers and farm advisers to "have a dialogue" with the computer and to apply mathematical models with a minimum of mathematical schooling and expert knowledge.

The costs of computer and extension services, moreover, will not be higher than those of simpler methods which require considerable calculations by the farm adviser himself, whereas the potential of linear programming as to scope and complexity of management problems is much bigger. The realization of such a scheme requires close cooperation between technical and economic scientists and good instruction of farm advisers (who have to be convinced of the potential advantages of such a system).

The time seems to be ripe for these developments. The increasing interest from the side of the farmers is brought about by rapid changes in social, economical, and technical conditions. Farmers are increas-

ingly confronted with the necessity of radical changes. These changes
perhaps motivate farmers as much or more than do the advances made
by the extension services themselves.

Chapter 26-27 ☜☞ DISCUSSION

Lazlo Enese, *Institute of Agricultural Economics* (Hungary)

PERHAPS the point of this discussion seems to be less scientific,
but I believe it is more exciting and interesting. The question, not
the least important, is whether and how all efforts, labor, and success performed by the excellent representatives of this discipline could
be turned to the advantage of the society in which we are working. My
opinion is that the extension of economic models and quantitative methods applied in farm management provides us with especially serious
tasks.

There are many kinds of farm management decisions to be made in
agricultural production. Categories and levels of these decisions, as
well as those persons who make them, have been dealt with in several
papers. Referring principally to Hungarian large-scale farms, but considering also other types of farms, I would proceed as follows in grouping those methods and decisions which should be extended in farming
practice.

The first group of farm decisions is represented by fundamental
economic decisions: the establishment of economic goals, farm planning for one or several years, the development of production structure,
decisions on investments, the allocation of resources among different
enterprises, marketing policy, the utilization of incomes for labor remuneration (i.e., for consumption) and for accumulation. In relation to
such decisions, techniques discussed here can play a considerable part.
I think, however, that for a long while this task will surpass the potentialities of farm managers.

The second group of decisions perhaps could be called technical
decisions containing also technological, zootechnical, and agronomical
decisions (e.g., the optimum solving of feeding, of crop rotation, or of
location of crops within the farm area, the selection of technologies,
machine systems, etc.). In my opinion the making of such decisions
proves to be more simple. Therefore simpler methods also can be applied and include simple forms of linear programming, graph techniques,
and the like.

The third group of decisions could be called decisions of an organizational order. The organization of linking production processes and of

actual labor processes belongs to this group. In the organization of labor especially, network diagram planning methods can be applied very well, as outlined by Professor Reisch and discussed also by my Hungarian colleagues who demonstrated at the same time their own initiatives in this field. Here again we have to attain solution of these problems in the farms, with more or less assistance in planning, and farm managers should develop their own means for making decisions.

Decisions belonging to each of these three groups have, of course, economic content and economic effects. Yet the decisions of a technical and organizational order are subordinated to fundamental economic ones, being thus restricted to a certain extent. I think that our methods and techniques should be classified according to the purposes of their utilization and according to the following criteria: which methods, administered in what way, and with what exterior assistance should be applied to various kinds of planning decisions? In this way, perhaps, a broader extension and use of techniques elaborated by and available from science can be achieved. I may only confirm the statements made by several colleagues that our methods do not as yet extend so far.

Looking to our work ahead, please allow me an irregular approach. Why should we not aim at the elaboration of a "strategic model" for our discipline? What should this model contain? I think it should contain all efforts concerning the development of theory. Certainly there are excellent econometricians in the world highly ambitious to develop theory reaching toward magnificent results and meriting thereby the admiration of those who are dealing with practical problems. The "model" certainly will contain techniques for solving national and regional economic problems. These will probably be very complicated methods again; practical application, however, will not be very difficult because even in such a small country as Hungary there will be some econometricians who will understand these methods without any difficulty and who will be anxious to act in their practical application.

In my opinion the following question seems to be more problematic: What should be done for the extension in farming practice of the achievements, methods, and techniques of this discipline? I am firmly convinced that decisive efforts should be made to educate the managers of the farms, so that they may master the application of these methods. Here in Hungary only 3,000 large-scale farms exist and yet it is certain that in the next decade there will not be an expert on any of these 3,000 farms able to apply even the simplest of the methods discussed here. I think if we do not want to waste this decade, or future decades, then we must adapt ourselves to the experts and managers working on farms. Unfortunately the situation in this respect is very disadvantageous. Reading the articles published in the periodicals and journals, I have the impression that papers presenting even the solution of very simple and solid problems are written for the level of participants of this seminar, and not to the managers and agronomists on farms. I am afraid that if the most excellent representatives of this field of science do not set examples of simple and commonly comprehensible descriptions

of the application of such techniques, not for economists and mathema-
ticians but for agronomists and farmers, then our methods will not extend into practice for a long while.

In a discussion between Mr. Reisegg and Mr. de Benedictis, Mr.
Reisegg expressed his wish that models and techniques should be simpler even if they present only a rougher approach. On the contrary,
Mr. de Benedictis said that labor should never be skimped but most
complete results always should be the aim. I think that the simplicity
or complexity of any solution depends largely upon the problem to be
solved. But whether techniques and results of a solution are simple or
complex, they must in any case be presented very clearly and compre-
hensively to those who are expected to use and apply them. Therefore
I should like to emphasize again the importance of the example, or of the
additional example, set by the excellent representatives of this scientific
seminar who present results in a comprehensible and applicable manner
for farm managers.

While I am agitating for the extension of microeconomic models
and quantitative methods applicable to agriculture, I believe that colleagues dealing with macroeconomic problems also could much profit
from this consideration. The amount of uncertainty contained in calculations and models trying to approach the responses of producers has
been discussed broadly. Several critical opinions were also expressed
on the fact that there are frequently considerable gaps between the results of such calculations and the facts. Considering only 3,000 large-
scale farms, I believe that if an optimum program could be elaborated
for the majority of them, then very probably the assessment of responses originated by diverse measures of economic policy or by economic changes among producers also will be easier and more exact.
Thus macroeconomic calculations will become more reliable too, increasing thereby the esteem of this discipline. I think that the most
decisive field of practical application of scientific results in the forthcoming period will be at the micro level. If these methods will afford
certain success in farming practice, then the general opinion and also
the leaders of agriculture will have confidence in applications at national
and regional levels of those planning procedures which have been discussed here. The following consequence can be drawn in summary:
purposeful and broad extension of microeconomic methods must play
an important part within the "strategic model" of this discipline conceived for the next period.

Chapter 26-27 ☞☜ DISCUSSION

J. C. Tirel, *Center for Rural Economic Study*
            (France)

THE TWO PAPERS by Eremias and de Veer dealing with problems
of planning in the activity of advisory and administrative services
illustrate the need for coherence and continuity in the general process of planning.

In my belief, tools such as linear programming and the theory of
decomposition can help us clear some aspects of interdependence between the problems of planning at different levels, even if they are not
able to solve them perfectly.

First, whenever we try to solve a problem at the technical unit
level, farm level, regional level, and other levels, we have to suppose
that this technical or economic unit can be isolated from its technological and economic environment. That is to say, we have to set up a hypothesis about the interrelations existing between the considered unit
and its environment. For instance, in solving a problem at the farm
level we use a set of prices for goods which can be bought or sold on
the market, but also we consider in the model a set of activities which
constitute a subset as compared with all the technological possibilities
which are available. Doing this, we make a choice, using *implicitly* a
system of prices for limiting factors, such as arable land, pasture,
buildings, or such intermediary goods as green forage or silage. That
is, we consider only one or a few solutions of each problem which has
to be solved at the technical unit level. What is the optimal quantity of
water for irrigated crops? What is the optimal level of mechanization
for harvesting cereals or sugar beets? Therefore each linear programming at the farm level, referring to the general theory of decomposition,
is no more than the reduced form of the main problem, activities of
which would be alternative solutions of implicit subproblems at the technical unit level.

But this theory tells us that the solution of the farm problem is optimal only if the set of internal prices (shadow prices) given by the dual
solution is the same which might have been used to choose the alternative solutions of technical subproblems. If not, this so-called optimal
solution for the farm is no more than the best answer to a wrong question. Fortunately, and this is an important advantage of linear programming, the dual solution gives the system of internal prices which can be
used to check the validity of technical choices and to appreciate the opportunity to complete the matrix with new activities dealing with new
crops or new technical processes.

As individual farm planning is considered, we can see from the theoretical approach what should be the role of economist and technical

advisers, what should be the dialogue between economist and agricultural scientists, and the necessity of interdisciplinary and cooperative research.

As we remain at the *individual* farm level, the validity of the second set of hypotheses about market prices for inputs and outputs can be found in the classical theory. But if we leave this level — as the extension and advisory services do whenever they try to build up a development program at regional or national levels — this hypothesis is no longer valid. At the regional level, for instance, we find again a similar situation: we need two series of hypotheses about the interrelation existing between the region and the rest of the economy, and between the region as a unit and decision makers at the firm level. A regional model can be considered as a reduced form of the main problem, activities of which are no more than alternative solutions of subproblems at the firm level. Even if the price system describing the situation of the region in the economy were available, the solution of the regional model would have to be checked by comparing the price system given by the dual solution and the price system used to choose the different production plans for farms for instance.

Of course, as we saw during this seminar, it is possible to build regional and interregional models including farm level constraints and activities, but generally such models can be both oversimplified and hardly manageable. So it seems to me that it can be interesting to use programming tools of limited size at each level and to define the place and the part of each one in the general process of planning. For me the most important is that all persons should be conscious that each problem includes two aspects: it can be considered as a main problem regarding subproblems lying at a lower level, and as one subproblem regarding a main problem at the upper level. The point then is to secure a good circulation of the needed information and the existence of a permanent dialogue between the different levels in this decentralized system. This scheme is a theoretical approach. But even if such organization is built up in a very rough way, it seems that its main interest is to fix the possibilities and limits of each link of the chain and to define the role of each one — research worker, adviser, regional leaders, officers, national leaders. This also allows us to stress the need for integrated and general planning, of which each project of extension or development is only an element. Then we can seriously speak about administrative organization of a planning system for agriculture.

It seems that these general principles hold true whatever the economic system is; the differences lie in the level of efficiency of the different ways which are used to incite the economic agents to apply the plan. Considering the papers of the two speakers and the converging efforts made by the different countries, however, we can suppose that the basic economic problems of countries with varied economic and social systems are not really different.

PARTICIPANTS

Ackermann, J.
Farm Foundation
Chicago, Illinois
U.S.A.

Aidin, V.
Lenin Academy of Agricultural
  Sciences
U.S.S.R.

Akkelj, T.
Scientific Research Institute for
  Agriculture and Soil Science
U.S.S.R.

Ashton, J.
University of Newcastle upon Tyne
Newcastle upon Tyne
U.K.

Baker, C.
University of Illinois
Urbana, Illinois
U.S.A.

Bacskay, Z.
Keszthely College of Agriculture
Keszthely
Hungary

Borlin, M.
Center for Research
Geneva
Switzerland

Brandes, W.
Institute of Agriculture
Gottingen
German Federal Republic

Braslavec, M.
Agricultural Institute of the
  Academy of Science
Odessa
U.S.S.R.

Candela, V.
Research Institute of Agricultural
  Economics
Bucharest
Romania

Csepinszky, A.
Central Bureau of Statistics
Budapest
Hungary

Dean, G.
University of California
Davis, California
U.S.A.

De Benedictis, M.
Center for Agricultural Economic
  Research
University of Naples
Portici
Italy

De Veer, J.
Institute for Land Economics
The Hague
Netherlands

Djordjev, T.
University of Skopje
Skopje
Yugoslavia

Dobos, K.
University of Agricultural Sciences
Godollo
Hungary

Dumitru, D.
Institute of Agricultural Economics
Bucharest
Romania

Edemsky, V.
Central Economic-Mathematical
    Institute
Academy of Sciences
Moscow
U.S.S.R.

Enese, L.
Research Institute for Agricultural
    Economics
Budapest
Hungary

Erdei, F.
Research Institute for Agricultural
    Economics
Budapest
Hungary

Eremias, V.
Research Institute for Agricultural
    Economics
Prague
Czechoslovakia

Fecske, M.
Research Institute for Economic
    Trends
Budapest
Hungary

Fekete, F.
Research Institute for Agricultural
    Economics
Budapest
Hungary

Folkesson, L.
Institute of Agricultural and
    Forestry Economics
Agricultural College of Sweden
Uppsala
Sweden

Gavrilov, G.
All-Union Scientific Institute for
    Agricultural Economics
Moscow
U.S.S.R.

Gorfan, C.
Central Economic-Mathematical
    Institute
Academy of Sciences
Moscow
U.S.S.R.

Gruber, J.
Institute of Agricultural Policy
    and Marketing
University of Munich
Freising
German Federal Republic

Habr, J.
Czechoslovakia Academy
Prague
Czechoslovakia

Hall, H.
University of Kentucky
Lexington, Kentucky
U.S.A.

Havlicek, J.
Research Institute for Economic
    Planning
Prague
Czechoslovakia

Heady, E.
Iowa State University
Ames, Iowa
U.S.A.

Heidhues, Th.
Georg-August University
Gottingen
German Federal Republic

Heinrichsmeyer, W.
University of Hohenheim
Stuttgart-Hohenheim
German Federal Republic

Herer, W.
Institute of Planning
Poland

Hoose, J.
Karl Marx University of
  Economics
Budapest
Hungary

Hrabe, S.
Ministry for Economic Planning
Prague
Czechoslovakia

Janko, J.
Agricultural College
Mosonmagyarovar
Hungary

Kadlec, V.
Ministry of Education
Prague
Czechoslovakia

Kazareczki, K.
Ministry of Agriculture and Food
Budapest
Hungary

Kelemen, Z.
Institute for National Economy
Budapest
Hungary

Kiselev, V.
Central Economic-Mathematical
  Institute
Academy of Sciences
Moscow
U.S.S.R.

Kiss, A.
University of Agricultural Sciences
Godollo
Hungary

Kopetz, H.
Board of Agriculture
Schloss-Tollea
Austria

Kovacs, G.
Keszthely College of Agriculture
Keszthely
Hungary

Kravtchenko, R.
All-Union Scientific Institute
  for Agricultural Economics
Moscow
U.S.S.R.

Kubas, P.
Research Institute for Agricultural
  Economics
Bratislava
Czechoslovakia

Kulin, S.
Keszthely College of Agriculture
Keszthely
Hungary

Love, H.
University of Alberta
Edmonton, Alberta
Canada

McFarquhar, A.
Cambridge University
Cambridge
U.K.

Mash, V.
Central Economic-Mathematical
  Institute
Academy of Sciences
Moscow
U.S.S.R.

Miloserdov, V.
All-Union Scientific Institute for
  Agricultural Economics
Moscow
U.S.S.R.

Miric, S.
Agricultural University of Zemun
Zemun
Yugoslavia

Nagy, G.
Postgraduate Training Institute
of Agricultural Engineers
Budapest
Hungary

Nagy, J.
Research Institute for Agricultural
Economics
Budapest
Hungary

Nagy, L.
Keszthely College of Agriculture
Keszthely
Hungary

Olejnik-Ovod, Y.
Central Economic-Mathematical
Institute
Academy of Sciences
Moscow
U.S.S.R.

Orazem, F.
Kansas State University
Manhattan, Kansas
U.S.A.

Oury, B.
Economics Department
International Bank for
Reconstruction and Development
Paris
France

Pallos, L.
Ministry of Finances
Budapest
Hungary

Pejin, D.
Agricultural University of Zemun
Zemun
Yugoslavia

Pic, J.
College of Agriculture
Prague
Czechoslovakia

Porwit, K.
Institute of Planning
Poland

Poscus, V.
Agricultural Academy of the
U.S.S.R.
Vilna
U.S.S.R.

Potsubay, J.
Keszthely College of Agriculture
Keszthely
Hungary

Radovics, G.
Research Institute for Agricultural
Economics
Budapest
Hungary

Regan, D.
Institute of Agricultural Economics
Kaciceva
Yugoslavia

Reisch, E.
University of Hohenheim
Stuttgart-Hohenheim
German Federal Republic

Reisegg, F.
Norwegian Institute for Agricultural
Economics
Oslo
Norway

Renborg, U.
Agricultural College of Sweden
Uppsala
Sweden

Rosenberg, V.
Agricultural Academy of the
U.S.S.R.
Tartu
U.S.S.R.

Rychlik, T.
Institute of Agricultural Economics
Warsaw
Poland

Schultz, T.
University of Chicago
Chicago, Illinois
U.S.A.

Sebestyen, J.
Research Institute for Agricultural
    Economics
Budapest
Hungary

Stern, V.
Agricultural Institute of Slovenia
Ljubliana
Yugoslavia

Stipetic, V.
University of Zagreb
Zagreb
Yugoslavia

Swanson, E.
University of Illinois
Urbana, Illinois
U.S.A.

Szakolczai, G.
Central Bureau of Statistics
Budapest
Hungary

Szikszai, B.
Research Institute for Agricultural
    Economics

Theisz, E.
Central Bureau of Statistics
Budapest
Hungary

Tintner, G.
University of Southern California
Los Angeles, California
U.S.A.

Tirel, J.
Center for Rural Economic Study
Grignon
France

Toth, J.
Agricultural College
Debrecen
Hungary

Toth, M.
Ministry of Agriculture and Food
Budapest
Hungary

Tulenev, A.
Central Economic-Mathematical
    Institute
Academy of Sciences
Moscow
U.S.S.R.

Tweeten, L.
Oklahoma State University
Stillwater, Oklahoma
U.S.A.

Venezian, E.
Ford Foundation
Mexico City
Mexico

Vever, E.
Scientific Research Institute for
    Agriculture
Riga
U.S.S.R.

Vincek, Z.
Institute for Agricultural
    Economics
Zagreb
Yugoslavia

Weckman, K.
Helsingfors University
Helsinki
Finland

Weinschenk, G.
University of Hohenheim
Stuttgart-Hohenheim
German Federal Republic

INDEX